Denizations and Naturalizations in the British Colonies in America, 1607–1775

D1453620

Denizations and Naturalizations in the British Colonies in America, 1607–1775

Lloyd deWitt Bockstruck

Contents

Introduction

The status of English colonists who left the Mother Country to settle in North America became an important issue after the founding of the British Empire at Jamestown in 1607. The English took the position that colonists did not forfeit their status as citizens and that children born in the colonies were on an equal footing with those born in England.

The colonial charters provided that ". . . all and every the Persons being our Subjects, which shall dwell and inhabit within every or any the said several Colonies and Plantations, and every of their children, which shall happen to be born within any of the Limits and Precincts of the said several Colonies and Plantations, shall HAVE and enjoy all Liberties, Franchises, and Immunities, within any of our other Dominions, to all Intents and Purposes, as if they had been abiding and born, within this our Realm of *England*, or any other of our said Dominions."[1]

The American colonies from the beginning needed settlers for military security, economic prosperity, and population growth. Since there were not enough English colonists to fulfill these demands, the English colonies had to invite foreigners to do so. Since some of the colonists were non-English, the question of citizenship arose early in the American colonial experience. Many aliens sought citizenship before leaving England. Still others sought an English grant after their arrival.

There were two avenues to English citizenship available. One was naturalization; the other was denization. In England, Parliament could grant the former by private act; the King could grant the latter by letters patent. Naturalization was more costly for the alien, but it did convey a higher status and more rights. Because it was more difficult to qualify for parliamentary naturalizations than royal denizations, aliens often opted to be endenized. Because denizations were granted by letters patent, however, they could be withdrawn by the authority that issued them. Colonial governors and legislative assemblies followed the pattern of their counterparts in England. There was also a third means of becoming an English subject in the New World. It was by the annexation of former colonies of other European powers, as in the case of the acquisition of New Netherland (which earlier had absorbed New Sweden), Acadia, Quebec, East Florida, and West Florida. In conjunction with annexation there may have been additional requirements such as oaths of allegiance.

In the colonial period both denization and naturalization conferred civil but not political rights. They primarily involved the ownership and transfer of realty. Denization conferred limited rights of inheritance, but naturalization was complete. A denizen was allowed to buy and devise land while an alien could not. Neither an alien nor any of his children could inherit land. He could not hold any office of trust or receive grants of land from the Crown. In most cases suffrage was not connected

---

[1] Francis Newton Thorpe, *The Federal and State Constitutions, Colonial Charters, and Other Organic Laws of the States, Territories, and Colonies Now Heretofore Forming the United States of America* (Washington, D.C., 1909) VII, 3788.

to either. In the event that an alien who had been endenized died intestate with a son born prior to his denization and a son born after it, the younger son would inherit the father's land because the father had no inheritable blood to communicate to his first-born son. If the father instead had opted to be naturalized, his eldest son would have been his heir because naturalization had retrospective energy.

It should be noted that Jews were admitted to English colonies in the New World earlier than in England. Under Cromwell Jews could gain legal entry into England in 1655. In many of the records they are identified by religion. In others, however, their identity is more subtly revealed. Whereas Christians subscribed to oaths of allegiance or affirmed when it was appropriate by placing their hand on the Bible, Jews did so by placing their hand on the Old Testament. The sacred text, therefore, indicated their religion.

The first instance of a blanket policy of denization for aliens was the 1681 announcement by King Charles II granting the Huguenot refugees denization without charge. Some of the refugees sought denizations or naturalizations in England before leaving for the colonies. Such action gave them imperial status. One of the earliest such examples was Nicholas Martiau who came to Jamestown, Virginia in the spring of 1620.[2] The earliest example of a stranger being admitted to citizenship in the colonies was that of George Hacke in 1653 in Northampton County, Virginia.

On 18 January 1699/1700 by an order-in-council, the English government banned the granting of denizations in the colonies by governors unless expressly authorized to do so in their commissions. By the statute of 11 and 12 William III, all persons being natural-born subjects of the king could inherit from ancestors, lineal and collateral, even though their forebear was born out of the king's allegiance.

In 1709 Parliament provided for naturalization in both a timely and inexpensive manner. Applicants had to take and subscribe the oaths of allegiance and supremacy and to disavow the Roman Catholic doctrine of transubstantiation in open court. At the same time they had to present proof that they had taken the Sacrament within the last three months according to Anglican form. The fee was a modest one shilling. This legislation was prompted by the arrival of some 15,000 Palatines who had flocked to Great Britain during the reign of Queen Anne.

The 1709 act permitted great numbers of foreign Protestants to acquire British citizenship. Response among the German Palatines was so overwhelming that Parliament once again under Tory control repealed the law just three years later in January 1711/12. The only avenue remaining available for naturalization was a private act. It should be pointed out that the 1709 law did not apply to the colonies. Those seeking to benefit under its terms had to do so in Great Britain.

The question of individual colonial naturalizations was clarified in 1736 when it was determined that an alien naturalized in one colony was to be considered an Englishman in that colony only; elsewhere, he retained his alien status.

It was not until 1740 that Parliament provided for imperial naturalization. The act required an applicant to reside seven or more years in a colony without being absent for more than two consecutive months. The applicant had to take the oath of allegiance and subscribe his profession in the Christian belief before the chief justice or some other colonial judge in open court, and he had to submit a certificate signed by two witnesses proving that he had taken the Sacrament within the last three months in a Protestant or Reformed congregation within Great Britain or the American colo-

---

[2] Numbered among his notable descendants are Her Majesty, Queen Elizabeth II, and the first President of the United States, George Washington.

nies. The act exempted Quakers and Jews from complying with the sacramental requirement and substituted oaths accommodating their respective faiths. The name of each person was to be entered in the local court record and in the official book of the colony's secretary. Annual lists of the names of those naturalized were to be transmitted to the Lords Commissioners of Trade. Such naturalizations were valid throughout the Empire. The act excluded Roman Catholics. In 1747 the act was amended to accommodate Protestants such as Moravians from having to avoid compromising their scruples against taking oaths.

During the French and Indian War Parliament established another means of naturalization. By the 1756 act the King could commission foreigners as officers (except the colonel of a regiment) and engineers in colonial regiments who could assist with the foreign-born subjects—particularly in Pennsylvania and Maryland. Each alien was to take the oath of allegiance and the Sacrament six months prior to his commissioning. These naturalized officers and engineers, however, could serve only in America.

Parliament took especial note of the contributions of these foreign-born soldiers in America and in 1761 provided for granting naturalization to aliens who were officers and common soldiers in the Royal American Regiment and Engineers. Any foreign Protestant who had served or would serve two years in the British forces in North America, would take the oaths and declarations, and had taken the Sacrament within six months prior to admission could be naturalized. If they had purchased estates since the earlier act of 1756, these were to be confirmed.

The acts of 1740 and 1761 qualified naturalized subjects to hold military and civil offices but barred them from serving in Parliament, the Privy Council, and offices in the Kingdoms of Great Britain and Ireland. Accordingly, the act of 1773 removed such impediments. An order in council in 1773 banned local admission to citizenship in the colonies.

This volume is a compilation of naturalization and denization records in the British colonies in America between 1607 and 1775. In these records are a number of interesting examples that illuminate the prevailing practices in the colonies. An English subject was one of English descent born on English soil. The offspring of Englishmen born abroad, even though of English descent, were not citizens and had to undergo naturalization if they intended to acquire realty and transmit it to their heirs. Examples include the family of Captain James Neale in Maryland in 1666, Edward Broughton in Jamaica in 1690, the brothers John and William Custis in Virginia in 1658, Col. Walter Hamilton of Nevis in 1703, Anna Vassal in Jamaica, and Gideon Harvey in Northumberland County, Virginia in 1656. While the latter was born in The Hague, Holland, his citizenship record identified his parents' place of origin as Westminster, Middlesex, England. The only exception were those children born of parents who followed Charles II into exile during 1641–1660.

Josiah James Hanses was born of English parents on the high seas in an English bottom. Since he was not, however, born on English soil, it was necessary for him to be naturalized in Jamaica on 11 November 1703. He was still a minor. Finally, it was not enough simply to be born in the British Empire. Children of aliens born in the colonies were still aliens. That situation changed in 1700 during the reign of William III, when legislation allowed natural-born subjects the right to inherit from alien parents or more remote ancestors. Accordingly, there was no longer a distinction between an Englishman and a colonial in the matter of inheritance.

Prior to the Act of Union of 1707, uniting the Kingdoms of England and Scotland, the status of Scots was one of strangers. There was one important exception. Scots could take up residence in certain American colonies before the Act of Union if the Royal charter for a colony specified their eligibility. Such was the case in the Royal grant to Sir Fernando Gorges in 1639, which deemed Scots as natural-born subjects. Otherwise, they had to undergo denization or naturalization in the colonies, as in the case of John Pouston of Massachusetts in 1664. People born in a former colony of another European power annexed by England were also aliens. Jacob Lookerman of New York was such an individual in 1678. He had been born in New York when it was under Dutch control. Among those foreigners taking advantage of serving in the military in order to become a British subject was Col. Henry Bouquet. Denizations and naturalizations by a colony were not valid outside of the granting colony. If a citizen of such a colony removed to another colony, he or she was obligated to reapply under the terms of the statutes of his or her new colony of residence. Accordingly, Peter Hendrick Striepers was naturalized in New Jersey in 1765 and in Pennsylvania in 1766.

Whether it was the cost of obtaining citizenship, geographical proximity, loop holes in the law, or ignorance that prompted colonists to travel to another colony to obtain citizenship, it was not unusual to find aliens from Maryland and New Jersey being naturalized in the neighboring colony of Pennsylvania. The value of a compilation of naturalizations for all of the English colonies is best exemplified by the case of David Law of Orange County, North Carolina who was naturalized in Pennsylvania in April 1761. Why he did so is unclear. Perhaps he was back in Pennsylvania on business and decided to take advantage of the situation available to him. Because the British colonies, notably those that united to form the United States in 1776, are no longer in the Commonwealth, this composite index may serve to indicate the whereabouts of individuals in colonies seemingly having no geographical relevance. Sebastian Zouberbuhler, for example, lived in Massachusetts and South Carolina many years before eventually settling in Nova Scotia, where he finally took out citizenship.

The status of alien women being endenized and naturalized might seem to imply that they were unmarried or widowed, since married women were the property of their husbands. Michael Reis was naturalized in April 1744 in Pennsylvania. His wife, Margaret Reis, was naturalized five months later, so care should be exercised in deducing the status of females in these records. While one might presume that an applicant for citizenship would have been an adult, the case of eleven-and-a-half-year-old Jacob Sickneer in New York in 1715/6 demonstrates the contrary. It will be necessary to interpret each case in light of the law in the colony involved.

While Protestants and Jews, as well as Roman Catholics in certain instances, became British subjects, American Indians could also be made citizens as in the case of Abimelech in 1695 in Connecticut. Aliens born in Africa were also admitted to citizenship; Jamaica had the greatest number.

During the seventeenth and the first decade of the eighteenth century French Huguenots accounted for the majority of non-English stock seeking citizenship. German colonists, however, surpassed their number thereafter. While Germans accounted for the largest number of aliens becoming British between 1607 and 1776, others were from Bohemia, Denmark, France, Greece, Italy, Luxembourg, Norway, the Netherlands, Portugal, Spain, Sweden, and Switzerland.

It is imperative to be acquainted with the statutes of each colony for the appropriate period in order to ascertain the status of the foreign born. While suffrage was restricted to citizens in certain colonies, there were exceptions. In South Carolina, for example, an alien could vote provided that he owned the requisite amount of land, but he could not hold political office.

The location of colonial denization and naturalization records varies from one colony to another. They may be found at the local jurisdictional level as well as the colonial level. They may be found in court minutes, government records, deed books, legislative journals, statutes, private papers of proprietors such as William Penn, and land patents as in Jamaica and Pennsylvania.

More so in England than in the colonies the question of naturalization was one that generated opposition. The English coveted their commercial privileges and were reluctant to share those benefits with others. Xenophobia, religious differences, fear of loss of political power, and military security influenced naturalization policy and legislation. In England, Parliament sought to maintain its powers by refusing to allow the monarch too much authority in the area of naturalization.

Special occupational categories at various times received favored treatment in the area of naturalization. People involved in the linen industry did so in 1663. Foreigners serving on English men-of-war or merchant ships in times of war did so in 1667. In neither instance were applicants under these statutes subject to the Sacramental test. In 1749 foreign Protestants in whaling could become English subjects, although they could not be absent for more than a year from Great Britain, Ireland, or the colonies.

The list of denization and naturalization records in this book has been compiled from a large body of published literature (see below), then expanded and improved by the examination of original source material not previously available to scholars.

The literature may treat aliens from the point of view of ethnicity or religion; examples are Charles W. Baird's *History of the Huguenot Emigration in America* (1885) or Arthur Henry Hirsh's *The Huguenots of Colonial South Carolina* (1928). In addition to monographic studies, periodicals of the same ilk, e.g. the American Jewish Historical Society's *Publications* and the Jewish Historical Society of England's *Transactions*, are replete with lists and examples of denizations and naturalizations.

The following are publications and sources, listed by locality, that contain denization and naturalization records:

England

The most important published works for England are William A. Shaw's *Letters of Denization and Acts of Naturalizations for Aliens in England and Ireland, 1603– 1700 [and] 1701–1800*, 2 volumes (1911–23), *A Supplement to Dr. W. A. Shaw's Letters of Denization and Acts of Naturalizations* (1932), Montague S. Giuseppi's *Naturalization of Foreign Protestants in the American and West Indian Colonies (Pursuant to Statute 13 George II, c.7)* (1921), *Calendar of State Papers, Colonial Series America and West Indies, 1574–1730* (1860–1939), Leo Francis Stock's *Proceedings and Debates of the British Parliament Respecting North America*, I, 314– 15 (1924), and William L. Grant's *Acts of the Privy Council of England, Colonial Series*, II, 95–96 (1908–12). Many of the entries in these works specify the colony of residence of the alien.

Connecticut

Public Records of the Colony of Connecticut, 15 volumes (1884–1967), contain the records created at the colony level.

Delaware

Records of the Court of New Castle on Delaware, II, 1676–1699 Land and Probate Abstract Only (1904–34) and Craig W. Horle's *Records of the Courts of Sussex County Delaware 1677–1710* (1991) include denizations and naturalizations.

Florida, East and West

"A List of the Inhabitants of Mobile in West Florida, Who Have Taken the Oaths of Allegiance and Fidelity to His Britannick Majesty, King George the Third," appears in the *Mississippi Provincial Archives English Dominion: Transcripts of Archives Public Record Office, London, England,* I, 201–2. The latter has been microfilmed.

Georgia

Very few naturalizations survive for the only Hanoverian planted colony. Mary Bondurant Warren and Jack Moreland Jones' *Georgia Governor and Council Journals 1753–1760* (1991) is one of the few original records of aliens taking the oath of citizenship.

Jamaica

Naturalizations and denizations were routinely entered in the volumes of land patents of the colony, and records from volumes 1–32, 1661–1774, are included herein. These manuscripts have been microfilmed.

Maryland

"Early Maryland Naturalizations, Kilty's Laws" appeared in Gaius Marcus Brumbaugh's *Maryland Records: Colonial, Revolutionary, County and Church from Original Sources,* II, 311–13 (1928). Jeffrey A. and Florence L. Wyand's *Colonial Maryland Naturalizations* (1975) was a more nearly complete compilation. Scattered throughout the series, *The Archives of Maryland,* 72 volumes (1883–1972), were many denizations and naturalizations. The digitization of the series permitted retrieval of all of the relevant references. Commission Book No. 82 contains all sorts of miscellaneous entries including denizations and naturalizations. Abstracts appear in *Maryland Historical Magazine,* XXVI–XXVII (1931–32).

Massachusetts

Joseph Willard's "Naturalizations in the American Colonies, with More Particular Reference to Massachusetts," *Massachusetts Historical Society Proceedings,* IV (1858–60) 337–64, contains the entries from the Superior Court of the Province between 1740 and the Revolution. *Report of the Record Commissioners of the City of Boston,* X (1886) 62, gives a list of Frenchmen admitted into the colony by the governor and council in 1691/2. The Colonial Society of Massachusetts' *Publications,* III (1895–97) 241–42, has the 1730 petition for six aliens.

New Hampshire

New Hampshire was the only colony that failed to provide by statute a means for aliens to be endenized or naturalized.

New Jersey

Dr. John R. Stevenson's "Persons Naturalized in New Jersey Between 1702 and 1776," *The New York Genealogical and Biographical Record,* XXVIII (1897) 86–89, contains names of aliens naturalized in the colony between the reign of Queen

Anne and the Revolutionary War. Dr. Peter A. Winkel's "Naturalizations Province of New Jersey, 1747–1775," *The Genealogical Magazine of New Jersey,* LXV (1990) 1–8 and 59–66, based primarily upon petitions to the Supreme Court of the colony, is another noteworthy contribution. The New Jersey Historical Records Program prepared *Guide to Naturalization Records in New Jersey* (1941), which included entries taken from *Acts of the General Assembly of the Province of New Jersey, 1702–1778.* In the first series of the *New Jersey Archives* is the sub-series *Journal of the Governor and Council, 1682–1755,* volumes 13–16 (1890–91) containing bills of naturalization. The third series of *New Jersey Archives,* the *Laws of the Royal Colony in New Jersey,* volumes 2–5 (1977–1986) by Bernard Bush, have the most accurate renderings of the names of those seeking to become English subjects.

New York

The five-volume set *The Colonial Laws of New York from the Year 1664 to the Revolution* (1894–96) is one of the richest sources of records granting citizenship to aliens. Also useful are "The Oaths of Abjuration, 1715–1716," *Quarterly Bulletin of the New York Historical Society,* III (1919) 35–40, Kenn Stryker-Rodda's "Ulster County Naturalizations, 1715," *The New York Genealogical and Biographical Record,* CXIII (1972) 85–88, and Richard J. Wolfe's "The Colonial Naturalization Act of 1740 with a List of Persons Naturalized in New York Colony, 1740–1769," *The New York Genealogical and Biographical Record,* XCIV (1963) 132–47. E. B. O'Callaghan's *Calendar of Historical Manuscripts in the Office of the Secretary of State, Albany, N.Y.* (1865–66) and *Documents Relative to the Colonial History of the State of New York* (1856–1887) are also quite useful. The best compilation heretofore for New York is Kenneth Scott and Kenn Stryker-Rodda's *Denizations, Naturalizations, and Oaths of Allegiance in Colonial New York* (1975).

North Carolina

William L. Saunders included such records in *The Colonial Records of North Carolina,* 10 volumes (1886–1890). Additional and more accurately interpreted entries appear in the second series, *The Colonial Records of North Carolina,* 10 volumes (1963–99). Court minutes of counties with sizable foreign-born populations, e.g. Rowan and Tryon, contain additional relevant references for the eighteenth century.

Nova Scotia

The 1720 oath of allegiance of the Acadians is found in *Collections de documents inedits sur le Canada et l'Amerique,* I, 186–88. *Memoires de la Societe Genealogique Canadienne-Francaise,* VI (1954) 316–17 features the 1695 oath from the Massachusetts Archives. There is both a copy of the original and a transcript. Placide Gaudet's *Acadian Genealogy and Notes Concerning the Expulsion* (1996) contains the 1729 petition and 1730 list of those taking the oath of allegiance. The 1730 oath is also included in Thomas B. Akins' *Acadia and Nova Scotia: Documents Relating to the Acadian French and the First British Colonization of the Province, 1714–1758,* between pages 84 and 85. Dr. Terrence M. Punch's "An Acadian Oath of Allegiance of 1765," *The Nova Scotia Genealogist,* VI (1986) 4–5, is still a later record involving the complex status of the Acadians within the Empire. Richard Bell Winthrop's *The "Foreign Protestants" and the Settlement of Nova Scotia: The History of a Piece of Arrested British Colonial Policy in the Eighteenth Century* (1961) is essential for understanding the situation in the colony and includes a number of instances of naturalization. Kenneth S. Paulsen's "The Provincial Election of 1768: The First Vote in Lunenburg, Nova Scotia," *The New England Historical and Ge-*

nealogical Register, CLVI (2002) 159–64, contains relevant data about the foreign Protestants. Dr. Terrence M. Punch's "Naturalization of Foreign Protestants, Nova Scotia, 1758," *The Nova Scotia Genealogist,* XXI (2003) 61–66, is a superior work of genealogical scholarship.

Pennsylvania

The Papers of William Penn, I, 347–49 (1981) has the naturalizations of residents of the former New Sweden including Swedes, Finns, and Dutch. *The Colonial Records of Pennsylvania,* 10 volumes (1838–52) featuring the Minutes of the Provincial Council constitute another important source. The statutes of the colony are equally valuable. *Persons Naturalized in the Province of Pennsylvania* appeared in *The Pennsylvania Archives,* Second Series, II, 293–415. This work included those who were naturalized between 1740 and the eve of the Revolution. *Statutes at Large of Pennsylvania from 1682 to 1801* (1898–1911). *Abstracts of Pennsylvania Records of Naturalizations 1695–1773 Found in Colonial Records (Minutes of the Provincial Council), Volumes 1, 2, 3, 9, & 10; the Statutes at Large of Pennsylvania, volumes II, III, IV, VI, VII, & VIII; Pennsylvania Archives, Series I, Volumes 1, 3, & 4 with Surname Index* (1983) brought together the records from lesser known and underutilized sources. Cindy Crocker Livengood's *Genealogical Abstracts of the Laws of Pennsylvania and the Statutes at Large* (1990) has abstracts from both sources. In record group 17 of the Pennsylvania Land Records, the early patent and commission books contain naturalizations that routinely report the place of birth and parentage. These date from the first two decades of the eighteenth century. The records have been microfilmed.

Rhode Island and Providence Plantations

Sidney S. Rider's *The History of Denization and Naturalization in the Colony of Rhode Island 1636–1790* (1905?) was the earliest study for the state. Additional examples appeared in *Records of the Colony of Rhode Island and Providence Plantations in New England,* 10 volumes (1856–65).

South Carolina

Daniel Ravenel's *Liste des Francois et Suisses from an Old Manuscript List of French and Swiss Protestants Settled in Charleston, on the Santee and at the Orange Quarter in Carolina Who Desired Naturalization Prepared about 1695–1696* (1888) is the most important source for the colony's earliest naturalizations. *The Statutes at Large of South Carolina* by Thomas Cooper, II, 132–33 (1837) is complementary. Others appear in the Miscellaneous Records, Main Series, volumes EE and FF. In the *Records in the British Public Record Office Relating to South Carolina,* XX, 547–48 and XXIII, 263–64 are transcripts of naturalization records. Both of the latter two sources are on microfilm. The Provincial Court Record Book, 1694–1704, also contains a number of entries involving the early Huguenot colonists.

Virginia

An earlier attempt to compile a list of naturalizations and denizations in the Old Dominion was Lloyd de Witt Bockstruck's "Naturalizations and Denizations in Virginia," *National Genealogical Society Quarterly,* LXXIII (1985) 109–16. *The Journals of the House of Burgesses of Virginia 1619–1776,* 13 volumes, (1895–1905) have petitions for naturalizations. William Waller Hening's *The Statutes at Large; Being a Collection of All the Laws of Virginia from the First Session of the Legislature in the Year 1619,* volumes 1–8 (1819–23), contains the texts of the laws bestowing citizenship upon aliens. The lesser known *The Laws of Virginia Being a Supplement to Hening's The Statutes at Large 1700–1750,* pp. 39–41 (1975), contains naturalizations for the Manakin Huguenots. County records, notably deed books and court orders, are also rich sources for naturalizations and denizations. These records have been microfilmed.

Quebec

The Appendix is an index of naturalizations granted by the French in Quebec; most of the individuals were from the English colonies. It is based upon "Les Lettres de Naturalite sous le Regime Francais," *Le Bulletin des Recherches Historiques,* XXX (1924) 223–32. It has been included in this work to indicate that former British subjects may be found amongst the records of the colonies of other European nations.

The spellings of place names, personal names, and occupations found in the original records have been retained. Therefore, you will encounter some inconsistencies, sometimes even within the same record. It is important to search for relevant entries under variant spellings. Additions and corrections will be most welcomed by the author.

Finally I would like to thank the following individuals for their assistance and counsel: Brent H. Holcomb; John Frederick Dorman, FASG; Peter Stebbins, FASG; Steve Myers of the Allen County Public Library; Mary Bondurant Warren; Winston De Ville, FASG; Henry B. Huff, FASG; Terrence M. Punch, FRSAI; Claire Mire Bettag; and Susan Kaufman of the Allen County Public Library.

Lloyd deWitt Bockstruck, FNGS
Dallas, Texas, U.S.A.
A.D. MMIV

Note: **In a number of instances, most notably those involving Acadians, there are multiple entries for people of the same name in a record of the same date. Each entry pertains to a separate individual. In April 1730, for example, three Pierre Doucets took the oath of allegiance in Nova Scotia.**

Denizations and
Naturalizations
in the
British Colonies
in America,
1607–1775

Denizations and Naturalizations
in the British Colonies in America, 1607–1775

[no surname], Abimelech. He was naturalized in Connecticut 16 Oct. 1695. He was an American Indian and the grandson of Uncas.

[no surname], Bertrain. He was endenized 3 Oct. 1667 in Virginia. He was a servant and freeman and had lived in the colony a number of years. He belonged to the Reformed faith.

[no surname], Eva Maria. She was naturalized in Jamaica 11 Dec. 1729. She was a free Negro.

[no surname], Philip. He was naturalized in Jamaica 3 Nov. 1714. He was a free Negro and alien born.

[— ? —], Hendrick. He took the oath of naturalization in New York 1 Sep. 1687 in Ulster County.

Aache, George. He was naturalized in Pennsylvania 24–25 Sep. 1764. He was from Cocalico Township, Lancaster County.

Aache, Henry. He was naturalized in Pennsylvania 24–25 Sep. 1764. He was from Cocalico Township, Lancaster County.

Aadig, Ernest. He was naturalized in New York 24 Mar. 1772.

AaronHart, Killian. He was naturalized in North Carolina 23 Mar. 1765. He was from Rowan County.

AaronHart, Phillip. He was naturalized in North Carolina 23 Mar. 1765. He was from Rowan County.

Aaton, Adriaen Hend. He took the oath of allegiance in Flackbush, Kings County, New York 26–30 Sep. 1687. He had been in the colony 36 years.

Aaton, Hendrick. He took the oath of allegiance in Breucklijn, Kings County, New York 26–30 Sep. 1687. He was a native of the colony.

Aaton, Thomas. He took the oath of allegiance in Flackbush, Kings County, New York 26–30 Sep. 1687. He was a native of the colony.

Abaranel, Phineas. He sought to be made a denizen 30 Aug. 1692. He was from Jamaica.

Abaugh, John. He was naturalized in Maryland 15 Sep. 1762. He was a German from Frederick County.

Abaz, Isaac. He was naturalized in Jamaica 23 Nov. 1688.

Abbot, John James. He was naturalized in New York 23 Dec. 1765.

Abel, Andrew. He was naturalized in New Jersey in 1750. He was from Hunterdon County.

Abel, Jacob. He was naturalized in New York 3 May 1755.

Abel, Leonard. He was naturalized in Pennsylvania 10 Apr. 1760.

Abel, Michael. He was naturalized in New Jersey in 1759.

Abelain, John. He was endenized in London 24 June 1703. He came to New York.

Abelain, John. He was endenized in London 24 June 1703. He was the son of John Abelain. He came to New York.

Abendana, Raphael. He was endenized in Barbados 9 Mar. 1693/4.

Abendshen, Reinhot. He was naturalized in Pennsylvania 24 Sep. 1755. He was from Berks County.

Aberlae, John. He was naturalized in Maryland 11 Apr. 1760.

Aberlee, Henry. He was naturalized in Pennsylvania 11–12 Apr. 1744. He was from Lancaster County.

Abette, Jan Salomnse. He was naturalized in New York 13 Mar. 1715/6. He was from Albany County.

Abight, Ernest Frederick. He was naturalized in New York 22 Apr. 1772. He was a tanner in New York City. He was a German.

Aboad, Isaac. He was naturalized in Jamaica 30 Sep. 1742.

Aboad, Joshua. He was naturalized in Jamaica 27 Feb. 1749/50. He was a Jew.

Aboad, Moses. He was granted a license to trade in New York 25 June 1684.

Abraham, Guillaume. He was an Acadian and took the oath to the King at the Mines, Pisiquit, Nova Scotia 31 Oct. 1727.

Abraham, John. He was endenized in Virginia 1 Apr. 1658.

Abraham, John. He was naturalized in Augusta County, Virginia 22 Aug. 1770. He was a Dutchman.

Abrahams, Isaac. He was naturalized in New York 21 Sep. 1744.

Abrahams, Solomon. He was naturalized in Jamaica 27 Feb. 1745/6. He was a Jew.

Abram, Nathan. He was naturalized in Jamaica 29 Dec. 1735.

Abrams, Chapman. He was naturalized in New York 3 May 1755.

Abramse, Frans. He took the oath of allegiance in Breucklijn, Kings County, New York 26–30 Sep. 1687. He was a native of the colony.

Abramsz, Hendrick. He took the oath of allegiance 26 Sep. 1687 in Orange County, New York.

Arbrahamzen, Isaac. He took the oath to the King 21–26 Oct. 1664 after the conquest of New Netherland.

Abrahamzen, Willem van der Borden. He took the oath to the King 21–26 Oct. 1664 after the conquest of New Netherland.

Abrathar, Joseph. He was naturalized in Jamaica 26 Feb. 1740/1. He was a Jew.

Abrinck, Peter. He expressed his desire to be naturalized in New Castle County, Delaware 21 Feb. 1682/3.

Abudient, Samson. He was endenized in Barbados 19 Aug. 1688.

Abudiente, Abraham. He was endenized in Barbados 19 Aug. 1688.

Abudiente, Rowland. He was endenized in Barbados 19 Aug. 1688.

Abuquerques, Daniel. He was naturalized in Jamaica 27 Feb. 1749/50.

Accree, John. He was naturalized in Pennsylvania 11–13 Apr. 1743. He was from Philadelphia County.

Acer, Adam. He was naturalized in Maryland 15 Apr. 1761.

Achee, Cyprien. He took the oath of allegiance at Harbour Amhurst in the Magdalen Islands, Gulf of Saint Lawrence on 31 Dec. 1765. He was a native of Nova Scotia.

Achee, Jacque. He took the oath of allegiance at Harbour Amhurst in the Magdalen Islands, Gulf of Saint Lawrence on 31 Dec. 1765. He was a native of Nova Scotia.

Achee, Joseph. He took the oath of allegiance at Harbour Amhurst in the Magdalines, Gulf of Saint Lawrence on 31 Dec. 1765. He was a native of Nova Scotia.

Achilles, Peter. He was naturalized in Maryland in Feb. 1674. He was born in Amsterdam, Holland. He also appeared as Peter Achillis.

Acker, Casper. He was naturalized in Pennsylvania in 1730–31. He was from Chester County.

Acker, Henry. He was naturalized in Pennsylvania 26–27 Sep. 1743. He was from Bucks County.

Acker, Jacob. He was naturalized in Pennsylvania in 1730–31. He was from Chester County.

Ackre, Andrew. He was naturalized in Pennsylvania 26–27 Sep. 1743. He was from Bucks County.

Ackre, Philip Jacob. He was naturalized in Pennsylvania 26–27 Sep. 1743. He was from Bucks County.

Adam, Johannes. He was naturalized in Maryland 11 Sep. 1765.

Adam, John. He was naturalized in Maryland 11 Sep. 1765. He was a German from Frederick County.

Adam, Martin. He was naturalized in Maryland in Apr. 1749. He was from Frederick County.

Adams, John. He was naturalized in Pennsylvania 11–13 Apr. 1743. He was from Philadelphia County.

Adams, Valentine. He was naturalized in Maryland 13 Apr. 1763. He was a German.

Adamzen, Abraham. He took the oath to the King 21–26 Oct. 1664 after the conquest of New Netherland.

Adamzen, Jan. He took the oath to the King 21–26 Oct. 1664 after the conquest of New Netherland.

Admire, George. He was naturalized in North Carolina 24 Sep. 1766. He was from Rowan County. His name has been mistakenly interpreted as George Adwicke.

Adolphus, Isaac. He was naturalized in New York 27 July 1758. He was a Jew.

Adolphus, Joseph. He was naturalized in Jamaica 13 Aug. 1733.

Adriaens, Lammert. He took the oath of allegiance in Orange County, New York 26 Sep. 1687.

Adriaense, Elbert. He took the oath of allegiance in Flackbush, Kings County, New York 26–30 Sep. 1687. He was a native of the colony.

Adriaense, Marten. He took the oath of allegiance in Flackbush, Kings County, New York 26–30 Sep. 1687. He was a native of the colony.

Aertse, Garret. He was naturalized in New York 8–9 Sep. 1715. He was from Ulster County.

Aertse, William. He was endenized in New York 8 Nov. 1698.

Aertsen, Jacob. He was naturalized in New Castle County, Delaware 21 Feb. 1682/3.

Aertsen, Jan. He took the oath of allegiance in Breucklijn, Kings County, New York 26–30 Sep. 1687. He had been in the colony 26 years.

Aertsen, Reynier. He took the oath of allegiance in Flackbush, Kings County, New York 26–30 Sep. 1687. He had been in the colony 34 years.

Aertsen, Simon. He took the oath of allegiance in Breucklijn, Kings County, New York 26–30 Sep. 1687. He had been in the colony 23 years.

Aettinger, Caspar. He was naturalized in New York 3 July 1759.

Affarina, Aaron. He was naturalized in Jamaica 6 July 1709.

Afiello, Mordohay. He was naturalized in Jamaica 30 Mar. 1703.

Agbortsin, Gerrit. He took the oath of naturalization in New York 1 Sep. 1687 in Ulster County.

Agee, Adam. He was naturalized in New Jersey 20 Aug. 1755.

Ageron, Peter. He was naturalized in Jamaica 3 May 1703.

Aguilar, Abraham. He was naturalized in Jamaica 28 Nov. 1706.

Aguilar, Esther. She was naturalized in Jamaica 31 Oct. 1737.

Aguilar, Moses. He was naturalized in Jamaica 27 May 1745. He was a Jew.

Aguilar, Rachel. She was naturalized in Jamaica 31 Oct. 1737.

Aguilar, Rebeckah. She was naturalized in Jamaica 24 Oct. 1718. She was the wife of Abraham Aguilar.

Aguylar, Jacob. He was naturalized in Jamaica 28 Feb. 1703.

Ahlbach, William. He was naturalized in New Jersey in 1750. He was from Hunterdon County.

Ahler, Henry. He was naturalized in Virginia 19 Apr. 1745. He was a native of Wurttemberg, Germany.

Aigler, Simon. He was naturalized in Pennsylvania 10 Sep. 1761. He was from Berks County. He was a Moravian.

Aimes, Georg. He was naturalized in New York 3 July 1759.

Ainusheffer, Johan Wilhelm. He was naturalized in New York 8–9 Sep. 1715. He was from Ulster County.

Aister, Jacob. He was naturalized in Pennsylvania 29 May 1739. He was from Philadelphia County.

Akeley, Jacob. He was naturalized in New Jersey 6 Dec. 1769.

Akerman, Jacob. He was naturalized in New Jersey in 1750. He also appeared as Jacob Ackerman. He was from Hunterdon County.

Alancet, Francois. He took the oath of allegiance at Mobile, West Florida 2 Oct. 1764.

Albaugh, William. He was naturalized in Maryland 11 Sep. 1765.

Alber, Mathias. He was naturalized in Pennsylvania 10 & 23 Sep. 1764. He was from Cocalico Township, York County.

Albert, John Jacob. He was naturalized in Maryland 14 Sep. 1763. He was a German.

Albert, John Matthias. He was naturalized in Pennsylvania 11 Apr. 1761. He was from Lancaster County.

Albert, Michael. He was naturalized in Pennsylvania 19 May 1739. He was from Lancaster County.

Albert, Philip. He was naturalized in Pennsylvania 10 & 23 Apr. 1764. He was from Hempfield Township, Lancaster County.

Albert, William. He was naturalized in Pennsylvania 11 Apr. 1763. He was from Salisburg Township, Northampton County.

Albert, William. He was naturalized in Pennsylvania 19 May 1739. He was from Lancaster County.

Alberts, Otto. He was naturalized in Jamaica 25 Feb. 1761.

Albertsa, Hendrick. He took the oath of naturalization in New York 1 Sep. 1687 in Ulster County.

Albertse, Ruth. She took the oath of allegiance in Flackbush, Kings County, New York 26–30 Sep. 1687. She had been in the colony 25 years.

Albertzen, Ebgert. He took the oath to the King 21–26 Oct. 1664 after the conquest of New Netherland. He was from Amsterdam.

Albin, Abraham Henriques. He was naturalized in Jamaica 14 Apr. 1693.

Albin, Isaac Henriques. He was naturalized in Jamaica 25 July 1687.

Albin, Mosek Lopez. He was naturalized in Jamaica 16 Dec. 1690.

Albortsa, Gisbort. He took the oath of naturalization in New York 1 Sep. 1687 in Ulster County.

Albrandt, John. He was naturalized in New York 11 Sep. 1761.

Albrant, Hannis. He was naturalized in New York 27 Jan. 1770.

Albrecht, Jacob. He was naturalized in Pennsylvania 24 Sep. 1766.

Albrespy, Guilleaume. He was naturalized in Rhode Island 4 Aug. 1756 and took the oath on 25 Aug. He was from France, had previously been an inhabitant of New York City, and was a resident of Newport.

Albright, Christian. He was naturalized in Pennsylvania 11 Apr. 1761. He was from Berks County.

Albright, George. He was naturalized in Pennsylvania 25–27 Sep. 1740. He was from Philadelphia.

Albright, Jacob. He was naturalized in Pennsylvania 11 Apr. 1761. He was from Berks County.

Albright, Jacob. He was naturalized in New Jersey 3 June 1763.

Albright, Joseph. He was naturalized in Pennsylvania 11–13 Apr. 1743. He was from Bucks County.

Albright, Lodowick. He was naturalized in North Carolina 23 Mar. 1763. He was from Rowan County.

Albright, Maria Catharine. She was naturalized in Pennsylvania 10 Apr. 1760.

Alderfer, Frederick. He was naturalized in Pennsylvania 11–13 Apr. 1743. He was from Philadelphia County.

Aldricks, Peter. He took the oath to the King 21–26 Oct. 1664 after the conquest of New Netherland.

Alendorph, Henry. He was naturalized in New York 3 May 1755.

Alex, Michael. He was naturalized in Maryland 15 Apr. 1761.

Alexander, Francis. He was naturalized in Jamaica on 24 [torn] 1692.

Alexander, Francois. He took the oath of allegiance in Mobile, West Florida 2 Oct. 1764.

Alexander, Isabell. She took the oath of allegiance in Mobile, West Florida 2 Oct. 1764.

Alexandre, Jean Baptist. He took the oath of allegiance in Mobile, West Florida 2 Oct. 1764.

Alforino, Phineas. He was Jewish and was naturalized in Maryland 18 Oct. 1742. He was born in Florence and lived in Talbot County.

Algajer, Jacob. He was naturalized in New York 3 July 1759.

Alin, Louis. He took the oath of allegiance at Port Royal, Nova Scotia 16 Aug. 1695.

All, Adam. He was naturalized in New York 19 Apr. 1769. He was a yeoman in New York City.

Allain, Louis. He was an Acadian who took the oath at Annapolis River in Dec. 1729.

Allain, Pierre. He was an Acadian who took the oath to George II at the Mines, Pisiquit 31 Oct. 1727.

Allain, Pierre. He was an Acadian who took the oath of allegiance in Apr. 1730.

Allaire, Alexander. He petitioned to be naturalized in New York 19 Aug. 1687.

Allaire, Alexander. He was endenized in New York 6 Feb. 1695/6.

Allare, Louis. He was admitted into the colony of Massachusetts 1 Feb. 1691. He was French.

Allebach, Christian. He was naturalized in Pennsylvania 11–13 Apr. 1743. He was from Philadelphia County.

Allen, Elizabeth. She was naturalized in New York 27 Jan. 1770.

Aller, Peter. He was naturalized in New Jersey in 1763. He was born in Germany and had been in the colony seven years.

Aller, Ulrick. He was naturalized in Pennsylvania 29 Mar. 1735. He was from Philadelphia.

Allgayer, Jacob. He was naturalized in Maryland 19 Sep. 1761.

Allgeyer, Johannes. He was naturalized in Maryland 12 Sep. 1759.
Allison, John. He was naturalized in New Jersey 7 Apr. 1761.
Almeida, Abraham. He was naturalized in Jamaica 1 May 1710.
Almeyda, David. He was naturalized in Jamaica 11 Oct. 1714.
Almeyda, Isaac Campos. He was naturalized in Jamaica 30 Aug. 1743. He was a Jew.
Almeyda, Jacob. He was naturalized in Jamaica 13 Oct. 1718.
Almeyda, Rica Campos. He was naturalized in Jamaica 27 Aug. 1745. He was a Jew.
Alrichs, Peter. He was naturalized in New Castle County, Delaware 21 Feb. 1682/3.
Alsback, Henry. He was naturalized in Pennsylvania 10 Sep. 1761. He was from Berks County.
Alsdorf, Lawrence. He was naturalized in New York 29 July 1752.
Alshouse, Henry. He was naturalized in Pennsylvania 11 Apr. 1761. He was from Northampton County.
Alspack, David. He was naturalized in Pennsylvania 10–12 Apr. 1762. He was from Berks County.
Alstat, Martin. He was naturalized in Pennsylvania 24 Sep. 1760. He was from Berks County.
Alstat, Nicholas. He was naturalized in Pennsylvania 24 Sep. 1760. He was from Berks County.
Alt, Hanis. He was naturalized in New York 27 Jan. 1770.
Alt, John. He was naturalized in New York 11 Sep. 1761.
Alt, John. He was naturalized in Pennsylvania 11 Apr. 1763. He was from Marlborough Township, Philadelphia County.
Althouse, John. He was naturalized in Pennsylvania 11 Apr. 1761. He was from Berks County.
Alvares, Aaron. He was naturalized in Jamaica 17 Jan. 1728/9.
Alvares, Abraham. He was naturalized in Jamaica 4 Feb. 1696. He was a merchant.
Alvares, Abraham. He was naturalized in Jamaica 26 Apr. 1757.
Alvares, Jacob. He was naturalized in Jamaica 19 Aug. 1700.
Alvares, Jacob. He was endenized in London 30 June 1725. He was a merchant from Nevis.
Alvares, Judith. She was naturalized in Jamaica 27 Jan. 1696. She was the wife of Jacob Alvares, merchant.
Alvares, Moses. He was naturalized in Jamaica 24 Feb. 1741/2. He was a Jew.
Alvarez, Abraham. He was naturalized in Jamaica 26 Nov. 1678.
Alvarez, David. He was naturalized in Jamaica 2 Oct. 1678.
Alvarez, Jacob. He was naturalized in Jamaica 26 Apr. 1688.
Alvarez, Jacob. He was naturalized in Nevis 14 Apr. 1725.
Alvarez, Moses. He was naturalized in Jamaica 23 Dec. 1717.
Alvarez, Rachell. She was naturalized in Jamaica 30 Nov. 1696. She was a widow.
Alvaringa, Abigaile DaCosta. She was naturalized in Jamaica 24 May 1700.
Alvaringa, Daniel DeCosta. He was declared to be naturalized in Jamaica 8 Apr. 1700. He was the son of Joseph DeCosta Alvaringa, merchant, deceased, and his wife Abigail, and was born at Port Royall. David Lopez Narbona, aged 70, and Moses Yezurum Cardosa, aged 43, swore that they recalled his birth and circumcision. Jacob Mendez Guterez, aged 80, was his godfather at his circumcision, and Leah Mendez Guterez, aged 65, also attested his birth. Ellinor Robellard, aged 45 and a Christian, also testified to his birth.
Alvaringa, Ester DaCosta. She was naturalized in Jamaica 23 Feb. 1742/3. She was a Jewess.
Alvaringa, Dr. Isaac DaCosta. He was naturalized in Jamaica 4 Aug. 1718.
Alvaringa, Joseph DaCosta. He was naturalized in Jamaica 28 June 1675.
Alvaringa, Rachel. She was naturalized in Jamaica 23 Feb. 1742/3. She was a Jewess.
Alvaringa, Rachel DaCosta. She was naturalized in Jamaica 23 Feb. 1742/3. She was a Jewess.
Alverson, Teleife. He was naturalized in Virginia ca. 1704. He also appeared as Teleife Alverton.
Alvin, Abraham Lopes. He was naturalized in Jamaica 18 Jan. 1694/5.
Alward, John. He was naturalized in Maryland 13 May 1682. He lived in Charles County.
Alwinkle, Hannah. She was naturalized in Jamaica 8 July 1690.
Ambrose, Abraham. He and his son, Abraham Ambrose, were naturalized in Maryland 18 Oct. 1694.
Ambrose, Jacob. He was naturalized in Maryland in Apr. 1749. He was from Frederick County.
Ambrose, Jacob. He was naturalized in Maryland 9 Sep. 1761.
Ambrose, Mateas. He was naturalized in Maryland 19 Oct. 1743.

Amend, John. He was naturalized in Pennsylvania 10 Sep. 1761. He was from York County.

Ament, Pieter. He was naturalized in New York 23 Aug. 1715. He was a cooper in New York City.

Amiel, John. He was naturalized in Rhode Island in June 1756 and took the oath on 10 June. He had been a resident of the colony for many years and had married an English wife.

Amirau, François. He was an Acadian and took the oath to George II in the winter of 1730 at Annapolis River, Nova Scotia.

Amirau, Joseph. He was an Acadian and took the oath to George II in the winter of 1730 at Annapolis River, Nova Scotia.

Amiraul, Jacques. He was an Acadian who took the oath of allegiance in Apr. 1730.

Amiraul, Pierre. He was an Acadian who took the oath of allegiance in Apr. 1730.

Amirault, Francois. He was an Acadian who took the oath at Annapolis River in Dec. 1729.

Amirault, Joseph. He was an Acadian who took the oath at Annapolis River in Dec. 1729.

Amma, Conrad. He was naturalized in Pennsylvania 10 Apr. 1760.

Amma, Daniel. He was naturalized in Pennsylvania 18 Nov. 1768. He was from Paradise Township, York County.

Ammerman, Dirck Janssen. He took the oath of allegiance in Kings County, New York 26–30 Sep. 1687. He was from Flackland.

Ammond, George. He was naturalized in Pennsylvania 11–12 Apr. 1744. He was from Lancaster County.

Amon, Jacco. He took the oath of allegiance at Mobile, West Florida 2 Oct. 1764.

Amonet, Jacob. He was naturalized in Virginia 12 May 1705.

Amstmeyer, George. He was naturalized in Pennsylvania 10 Apr. 1757.

Amweg, John Michael. He was naturalized in Pennsylvania 10 Apr. 1760.

Anckten, Peter. He was naturalized in New York 16 Feb. 1771.

Ancoin, Martin. He was an Acadian and took the oath to the King at the Mines, Pisiquit, Nova Scotia 31 Oct. 1727.

Ancoin, Martin. He was an Acadian and took the oath to the King at the Mines, Pisiquit, Nova Scotia 31 Oct. 1727.

Ancoin, Rene. He was an Acadian and took the oath to the King at the Mines, Pisiquit, Nova Scotia 31 Oct. 1727.

Andeas, Michael. He was naturalized in Pennsylvania 11 Apr. 1761. He was from Lancaster County.

Anders, Patron. He was naturalized in New York 17 Jan. 1715/6. He was from Albany County.

Anderson, Jacob. He was naturalized in Jamaica 30 Nov. 1762.

Anderson, John. He was naturalized in New York 24 Nov. 1750.

Anderson, Lasey. He was naturalized in Pennsylvania 11 Jan. 1683. He was formerly of New Sweden.

Anderson, Mounts. He was naturalized in Maryland 6 June 1674. He was Swedish.

Anderson, Robert. He was naturalized in Jamaica 5 Aug. 1681.

Anderson, Rowland. He was naturalized in Virginia in Oct. 1673.

Andre, Peter. He was naturalized in Maryland 11 Sep. 1705.

Andreas, Barnett. He was naturalized in Jamaica 28 Jan. 1677/8.

Andreas, Michael. He was naturalized in Pennsylvania 11 Apr. 1761. He was from Lancaster County.

Andrews, Abraham. He was naturalized in Pennsylvania 22 Apr. 1762. He was a Jewish shopkeeper in New York City.

Andrews, Anna. She was naturalized in Pennsylvania 11 Apr. 1763. She was from Towamensing Township, Philadelphia County.

Andrews, George. He was naturalized in Pennsylvania 10 Apr. 1755. He was from Philadelphia County.

Andrews, William. He was naturalized in Maryland 13 Apr. 1763. He was a German from Frederick County.

Andries, Jacobus. He was naturalized in New Castle County, Delaware 21 Feb. 1682/3.

Andries, Roelof. He was naturalized in New Castle County, Delaware 21 Feb. 1682/3.

Andriessen, Christiaen. He expressed his desire to be naturalized in New Castle County, Delaware 21 Feb. 1682/3.

Andriessen, Claes. He expressed his desire to be naturalized in New Castle County, Delaware 21 Feb. 1682/3.

Andriessen, Hendrick. He expressed his desire to be naturalized in New Castle County, Delaware 21 Feb. 1682/3.

Andriezen, Ariaan. He took the oath to the King 21–26 Oct. 1664 after the conquest of New Netherland.

Andriezen, Lucas. He took the oath to the King 21–26 Oct. 1664 after the conquest of New Netherland.

Andriezen, Paulus. He took the oath to the King 21–26 Oct. 1664 after the conquest of New Netherland.

Andrizen, Andries. He took the oath to the King 21–26 Oct. 1664 after the conquest of New Netherland.

Angell, Anthony. He was naturalized in Jamaica 23 May 1717. He was a mariner.

Angene, Devold. He was naturalized in Maryland 11 Sep. 1765.

Angle, Coenradt. He was naturalized in New York 3 May 1755.

Angle, Nicholas. He was naturalized in New Jersey 3 June 1763.

Angola, Francesco. He was naturalized in Jamaica 26 Sep. 1690. He was a "Spanish Negro."

Angola, Lewis. He was naturalized in Jamaica 26 Sep. 1690. He was a "Spanish Negro."

Angst, Hans Ulrick. He was naturalized in Pennsylvania 10–12 Apr. 1762. He was from Philadelphia County.

Angstat, George. He was naturalized in Pennsylvania 24 Sep. 1762. He was from Berks County.

Anleton, Peter. He was naturalized in Maryland 6 Nov. 1683. He also appeared as Peter Auesone and Peter Auelson.

Annsbach, Baltus. He was naturalized in New York 3 Jan. 1715/6. He was from Albany County.

Anschutz, Paul. He was naturalized in Nova Scotia 5 July 1758.

Anspachen, Magdalen. She was naturalized in Pennsylvania 26 Sep. 1748. She was from Bucks County and was the wife of Peter Anspachen.

Antes, Frederick. He was naturalized in Pennsylvania 24 Sep. 1742. He was from Philadelphia County.

Anthony, Abraham. He was naturalized in Jamaica 12 Mar. 1716/7.

Anthony, Allard. He took the oath to the King 21–26 Oct. 1664 after the conquest of New Netherland.

Anthony, Francis. He was naturalized in Jamaica 12 July 1764.

Anthony, Joseph. He was naturalized in New York 22 Apr. 1762. He was a French Protestant and a merchant in Westchester County.

Anthony, Nicolas. He took the oath of naturalization in New York 1 Sep 1687 in Ulster County.

Anthony, Paul. He was naturalized in Pennsylvania 25 Sep. 1752. He was from Philadelphia County.

Anthony, Allard. He was endenized in New York 16 Jan. 1664/5.

Antis, Henry. He was naturalized in Pennsylvania 6 Feb. 1730/1. He was from Philadelphia County.

Antonsi, Jacob. He was naturalized in New Jersey 28 Nov. 1760. He also appeared as Jacob Anthoni. He had been in the colony eleven years. He was born in Alsace. He lived in Hunterdon County.

Apell, Hendrick. He was endenized in New York 3 Sep. 1694.

Appel, Anton. He was naturalized in New York 20 Apr. 1769. He was a baker in New York City.

Appel, Catharina. She was naturalized in Maryland 7 May 1767. She was German and lived in Frederick County.

Appel, Hannes. He was naturalized in New York 11 Sep. 1761.

Appell, Arien. He took the oath to the King 21–26 Oct. 1664 after the conquest of New Netherland.

Appiar, John. He was naturalized in Jamaica 24 Feb. 1742/3. He was a free Negro.

Apple, Adam. He was naturalized in Pennsylvania 10 Sep. 1761. He was from Berks County.

Apple, Anthony. He was naturalized in New York 20 May 1769.

Apple, Christian. He was naturalized in Maryland 13 Apr. 1761.

Apple, John. He was naturalized in Pennsylvania 11 Apr. 1761. He was from Northampton County.

Apple, Martin. He was naturalized in Pennsylvania 11 Apr. 1761. He was from Northampton County.

Apple, Peter. He was naturalized in Maryland in Apr. 1749. He was from Frederick County.

Apple, Peter. He was naturalized in Maryland 14 Sep. 1763. He was a German.

Appleman, John. He was naturalized in Pennsylvania 11 Apr. 1761. He was from York County.

Appler, Adam. He was naturalized in New York 3 May 1755.

Arbegast, Christopher. He was naturalized in Maryland 9 Sep. 1772. He was a German.

Arbo, John. He was naturalized in Pennsylvania 24–29 Sep. 1768. He was from Bethlehem Township, Northampton County.

Arbocoast, Michael. He was naturalized in Augusta County, Virginia 22 Aug. 1770.

Archambeau, Timothy. He was endenized in England 31 Jan. 1689/90. He came to New York.

Archbold, Joanna Williamina. She was naturalized in Jamaica 7 Oct. 1695. She was the wife of Henry Archbold.

Ardell, Henry. He was naturalized in Pennsylvania 11 Apr. 1763. He was from Richmond Township, Berks County.

Ardnold, John George. He and his sons, John Ardnold, Daniel Ardnold, Samuel Ardnold, and Andrew Ardnold, were naturalized in Maryland 15 Jan. 1739. He was from Prince George's County and was born in Germany.

Arenberg, Friedrich. He was naturalized in Nova Scotia 5 July 1758.

Arenson, Cornelius. He was naturalized in Maryland 6 June 1674. He was Dutch.

Arent, Jacob. He was naturalized in Pennsylvania in Sep. 1740. He was from Philadelphia County.

Arents, Hartwyck. He was naturalized in New York 20 Mar. 1762.

Arents, Jacob. He and his children, Nicholas Arents, Mary Arents, and Margaret Arents, were naturalized in New Jersey 26 Jan. 1716/7. They were born in Germany.

Arenzen, Frederic. He took the oath to the King 21–26 Oct. 1664 after the conquest of New Netherland.

Arianzen, Jan. He took the oath to the King 21–26 Oct. 1664 after the conquest of New Netherland.

Armbrister, Christopher. He was naturalized in New York 3 May 1755.

Armbrister, Johan Christopher. He was naturalized in New York 11 Sep. 1761. He was an inn holder in New York City.

Armon, Philip. He took the oath of allegiance at Mobile, West Florida 2 Oct. 1764.

Arnald, Jacque[s]. He took the oath of allegiance at Mobile, West Florida 2 Oct. 1764.

Arnault, John. He was naturalized in Massachusetts 18 Aug. 1732. He was a furrier from Boston.

Arnest, Jacob. He was naturalized in Lunenburg County, Virginia 7 July 1752.

Arnt, Henry. He was naturalized in Pennsylvania 24 Sep. 1760. He was from Philadelphia County.

Arnoldi, John. He was naturalized in New York 20 Mar. 1715/6. He was a physician in New York City.

Arrets, Lenartt. He was naturalized in Pennsylvania 29 Sep. 1709. He was from Philadelphia County.

Arreyn, Hendrick. He took the oath of naturalization in New York 1 Sep. 1687 in Ulster County.

Arsenaux, Alexandre. He took the oath of allegiance at Harbour Amhurst in the Magdalines, Gulf of Saint Lawrence on 31 Aug. 1765. He was a native of Nova Scotia.

Arsenoe, Abraham, Jr. He was an Acadian who took the oath of allegiance in Apr. 1730.

Arsenoe, Augustin. He was an Acadian who took the oath of allegiance in Apr. 1730.

Arsenoe, Charles. He was an Acadian who took the oath of allegiance in Apr. 1730.

Arsenoe, Francois. He was an Acadian who took the oath of allegiance in Apr. 1730.

Arsenoe, Pierre. He was an Acadian who took the oath of allegiance in Apr. 1730.

Arsenoe, Pierre. He was an Acadian who took the oath of allegiance in Apr. 1730.

Arsin, Gerritt. He took the oath of naturalization in New York 1 Sep. 1687 in Ulster County.

Arsin, Jacob. He took the oath of naturalization in New York 1 Sep. 1687 in Ulster County.

Arsneaux, Claud. He took the oath of allegiance at Harbour Amhurst in the Magdalen Islands, Gulf of Saint Lawrence on 31 Aug. 1765. He was a native of Nova Scotia.

Arsneaux, Cyprien. He took the oath of allegiance at Harbour Amhurst in the Magdalen Islands, Gulf of Saint Lawrence on 31 Aug. 1765. He was a native of Nova Scotia.

Arsneaux, Francois. He took the oath of allegiance at Harbour Amhurst in the Magdalen Islands, Gulf of Saint Lawrence on 31 Aug. 1765. He was a native of Nova Scotia.

Arsneaux, Joseph. He took the oath of allegiance at Harbour Amhurst in the Magdalen Islands, Gulf of Saint Lawrence on 31 Aug. 1765. He was a native of Nova Scotia.

Arsneaux, Joseph. He took the oath of allegiance at Harbour Amhurst in the Magdalen Islands, Gulf of Saint Lawrence on 21 Aug. 1765. He was a native of Nova Scotia.

Arsneaux, Jacque. He took the oath of allegiance at Harbour Amhurst in the Magdalen Islands, Gulf of Saint Lawrence on 31 Aug. 1765. He was a native of Nova Scotia.

Arsneaux, Jean. He took the oath of allegiance at Harbour Amhurst in the Magdalen Islands, Gulf of Saint Lawrence on 31 Aug. 1765. He was a native of Nova Scotia.

Arsneaux, Joseph. He took the oath of allegiance at Harbour Amhurst in the Magdalen Islands, Gulf of Saint Lawrence on 31 Aug. 1765. He was a native of Nova Scotia.

Arsneaux, Paul. He took the oath of allegiance at Harbour Amhurst in the Magdalen Islands, Gulf of Saint Lawrence on 31 Aug. 1765. He was a native of Nova Scotia.

Arsneaux, Pierre. He took the oath of allegiance at Harbour Amhurst in the Magdalen Islands, Gulf of Saint Lawrence on 31 Aug. 1765. He was a native of Nova Scotia.

Arthur, Michael. He was naturalized in Maryland 10 Apr. 1765. He was a German from Baltimore County.

Artz, Jacob. He was naturalized in Pennsylvania 24 Sep. 1762. He was from Berks County.

Artz, John. He was naturalized in Pennsylvania 10–12 Apr. 1762. He was from Berks County.

Arwogaust, Jacob. He was naturalized in Pennsylvania in Sep. 1740. He was from Bucks County.

Asby, Rudolph. He was naturalized in Maryland 30 Sep. 1762. He was a German from Frederick County.

Ascen, Jan. He took the oath to the King 21–26 Oct. 1664 after the conquest of New Netherland.

Ash, Henry. He was naturalized in Maryland 11 Sep. 1765.

Ash, Peter. He was naturalized in Pennsylvania 11–13 Apr. 1743. He was from Chester County.

Ash, William. He was naturalized in New York 3 July 1759.

Asher, Adam. He was naturalized in New York 3 May 1755.

Ashers, Sim. He was naturalized in Jamaica 8 Oct. 1706.

Ashleman, Daniel. He was naturalized in Pennsylvania 14 Feb. 1729/30. He was from Lancaster County.

Ashlir, John. He was naturalized in North Carolina 13 Sep. 1770. He was from Rowan County.

Ashman, Abraham. He was naturalized in Pennsylvania 11–13 Apr. 1743. He was from Philadelphia County.

Assuerus, Hendrick. He took the oath to the King 21–26 Oct. 1664 after the conquest of New Netherland.

Assum, Peter. He was naturalized in Pennsylvania 10 Sep. 1761. He was from Lancaster County.

Atchey, Herman. He was naturalized in Pennsylvania 10–12 Apr. 1762. He was from Philadelphia County.

Athias, Jacob Franco. He was naturalized in Jamaica 4 May 1691.

Auboyneau, John. He was naturalized in New York in 1740–41.

Aubry, Andrew. He was naturalized in Virginia 12 May 1705.

Auch, Georg. He was naturalized in New York 3 July 1759.

Aucoin, Joseph. He was an Acadian who took the oath of allegiance 31 Oct. 1727.

Aucoin, Martin. He was an Acadian who took the oath of allegiance 31 Oct. 1727.

Aucoin, Martin. He was an Acadian who took the oath of allegiance 31 Oct. 1727.

Aucoin, Rene. He was an Acadian who took the oath of allegiance 31 Oct. 1727.

Audier, Moise. He was naturalized in New York 6 Dec. 1746.

Augier, John. He was naturalized in Jamaica 5 Sep. 1693.

Aukenbrand, Christopher. He was naturalized in Pennsylvania in Sep. 1740. He was from Philadelphia County.

Aulenbacker, Andrew. He was naturalized in Pennsylvania 24 Sep. 1762. He was from Berks County.

Aunaut, Jean. He was born at Nisme, France, the son of Jean Aunaut and Sibelle Dumas. His wife was Marie Soyer, a native of Diepe, Normandie, France. They were naturalized in South Carolina 10 Mar. 1696/7. He was a silk throwster. He also appeared as Jean Aunant.

Aupvin, Isaac Zacharias. He was endenized in New York 12 Dec. 1685.

Avary, Ephraim. He was naturalized in Jamaica 14 Mar. 1691.

Avary, Joseph. He was naturalized in Jamaica 14 Mar. 1683.

Avey, Henry. He was naturalized in Maryland 20 Oct. 1747.

Avila, —. He was naturalized in South Carolina 10 Mar. 1696/7. He was a merchant.

Awlem, Jacob. He was naturalized in Pennsylvania 10 Apr. 1765. He was from Haycock Township, Bucks County.

Ax, John Frederick. He was naturalized in Pennsylvania 14 Feb. 1729/30. He was from Philadelphia.

Axer, Michael. He was naturalized in Pennsylvania 25–26 Sep./4 Oct. 1749. He was from Lancaster County.

Axon, Elizabeth. She was naturalized in New York 18 Oct. 1750. She was a widow from New York City.

Aybe, John. He was naturalized in Pennsylvania 14 Feb. 1729/30. He was from Lancaster County.

Aybe, Peter. He was naturalized in Pennsylvania 14 Feb. 1729/30. He was from Lancaster County.

Ayler, Gertrude. She was naturalized in Jamaica 7 Oct. 1720.

Ayrault, Daniel. He was naturalized in Rhode Island 3 July 1701. He was from East Greenwich and was a French Protestant.

Ayrer, Frederick. He was naturalized in New York 8 Mar. 1773.

Azamarin, Juliet de Brose. She took the oath of allegiance at Mobile, West Florida 2 Oct. 1764.

Azeuedo, Abraham. He was naturalized in Jamaica 29 Dec. 1696.

Baal, Johan Peter. He was naturalized in New York 13 Mar. 1715/6. He was from Albany County.

Baam, Philip. He was naturalized in New York 11 Sep. 1761.

Bab, Conrad. He was naturalized in Pennsylvania 10 Sep. 1761. He was from Berks County.

Babin, Charles. He was an Acadian and took the oath to the King at the Mines, Pisiquit, Nova Scotia 31 Oct. 1727.

Babin, Charles. He was an Acadian who took the oath of allegiance in Apr. 1730.

Babin, Charles. He was an Acadian who took the oath of allegiance in Apr. 1730.

Babin, Claude. He was an Acadian and took the oath to the King at the Mines, Pisiquit, Nova Scotia 31 Oct. 1727.

Babin, Claude. He was an Acadian who took the oath of allegiance in Apr. 1730.

Babin, Francois. He was an Acadian who took the oath of allegiance in Apr. 1730.

Babin, Jermain. He was an Acadian who took the oath of allegiance in Apr. 1730.

Babin, Jean. He was an Acadian and took the oath to the King at the Mines, Pisiquit, Nova Scotia 32 Oct. 1727.

Babin, Jean [second of the name]. He was an Acadian and took the oath to the King at the Mines, Pisiquit, Nova Scotia 31 Oct. 1727.

Babin, Jean [third of the name]. He was an Acadian and took the oath to the King at the Mines, Pisiquit, Nova Scotia 31 Oct. 1727.

Babin, Jean. He was an Acadian who took the oath of allegiance in Apr. 1730.

Babin, Jean. He was an Acadian who took the oath of allegiance in Apr. 1730.

Babin, Jean, Jr. He was an Acadian who took the oath of allegiance in Apr. 1730.

Babin, Joseph. He was an Acadian and took the oath to the King at the Mines, Pisiquit, Nova Scotia 31 Oct. 1727.

Babin, Joseph. He was an Acadian who took the oath of allegiance in Apr. 1730.

Babin, Joseph. He was an Acadian who took the oath of allegiance in Apr. 1730.

Babin, Paul. He was an Acadian who took the oath of allegiance in Apr. 1730.

Babin, Pierre. He was an Acadian and took the oath to the King at the Mines, Pisiquit, Nova Scotia 31 Oct. 1727.

Babin, Pierre. He was an Acadian and took the oath to the King at the Mines, Pisiquit, Nova Scotia 31 Oct. 1727.

Babin, Pierre. He was an Acadian who took the oath of allegiance in Apr. 1730.

Babin, Pierre. He was an Acadian who took the oath of allegiance in Apr. 1730.

Babin, Rene. He was an Acadian who took the oath of allegiance in Apr. 1730.

Babin, Rene. He was an Acadian who took the oath of allegiance in Apr. 1730.

Babin, Vincent. He was an Acadian and took the oath to the King at the Mines, Pisiquit, Nova Scotia 31 Oct. 1727.

Babin, Vincent. He was an Acadian and took the oath of allegiance in Apr. 1730.

Babinot, Jean. He took the oath of allegiance at Port Royal, Nova Scotia 16 Aug. 1695.

Babinot, Jean. He was an Acadian who took the oath of allegiance in Apr. 1730.

Babinot, Clement. He was an Acadian and took the oath to George II at Annapolis River, Nova Scotia in Dec. 1729. He also appeared as Clement Babineau.

Bach, Adam. He was naturalized in Pennsylvania 10 Apr. 1767. He was from Lebanon Township, Lancaster County.

Bach, Jacob. He was naturalized in Pennsylvania 11–13 Apr. 1743. He was from Chester County.

Bacher, Theobald. He was naturalized in New York 8 Mar. 1773.

Bachman, Felix. He was naturalized in Pennsylvania 24 Sep. 1762. He was from Lancaster County.

Bachman, George. He was naturalized in Pennsylvania in 1730–31. He was from Bucks County.

Bachus, Johan Ernst. He was naturalized in New York 8–9 Sep. 1715. He was from Ulster County.

Bachus, Johanis. He was naturalized in New York 8–9 Sep. 1715. He was from Ulster County.

Back, Balthasar. He was naturalized in Maryland 16 Apr. 1760. He lived in Frederick, Maryland.

Backenstoose, John. He was naturalized in Pennsylvania 10–12 Apr. 1762. He was from Lancaster County.

Backer, Claes Janssen. He took the oath to the King 21–26 Oct. 1664 after the conquest of New Netherland.

Backer, Jacob. He took the oath to the King 21–26 Oct. 1664 after the conquest of New Netherland.

Backer, Peter. He was naturalized in Pennsylvania 20 Apr. 1753. He was from Philadelphia County.

Backer, Reinier Willemzen. He took the oath to the King 21–26 Oct. 1664 after the conquest of New Netherland.

Backle, Frederick. He was naturalized in Pennsylvania 10 Sep. 1761. He was from Northampton County.

Backus, John. He was naturalized in New York 3 May 1755.

Bacot, Pierre. He was born in Tours, France, the son of Pierre Bacot and Jeanne Moreau. His wife was Jacquine Mercier, daughter of Alexander Mercier and Jacquine Selipeaux. Their children were Pierre Bacot, Daniel Bacot, and Elizabeth Bacot. Their sons were born in Tours, France, and their daughter was born in South Carolina. They were naturalized in South Carolina ca. 1696.

Badhauer, Andrew. He was naturalized in Maryland 7 May 1767. He was a German from Frederick County.

Badheimer, William. He was naturalized in Maryland 1 Oct. 1767. He was a German.

Badon, Joseph. He took the oath of allegiance at Mobile, West Florida 2 Oct. 1764.

Bagenpok, Casper. He was naturalized in Maryland 10 Apr. 1760. He lived in Frederick County.

Bagentoss, Ulrick. He was naturalized in Pennsylvania 11 Apr. 1761. He was from Berks County.

Bager, Rev. George. He was naturalized in Maryland 10 Sep. 1762.

Bags, George. He was naturalized in Maryland 16 Sep. 1762. He was a German from Frederick County.

Baham, Jean. He took the oath of allegiance at Mobile, West Florida 2 Oct. 1764.

Baillergeau, Jacob. He was born at Loudun, Tourene, France, the son of Jacob and Margueritt Baillergeau. He was endenized in England 5 Apr. 1700. He came to New York.

Bailer, Michael. He was naturalized in New Jersey in 1750.

Baillie, Dorcas. She was naturalized in Jamaica 28 Nov. 1738.

Bailliet, Paul. He was naturalized in Pennsylvania 10 Apr. 1759.

Bailly, George Frederick. He was naturalized in Nova Scotia 1 Apr. 1761. He was a French schoolmaster.

Baish, George Frederick. He was naturalized in Pennsylvania 11 Apr. 1761. He was from Lancaster County.

Bake, Philip. He was naturalized in Pennsylvania 10 Sep. 1761. He was from Lancaster County.

Baker, Ambroos. He was naturalized in Delaware 21 Feb. 1682/3. He was from New Castle County.

Baker, Frederick. He was naturalized in Pennsylvania 11–13 Apr. 1743. He was from Philadelphia County.

Baker, Frederick. He was naturalized in Pennsylvania 25 Sep. 1752. He was from Philadelphia.

Baker, Henry. He was naturalized in Jamaica 17 Aug. 1714.

Baker, Henry. He was naturalized in Frederick County, Virginia 4 Sep. 1765.

Baker, Henry. He was naturalized in Pennsylvania 10 Sep. 1761. He was from Philadelphia County.

Baker, Henry. He was naturalized in Maryland 4 May 1774. He was a German.

Baker, Johan. He was naturalized in Pennsylvania 6 Feb. 1730/1. He was from Philadelphia.

Baker, John. He was naturalized in New Jersey 20 Aug. 1755.

Baker, John. He was naturalized in Pennsylvania 23–24 November 1773. He was from Lancaster County.

Baker, John. He was naturalized in Pennsylvania 11 Apr. 1763. He was from Plymouth Township, Lancaster County.

Baker, John Philip. He was naturalized in Pennsylvania 24 Sep. 1762. He was from Lancaster County.

Baker, Peter. He was endenzied in Maryland 16 Aug. 1773. He was born in Germany.

Baker, Peter. He was naturalized in Pennsylvania 25–26 Sep./4 Oct. 1749. He was from Lancaster County.

Baker, Valentine. He was naturalized in Pennsylvania 11–13 Apr. 1743. He was from Lancaster County.

Baker, William. He was naturalized in Pennsylvania 10 Apr. 1755. He was from Philadelphia.

Balchemire, Henry. He was naturalized in Maryland 13 Apr. 1761.

Balck, Jacob. He petitioned to be endenized in New York 21 Mar. 1702.

Baldt, Jacob. He was naturalized in Pennsylvania 11–13 Apr. 1743. He was from Philadelphia County.

Baldt, Johannes. He was naturalized in Pennsylvania 11–13 Apr. 1743. He was from Philadelphia County.

Bale, Vincent. He took the oath of allegiance 26–30 Sep. 1687 in Kings County, New York. He was from Boswijck.

Balio, Peter. He was naturalized in Pennsylvania 6 Feb. 1730/1. He was from Philadelphia County.

Ballareaux, Jean. She was naturalized in New York 17 June 1726.

Balmir, George Michael. He was naturalized in Pennsylvania 24 Sep. 1762. He was from Lancaster County.

Balsbach, Peter. He was naturalized in Pennsylvania 24 Sep. 1741. He was from Lancaster County.

Bamberger, Arnold. He was naturalized in Pennsylvania 5 Mar. 1725/26. He was born in Germany.

Bamper, Lodwyck. He was naturalized in New York 24 Nov. 1750.

Bamper, Margaret. She was naturalized in New York 24 Nov. 1750.

Bancker, Jacob. He was naturalized in Maryland 10 Sep. 1760.

Bander, Peter. He was naturalized in Maryland 15 Sep. 1762. He was from Frederick County.

Bander, Leonard. He was naturalized in Maryland 11 Sep. 1765. He was a German from Frederick County.

Baner, Adam. He was naturalized in Maryland 11 May 1774. He was a German.

Baney, Jacob. He was naturalized in Maryland 10 Sep. 1761.

Bangel, Adam. He was naturalized in New York 31 Dec. 1768.

Bapp, Conrad. He was naturalized in Pennsylvania 10 Apr. 1757.

Baptiste, Jean. He was an Acadian and took the oath to the King at the Mines, Pisiquit 31 Oct. 1727.

Baptiste, John. He was naturalized in Jamaica 27 July 1714. He was a free Negro.

Barailleau, Peter. He was naturalized in London in 1699. It was recorded in Jamaica 8 Apr. 1699. He was born at Montague, Poitou, France, the son of Henry Barailleau and his wife Frances.

Barand, Lazare. He was endenized in New York 22 Oct. 1697.

Barandon, Rachell. She was naturalized in Jamaica 15 Jan. 1710/11.

Barba, Francois. He took the oath of allegiance at Mobile, West Florida 2 Oct. 1764.

Barbarie, John. He and his sons, John Peter Barbarie and Peter Barbarie, were endenized in London 16 Dec. 1687. They came to New York.

Barbauld, Ezekiel. He was endenized in England in 1709. He came to New York.

Barbery, Thomas. He was made a denizen in Maryland 12 Oct. 1666. He was Portuguese.

Barbould, Ezekiel. He was naturalized in Jamaica 22 Sep.1713.

Barbut, William. He was admitted into the colony of Massachusetts 1 Feb. 1691. He was French. He was naturalized in England 31 Jan. 1690.

Bard, Henry. He was naturalized in Pennsylvania 25–27 Sep. 1740. He was from Philadelphia County.

Bard, Peter. He was naturalized in Pennsylvania 3 Oct. 1704. He was born at St. Paul, Trois Chateau, France, the son of Bennett Bard. He was a Protestant.

Bard, Peter. He was naturalized in New Jersey 11 Mar. 1713/4. He was a native of France.

Bare, Bernard. He was naturalized in Pennsylvania 11 Apr. 1761. He was from Northampton County.

Bare, Henry. He was naturalized in Pennsylvania 14 Feb. 1729/30. He was from Lancaster County.

Bare, Jacob. He was naturalized in Pennsylvania 24–25 Sep. 1764. He was from Philadelphia.

Bare, Jacob, Jr. He was naturalized in Pennsylvania 14 Feb. 1729/30. He was from Lancaster County.

Bare, Jacob, Jr. He was naturalized in Pennsylvania 19 May 1739. He was from Lancaster County.

Bare, John Henry. He was naturalized in Pennsylvania 14 Feb. 1729/30. He was from Lancaster County.

Bared, Anthony DaCosta. He was naturalized in Jamaica 25 Feb. 1746/7.

Barens, Joseph. He was naturalized in New Castle County, Delaware 21 Feb. 1682/3.

Barense, Jan. He took the oath of allegiance in Gravens End, Kings County, New York 26–30 Sep. 1687. He had been in the colony 30 years. He was from Zutphen.

Barent, Hannes. He was naturalized in New York 11 Sep. 1761.

Barentsen, John. He was naturalized in New Castle County, Delaware 21 Feb. 1682/3.

Barentzen, Cornelius van der Kuyl. He took the oath to the King 21–26 Oct. 1664 after the conquest of New Netherland.

Barentzen, Simon. He took the oath to the King 21–26 Oct. 1664 after the conquest of New Netherland.

Bares, Solomon. He was naturalized in New York in 1740–41. He was a Jew.

Barge, George. He was naturalized in Pennsylvania 25 May 1770. He was from Philadelphia.

Barge, Jacob. He was naturalized in Pennsylvania 10 Apr. 1760.

Barge, Jean. He petitioned to be endenized in New York 28 Sep. 1695.

Barier, John. He took the oath of allegiance in Orange County, New York 26 Sep. 1687.

Bario, Antoine. He was an Acadian and took the oath to the King at the Mines, Pisiquit 31 Oct. 1727.

Barlet, Frederick. He was naturalized in Pennsylvania 10 Sep. 1761. He was from Berks County.

Barnard, Francois. He took the oath of allegiance at Mobile, West Florida 2 Oct. 1764.

Barner, Hans Jury. He was naturalized in New York 13 Mar. 1715/6. He was from Albany County.

Barnerd, John. He was naturalized in Pennsylvania 24 Sep. 1754. He was from Philadelphia County.

Barnes, Conradt. He was naturalized in New York 19 Oct. 1763. He was a hatter from New York City.

Barnets, Daniel. He was naturalized in Maryland 26 Apr. 1750.

Baron, Anthony. He was naturalized in New York 24 Mar. 1772.

Barr, Christopher. He was naturalized in Pennsylvania 11 Apr. 1761. He was from Northampton County.

Barr, George. He was naturalized in Maryland 22 June 1760.

Barr, George. He was naturalized in Maryland 17 Apr. 1761.

Barr, Jeremiah. He was naturalized in Pennsylvania 10 Sep. 1761. He was from Berks County.

Barr, John. He was naturalized in Pennsylvania 24 Sep. 1753. He was from Lancaster County.

Barr, Melchior. He was naturalized in Pennsylvania 11 Apr. 1763. He was from Northampton County.

Barral, Esprit. He was naturalized in Jamaica 19 May 1768.

Barre, Charles. He was naturalized in Jamaica 4 June 1680.

Barreau, Lazare. He petitioned for denization in New York 14 Oct. 1697. He was a French Protestant.

Barreau, Nicholas. He was endenized in New York 12 Oct. 1688.

Barrenzen, Meindert. He took the oath to the King 21–26 Oct. 1664 after the conquest of New Netherland.

Barriere, Anthony. He was endenized in Maryland 26 Apr. 1768. He was born in France.

Barringer, Conraed. He was naturalized in New York 17 Jan. 1715/6. He was from Albany County.

Barringer, David. He was naturalized in Pennsylvania 10 Apr. 1755. He was from Northampton County.

Barrios, Daniel Lopes. He was naturalized in Jamaica Feb. 1748/9. He was a Jew.

Barrios, Jacob Levi. He was naturalized in Jamaica 9 June 1708.

Barriot, Jacques. He was an Acadian who took the oath of allegiance in Apr. 1730.

Barrow, Moses. He was naturalized in Jamaica 30 Jan. 1699/1700.

Barrs, Derrick. He was naturalized in Jamaica 30 Apr. 1700.

Bartel, Andries. He was naturalized in New York 22 Nov. 1715. He was from Albany County.

Bartel, Philip. He was naturalized in New York 22 Nov. 1715. He was from Albany County.

Bartells, Senwes. He and his son, Henry Bartells, were naturalized in Pennsylvania 29 Sep. 1709. They were from Philadelphia County.

Bartelzen, Jonas. He took the oath to the King 21–26 Oct. 1664 after the conquest of New Netherland.

Barth, Peter. He was naturalized in Maryland 15 Apr. 1761.

Barth, Zachary. He was naturalized in Pennsylvania 10 Apr. 1765. He was from Lampeter Township, Lancaster County.

Bartholomew, George. He was naturalized in New York 8 Mar. 1773.

Bartholomew, John. He was naturalized in New York 16 Feb. 1771.

Bartholomew, John. He was naturalized in Pennsylvania 25–27 Sep. 1740. He was from Philadelphia County.

Bartholomew, Manuall. He was naturalized in Jamaica 11 Sep. 1704.

Bartholomey, Juanico. He was naturalized in Jamaica 12 Oct.1731.

Bartlet, John, Jr. He was naturalized in Pennsylvania 11–13 Apr. 1743. He was from Philadelphia County.

Bartolet, Abraham. He was naturalized in Pennsylvania 11–13 Apr. 1743. He was from Philadelphia County.

Bartolett, Jean. He was naturalized in Pennsylvania in 1730–31. He was from Philadelphia County.

Baruk, Isaque Moses. He sought to be made a denizen 30 Aug. 1692. He was from Jamaica.

Barwick, William. He was naturalized in New Jersey 21 Oct. 1754.

Basbon, George. He was naturalized in Pennsylvania 24 Sep. 1762. He was from Philadelphia County.

Basdrau, John Baptist. He took the oath of allegiance at Mobile, West Florida 2 Oct. 1764.

Basque, François. He was an Acadian and took the oath to George II at Annapolis River, Nova Scotia in Dec. 1729.

Basseler, Henry. He was naturalized in Pennsylvania 19 May 1739. He was from Lancaster County.

Basseler, John Henry. He was naturalized in Pennsylvania 19 May 1739. He was from Lancaster County.

Basset, Doctor —. He was admitted into the colony of Massachusetts 1 Feb. 1691. He was French.

Bassett, Francis. He, his wife Mary Magdalen Bassett, and his daughters, Susanna Magdalen Bassett and Susanna Bassett, were naturalized in England 25 Apr. 1693. They were born beyond the seas. They had their naturalization recorded in New York City 23 Sep. 1693 and in Pennsylvania in 1698.

Bassinger, Charles. He was naturalized in North Carolina 22 Mar. 1764. He was from Rowan County and a German.

Bast, Hendrick. He was naturalized in New Jersey 8 July 1730. He was born in Germany.

Bast, John. He was naturalized in Pennsylvania 10–12 Apr. 1762. He was from Berks County.

Bast, Joseph. He was naturalized in New Jersey 8 July 1730. He was born in Germany.

Bast, Lawrence. He was naturalized in Pennsylvania 11–13 Apr. 1743. He was from Philadelphia County.

Bast, Valentine. He was naturalized in Maryland 15 Sep. 1762. He was from Frederick County.

Bastarache, Jean. He was an Acadian and took the oath to George II at Annapolis River, Nova Scotia in Dec. 1729.

Bastarache, John. He took the oath of allegiance at Port Royal, Nova Scotia 16 Aug. 1695.

Bastarache, Pierre. He was an Acadian and took the oath to George II at Annapolis River, Nova Scotia in Dec. 1729.

Basteon, Andrew. He was naturalized in Maryland 13 Apr. 1763. He was a German from Frederick County.

Bastian, Matthias. He was naturalized in Pennsylvania 10 Apr. 1765. He was from Hereford Township, Berks County.

Bastiank, Hans Jacob. He was naturalized in New York 11 Sep. 1761.

Bastianse, Johannis. He was naturalized in New York 11 Sep. 1761.

Bastian, Christopher. He was naturalized in Pennsylvania 11–13 Apr. 1743. He was from Philadelphia County.

Baton, Isaac. He was born at Leschelle, Picardie, France, the son of Corneille Baton and Judith Voyenne. He was naturalized in South Carolina 10 Mar. 1696/7. His wife, Marie DeLome, a native of Vadenouste, France, was deceased. He was a weaver.

Baton, Isaac. He was born in London, England. He was the son of Isaac Baton and Marie DeLorme. He was naturalized in South Carolina 10 Mar. 1696/7. He was also reported to have been born in South Carolina.

Baton, Jacques. He was born in London, England. He was the son of Isaac Baton and Marie DeLorme. He was naturalized in South Carolina ca. 1696.

Battar, Ignatius. He was naturalized in Rhode Island in May 1756. He had lived in New London, Connecticut for six years and for some time in Newport. [His name is incorrectly given as Nicholas Battar in some printed accounts.]

Battorff, Martin. He was naturalized in Pennsylvania 10 Sep. 1761. He was from Lancaster County.

Bauccus, William. He was naturalized in Pennsylvania 24–25 Sep. 1764. He was from Northern Liberties Township, Philadelphia County.

Bauer, Casper. He was naturalized in New York 11 Sep. 1761.

Bauer, Diel. He was naturalized in Pennsylvania 10 Apr. 1760.

Baulden, Elizabeth. She was naturalized in Jamaica 30 Apr. 1731.

Baulus, Andreas. He was naturalized in Maryland 14 Apr. 1762. He was a German from Frederick County.

Baulus, Nicholas. He was naturalized in Maryland 7 May 1767. He was a German from Frederick County.

Baum, George Peter. He was naturalized in Maryland 31 Aug. 1757.

Baum, George Peter. He was naturalized in Maryland 9 Sep. 1761.

Baum, George Simon. He was naturalized in Maryland 11 Apr. 1759.

Baum, Henry. He was naturalized in Pennsylvania 24 Sep. 1762. He was from York County.

Baum, Simon. He was naturalized in Maryland 31 Aug. 1757.

Bauman, Johan Ditterig. He was naturalized in Pennsylvania 19 May 1739. He was from Philadelphia County.

Bauman, William. He was naturalized in Pennsylvania 10 Apr. 1758.

Baumgartner, Valentine. He was naturalized in Pennsylvania 10–12 Apr. 1762. He was from Berks County.

Baumgertel, Erhard. He was naturalized in Maryland 1 Oct. 1767. He was a German from Frederick County.

Bausley, Peter. He was naturalized in New York 3 July 1759.

Bauyesen, Christopher. He was naturalized in New Jersey 28 Nov. 1760.

Bawn, Theowald. He was naturalized in Pennsylvania 11 Apr. 1741. He was from Philadelphia County.

Bayard, Nicholas. He took the oath to the King 21–26 Oct. 1664 after the conquest of New Netherland.

Bayard, Peter. He was naturalized in Maryland 26 Apr. 1684.

Bayard, Peter. He expressed his desire to be naturalized in New Castle County, Delaware 21 Feb. 1682/3.

Bayer, George. He was naturalized in Nova Scotia on 4 July 1758.

Bayer, Jacob. He was naturalized in Maryland 16 Apr. 1761.

Bayer, Jacob. He was naturalized in New York 17 Jan. 1715/6. He was from Albany County.

Bayer, Martin. He was naturalized in Pennsylvania 11 Apr. 1761. He was from Berks County.

Bayer, Melchoir. He was naturalized in Maryland 10 Sep. 1760.

Bayeux, Thomas. He was naturalized in New York 6 Mar. 1715/6. He was a merchant in New York City.

Beagler, Michael. He was naturalized in Pennsylvania 29–30 May 1772. He was from Codorus Township, York County.

Beaker, John. He was naturalized in New York 16 Jan. 1771. He was a baker in New York City.

Beakman, Gerraradus. He took the oath of allegiance in Flackbush, Kings County, New York 26–30 Sep. 1687. He was a native of the colony.

Beakman, William. He took the oath to the King 21–26 Oct. 1664 after the conquest of New Netherland. He was from Esopies.

Beal, John. He was naturalized in Maryland 15 Apr. 1772. He was a German.

Beam, Conradt. He was naturalized in Pennsylvania 24 Sep. 1755. He was from Berks County.

Beam, Gorg. He was naturalized in New York 8–9 Sep. 1715. He was from Ulster County.

Beam, Johan Albert. He was naturalized in New York 8–9 Sep. 1715. He was from Ulster County.

Beam, Michael. He was naturalized in North Carolina in Sep. 1767. He was from Rowan County and a German. His name has also been interpreted as Michael Buin.

Beam, Peter. He was naturalized in North Carolina in Sep. 1767. He was from Rowan County and a German.

Beam, Peter. He was naturalized in North Carolina 22 Sep. 1767. He was born in Germany.

Bear, John George. He and his son, John Bear, were naturalized in Maryland 3 May 1740. He was from Prince George's County and was born in Germany.

Bear, John. He was naturalized in Pennsylvania 12 Apr. 1750. He was from Chester County.

Bear, Henry. He was naturalized in Augusta Co., Va. 21 Aug. 1770.

Bear, Jurry. He was naturalized in New York 24 Mar. 1772.

Beard, John George. He was naturalized in Pennsylvania 29 Mar. 1735. He was from Lancaster County.

Beard, John Lewis. He was naturalized in Rowan County, North Carolina 15 July 1755.

Beard, Michael. He was naturalized in Pennsylvania 10 Apr. 1765. He was from Providence Township, Philadelphia County.

Beas, Michel. He was naturalized in New Jersey in 1759.

Beau, Anthoine. He was an Acadian who took the oath of allegiance in Apr. 1730.

Beau, Daniel. He was naturalized in New York 16 Aug. 1715. He was a mariner from New York City.

Beaudouin, Jeremiah. He was naturalized in New York 17 Jan. 1754. He was a staymaker in New York City and a French Protestant.

Beaver, John. He was endenized in Maryland 12 Feb. 1773. He was born in Germany.

Beaver, Matthias. He was naturalized in North Carolina 11 Oct. 1754. He was from Rowan County.

Beber, Dewald. He was naturalized in Pennsylvania 11 Apr. 1761. He was from Berks County.

Beber, John. He was naturalized in Pennsylvania 11 Apr. 1761. He was from Berks County.

Bebinger, Killian. He was naturalized in Pennsylvania 10 & 23 Apr. 1764. He was from Roseborough Township, York County.

Becclesheimer, John. He was naturalized in New Jersey 20 Aug. 1755.

Bechtel, Jacob. He was naturalized in Pennsylvania 24 Sep. 1762. He was from Berks County.

Bechtel, Martin. He was naturalized in Pennsylvania 12 Apr. 1750. He was from Philadelphia County.

Bechtley, George. He was naturalized in Pennsylvania 6 Feb. 1730/1.

Bechtley, Hans Jacob. He was naturalized in Pennsylvania in 1730–31. He was from Philadelphia County.

Bechtoe, Philip. He was naturalized in Pennsylvania 24 Sep. 1762. He was from Lancaster County.

Beck, Andrew. He was naturalized in Maryland 11 May 1774. He was a German.

Beck, Christian. He was naturalized in New Jersey 20 Aug. 1755.

Beck, Daniel. He was naturalized in Jamaica 16 Jan. 1701/2.

Beck, George. He was naturalized in New Jersey 10 Mar. 1762.

Beck, George. He was naturalized in Pennsylvania in Sep. 1740. He was from Philadelphia County.

Beck, George. He was naturalized in Pennsylvania 11 Apr. 1761. He was from York County.

Beck, Jacob. He was naturalized in New Jersey in 1762.

Beck, Jacob. He was naturalized in Pennsylvania 24–25 Sep. 1764. He was from Cocalico Township, Lancaster County.

Beck, John. He was naturalized in Pennsylvania 10 Apr. 1765. He was from Brecknock Township, Lancaster County.

Beck, John. He was naturalized in Pennsylvania 24–25 Sep. 1764. He was from Lancaster Township, Lancaster County.

Beck, John George. He was naturalized in Pennsylvania 10–12 Apr. 1762. He was from Philadelphia County.

Beck, Joseph. He was naturalized in Maryland 14 Sep. 1763. He was a German.

Beck, Mathias. He was naturalized in Pennsylvania 11–13 Apr. 1743. He was from Philadelphia County.

Beck, Peter. He was naturalized in Pennsylvania 10 Apr. 1765. He was from Earl Township, Lancaster County.

Beckburgh, Edward. He was naturalized in Jamaica 29 Oct. 1702.

Beckenbogh, Peter. He was naturalized in Maryland 15 Sep. 1762. He was from Frederick County.

Becker, Barnaby. He was naturalized in Pennsylvania 24 Sep. 1760. He was from Philadelphia County.

Becker, Frederick. He was naturalized in New York 22 June 1734.

Becker, George. He was naturalized in Pennsylvania 10 Apr. 1760.

Becker, Henry. He was naturalized in New York 8 Mar. 1773.

Becker, Jacob. He was naturalized in Pennsylvania 19 May 1739. He was from Lancaster County.

Becker, Jacob. He was naturalized in Pennsylvania 24 Sep. 1760. He was from Philadelphia County.

Becker, Jacob. He was naturalized in New York 27 Jan. 1770.

Becker, John Broerson. He took the oath of allegiance in New York 1 Sep. 1687 in Ulster County.

Becker, John Michael. He was naturalized in Pennsylvania 11 Apr. 1763. He was from Heidelberg Township, Lancaster County.

Becker, Johan Philip Leuring. He was naturalized in New York 24 July 1724.

Becker, Jonas. He was naturalized in Maryland 10 Sep. 1762.

Becker, Martin. He was naturalized in Pennsylvania 10 Apr. 1760.

Becker, Michael. He was naturalized in Pennsylvania 19 May 1739. He was from Lancaster County.

Becker, Michael. He was naturalized in Pennsylvania 26 Sep. 1748. He was from Northern Liberties, Philadelphia.

Becker, Peter. He was naturalized in New York 8–9 Sep. 1715. He was from Ulster County.

Becker, Philip. He was naturalized in Maryland 9 Sep. 1761.

Becker, Wendal. He was naturalized in Pennsylvania 24 Sep. 1760. He was from Philadelphia County.

Becker, William. He was naturalized in Maryland 11 Sep. 1765.

Becker, Zacharias. He was naturalized in New York in Oct. 1740. He was from Ulster County.

Beckerum, Frederick. He was naturalized in Maryland 16 Sep. 1773. He was a German.

Becking, Frederick. He was naturalized in Pennsylvania 11 Apr. 1763. He was from Lower Merrion Township, Philadelphia County.

Becksaker, Peter. He was naturalized in Pennsylvania 24 Sep. 1755. He was from Lancaster County.

Becktel, Burkhard. He was naturalized in Pennsylvania 24–25 Sep. 1764. He was from East Nantmele Township, Chester County.

Bectell, John. He was naturalized in Pennsylvania 10 Apr. 1759.

Bedinger, Nicholas. He was naturalized in Pennsylvania 10 Apr. 1760.

Bedinger, Peter. He was naturalized in Frederick County, Virginia 1 Aug. 1769.

Bedlo, Isaack. He was made a denizen in Maryland 23 Jan. 1662. He was Dutch and late of England.

Bedlow, Isaac. He took the oath to the King 21–26 Oct. 1664 after the conquest of New Netherland.

Beeber, George. He was naturalized in Pennsylvania 10 Sep. 1761. He was from Berks County.

Beeber, John. He was naturalized in Pennsylvania 10 Apr. 1760.

Beechtel, Christ. He was naturalized in Pennsylvania 10 Sep. 1761. He was from Berks County.

Beeckman, Joghim. He took the oath to the King 21–26 Oct. 1664 after the conquest of New Netherland.

Beegel, David. He was naturalized in Maryland 1 Oct. 1767. He was a German from Frederick County.

Beehler, David. He was naturalized in Pennsylvania 11–13 Apr. 1743. He was from Lancaster County.

Beekman, Hennery. He took the oath of naturalization in New York 1 Sep. 1687 in Ulster County. He was styled captain.

Beekman, Henr. He was naturalized in New York 8–9 Sep. 1715. He was from Ulster County.

Beekman, Tedeus. He was naturalized in New York 24 June 1719.

Beel, Peter. He was naturalized in Pennsylvania 11 Apr. 1761. He was from Berks County.

Beem, Adam. He was naturalized in Maryland 11 Sep. 1765. He was a German from Frederick County.

Been, Conrad. He was naturalized in Pennsylvania 24 Sep. 1760. He was from Berks County.

Beener, Jacob. He was naturalized in Pennsylvania 10 Apr. 1765. He was from Philadelphia.

Beener, Jurry. He was naturalized in New York 11 Oct. 1715. He was from Albany County.

Beer, Peter, Sr. He was naturalized in Pennsylvania 10–12 Apr. 1762. He was from Lancaster County.

Beerman, Johannis. He was naturalized in New York 22 Nov. 1715. He was from Albany County.

Beeser, John. He was naturalized in Pennsylvania 24 Sep. 1753. He was from Berks County.

Beffell, Paul. He was naturalized in Rowan County, North Carolina 13 July 1763.

Begon, John Francisco. He was naturalized in Jamaica 1 July 1729.

Begtol, Jacob. He was naturalized in Pennsylvania 24 Sep. 1759.

Begun, Lewis. He was naturalized in Jamaica 10 Oct. 1722.

Beher, Caspar. He was naturalized in New Jersey in 1762. He was from Germany and had been in the colony seven years.

Behinger, Joseph. He was naturalized in New Jersey in 1764.

Behm, Adam. He was naturalized in Pennsylvania 16 Nov. 1771. He was from Brecknock Township, Berks County.

Behm, Hans Henrich. He was naturalized in New York 8–9 Sep. 1715. He was from Ulster County.

Behm, John. He was naturalized in Pennsylvania 25 Mar. 1764. He was from North Wales Township, Philadelphia County.

Behm, John Philip. He was naturalized in Pennsylvania 11 Apr. 1741. He was from Philadelphia County.

Behm, Philip. He was naturalized in Pennsylvania 11 Apr. 1761. He was from Philadelphia County.

Behm, Rudolph. He was naturalized in Pennsylvania 26–27 Sep. 1743. He was from Lancaster County.

Behr, Caspar. He was naturalized in New Jersey in 1763. He was from Germany. He had lived in the colony seven years. He also appeared as Caspar Bier.

Beidleman, Elias. He was naturalized in Pennsylvania 10–14 Apr. 1747. He was from Bucks County.

Beidleman, Jacob. He was naturalized in Pennsylvania 10–11 Apr. 1745. He was from Bucks County.

Beidler, Christian. He was naturalized in Pennsylvania 11–13 Apr. 1743. He was from Philadelphia County.

Beidler, Peter. He was naturalized in Pennsylvania 11–13 Apr. 1743. He was from Philadelphia County.

Beidler, Ulrick. He was naturalized in Pennsylvania 11–13 Apr. 1743. He was from Philadelphia County.

Beighley, George. He was naturalized in Pennsylvania 11–13 Apr. 1743. He was from Philadelphia County.

Beighnen, Henry. He was endenized in New York 6 Feb. 1695/6.

Beiser, Jacob. He was naturalized in Pennsylvania 10 Apr. 1765. He was from Hatfield Township, Philadelphia County.

Beisser, John. He was naturalized in Pennsylvania 10 Apr. 1760.

Beitzell, John. He was naturalized in Pennsylvania 11 Apr. 1761. He was from York County.

Beker, Hilarius. He was naturalized in Pennsylvania 11 Apr. 1763. He was from Germantown, Philadelphia County.

Beker, Ludwick. He was naturalized in Pennsylvania 11 Apr. 1761. He was from Lancaster County.

Beker, Samuel. He was naturalized in Maryland 14 Apr. 1761.

Bekle, Tobias. He was naturalized in Pennsylvania 24 Sep. 1755. He was from Lancaster County.

Bekner, Henry. He was naturalized in Maryland 20 Apr. 1771. He was a German.

Bekner, Johannes. He was naturalized in Pennsylvania 11–13 Apr. 1743. He was from Philadelphia County.

Belain, Alard. He was naturalized in South Carolina ca. 1696.

Belamie, Bernard. He was naturalized in Jamaica 25 Oct. 1759.

Belemare, Jacques. He was an Acadian who took the oath of allegiance in Apr. 1730.

Belesvelt, Johannes. He was naturalized in New Jersey 29 May 1756.

Belinger, Peter. He was naturalized in New York 31 Jan. 1715/6. He was from Albany County.

Belitz, Lorence. He was naturalized in Pennsylvania in 1730–31. He was from Philadelphia County.

Belivet, James. He was naturalized in Virginia 12 May 1705.

Bell, Anthonius. He was naturalized in Maryland 12 Sep. 1764. He was a German from Frederick County.

Bell, Christopher. He was naturalized in New York 21 Apr. 1769. He was a farmer from Orange County.

Bell, Henry. He was naturalized in New York 3 May 1755.

Bell, John. He was naturalized in Jamaica 8 Jan. 1744/5.

Bell, John Fredrick. He was naturalized in New York 11 Oct. 1715. He was from Albany County.

Bell, Peter. He was naturalized in Maryland 11 Sep. 1765. He was a German from Frederick County.

Bell, William. He was naturalized in New York 17 Oct. 1764. He was from Orange County and was a cooper.

Bellanger, Philip. He was naturalized in New York 8 Mar. 1773.

Bellesfelt, Adam. He was naturalized in New Jersey 8 Dec. 1744.

Bellesfelt, Johann William. He was naturalized in New Jersey 8 Dec. 1744.

Bellesfelt, Peter. He was naturalized in New Jersey 8 Dec. 1744.

Bellesfelt, Willem. He was naturalized in New Jersey 8 July 1730. He was born in Germany.

Bellicane, Michael, Sr. He was naturalized in Maryland 9 May 1700. He lived in Cecil County and was born of Dutch parents. He also appeared as Michael Rattican.

Bellicane, Michael, Jr. He and his sons, James Bellicane and Christopher Bellicane, were naturalized in Maryland 9 May 1700. They lived in Cecil County. He was born of Dutch parents.

Bellinger, Frederick. He was naturalized in New York 22 Nov. 1715. He was from Albany County.

Bellis, Philip. He was naturalized in New Jersey in 1764. He was born in Germany.

Bellivau, Charles. He was an Acadian and took the oath to George II at Annapolis River, Nova Scotia in Dec. 1729.

Bellivau, Joseph. He was an Acadian and took the oath to George II at Annapolis River, Nova Scotia in Dec. 1729.

Bellivau, Pierre. He was an Acadian and took the oath to George II at Annapolis River, Nova Scotia in the Dec. 1729.

Bellivau, Pierre. He was an Acadian and took the oath to George II at Annapolis River, Nova Scotia in the Dec. 1729.

Bellivaux, Jean. He was an Acadian and took the oath to George II at Annapolis River, Nova Scotia in Dec. 1729.

Bellivaux, Joseph. He was an Acadian who took the oath of allegiance in Apr. 1730.

Belliveau, Antonie. He was an Acadian and took the oath at Annapolis River, Nova Scotia in Dec. 1729.

Belliveau, Jean. He took the oath of allegiance at Port Royal, Nova Scotia 16 Aug. 1695.

Belliveaux, Charles. He was an Acadian and took the oath to George II at Annapolis River, Nova Scotia in the winter of 1730.

Belliveaux, Charles. He was an Acadian and took the oath to George II at Annapolis River, Nova Scotia in the winter of 1730.

Bellmore, John. He sought naturalization in New Jersey in the 18th century.

Beloud, Louis. He was naturalized in Nova Scotia 5 July 1758.

Beltz, John. He was naturalized in Pennsylvania 24 Sep. 1763. He was from Passyunk Township, Philadelphia County.

Belzener, Simon. He was naturalized in Pennsylvania 11–13 Apr. 1743. He was from Philadelphia County.

Bem, Conrad. He was naturalized in Pennsylvania 25 Sep. 1758.

Bemer, Henry. He was naturalized in New Jersey 20 Aug. 1755.

Bemer, Philip. He was naturalized in New Jersey in 1768.

Benbenisle, Eliau. He was naturalized in Jamaica 1 June 1710.

Bender, George. He was naturalized in Maryland 16 Sep. 1765. He was a German.

Benaat, Garrrit. He took the oath to the King 21–26 Oct. 1664 after the conquest of New Netherland.

Bender, Johannes. He was naturalized in Pennsylvania 19 May 1739. He was from Philadelphia County.

Bender, John. He was naturalized in Pennsylvania 10 Sep. 1761. He was from Lancaster County.

Bender, Leonhart. He was naturalized in Pennsylvania 19 May 1739. He was from Lancaster County.

Bender, Ludwick. He was naturalized in Pennsylvania 24 Sep. 1762. He was from Berks County.

Bender, Margaret. She was naturalized in New York 29 Oct. 1730.

Bender, Philips. He was naturalized in New York 31 Jan. 1715/6. He was from Albany County.

Bender, Valatin. He was naturalized in New York 8–9 Sep. 1715. He was from Ulster County.

Bender, William. He was naturalized in New York 8 Mar. 1773.

Benedix, Israel. He was naturalized in Jamaica 8 Mar. 1735/6.

Benezet, Anthony. He was naturalized in Pennsylvania 29 Mar. 1735. He was from Philadelphia.

Bengle, Adam. He was naturalized in New York 8 Mar. 1773.

Benkele, Peter. He was naturalized in Maryland 11 Apr. 1764. He was from Monokosy and a German.

Benner, Bastian. He was naturalized in Pennsylvania 10 Apr. 1759.

Benner, Jacob. He was naturalized in Pennsylvania 11 Apr. 1763. He was from Worcester Township, Philadelphia County.

Benner, John. He was naturalized in Maryland 5 May 1768. He was a German from Frederick County.

Bennet, Paul. He was naturalized in Jamaica 28 Aug. 1675.

Bennit, Abriaen. He took the oath of allegiance in Breucklijn, Kings County, New York 26–30 Sep. 1687. He was a native of the colony.

Bennit, Jacob Willemse. He took the oath of allegiance in Breucklijn, Kings County, New York 26–30 Sep. 1687. He was a native of the colony.

Bennit, Jan. He took the oath of allegiance in Breucklijn, Kings County, New York 26–30 Sep. 1687. He was a native of the colony.

Bennitt, Willem. He took the oath of allegiance in Breucklijn, Kings County, New York 26–30 Sep. 1687. He was a native of the colony.

Bennoit, Claude. He was an Acadian who took the oath of allegiance in Apr. 1730.

Benoit, Abraham. He was an Acadian who took the oath of allegiance in Apr. 1730.

Benoit, Charles. He was an Acadian and took the oath to the King at the Mines, Pisiquit, Nova Scotia 31 Oct. 1727.

Benoit, Charles. He was an Acadian who took the oath of allegiance in Apr. 1730.

Benoit, Clement. He was an Acadian who took the oath to the King at the Mines, Pisiquit, Nova Scotia on 31 Oct. 1727.

Benoit, Clement. He was an Acadian who took the oath of allegiance in Apr. 1730.

Benoit, Claude. He was an Acadian who took the oath of allegiance in Apr. 1730.

Benoit, Guillaume. He was an Acadian who took the oath of allegiance in Apr. 1730.

Benoit, Jacques. He was the son of Jacques Benoit and Gabrielle Mercier and was born at Sussay, Poitou, France. His wife was Sara Mounie. His son, Jean Benoit, was born in France and his children, Jacques Benoit and Pierre Benoit, were born in South Carolina. They were naturalized in South Carolina ca. 1696.

Benoit, Jean. He was an Acadian who took the oath of allegiance in Apr. 1730.

Benoit, Jean. He was an Acadian who took the oath of allegiance in Apr. 1730.

Benoit, Martin. He was an Acadian who took the oath of allegiance in Apr. 1730.

Benoit, Paul. He was an Acadian who took the oath to George II at the Mines, Pisiquit 31 Oct. 1727.

Benoit, Paul. He was an Acadian who took the oath of allegiance in Apr. 1730.

Benoit, Pierre, Jr. He was an Acadian who took the oath to George II at the Mines, Pisiquit 31 Oct. 1727.

Benoit, Pierre. He was an Acadian who took the oath of allegiance in Apr. 1730.

Benoit, Pierre. He was an Acadian who took the oath of allegiance in Apr. 1730.

Benoit, Pierre, Sr. He was an Acadian who took the oath of allegiance in Apr. 1730.

Benracth, John. He was naturalized in Maryland 7 May 1767. He was a German.

Bensel, Charles, Jr. He was naturalized in Pennsylvania 19 May 1739. He was from Philadelphia County.

Bensell, Charles. He was naturalized in Pennsylvania 25–27 Sep. 1740. He was from Philadelphia County.

Bensell, Conrad. He was naturalized in Pennsylvania 29 Mar. 1735. He was from Philadelphia County.

Bensell, George. He was naturalized in Pennsylvania 25–27 Sep. 1740. He was from Philadelphia County.

Benter, Matthias. He was naturalized in New York 14 Feb. 1775. He was a boy of 14 years of age and a cooper in New York City.

Bentser, Solomon. He was naturalized in Jamaica 17 June 1721. He was also appeared as Solomon Bulser.

Bentz, John. He was naturalized in Pennsylvania 11 Apr. 1761. He was from Lancaster County.

Bentz, John. He was naturalized in Pennsylvania 10 Sep. 1761. He was from York County.

Bentz, Michael. He was naturalized in Pennsylvania 10 Sep. 1761. He was from Lancaster County.

Bentzell, Johannes George. He was naturalized in Pennsylvania in 1730–31. He was from Philadelphia County.

Benzel, Adolphus. He was naturalized in New York 20 Dec. 1763.

Berand, Joseph. He was an Acadian who took the oath of allegiance in Apr. 1730.

Beranger, Jacques. He was naturalized in Jamaica in Aug. 1750.

Berard, Jean. He was an Acadian who took the oath of allegiance in Apr. 1730.

Berbauld, Ezekiel. He was naturalized in New York 20 Sep. 1728.

Berck, Christian. He was naturalized in New York 31 Jan. 1715/6. He was from Albany County.

Berg, Johan Diel. He was naturalized in New Jersey 8 Dec. 1744.

Berg, Johann William. He and his sons, Johannes Berg, Pieter Berg, and John Berg, were naturalized in New Jersey 8 July 1730. They were born in Germany.

Bergen, Jacob Hanssen. He took the oath of allegiance in Breucklijn, Kings County, New York 26–30 Sep. 1687. He was a native of the colony.

Berger, Adam. He was naturalized in Pennsylvania 11 Apr. 1761. He was from Lancaster County.

Berger, Christian. He was naturalized in Pennsylvania 11 Apr. 1761. He was from Berks County.

Berger, Henry. He was naturalized in Pennsylvania 24 Sep. 1762. He was from Berks County.

Berger, John. He was naturalized in Pennsylvania 11–13 Apr. 1743. He was from Lancaster County.

Berger, Michael. He was naturalized in Pennsylvania 29 Mar. 1735. He was from Philadelphia County.

Berger, Philip. He was naturalized in Maryland 11 Apr. 1764. He was a German.

Berger, Rudolph. He was naturalized in Pennsylvania 10 Apr. 1755. He was from Berks County.

Bergestock, John Justice Jacob. He was naturalized in Pennsylvania 10–11 Apr. 1746. He was from Bucks County. He was a clerk [i.e. a clergyman].

Bergey, Henry. He was naturalized in Pennsylvania 10–12 Apr. 1762. He was from Northampton County.

Bergh, Michael. He was naturalized in Jamaica 9 June 1675.

Bergman, Peter. He was naturalized in Nova Scotia on 4 July 1758.

Bergstraser, George. He was naturalized in Pennsylvania in Sep. 1740. He was from Bucks County.

Bering, Francis. He was naturalized in Virginia 12 May 1705.

Berk, Abraham. He was naturalized in New York 17 Jan. 1715/6. He was from Albany County.

Berk, Handel. He was naturalized in Maryland 11 Sep. 1765.

Berkenbeil, Christopher. He was naturalized in Pennsylvania 11 Apr. 1761. He was from Philadelphia County.

Berkman, Peter. He was naturalized in Maryland 18 Sep 1764. He was a German.

Berlet, John Wolf. He was naturalized in New York 3 July 1759.

Berlin, Abraham. He was naturalized in Pennsylvania 11 Apr. 1761. He was from Northampton County.

Bernard, Baptiste. He was an Acadian who took the oath of allegiance in Apr. 1730.

Bernard, David. He was naturalized in Virginia 12 May 1705.

Bernard, Rene. He was an Acadian who took the oath of allegiance in Apr. 1730.

Bernard, Stephen. He was naturalized in Pennsylvania 24 Sep. 1755. He was from Berks County.

Bernardt, Charles. He was naturalized in Jamaica 30 Mar. 1677.

Bernauer, Jacob. He was naturalized in Maryland 10 Sep. 1760.

Berndaller, Daniel. He was naturalized in Pennsylvania 25–27 Sep. 1740. He was from Philadelphia County.

Berndheisell, Valentine. He was naturalized in Pennsylvania 11 Apr. 1741. He was from Philadelphia County.

Bernhard, Andreas. He was naturalized in Pennsylvania in Sep. 1740. He was from Philadelphia County.

Bernhard, Jacob. He was naturalized in Pennsylvania 24 Sep. 1763. He was from Limerick Township, Philadelphia County.

Bernhard, Peter. He was naturalized in Pennsylvania 11–12 Apr. 1744. He was from Philadelphia County.

Bernhardus, George. He was naturalized in Pennsylvania 24 Sep. 1762. He was from Berks County.

Bernhart, Henry. He was naturalized in Pennsylvania 19 May 1739. He was from Bucks County.

Bernon, Gabriel. He was endenized in England 9 Apr. 1687. He went to Massachusetts and was admitted into the colony 1 Feb. 1691.

Berot, Frantz Ludwick. He was naturalized in Pennsylvania 11 Apr. 1761. He was from York County.

Berringer, Michael. He was naturalized in New York 2 Mar. 1772.

Berriot, Pierre. He was an Acadian who took the oath of allegiance in Apr. 1730.

Berriott, Nicholas. He was an Acadian who took the oath of allegiance in Apr. 1730.

Berritt, Joseph. He was naturalized in Pennsylvania 10 Sep. 1761. He was from Berks County.

Berry, Samuel. He was naturalized in Maryland 14 Nov. 1713. He lived in Kent County and was a carpenter. He was Swedish.

Berrey, Samuel. He took the oath of naturalization in New York 1 Sep. 1687 in Ulster County.

Bersinger, Andreas. He was naturalized in Pennsylvania 19 May 1739. He was from Lancaster County.

Bertain, Pierre. He was naturalized in New York 2 Aug. 1715. He was a cooper from New Rochelle.

Berte, Paul. He and his wife, Mary Berte, were naturalized in Maryland 19 Nov. 1686.

Bertreaud, Jean. He was an Acadian who took the oath of allegiance in Apr. 1730.

Berthold, Gebhart. He was naturalized in Pennsylvania 10 Apr. 1760.

Berthon, Michael. He was naturalized in New York 17 June 1726.

Bertnitz, Carl. He was naturalized in Maryland 17 Sep. 1751. He also appeared as Carl Bernitz.

Bertran, Jacques. He was an Acadian and took the oath to George II at Annapolis River, Nova Scotia in Dec. 1729.

Bertrand, Peter. He was endenized in London 11 Mar. 1699/1700. He came to New York.

Bertraud, Jean. He was born at St. Lo, France, the son of Jean Bertraud and Marguerite Robert. He was naturalized in South Carolina ca. 1696.

Besharn, Johan Jacob. He was naturalized in New York 31 Jan. 1715/6. He was from Albany County.

Besler, Jacob. He was naturalized in Pennsylvania 26–27 Sep. 1743. He was from Philadelphia County.

Besley, Nicholas. He was naturalized in New York 20 Dec. 1763.

Besley, Oliver. He was naturalized in New York 10 Jan. 1715/6. He was from New Rochelle.

Besly, Hester. She was naturalized in New York 25 Nov. 1727.

Bessilleu, Mark Anthony. He was naturalized in South Carolina 14 Aug. 1744.

Besson, Stephen. He was naturalized in Maryland 19 Apr. 1671. He lived in Dorchester County and was French.

Best, Jacob. He was naturalized in New York 17 Jan. 1715/6. He was from Albany County.

Best, Jury. He was naturalized in New York 8–9 Sep. 1715. He was from Ulster County.

Besteyansa, Jacob. He took the oath on naturalization in New York 1 Sep. 1687 in Ulster County.

Betellbrunt, Anthony. He was naturalized in New York 16 Feb. 1771.

Betiny, George Cunce. He was naturalized in Maryland in Apr. 1749.

Betser, Adam. He was naturalized in New York 24 Oct. 1741.

Betser, Marma. He was naturalized in New York 17 Jan. 1715/6. He was from Albany County. He also appeared as Harma Betser.

Betser, Peter. He was naturalized in New York 17 Jan. 1715/6. He was from Albany County.

Bettley, Mathias. He was naturalized in Pennsylvania 11–12 Apr. 1744. He was from Lancaster County.

Bettley, Michael. He was naturalized in Pennsylvania 26–27 Sep. 1743. He was from Lancaster County.

Beuf, Hendrick. He was naturalized in New Jersey 21 June 1754.

Beuf, Hendrick, Jr. He was naturalized in New Jersey 21 June 1754.

Bevyer, Louys. He was naturalized in New York 8–9 Sep. 1715/6. He was from Ulster County.

Beyer, Abraham, Jr. He was naturalized in Pennsylvania 19 May 1739. He was from Philadelphia County.

Beyer, Abraham. He was naturalized in Pennsylvania 11–13 Apr. 1743. He was from Philadelphia County.

Beyer, Andrew. He was naturalized in Pennsylvania 26–27 Sep. 1743. He was from Lancaster County.

Beyer, George Frederick. He was naturalized in Pennsylvania 25 Sep. 1758.

Beyer, Jacob. He was naturalized in Pennsylvania 26–27 Sep. 1743. He was from Lancaster County.

Beyer, Melchior. He was naturalized in Maryland 14 Apr. 1762. He was a German.

Beyer, Philip. He was naturalized in Pennsylvania 11–13 Apr. 1743. He was from Philadelphia County.

Beyle, John. He was naturalized in Pennsylvania 11–13 Apr. 1743. He was from Philadelphia County.

Beysell, Peter. He was naturalized in Pennsylvania 24 Sep. 1741. He was from Philadelphia County.

Bheme, Jacob. He was naturalized in Pennsylvania 14 Feb. 1729/30. He was from Lancaster County.

Bick, Christian. He was naturalized in Pennsylvania 24–25 Sep. 1764. He was from Philadelphia.

Bickenbach, John Adam. He was naturalized in Maryland 17 Sep. 1764. He was a German.

Bickinbachin, Anna Maria. She was naturalized in Maryland 12 Sep. 1764. She was a German.

Bickle, Francis. He was naturalized in New Jersey 20 Aug. 1755.

Bickle, Jacob. He was naturalized in New York 16 Feb. 1771.

Bidleman, Leonard. He was naturalized in Pennsylvania 10 Apr. 1760.

Bidler, John. He was naturalized in Pennsylvania 10 Sep. 1761. He was from Philadelphia County.

Biegler, Heinrick. He was naturalized in Maryland 12 Sep. 1759.

Bier, Philip. He was naturalized in Maryland 17 July 1765. He was a German.

Biere, Jacob. He was naturalized in Pennsylvania 14 Feb. 1729/30. He was from Lancaster County.

Biess, Henrich. He was naturalized in Maryland 12 Sep. 1759.

Bigler, Michael. He was naturalized in Maryland 21 Sep. 1763. He was a German from Frederick County.

Bilderbeck, David. He was naturalized in New Castle County, Delaware 21 Feb. 1682/3.

Billmyer, Jacob. He was naturalized in Pennsylvania 25 Sep. 1750. He was from York County.

Billmyer, Leonard. He was naturalized in Pennsylvania 25 Sep. 1750. He was from Lancaster County.

Binder, George. He was naturalized in New York 27 Jan. 1770.

Binder, Hans Ulrich. He was naturalized in New York 18 Oct. 1750. He was from Ulster County.

Binder, John Jacob. He was naturalized in Pennsylvania 10 Sep. 1761. He was from Philadelphia County.

Binder, Martin. He was naturalized in Pennsylvania 24 Sep. 1763. He was from York Township, York County.

Bindur, Hendrick. He was naturalized in New Jersey 8 Oct. 1750.

Bindur, Theophilus. He was naturalized in New Jersey 8 Oct. 1750.

Bingamon, Peter. He was naturalized in Pennsylvania 11–13 Apr. 1743. He was from Philadelphia County.

Biork, Erirus Tobias. He was naturalized in Pennsylvania 28 Oct. 1701. He was born in Koping, Sweden, the son of Tobias and Ann Biork.

Bird, Henry. He was naturalized in New York 20 Dec. 1763.

Birkinbile, Andrew. He was naturalized in Maryland 6 Sep. 1769. He was a German.

Bisch, George. He was naturalized in Pennsylvania 10 & 23 Sep. 1764. He was from Haycock Township, Bucks County.

Bisck, Jan. He expressed his desire to be naturalized in New Castle County, Delaware 21 Feb. 1682/3.

Biscon, Isaac. He and his wife were admitted into the colony of Massachusetts 1 Feb. 1691. They were French.

Bishop, Christopher. He was naturalized in New Jersey 6 Dec. 1769.

Bishop, Francis Michael. He was naturalized in Pennsylvania 10 Apr. 1760.

Bishop, Jacob. He was naturalized in Maryland 28 Aug. 1765. He was a German from Frederick County.

Bishop, John. He was naturalized in Maryland 10 Sep. 1762.

Bishop, John. He was naturalized in Pennsylvania 24 Sep. 1741. He was from Lancaster County.

Bishop, John. He was naturalized in Pennsylvania 24 Sep. 1759.

Bisset, Elias. He was born at St. Jean d'Angely, France, the son of Abraham Bisset and Marye Bitheur. His wife was Jeanne Poinsett. Their children, born in South Carolina, were Anne Bisset and Catherine Bisset. They were naturalized in South Carolina 10 Mar. 1696/7. He was a shammy-dresser.

Bittell, Nicholas. He was naturalized in Pennsylvania 11 Apr. 1751. He was from Philadelphia County.

Bitter, Lawrence. He was naturalized in Pennsylvania 10 Sep. 1761. He was from Lancaster County.

Bittinger, Henry. He was naturalized in Pennsylvania 20 May 1769. He was from Frederick County, Virginia.

Bittiner, Nicholas. He was naturalized in Pennsylvania 18 Nov. 1768. He was from Berwick Township, York County.

Bitting, John. He was naturalized in Pennsylvania 10 Apr. 1760.

Bitzell, Henry. He was naturalized in Maryland 14 Apr. 1760.

Blackwelder, John. His son Caleb Blackwelder, his daughter Elizabeth Blackwelder, his son John Blackwelder, his daughter Margaret Blackwelder, and his sister Catherine Blackwelder were naturalized in Brunswick County, Virginia 3 Apr. 1746. He was a native of the Marquisate of Durloch, Germany. They had previously been in Pennsylvania.

Blair, John. He was naturalized in Jamaica 2 Mar. 1695/6.

Blake, Christopher. He was naturalized in North Carolina 22 Sep. 1766. He was from Rowan County.

Blanc, Pierre. He was an Acadian and took the oath to the King at the Mines, Pisiquit, Nova Scotia 31 Oct. 1727.

Blanchard, Antoine. He was an Acadian and took the oath to George II at Annapolis River, Nova Scotia in the winter of 1730.

Blanchard, Charles. He was an Acadian and took the oath to George II at Annapolis River, Nova Scotia in the winter of 1730.

Blanchard, Francois. He was naturalized in New York 6 Dec. 1746.

Blanchard, Francois. He was an Acadian who took the oath of allegiance in Apr. 1730.

Blanchard, Francois. He was an Acadian who took the oath of allegiance in Apr. 1730.

Blanchard, Guillaume. He took the oath of allegiance at Port Royal, Nova Scotia 16 Aug. 1695.

Blanchard, Guillaume. He was an Acadian and took the oath to George II at Annapolis River, Nova Scotia in the winter 1730.

Blanchard, James. He was naturalized in New York 22 Apr. 1761. He was a French Protestant and a cooper in New York City.

Blanchard, Jean. He was an Acadian and took the oath to George II at Annapolis River, Nova Scotia in the winter of 1730.

Blanchard, John. He took the oath of naturalization in New York 1 Sep. 1687 in Ulster County.

Blanchard, Joseph. He was an Acadian who took the oath of allegiance in Apr. 1730.

Blanchard, Martin. He took the oath of allegiance at Port Royal, Nova Scotia 16 Aug. 1695.

Blanchard, Martin. He was an Acadian who took the oath of allegiance in Apr. 1730.

Blanchard, Paul. He was an Acadian and took the oath to George II at Annapolis River, Nova Scotia in Dec. 1729.

Blanchard, Pierre. He was an Acadian and took the oath to George II at Annapolis River, Nova Scotia in Dec. 1729.

Blanchard, Pierre. He was an Acadian who took the oath of allegiance in Apr. 1730.

Blanchard, Pierre. He was an Acadian who took the oath of allegiance in Apr. 1730.

Blanchard, Rene. He was an Acadian and took the oath to the King at the Mines, Pisiquit, Nova Scotia 31 Oct. 1727.

Blanchard, Rene. He was an Acadian and took the oath to the King at the Mines, Pisiquit, Nova Scotia 31 Oct.1727.

Blanchard, Rene. He was an Acadian who took the oath of allegiance at Annapolis River, Nova Scotia in Dec. 1729.

Blanchard, Rene. He was an Acadian who took the oath of allegiance in Apr. 1730.

Blanchard, Rene. He was an Acadian who took the oath of allegiance in Apr. 1730.

Blanchard, Toussaint. He was an Acadian who took the oath of allegiance in Apr. 1730.

Blanck, Frederick. He was naturalized in Maryland 6 Sep. 1765. He was a German from Frederick County.

Blanck, Johan. He was naturalized in New York 8–9 Sep. 1715. He was from Ulster County.

Blanck, Jurien. He took the oath to the King 21–26 Oct. 1664 after the conquest of New Netherland.

Blangey, Lewis. He was naturalized in Maryland 17 Sep. 1681.

Blank, Adam. He was naturalized in Pennsylvania 10 Apr. 1755. He was from Northampton County.

Blank, Frederick. He was naturalized in New York 11 Sep. 1761.

Blankenbacker, Zacheriah. He was naturalized in Orange County, Virginia 28 Jan. 1742/3. He was a native of Nieuberg in the Bishopric of Speyer, Germany.

Blankenstein, William. He was naturalized in Maryland 17 Nov. 1682. He lived in St. Mary's County.

Blanzan, Matthis, Jr. He took the oath of naturalization in New York 1 Sep. 1687 in Ulster County.

Blarick, —. He was naturalized in New York 8–9 Sep. 1715. He was from Ulster County.

Blass, Chrsr. He was naturalized in North Carolina 24 Sep. 1766. He was from Rowan County.

Blatner, Jacob. He was naturalized in New York 23 Aug. 1765. He was a miller from Albany County.

Blatt, Frederick. He was naturalized in Pennsylvania 10–12 Apr. 1762. He was from Berks County.

Bleck, Jacob. He was naturalized in Pennsylvania 10–12 Apr. 1762. He was from Frederick County, Maryland.

Bleeker, Jan Janse. He was naturalized in New York 11 Oct. 1715. He was from Albany County.

Bleikers, Johannes. He was naturalized in Pennsylvania 29 Sep. 1709. He was from Bucks County.

Bleimyer, Abraham. He was naturalized in Pennsylvania 13 May 1768. He was from York Township, York County.

Blemsan, Mattys. He was naturalized in New York 8–9 Sep. 1715. He was from Ulster County.

Blencoe, Mary. She was naturalized in Jamaica 15 Nov. 1720.

Blewlet, Abraham. He was naturalized in North Carolina 29 Oct. 1722. He was a native of Switzerland.

Blim, Christian. He was naturalized in Pennsylvania 12 Apr. 1750. He was from Philadelphia County.

Bliss, Emrich. He was naturalized in New York 17 Jan. 1715/6. He was from Albany County.

Blocq, Mary. She was naturalized in New Castle County, Delaware 21 Feb. 1682/3.

Bloet, Johannes Jong. He was naturalized in New York 8 Nov. 1735.

Blom, Claes Barentse. He took the oath of allegiance in Breucklijn, Kings County, New York 26–30 Sep. 1687. He was a native of the colony.

Blom, Jan Barense. He took the oath of allegiance in Flackbush, Kings County, New York 26–30 Sep. 1687. He was a native of the colony.

Bloom, John. He was naturalized in New Jersey 31 July 1704. He was born in Germany.

Blovet, Daniel. He was naturalized in Virginia 12 May 1705.

Blum, John. He was naturalized in Pennsylvania 19 May 1739. He was from Lancaster County.

Blumenschein, John. He was naturalized in Maryland 13 Apr. 1763. He was a German from Frederick County.

Boate, Nicholas. He was endenized in Virginia 13 Mar. 1659/60.

Boatsman, Jurian. He was naturalized in New Castle County, Delaware 21 Feb. 1682/3.

Bobin, James. He was naturalized in New York 3 Apr. 1716. He was a yeoman from Bushwick, Kings County.

Bobineau, Stephen. He, his wife Judith Bobineau, and daughter Mary Bobineau were endenized in England 9 Apr. 1687. They came to New England.

Bocard, Peter. He was naturalized in Virginia 12 May 1705.

Bochet, Abel. He was born at Nanteuil, France, the son of Nicholas Bochet and Marguerite Petit. He was naturalized in South Carolina 10 Mar. 1696/7. He was a planter.

Bochet, Nicholas. He was born at Nanteuil les Meaux [?], Brye, France, the son of Nicholas Bochet and Marguerite Petit. His wife was Suzanne Dehays from Magny Boutigny. Their daughter, Suzanne Bochet, was born in Fublainne, Brie, France and their sons, Pierre Bochet and Nicholas Bochet, were born in South Carolina. They were naturalized in South Carolina 10 Mar. 1696/7. He was a planter. He also appeared as Nicholas Bouchet.

Bockoven, George. He was naturalized in New Jersey in 1769. He also appeared as George Backofen.

Bocquet, Peter. He was naturalized in South Carolina 14 Oct. 1744.

Bockius, Godfried. He was naturalized in Pennsylvania 10 Apr. 1760.

Bodardo, Katherine. She and her husband, Stephen Bodardo, were endenized in London in Apr. 1663. They were from Antigua.

Bodardo, Stephen. He and his wife, Katherine Bodardo, were endenized in London in Apr. 1663. They were from Antigua.

Bodeker, Diederick William. He was naturalized in Maryland 18 Aug. 1739. He was a planter in Baltimore County and was born in Germany.

Bodien, Francis Ludolph. He and his children, Anne Bodien, Eliza Bodien, Hannah Bodien, Henry Augustus Bodien, and Sophie Sidonia Bodien, were naturalized in Maryland 30 Oct. 1727. He lived in Kent County and was a surgeon. He was a German.

Bodine, Peter. He was naturalized in New Jersey 8 July 1730. He was born in Germany.

Bodrot, Francois. He was an Acadian and took the oath to George II at Annapolis River, Nova Scotia in the winter of 1730.

Boeck, Martin. He was naturalized in New York 8–9 Sep. 1715. He was from Ulster County.

Boel, Henricus. He was naturalized in New York 3 July 1718.

Boel, Tobias. He was naturalized in New York 3 July 1718.

Boelen, Jacob. He was naturalized in New York 26 July 1715. He was a silversmith.

Boeler, Martin. He was naturalized in Pennsylvania 11 Apr. 1751. He was from Lancaster County. He was a Moravian.

Boeyar, Jan. He expressed his desire to be naturalized in New Castle County, Delaware 21 Feb. 1682/3.

Bogaert, Theunis Gysbertse. He took the oath of allegiance in Breucklijn, Kings County, New York 26–30 Sep. 1687. He had been in the colony 35 years.

Bogaert, William. He was naturalized in New York 14 Feb. 1715/6. He was a turner in New York City.

Bogan, Richard. He was naturalized in Northumberland County, Va. 17 Sep. 1656. He was the son of Richard Bogan and was born in France.

Bogard, Hendrick Cornelis. He took the oath of naturalization in New York 1 Sep. 1687 in Ulster County.

Bogardos, Cornelis. He took the oath of naturalization in New York 1 Sep. 1687 in Ulster County.

Bogardus, Willem. He took the oath to the King 21–26 Oct. 1664 after the conquest of New Netherland.

Bogart, Hendrick. He was naturalized in New York 8–9 Sep. 1715. He was from Ulster County.

Boger, Martin. He was naturalized in Pennsylvania 10 Apr. 1755. He was from Berks County.

Bohm, Anthony. He was naturalized in Pennsylvania 29 Mar. 1735. He was from Philadelphia County.

Bohm, John Philip. He was naturalized in Pennsylvania 14 Feb. 1729/30. He was from Philadelphia.

Bohman, John. He was naturalized in Pennsylvania 14 Feb. 1729/30. He was from Lancaster County.

Bohman, Michael. He was naturalized in Pennsylvania 14 Feb. 1729/30. He was from Lancaster County.

Bohn, John. He was naturalized in New Jersey 6 Dec. 1769.

Bohr, Michael. He was naturalized in Pennsylvania 10 Sep. 1761. He was from Lancaster County.

Bohrer, Peter. He was naturalized in Maryland 7 May 1767. He was a German.

Boisbilland, John. He was endenized in New York 2 Sep. 1685. He had lived in Gravesend two years when he took the oath and received his letters of denization 26–30 Sep. 1687. He also appeared as John Boisbillaud.

Boisseau, Jean. He was born at Maraine, France and was the son of Jacques Boisseau and Marie LaCourt. His wife was Marie Postel. They were naturalized in South Carolina ca. 1696.

Bollinger, Henry. He was naturalized in Pennsylvania 10 & 23 Apr. 1764. He was from Long Swamp Township, Berks County.

Bollinger, Rudy. He was naturalized in Pennsylvania 11 Apr. 1761. He was from Lancaster County.

Bollman, Abraham. He was naturalized in Pennsylvania 10 Apr. 1767. He was from Heidelberg Township, Lancaster County.

Bollman, Adam. He was naturalized in Pennsylvania 11 Apr. 1761. He was from Lancaster County.

Bolthouse, Conrad. He was naturalized in Pennsylvania 11 Apr. 1761. He was from Lancaster County.

Boltz, George. He was naturalized in Pennsylvania 10 & 23 Apr. 1764. He was from Tulpehocken Township, Berks County.

Boltz, Michael. He was naturalized in Pennsylvania 24 Sep. 1763. He was from Lebanon Township, Lancaster County.

Boltzel, Henry. He was naturalized in Maryland 11 Sep. 1765.

Boltzel, Jacob. He was naturalized in Maryland 11 Sep. 1765.

Boltzel, Peter. He was naturalized in Maryland 11 Sep. 1765.

Bombarger, Henry. He was naturalized in Pennsylvania 11 Apr. 1763. He was from Upper Salford Township, Philadelphia County.

Bomberger, Charles. He was naturalized in Pennsylvania 10 Apr. 1765. He was from Tulpehocken Township, Berks County.

Bomgardener, Frederick. He was naturalized in Orange County, Virginia 28 Jan. 1742/3. He was a native of Wurttemberg.

Bomont, Giles de. He was endenized in England 5 Jan. 1624/5. He was born in France. He intended to go to Virginia. He also appeared as Giles de Beaumont.

Bomper, Abraham. He was naturalized in Pennsylvania 10 Sep. 1761. He was from Northampton County.

Bomper, Jacob. He was naturalized in New York 25 Nov. 1727.

Bomer, Philip Jacob. He took the oath in New York City 9 Sep. 1729.

Bomser, Estienne. He petitioned 19 Aug. 1687 for naturalization.

Bonamiz, James. He took the oath of naturalization in New York 1 Sep. 1687 in Ulster County.

Bonan, Samaiah. He was naturalized in Jamaica 27 Dec. 1759. He also appeared as Samaiah Bonner.

Bonder, Elias. He was naturalized in Pennsylvania 11 Apr. 1752. He was from Bucks County.

Bondurand, John Peter. He was naturalized in Virginia 12 May 1705.

Bonfee, Peter. He was naturalized in Jamaica 15 Jan. 1724.

Bonfils, John. He was naturalized in Jamaica 11 Oct. 1726.

Bonfils, Thomas. He was naturalized in Jamaica 16 June 1725.

Bongarden, Philip. He was naturalized in Massachusetts 7 Dec. 1731.

Bongrand, Lewis. He was endenized in England 19 Aug. 1688. He came to New York.

Bonhoste, Jonas. He was born in Paris, France, the son of Pierre Bonhoste and Marie Garlin. His wife was Catherine Alaire. Their son was Jonas Bonhoste born in South Carolina. They were naturalized in South Carolina 10 Mar. 1696/7. He was a wheelwright.

Bonito, Abraham Mendes. He was naturalized in Jamaica 12 Nov. 1770.

Bonn, Solomon Heim. He was naturalized in Pennsylvania 25 Sep. 1752. He was from Philadelphia. He was a Jew.

Bonnain, Elias. He was naturalized in New York 24 Nov. 1750.

Bonneau, Anthoine. He was born at LaRochelle, France, the son of Jean Bonneau and Catherine Roi. His wife was Catherine DuBliss. Their children were Anthonie Bonneau, Jean Henri Bonneau, and Jacob Bonneau. Their first and second children were born in France and the last child was born in South Carolina. They were naturalized in South Carolina 10 Mar. 1696/7. He was a cooper. His son, Anthony Bonneau, Jr., was a gunsmith.

Bonnefoy, David. He was endenized in New York 6 Feb. 1695/6.

Bonnel, Daniel. He was the son of Jean Bonnel and Marie Lalon. His wife was Marie Izambert. Their daughter was Susanne Bonnel who was born in South Carolina. They were naturalized in South Carolina ca. 1696.

Bonner, Conrad. He was naturalized in Pennsylvania 24 Sep. 1760. He was from Philadelphia County.

Bonner, Philip. He was naturalized in Maryland 14 Sep. 1763. He was a German.

Bonner, Rudolph. He was naturalized in Pennsylvania 19 May 1739. He was from Philadelphia County.

Bonnerie, Benjamin. He was naturalized in Jamaica 17 Feb 1718/9.

Bonnett, John. He was naturalized in Pennsylvania 11 Apr. 1761. He was from Lancaster County.

Bonnesteel, Niecolas. He was naturalized in New York 17 Jan. 1715/6. He was from Albany County.

Bonnet, Daniel. He was naturalized in New York 27 Sep. 1715. He was a yeoman from New Rochelle.

Bonnevie, Jacques. He was an Acadian and took the oath to George II at Annapolis River, Nova Scotia in Dec. 1729.

Bontecou, Daniel. He was naturalized in New York 12 July 1715. He was a cooper.

Bontecou, Daniel. He was naturalized in New York 31 July 1741. He was a merchant from New York City.

Bonticou, Marinne. She was naturalized in New York 17 June 1726. She was the wife of Daniel.

Bonwer, Pieter. He was naturalized 8–9 Sep. 1715 in New York. He was from Ulster County.

Boo, Stoffell. He was naturalized in North Carolina 26 Sep. 1767. He was from Rowan County.

Boobinger, Florian. He was naturalized in Pennsylvania 11–13 Apr. 1743. He was from Philadelphia County.

Boochstaver, Jacob. He was naturalized in New York 8 Nov. 1735.

Booe, Gasper. He was naturalized in North Carolina 22 Sep. 1763. He was from Rowan County and a German.

Booe, Jacob. He was naturalized in North Carolina 22 Sep. 1763. He was from Rowan County and a German.

Book, Christian. He was naturalized in Pennsylvania 11 Apr. 1761. He was from Lancaster County.

Boom, Christian. He was naturalized in Jamaica 25 Sep. 1729. [His name may have been Christian Boor.]

Boom, Hendrik. He was naturalized in New York 11 Sep. 1761.

Boomgaert, Gijsbert. He took the oath of allegiance in Breucklijn, Kings County, New York 26–30 Sep. 1687. He was a native of the colony.

Boon, Francis. He took the oath to the King 21–26 Oct. 1664 after the conquest of New Netherland.

Boon, John. He was naturalized in New Jersey in 1759. He was born in Germany. He also appeared as John Bounn.

Boon, Nichole. He was naturalized in Maryland 11 Sep. 1765.

Boone, Adam. He was naturalized in Pennsylvania 10 Apr. 1760.

Boorehanc, John. He took the oath of naturalization in New York 1 Sep. 1687 in Ulster County.

Boos, Christ. He sought naturalization in New Jersey in the 18th century.

Boos, Wendel. He was naturalized in New York 21 Apr. 1762. He was a baker from New York City.

Boosse, John Paul. He was naturalized in Pennsylvania 11 Apr. 1763. He was from Bristol Township, Bucks County.

Bop, Conrad. He was naturalized in Pennsylvania 25 Sep. 1751. He was from Philadelphia County.

Borcklo, Willem Willemse. He took the oath of allegiance in Flackland, Kings County, New York 26–30 Sep. 1687. He was a native of the colony.

Border, Conradth. He was naturalized in Pennsylvania 11–13 Apr. 1743. He was from Philadelphia County.

Bordner, Jacob. He was naturalized in Pennsylvania 11 Apr. 1761. He was from Berks County.

Bording, Christian. He petitioned for naturalization in New York 16 Nov. 1739.

Borkly, George. He was naturalized in Maryland 10 Apr. 1771. He was a German.

Born, Adam. He was naturalized in Maryland 10 Sep. 1760.

Born, Daniel. He was naturalized in Pennsylvania 10 Sep. 1761. He was from Lancaster County.

Born, George. He was naturalized in Maryland 10 Sep. 1760.

Born, George. He was naturalized in Pennsylvania 24 Sep. 1762. He was from Berks County.

Born, Michael. He was naturalized in Maryland 31 Aug. 1757.

Borrell, Mathias. He was naturalized in New York 17 June 1726.

Bort, Nicholas. He was naturalized in Maryland 17 Apr. 1761.

Bos, Hendrick. He took the oath to the King 21–26 Oct. 1664 after the conquest of New Netherland.

Bos, Peter. He was naturalized in New York 16 Feb. 1771. He was a farmer from Bergen County, New Jersey.

Bosard, John. He was naturalized in Virginia 12 May 1705.

Boshaer, Jorg. He was naturalized in New York 8–9 Sep. 1715. He was from Ulster County.

Boshart, Jacob. He was naturalized in New York 21 Apr. 1752. He was a stone cutter from New York City.

Boshart, John. He, his wife Anna Rosina Boshart, son Christopher Boshart, and daughter Dorothy Boshart were naturalized in New Jersey 10 Feb. 1727/8. They were born in Germany.

Bosmon, Francois. He was endenized in New York 16 Aug. 1686.

Boss, Jacob. He was naturalized in New York 24 June 1734.

Bossard, John. He was naturalized in Virginia 12 May 1705.

Bott, Adam. He was naturalized in Pennsylvania 10 Sep. 1761. He was from York County.

Bott, Emrich. He was naturalized in Maryland 12 Sep. 1765. He was a German from Frederick County.

Bott, Henry. He was naturalized in Pennsylvania 11 Apr. 1761. He was from York County.

Bott, Henry. He was naturalized in Pennsylvania 10–12 Apr. 1762. He was from Lancaster County.

Bott, Herman. He was naturalized in Pennsylvania 25 Sep. 1750. He was from York County.

Bott, Jacob. He was naturalized in Pennsylvania 11 Apr. 1761. He was from York County.

Bott, Wendel. He was naturalized in Maryland 11 Sep. 1763. He was a German from Frederick County.

Botts, Rynhard. He was naturalized in Pennsylvania 11 Apr. 1761. He was from York County.

Bouch, Elizabeth. She was naturalized in New York 6 July 1723.

Boucher, Benjamin. He was naturalized in Pennsylvania 10–11 Apr. 1745. He was from Lancaster County.

Boucher, Elias. He was endenized in England 31 Jan. 1689/90. He came to Massachusetts.

Boucher, Louis. He was naturalized in England 20 Mar. 1686. He came to Massachusetts.

Boucher, Michael. He was naturalized in Virginia 5 May 1747. He was from Frederick County.

Boucher, Phillip. He was naturalized in Virginia 5 May 1747. He was from Frederick County.

Bouchet, Nicholas. He was a native of Nantheil, Les Meaux, France. His wife was Susanne Deshais born at Magny Poroisse, Bountigny, France. His daughter was Susanna Bouchet born at Fublainne, Brie, France. They were naturalized in South Carolina ca. 1696.

Bouderaux, Francois. He took the oath of allegiance at Harbour Amhurst in the Magdalen Islands, Gulf of Saint Lawrence on 31 Aug. 1765. He was a native of Nova Scotia.

Bouderaux, Francois. He took the oath of allegiance at Harbour Amhurst in the Magdalen Islands, Gulf of Saint Lawrence 31 Aug. 1765. He was a native of Nova Scotia.

Bouderaux, Joseph. He took the oath of allegiance at Harbour Amhurst in the Magdalen Islands, Gulf of Saint Lawrence on 31 Aug. 1765. He was a native of Nova Scotia.

Bouderaux, Joseph. He took the oath of allegiance at Harbour Amhurst in the Magdalen Islands, Gulf of Saint Lawrence on 31 Aug. 1765. He was a native of Nova Scotia.

Boudin, John. He and his wife, Ester Boudin, were endenized in England 14 Oct. 1681. They came to New York.

Boudinot, Elias. He and his children, Peter Boudinot, Elias Boudinot, John Boudinot, and Mary Boudinot, were endenized in England 5 Mar. 1685/6. The family came to New York.

Boudrot, Anselme. He was an Acadian who took the oath of allegiance in Apr. 1730.

Boudrot, Antoine. He was an Acadian and took the oath to George II at the Mines, Pisiquit 31 Oct. 1727.

Boudrot, Antoine. He was an Acadian who took the oath of allegiance in Apr. 1730.

Boudrot, Chale. He was an Acadian and took the oath to George II at Annapolis River, Nova Scotia in Dec. 1729.

Boudrot, Charles. He was an Acadian who took the oath to George II at the Mines, Pisiquit 31 Oct. 1727.

Boudrot, Charles. He was an Acadian who took the oath of allegiance at Annapolis River in Dec. 1729.

Boudrot, Charles. He was an Acadian who took the oath of allegiance in Apr. 1730.

Boudrot, Charles. He was an Acadian who took the oath of allegiance in Apr. 1730.

Boudrot, Claude. He was an Acadian who took the oath of allegiance in Apr. 1730.

Boudrot, Claude. He was an Acadian who took the oath of allegiance in Apr. 1730.

Boudrot, Claude. He was an Acadian who took the oath of allegiance in Apr. 1730.

Boudrot, Dennis. He was an Acadian who took the oath of allegiance in Apr. 1730.

Boudrot, Etienne. He was an Acadian and took the oath to George II at the Mines, Pisiquit 31 Oct. 1727.

Boudrot, Etienne. He was an Acadian who took the oath of allegiance in Apr. 1730.

Boudrot, Francois. He was an Acadian and took the oath to George II at the Mines, Pisiquit 31 Oct. 1727.

Boudrot, Francois. He was an Acadian who took the oath of allegiance in Apr. 1730.

Boudrot, Fancois. He was an Acadian who took the oath of allegiance in Apr. 1730.

Boudrot, Jean. He was an Acadian who took the oath of allegiance in Apr. 1730.

Boudrot, Jean. He was an Acadian who took the oath of allegiance in Apr. 1730.

Boudrot, Joseph. He was an Acadian who took the oath to George II at the Mines, Pisiquit 31 Oct. 1727.

Boudrot, Joseph. He was an Acadian who took the oath of allegiance in Apr. 1730.

Boudrot, Joseph. He was an Acadian who took the oath of allegiance in Apr. 1730.

Boudrot, Michel. He was an Acadian and took the oath to George II at the Mines, Pisiquit 31 Oct. 1727.

Boudrot, Michel. He was an Acadian and took the oath to George II at Annapolis River, Nova Scotia in Dec. 1729.

Boudrot, Ollevier. He was an Acadian who took the oath of allegiance in Apr. 1730.

Boudrot, Paul. He was an Acadian who took the oath of allegiance in Apr. 1730.

Boudrot, Paul. He was an Acadian who took the oath of allegiance in Apr. 1730.

Boudrot, Paul. He was an Acadian who took the oath of allegiance in Apr. 1730.

Boudrot, Pierre. He was an Acadian and took the oath to George II at Annapolis River, Nova Scotia in the Dec. 1729.

Boudrot, Pierre. He was an Acadian who took the oath of allegiance in Apr. 1730.

Boudrot, Pierre. He was an Acadian who took the oath of allegiance in Apr. 1730.

Boudrot, Pierre. He was an Acadian who took the oath of allegiance in Apr. 1730.

Boudrot, Rene. He was an Acadian and took the oath to George II at the Mines, Pisiquit 31 Oct. 1727.

Boudrot, Rene. He was an Acadian who took the oath of allegiance in Apr. 1730.

Bougeaud, Louis. He petitioned to be naturalized in New York 19 Aug. 1687.

Bougenon, Joseph. He took the oath of allegiance at Mobile, Alabama 2 Oct. 1764.

Bougher, John. He was naturalized in Pennsylvania 11 Apr. 1763. He was from Lancaster County.

Bougher, John. He was naturalized in Pennsylvania 11 Apr. 1761. He was from Lancaster County.

Boughtall, Henry. He was naturalized in Maryland 19 Apr. 1743.

Bouher, Martin. He was naturalized in Pennsylvania 10 Sep. 1761. He was from Lancaster County.

Bouier, Lowies. He took the oath of naturalization in New York 1 Sep. 1687 in Ulster County.

Bouin, Aman. He was endenized in England 16 Dec. 1687. He came to New York.

Bouin, Gabriel. He was endenized in England 29 Sep. 1698. He came to New York.

Boullon, Andre. He took the oath of allegiance at Mobile, West Florida 2 Oct. 1764.

Boulus, Nicholas. He was naturalized in Maryland 11 Sep. 1765. He was a German from Frederick County.

Boum, Jacob. He was naturalized in New Jersey 20 Aug. 1755.

Bouman, Golliep. He was naturalized in New Jersey 20 Mar. 1762.

Bouman, Simon. He was naturalized in Maryland 11 Sep. 1765. He was a German from Frederick County.

Bounin, Aaman [?]. He was naturalized in England and had it recorded in New York 21 Apr. 1691, Barbados 3 July 1694, and South Carolina 1 Nov. 1698.

Bouquet, Col. Henry. He was naturalized in Maryland 24 Apr. 1762. He served in the 6th or Royal Regiment.

Bouquet, Henry. He was naturalized in Pennsylvania 10 Apr. 1765. He was from Bucks County. He was a colonel in the Royal American Regiment.

Bouquet, Peter. He was naturalized in South Carolina 14 Aug. 1744.

Bourdet, Pierre. He was endenized in New York 10 Mar. 1686.

Bourdet, Samuel. He was endenized in London 5 Jan. 1686/7. He came to New York.

Bourdillon, Rev. Benedict. He, his wife Johanna Gertruij Bourdillon, and son Andrew Bourdillon were naturalized in Maryland 24 July 1769. He was a native of Geneva, Switzerland and was minister of St. Paul's Parish in Baltimore County.

Boureau, Antoine. He was born at Lusinain, Poitou, France, the son of Jean Boureau and Marguerit Gourdain. His wife was Jeanne Boureau, was born in England. They were naturalized in South Carolina ca. 1696.

Bourg, Abraham. He took the oath of allegiance at Port Royal, Nova Scotia 16 Aug. 1695.

Bourg, Abraham. He was an Acadian and took the oath to George II at Annapolis River, Nova Scotia in Dec. 1729.

Bourg, Abraham. He was an Acadian who took the oath of allegiance in Apr. 1730.

Bourg, Abraham. He was an Acadian who took the oath of allegiance in Apr. 1730.

Bourg, Alexandre. He took the oath of allegiance at Port Royal, Nova Scotia 16 Aug. 1695.

Bourg, Alexandre. He was an Acadian who took the oath of allegiance in Apr. 1730.

Bourg, Alexandre, Jr. He was an Acadian who took the oath of allegiance in Apr. 1730.

Bourg, Ambroise. He was an Acadian who took the oath of allegiance in Apr. 1730.

Bourg, Bernard. He took the oath of allegiance at Port Royal, Nova Scotia 16 Aug. 1695.

Bourg, Charles. He was an Acadian who took the oath of allegiance in Apr. 1730.

Bourg, Claude. He was an Acadian and took the oath to George II at Annapolis River, Nova Scotia in Dec. 1729.

Bourg, Francois. He was an Acadian who took the oath of allegiance in Apr. 1730.

Bourg, Francois. He was an Acadian who took the oath of allegiance in Apr. 1730.

Bourg, Francois. He was an Acadian who took the oath of allegiance in Apr. 1730.

Bourg, J. He was an Acadian who took the oath to the King at the Mines, Pisiquit, Nova Scotia 31 Oct. 1737.

Bourg, Jean. He took the oath of allegiance at Port Royal, Nova Scotia 16 Aug. 1695.

Bourg, Jean. He was an Acadian who took the oath of allegiance in Apr. 1730.

Bourg, John. He was an Acadian who took the oath of allegiance in Apr. 1730.

Bourg, Joseph. He was an Acadian and took the oath to George II at Annapolis River, Nova Scotia in Dec. 1729.

Bourg, Joseph. He was an Acadian and took the oath to George II at Annapolis River, Nova Scotia in Dec. 1729.

Bourg, Joseph. He was an Acadian and took the oath to George II at Annapolis River, Nova Scotia in Dec. 1729.

Bourg, Joseph. He was an Acadian who took the oath of allegiance in Apr. 1730.

Bourg, Louis. He was an Acadian who took the oath of allegiance in Apr. 1730.

Bourg, Martin. He took the oath of allegiance at Port Royal, Nova Scotia 16 Aug. 1695.

Bourg, Michel. He was an Acadian who took the oath of allegiance in Apr. 1730.

Bourg, Michel. He was an Acadian who took the oath of allegiance in Apr. 1730.

Bourg, Pierre. He was an Acadian and took the oath to the King at the Mines, Pisiquit, Nova Scotia 31 Oct. 1727.

Bourg, Pierre. He was an Acadian who took the oath of allegiance in Apr. 1730.

Bourg, Pierre. He was an Acadian who took the oath of allegiance in Apr. 1730.

Bourgeois, Charles. He was an Acadian who took the oath of allegiance in Apr. 1730.

Bourgeois, Charles. He was an Acadian who took the oath of allegiance in Apr. 1730.

Bourgeois, Claude. He was an Acadian and took the oath to George II at Annapolis River, Nova Scotia in Dec. 1729.

Bourgeois, Claude. He was an Acadian who took the oath of allegiance in Apr. 1730.

Bourgeois, G. He was an Acadian and took the oath to George II at Annapolis River, Nova Scotia in the Dec. 1729.

Bourgeois, Guillaume. He was an Acadian who took the oath of allegiance in Apr. 1730.

Bourgeois, Henry. He was an Acadian who took the oath of allegiance in Apr. 1730

Bourgeois, Jean Baptiste. He was an Acadian who took the oath of allegiance in Apr. 1730.

Bourgeois, Joseph. He was an Acadian and took the oath to George II at Annapolis River, Nova Scotia in Dec. 1729.

Bourgeois, Michel. He was an Acadian and took the oath to George II at Annapolis River, Nova Scotia in Dec. 1729.

Bourgeois, Michel. He was an Acadian who took the oath of allegiance in Apr. 1730.

Bourgeois, Paul. He was an Acadian who took the oath of allegiance in Apr. 1730.

Bourgeois, Pierre. He was an Acadian who took the oath of allegiance in Apr. 1730.

Bourget, Daniel. He was naturalized in South Carolina 20 Jan. 1741. He also appeared as Daniel Bourzet.

Bourie, Nicholas. He took the oath of allegiance at Mobile, West Florida 2 Oct. 1764.

Boussel, Francois. He was an Acadian who took the oath of allegiance in Apr. 1730.

Boutellier, Jean. He petitioned to be naturalized in New York 19 Aug. 1687.

Boutineau, Stephen. He was endenized in London 24 June 1703. He came to New York.

Bouton, Johann Daniel. He was naturalized in Pennsylvania 10–14 Apr. 1747. He was from Philadelphia.

Bouwman, Abraham. He was naturalized in New York 20 Mar. 1762.

Bouyer, John. He was endenzied in New York 2 Oct. 1695.

Bouzage, Joseph. He took the oath of allegiance at Mobile, West Florida 2 Oct. 1764.

Bower, George. He was naturalized in New York 8 Mar. 1773.

Bower, George. He was naturalized in Pennsylvania 10 Sep. 1761. He was from Bucks County.

Bower, Jacob. He was naturalized in Pennsylvania 10 Apr. 1765. He was from Philadelphia.

Bower, Michael. He was naturalized in Pennsylvania 10 Apr. 1767. He was from Amity Township, Philadelphia County.

Bowman, Casper. He was naturalized in Pennsylvania 11–13 Apr. 1743. He was from Philadelphia County.

Bowman, Christian. He was naturalized in Pennsylvania 6 Feb. 1730/1. He was from Philadelphia County.

Bowman, Henry. He was naturalized in Pennsylvania 11 Apr. 1749. He was from Lancaster County.

Bowman, Jacob. He was naturalized in Pennsylvania 29 Mar. 1735. He was from Philadelphia County.

Bowman, John. He was naturalized in Pennsylvania 24 Sep. 1753. He was from Lancaster County.

Bowman, John. He was naturalized in Pennsylvania 11 Apr. 1761. He was from Lancaster County.

Bowman, Mathew. He was naturalized in New York 28 July 1749. He was from New York City and a yeoman.

Bower, Adam. He was naturalized in Pennsylvania 24 Sep. 1762. He was from Berks County.

Bower, Christian. He was naturalized in Maryland 11 Sep. 1765.

Bower, Christian. He was naturalized in Pennsylvania 29–30 May 1772. He was from Frederick County, Maryland.

Bower, Daniel. He was naturalized in Maryland 8 Sep. 1768. He was a German.

Bower, John. He was naturalized in New Jersey in 1770.

Bower, John. He was naturalized in Pennsylvania 11–13 Apr. 1743. He was from Philadelphia County.

Bower, Samuel. He was naturalized in Pennsylvania 11–13 Apr. 1743. He was from Philadelphia County.

Bower, Martin. He was naturalized in Pennsylvania 11 Apr. 1751. He was from York County.

Bower, Michael. He was naturalized in Pennsylvania 10 Sep. 1761. He was from York County.

Bower, Michael. He was naturalized in Pennsylvania 11 Apr. 1767. He was from Amity Township, Philadelphia County.

Bower, Stephen. He was naturalized in Maryland 14 Apr. 1762.

Bowles, John. He was naturalized in Pennsylvania 11 Jan. 1683. He was formerly of New Sweden.

Bowman, Christian. He was naturalized in Pennsylvania in 1730–31. He was from Philadelphia County.

Bowman, Henry. He was naturalized in Pennsylvania 10 Sep. 1761. He was from York County.

Bowman, Jacob. He was naturalized in Pennsylvania in 1735. He was from Philadelphia County.

Bowman, Jacob. He was naturalized in Frederick County, Virginia 3 June 1767.

Bowman, Jacob. He was naturalized in Pennsylvania 24–25 Sep./5 Oct. 1767. He was from Frederick County, Maryland.

Bowman, John. He was naturalized in Pennsylvania in 1730–31. He was from Philadelphia County.

Bowman, Valentine. He was naturalized in Pennsylvania 24 Sep. 1760. He was from Lancaster County.

Bowse, John. He was naturalized in Pennsylvania 10 Sep. 1761. He was from Bucks County.

Bowshard, Andrew. He was naturalized in Pennsylvania 24–25 Sep. 1764. He was from Philadelphia.

Bowsman, Michael. He was naturalized in Pennsylvania 10 & 23 Apr. 1764. He was from Lancaster Township, Lancaster County.

Bowyer, Gabriel. He was naturalized in Pennsylvania 11–13 Apr. 1743. He was from Philadelphia County.

Bowyer, Etienne. He was endenized in New York 29 July 1686.

Boyd, Jacques. He was the son of Jean and Jeanne Boyd of Bordeaux, Guienne, France. He was naturalized in South Carolina ca. 1696.

Boyd, Jean. He was the son of Jean and Jeanne Boyd of Bordeaux, Guienne, France. He was naturalized in South Carolina ca. 1696.

Boyd, Gabriel. He was the son of Jean and Jeanne Boyd of Bordeaux, Guienne, France. He was naturalized in South Carolina ca. 1696.

Boyd, Jeanne. She was the wife [i.e. widow] of Jean Boyd and daughter of Elie Berchaud and Jeane Berchaud of LaRochelle, d'Onis, France. Her younger children were Jeanne Boyd, Elizabeth Boyd, Jacques Boyd, and Jean Auguste Boyd who were born in South Carolina. They were naturalized in South Carolina ca. 1696.

Boyer, Andreas. He was naturalized in Pennsylvania 11 Apr. 1761. He was from Northampton County.

Boyer, Andrew. He was naturalized in Pennsylvania 11 Apr. 1749. He was from Philadelphia County.

Boyer, Andrew. He was naturalized in Pennsylvania 10 Apr. 1754. He was from Berks County.

Boyer, Andrew. He was naturalized in Pennsylvania 24 Sep. 1755. He was from Philadelphia County.

Boyer, Christopher. He was naturalized in Pennsylvania 10 Sep. 1761. He was from Berks County.

Boyer, Jacob. He was naturalized in Pennsylvania 24 Sep. 1760. He was from Berks County.

Boyer, John. He was naturalized in Pennsylvania 10 Apr. 1754. He was from Berks County.

Boyer, Malacki. He was naturalized in Maryland 11 Apr. 1771. He was a German.

Boyer, Nicholas. He was naturalized in Pennsylvania 24 Sep. 1759.

Boyer, Philip. He was naturalized in Pennsylvania 10–12 Apr. 1762. He was from Philadelphia County.

Boyerle, Conrod. He was naturalized in Maryland 11 Apr. 1764. He was a German.

Boyerle, Ludy. He was naturalized in Maryland 11 Apr. 1764.

Boyle, Baltzer. He was naturalized in Pennsylvania 11 Apr. 1761. He was from Northampton County.

Boys, Cornelius. He was naturalized in Maryland 17 Sep. 1681.

Boythyman, Jacob. He was naturalized in Pennsylvania 24–25 Sep. 1764. He was from Northern Liberties Township, Philadelphia County.

Braambos, Willemina. She was naturalized in New York 6 Dec. 1746.

Braambos, William. He was naturalized in New York 6 Dec. 1746.

Braambos, William, Jr. He was naturalized in New York 6 Dec. 1746.

Brack, Hans Michall. He was naturalized in New York 22 Nov. 1715. He was from Albany County.

Brader, John. He was naturalized in New York 27 Jan. 1770.

Bradhour, Nicholas. He was naturalized in New York 27 Jan. 1770.

Bradon, Isaque Pereyra. He was naturalized in Jamaica 2 Feb. 1708/9.

Bradonneau, Henry. He was naturalized in Virginia 12 May 1705.

Bradshaw, Mary. She was naturalized in Jamaica 17 June 1696.

Braker, John. He was naturalized in Maryland 11 Sep. 1765.

Brand, Adam. He was naturalized in Pennsylvania 14 Feb. 1729/30. He was from Lancaster County.

Brand, Adam. He was naturalized in Maryland 17 July 1765. He was a German from Frederick, Md.

Brand, Martin. He was naturalized in Pennsylvania 10 Apr. 1755. He was from Philadelphia County.

Brand, Michael. He was naturalized in Pennsylvania 11 Apr. 1761. He was from Philadelphia County.

Brand, Paulus. He was naturalized in New York 20 Mar. 1762.

Brandas, Isaack. He was naturalized in Jamaica 29 July 1690.

Brandau, Nicolas. He was naturalized in New York 8-9 Sep. 1715 He was from Ulster County.

Brandau, Wilhelminus. He was naturalized in New York 8-9 Sep. 1715. He was from Ulster County.

Brandiman, Christian. He was naturalized in Pennsylvania 11-13 Apr. 1743. He was from Philadelphia County.

Brandon, Abigail. She was naturalized in Jamaica 3 Feb. 1731/2.

Brandon, Easter. She was naturalized in Jamaica 3 Jan. 1732/3. She was a widow.

Brandon, Esther Pinto. She was naturalized in Jamaica 27 Aug. 1745. She was a Jewess.

Brandon, Isaac Peirera. He was naturalized in Jamaica 26 May 1709.

Brandon, Isaac Pereria, Jr. He was naturalized in Jamaica 25 Mar. 1728/9.

Brandon, Isaac Pinton. He was naturalized in Jamaica 26 Oct. 1736.

Brandon, Jacob. He was naturalized in Jamaica 17 Aug. 1709.

Brandon, Jacob. He was naturalized in Jamaica 14 Apr. 1712.

Brandon, Jacob. He was naturalized in Jamaica 24 Nov. 1741. He was a Jew.

Brandon, Jacob Pinto. He was naturalized in Jamaica 25 Nov. 1740. He was a Jew.

Brandon, Joshua. He was naturalized in Jamaica 14 Aug. 1710.

Brandon, Sarah. She was naturalized in Jamaica 8 Oct. 1735.

Brandonneau, Henry. He was naturalized in Virginia 12 May 1705.

Brandt, Johannes. He was naturalized in Pennsylvania 11-13 Apr. 1743. He was from Philadelphia County.

Brant, Albertus. He was endenized in New York 14 July 1686.

Branner, Henry. He and his son, John Branner, were naturalized in Maryland 3 May 1740. He was from Prince George's County and was born in Germany.

Branner, Jacob. He and his children, Peter Branner, Michael Branner, John Branner, Jacob Branner, Mary Branner, and Elizabeth Branner, were naturalized in Maryland 3 May 1740. He was from Prince George's County and was born in Germany.

Branner, John. He and his children, John Branner, Jacob Branner, Catherine Branner, Barbara Branner, and Mary Branner, were naturalized in Maryland 3 May 1740. He was from Prince George's County and was born in Germany.

Branner, Joseph. He and his son, Elias Branner, were naturalized in Maryland 3 May 1740. He was from Prince George's County and was born in Germany.

Branner, Paul. He was naturalized in Pennsylvania 11-13 Apr. 1743. He was from Philadelphia County.

Braquet, Jean Seben. He took the oath of allegiance at Mobile, West Florida 2 Oct. 1764.

Brasseuir, Benojs. He, his wife, and children were made denizens in Maryland 4 Dec. 1661. He was French and was late of Virginia. He also appeared as Benjamin Brasseuir.

Brassier, Matthurin. He was an Acadian who took the oath of allegiance in Apr. 1730.

Brassillon, Tourangau die [sic]. He took the oath of allegiance at Mobile, West Florida 2 Oct. 1764.

Brathouwer, Nicholas. He was naturalized in New York 20 Mar. 1762.

Braun, Georg Frederick. He was naturalized in Maryland 9 Apr. 1760. He lived in Baltimore, Maryland.

Braun, Simon. He was naturalized in Pennsylvania 20 Mar. 1762.

Braux, Antoine. He was an Acadian who took the oath to the King 31 Oct. 1727.

Braux, Jean. He was an Acadian who took the oath to the King at the Mines, Pisiquit, Nova Scotia 31 Oct. 1727.

Braux, Pierre. He was an Acadian who took the oath to the King at the Mines, Pisiquit on 31 Oct. 1727.

Bravet, John. He was naturalized in Jamaica 27 Jan. 1723/4.

Bravo, Benjamin. He was naturalized in Jamaica 30 Nov. 1740. He was a Jew.

Bravo, David. He was naturalized in Jamaica 30 July 1706.

Bravo, David. He was naturalized in Jamaica in 30 Nov. 1740. He was a Jew.

Bravo, Isaac. He was naturalized in Jamaica 31 May 1710.

Breack, David. He was naturalized in Pennsylvania 24 Sep. 1755. He was from Lancaster County.

Breau, Alexandre. He was an Acadian and took the oath of allegiance in Apr. 1730.

Breau, Ambroise. He was an Acadian and took the oath to George II at Annapolis River, Nova Scotia in Dec. 1729.

Breau, Charles. He was an Acadian who took the oath of allegiance in Apr. 1730.

Breau, Francois. He was an Acadian who took the oath of allegiance in Apr. 1730.

Breau, Jean. He was an Acadian and took the oath to George II at Annapolis River, Nova Scotia in Dec. 1729.

Breau, Jean. He was an Acadian who took the oath of allegiance in Apr. 1730.

Breau, Jean. He was an Acadian who took the oath of allegiance in Apr. 1730.

Breau, Jean. He was an Acadian who took the oath of allegiance in Apr. 1730.

Breau, Jean. He was an Acadian who took the oath of allegiance in Apr. 1730.

Breau, Joseph. He was an Acadian who took the oath of allegiance in Apr. 1730.

Breau, Pierre. He was an Acadian who took the oath of allegiance in Apr. 1730.

Breau, Pierre. He was an Acadian who took the oath of allegiance in Apr. 1730.

Breau, Pierre. He was an Acadian who took the oath of allegiance in Apr. 1730.

Breau, Pierre. He was an Acadian who took the oath of allegiance in Apr. 1730.

Breaunea, Maran. He took the oath of allegiance at Mobile, West Florida 2 Oct. 1764.

Brechel, Andrew. He was naturalized in Pennsylvania 10 Apr. 1759.

Brecht, John. He was naturalized in Pennsylvania 29 Mar. 1735. He was from Bucks County.

Brecht, Michael. He was naturalized in Pennsylvania 25 Sep. 1744. He was from Lancaster County.

Brecht, Stephen. He was naturalized in Pennsylvania 11 Apr. 1741. He was from Lancaster County.

Brecht, Wentzel. He was naturalized in Maryland 12 Sep. 1759.

Brecker, Peter. He was naturalized in Pennsylvania 11–13 Apr. 1743. He was from Lancaster County.

Brehm, Phillip. He was naturalized in Nova Scotia on 4 July 1758.

Breikbill, John Wendell. He was naturalized in Pennsylvania in Sep. 1740. He was from Philadelphia.

Breitenback, Philip. He was naturalized in Pennsylvania 11 Apr. 1761. He was from Lancaster County.

Breitenbeger, Baltus. He was naturalized in New York 8 Mar. 1773.

Bremar, Solomon. He was born in Anseme, Picardie, France and was the son of Jacque Bremar and Marthe LeGrande. His wife was Marie Sauvagot who was born at D'alleurs, pais Saintonge, France. She was the daughter of Jean Sauvagot and Madelenne Potet. They were naturalized in South Carolina 10 Mar. 1696/7. He was a weaver.

Brendel, George. He was naturalized in Pennsylvania 10 Sep. 1761. He was from Berks County. He was a Moravian.

Breneaux, Pierre. He took the oath of allegiance at Mobile, West Florida 2 Oct. 1764.

Breneison, Rudolph. He was naturalized in Pennsylvania 10 Apr. 1760.

Brenner, Philip. He was naturalized in Pennsylvania 16 May 1769. He was from Donegal Township, Lancaster County.

Brenor, Garrard. He was naturalized in Pennsylvania 24 Sep. 1753. He was from Lancaster County.

Brenser, Christian. He was naturalized in Pennsylvania 11 Apr. 1761. He was from Lancaster County.

Brescher, Philip. He was naturalized in Pennsylvania 10 & 23 Apr. 1764. He was from Macungy Township, Northampton County.

Bresse, Gerrit Hendrickse. He took the oath of allegiance in Flackland, Kings County, New York 26–30 Sep. 1687. He was a native of the colony.

Bretter, Anthony. He was naturalized in Pennsylvania 19 May 1739. He was from Lancaster County.

Brewback, Adam. He was naturalized in Frederick County, Virginia 1 Nov. 1768.

Brewer, Johannes. He was naturalized in Pennsylvania 11–13 Apr. 1743. He was from Philadelphia County.

Brevet, Phillip. He was naturalized in Jamaica 17 Sep. 1741. He was a free Negro.

Breyfogel, Peter. He was naturalized in Pennsylvania 16 Nov. 1771. He was from Maiden Creek Township, Berks County.

Breytigam, Frederick. He was naturalized in New York 26 July 1769. He was a baker from New York City.

Brez, Jean Peter. He was naturalized in South Carolina 24 Oct. 1741.

Bricard, Henry. He was naturalized in New York 10 Jan. 1715/6. He was from New York City and a merchant.

Bricker, Jacob. He was naturalized in Pennsylvania 10 Apr. 1760.

Bridlife, Henrich. He was naturalized in New York 20 Mar. 1762.

Bridon, Francis. He, his wife Jeanne Bridon, son John Bridon, and daughter Susanna Bridon, were endenized in England 8 Mar. 1681/2. They came to Massachusetts.

Briell, Toussein. He took the oath to the King 21–26 Oct. 1664 after the conquest of New Netherland.

Brimmer, Martin. He was naturalized in Massachusetts 12 Apr. 1731. He was a German.

Brindle, Philip. He was naturalized in Pennsylvania 10 Sep. 1761. He was from Lancaster County.

Bringier, Marie. She was naturalized in New York 1740–1741.

Bringle, Christian. He was naturalized in Maryland 11 May 1774. He was a German.

Brinihol, David. He was naturalized in London 5 June 1707. He was the son of Stephen Brinihol by his wife Jane. He was born at Clariat in France. The record was recorded in Jamaica in 1709.

Brining, David. He was naturalized in Pennsylvania 10–12 Apr. 1762. He was from Berks County.

Brinker, Henry. He was naturalized in Frederick County, Virginia 5 Sep. 1754.

Brisant, John. He was naturalized in Jamaica 12 Aug. 1734. He was a sugar baker.

Brispoe, Anthony. He was naturalized in Maryland in Feb. 1674. He was born in Spain.

Britt, William. He was naturalized in New York 24 Apr. 1767. He was a farmer from Westchester County.

Brock, Rudy. He was naturalized in Frederick County, Virginia 4 Aug. 1747.

Brodbeck, Bernard. He was naturalized in Pennsylvania 10 Sep. 1761. He was from Lancaster County.

Brohx, Pierre. He was an Acadian who took the oath to the King 31 Oct. 1727.

Brok, Moses. He was naturalized in Virginia 12 May 1705.

Brolliar, Emanuel. He was naturalized in Pennsylvania 10 Sep. 1761. He was from Lancaster County.

Bronce, George. He was naturalized in New York 27 Jan. 1770.

Bronck, Henrich. He was naturalized in New York 8–9 Sep. 1715. He was from Ulster County.

Brooker, Peter. He was naturalized in Pennsylvania 11 Apr. 1761. He was from Berks County.

Brookhart, Julius. He was naturalized in Pennsylvania 24 Sep. 1763. He was from Helm Township, York County.

Brooks, John. He was naturalized in New York 20 May 1769.

Brooks, Michael. He was naturalized in Pennsylvania 24 Sep. 1745. He was from Lancaster County.

Broord, James. He and his sons, James Broord, John Broord, and Solomon Broord, were naturalized in Maryland 25 Mar. 1702. They lived in Kent County.

Brosis, Abraham. He was naturalized in Pennsylvania 25 Sep. 1758.

Brosius, George. He was naturalized in Pennsylvania 10–14 Apr. 1747. He was from Lancaster County.

Brosman, Frances. He was naturalized in Pennsylvania 10 Sep. 1761. He was from Lancaster County.

Brossius, Sebastian. He was naturalized in Pennsylvania 24–25 Sep. 1764. He was from Tulpehocken Township, Berks County.

Brosst, Adam. He was naturalized in Pennsylvania 24 Sep. 1762. He was from Northampton County.

Brost, Conrod. He was naturalized in Maryland 12 Sep. 1759.

Brotzman, Conrad. He was naturalized in Pennsylvania 11 Apr. 1768. He was from Providence Township, Philadelphia County.

Brough, Matthew. He was naturalized in New York 3 May 1755.

Broughton, Edward. He was naturalized in London in 1690. He was born at The Hague, Holland, the son of Edward Broughton late of March Weild in Denbigh and his wife Alice. It was recorded in Jamaica in Feb. 1690.

Broulaet, Bourgon. He took the oath of allegiance in Breucklijn, Kings County, New York 26–30 Sep. 1687. He had been in the colony 12 years.

Broussard, Francois. He took the oath of allegiance at Port Royal, Nova Scotia 16 Aug. 1695.

Broussard, Saviott. He petitioned for denization 12 Mar. 1695/6 in New York. He was also known as Saviott Deschamps.

Brossard, Claude. He was an Acadian and took the oath to the King at the Mines, Pisiquit, Nova Scotia 31 Oct. 1727.

Brousse, James. He was naturalized in Virginia 12 May 1705.

Brouwer, Abram. He took the oath of allegiance in Breucklijn, Kings County, New York 26–30 Sep. 1687. He was a native of the colony.

Brouwer, Adam. He took the oath of allegiance in Breucklijn, Kings County, New York 26–30 Sep. 1687. He had been in the colony 45 years.

Brouwer, Adam, Jr. He took the oath of allegiance in Breucklijn, Kings County, New York 26–30 Sep. 1687. He was a native of the colony.

Brouwer, Dirck. He took the oath of allegiance in Flackland, Kings County, New York 26–30 Sep. 1687. He was a native of the colony.

Brouwer, Hendrick. He took the oath of allegiance in Flackland, Kings County, New York 26–30 Sep. 1687. He was a native of the colony.

Brouwer, Jacob. He took the oath of allegiance in Breucklijn, Kings County, New York 26–30 Sep. 1687. He was a native of the colony.

Brouwer, Johannis. He took the oath of allegiance in Gravens End, Kings County, New York 26–30 Sep. 1687. He was a native of the colony.

Brouwer, Pieter. He took the oath of allegiance in Breucklijn, Kings County, New York 26–30 Sep. 1687. He was a native of the colony.

Brouwer, Pieter. He took the oath of allegiance in Flackland, Kings County, New York 26–30 Sep. 1687. He was a native of the colony.

Browbraker, John. He was naturalized in Pennsylvania 24 Sep. 1760. He was from Lancaster County

Brower, Christian. He was naturalized in Pennsylvania 11–13 Apr. 1743. He was from Chester County.

Brower, Frederick. He was naturalized in North Carolina 22 Sep. 1763. He was from Rowan County and a German.

Brower, Jan. He took the oath of allegiance in Kings County, New York 26–30 Sep. 1687. He was from Flackland and had been in the colony 30 years.

Brower, Matthis. He took the oath of allegiance in Orange County, New York 26 Sep. 1687.

Brown, Conrad. He was naturalized in Pennsylvania 10 Apr. 1760.

Brown, Conrad. He was naturalized in Pennsylvania 10 Sep. 1761. He was from Berks County.

Brown, Derick. He was naturalized in Maryland 19 Nov. 1686.

Brown, Frederick. He was naturalized in Jamaica 4 June 1762.

Brown, George. He was naturalized in New York 8 Mar. 1773.

Brown, Godfrey. He was naturalized in Pennsylvania 25 Sep. 1744. He was from Lancaster County.

Brown, Henry. He was naturalized in Maryland 11 Sep. 1765. He was a German from Pint-Run Hundred, Frederick County.

Brown, Jacob. He was naturalized in New Jersey in 1755.

Brown, Jacob. He was naturalized in North Carolina 23 Mar. 1763. He was from Rowan County.

Brown, Jacob. He was naturalized in Pennsylvania 24–25 Sep. 1764. He was from Philadelphia.

Brown, Jacob Frederick. He was naturalized in Maryland 14 Apr. 1762. He was a German.

Brown, James. He was naturalized in Jamaica 20 Jan. 1750/1. He was a free Negro.

Brown, John. He was naturalized in Massachusetts 7 Dec. 1731.

Brown, John. He was naturalized in Pennsylvania 11–13 Apr. 1743. He was from Philadelphia County.

Brown, John. He was naturalized in Pennsylvania 24 Sep. 1763. He was from Lancaster Township, Lancaster County.

Brown, John Engle. He was naturalized in Pennsylvania 11 Apr. 1761. He was from Berks County.

Brown, John Henrick. He was naturalized in New York 25 July 1752. He was a wheelwright from Albany County.

Brown, Joseph. He was endenized in New York 12 May 1686.

Brown, Michael. He was naturalized in North Carolina 22 Sep. 1763. He was from Rowan County and a German.

Brown, Peter. He was naturalized in New Jersey 6 Dec. 1769.

Brown, Philip. He was naturalized in Pennsylvania 24 Sep. 1755.

Brown, Robert. He was naturalized in Jamaica 6 June 1710. He was a free Negro.

Brown, Sarah. She was naturalized in Jamaica 25 Sep. 1724.

Brown, Sarah. She was naturalized in Jamaica 23 Sep. 1725. She was the daughter of Abraham Lopez Laguna.

Brown, Stofold. He was naturalized in Maryland 24 Sep. 1765. He was a German.

Brown, William. He was naturalized in New York 25 July 1757.

Brownback, Garratt. He was naturalized in Pennsylvania 29 Mar. 1735. He was from Chester County.

Browne, Emanuel. He was naturalized in Jamaica 24 Dec. 1702.

Brownhill, James. He was naturalized in Jamaica 19 Aug. 1701.

Broyle, Conrad. He was naturalized in Orange County, Virginia 23 Feb. 1742/3. He was a native of Wurttemberg. He had been in the colony seven years. He also appeared as Conrad Broil.

Brua, Jacob. He was naturalized in Pennsylvania 12 Apr. 1750. He was from Lancaster County.

Brubagh, Michael. He was naturalized in Pennsylvania 11–13 Apr. 1743. He was from Lancaster County.

Brubaker, John. He was naturalized in Pennsylvania 14 Feb. 1729/30. He was from Lancaster County.

Brubecker, Rudulphus. He was naturalized in Maryland 9 Sep. 1761.

Brucker, Jacob. He was naturalized in Pennsylvania 24 May 1771. He was from Lebanon Township, Lancaster County.

Bruder, Henry. He was naturalized in Maryland 23 Sep. 1772. He was a German from Frederick County.

Bruder, Tobias. He was naturalized in Maryland 1 Oct. 1767. He was a German and a Dunker.

Brugman, Cornelius. He was naturalized in New York 3 Apr. 1716. He was a periwig maker from New York City.

Brugman, Gotfried. He was naturalized in New York 21 Oct. 1765. He was a mason from New York City.

Brugman, Henry. He was naturalized in New York 18 Oct. 1715. He was a rope maker from New York City.

Brugnet, Marye. She was the widow of Nicholas Potell. She was born at Diepe, France. She was naturalized in South Carolina ca. 1696.

Bruier, Peter. He was naturalized in New Jersey 28 Mar. 1749.

Bruin, Anth. He was an Acadian and took the oath of allegiance in Apr. 1730.

Brun, Antoine. He was an Acadian and took the oath to George II at Annapolis River, Nova Scotia in Dec. 1729.

Brun, Claud. He was an Acadian and took the oath to George II at Annapolis River, Nova Scotia in Dec. 1729.

Brun, Jean. He was an Acadian and took the oath to George II at Annapolis River, Nova Scotia in Dec. 1729.

Brun, Joseph. He was an Acadian and took the oath to George II at Annapolis River, Nova Scotia in Dec. 1729.

Brun, Vincent. He was an Acadian and took the oath to George II at Annapolis River, Nova Scotia in Dec. 1729.

Brunckhorst, John. He was naturalized in New York 20 May 1769. He was a sugar refiner in New York City.

Bruneau, Paul. He was the son of Arnaud Bruneau of Chabossiere and was born in La Rochelle, d'Onis, France. He was naturalized *ca.* 1696 in South Carolina.

Bruneau, Henri. He was the son of Henri and Marie Bruneau, and was born in La Rochelle, d'Onis, France. He was naturalized *ca.* 1696 in South Carolina.

Bruner, George. He was naturalized in North Carolina 23 Mar. 1763. He was from Rowan County.

Bruner, Henry. He was naturalized in North Carolina 23 Mar. 1763. He was from Rowan County.

Bruner, Peter. He was naturalized in Maryland 1 Oct. 1767. He was a German.

Brunesholtz, Christian. He was naturalized in Pennsylvania 10 Sep. 1761. He was from Lancaster County.

Brunner, Caspar. He was naturalized in Pennsylvania 10 Apr. 1765. He was from Lancaster Township, Lancaster County.

Brunner, Feliz. He was naturalized in Pennsylvania 11 Apr. 1749. He was from Bucks County.

Brunner, Henry. He was naturalized in Pennsylvania 10 Apr. 1760.

Brunner, Henry. He was naturalized in Pennsylvania 11 Apr. 1761. He was from Northampton County.

Brunner, Henry. He was naturalized in Pennsylvania 10 Sep. 1761. He was from Lancaster County.

Brunner, Jacob. He was naturalized in New York 3 July 1759.

Brunner, Peter. He was naturalized in Pennsylvania 10 Apr. 1765. He was from Lancaster Township, Lancaster County.

Brunnet, Henry. He was naturalized by Lord Culpeper in Virginia under the act of 1680. He was born in Rochelle, France.

Brussar, Clause. He was an Acadian who took the oath of allegiance in Apr. 1730.

Brussar, Jean. He was an Acadian and took the oath to George II at Annapolis River, Nova Scotia in Dec. 1729.

Brussar, Pierre. He was an Acadian and took the oath to George II at Annapolis River, Nova Scotia in Dec. 1729.

Brussar, Pierre. He was an Acadian and took the oath to George II at Annapolis River, Nova Scotia in Dec. 1729.

Brutel, John. He was naturalized in Jamaica 29 Dec. 1693.

Bruter, Jacob. He was naturalized in Maryland 12 Sep. 1764. He was a German.

Bruynenburgh, Jan Hanssen. He took the oath of allegiance 26–30 Sep. 1687 in Kings County, New York. He was from New Uijtrecht.

Bruynsen, Ruth. She took the oath of allegiance in Flackland, Kings County, New York 26–30 Sep. 1687. She had been in the colony 34 years.

Bryant, Anthony. He expressed his desire to be naturalized in New Castle County, Delaware 21 Feb. 1682/3.

Bryder, Abraham. He was naturalized in Pennsylvania 11–13 Apr. 1743. He was from Bucks County.

Bryell, Peter. He was naturalized in Pennsylvania 11 Apr. 1761. He was from Berks County.

Bryer, Francis. He was naturalized in New York 11 Sep. 1761.

Bryer, Jacob. He was naturalized in Pennsylvania 1740. He was from Bucks County.

Bryn, Jacobus. He was naturalized in New York 8–9 Sep. 1715. He was from Ulster County.

Bryninger, John Godlit. He was naturalized in Pennsylvania 10 Sep. 1761. He was from Berks County.

Bryninger, John Martin. He was naturalized in Pennsylvania 10 Sep. 1761. He was from Berks County.

Brytenhart, Christopher. He was naturalized in Pennsylvania 10 Sep. 1761. He was from Lancaster County.

Bsheere, Jacob. He was naturalized in New York 22 Nov. 1715. He was from Albany County.

Buch, Daniel. He was naturalized in New York 17 Jan. 1715/6. He was from Albany County.

Buch, John Hend. He was naturalized in New York 17 Jan. 1715/6. He was from Albany County.

Bucher, John. He was naturalized in Pennsylvania 11–13 Apr. 1743. He was from Lancaster County.

Bucher, Jacob. He was naturalized in Pennsylvania 11 Apr. 1761. He was from Lancaster County.

Bucher, John Ulrich. He was naturalized in Frederick County, Virginia 5 Nov. 1746.

Bucher, Peter. He was naturalized in Maryland 21 Sep. 1762. He was a German.

Bucher, Philip. He was naturalized in Maryland 4 Sep. 1765. He was a German from Frederick County.

Bucholtz, Henry. He was naturalized in Pennsylvania 29 Sep. 1709. He was from Philadelphia County.

Buck, Leonard. He was naturalized in Pennsylvania 11–13 Apr. 1743. He was from Philadelphia County.

Buckenmeyer, Erasmus. He was naturalized in Pennsylvania 19 May 1739. He was from Lancaster County.

Buckert, Johan Dedrick. He was naturalized in Pennsylvania 11 Apr. 1741. He was from Philadelphia County.

Buckhaus, John. He was naturalized in Pennsylvania 24 Sep. 1755. He was from Philadelphia County.

Buckner, John. He sought naturalization in New Jersey in the 18th century.

Bucks, John. He was naturalized in Pennsylvania 26 Sep. 1748. He was from Lancaster County.

Buckwalter, Jacob. He was naturalized in Pennsylvania 11–13 Apr. 1743. He was from Philadelphia County.

Buckwalter, Johannes. He was naturalized in Pennsylvania 6 Feb. 1740/1. He was from Philadelphia County.

Buckwalter, Joseph. He was naturalized in Pennsylvania 14 Feb. 1729/30. He was from Lancaster County.

Buckwalter, Turst. He was naturalized in Pennsylvania 19 May 1739. He was from Lancaster County.

Bud, Nicholas. He was naturalized in New Jersey 31 July 1740. He was born in Norway.

Budd, Nicholas. He was naturalized in Massachusetts 17 Nov. 1741. He was a native of Norway and had been in the colony for more than seven years.

Bueno, Jacob. He was naturalized in Jamaica 29 July 1682.

Bueno, Joseph. He may have been the one of the name endenized in London 2 Oct. 1662. He came to New York. One of that name was also in Barbados.

Buffenmyer, Matthew. He was naturalized in Pennsylvania 10 Apr. 1765. He was from Hempfield Township, Lancaster County.

Bugeauld, Joseph. He was an Acadian who took the oath to George II at the Mines, Pisiquit 31 Oct. 1727.

Bugeauld, Joseph. He was an Acadian who took the oath of allegiance in Apr. 1730.

Buger, Peter. He was naturalized in Pennsylvania 10 Apr. 1760.

Buijs, Jan. He took the oath of allegiance in Breucklijn, Kings County, New York 26–30 Sep. 1687. He had been in the colony 39 years.

Bujeau, Allain. He was an Acadian who took the oath of allegiance in Apr. 1730.

Bujeau, Amant. He was an Acadian who took the oath of allegiance in Apr. 1730.

Buke, Matthew. He was naturalized in Maryland 11 Sep. 1760.

Buker, Peter. He was naturalized in Pennsylvania 24 Sep. 1760. He was from Lancaster County.

Bullinger, Jacob. He was naturalized in Pennsylvania 10 Sep. 1761. He was from Lancaster County.

Bullman, John. He was naturalized in Pennsylvania 11 Apr. 1761. He was from Berks County.

Bullon, Conrod. He was naturalized in North Carolina 22 Sep. 1763. He was from Rowan County and was a German.

Bumbarger, Martin. He was naturalized in Pennsylvania 24 Sep. 1753. He was from Lancaster County.

Bumberger, Henry. He was naturalized in Pennsylvania 24 Sep. 1753. He was from Bucks County.

Bumgardner, John. He was naturalized in Virginia 20 Oct. 1744. He was a native of Risenbach, Sweden.

Bumgardner, Mathias. He was naturalized in Pennsylvania 10 Apr. 1755. He was from Lancaster County.

Bumgarner, Peter. He was naturalized in Pennsylvania 14 Feb. 1729/30. He was from Lancaster County.

Bumper, Philip Jacob. He was naturalized in New York 12 July 1728.

Bunn, Peter. He was naturalized in Pennsylvania 11–12 Apr. 1744. He was from Philadelphia County.

Buretel, Pierre. He was born at LaRochelle, France, the son of Charles Buretel and Sara Bouhier. His wife was Elizabeth Chintrie. They were naturalized in South Carolina ca. 1696.

Burger, Conrad. He was naturalized in Nova Scotia 10 July 1758.

Burger, Marten. He was naturalized in New York 8–9 Sep. 1715. He was from Ulster County.

Burger, Peter. He was naturalized in New York 17 Jan. 1715/6. He was from Albany County.

Burger, Samuel. He was naturalized in Pennsylvania 10 Apr. 1755. He was from Berks County.

Burgher, Hans Ulrick. He was naturalized in Pennsylvania 11–13 Apr. 1743. He was from Philadelphia County.

Burgher, Matthias. He was naturalized in Pennsylvania 24 Sep. 1760. He was from Lancaster County.

Burgoon, Jacob. He was endenized in Maryland 30 Sep. 1771. He was born in Germany.

Burgos, Irmiahu. He was endenized in England 10 Dec. 1695. He settled in Barbados. He also appeared as Jeremiah Burges.

Burgunt, Simon. He was naturalized in Maryland 6 Sep. 1765. He was a German from Frederick County.

Burkhalter, Ulrick. He was naturalized in Pennsylvania 11–13 Apr. 1743. He was from Bucks County.

Burkhard, George. He was naturalized in Pennsylvania 10 Apr. 1760.

Brukhard, George. He was naturalized in Pennsylvania 10–12 Apr. 1762. He was from Lancaster County.

Burkhard, John Philip. He was naturalized in Pennsylvania 10 Apr. 1760.

Burkhardt, Nicholas. He was naturalized in Pennsylvania 10–12 Apr. 1762. He was from Philadelphia County.

Burkheimer, Leonard. He was naturalized in Pennsylvania 24 Sep. 1762. He was from Philadelphia County.

Burkholder, Abraham. He was naturalized in Pennsylvania 14 Feb. 1729/30. He was from Lancaster County.

Burkholder, John. He was naturalized in Pennsylvania 14 Feb. 1729/30. He was from Lancaster County.

Burkholder, John, Jr. He was naturalized in Pennsylvania 14 Feb. 1729/30. He was from Lancaster County.

Burkholder, Martin. He was naturalized in Pennsylvania 10 Apr. 1760.

Burkholder, Peter. He was naturalized in Pennsylvania 11 Apr. 1761. He was from Northampton County.

Burkey, Michael. He was naturalized in Pennsylvania 10 & 23 Apr. 1764. He was from York Township, York County.

Burkitt, George. He was naturalized in Maryland 12 Sep. 1753.

Burkitt, Matthais. He was naturalized in Maryland 12 Sep. 1753.

Burkitt, Michael. He was naturalized in Maryland 19 July 1765. He was from Frederick County.

Burneman, Daniel. He was naturalized in Pennsylvania 24 Sep. 1755. He was from Philadelphia County.

Burnett, John Straw. He was naturalized in Jamaica 14 Mar. 1749/50. He was a free Negro.

Burrey, Joseph. He was naturalized in Pennsylvania 10 Apr. 1755. He was from Berks County.

Burtell, Pierre. He was endenized in New York 18 Aug. 1686.

Bury, John. He was naturalized in New York 24 Nov. 1750.

Busch, Johann Henrich. He was naturalized in New York 22 Oct. 1750. He was a blacksmith from Ulster County.

Busel, John. He was naturalized in New Jersey in 1772. He was born in Germany.

Bush, George. He was naturalized in Augusta County, Virginia 21 June 1763.

Bush, George. He was naturalized in Pennsylvania 10 Apr. 1760.

Bush, Henry. He was naturalized in Pennsylvania 11 Apr. 1761. He was from Northampton County.

Bush, Johanas. He took the oath of naturalization in New York 1 Sep. 1687 in Ulster County.

Bush, Julius. He was naturalized in New York 8 Mar. 1773.

Bush, Mathias. He was naturalized in Pennsylvania 11 Apr. 1751. He was from Philadelphia County. He was a Jew.

Bush, Philip. He was naturalized in Pennsylvania 2 Feb. 1765. He was from Blockley Township, Philadelphia County and an inn holder. He had come into the province as an infant from Germany.

Bush, William. He was naturalized in Pennsylvania 10 Apr. 1760.

Bushung, John. He was naturalized in Pennsylvania 19 May 1739. He was from Lancaster County.

Bushung, Philip. He was naturalized in Pennsylvania 10 Sep. 1761. He was from Lancaster County.

Busler, William. He was naturalized in Pennsylvania 11 Apr. 1763. He was from Windsor Township, Berks County.

Bussard, Hendrick. He was naturalized in New York 11 Sep. 1761.

Bussard, John. He was naturalized in North Carolina 22 Sep. 1763. He was from Rowan County and a German.

Bussart, Daniel. He was naturalized in Pennsylvania 10 & 23 Apr. 1764. He was from Cumru Township, Berks County.

Bussart, Jacob. He was naturalized in Pennsylvania 11–13 Apr. 1740. He was from Chester County.

Bussinberger, John. He was naturalized in Pennsylvania 24–25 Sep. 1764. He was from Amwell, Hunterdon County, New Jersey.

Butser, John. He was naturalized in Pennsylvania 10 Sep. 1761. He was from Lancaster County.

Button, George. He was naturalized in Pennsylvania 24 Sep. 1754. He was from Philadelphia County.

Buvelot, Jacques Gabriel. He was naturalized in New York 20 Sep. 1728.

Buvelot, James. He was naturalized in New York 31 July 1741. He was a brasier from New York City.

Buys, Cornelis. He took the oath of allegiance in Gravens End, Kings County, New York 26–30 Sep. 1687. He was a native of the colony.

Buzzard, Andreas. He was naturalized in Pennsylvania 11–13 Apr. 1743. He was from Philadelphia County.

Byar, Blessius. He was naturalized in Pennsylvania in Sep. 1740. He was from Philadelphia.

Byar, Carl. He was naturalized in Pennsylvania 24 Sep. 1754. He was from Philadelphia County.

Byard, Adam. He was naturalized in Maryland 1 May 1736. He was a planter from Baltimore County and a native of Germany.

Bydeman, Simon. He was naturalized in New York 8 Mar. 1773.

Byer, Hubertus. He was naturalized in Maryland 18 Sep. 1764. He was a German.

Byer, John. He was naturalized in Pennsylvania 26–27 Sep. 1743. He was from Lancaster County.

Byer, Samuel. He was naturalized in Pennsylvania 26–27 Sep. 1743. He was from Lancaster County.

Byerle, John Henrick. He was naturalized in Pennsylvania 10 Sep. 1761. He was from Berks County.

Byerly, Jacob. He was naturalized in Pennsylvania 29 Mar. 1735. He was from Chester County.

Byerly, John Michael. He was naturalized in Pennsylvania 24 Sep. 1753. He was from Lancaster County.

Byerly, Michael. He was naturalized in Pennsylvania 29 Mar. 1735. He was from Chester County.

Bylestine, Jacob. He was naturalized in Pennsylvania 24–25 Sep. 1764. He was from Bart Township, Lancaster County.

Byndlos, Anna Petronella. She was naturalized in Jamaica 22 Nov. 1681.

Byrkey, Jacob. He was naturalized in New York 8 Mar. 1773.

Byrkey, Jacob, Jr. He was naturalized in New York 8 Mar. 1773.

Byrkey, Peter. He was naturalized in New York 8 Mar. 1773.

Bysher, Matthias. He was naturalized in Pennsylvania 10 Sep. 1761. He was from York County.

Caaf, Christian. He was naturalized in New York 11 Sep. 1761.

Cabany, Henry. He was naturalized in Virginia 12 May 1705. [He was Henry Cabiness.]

Cackley, Jacob. He was naturalized in Frederick County, Virginia 1 Aug. 1760.

Caillabeuf, Isaac. He was born at Ste. Soline, France, the son of Louis Caillabeuf and Marie Charuyer. His wife was Rachel Fanton. Their children were Isaac Caillabeuf, Etienne Caillabeuf, and Anne Calliabeuf who were born in South Carolina. They were naturalized in South Carolina *ca.* 1696.

Caillard, Isaaq. He was endenized in New York 6 Feb. 1695/6.

Caillard, Peter. He was naturalized in Jamaica 5 Sep. 1693.

Cain, Peter. He was naturalized in North Carolina 24 Mar. 1764. He was from Rowan County and was a German.

Cajot, Piere. He took the oath of allegiance at Mobile, West Florida 2 Oct. 1764.

Calame, Peter Frederick. He was naturalized in Jamaica 6 Dec. 1744.

Calco, Nicholas. He took the oath of allegiance at Mobile, West Florida 2 Oct. 1764.

Callard, Isaac. He was endenized in New York 6 Feb. 1695/6.

Calback, Adam. He was naturalized in Pennsylvania 18–20 May 1772. He was from Tulpehocken Township, Berks County.

Callman, Michael. He was naturalized in New York 28 Feb. 1715/6. He was a merchant from New York City.

Callot, Joseph. He was naturalized in Virginia 12 May 1705.

Calman, John Rudy. He was naturalized in Maryland 13 Apr. 1763. He was a German.

Calman, Mathias. He was naturalized in Maryland 13 Apr. 1763. He was a German.

Calvert, John. He was naturalized in Virginia 12 May 1705.

Calvet, Peter. He was naturalized in South Carolina 20 Jan. 1741.

Cambel, John. He was naturalized in Virginia 12 May 1705.

Cambree, John. He was naturalized in Pennsylvania 11–12 Apr. 1744. He was from Philadelphia County.

Camel, Adam. He was naturalized in Pennsylvania 10–12 Apr. 1762. He was from Philadelphia County.

Camer, Nicoles. He was naturalized in New Jersey in 1759.

Caminada, Francois. He took the oath of allegiance at Mobile, West Florida 2 Oct. 1764.

Cammerdinger, Ludwig. He was naturalized in New York 21 Oct. 1765. He was a tailor from New York City.

Cammerel, Andrew. He was naturalized in Pennsylvania 10 Sep. 1761. He was from Lancaster County.

Cammerer, Ludwig. He was naturalized in Maryland 12 Sep. 1764. He was a German from Frederick County.

Campos, Isaac Henriques. He was naturalized in Jamaica 8 May 1734.

Campos, Isaac Henriques. He was naturalized in Jamaica 26 Feb. 1740/1. He was a Jew.

Campos, Judith Henriques. She was naturalized in Jamaica 28 Nov. 1749. She was a Jewess.

Camper, Wilpert. He was naturalized in Pennsylvania 11 Apr. 1763. He was from Lancaster Township, Lancaster County.

Camperson, Leonard. He was naturalized in Maryland 22 May 1695.

Canche, Ayme. He was endenized in New York 10 Sep. 1686.

Canchi, Aimi. He took the oath of naturalization in New York 1 Sep. 1687 in Ulster County.

Candle, Nicholas. He was naturalized in Pennsylvania 19 May 1739. He was from Lancaster County.

Canon, Andre. He and his son Abraham Canon were endenized in London 3 July 1701. They came to New York.

Cantain, Moyse. He was naturalized in New York 8–9 Sep. 1715. He was from Ulster County.

Cantepie, Michel. He was naturalized in Virginia 12 May 1705.

Canter, George. He was naturalized in Pennsylvania 11 Apr. 1761. He was from Berks County.

Cantine, Moses. He took the oath of naturalization in New York 1 Sep. 1687 in Ulster County.

Capell, Charles. He was naturalized in Jamaica 26 Nov. 1717.

Capon, Jacob. He was naturalized in Virginia 12 May 1705.

Caparond, Martin. He was an Acadian who took the oath to the King at the Mines, Pisiquit 31 Oct. 1727.

CapPrimo, Mose DeCampo. He was naturalized in Jamaica 26 Sep. 1690. He was a Spanish Negro.

Capue, John. He was naturalized in Jamaica 25 Oct. 1732.

Carasquillah, Anthony. He was naturalized in Jamaica 8 Dec. 1722.

Carbeck, Valentine. He was naturalized in Maryland 4 Sep. 1773. He was a German from Baltimore County.

Carcas, Abraham. He was naturalized in New York 17 June 1726.

Cardosa, Abraham. He was naturalized in Jamaica 15 Apr. 1725.

Cardosa, Abraham alias Gaspar. He was naturalized in Jamaica 24 Mar. 1693/4.

Cardosa, Daniel Fernandes. He and his mother, Rachell Fernandes Cardosa, were naturalized in Jamaica 17 Sep. 1730.

Cardosa, David. He was naturalized in Jamaica 5 Jan. 1724/5.

Cardosa, Isaque. He was naturalized in Jamaica 24 Apr. 1704.

Cardosa, Moses. He was naturalized in Jamaica 9 Dec. 1725.

Cardosa, Rachell Fernandes. She and her son, Daniel Fernandes Cardosa, were naturalized in Jamaica 17 Sep. 1730.

Cardosa, Rachaell. She was naturalized in Jamaica 2 Mar. 1740/1. She was a Christian.

Cardosa, Rebecca Yezurum. She was naturalized in Jamaica 4 Jan. 1725/6. She was the wife of Yezurum Cardoza.

Cardoso, Easther. She was naturalized in Jamaica 27 July 1761.

Cardoso, Isaac Lopes. He was naturalized in Jamaica 16 Dec. 1733.

Cardosso, Esther. She was the wife of Jacob Yezurum Cardosso, merchant, of Port Royal. She was naturalized in Jamaica 1 Sep. 1737.

Cardoza, Daniel. He was naturalized in Jamaica 24 Sep. 1728.

Cardoza, Abraham. He was naturalized in Jamaica 8 Jan. 1732/3.

Cardoza, Jacob Aboah. He was naturalized in Jamaica 1 July 1755.

Cardoza, Solomon. He was endenized in London 29 May 1663. He was from Barbados.

Cardoza, Abraham Roiz. He was naturalized in Jamaica 26 Feb. 1744/5. He was a Jew.

Cardozo, Daniel. He was naturalized in Jamaica 1 Dec. 1742. He was a Jew.

Cardozo, Jacob. He was naturalized in Jamaica 26 Nov. 1735.

Cardozo, Leah. She was naturalized in Jamaica 31 May 1743. She was a Jewess.

Cardozo, Mosce Geshuran. He was naturalized in Jamaica 12 June 1675.

Cardozo, Mosseh Yesurun. He was endenized in England 15 Apr. 1672.

Cardozo, Sarah. She was naturalized in Jamaica 31 May 1743. She was a Jewess.

Carelezen, Joost. He took the oath to the King 21–26 Oct. 1664 after the conquest of New Netherland.

Caricis, William. He was naturalized in Pennsylvania 11–13 Apr. 1743. He was from Philadelphia County.

Cario, Michael. He was naturalized in New York 12 July 1729.

Carion, —. He was naturalized in South Carolina ca. 1696.

Carion, Moise. He was born at Faugere, Languedoc, France, the son of Andre Carion and Marie Fascal. His wife was Anne Ribouteau. Their son was Moise Carion. They were naturalized in South Carolina 10 Mar. 1696/7. He was a joiner.

Carl, Nicholas. He was naturalized in Pennsylvania 24 Sep. 1771. He was from Upper Dublin Township, Philadelphia County.

Carle, John. He was naturalized in New York 21 Apr. 1762. He was a French Protestant in New York City.

Carll, Simon. He was naturalized in Pennsylvania 25 Sep. 1751. He was from Lancaster County.

Carn, Conrod. He was naturalized in North Carolina 22 Mar. 1763. He was from Rowan County and a German.

Carne, Dewald. He was naturalized in Pennsylvania 10 Apr. 1755. He was from Berks County.

Carnell, Jane. She was naturalized in Jamaica 13 Dec. 1739.

Caron, Nicolas. He was naturalized in New York 3 July 1718.

Carpenter, Emanuel. He was naturalized in Pennsylvania 14 Feb. 1729/30. He was from Lancaster County.

Carpenter, Gabriel. He was naturalized in Pennsylvania 14 Feb. 1729/30. He was from Lancaster County.

Carpenter, Henry. He was naturalized in Pennsylvania 14 Feb. 1729/30. He was from Lancaster County.

Carpenter, John. He was naturalized in Tryon County, North Carolina Oct. 1772.

Carr, Ann. She was naturalized in Jamaica 29 July 1731.

Carr, John. He was naturalized in Pennsylvania 10 Apr. 1766. He was from Whiteland Township, Chester County.

Carriere, Jean. He was born in Normandie, France, the son of Jean Carriere. He was naturalized in South Carolina 10 Mar. 1696/7. He was a cooper.

Carriere, Louis. He took the oath of allegiance at Mobile, West Florida 2 Oct. 1764.

Carrmar, Abraham. He took the oath of naturalization in New York 13 June 1687.

Carron, Claude. He was born at Tours, France, the son of Michel Carron and Elizabeth Belong. He was naturalized in South Carolina 10 Mar. 1696/7. He was a planter.

Carstens, Johannes Lorents. He was naturalized in New York 14 Oct. 1737. He was of St. Thomas.

Carstense, Jan. He took the oath of allegiance in Gravens End, Kings County, New York 26–30 Sep. 1687. He was a native of the colony.

Carter, Jacob. He was naturalized in Pennsylvania 24 Sep. 1763. He was from Springfield Township, Philadelphia County.

Cartier, John. He petitioned for denization in New York 6 June 1695. He was from New Rochelle.

Cartwright, Matthew. He was naturalized in Maryland 19 Apr. 1671. He lived in St. Mary's County and was born in Middlebrough, Zealand.

Cartwright, Mary. She was naturalized in New York 29 Dec. 1660. She was born in Amsterdam, the Netherlands, the daughter of Giles and Mary Silvester. Her parents were English.

Carvalho, Hester. She was naturalized in Jamaica 12 Feb. 1711/2.

Carvallo, Benjamin Baru. He was naturalized in Jamaica 29 May 1683.

Carvallo, Joseph. He was naturalized in Jamaica 14 May 1691.

Carvallo, Samuel. He was naturalized in Jamaica 15 June 1708.

Carvalo, Daniel. He was naturalized in Jamaica 2 July 1712.

Carvello, Jacob. He was naturalized in Jamaica 19 Aug. 1751.

Carver, Jacob. He was naturalized in Pennsylvania 24 Sep. 1760. He was from Philadelphia County.

Carver, John. He was naturalized in Pennsylvania 10 Sep. 1761. He was from Berks County.

Carver, Nicholas. He was naturalized in Pennsylvania 11–12 Apr. 1744. He was from Chester County.

Case, Peter. He was naturalized in New Jersey 20 Aug. 1755.

Case, Tunis. He was naturalized in New Jersey 20 Aug. 1755.

Caslar, Lewis. He was naturalized in Pennsylvania 24 Sep. 1757.

Casler, Michael. He was naturalized in New Jersey in 1750. He was from Hunterdon County.

Casparus, Johannes Valentine. He was naturalized in New York 11 Sep. 1761.

Caspel, Isaac Van Haaren. He was naturalized in New York 1 Aug. 1751. He was a chirurgeon from New York City.

Caspars, Melchior. He took the oath of allegiance in Orange County, New York 26 Sep. 1687.

Casper, Casper. He was naturalized in New York 24 Oct. 1755.

Casperse, Johannis. He took the oath of allegiance in Breucklijn, Kings County, New York 26–30 Sep. 1687. He had been in the colony 35 years.

Casperse, Joost. He took the oath of allegiance in Breucklijn, Kings County, New York 26–30 Sep. 1687. He had been in the colony 35 years.

Cassel, Christian. He was naturalized in Pennsylvania 10 Apr. 1760.

Casselman, And: Lodwick. He was naturalized in New York 17 Jan. 1715/6. He was from Albany County.

Casset, Joseph. He was naturalized in New York 24 Nov. 1750.

Castang, Gideon. He was naturalized in New York 16 Aug. 1715. He was a rope maker in New York City.

Castelo, David. He was endenized in England 9 Mar. 1693/4. He settled in Barbados.

Castige, Paul. He was naturalized in Virginia 12 May 1705.

Casy, Jean. He was an Acadian who took the oath of allegiance in Apr. 1730.

Casy, Pierre. He was an Acadian who took the oath of allegiance in Apr. 1730.

Catelman, Christian. He was naturalized in New York 8–9 Sep. 1715. He was from Ulster County.

Caubal, Abraham. He was naturalized in Pennsylvania 10–12 Apr. 1762. He was from Lancaster County.

Cauche, Aime. He petitioned to be naturalized in New York 19 Aug. 1687.

Caudet, Pierre, Jr. He was an Acadian who took the oath of allegiance in Apr. 1730.

Causine, Ignatius. He petitioned to be naturalized in Maryland in Apr. 1671. He was the son of Nicholas Causine, a subject of the Crown of France and of a English mother. He was born at his father's home in St. George's River in Maryland. His father had his land surveyed in his lifetime. The land was patented by the said Ignatius after his father's death. It was declared that Ignatius Causine was a free denizen of the Kingdom of England and needed no naturalization being born in Maryland. His father's certificate of the survey was only a chattel read of which his mother was seized and made over to her son. Since he obtained the grant from the proprietor and held nothing by descent, he had as much security for his lands as any other person in the province. The proprietor could grant nothing more.

Cavalier, John. He was naturalized in Jamaica 28 May 1728.

Caville, Abraham. He was naturalized in Jamaica in Feb. 1748/9. He was a Jew.

Cazered, Jacob David de. He sought to be a denizen 30 Aug. 1692. He was from Jamaica.

Cebe, Mariane. She petitioned to be naturalized in New York 16 Nov. 1739.

Cebe, Paul Francis. He petitioned to be naturalized in New York 16 Nov. 1739.

Celestin, Anth. He was an Acadian who took the oath of allegiance in Apr. 1730.

Cerman, Jacob. He was naturalized in New York 14 Feb. 1715/6. He was from Albany County.

Ceywids, Frederick. He was naturalized in New York 11 Sep. 1761.

Chaburn, Charles. He was naturalized in Jamaica 11 Aug. 1704.

Chaigneau, Peter. He was endenized in England 25 Mar. 1688. He came to New York.

Chalmas, Stephen. He was naturalized in New Jersey 17 Mar. 1713/4. He was a native of France.

Chambers, John. He was naturalized in Jamaica 28 Sep. 1690.

Chambers, Richard. He was naturalized in Jamaica 28 Sep. 1690.

Chambers, Thomas. He took the oath to the King 21–26 Oct. 1664 after the conquest of New Netherland.

Chambert, Jacob. He was naturalized in Maryland 15 Sep. 1762. He was from Frederick County.

Chambon, Gideon. He was naturalized in Virginia 12 May 1705.

Champagne, James. He was naturalized in Virginia 12 May 1705. He was born in France.

Champeign, Nicholas. He took the oath of allegiance at Mobile, West Florida 2 Oct. 1764.

Chappelle, John Peter. He was naturalized in New York 22 Apr. 1761. He was a French Protestant from New York City.

Chappelle, John Peter, Jr. He was naturalized in New York 20 Apr. 1769. He was a French Protestant and a stocking weaver in New York City.

Charbouneaw, Peter. He was endenized in Pennsylvania 21 Feb.1694/5. He was a ship's carpenter from France.

Chardaveyne, Elias. He was naturalized in New York 26 July 1715. He was a victualer in New York City.

Chardon, Peter. He was endenized in England 9 Apr. 1687. He came to Massachusetts.

Charles, Adam. He was naturalized in Jamaica 10 Mar. 1738/9.

Charles, Michael. He was naturalized in North Carolina 22 Sep. 1763. He was from Rowan County and a German.

Charrier, Benjamin. He was naturalized in Pennsylvania 1 Mar. 1702. He was the son of Benjamin Charrier and was born in the barony of Cossonay, canton of Berne, Switzerland.

Charrier, Francis. He was naturalized in Pennsylvania 1 Mar. 1704. He was the son of John Baptist Charrier, Seigneur of [–?–] and Castellain, barony of Cossonay, canton of Berne, Switzerland. He was styled Captain.

Chason, Jean. He was an Acadian who took the oath of allegiance in Apr. 1730.

Chasper, Conrad. He was naturalized in New Jersey in 1750. He was from Hunterdon County. He also appeared as Conrad Casper.

Chasson, Jean. He took the oath of allegiance at Harbour Amhurst in the Magdalen Islands, Gulf of Saint Lawrence on 31 Aug. 1765. He was a native of Nova Scotia.

Chastang, Joseph. He took the oath of allegiance at Mobile, West Florida 2 Oct. 1764.

Chatagner, Alexandre These. He was the son of Roch Chatagner and Jeanne de Chatagner. He was born in LaRochelle, d'Onis, France. His wife, Elizabeth Chatagner, was the daughter of Pierre

Buretel and Elizabeth Buretel. Their children, Alexandre Chatagner and Elizabeth Madeleine Chatagner, were born in South Carolina. They were naturalized in South Carolina ca. 1696.

Chatagner, Henry Auguste. He was the son of Roch Chatagner and Jeanne de Chatagner. He was born in LaRochelle, d'Onis, France. He was naturalized in South Carolina ca. 1696.

Chastain, Stephen. He was naturalized in Virginia 12 May 1705.

Chataigmer, Peter. He was naturalized in Virginia 12 May 1705.

Chatain, Peter. He was naturalized in Virginia 12 May 1705.

Chauvaux, Adrian. He was naturalized in Jamaica 20 Oct. 1740.

Chauvet, Charles. He was an Acadian who took the oath of allegiance to the King at the Mines, Pisiquit, Nova Scotia 31 Oct. 1727.

Chauvet, Charles. He was an Acadian who took the oath of allegiance in Apr. 1730.

Chavet, Charles. He was an Acadian who took the oath of allegiance in Apr. 1730.

Cheek, Ludwick. He was naturalized in Maryland 15 Sep. 1773. He was a German.

Chene, Jean. He was an Acadian who took the oath of allegiance in Apr. 1730.

Chenerard, Isaac Henry Albert. He was naturalized in Jamaica 15 Apr. 1726.

Chenette, Francois. He took the oath of allegiance at Mobile, West Florida 2 Oct. 1764.

Cherbacher, John. He was naturalized in New York 20 May 1769.

Chermeson, Joseph. He was naturalized in Virginia 12 May 1705.

Chierts, David. He was naturalized in New Jersey 22 Nov. 1715. He was from Albany County.

Chintrier, Marie. She was endenized in New York 12 Mar. 1695/6. She was the now wife of Saviott Broussard alias Deschamps.

Chopard, Daniel. He was naturalized in South Carolina 14 Aug. 1744.

Chriest, Henry. He was naturalized in Pennsylvania 11–13 Apr. 1743. He was from Philadelphia County.

Chrisman, Peter. He was naturalized in Virginia 1 May 1770. He was from Frederick County.

Christ, Hendrick. He was naturalized in New York 8 Nov. 1735.

Christ, Henry. He was naturalized in Pennsylvania 10 Apr. 1755. He was from Berks County.

Christ, Johannes. He was naturalized in New York 1740–41. He also appeared as Johannes Christee.

Christ, Lawrence. He was naturalized in New York 8 Nov. 1735.

Christ, Philip. He was naturalized in Pennsylvania 18 Nov. 1768. He was from Paradise Township, York County.

Christ, Stephanus. He was naturalized in Pennsylvania 8 Nov. 1735.

Christiaense, Jacob. He took the oath of allegiance in New Uijtreceht, New York 26–30 Sep. 1687. He was a native of the colony.

Christian, Cornelius. He was made a free denizen in New York City. He had his denization recorded in Jamaica 30 Oct. 1678. He was a brother of Peter Christian.

Christian, George. He was naturalized in Pennsylvania 10–12 Apr. 1762. He was from Berks County.

Christian, Lawrence. He was naturalized in Maryland 6 June 1674. He was a German.

Christian, Martin. He was naturalized in Pennsylvania 10–12 Apr. 1762. He was from Berks County.

Christian, Peter. He was a free denizen in New York City. He had his denization recorded in Jamaica 30 Oct. 1678. He was a brother of Cornelius Christian and was master of the sloop, *Dolphin*.

Christiana, David. He was naturalized in South Carolina 20 Jan. 1741.

Christianse, David. He was endenized in New York 29 Jan. 1693/4.

Christiansen, Peter. He was naturalized in New York 6 Mar. 1715/6. He was a boatman from New York City.

Christle, Theobald. He was naturalized in Orange County, Virginia 28 Jan. 1742/3.

Christler, Leonhart. He was naturalized in Pennsylvania 19 May 1739. He was from Philadelphia County.

Christman, Jacob. He was naturalized in Virginia 23 Oct. 1745. He was a native of Worms, Germany.

Christman, Johans. He was naturalized in New York 17 Jan. 1715/6. He was from Albany County.

Christopher, Charles. He was naturalized in Pennsylvania 14 Feb. 1729/30. He was from Lancaster County.

Christy, John. He was naturalized in Pennsylvania 25 Sep. 1750. He was from Lancaster County.

Chryselar, Gorg. He was naturalized in New York 8–9 Sep. 1715. He was from Ulster County.

Chryselar, Johan Phillip. He was naturalized in New York 8–9 Sep. 1715. He was from Ulster County.

Chryster, Jacob. He was naturalized in Pennsylvania 24 Sep. 1755. He was from Philadelphia.

Chudy, Martin. He was naturalized in Maryland 14 Sep. 1763. He was a German.

Churts, Jacob. He was naturalized in Pennsylvania 14 Feb. 1729/30. He was from Lancaster County.

Cimmerman, Sebastian. He was naturalized in Pennsylvania 11–13 Apr. 1743. He was from Philadelphia County.

Circle, Henry. He was naturalized in Pennsylvania 11–13 Apr. 1743. He was from Philadelphia County.

Cirkle, Ludowick. He was naturalized in Pennsylvania 19 May 1739. He was from Philadelphia County.

Claaesen, Hendrick. He took the oath of allegiance in Breucklijn, Kings County, New York 26–30 Sep. 1687. He had been in the colony 33 years.

Claassen, Jacob. He expressed his desire to be naturalized in New Castle County, Delaware 21 Feb. 1682/3.

Claassen, Peter. He was naturalized in Delaware 21 Feb. 1682/3. He was from New Castle County.

Claerhoudt, Walraven. He took the oath to the King 21–26 Oct. 1664 after the conquest of New Netherland.

Claes, Hendrick. He took the oath of naturalization in New York 1 Sep. 1687 in Ulster County.

Claesen, Andries. He took the oath to the King 21–26 Oct. 1664 after the conquest of New Netherland.

Claesen, Sibout. He took the oath to the King 21–26 Oct. 1664 after the conquest of New Netherland.

Claesz, Cornelis. He took the oath of allegiance in Orange County, New York 26 Sep. 1687.

Clajont, William. He was naturalized in New York 27 Oct. 1775. He was a French Protestant.

Clampferr, Adam. He was naturalized in Pennsylvania 13–15 Apr. 1748. He was from Philadelphia County.

Clampferr, William. He was naturalized in Pennsylvania 13–15 Apr. 1748. He was from Philadelphia County.

Clantz, Jacob. He was naturalized in Maryland 15 Apr. 1771. He was a German.

Clap, Lodowick. He was naturalized in North Carolina 23 Mar. 1763. He was from Rowan County.

Clapier, Francis. He was naturalized in Virginia 12 May 1705.

Clapp, George Valentine. He was naturalized in North Carolina 22 Sep. 1763. He was from Rowan County and a German.

Clappert, Herman. He was naturalized in Maryland 10 Sep. 1772.

Clarck, Ellick. He was naturalized in New York 27 Mar. 1716. He was a mariner from New York City.

Clarcke, Daniel. He took the oath of allegiance in Orange County, New York 26 Sep. 1687.

Clarke, Elizabeth. She was naturalized in Jamaica 15 July 1717.

Clasen, Baudoin. He was endenized in London 3 July 1671. He was a merchant from Jamaica.

Classen, Henrick. He was naturalized in Nova Scotia 5 July 1758.

Classen, Peter. He was naturalized in New Castle County, Delaware 21 Feb. 1682/3.

Claud, Philipe. He was naturalized in Virginia 12 May 1705.

Claudi, Jean. He was naturalized in New York 24 July 1724.

Clauer, William. He was naturalized in Pennsylvania 11 Apr. 1771. He was from Philadelphia.

Claus, Bowden. He was naturalized in Jamaica 5 Apr. 1676.

Claus, William. He was naturalized in Pennsylvania 24–25 Sep./5 Oct. 1767. He was from Upper Dublin Township, Philadelphia County.

Clauser, Jacob. He was naturalized in New York 3 July 1759.

Clauson, Jacob. He was made a denizen in Maryland 30 July 1661. He was Dutch and was late of New Amstel.

Clauson, Katherine. She was naturalized in Jamaica 9 July 1684.

Clava, Benjamin Moses. He was naturalized in Pennsylvania 24 Sep. 1762. He was a Jew.

Clear, John. He was naturalized in New York 19 Dec. 1766.

Cleem, Christian. He was naturalized in Nova Scotia 10 July 1758.

Clem, George. He was naturalized in Maryland in Apr. 1749.

Clem, George. He was naturalized in Maryland 16 Apr. 1760. He was from Frederick County.

Clemens, Jacob. He was naturalized in Pennsylvania 11–13 Apr. 1743. He was from Philadelphia County.

Clemens, John. He was naturalized in Pennsylvania 11–13 Apr. 1743. He was from Philadelphia County.

Clemens, Matthias. He was naturalized in New York 8 Mar. 1773.

Clemens, Philip. He was naturalized in New York 8 Mar. 1773.

Clemensen, Oele. He expressed his desire to be naturalized in New Castle County, Delaware 21 Feb. 1682/3.

Clement, Jan. He took the oath of allegiance in New Uijtrceht, Kings County, New York 26–30 Sep. 1687. He had been in the colony 22 years.

Clement, Moses. He was naturalized in New York 16 Apr. 1755. He was a cabinetmaker from New York City.

Clements, Andrew. He was naturalized in Maryland 6 June 1674. He was Swedish.

Clements, Gerhard. He was naturalized in Pennsylvania in 1730–31. He was from Philadelphia County.

Clementsen, Jacob. He expressed his desire to be naturalized in New Castle County, Delaware 21 Feb. 1682/3.

Clementson, Andrew. He was made a denizen in Maryland 29 July 1661. He was Swedish and was late of New Amstel.

Clementz, Leonard. He was naturalized in Maryland 27 Apr. 1763. He was a German from Frederick County.

Clementz, Valentine. He was naturalized in Maryland 5 Sep. 1762. He was from Frederick County.

Clenpetre, Philip. He took the oath of allegiance at Mobile, West Florida 2 Oct. 1764.

Clentz, Henry. He was naturalized in Maryland 13 Apr. 1763. He was a German.

Clerembault, Francis. He was naturalized in New York 24 July 1724.

Clesdale, Christoph. He was naturalized in Nova Scotia 15 Sept. 1758.

Clever, Peter. He was naturalized in Pennsylvania 29 Sep. 1709. He was from Philadelphia County.

Clindman, Til. He was naturalized in Maryland 11 Sep. 1765.

Cline, Boston. He was naturalized in Rowan County, North Carolina 16 July 1755.

Cline, John. He was naturalized in Pennsylvania 10 & 23 Apr. 1764. He was from Warwick Township, Lancaster County.

Cline, John Henry. He was naturalized in Pennsylvania 11 Apr. 1761. He was from Philadelphia County.

Cline, John Herick. He was naturalized in Pennsylvania 11 Apr. 1761. He was from York County.

Cline, Leonard. He was naturalized in Pennsylvania 24 Sep. 1760. He was from Lancaster County.

Cline, Mathias. He was naturalized in Pennsylvania 10 Apr. 1754. He was from Philadelphia County.

Cline, Michael. He was naturalized in Pennsylvania 11 Apr. 1761. He was from Bucks County.

Cline, William. He was naturalized in New York 20 May 1769.

Clineyenny, Johannes. He was naturalized in Pennsylvania 11 Sep. 1761. He was from Berks County.

Cling, George. He was naturalized in New York 11 Sep. 1761.

Clingerman, Alexander. He was naturalized in North Carolina 11 Oct. 1754. He was from Rowan County.

Clock, Abraham. He took the oath to the King 21–26 Oct. 1664 after the conquest of New Netherland.

Clock, Casper. He was naturalized in New York 3 July 1759.

Clock, Hans Hendrick. He was naturalized in New York 3 Jan. 1715/6. He was from Albany County.

Cloistre, Pierre. He was an Acadian who took the oath of allegiance in Apr. 1730.

Clom, Philip. He was naturalized in New York 31 Jan. 1715/6. He was from Albany County.

Clont, Jacob. He was naturalized in Maryland 29 Sep. 1751.

Clop, Peter. He was naturalized in New York 17 Jan. 1715/6. He was from Albany County.

Clopper, Cornelis Yanzen. He took the oath to the King 21–26 Oct. 1664 after the conquest of New Netherland.

Clopper, Hendrick. He was naturalized in New York 8–9 Sep. 1715. He was from Ulster County.

Closs, Heinrich. He was naturalized in New York 3 July 1759.

Clots, Lewis. He was naturalized in Pennsylvania 10 Apr. 1753. He was from Northampton County.

Clover, Peter. He was naturalized in Pennsylvania 10 Apr. 1766. He was from Hunterdon County, New Jersey.

Clows, William. He was naturalized in Maryland 14 Sep. 1763. He was a German.

Clug, John James. He was from Annapolis, Maryland and petitioned for naturalization 20 Aug. 1731.

Clump, Peter. He was naturalized in New York 23 Dec. 1765.

Clyne, Andrew. He was naturalized in Pennsylvania 24 Sep. 1762. He was from Lancaster County.

Cobble, Anthony. He was naturalized in North Carolina 23 Mar. 1763. He was from Rowan County.

Cobell, Adam. He was naturalized in North Carolina 22 Sep. 1763. He was from Rowan County and a German.

Cobell, George. He was naturalized in North Carolina 22 Sep. 1763. He was from Rowan County and a German.

Cobell, Jacob. He was naturalized in North Carolina 22 Sep. 1763. He was from Rowan County and a German.

Coblens, Philip. He was naturalized in Maryland 13 Apr. 1763. He was a German from Frederick County.

Cock, Erick. He was naturalized in Pennsylvania 11 Jan. 1683. He was formerly of New Sweden.

Cock, Gerhard Daniel. He was naturalized in New York 29 July 1773. He was the minister at the German Reformed Church at Rhinebeck.

Cock, Jan Eskelsen. He expressed his desire to be naturalized in New Castle County, Delaware 21 Feb. 1682/3.

Cock, John. He was endenized in New York 12 Dec. 1695.

Cock, Lasey. He was naturalized in Pennsylvania 11 Jan. 1683. He was formerly of New Sweden.

Cock, Mounts. He was naturalized in Pennsylvania 11 Jan. 1683. He was formerly of New Sweden.

Cock, Nicholas. He was endenized in Northumberland County, Virginia 20 Sep. 1664.

Cock, Nicholas. He was naturalized in Virginia 20 Sep. 1673.

Cock, Peter, Jr. He was naturalized in Pennsylvania 11 Jan. 1683. He was formerly of New Sweden.

Cock, Peter Eskelsen. He was naturalized in New Castle County, Delaware 21 Feb. 1682/3.

Cock, Symon Eskelsen. He expressed his desire to be naturalized in New Castle County, Delaware 21 Feb. 1682/3.

Cocke, Andreas. He was naturalized in Virginia 12 May 1705.

Cockevaer, Alezander. He took the oath of allegiance in Boswijck, Kings County, New York 26–30 Sep. 1687. He had been in the colony 30 years.

Coderus, Hans. He was naturalized in New Castle County, Delaware 21 Feb. 1682/3.

Codwise, John Conrad. He was naturalized in New York 12 July 1715. He was a schoolmaster.

Cody, William. He and his children were naturalized in Maryland 3 Nov. 1711. He lived in Charles County and was a tailor.

Coelie, Henry. He was naturalized in New York 27 Apr. 1715. He was a tailor from New York City.

Coenrad, Frederick. He was naturalized in New York 11 Sep. 1761.

Coenraats, Octavo. He was naturalized in New York 19 July 1715. He was a merchant.

Coenraet, Hendrick. He was naturalized in New York 14 Feb. 1715/6. He was from Albany County.

Coens, Jacob. He was naturalized in New York 15 Feb. 1715/6. He was from Albany County.

Coens, Johannis. He was naturalized in New York 31 Jan. 1715/6. He was from Albany County.

Coens, Mathys. He was naturalized in New York 14 Feb. 1715/6. He was from Albany County.

Coens, Peter. He was naturalized in New Jersey 20 Aug. 1755. He also appeared as Peter Covns.

Coens, Philip. He was naturalized in New York 14 Feb. 1715/6. He was from Albany County.

Coessart, John. He was endenized in New York 4 Nov. 1692.

Coeymans, Gertruyd. She was naturalized in New York 6 July 1723.

Coffman, Andrew. He was naturalized in Pennsylvania 14 Feb. 1729/30. He was from Lancaster County.

Coffman, Isaac. He was naturalized in Pennsylvania 14 Feb. 1729/30. He was from Lancaster County.

Coffman, John. He was naturalized in Pennsylvania 14 Feb. 1729/30. He was from Lancaster County.

Coffman, Michael. He was naturalized in Pennsylvania 14 Feb. 1729/30. He was from Lancaster County.

Cogar, James. He was naturalized in Halifax County, Virginia 18 Nov. 1756.

Cohall, George. He was naturalized in Jamaica 8 Feb. 1730/1.

Coghnot, John Everhart. He was naturalized in New York 27 Jan. 1770.

Cohen, Abraham. He was endenized in England 19 Aug. 1688. He settled in Barbados and was a Jew.

Cohen, Abraham Meyers. He was naturalized in New York 16 Dec. 1737.

Cohen, Abraham Meyers. He was naturalized in New York in 1740–41. He was a Jew. He was a merchant in New York City.

Cohen, Daniel. He was endenized 12 Apr. 1700 probably in London. He came to Nevis.

Cohen, Hayam. He was naturalized in Jamaica 14 [?19] Nov. 1720.

Cohen, Jonathan. He was naturalized in Jamaica 17 Oct. 1706.

Cohen, Moses. He was naturalized in Jamaica 18 Nov. 1681.

Cohen, Samuel Myers. He was naturalized in New York in 1740–41. He was a Jew. He was a merchant in New York City.

Coil, Valentine. He was naturalized in Augusta County, Virginia 22 Aug. 1764.

Coleck, Jonas N. He was naturalized in New York 23 Apr. 1744. He was a baker in New York City.

Colie, Henry. He was naturalized in New York 27 Sep. 1715. He was a tailor from New York City.

Colin, Francois. He took the oath of allegiance at Mobile, West Florida 2 Oct. 1764.

Colke, Oliver. He was naturalized in Maryland 6 June 1674. He was Swedish.

Coll, Barrant. He took the oath of naturalization in New York 1 Sep. 1687 in Ulster County.

Collickman, Derrick. He was naturalized in Maryland 25 Mar. 1702. He lived in Cecil County and was born of Dutch parents.

Collier, Henry. He was endenized in England 8 Mar. 1681/2. He came to New York.

Collin, Daniel. He was naturalized in New York 3 Feb. 1768.

Collin, Pierre. He was born at L'Isle de Re, France, the son of Jean Collin and Judith Vasleau. He was naturalized in South Carolina 10 Mar. 1696/7. He was a merchant.

Collin, William. He was naturalized in Jamaica 25 Aug. 1753. He was a free Negro.

Collineau, Mathew. He was born at Paris, France, the son of Mathew and Jane Collineau. He was endenized in England 19 Aug. 1688. He was endenized in New York 12 July 1694.

Collins, James. He was naturalized in Jamaica 9 Sep. 1736.

Collins, Sarah. She was naturalized in Jamaica 8 Sep. 1736.

Collman, Jacob. He was naturalized in Pennsylvania 25–27 Sep. 1740. He was from Philadelphia County.

Colomb, Joseph. He took the oath of allegiance at Mobile, West Florida 2 Oct. 1764.

Colon, George. He was naturalized in New York 27 Jan. 1770.

Colon, James. He was naturalized in New York 27 Jan. 1770.

Colon, Jean. He was naturalized in New York 17 Apr. 1750. He was a felt maker from Schenectady, Albany County.

Colon, John. He was naturalized in New York 24 Nov. 1750.

Colon, Jonas. He was naturalized in New York 27 Jan. 1770.

Colonge, Mary Elizabeth. She was naturalized in New York 25 Nov. 1751. She was the widow of Disleau Colonge.

Colsher, Peter. He was naturalized in New Jersey in 1768.

Comages, Cornelius. He was made a denizen in Maryland 30 July 1661. He was Dutch and was late of New Amstel.

Combe, Mary. She was the wife of William Combe, merchant of Port Royal. She was naturalized in Jamaica 5 Oct. 1699.

Come, Adam. He was naturalized in Maryland 18 July 1759.

Comeau, Abraham. He was an Acadian who took the oath of allegiance in Dec. 1729.

Comeau, Alexander. He was an Acadian who took the oath of allegiance in Dec. 1729.

Comeau, Alexandre. He was an Acadian who took the oath of allegiance in Apr. 1730.

Comeau, Ambroise. He was an Acadian who took the oath of allegiance in Apr. 1730.

Comeau, Augustin. He was an Acadian who took the oath of allegiance in Dec. 1729.

Comeau, Claude. He was an Acadian who took the oath of allegiance in Apr. 1730.

Comeau, Estienne. He was an Acadian and took the oath to the King at the Mines, Pisiquit, Nova Scotia 31 Oct. 1727.

Comeau, Estienne. He was an Acadian who took the oath of allegiance in Apr. 1730.

Comeau, Etienne. He was an Acadian who took the oath of allegiance in Apr. 1730.

Comeau, Francois. He was an Acadian who took the oath of allegiance in Apr. 1730.

Comeau, J. B. He was an Acadian who took the oath of allegiance in Apr. 1730.

Comeau, Jean. He was an Acadian and took the oath to the King at the Mines, Pisiquit, Nova Scotia 31 Oct. 1727.

Comeau, Jean. He was an Acadian and took the oath to the King at the Mines, Pisiquit, Nova Scotia 31 Oct. 1727.

Comeau, Jean Baptiste. He was an Acadian who took the oath of allegiance in Apr. 1730.

Comeau, Joseph. He was an Acadian who took the oath of allegiance in Apr. 1730.

Comeau, Maurice. He was an Acadian who took the oath of allegiance in Apr. 1730.

Comeau, Pierre. He was an Acadian who took the oath of allegiance in Dec. 1729.

Comeau, Pierre. He was an Acadian who took the oath of allegiance in Dec. 1729.

Comeau, Pierre. He was an Acadian who took the oath of allegiance in Apr. 1730.

Comeau, Pierre. He was an Acadian who took the oath of allegiance in Apr. 1730.

Comegys, Cornelius. He and his wife, Millementy Comegys, were naturalized in Maryland 20 Oct. 1671. He was born in Lexmont, Holland, and she was born in Barnevelt, Holland.

Comet, Peter. He was naturalized in Jamaica 12 Apr. 1744.

Comegys, Cornelius, Jr. He, his wife Elizabeth Comegys, and their children, Hannah Comegys and William Comegys, were naturalized in Maryland 20 Oct. 1671. He was born in Virginia.

Comfort, Andrew. He was naturalized in Pennsylvania 24 Sep. 1762. He was from York County.

Comfort, John. He was naturalized in Pennsylvania 24 Sep. 1762. He was from York County.

Commau, Abraham. He was an Acadian and took the oath to George II at Annapolis River, Nova Scotia in the winter of 1730.

Commeau, Piere. He was an Acadian and took the oath to George II at Annapolis River, Nova Scotia in the winter of 1730.

Commeaux, Etienne. He took the oath of allegiance at Port Royal, Nova Scotia 16 Aug. 1695.

Commeaux, Jean. He took the oath of allegiance at Port Royal, Nova Scotia 16 Aug. 1695.

Commeaux, Pierre. He took the oath of allegiance at Port Royal, Nova Scotia 16 Aug. 1695.

Commeaux, Pierre. He took the oath of allegiance at Port Royal, Nova Scotia 16 Aug. 1695.

Como, Alexr. He was an Acadian and took the oath to George II at Annapolis River, Nova Scotia in the winter of 1730.

Como, Augustin. He was an Acadian and took the oath to George II at Annapolis River, Nova Scotia in the winter of 1730.

Como, Jean. He was an Acadian who took the oath of allegiance in Apr. 1730.

Como, Piere. He was an Acadian and took the oath to George II at Annapolis River, Nova Scotia in the winter of 1730.

Conaway, Hannah. She was naturalized in Jamaica 20 Aug. 1720.

Congle, Andrew. He was naturalized in New Jersey 6 Dec. 1769.

Coninck, Aldert. He took the oath to the King 21–26 Oct. 1664 after the conquest of New Netherland.

Coninck, Thomas. He took the oath to the King 21–26 Oct. 1664 after the conquest of New Netherland.

Conjes, Jacob. He was naturalized in New York 24 Mar. 1772.

Conrad, George. He was naturalized in Pennsylvania 25 Mar. 1764. He was from Paradise Township, York County.

Conrad, George. He was naturalized in Pennsylvania 10 & 23 Apr. 1764. He was from Conawawga Township, York County.

Conrad, Henrick. He was naturalized in Pennsylvania 10–12 Apr. 1762. He was from Philadelphia County.

Conrad, Jacob. He was naturalized in Pennsylvania 10 Apr. 1765. He was from Lebanon Township, Lancaster County.

Conrad, Stephen. He was naturalized in Pennsylvania 11 Apr. 1751. He was from Lancaster County.

Conradi, Conrad. He was naturalized in Maryland 9 Apr. 1760. He lived in Baltimore, Maryland.

Conradt, Peter. He was naturalized in Pennsylvania 11–13 Apr. 1743. He was from Philadelphia County.

Constant, Jean. He was endenized in New York 6 Feb. 1695/6.

Constantin, Coenraet. He was naturalized in New Castle County, Delaware 21 Feb. 1682/3.

Contenho, Isaac Pereira. He was endenized in England 14 Dec. 1666. He settled in Barbados and was a Jew.

Conterman, Johan Coenrart. He was naturalized in New York 8–9 Sep. 1715. He was from Ulster County.

Conterman, Johan Friedrich. He was naturalized in New York 8–9 Sep. 1715. He was from Ulster County.

Conterman, Johan Georg. He was naturalized in New York 8–9 Sep. 1715. He was from Ulster County.

Continho, Ester. She was naturalized in Jamaica in July 1711.

Continho, Isaac. He was naturalized in Jamaica 10 Nov. 1681.

Co[n]tinho, Moses. He was naturalized in Jamaica 22 Mar. 1681/2.

Contryman, Andries. He was naturalized in New York 8–9 Sep. 1715. He was from Ulster County.

Coob, Joseph. He was naturalized in Pennsylvania 19 May 1739. He was from Philadelphia County.

Coob, Nicholas, Jr. He was naturalized in Pennsylvania 25–27 Sep. 1740. He was from Philadelphia County.

Cooher, John Peter. He was naturalized in Pennsylvania 19 May 1739. He was from Lancaster County.

Cook, George. He was naturalized in New York 24 Mar. 1772.

Cook, Henry. He was naturalized in New Jersey 28 Apr. 1762.

Cook, Henry Mickael. He was naturalized in New York 6 July 1723.

Cook, John. He was naturalized in Pennsylvania 24 Sep. 1757.

Cook, John. He was naturalized in New York 16 Feb. 1771.

Cooke, Peter. He was naturalized in New York 27 July 1774.

Cooke, Philip Christopher. He was naturalized in Jamaica 8 Nov. 1733.

Cookenham, Johan Jury. He was naturalized in New York 11 Sep. 1761.

Cookenheim, Daniel. He was naturalized in New York 3 July 1766.

Cooker, Bartle. He was naturalized in Pennsylvania 24 Sep. 1741. He was from Philadelphia County.

Cooker, John Peter. He was naturalized in Pennsylvania in 1739. He was from Lancaster County.

Cool, Cornelis. He took the oath of naturalization in New York 1 Sep. 1687 in Ulster County.

Cool, Cornelis. He was naturalized in New York 8–9 Sep. 1715. He was from Ulster County.

Cool, Jacob. He took the oath of naturalization in New York 1 Sep. 1687 in Ulster County.

Cool, Lendert. He took the oath of naturalization in New York 1 Sep. 1687 in Ulster County.

Cool, Philip. He was naturalized in New York 8 Mar. 1773.

Cool, Symon. He took the oath of naturalization in New York 1 Sep. 1687 in Ulster County.

Coon, Michael. He was naturalized in North Carolina 22 Sep. 1763. He was from Rowan County and a German.

Coone, Nicholas. He was naturalized in North Carolina 22 Sep. 1763. He was from Rowan County and a German.

Coonrod, Woolrich. He was naturalized in Augusta County, Virginia 18 May 1762.

Coonst, Joose. He was naturalized in New York 24 Mar. 1772.

Coontz, George. He and his children, John Coontz, Eve Coontz, and Catherine Coontz, were naturalized in Maryland 4 June 1738. He was from Baltimore County and was born in Germany.

Coop, Nichlaus. He was naturalized in Maryland 12 Apr. 1758.

Cooper, Christian. He was naturalized in New York 11 Sep. 1761.

Cooper, George. He was naturalized in New Jersey 8 Oct. 1750.

Cooper, Daniel. He was naturalized in Maryland 15 Sep. 1762. He was from Frederick County.

Cooper, Eliza. She was naturalized in Jamaica 15 Aug. 1716.

Cooper, Lawrence. He was naturalized in Pennsylvania 24–25 Sep./5 Oct. 1767. He was from Amity Township, Berks County.

Cooper, Philip. He was naturalized in New Jersey 8 Oct. 1750.

Coplenz, Peter. He was naturalized in Maryland 28 Sep. 1762. He was a German from Frederick County.

Coppersmith, John. He was naturalized in Maryland 15 Sep. 1763. He was a German.

Coquelin, Detrick. He was naturalized in Pennsylvania 24 Sep. 1760. He was from Lancaster County.

Coquelin, John. He was naturalized in Pennsylvania 24 Sep. 1760. He was from Lancaster County.

Coranflow, George. He was naturalized in Maryland 1 Oct. 1767. He was a German.

Corcilius, Peter. He was naturalized in New York 8 Nov. 1735.

Corcilius, William. He was naturalized in New York 8 Nov. 1735.

Corche, Elias Fernandes. He was naturalized in Jamaica 26 Feb. 1740/1. He was a Jew.

Corche, Moses Alvares. He was naturalized in Jamaica 26 Feb. 1740/1. He was a Jew.

Corcho, Elias Fernandes. He was naturalized in Jamaica 8 Jan. 1728/9.

Corcho, Jospeh Alvares. He was naturalized in Jamaica 8 Jan. 1728/9.

Corcho, Joseph Alvares. He was naturalized in Jamaica 29 Nov. 1743. He was a Jew.

Corcho, Moses Alvares. He was naturalized in Jamaica 8 Jan. 1728/9.

Cordaback, James. He took the oath of naturalization in New York 1 Sep. 1687 in Ulster County.

Cordea, Hester. She was naturalized in Maryland 6 June 1674. She was born in Deepe, Normandy, France.

Cordea, Marke. He was naturalized in Maryland 19 Apr. 1671. He lived in St. Mary's County, Maryland and was born in Normandy, France.

Cordes, Anthoine. He was born at Bazamet, Languedoc, France, the son of Paul Cordes and Marie Depeuch. His wife was Ester Madeleine Balluet. Their children were Isaac Cordes, Madeleine Cordes, and Ester Cordes who were born in South Carolina. They were naturalized in South Carolina ca. 1696.

Cordosa, David DaSilva. He was naturalized in Jamaica 15 Jan. 1685/6.

Cordoso, Jacob. He was naturalized in Jamaica 29 Nov. 1743. He was a Jew.

Cordoso, Rachael. She was naturalized in Jamaica 29 Nov. 1743. She was a Jewess.

Cordoza, Rebecca. She was the wife of Moses Jesurin Cordoza, merchant, and was naturalized in Jamaica 8 Jan. 1696.

Cordoza, Solomon. He was endenized in England 29 May 1663. He lived in Barbados and was a Jew.

Cordt, Arent Flaake. He was naturalized in New York 24 Nov. 1750.

Cordt, Marchard. He was naturalized in Virginia 24 Nov. 1750.

Cormier, Alexis. He was an Acadian who took the oath of allegiance in Apr. 1730.

Cormier, Francois. He was an Acadian who took the oath of allegiance in Apr. 1730.

Cormier, Jermain. He was an Acadian who took the oath of allegiance in Apr. 1730.

Cormier, Michel. He was an Acadian who took the oath of allegiance in Apr. 1730.

Cormier, Pierre. He was an Acadian who took the oath of allegiance in Apr. 1730.

Cormier, Pierre. He was an Acadian who took the oath of allegiance in Apr. 1730.

Cormier, Pierre. He was an Acadian who took the oath of allegiance in Apr. 1730.

Cornee, Peter. He was naturalized in New York 29 Oct. 1730.

Cornelis, Gerrit. He took the oath of naturalization in New York 1 Sep. 1687 in Ulster County.

Cornelis, John. He was naturalized in New York 26 Aug. 1696.

Cornelis, Petter. He took the oath of naturalization in New York 1 Sep. 1687 in Ulster County.

Cornelisen, Garret. He was naturalized in New York 17 June 1726.

Cornelisen, Matthys. He took the oath of allegiance in Breucklijn, Kings County, New York 26–30 Sep. 1687. He had been in the colony 24 years.

Cornelison, Mathias. He was endenized in Maryland 29 July 1661. He was Swedish.

Cornelius, Christian. He was naturalized in New Jersey 8 July 1730. He was born in Germany.

Cornelius, John. He was naturalized in New York 26 Aug. 1696.

Cornelius, Lawrence. He sought denization in Pequot, Connecticut 26 Feb. 1656/6. He was a Dutchman.

Cornelius, Lawrence. He was naturalized in Pennsylvania 11–13 Apr. 1743. He was from Philadelphia County.

Cornelius, Mathias. He was made a denizen in Maryland 29 July 1661. He was Swedish and was late of New Amstel.

Cornelius, Samuel. He was naturalized in Jamaica 7 Sep. 1748.

Cornifleau, Laurens. He petitioned to be endenized in New York in 1691. He was a French Protestant.

Corning, Johan Lodolph. He was naturalized in New York 31 Jan. 1715/6. He was from Albany County.

Cornman, John. He was naturalized in Pennsylvania 24–25 Sep. 1767/5 Oct. 1767. He was from Philadelphia. He was a Moravian.

Cornman, Lodowick. He was naturalized in Pennsylvania 25–26 Sep./4 Oct. 1749. He was from Lancaster County.

Corporon, Francois. He was an Acadian and took the oath to George II at Annapolis River, Nova Scotia in the winter of 1730.

Corporon, Francois. He was an Acadian who took the oath of allegiance in Apr. 1730.

Corporon, Francois. He was an Acadian who took the oath of allegiance in Apr. 1730. [second of the name]

Corporon, Jean. He took the oath of allegiance at Port Royal, Nova Scotia 16 Aug. 1695.

Corporon, Martin. He was an Acadian who took the oath of allegiance in Apr. 1730.

Corporon, Paul. He was an Acadian who took the oath of allegiance in Apr. 1730.

Correa, Isaac Alvarez. He was naturalized in Jamaica in 1721.

Correa, Moses Alvares. He was naturalized in Jamaica 21 May 1743. He was a Jew.

Corrier, Emanuell. He was naturalized in Jamaica 21 Nov. 1688.

Corselius, Peter. He was naturalized in New York 8 Nov. 1735.

Corselius, William. He was naturalized in New York 8 Nov. 1735.

Corsen, Pieter. He took the oath of allegiance in Breucklijn, Kings County, New York 26–30 Sep. 1687. He was a native of the colony.

Corteljou, Cornelis. He took the oath of allegiance in New Uijtrceht, Kings County, New York 26–30 Sep. 1687. He was a native of the colony.

Corteljou, Jacques. He took the oath of allegiance in New Uitjrceht, Kings County, New York 26–30 Sep. 1687.

Corteljou, Jacques, Jr. He took the oath of allegiance in New Uitjrceht, Kings County, New York 26–30 Sep. 1687. He was a native of the colony.

Corteljou, Pieter. He took the oath of allegiance in New Uitjrceht, Kings County, New York 26–30 Sep. 1687. He was a native of the colony.

Corteljouw, Willem. He took the oath of allegiance in New Uitjrceht, Kings County, New York 26–30 Sep. 1687. He was a native of the colony.

Cosins, John. He was naturalized in Maryland 16 Nov. 1683.

Cosman, John. He was naturalized in New Jersey 6 Dec. 1769.

Cosard, Lees. He promised allegiance to the King and obedience to William Penn in Pennsylvania 10 Sep. 1683.

Cossar, Jacob. He took the oath to the King 21–26 Oct. 1664 after the conquest of New Netherland.

Cossman, Johannis. He was naturalized in New York 25 Nov. 1751.

Cost, Felty. He was naturalized in Maryland 11 Sep. 1765.

Cost, George. He was naturalized in Maryland 11 Sep. 1765.

Coster, Jan. He took the oath to the King 21–26 Oct. 1664 after the conquest of New Netherland.

Costurier, Jacques. He took the oath to the King 21–26 Oct. 1664 after the conquest of New Netherland.

Cothonneau, Guilleaume. He was endenized in New York 6 Feb. 1695/6. He was a son of Marie Cothonneau.

Cothonneau, Jeremie. He was born at LaRochelle, France, the son of Germain Cothonneau and Elizabeth Nombret. His wife was Mayre Billon. Their children, Germain Cothonneau and Pierre Cothonneau, were born at LaRochelle and their daughter, Ester Marthe Cothonneau, was born in South Carolina. They were naturalized in South Carolina 10 Mar.1696/7. He was a cooper.

Cothonneau, Marie. She was endenized in New York 6 Feb. 1695/6.

Cottin, Jean. He was naturalized in New York 8–9 Sep. 1715. He was from Ulster County.

Cottin, Jean. He took the oath of allegiance in New York 2 Dec. 1687. He was from Ulster County.

Cottin, John. He took the oath of naturalization in New York 1 Sep. 1687 in Ulster County.

Cottrell, Elizabeth. She was naturalized in Jamaica 14 Nov. 1720.

Couillandeau, Pierre. He was born at LaTramblade, France, the son of Pierre Couillandeau and Marie Fougeraut. He was naturalized in South Carolina ca. 1696.

Couns, George Necol. He was naturalized in New York 29 Oct. 1730.

Countinho, Moses. He was endenized in England 9 Mar. 1693/4. He settled in Barbados.

Countryman, Andries. He was naturalized in New York 8–9 Sep. 1715. He was from Ulster County.

Couperight, George Peter. He was naturalized in Maryland 29 Sep. 1762. He was a German from Frederick County.

Course, Barren. He took the oath to the King 21–26 Oct. 1664 after the conquest of New Netherland.

Cousseau, Jasper. He took the oath to the King 21–26 Oct. 1664 after the conquest of New Netherland.

Cousalmet, Johan. He was naturalized in New York 8–9 Sep. 1715. He was from Ulster County.

Coustarier, Hendrick. He was endenized in New York 8 July 1672.

Coutanseau, Jacob. He was endenized in England 22 Dec. 1632. He came to Virginia. His son, Jacob Coutanseau, requested the Virginia Assembly to confirm the said paper. In Oct. 1669 the Assembly responded that the record granted in England was better than anything they could give.

Coutino, Moses. He sought to be made a denizen 30 Aug. 1692.

Couttinho, David. He was endenized in England 13 Jan. 1695/6. He settled in Barbados and was a Jew.

Couttinho, Isaque. He was endenized in England 13 Jan. 1695/6. He settled in Barbados and was a Jew.

Couty, Rabba. He was endenized in New York ante 1671.

Covert, Johannes. He was naturalized in New York 11 Sep. 1761.

Couverts, Jan. He took the oath of allegiance in Breucklijn, Kings County, New York 26–30 Sep. 1687. He had been in the colony 35 years.

Couverts, Luijcas. He took the oath of allegiance in Breucklijn, Kings County, New York 26–30 Sep. 1687. He had been in the colony 24 years.

Couverts, Mauritius. He took the oath of allegiance in Breucklijn, Kings County, New York 26–30 Sep. 1687. He was a native of the colony.

Courverts, Theunis Janse. He took the oath of allegiance in Breucklijn, Kings County, New York 26–30 Sep. 1687. He had been in the colony 36 years.

Coxe, Henry Michael. He was naturalized in New York 6 July 1723.

Craford, Mungo. He was given a certificate to trade and deal and enjoy liberties and privileges as other of his Majesty's subjects in Boston, Massachusetts 20 July 1686. He was a Scotsman and had been an inhabitant of Boston for many years.

Craft, Martin. He was naturalized in Pennsylvania 11 Apr. 1761. He was from Berks County.

Craismig, Jasper. He was naturalized in Maryland 13 Apr. 1761.

Craler, Peter. He was naturalized in New York 22 June 1734.

Crall, Christian. He was naturalized in Pennsylvania 11–13 Apr. 1743. He was from Bucks County.

Cramer, Anthony. He was naturalized in New York 8–9 Sep. 1715. He was from Ulster County.

Cramer, Christopher. He was naturalized in New York 3 May 1755.

Cramer, George. He was naturalized in New York 31 Dec. 1761.

Cramer, George. He was naturalized in New York 24 Dec. 1772.

Cramer, Matthias. He was naturalized in New Jersey in 1750.

Cramer, Michael. He was naturalized in New York 22 Nov. 1715. He was a boatman from New York City.

Cramlick, Jacob. He was naturalized in Maryland 10 Sep. 1762.

Crane, Josiah. He was naturalized in New York 21 Apr. 1752. He was a tobacconist merchant in New York City.

Craner, Michael. He was naturalized in Maryland 15 Apr. 1763. He was a German.

Crasper, Casper. He was naturalized in New York 3 May 1755.

Crasper, Isaac. He was naturalized in New York 3 May 1755.

Crasper, John. He was naturalized in New York 3 May 1755.

Crasper, Uldrick. He was naturalized in New York 3 May 1755.

Cratho, John. He was naturalized in Pennsylvania in 1724. He was from Germany.

Cratser, Leanhart. He was naturalized in Pennsylvania 31 Dec. 1768.

Cratzer, Philip. He was naturalized in Pennsylvania 11 Apr. 1761. He was from Northampton County.

Cratzinberger, Coenraedt. He was naturalized in New York 3 July 1759.

Craw, Conrad. He was naturalized in Maryland 24 Sep. 1765. He was a German.

Cray, Teunis. He took the oath to the King 21–26 Oct. 1664 after the conquest of New Netherland.

Creature, Moritz. He was naturalized in New Jersey in 1750. He was from Hunterdon County. He also appeared as Moritz Kreder.

Creeble, Melchoir. He was naturalized in Pennsylvania 25–26 Sep./4 Oct. 1749. He was from Philadelphia County.

Creek, Francis. He was naturalized in Pennsylvania 25–26 Sep./4 Oct. 1749. He was from Lancaster County.

Creesermer, Casper. He was naturalized in Pennsylvania 10–11 Apr. 1745. He was from Philadelphia County.

Creesman, George. He was naturalized in Pennsylvania 19 May 1739. He was from Philadelphia County.

Cregier, Martin. He took the oath to the King 21–26 Oct. 1664 after the conquest of New Netherland.

Creighoff, Jacob. He was naturalized in New York 16 Feb. 1771.

Creitz, Han Ury. He was naturalized in New York 27 Jan. 1770.

Creitz, Hans Georg. He was naturalized in New York 3 July 1759.

Crell, Joseph. He was naturalized in Pennsylvania 11–12 Apr. 1744. He was from Philadelphia.

Cremer, Johan N. He was naturalized in New York 24 Mar. 1772.

Crepel, Peter. He was naturalized in Maryland 15 Sep. 1762. He was from Frederick County.

Crepper, Karel. He was naturalized in New York 11 Sep. 1761.

Cresh, George. He was naturalized in Pennsylvania 10 Apr. 1765. He was from Douglass Township, Berks County.

Creson, Isaac. He was naturalized in North Carolina 23 Mar. 1763. He was from Rowan County.

Cressman, Frederick. He was naturalized in Pennsylvania 24 Sep. 1755. He was from Philadelphia County.

Cressman, John. He was naturalized in Pennsylvania 25–27 Sep. 1740. He was from Philadelphia County.

Cressman, Valentine. He was naturalized in Pennsylvania 11–13 Apr. 1743. He was from Philadelphia County.

Creutz, Christopher Godlieb. He was naturalized in New York 1 Aug. 1748. He was a baker from New York City.

Creutzer, Andrew. He was naturalized in Pennsylvania 25–26 Sep./4 Oct. 1749. He was from Lancaster County.

Crime, Jacob. He was naturalized in Pennsylvania 11 Apr. 1761. He was from Berks County.
Crime, Sebastian. He was naturalized in Pennsylvania 11 Apr. 1761. He was from Berks County.
Crisma, [—]. He was naturalized in Virginia 23 Oct. 1745.
Crismand, Joseph. He was naturalized in Maryland 15 Nov. 1712. He lived in Charles County.
Crist, Jacob. He was naturalized in Maryland 24 Sep. 1765. He was a German.
Crist, Johannis. He sought naturalization in New York 31 Oct. 1769.
Crist, Michael. He was naturalized in Maryland 24 Sep. 1765. He was a German.
Crist, Philip. He was naturalized in Maryland 24 Sep. 1765. He was a German.
Cristen, Jacob. He was naturalized in Maryland 10 Apr. 1760. He lived in Frederick County.
Critz, Herman. He was naturalized in Virginia 18 Sep. 1753. He was from Halifax County.
Criupill, Anthony. He took the oath of naturalization in New York 1 Sep. 1687 in Ulster County.
Criupill, Petter. He took the oath of naturalization in New York 1 Sep. 1687 in Ulster County.
Croaner, George. He was naturalized in Pennsylvania 11–12 Apr. 1744. He was from Bucks County.
Crocheron, Jean. He was naturalized in New York 23 Aug. 1715. He was a yeoman from Staten Island.
Crock, Coenradt. He was naturalized in New York 21 Mar. 1772.
Croe, Mathew. He was naturalized in Jamaica 5 Sep. 1745.
Croesie, William. He expressed his desire to be naturalized in New Castle County, Delaware 21 Feb. 1682/3.
Croesman, Philip Balshazar. He was naturalized in Pennsylvania 13–15 Apr. 1748. He was from Philadelphia County.
Croffern, Christopher. He was naturalized in Pennsylvania 10–14 Apr. 1747. He was from Lancaster County.
Croft, William. He was naturalized in Pennsylvania 24–29 Sep. 1768. He was from Tewksbury, Hunterdon County, New Jersey.
Crolges, William. He was naturalized in New York 17 June 1726.
Croll, Christian. He was naturalized in Pennsylvania 11–12 Apr. 1744. He was from Lancaster County.
Crom, Florus. He took the oath of allegiance in Orange County, New York 26 Sep. 1687.
Crommelin, Daniel. He was born at Saint Quentin, France, the son of John Crommelin and Rachel Tazzet. He was naturalized in England 13 June 1685. He came to New York.
Cron, Nicholas. He was naturalized in Pennsylvania 10–14 Apr. 1747. He was from Philadelphia County.
Crone, John. He was naturalized in Pennsylvania 11 Apr. 1763. He was from Windsor Township, York County.
Cronice, George. He was naturalized in Maryland 10 Apr. 1760. He lived in Frederick County.
Cronmiller, Martin. He was naturalized in Pennsylvania 10–12 Apr. 1762. He was from York County.
Croo, Henry. He was naturalized in New Jersey 6 June 1751.
Croob, Nicholas. He was naturalized in New York 21 Apr. 1762. He was a cordwainer from New York City.
Croois, Christopher. He was naturalized in Maryland 3 Sep. 1765. He was a German from Sharpsburgh, Maryland.
Crooner, John Jacob. He was naturalized in North Carolina 13 Sep. 1770.
Cross, Lewis. He was naturalized in Jamaica 21 Dec. 1720.
Crosskop, John George. He was naturalized in New York 20 Apr. 1763. He was a baker from New York City.
Crossman, George. He was naturalized in Pennsylvania 25–27 Sep. 1740. He was from Philadelphia County.
Croup, Christian. He was naturalized in Pennsylvania 12 Apr. 1750. He was from Lancaster County.
Crow, Leonard. He was naturalized in Pennsylvania 11–13 Apr. 1743. He was from Lancaster County.
Crowl, Jacob. He was naturalized in Pennsylvania 24 Sep. 1763. He was from Reading Township, Berks County.

Crox, John William. He was naturalized in Pennsylvania 11–13 Apr. 1743. He was from Philadelphia County.

Croyder, John. He was naturalized in Pennsylvania 14 Feb. 1729/30. He was from Lancaster County.

Cruger, John. He was naturalized in New York 20 Mar. 1715/6. He was a merchant.

Cruger, John. He was endenized in New York 30 Mar. 1694/5.

Crumryne, Hans Michael. He was naturalized in Pennsylvania 9 Apr. 1741. He was from Philadelphia County.

Crush, John. He was naturalized in Pennsylvania 10–12 Apr. 1762. He was from Lancaster County.

Crush, Peter. He was naturalized in Maryland 23 Apr. 1772. He was a German.

Cruyslear, Johannis. He was naturalized in New York 8–9 Sep. 1715. He was from Ulster County.

Cryder, Martin. He was naturalized in Frederick County, Virginia 3 Mar. 1768.

Crysman, John George. He was naturalized in Pennsylvania 25 Sep. 1747. He was from Philadelphia County.

Cubber, John. He was naturalized in Pennsylvania 10 Apr. 1754. He was from Philadelphia County.

Cugnet, John Peter. He was naturalized in Pennsylvania 24 Sep. 1762. He was from Lancaster County.

Cuinst, Barrant. He took the oath of naturalization in New York 1 Sep. 1687 in Ulster County.

Cuikes, Hendrick. He was naturalized in Maryland 29 Sep. 1752.

Culluck, Jacob. He was naturalized in Pennsylvania 17 Sep. 1701. He was born in Thurgow, South Holland, son of George Culluck. He was a cordwainer and a Protestant.

Cumerah, Jacob. He was naturalized in Pennsylvania 24 Sep. 1763. He was from Maxatawny Township, Berks County.

Cun, John Christopher. He was naturalized in Pennsylvania 10–14 Apr. 1747. He was from Philadelphia County.

Cuna, Isaac Henriques. He was naturalized in Jamaica 31 May 1743. He was a Jew.

Cuncle, Adam. He was naturalized in New Jersey in 1764. He also appeared as Adam Cunckel.

Cunha, Abraham Rodriques. He was naturalized in Jamaica 16 July 1734.

Cunha, Isaac Mendes. He was naturalized in Jamaica 31 Dec. 1734.

Cunha, Isaac Mendes. He was naturalized in Jamaica 29 Nov. 1743. He was a Jew.

Cunius, Philip. He was naturalized in Pennsylvania 25 Sep. 1751. He was from Philadelphia County.

Cunnus, John. He was naturalized in Pennsylvania 24 Sep. 1760. He was from Berks County.

Cunrads, John, Sr. He was naturalized in Pennsylvania 29 Sep. 1709. He was from Philadelphia County.

Cuntra, Rachel Henriques. She was naturalized in Jamaica 28 Nov. 1749. She was a Jewess.

Curfiss, Christopher. He was naturalized in Pennsylvania 10 Sep. 1761. He was from Philadelphia County.

Curiel, Solomon. He was naturalized in Jamaica 30 June 1714.

Curiel, Solomon. He was naturalized in Jamaica 26 May 1741. He was a Jew.

Curriel, Isaac. He was naturalized in Jamaica 8 Aug. 1717.

Curtis, Michael. He was naturalized in Maryland 19 Oct. 1695. He lived in St. Mary's County.

Custis, John. He was naturalized in Virginia 1 Apr. 1658. He was of English parentage.

Custis, William. He was naturalized in Virginia 1 Apr. 1658. He was of English parentage.

Cutts, Nicholas. He was naturalized in Pennsylvania 19 May 1739. He was from Lancaster County.

Cutwalt, Adam. He was naturalized in Pennsylvania 10 Apr. 1760.

Cyffer, William. He was naturalized in New York 18 Oct. 1750. He was a farmer from Dutchess County.

DaAndrade, Raphael. He was naturalized in Jamaica 18 June 1717.

DaCosta, Abraham Nunez. He was naturalized in Jamaica 31 May 1743. He was a Jew.

DaCosta, Daniel Albuquerque. He was naturalized in Jamaica 3 July 1733.

DaCosta, Daniel Mendes. He was naturalized in Jamaica 20 Aug. 1716.

DaCosta, Daniel Nunes. He was naturalized in New York 25 Nov. 1727.

DaCosta, Daniel Nunes. He was naturalized in New York 20 Sep. 1728.
DaCosta, David. He was endenized in London 8 Mar. 1662/3. He was from Barbados.
DaCosta, David. He applied for endenization in Jamaica in Feb. 1663.
DaCosta, Del. Mz. He was naturalized in Jamaica 25 Nov. 1740. He was a Jew.
DaCosta, Isaac. He was endenized in New York 29 July 1686.
DaCosta, Isaac Nunez. He was naturalized in Jamaica 25 Aug. 1741. He was a Jew.
DaCosta, Jacob. He was naturalized in Jamaica 2 Oct. 1678.
DeCosta, Jacob. He was naturalized in Jamaica 2 Sep. 1735.
DaCosta, Jacob Nunez. He was naturalized in Jamaica 25 Aug. 1741. He was a Jew.
DaCosta, Mathias. He was naturalized in Maryland 20 Oct. 1671. He lived in St. Mary's County and was Portuguese. He was born in Fiall [Fayall], Azores.
DaCosta, Moses Nunez. He was naturalized in Jamaica 30 Aug. 1743. He was a Jew.
DaCosta, Moses Pera. He was naturalized in Jamaica 26 Aug. 1746. He was a Jew.
DaCuna, Sarah. She was naturalized in Jamaica 1 Jan. 1711/2.
Daet, Hans Bernhard. He was naturalized in New York 14 Feb. 1715/6. He was from Albany County.
Daet, Johannis. He was naturalized in New York 14 Feb. 1715/6. He was from Albany County.
Daggenbach, Martin. He was naturalized in Pennsylvania 24–25 Sep. 1764. He was from Hannover Township, Philadelphia County.
Dahne, Philip Henry. He was naturalized in Pennsylvania 10 Sep. 1761. He was from Lancaster County.
Dahlberg, Nicholas. He was naturalized in New Jersey 31 July 1740. He was born in Sweden.
Daigre, Abraham. He was an Acadian who took the oath to George II at the Mines, Pisiquit 31 Oct. 1727.
Daigre, Bernard. He was an Acadian who took the oath to George II at the Mines, Pisiquit 31 Oct. 1727.
Daigre, Bernard. He was an Acadian who took the oath to George II at the Mines, Pisiquit 31 Oct. 1727.
Daigre, Francois. He was an Acadian who took the oath to George II at the Mines, Pisiquit 31 Oct. 1727.
Daigre, Pierre. He was an Acadian who took the oath to George II at the Mines, Pisiquit 31 Oct. 1727.
Daiser, Michael. He was naturalized in Pennsylvania 10 Apr. 1754. He was from Lancaster County.
Dalbo, Lasey. He was naturalized in Pennsylvania 11 Jan. 1683. He was formerly of New Sweden.
Dalep, Isaac. He was naturalized in Pennsylvania 10 Apr. 1755. He was from Northampton County.
Dalgas, Francis. He was naturalized in South Carolina 20 Jan. 1741.
Dalis, Johan Willem. He was naturalized in New York 17 Jan. 1715/6. He was from Albany County.
Damen, Jan. He took the oath of allegiance in Breucklijn, Kings County, New York 26–30 Sep. 1687. He had been in the colony 37 years.
Damer, Christian. He was naturalized in Maryland 15 Sep. 1762. He was from Baltimore County.
Damouvel, Samuel. He was naturalized in Westmoreland County, Virginia 24 Apr. 1712. He was a Frenchman.
Danbach, Frederick. He was naturalized in Maryland 9 Sep. 1761.
Dandler, Uldrich. He was naturalized in New York 31 Jan. 1715/6. He was from Albany County.
Dangerman, Christopher. He was naturalized in Maryland 25 May 1705. He was a saddler and lived in Calvert County. He was born in Hannover in the county of Liningburg, Germany.
Daniel, Pieter. He took the oath of allegiance in Boswijck, Kings County, New York 26–30 Sep. 1687. He had been in the colony 10 years.
Danielzen, Jacob. He took the oath to the King 21–26 Oct. 1664 after the conquest of New Netherland.
Dannahower, George. He was naturalized in Pennsylvania 10 Apr. 1766. He was from Robinson Township, Berks County.
Dannehauer, George. He was naturalized in Pennsylvania 10–14 Apr. 1747. He was from Philadelphia County.

Dannehower, Abraham. He was naturalized in Pennsylvania 11 Apr. 1761. He was from Northampton County.

Danner, Dieter. He was naturalized in Maryland 10 Sep. 1760.

Danner, Jacob. He was naturalized in Maryland 10 Sep. 1760.

Danner, Martin. He was naturalized in Pennsylvania 10 Apr. 1760.

Danner, Michael. He was naturalized in Maryland 14 Sep. 1763. He was a German from Frederick County.

Danswick, William. He took the oath of naturalization in New York 1 Sep. 1687 in Ulster County.

Dantfeltzer, Wendel. He was naturalized in Pennsylvania 24 Sep. 1770. He was from Nantmill Township, Chester County.

Danzy, John. He was naturalized in Virginia 7 June 1704. He was a German.

Daran, Francois. He took the oath of allegiance at Mobile, West Florida 2 Oct. 1764.

Darfer, John Derved. He was naturalized in Pennsylvania 11–13 Apr. 1743. He was from Lancaster County.

Darr, George. He was naturalized in Maryland 24 Sep. 1762. He was a German from Frederick County.

Darr, Sebastian. He was naturalized in Maryland 15 Apr. 1761.

Das, Pierre. He was endenized in New York 6 Jan. 1695/6. His name may have been Pierre Vas.

DaSilva, Aaron Mendez. He was naturalized in Jamaica 15 Jan. 1696.

DaSilva, Daniel. He was naturalized in Jamaica 1 Dec. 1742. He was a Jew.

DaSilva, Jacob. He was naturalized in Jamaica 26 Feb. 1740/1. He was a Jew.

DaSilva, Isaac Henriques. He was naturalized in Jamaica 25 May 1732.

DaSilva, Joseph. He was naturalized in Jamaica 1 Sep. 1738.

DaSilva, Judica. She was naturalized in Jamaica 26 Aug. 1746. She was a Jewess.

DaSilva, Moses. He was naturalized in Jamaica 6 Nov. 1719.

DaSilva, Rica. She was naturalized in Jamaica 26 Aug. 1746. She was a Jewess.

Dats, Peter. He was naturalized in New York 16 Aug. 1715. He was a yeoman from New Rochelle.

Datweiller, Hans. He was naturalized in Pennsylvania 6 Feb. 1730/1. He was from Philadelphia County.

Daubendisteil, Jacob. He was naturalized in Pennsylvania 24–25 Sep. 1764. He was from Philadelphia.

Dauison, Daniel, Sr. He was naturalized in Maryland 1 Mar. 1694. He was from Calvert County.

Dauison, Daniel, Jr. He was naturalized in Maryland 1 Mar. 1694. He was the son of Daniel Dauison, Sr. He was from Calvert County.

Daunces, Jasper. He was naturalized in Maryland 26 Apr. 1684. He also appeared as Jasper Dauncres.

Davene, John. He was endenized in New York 17 Sep. 1685.

David, Hayman. He petitioned for naturalization in New York 27 Nov. 1756.

David, Jacob. He was naturalized in Jamaica 15 Aug. 1740.

David, James. He took the oath to the King 21–26 Oct. 1664 after the conquest of New Netherland.

David, Jean Baptiste. He was an Acadian and took the oath to the King at the Mines, Pisiquit, Nova Scotia 31 Oct. 1727.

David, John. He took the oath of naturalization in New York 1 Sep. 1687 in Ulster County.

David, John Henry. He was naturalized in Pennsylvania 29–30 May 1772. He was from Baltimore, Maryland.

Davies, Willem. He took the oath of allegiance in Flackland, Kings County, New York 26–30 Sep. 1687. He had been in the colony 34 years.

Davis, Johannes. He was naturalized in Maryland 21 Sep. 1764. He was a German.

DeAbila, Isaque. He was naturalized in Jamaica 4 Dec. 1704.

D'Aiger, Joseph. He was an Acadian and took the oath of allegiance in Apr. 1730.

D'Aiger, Ollivier. He was an Acadian and took the oath of allegiance in Apr. 1730.

D'Aigle, Bernard. He was an Acadian and took the oath of allegiance in Apr. 1730.

D'Aigle, Rene. He was an Acadian and took the oath of allegiance in Apr. 1730.

[D']Aigre, Abraham. He was an Acadian and took the oath of allegiance in Apr. 1730.

D'Aigre, Amant. He was an Acadian and took the oath of allegiance in Apr. 1730.

D'Aigre, Charles. He was an Acadian and took the oath of allegiance in Apr. 1730.

D'Aigre, Francois. He was an Acadian and took the oath of allegiance in Apr. 1730.

D'Aigre, Jean. He was an Acadian and took the oath of allegiance in Apr. 1730.

D'Aigre, Pierre. He was an Acadian and took the oath of allegiance in Apr. 1730.

D'Aigre, Rene. He was an Acadian and took the oath of allegiance in Apr. 1730.

D'Aroits, Paul. He was an Acadian who took the oath of allegiance in Apr. 1730.

Deacanhalt, Henry. He was naturalized in Pennsylvania 25 Sep. 1758.

DeAcurria, Joseph. He was naturalized in Jamaica 16 Feb. 1718/9.

Deafisback, Adam. He was naturalized in Pennsylvania 10 Sep. 1761. He was from Lancaster County.

DeAguilar, Isaac. He was naturalized in Jamaica 1 Aug. 1693.

Deal, Caspar. He was naturalized in Pennsylvania 24–25 Sep. 1764. He was from Carnarvon Township, Lancaster County.

Deal, John. He was naturalized in Pennsylvania 24 Sep. 1760. He was from Berks County.

Deal, Peter. He was naturalized in Pennsylvania 10 Apr. 1760.

Dealing, John. He was naturalized in New York 20 Apr. 1768. He was a shopkeeper from New York City.

DeAlmeida, Daniel. He was naturalized in Jamaica 1 July 1700.

DeAlmeida, Isaac. He was naturalized in Jamaica 1 July 1700.

Deame, John. He was naturalized in Maryland 21 Sep. 1762. He was a German.

DeAndrada, Rebeccah Rodriques. She was naturalized in Jamaica 12 July 1726. She was the wife of Raphael DeAndrada.

DeAndrada, Rodriques. He was naturalized in Jamaica 12 July 1726.

Deangaud, John. He was naturalized in New York 17 June 1726.

Deany, John. He was naturalized in Pennsylvania 11–13 Apr. 1743. He was from Philadelphia County.

Dearner, Jacob. He was naturalized in Maryland 10 Apr. 1760. He lived in Frederick County.

Debaene, Joost. He took the oath of allegiance in New Uijtrceht, Kings County, New York 26–30 Sep. 1687. He had been in the colony 4 years.

DeBallile, Routier. He was naturalized in Jamaica 5 Mar. 1756.

DeBarrette, Isaac. He was naturalized in Maryland 8 May 1669. He was born in Harlem, Holland.

D'Beauvois, Jacobus. He took the oath of allegiance in Breucklijn, Kings County, New York 26–30 Sep. 1687. He had been in the colony 28 years.

Debele, John George. He was naturalized in New York 31 Oct. 1745. He was a gardener from New York City.

Debler, Melchor. He was naturalized in Pennsylvania 11 Apr. 1761. He was from Berks County.

DeBertholt, John Philip. He was naturalized in Pennsylvania 25 Sep. 1744. He was from Philadelphia County.

Debodent, Jean Baptist. He took the oath of allegiance at Mobile, West Florida 2 Oct. 1764.

Deboijs, Abraham. He took the oath of naturalization in New York 1 Sep. 1687 in Ulster County.

DeBonrepos, David. He was endenized in New York 6 Feb. 1695/6.

DeBonrepos, Elias. He, his wife Ester DeBonrepos, son Elias DeBonrepos, and son Alexander DeBonrepos were endenized in England 31 Jan. 1689/90. He was naturalized in Massachusetts in 1686–1687.

DeBourdeau, Jacques. He was born at Grenoble, France, the son of Evermond DeBourdeau and Catherine Fresne. His wife was Madeleine Garillond. Their children were Madeleine DeBourdeau and Judith DeBourdeau who were born at Grenoble; Anthoine DeBourdeau, Jacques DeBourdeau, and Israel DeBourdeau born in South Carolina. They were naturalized in South Carolina *ca.* 1696.

Deboyes, David. He took the oath of naturalization in New York 1 Sep. 1687 in Ulster County.

Deboyes, Isack. He took the oath of naturalization in New York 1 Sep. 1687 in Ulster County.

Deboyes, Jacob. He took the oath of naturalization in New York 1 Sep. 1687 in Ulster County.

Deboyes, Lowies, Sr. He took the oath of naturalization in New York 1 Sep. 1687 in Ulster County.

Deboyes, Sallomon. He took the oath of naturalization in New York 1 Sep. 1687 in Ulster County.

Debruler, John. He and his sons, John Debruler and William Debruler, together with other sons and daughters born in Maryland were naturalized there 17 May 1701. They lived in Baltimore County. He also appeared as John Debruter.

DeCamp, Laurens Janse. He took the oath of allegiance in New Uijtrceht, Kings County, New York 26–30 Sep. 1687. He had been in the colony 23 years.

DeCampos, Abraham. He was naturalized in Jamaica 26 Feb. 1744/5. He was a Jew.

DeCasserez, Abraham. He was naturalized in New York 3 July 1718.

DeCastro, Daniel Mendez. He was naturalized in Jamaica 23 June 1759.

DeCastro, Jacob. He was naturalized in Jamaica 28 May 1707.

DeCastro, Samuel. He was naturalized in Jamaica 3 June 1717.

Decatur, Stephen. He was naturalized in Rhode Island in Feb. 1752/3. He was born in France and lived in Newport, R.I.

DeCausse, Leonard. He was a native of Switzerland and sought naturalization in Maryland 2 Apr. 1735. He was a resident of Anne Arundel County. He was naturalized 29 Apr. 1735.

DeChavis, David. He was naturalized in Jamaica 13 Dec. 1716.

Deck, Jacob. He was naturalized in Pennsylvania 10 Apr. 1754. He was from Northampton County.

Decker, Christopher, Jr. He was naturalized in Maryland 9 Sep. 1761.

Decker, Gerritt Jansa. He took the oath of naturalization in New York 1 Sep. 1687 in Ulster County.

Decker, Harmanus. He was naturalized in New York 8–9 Sep. 1715. He was from Ulster County.

Decker, Jacob. He took the oath of naturalization in New York 1 Sep. 1687 in Ulster County.

Decker, Jacob. He was naturalized in New York 8–9 Sep. 1715. He was from Ulster County.

Decker, Jacob. He was naturalized in Pennsylvania 23 Nov. 1771. He was from Lancaster, Lancaster County.

Decker, John Broerson. He took the oath of naturalization in New York 13 June 1687.

Decker, Rudolph. He was naturalized in Maryland 31 Aug. 1757.

DeConsilie, Jean. He took the oath of allegiance in Boswijck, Kings County, New York 26–30 Sep. 1687. He had been in the colony twenty-five years.

DeConte & Gravinia, Don Peter Marquis. He was naturalized in Nova Scotia 15 Sep. 1758. [He was a Sicilian.]

DeCommink, Peter. He was naturalized in New Castle County, Delaware 21 Feb. 1682/3.

Decoppet, John Francis. He was naturalized in Virginia 12 May 1705.

Decor, Pierre. He was endenized in New York 16 Aug. 1686. His name may have been Pierre Lecor.

DeCordova, Joshua Hesquia. He was naturalized in Jamaica 1 July 1755.

Decotay, Ami. He was naturalized in Rhode Island in Feb. 1754. He was a merchant in Newport. He was born in Genoa, Italy.

DeCramache, Henry Augustus Chastaigne. He was endenized in England 9 Apr. 1687. He came to South Carolina.

DeCrasto, Jacob. He was naturalized in Jamaica 12 Dec. 1690.

DeCrasto, Jacob Lopez. He was naturalized in Jamaica 1740–41. He was a Jew.

DeCuna, Elias. He was naturalized in Jamaica 29 July 1690.

Dederich, Christopher. He was naturalized in New York 17 Jan. 1715/6. He was from Albany County.

Dedier, John. He was naturalized in Pennsylvania 24 Sep. 1757.

Dedrich, Fredrich. He was naturalized in New York 8–9 Sep. 1715. He was from Ulster County.

Dedrich, Johan Wilhelm. He was naturalized in New York 8–9 Sep. 1715. He was from Ulster County.

Dedrick, Christian. He was naturalized in New York 8–9 Sep. 1715. He was from Ulster County.

Dedrick, Johan Christian. He was naturalized in New York 8–9 Sep. 1715. He was from Ulster County.

Dee Koch Brune, Lewis. He was naturalized in Maryland 18 Oct. 1694.

Deeden, John. He was naturalized in Pennsylvania 29 Sep. 1709. He was from Philadelphia County.

Deeds, Christian. He was naturalized in New Jersey in 1750. He was from Hunterdon County. He also appeared as Christian Dieds.

Deefenback, Christian. He was naturalized in Maryland 7 May 1767. He was from Germany Township, York County, Pennsylvania and was a German. He also appeared as Christopher Deefenback.

Deel, Adam. He was naturalized in Pennsylvania 10 & 23 Apr. 1764. He was from Dover Township, York County.

Deel, George. He was naturalized in Pennsylvania 10 & 23 Apr. 1764. He was from Dover Township, York County.

Deem, Jacob. He was naturalized in Pennsylvania 10–12 Apr. 1762. He was from Berks County.

Deem, Thomas. He was naturalized in Pennsylvania 11 Apr. 1763. He was from Reading Township, Berks County.

Deener, John. He was naturalized in Maryland 15 Sep. 1762. He was from Frederick County.

Deer, George. He was naturalized in Pennsylvania 10 Apr. 1760.

Deer, John. He was naturalized in Pennsylvania 24 Sep. 1762. He was from Lancaster County.

Deeringer, Henry. He was naturalized in Pennsylvania 19 May 1739. He was from Philadelphia County.

Deets, Adam. He was naturalized in New York 11 Sep. 1761.

Deets, Hendrick. He was naturalized in New York 20 Mar. 1762.

Deetz, Adam. He was naturalized in Maryland 7 May 1767. He was a German from Frederick County.

Deetz, Frederick. He was naturalized in New York 29 July 1762. He was a tailor from New York City.

Defenne, Francis. He was endenized in New York 1 June 1698.

Deffour, Benjamin. He was naturalized in Maryland 17 Dec. 1708. He lived in Anne Arundel County and was French.

DeFlandre, Louis. He took the oath of allegiance at Mobile, West Florida 2 Oct. 1764.

DeFonseca, Isaac. He was naturalized in Jamaica 29 June 1675.

DeForrest, Isaac. He took the oath to the King 21–26 Oct. 1664 after the conquest of New Netherland.

DeForest, Rene. He took the oath of allegiance at Port Royal, Nova Scotia 16 Aug. 1695.

Deforet, Rene. He was an Acadian and took the oath to George II at Annapolis River, Nova Scotia in Dec. 1729.

Deforrais, Pierre. He was an Acadian who took the oath of allegiance to the King at the Mines, Pisiquit, 31 Oct. 1727.

DeFosse, John Aaron. He was naturalized in Jamaica 6 Oct. 1741.

DeFranck, Juan. He was naturalized in Jamaica 26 Sep. 1690. He was a Spanish Negro.

DeFreidenbergh, Charles. He was naturalized in New York 3 July 1766.

Deg, Andreas. He was naturalized in New York 3 July 1759.

DeGam, Moses. He expressed his desire to be naturalized in New Castle County, Delaware 21 Feb. 1682/3.

DeGay, Peter. He was naturalized in Jamaica 18 July 1715.

Dege, Hendrick. He was naturalized in New York 11 Sep. 1761.

DeGraaf, Johannis. He was naturalized in New York 23 Dec. 1765.

DeGroot, Staes. He took the oath of allegiance in Orange County, New York 26 Sep. 1687.

DeHaart, Balthazar. He took the oath to the King 21–26 Oct. 1664 after the conquest of New Netherland.

DeHaen, George. He was naturalized in London 26 Apr. 1710. He was of St. Gabriel Street. He was son of Abraham DeHaen and Goose Taber. He removed to Jamaica and died there.

DeHaen, Justa Andries. He was naturalized in New Castle County, Delaware 21 Feb. 1682/3.

Dehamseville, Peter. He was naturalized in Jamaica 4 Apr. 1680.

D'Harriette, Anna. She sought naturalization in New York 4 Sep. 1731. She was the wife of Benjamin D'Harriette.

DeHart, Balthazer. He was endenized in New York 16 Jan. 1664/5.

DeHayen, Isaac. He took the oath to the King 21–26 Oct. 1664 after the conquest of New Netherland.

Dehl, Charles. He was naturalized in Pennsylvania 24 Sep. 1763. He was from Shrewsbury Township, York County.

Dehl, Daniel. He was naturalized in Pennsylvania 11 Apr. 1761. He was from York County.

Dehoff, Henry. He was naturalized in Pennsylvania 11 Apr. 1761. He was from Lancaster County.

Dehogos, Johanas. He took the oath of naturalization in New York 1 Sep. 1687 in Ulster County.

Dehon, Theodore. He was naturalized in Massachusetts 17 Nov. 1741. He resided in Boston and had been in the colony more than seven years.

DeHonde, Courtrie Daniel. He took the oath to the King 21–26 Oct. 1664 after the conquest of New Netherland.

D'Heurtin, Peter Francis. He was naturalized in Rhode Island in June 1753. He was a merchant from Newport and had been in the colony ten years.

DeHonneur, Guillaume. He took the oath to the King 21–26 Oct. 1664 after the conquest of New Netherland.

Dehr, Lawrence. He was naturalized in Pennsylvania 11 Apr. 1749. He was from Philadelphia County.

Deihl, Peter. He was naturalized in Pennsylvania 16 May 1769. He was from Donegal Township, Lancaster County.

Dein, Jean. He was an Acadian who took the oath to the King at the Mines, Pisiquit 31 Oct. 1727.

Deinig, Henry. He was naturalized in Pennsylvania 19 May 1739. He was from Philadelphia County.

Deiter, John. He was naturalized in Pennsylvania 10 Apr. 1755. He was from Berks County.

Deitrick, Christian. He was naturalized in Pennsylvania 24–25 Sep. 1764. He was from Philadelphia.

Deitrick, Jacob. He was naturalized in Pennsylvania 10 Apr. 1760.

Deitz, John. He was naturalized in Pennsylvania 10 Sep. 1761. He was from Lancaster County.

DeJarnat, Jean. He was naturalized in Apr. 1705 in Virginia. He also appeared as Jean de Jarnal.

DeJoncourt, Jane. She was naturalized in New York 20 Jan. 1768. She was a widow from New York City.

DeKlerck, Daniel. He was naturalized in New York 23 Aug. 1715. He was a yeoman from Tappan.

DeKlerck, Jacobus. He was naturalized in New York 23 Aug. 1715. He was a yeoman from Tappan.

DeKleyn, Leendert Huygen. He was naturalized in New York 13 Dec. 1715. He was a merchant from New York City.

DeLaChesnaye, Charles Aubert. His vessel was licensed to import goods from Quebec to New York and to trade and traffic in the city 13 May 1684.

Delagard, Ann Gabriel. She was naturalized in Jamaica 27 Apr. 1720.

DeLagarde, Isaac. He was born in Laroche Chaley, Perigord, France, the son of Abraham and Mary DeLagarde. He was endenized in England 5 Apr. 1699/1700. He came to New York.

DeLage, Peter. He was naturalized in New York 17 June 1766.

DeLaGrange, Arnoldus. He was naturalized in Maryland 26 Apr. 1684. He also appeared as Arnoldas DeLaGrange.

DeLaGrange, Arnoldus. He was naturalized in New Castle County, Delaware 21 Feb. 1682/3.

DeLaGrangie, Omy. He was naturalized in New York 3 Jan. 1715/6. He was from Albany County.

DeLaMaire, John. He was naturalized in Maryland 6 June 1674. He was born in Anjou, France.

DeLaMare, Francis. He sought denization in North Carolina. He was a French Protestant and had been in the colony eleven years. It was probably in the last quarter of the seventeenth century.

DelaMontagne, Johannes. He took the oath to the King 21–26 Oct. 1664 after the conquest of New Netherland. He was from Albany.

DelaMontagne, William. He took the oath to the King 21–26 Oct. 1664 after the conquest of New Netherland. He was from Albany.

DelaMontaigne, Nicholas. He was naturalized in Maryland 18 Oct. 1694.

DeLamontanij, William. He took the oath of naturalization in New York 1 Sep. 1687 in Ulster County.

DeLancey, Stephen. He was endenized in London 5 Mar. 1685/6. He came to New York.

DeLancey, Stephen. He was naturalized in New York in 1740–41. He was a merchant from New York City.

DeLannay, Joseph. He was naturalized in South Carolina on or about 1 June 1602.

DeLaPehna, Isaac. He was naturalized in Jamaica 26 Feb. 1740/1. He was a Jew.

DeLaPehna, Isaac. He was endenized in London 3 June 1699. He was from Barbados.

Delapeire, John. He was naturalized in Jamaica 11 Sep. 1680.

Delapena, Isaac. He was naturalized in Jamaica 21 Nov. 1740.

Delapenha, Isaac. He was endenized in England 3 June 1699. He settled in Barbados and was a Jew.

DeLaPenha, Jacob. He was naturalized in Jamaica 26 Feb. 1740/1. He was a Jew.

DelaPlaine, Nicolas. He took the oath to the King 21–26 Oct. 1664 after the conquest of New Netherland.

Delara, Daniel Cohen. He was naturalized in Jamaica 30 Nov. 1686.

Delara, Jacob Nunes. He was naturalized in Jamaica 27 Feb. 1749/50. He was a Jew.

Delara, Moses Cohen. He was naturalized in Jamaica 20 June 1726.

Delara, Moses Cohen. He was naturalized in Jamaica 25 Nov. 1740. He was a Jew.

Delater, David. He was naturalized in Maryland in Apr. 1749. He was from Frederick County.

Delaterre, Jacob. He was naturalized in Maryland 10 Apr. 1762. He was a German from Anne Arundel County.

Delauder, Lawrance. He was naturalized in Maryland 26 Sep. 1765. He was a German.

Delaune, Jean. He was naturalized in Virginia 12 May 1705.

Delaza, David Cohen. He was naturalized in Jamaica 23 Oct. 1717.

DelCastillo, Dr. Saint Jago. He was naturalized in Jamaica 21 Mar. 1684/5. He was from Barcelona, Spain.

DeLeao, Benjamin Pereyra. He was endenized in England 10 Dec. 1695. He settled in Barbados and was a Jew.

DeLeas, Abraham. He was naturalized in New York 27 Apr. 1742. He was a Jew.

DeLeere, Anthony Regerson. He was endenized in London 29 May 1663. He was from Antigua.

DeLeon, Abraham Cohen. He was naturalized in Jamaica 23 Dec. 1681.

DeLeon, Abraham Rodriques. He was naturalized in Jamaica 2 Dec. 1701.

DeLeon, Abram de Moses. He was naturalized in Jamaica 5 Apr. 1693.

DeLeon, Estar Cohen. She was naturalized in Jamaica 23 Nov. 1704. She was the wife of Moses Cohen DeLeon.

DeLeon, Esther Rodriques. She was naturalized in Jamaica 17 Dec. 1723. She was the wife of Jacob Rodriques DeLeon.

DeLeon, Isaac de Moses. He was naturalized in Jamaica 25 June 1690.

DeLeon, Jacob. He was naturalized in Jamaica 17 Nov. 1681.

DeLeon, Jacob de Moses. He was naturalized in Jamaica 7 July 1690.

DeLeon, Jacob Rodriques. He was naturalized in Jamaica 10 Nov. 1681.

DeLeon, Jael Machorro. She was naturalized in Jamaica 11 Jan. 1696. She was a widow.

DeLeon, John. He was naturalized in Jamaica 13 Feb. 1733/4.

DeLeon, Michael. He was naturalized in Jamaica 20 Dec. 1758.

DeLeon, Moses Rodriques. He was naturalized in Jamaica 2 Dec. 1701.

DeLeon, Rachell Hannah Roderiques. She was naturalized in Jamaica 12 Sep. 1709. She was the widow of Jacob Roderiques DeLeon.

Deleon, Solomon. He was naturalized in Jamaica 6 Sep. 1675.

DeleRoche, Charles. He was naturalized in Maryland 8 May 1669. He was French.

Delgado, Abraham Morena. He was naturalized in Jamaica 7 Jan. 1750/1.

Delgarde, Michael. He was naturalized in Jamaica 1 Jan. 1707. He also appeared as Michael Vie.

Delille, Nicholas. He took the oath of allegiance at Mobile, West Florida 2 Oct. 1764.

DeLisle, John. He was naturalized in New York 11 Sep. 1761.

Delivot, Henret. He took the oath of allegiance at Mobile, West Florida 20 Oct. 1764.

Dellar, John. He was naturalized in New Jersey 7 Dec. 1763.

Dellenor, John George. He was naturalized in Frederick County, Virginia 5 May 1747.

Delmestre, Peter. He was naturalized in South Carolina 12 Nov. 1741.

DeLongemare, Nicholas. He was born at Forer, Lyone, Normandy, France, the son of Jacques de Longemare and of Adrienne Arachegunne. He was naturalized in South Carolina on 10 Mar. 1696/7. He was a watchmaker. His wife, Anne LeRoy, was deceased. He also appeared as Nicholas de Longuemare.

DeLongemare, Nicholas, Jr. He was born at Dieppe, France, the son of Nicholas Longemare and Anne LeRoy. He was naturalized in South Carolina 10 Mar. 1696/7. He was a goldsmith. He also appeared as Nicholas Longuemare.

Delony, Jacob. He was naturalized in Virginia 12 May 1705.

Delony, John. He was naturalized in Virginia 12 May 1705.

Delor, Jullien. He was naturalized in Jamaica 18 Mar. 1760.

DeLossa, Moses. He was naturalized in Jamaica 7 Nov. 1704.

DeLucena, Moses. He was naturalized in Jamaica 2 Oct. 1678.

Demarest, William. He was naturalized in Jamaica 27 Apr. 1743.

Demarr, Petter. He took the oath of naturalization in New York 1 Sep. 1687. He was from Ulster County.

DeMaxchena, Jacob. He was naturalized in Jamaica 1 Jan. 1684/5.

DeMedina, Jacob. He was endenized in England 14 Dec. 1694. He settled in Barbados and was a Jew.

DeMercado, Abraham. He was endenized in England 11 Oct. 1687. He settled in Barbados and was a Jew.

DeMercado, David Raphale. He was endenized in Barbados in 1661.

DeMercado, David Raphael. He was endenized in England 11 July 1678. He was a merchant from Barbados.

DeMercado, Isaak. He was naturalized in Jamaica 5 Sep. 1687. He was also known as Issak Cohen.

DeMercado, Moses His Kiaugh. He was a doctor of physic and was endenized in England in Jan. 1679/80. He settled in Barbados and was a Jew.

Demesqueta, Abraham Buena. He was endenized in Jamaica 14 Dec. 1694.

Demesqueta, David Pereira. He was naturalized in Jamaica 20 May 1736.

DeMesquita, Abraham Bueno. He was endenized in England 2 Feb. 1695. He settled in Barbados and was a Jew.

DeMesquita, Abraham Fernandez. He was naturalized in Jamaica 29 June 1732.

DeMesquito, Benjamin Bueno. He was endenized in England 24 Oct. 1664. He resided in Jamaica and later in Barbados. He was a Jew.

DeMessmaker, Charles. He was naturalized in Jamaica 6 Jan. 1700/1.

DeMetz, Benjamin. He was naturalized in New York 8–9 Sep. 1715. He was from Ulster County.

DeMeyer, Nicholas. He was endenized in New York 21 Mar. 1664/5.

DeMilt, Anthony. He took the oath to the King 21–26 Oct. 1664 after the conquest of New Netherland.

Demiranda, Rebecca Nunez. She was naturalized in Jamaica 3 Feb. 1737/8.

Demon, Peter. He was naturalized in New Jersey 16 Aug. 1733. He lived in Monmouth County.

DeMont, Wallraven, Jr. He took the oath of naturalization in New York 1 Sep. 1687 in Ulster County.

DeMontes, David. He was naturalized in Jamaica 13 Jan. 1761.

DeMonville, Samuel. He sought naturalization in Virginia in 1704.

DeMoreno, Mathatudo. He was naturalized in Jamaica 26 Jan. 1705/6.

DeMorsier, Jean Francois. He took the oath of allegiance at Mobile, West Florida 2 Oct. 1764.

DeMounderer, Anthony. He was naturalized in Maryland 19 Apr. 1671. He lived in Anne Arundel County and was French.

Demoux, Orbame. He took the oath of allegiance at Mobile, West Florida 2 Oct. 1764.

DeMusquita, Abraham Pereira. He was naturalized in Jamaica 2 May 1728.

Demyr[e]s, William. He took the oath of naturalization in New York 1 Sep. 1687 in Ulster County.

Dencker, Hendrick. He was naturalized in Pennsylvania 11 Sep. 1761.

Deneufville, Jean. He petitioned to be naturalized in New York 19 Aug. 1687.

Dengler, John. He was naturalized in Pennsylvania 10 Sep. 1761. He was from Berks County.

Denisse, Peter. He was naturalized in Jamaica 17 May 1759.

Dennis, John. He was naturalized in Jamaica 28 Aug. 1713.

Dennius, Philip. He was naturalized in Pennsylvania 11 Apr. 1761. He was from Lancaster County.

Denny, Peter. He was naturalized in Pennsylvania 11 Apr. 1761. He was from Lancaster County.

DeNormandie, Abraham. He was a merchant and naturalized in London 28 Apr. 1711. He had his certificate recorded in Pennsylvania 3 June 1738.

DeNos, Mathias. He was naturalized in New Castle County, Delaware 21 Feb. 1682/3.

DeNoyelles, John. He was naturalized in New York 18 Jan. 1769. He was from Orange County.

Dentlinger, Henry. He was naturalized in Pennsylvania 11–13 Apr. 1743. He was from Philadelphia County.

Dentzeller, Jacob. He was naturalized in Pennsylvania 24–25 Sep. 1764. He was from Rockland Township, Bucks County.

Deny, Michael. He was naturalized in Pennsylvania 11 Apr. 1761. He was from Chester County.

Dep, John. He was naturalized in Virginia 12 May 1705.

Depais, Rachel Lopez. She was naturalized in Jamaica 26 Nov. 1746.

DePaul, Asher Michelle. He was endenized in New York 8 Feb. 1683.

DePaz, Benjamin Abab. He was naturalized in Jamaica 2 Oct. 1678.

DePaz, Aaron Lopez. He was naturalized in Jamaica 7 July 1690.

DePaz, Esther Lopes. She was naturalized in Jamaica 28 Jan. 1716/7. She was the wife of Lopez Depaz.

DePax, Rebecca Lopez. She was naturalized in Jamaica 18 Feb. 1716/7.

DePeister, Johannes. He took the oath to the King 21–26 Oct. 1664 after the conquest of New Netherland.

Depeyster, Catherine. She was naturalized in New York 6 July 1723.

DePleinville, James. He was naturalized in Jamaica 27 July 1682.

DePrado, Isaac Rodriques. He was naturalized in Jamaica 10 Apr. 1682.

Depuis, Moses. He took the oath of naturalization in New York 1 Sep. 1687 in Ulster County.

DePutter, Peter. He was endenized in London 20 Feb. 1662/3. He was from Barbados.

Depoy, Jacob. He was naturalized in Jamaica 27 Nov. 1729.

DeRaquett, Alexander. He was naturalized in South Carolina on or about 1 June 1702.

D'Rapale, Daniel. He took the oath of allegiance in Breucklijn, Kings County, New York 26–30 Sep. 1687. He was a native of the colony.

D'Rapale, Jeronimus. He took the oath of allegiance in Breucklijn, Kings County, New York 26–30 Sep. 1687. He was a native of the colony.

Derder, Anthony. He was naturalized in Pennsylvania 25 Sep. 1758.

DeRespaldiza, Joseph. He was naturalized in Jamaica 29 Sep. 1761.

DeRichbourg, Claud Phillippe. He was naturalized in Virginia 12 May 1705. He was born in France.

DeRing, Hans Jacob. He was naturalized in Maryland 19 Apr. 1671. He was Dutch.

DeRing, Jacob Clause. He was naturalized in Maryland 19 Apr. 1671. He was Dutch.

DeRingh, Aemilius. He expressed his desire to be naturalized in New Castle County, Delaware 21 Feb. 1682/3.

DeRingh, Mathias. He expressed his desire to be naturalized in New Castle County, Delaware 21 Feb. 1682/3.

DeRivera, Abraham Rodriques. He was naturalized in 1740–41. He was a Portuguese Jew.

Dern, William. He was naturalized in Maryland 17 Apr. 1760.

Dernie, Philip. He was naturalized in New York 12 July 1715. He was a mariner.

Deronde, Adrian. He was naturalized in New York 20 May 1769.

DeRonde, Mattheus. He was naturalized in New York 20 May 1769.

DeRonde, Nicholas. He was naturalized in New York 3 July 1759.

DeRosseau, Theodore. He was naturalized in Virginia 12 May 1705.

DeRousserie, Francois. He was born at Montpelier, France, the son of Alexandre DeRousserye and Marie Suranne. He was naturalized in South Carolina ca. 1696.

DeRousserve, Francois. He was born at Montpelier, France. He was naturalized in South Carolina ca. 1696.

DeRouvell, Sr. Chv. He took the oath of allegiance at Mobile, West Florida 2 Oct. 1764.

Derr, Henry. He was naturalized in Pennsylvania 11 Apr. 1761. He was from Berks County.

Derr, Johan Martin. He was naturalized in Pennsylvania 11–13 Apr. 1743. He was from Philadelphia County.

Derr, Sebastian. He was naturalized in Pennsylvania 11–13 Apr. 1743. He was from Bucks County.

Derter, Balthasar. He was naturalized in Pennsylvania 11 Apr. 1763. He was from Heidelberg Township, Lancaster County.

Deruche, Felix. He took the oath of allegiance at Harbour Amhurst in the Magdalines, Gulf of Saint Lawrence on 31 Aug. 1765. He was a native of Nova Scotia.

Desbrosses, James. He was endenized in London 24 June 1703. He came to New York.

DeScer, Paulus. He was naturalized in New York 17 June 1726.

DeSeivra, Antony. He was naturalized in Jamaica 26 Sep. 1690. He also appeared as Antony DeLeivra.

DesImbres, Rene Fesan. He was endenized in New York 18 Sep. 1686.

Desch, John Baltus. He was naturalized in New York 3 July 1759. He also appeared as John Baltus Disch.

Deshler, Adam. He was naturalized in Pennsylvania 10 Apr. 1755. He was from Northampton County.

Deshler, Anthony. He was naturalized in Pennsylvania 10 Apr. 1753. He was from Philadelphia.

Deshler, David. He was naturalized in Pennsylvania 19 May 1739. He was from Philadelphia County.

Deshler, David. He was naturalized in Pennsylvania 25–27 Sep. 1740. He was from Philadelphia.

Desille, Lourens. He took the oath to the King 21–26 Oct. 1664 after the conquest of New Netherland.

Deshler, David. He was naturalized in Pennsylvania 11 Apr. 1761. He was from Northampton County.

Desille, Lourens. He took the oath to the King 21–26 Oct. 1664 after the conquest of New Netherland.

DeSilva, Aaron. He was endenized in England 12 July 1661. He settled in Barbados.

DeSilva, Isaac Gomez. He was naturalized in Jamaica 5 Mar. 1723/4.

DeSilva, Jacob. He was naturalized in Jamaica 3 June 1685.

Desjardines, John. He was naturalized in Maryland 6 June 1674. He was French.

DesMaizeaux, Peter. He was naturalized in New York in 1707–8. He was born at Paillat, Auvergne, France. He was the son of Lewis and Magdaline DesMaizeaux.

Desmoulins, John. He was naturalized in Jamaica 29 July 1690.

DeSoer, Paulus. He was naturalized in New York 17 June 1726.

Desosamendes, Abraham. He was licensed to trade and traffic in New York 8 Feb. 1683.

DeSossa, Issac Rodriques. He was naturalized in Jamaica 25 June 1690.

DeSousa, Abraham Henriques. He was naturalized in Jamaica 22 Aug. 1715.

Dessis, Thomas. He was naturalized in Jamaica 23 June 1719. He was a surgeon.

DeStapleton, Leopold. He was naturalized in Jamaica 11 Mar. 1706/7.

DeSylva, Mordecay. He was naturalized in Jamaica 6 Dec. 1681.

DeSylva, Joseph. He was naturalized in New Jersey in 1775. He lived in Middlesex County.

Deter, Matthias. He was naturalized in Pennsylvania 24 Sep. 1760. He was from Berks County.

Detloff, Henry. He was naturalized in New York 24 Apr. 1767. He was a cartman from New York City.

Detmers, Ferdinand Jacob. He was naturalized in Pennsylvania 24–29 Sep. 1768. He was from Bethlehem Township, Northampton County.

DeTores, Jacob. He was endenized in Jamaica 5 May 1671.

DeTorres, Jacob. He was endenized in London 25 May 1671. He was a merchant from Jamaica.

DeTorres, Jacob. He was naturalized in Jamaica 19 Sep. 1671.

Dettenburn, Ludowick. He was naturalized in Pennsylvania 19 May 1739. He was from Lancaster County.

Detter, Matthias. He was naturalized in Pennsylvania 21 May 1770. He was from Manchester Township, York County.

Dettermer, Hartman. He was naturalized in Pennsylvania 19 May 1739. He was from Philadelphia County.

Detrick, Elias. He was naturalized in Pennsylvania 24 Sep. 1754. He was from Northampton County.

Detry, Conrad. He was naturalized in Pennsylvania 10–12 Apr. 1762. He was from Philadelphia County.

DeVale, Sarah Rodriques. She was naturalized in Jamaica 9 Apr. 1725.

Devalle, Isaac. He was naturalized in Jamaica 25 Aug. 1741. He was a Jew.

DeVagha, John. He was naturalized in Maryland 18 Oct. 1694.

Devaux, Frederick. He was naturalized in New York 2 Aug. 1715. He was a husbandman from Westchester.

Devaux, Peter. He, his wife, and daughter were admitted into the colony of Massachusetts 1 Feb. 1691.

DeVerde, Paul Jansen. He was endenized in England 27 Dec. 1662. He settled in Barbados and was a Jew.

DeVerney, Anthony. He took the oath of allegiance at Mobile, West Florida 2 Oct. 1764.

DeVesaz, Paul. He was naturalized in Virginia 12 May 1705.

Devilsbit, Casper. He was naturalized in Pennsylvania 24 Sep. 1762. He was from Frederick County, Maryland.

Devot, Michel. He was an Acadian and took the oath of allegiance in Apr. 1730.

DeVries, Jean. He took the oath of allegiance in Orange County, New York 26 Sep. 1687.

DeVylder, John. He was naturalized in Jamaica 28 Mar. 1751.

Dewald, Daniel. He was naturalized in Pennsylvania 11 Apr. 1761. He was from York County.

Dewald, Henrick. He was naturalized in Pennsylvania 11 Apr. 1741. He was from Philadelphia County.

Dewald, Michael. He was naturalized in Pennsylvania 10–12 Apr. 1762. He was from Berks County.

DeWeerhem, Ambrosius. He took the oath to the King 21–26 Oct. 1664 after the conquest of New Netherland.

DeWeissenfels, Frederick. He was naturalized in New York 20 Dec. 1763.

DeWiit, Johannes. He took the oath to the King 21–26 Oct. 1664 after the conquest of New Netherland.

DeWilde, John. He took the oath of denization in New York 17 Feb. 1697/8.

DeWint, John. He was naturalized in New York 29 Oct. 1730.

DeWint, John. He was naturalized in New York 14 Oct. 1732.

DeWint, Pieter. He was naturalized in New York 21 Sep. 1744.

Dewit, John. He was naturalized in New Jersey in 31 July 1740. He was from Holland.

Dewitt, Andries. He took the oath of naturalization in New York 1 Sep. 1687 in Ulster County.

DeWitt, Jacob. He was naturalized in New York 8–9 Sep. 1715. He was from Ulster County.

Dewitt, John. He took the oath of naturalization in New York 1 Sep. 1687 in Ulster County.

DeWitt, Peter. He was naturalized in New Castle County, Delaware 21 Feb. 1682/3.

DeWitt, Pieter Janse. He took the oath of allegiance in Bowsijck, Kings County, New York 26–30 Sep. 1687. He had been in the colony 35 years.

DeWulffen, Johanis. He was naturalized in New York 8–9 Sep. 1715. He was from Ulster County.

DeWulfsen, Godfrid. He was naturalized in New York 8–9 Sep. 1715. He was from Ulster County.

Deybertsyer, George. He was naturalized in New York 20 Apr. 1769. He was a chimney sweeper from New York City.

Deygert, Sefreen. He was naturalized in New York 31 Jan. 1715/6. He was from Albany County.

Deygert, Warner. He was naturalized in New York 11 Oct. 1715. He was from Albany County.

DeYoung, Aaron. He was naturalized in New York 3 Feb. 1768.

DeYoung, Jacob Clause. He was naturalized in Maryland 19 Apr. 1671. He was from Baltimore County and was Dutch.

DeYoung, John. He was endenized in Virginia 7 Nov. 1666. He was a Dutchman.

DeYoung, John. He was naturalized in Virginia 12 May 1705.

Dhyniossa, Alexander. He, his wife Margaretta Dhyniossa, and children, Alexander Dhyniossa, Barbara Dhyniossa, Christina Dhyniossa, Johanna Dhyniossa, Johannes Dhyniossa, Maria Dhyniossa, and Peter Dhyniossa, were naturalized in Maryland 19 Apr. 1671. They lived in Talbot County and were Dutch.

Diamond, Constantine. He was naturalized in Jamaica 6 Aug. 1728. He was a fisherman. He had served as a mariner on H.M.S. *L'Amour* under Capt. Thomas Gordon.

Diarce, Alexander. He was naturalized in New York 3 July 1766.

Diarce, Alexander. He was naturalized in New York 3 Feb. 1768.

Dias, Luis. He was endenized in Barbados 2 Aug. 1661.

Dias, Isaque Fernandez. He sought to be made a denizen 30 Aug. 1692. He was from Jamaica.

Dias, Issac Vernandes. He was endenized in England 9 Mar. 1693/4. He settled in Barbados.

Dibbindurfer, Alexander. He was naturalized in Pennsylvania 25–27 Sep. 1740. He was from Bucks County.

Dibois, Isack. He took the oath of naturalization in New York 1 Sep. 1687 in Ulster County.

Dick, Adam. He was naturalized in Pennsylvania 18 Nov. 1768.

Dick, Conrad. He was naturalized in Maryland 10 Sep. 1760.

Dick, Dederick. He was naturalized in New York 16 Dec. 1737.

Dick, Paul. He was naturalized in New York 16 Dec. 1737.

Dick, Peter. He was naturalized in Pennsylvania 10 Apr. 1760.

Dick, Peter. He was naturalized in Maryland 16 Apr. 1761.

Dick, Philip. He was naturalized in Pennsylvania 10 Apr. 1760.

Dickman, John. He was naturalized in Jamaica 5 July 1687.

Dieder, Lourens. He was naturalized in New York 8–9 Sep. 1715. He was from Ulster County.

Diederigh, Christian. He was naturalized in New York 17 Jan. 1715/6. He was from Albany County.

Dieffedorf, Hendrick. He was naturalized in New York 11 Sep. 1761.

Dieffedorf, Hannes. He was naturalized in New York 11 Sep. 1761.

Dieffedorf, Jorg. He was naturalized in New York 11 Sep. 1761.

Diegert, Johan Pieter. He was naturalized in New York 31 Jan. 1715/6. He was from Albany County.

Diehl, George. He was naturalized in Pennsylvania 11 Apr. 1761. He was from Berks County.

Diehm, Peter. He was naturalized in Pennsylvania 24 Sep. 1762. He was from Berks County.

Diek, Jacob. He was naturalized in Pennsylvania 11 Apr. 1761. He was from Berks County.

Diekenshat, Christopher. He was naturalized in Pennsylvania 24 Sep. 1755. He was from Philadelphia.

Diel, Adolf. He was naturalized in New York 8–9 Sep. 1715. He was from Ulster County.

Diel, Laurentz. He was naturalized in New York 19 Oct. 1743. He was a yeoman from Dutchess County.

Diel, Nicholas. He was naturalized in Maryland 14 Apr. 1762. He was a German.

Dieler, Philip Adam. He was naturalized in Pennsylvania 11 Apr. 1761. He was from Lancaster County.

Diels, Adam. He was naturalized in New Jersey 8 Dec. 1744.

Diels, Hendrick. He was naturalized in New Jersey 8 Dec. 1744.

Diemer, Jacob. He was naturalized in Pennsylvania 24 Sep. 1770. He was from Earl Township, Lancaster County.

Diemer, John. He was naturalized in Pennsylvania 29 Mar. 1735. He was from Philadelphia.

Dierchenz, John. He was naturalized in Jamaica 14 July 1701.

Dieter, Hendrick. He was naturalized in New York 17 Oct. 1744. He was a farmer from Dutchess County.

Dieter, Theobald. He was naturalized in Maryland 12 Apr. 1758.

Dieterich, John. He was naturalized in Pennsylvania 6 Feb. 1730/1. He was from Philadelphia County.

Dietrich, Jacob. He was naturalized in New York 20 Mar. 1762.

Dietrick, Jacob. He was naturalized in Pennsylvania 10 Sep. 1761. He was from Berks County.

Dietz, John. He was naturalized in New York 28 July 1773. He was a yeoman from New York City.

Dietz, Michael. He was naturalized in Maryland 14 Apr. 1762. He was a German.

Diffidaffy, Henry. He was naturalized in New Jersey 28 Apr. 1762.

Diffenbach, Michael. He was naturalized in Maryland 9 Apr. 1760. He lived in Baltimore, Maryland.

Diffiderfer, Michael. He was naturalized in Pennsylvania 24 Sep. 1759.

Digon, Allain. He was an Acadian who took the oath to the King at the Mines, Pisiquit 31 Oct. 1727.

Dihl, Alexander. He was naturalized in Pennsylvania 29 Mar. 1735. He was from Philadelphia County.

Dihm, Andrew. He was naturalized in Pennsylvania 10 Apr. 1770. He was from Cumry Township, Berks County.

Dike, Philip. He was naturalized in Maryland 19 Sep. 1761.

Dilbeck, Isaac. He and his son, Jacobus Dilbeck, were naturalized in Pennsylvania 29 Sep. 1709. They were from Philadelphia County.

Dill, John Michael. He was naturalized in Pennsylvania 25–27 Sep. 1740. He was from Philadelphia.

Dilli, Johann. He was naturalized in Maryland 14 Apr. 1762. He was a German.

Dillo, Michael Hartman. He was naturalized in Pennsylvania 11 Apr. 1761. He was from Northampton County.

Dills, Johan William. He was naturalized in New Jersey in 1750. He was from Hunterdon County. He also appeared as William Dils.

Dinckle, Daniel. He was naturalized in Pennsylvania 24–25 Sep. 1764. He was from York Township, Philadelphia County.

Ding, Adam. He was naturalized in New York 17 Jan. 1715/6. He was from Albany County.

Dingman, Adam. He was naturalized in New York 27 Apr. 1716. He was from Albany County.

Dings, Johan Jacob. He was naturalized in New York 8–9 Sep. 1715. He was from Ulster County.

Dinser, Paul. He was naturalized in New York 11 Oct. 1715. He was from Albany County.

Dinshirtz, Joseph. He was naturalized in Pennsylvania 10–12 Apr. 1762. He was from Lancaster County.

Dipel, Johan Pieter. He was naturalized in New York 8–9 Sep. 1715. He was from Ulster County.

Dirckse, Paulus. He took the oath of allegiance in Breucklijn, Kings County, New York 26–30 Sep. 1687. He had been in the colony 36 years.

Dirckse, Stoffel. He took the oath of allegiance in Flackland, Kings County, New York 26–30 Sep. 1687. He was a native of the colony.

Dirckse, Volkert. He took the oath of allegiance in Boswijck, Kings County, New York 26–30 Sep. 1687. He was a native of the colony.

Dirckzen, Lucas. He took the oath to the King 21–26 Oct. 1664 after the conquest of New Netherland.

Dirckzen, Meyer Jan. He took the oath to the King 21–26 Oct. 1664 after the conquest of New Netherland.

Dirdorf, Anthony. He and his sons, Peter Dirdorf, John Dirdorf, Anthony Dirdorf, and Christian Dirdorf, were naturalized in New Jersey 8 July 1730. They were born in Germany.

Dirdorf, Hendrick. He was naturalized in New Jersey 8 July 1730. He was born in New Jersey.

Dirsten, Michael. He was naturalized in Pennsylvania 11–13 Apr. 1743. He was from Bucks County.

Dittis, Tobias. He was naturalized in Pennsylvania 10 Apr. 1766. He was from Salisbury Township, Lancaster County.

Ditz, Johan Wilhelm. He was naturalized in New York 3 Feb. 1768.

Ditz, Johan Wilhelm. He was naturalized in New York 29 July 1752. He was a shoemaker from Schohary, Albany County.

Dlaski, John Daniel. He was naturalized in Jamaica 28 Feb. 1737/8.

Dobb, Johannes. He was naturalized in New York 8–9 Sep. 1715/6. He was from Ulster County.

Dobeler, Yodocus. He was naturalized in Pennsylvania 24 Sep. 1763. He was from Lancaster Township, Lancaster County.

Dobler, Jacob. He was naturalized in Pennsylvania 10 Sep. 1761. He was from Lancaster County.

Doctor, George. He was naturalized in Pennsylvania 24–25 Sep. 1764. He was from Upper Salford Township, Philadelphia County.

Dodererer, Michael. He was naturalized in Pennsylvania 24 Sep. 1753. He was from Berks County.

Dodine, Anthony. He was naturalized in New York 20 May 1769.

Doeckles, William. He took the oath to the King 21–26 Oct. 1664 after the conquest of New Netherland.

Doeron, Noel. He was an Acadian and took the oath of allegiance in Apr. 1730.

Doeron, Pierre. He was an Acadian and took the oath of allegiance in Apr. 1730.

Dofgel, Peter. He was naturalized in New Jersey 8 Dec. 1744.

Doher, Georg. He was naturalized in New York 8–9 Sep. 1715.

Doiront, Paul. He was an Acadian who took the oath of allegiance in Apr. 1730.

Dold, John Philip. He was naturalized in Pennsylvania 10–14 Apr. 1747. He was from Philadelphia County.

Dolhagen, Denys. He was naturalized in New York 23 Aug. 1715. He was a victualer from New York City.

Doll, Christian. He was naturalized in Pennsylvania 10 Apr. 1755. He was from Philadelphia.

Doll, Conrad. He was naturalized in Maryland 14 Apr. 1762. He was a German.

Doll, Henry. He was naturalized in New Castle County, Delaware 21 Feb. 1682/3.

Doll, Jacob. He was naturalized in Maryland 14 Apr. 1762. He was a German.

Doll, John. He was naturalized in Pennsylvania 10–12 Apr. 1762. He was from Lancaster County.

Dollinger, George. He was naturalized in Pennsylvania 25 Sep. 1751. He was from Lancaster County.

Domer, Michael. He was naturalized in Maryland 11 Sep. 1765. He was a German from Frederick County.

Dompsback, Franz. He was naturalized in New York 17 Jan. 1715/6. He was from Albany County.

Dompsback, Jost Hend. He was naturalized in New York 17 Jan. 1715/6. He was from Albany County.

Donatt, George. He was naturalized in Pennsylvania 29 Mar. 1735. He was from Chester County.

Doneder, Michael. He was naturalized in Pennsylvania 14 Feb. 1729/30. He was from Lancaster County.

Dondle, Jacob. He was naturalized in Pennsylvania 10 Apr. 1757.

Donig, Johannes. He was naturalized in Nova Scotia 5 July 1758.

Donnacre, Christian. He was naturalized in Pennsylvania 11 Apr. 1761. He was from Philadelphia County.

Doodes, Minor. He was naturalized in Virginia in Oct. 1673.

Doolhagen, Denys. He was naturalized in New York 23 Aug. 1715. He was a victualer from New York City.

Doon, Priviego. He took the oath of naturalization in New York 1 Sep. 1687 in Ulster County.

Doorn, Artt Martenson. He took the oath of naturalization in New York 1 Sep. 1687 in Ulster County.

Doorn, Georg Michael. He was naturalized in Maryland 14 Sep. 1763. He was a German from Frederick County.

Dopp, Johann Peter. He was naturalized in New York 8–9 Sep. 1715. He was from Ulster County.

Dopp, Johannes Peter, Jr. He was naturalized in New York 8–9 Sep. 1715. He was from Ulster County.

Dopui, Piere. He was an Acadian and took the oath to George II at Annapolis River, Nova Scotia in the winter of 1730.

Dopzen, Joris. He took the oath to the King 21–26 Oct. 1664 after the conquest of New Netherland.

Doremus, Johannes. He was naturalized in New Jersey 21 June 1754.

Dorig, John Erdman. He was naturalized in Pennsylvania 10 Apr. 1772. He was from Monackeste Township, Frederick County, Maryland.

Dorin, Ann Mary. She was naturalized in Pennsylvania 10 Apr. 1769. She was from Philadelphia.

Dorland, Jan Gerrise. He took the oath of allegiance in Breucklijn, Kings County, New York 26–30 Sep. 1687. He had been in the colony 35 years.

Dorlant, Gerrit. He took the oath of allegiance in Flackbush, Kings County, New York 26–30 Sep. 1687. He was a native of the colony.

Dorlant, Gerrit. He took the oath of allegiance in Breucklijn, Kings County, New York 26–30 Sep. 1687. He was a native of the colony.

Dormer, Thomas. He was naturalized in Pennsylvania 11 Apr. 1752. He was from Philadelphia.

Dormindo, Manuel Martinez. He was endenized in London in 1677.

Dorn, Daniel. He was naturalized in New Jersey 3 June 1763.

Dornbach, Christofell. He was naturalized in Maryland 9 Apr. 1760. He lived in Baltimore County, Maryland.

Dornback, Matthias. He was naturalized in Pennsylvania 11 Apr. 1761. He was from Berks County.

Dorschheimer, Martin. He was naturalized in New Jersey in 1761.

Dorvo, Michael. He was naturalized in Jamaica 2 Feb. 1730/1.

Dory, Mary. She was naturalized in Jamaica 1 May 1710. She was a free Negro.

Dosch, George. He was naturalized in Pennsylvania 16 May 1769. He was from Mannor Township, Lancaster County.

Dotterer, Bernhard. He was naturalized in Pennsylvania 19 May 1739. He was from Philadelphia County.

Dotterer, Conrath. He was naturalized in Pennsylvania 19 May 1739. He was from Philadelphia County.

Dotterer, George Philip. He was naturalized in Pennsylvania 19 May 1739. He was from Philadelphia County.

Dotterer, Michael. He was naturalized in Pennsylvania 19 May 1739. He was from Philadelphia County.

Doublet, Jean. He was endenized in New York 23 Dec. 1695.

Doucet, Charles. He was an Acadian who took the oath of allegiance at Annapolis River in Dec. 1729.

Doucet, Charles. He was an Acadian who took the oath of allegiance in Apr. 1730 at Annapolis River.

Doucet, Claude. He was an Acadian and took the oath to George II at Annapolis River, Nova Scotia in Dec. 1729.

Doucet, Francois. He was an Acadian who took the oath of allegiance in Apr. 1730.

Doucet, Francois. He was an Acadian who took the oath of allegiance in Apr. 1730.

Doucet, Jean. He was naturalized in South Carolina ca. 1696.

Doucet, Jean. He was an Acadian and took the oath to George II at the Mines, Pisiquit 31 Oct. 1727.

Doucet, Jean. He was an Acadian and took the oath to George II at the Mines, Pisiquit 31 Oct. 1727.

Doucet, Jean. He was an Acadian and took the oath to George II at the Mines, Pisiquit 31 Oct. 1727.

Doucet, Jean. He was an Acadian and took the oath to George II at Annapolis River, Nova Scotia in Dec. 1729.

Doucet, Jean. He was an Acadian who took the oath of allegiance in Apr. 1730.

Doucet, Jean. He was an Acadian who took the oath of allegiance in Apr. 1730.

Doucet, Jean. He was an Acadian who took the oath of allegiance in Apr. 1730.

Doucet, Joseph. He was an Acadian and took the oath to George II at Annapolis River, Nova Scotia in Dec. 1729.

Doucet, Joseph. He was an Acadian and took the oath to George II at Annapolis River, Nova Scotia in Dec. 1729.

Doucet, Laurans. He took the oath of allegiance at Port Royal, Nova Scotia 16 Aug. 1695.

Doucet, Louis. He was an Acadian who took the oath of allegiance in Apr. 1730.

Doucet, Pierre. He was an Acadian and took the oath to George II at Annapolis River, Nova Scotia in Dec. 1729.

Doucet, Pierre. He took the oath of allegiance at Port Royal, Nova Scotia 16 Aug. 1695.

Doucet, Pierre. He was an Acadian who took the oath of allegiance in Apr. 1730.

Doucet, Pierre. He was an Acadian who took the oath of allegiance in Apr. 1730.

Doucet, Pierre. He was an Acadian who took the oath of allegiance in Apr.1730.

Doucett, Alexis. He was an Acadian and took the oath to George II at Annapolis River, Nova Scotia in Dec. 1729.

Doucett, Claude. He was an Acadian and took the oath to George II at Annapolis River, Nova Scotia in Dec. 1729.

Doucett, Germain. He was an Acadian and took the oath to George II at Annapolis River, Nova Scotia in Dec. 1729.

Doucett, Jacques. He was an Acadian and took the oath to George II at Annapolis River, Nova Scotia in Dec. 1729.

Doucett, Laurent. He was an Acadian and took the oath to George II at Annapolis River, Nova Scotia Dec. 1729.

Doucett, Mathieu. He was an Acadian and took the oath to George II at Annapolis River, Nova Scotia Dec. 1729.

Doucett, Michel. He was an Acadian and took the oath to George II at Annapolis River, Nova Scotia in Dec. 1729.

Doucett, Piere. He was an Acadian and took the oath to George II at Annapolis River, Nova Scotia in Dec. 1729.

Doucett, Piere. He was an Acadian and took the oath to George II at Annapolis River, Nova Scotia in Dec. 1729.

Doucett, Rene. He was an Acadian and took the oath to George II at Annapolis River, Nova Scotia in Dec. 1729.

Doueron, Charles. He was an Acadian who took the oath to the King at the Mines, Pisiquit 31 Oct. 1727.

Dousett, Joseph. He was an Acadian and took the oath to George II at Annapolis River, Nova Scotia in the winter of 1730.

Doussinet, Etienne. He was endenized in New York 17 Sep. 1685. As Stephen Doussinei, wife Susanna Doussinei, daughter Mary Ann Doussinei, and daughter Marianna Doussinei were endenized in England 8 Mar. 1681/2.

Douzen, Herman. He took the oath to the King 21–26 Oct. 1664 after the conquest of New Netherland.

Dovalle, Daniel. He was naturalized in Jamaica 26 Feb. 1740/1. He was a Jew.

Dovally, David. He was naturalized in Jamaica 17 Sep. 1694. He also appeared as David Dovalle.

Dovo, Petter. He took the oath of naturalization in New York 13 June 1687.

Dowdee, Peter. He was naturalized in Maryland 4 Apr. 1698. He lived in Somerset County and was French.

Dowdes, Minor. He was endenized in Isle of Wight County, Virginia 1 Apr. 1658. He was Dutch. He also appeared as John Dowdas.

Dowdle, Michael. He was naturalized in Pennsylvania 24–25 Sep. 1764. He was from York Township, York County.

Downey, Adam. He was naturalized in Pennsylvania 10 Apr. 1755. He was from Bucks County.

Dowsen, Harmen. He took the oath of allegiance in Orange County, New York 26 Sep. 1687.

Dowsen, Teunis. He took the oath of allegiance in Orange County, New York 26 Sep. 1687.

Doze, Andrew. He and his wife, Anne Doze, were endenized in Pennsylvania 21 Feb. 1694/5. They were from France.

Dozier, Leonard. He was naturalized in Westmoreland County, Virginia 28 Jan. 1683/4. He was born in France. His son, Richard Dozier, had his father's naturalization recorded 28 Jan. 1734.

Draiss, Peter. He was naturalized in Pennsylvania 11 Apr. 1763. He was from Philadelphia.

Drapier, Paul. He was naturalized in Virginia 24 Apr. 1704.

Draugh, Rudolph. He was naturalized in Pennsylvania 11–12 Apr. 1744. He was from Lancaster County.

Dreber, Justus. He was naturalized in Pennsylvania 24–25 Sep. 1764. He was from Lancaster Township, Lancaster County.

Dreess, Jacob. He was naturalized in Pennsylvania 10 Sep. 1761. He was from Berks County.

Dreher, Sebastian. He was naturalized in New York 8–9 Sep. 1715. He was from Ulster County.

Dreish, Jacob. He was naturalized in Maryland 10 Sep. 1760.

Dresback, Martin. He was naturalized in Pennsylvania 10 Apr. 1760.

Dresher, Christopher. He was naturalized in Pennsylvania 11–13 Apr. 1743. He was from Philadelphia County.

Dresher, George. He was naturalized in Pennsylvania 11–13 Apr. 1743. He was from Philadelphia County.

Dreths, Josias. He took the oath of allegiance in Breucklijn, Kings County, New York 26–30 Sep. 1687. He had been in the colony 26 years.

Drewid, John Christian. He was naturalized in New York 22 Nov. 1715. He was from Albany County.

Driesh, Frederick. He was naturalized in Pennsylvania 10 Sep. 1761. He was from Philadelphia County.

Driestle, John. He was naturalized in Pennsylvania 6 Feb. 1730/1. He was from Chester County.

Drisius, Samuel. He took the oath to the King 21–26 Oct. 1664 after the conquest of New Netherland.

Drom, Johan Andries. He was naturalized in New York 22 Nov. 1715. He was from Albany County.

Drolinger, Henry. He was naturalized in North Carolina 22 Sep. 1764. He was from Rowan County and a German.

Dropler, Barney. He was naturalized in North Carolina 22 Sep. 1764. He was from Rowan County and a German.

Drout, John. He was naturalized in Pennsylvania 10–14 Apr. 1747. He was from Philadelphia County.

Drullinger, Adam. He was naturalized in Pennsylvania 12 Apr. 1750. He was from Bucks County.

Drum, George. He was naturalized in Pennsylvania 24 Sep. 1762. He was from Berks County.

Duberte, Lewis. He was naturalized in Virginia 12 May 1705.

Dubes, Jacob. He was naturalized in Pennsylvania 11 Apr. 1749. He was from Bucks County.

DuBois, Gualtherus. He was naturalized in New York 19 July 1715. He was a minister.

DuBois, Jacob. He was naturalized in New York 8–9 Sep. 1715. He was from Ulster County.

DuBois, Jean. He was an Acadian who took the oath of allegiance in Apr. 1730.

DuBois, John. He was naturalized in New York 29 Dec. 1763.

DuBois, Louis, He sought naturalization in New York 12 Nov. 1748.

Dubosc, Isaac. He was the son of Louis Dubosc and Anne Dubosc of Dieppe, Normandie, France. His wife was Suzanne Dubosc, the daughter of Pierre Couillandeau and Susane Couillandeau, and was born at LaTramblade, Xaintonge, France. They were naturalized in South Carolina *ca.* 1696.

DuBose, Jacques. He was born at St. Ambroise, Languedoc, France and was the son of Andre DuBose and Marie LeStroade. His wife was Marie Dugue. Their daughter was Marie DuBose born in South Carolina. They were naturalized in South Carolina 10 Mar. 1696/7. He was a merchant.

DuBourdieu, Samuel. He was born at Vitre, Bretagne, France, the son of Olivier DuBourdieu and Marie Genne. His wife was Judith Dugue. His son, Louis Philipe DuBourdieu, was by his previous wife Louise Thoury. His son, Samuel DuBourdieu, was by Judith Dugue. Both of the children were born in South Carolina. They were naturalized in South Carolina *ca.* 1696.

Dubre, Jacob. He was endenized in Pennsylvania 21 Feb. 1694/5. He was from France and a carter.

Dubre, Jacob. He was naturalized in Pennsylvania 29 Mar. 1735. He was from Philadelphia County.

Dubree, Jacob. He was naturalized in Pennsylvania 24 Sep. 1762. He was from Berks County.

Dubroca, Valentine. He took the oath of allegiance at Mobile, West Florida 2 Oct. 1764.

Ducette, Charles. He took the oath of allegiance at Harbour Amhurst in the Magdalen Islands, Gulf of Saint Lawrence on 31 Aug. 1765. He was a native of Nova Scotia.

DuChaine, Anthonij. He took the oath of allegiance in New Uijtrceht, Kings County, New York 26–30 Sep.1687. He had been in the colony 24 years.

Duchart, Valerius. He applied in Maryland but died in 1756 before his citizenship was granted. He was born at Strasburg, Lorraine, France and came to New York via Holland and England in 1753. He came to Baltimore Co., Md. in 1754. He was survived by a widow and seven children.

Duchemin, Daniel. He petitioned to be naturalized in New York 19 Aug. 1687.

Duchemin, Daniel. He was naturalized in Virginia 12 May 1705.

Duchemin, Daniel. He was naturalized in New York 20 May 1769.

Duchezeaux, Adam. He was naturalized in Massachusetts 12 Apr. 1731.

Duchier, Jacobus. He, his wife Mary Duchier, son Arnold Duchier, and son Anthony Duchier were endenized in England 8 Mar. 1682. They came to New York.

Duckener, David. He was naturalized in Pennsylvania 10 Apr. 1760.

DuClose, John Oger. He was naturalized in Virginia 12 May 1705.

Dudin, James. He was naturalized in New Jersey 14 Apr. 1722.

Dueron, Charles. He was an Acadian who took the oath of allegiance in Apr. 1730.

Dueron, Charles. He was an Acadian who took the oath of allegiance in Apr. 1730.

Dueron, Joseph. He was an Acadian who took the oath of allegiance in Apr. 1730.

Dueron, Louis Mathieu. He was an Acadian who took the oath of allegiance in Apr. 1730.

Dureon, Paul. He was an Acadian who took the oath of allegiance in Apr. 1730.

Dueron, Pierre. He was an Acadian who took the oath of allegiance in Apr. 1730.

Dueron, Thomas. He was an Acadian who took the oath of allegiance in Apr. 1730.

Dueron, Vincent. He was an Acadian who took the oath of allegiance in Apr. 1730.

Duerr, Jacob. He was naturalized in Pennsylvania 24 Sep. 1763. He was from Upper Hannover Township, Philadelphia County.

Dufay, James. He was naturalized in South Carolina 2 Mar. 1699/1700. He was the son of James Dufay by Judith Dognier his wife and was born at Bologne, France.

Dufoy, Peter. He was naturalized in Virginia 12 May 1705.

Dugas, Alexandre. He was an Acadian who took the oath of allegiance in Apr. 1730.

Dugas, Charles. He was an Acadian and took the oath to George II at Annapolis River, Nova Scotia in Dec. 1729.

Dugas, Charles. He was an Acadian and took the oath to George II at Annapolis River, Nova Scotia in Dec. 1729.

Dugas, Charles. He was an Acadian who took the oath of allegiance in Apr. 1730.

Dugas, Claude. He took the oath of allegiance at Port Royal, Nova Scotia 16 Aug. 1695.

Dugas, Claude. He was an Acadian and took the oath to George II at Annapolis River, Nova Scotia in Dec. 1729.

Dugas, Claude. He was an Acadian who took the oath of allegiance in Apr. 1730.

Dugas, Claude. He was an Acadian who took the oath of allegiance in Apr. 1730.

Dugas, Claude. He was an Acadian who took the oath of allegiance in Apr. 1730.

Dugas, Jean. He was an Acadian who took the oath of allegiance in Apr. 1730.

Dugas, Joseph. He was an Acadian and took the oath at Annapolis River in the winter of 1730.

Dugas, Louis. He was an Acadian and took the oath to George II at Annapolis River, Nova Scotia in Dec. 1729.

Dugas, Francois. He was an Acadian and took the oath to George II at Annapolis River, Nova Scotia in Dec. 1729.

Dugas, Pierre. He was an Acadian who took the oath of allegiance in Apr. 1730.

Dugne, James. He was naturalized in South Carolina 30 Mar. 1696. [It is possible that he is the Jacques Dugue *infra*.]

Dugue, Peirre. He, his brother Isaac Dugue, and his sister Elizabeth Dugue were born at Besane, Bery, France. They were the children of Jacques Dugue and Elizabeth Dupuy. The trio were naturalized in South Carolina 10 Mar. 1696/7. He was a shipwright.

Duhattoway, Jacob. He was naturalized in Maryland in Feb. 1674. He was born in Dort, Holland.

Dui, Jacob. He was naturalized in Pennsylvania 11 Apr. 1761. He was from Lancaster County.

Dulgar, Hendrick. He expressed his desire to be naturalized in New Castle County, Delaware 21 Feb. 1682/3.

Dullivier, Maurice. He took the oath of allegiance at Mobile, West Florida 2 Oct. 1764.

DuMass, Jeremiah. He was naturalized in Virginia 12 May 1705.

Dumerneilt, Casper. He was naturalized in Pennsylvania 24 Sep. 1757.

Dumerneilt, David. He was naturalized in Pennsylvania 24 Sep. 1757.

Dumm, Adam. He was naturalized in New York 8 Mar. 1773.

Dumm, Melicher. He was naturalized in New York 8 Mar. 1773.

Dumm, Nicholas. He was naturalized in New York 8 Mar. 1773.

Dummin, Jacob. He was naturalized in Pennsylvania 11 Apr. 1761. He was from Lancaster County.

Dunckel, John Ludwig. He was naturalized in New York 3 July 1759.

Dunckell, Johannes. He was naturalized in Pennsylvania 24 Sep. 1741. He was from Philadelphia County.

Dunder, Jacob. He was naturalized in Pennsylvania 10 Apr. 1760.

Dunkle, John. He was naturalized in Augusta County, Virginia 18 May 1762.

Dunkleberry, Peter. He was naturalized in Pennsylvania 11–13 Apr. 1743. He was from Philadelphia County.

Dunshman, Johannes Gerardus. He was naturalized in New York 3 July 1759.

Duon, Jean. He was an Acadian and took the oath at Annapolis River in the winter of 1730.

Duon, V. T. He was an Acadian and took the oath to George II at Annapolis River, Nova Scotia in the winter of 1730.

Dupine, Peter Chevalier. He was endenized in New York 7 Oct. 1698.

Duponner, Ferdinand. He was naturalized in New York 3 July 1759.

DuPre, John. He was naturalized in Virginia 12 May 1705.

Dupis, Anth. He was an Acadian who took the oath of allegiance in Apr. 1730.

Dupont, Abraham. He was naturalized in South Carolina 10 Mar. 1696/7. He was a brazier.

Dupont, Jean Claude. He took the oath of allegiance at Mobile, West Florida 2 Oct. 1764.

Dupont, Pierre. He was naturalized in New York 3 July 1759.

Duppel, Maurice. He was naturalized in Pennsylvania 24 May 1771. He was from Heidelberg Township, Lancaster County.

Dupray, John. He was naturalized in Jamaica 22 Sep. 1714.

Dupre, Cornelius. He was naturalized in South Carolina 10 Mar. 1696/7. He was a planter.

DuPre, John. He was naturalized in Virginia 12 May 1705.

DuPre, Thomas. He was naturalized in Virginia 12 May 1705.

Dupree, Josias, Sr. He was naturalized in South Carolina 10 Mar. 1696/7. He was a merchant.

Dupree, Josias, Jr. He was naturalized in South Carolina 10 Mar. 1696/7. He was a shipwright.

DuPue, Francois. He took the oath of allegiance in Orange County, New York 26 Sep. 1687.

Dupuis, [——]. He took the oath of allegiance at Port Royal, Nova Scotia 16 Aug. 1695.

Dupuis, Antoine. He was an Acadian and took the oath to the King at the Mines, Pisiquit, Nova Scotia 31 Oct. 1727.

Dupuis, Charles. He was an Acadian and took the oath to the King at the Mines, Pisiquit, Nova Scotia 31 Oct. 1727.

Dupuis, Charles. He was an Acadian and took the oath to George II at Annapolis River, Nova Scotia in Dec. 1729.

Dupuis, Charles. He was an Acadian who took the oath of allegiance in Apr. 1730.

Dupuis, Charles. He was an Acadian who took the oath of allegiance in Apr. 1730.

Dupuis, Germain. He was an Acadian and took the oath to the King of the Mines, Pisiquit, Nova Scotia 31 Oct. 1727.

Dupuis, Jean. He was an Acadian and took the oath to the King at the Mines, Pisiquit, Nova Scotia 31 Oct. 1727.

Dupuis, Jean. He was an Acadian and took the oath to George II at Annapolis River, Nova Scotia in Dec. 1729.

Dupuis, Jean. He was an Acadian who took the oath of allegiance in Apr. 1730.

Dupuis, Jermain. He was an Acadian who took the oath of allegiance in Apr. 1730.

Dupuis, Joseph. He was an Acadian and took the oath of allegiance at Annapolis River, Nova Scotia in Dec. 1729.

Dupuis, Joseph. He was an Acadian who took the oath of allegiance in Apr. 1730.

Dupuis, Louis. He was an Acadian and took the oath to George II at Annapolis River, Nova Scotia in Dec. 1729.

Dupuis, Nicholas. He took the oath to the King 21–26 Oct. 1664 after the conquest of New Netherland.

Dupuis, Pierre. He was an Acadian and took the oath at Annapolis River in 1729.

Dupuit, Louis. He was an Acadian and took the oath to George II at Annapolis River, Nova Scotia in the winter of 1730.

Dupuy, Barthelemy. He was naturalized in Virginia 12 May 1705.

Dupuy, Andrew. He was endenized in London 29 Sep. 1698. He lost his papers in a shipwreck so he applied for re-endenization in New York 15 Oct. 1703. He was master of the *Jacob*.

Dupuy, Jubatiste. He was naturalized in New York 20 May 1769. He was a merchant in New York City.

Dupuy, Mosyes. He was naturalized in New York 8–9 Sep. 1715. He was from Ulster County.

Dupuy, Thomas. He was naturalized in Virginia 12 May 1705.

Duran, Charles. He was naturalized in New Jersey 31 July 1740. He was from France.

Durand, Peter. He was naturalized in New York 29 July 1762. He was a tailor from New York City. He was a French Protestant.

Durand, Moris. He took the oath of allegiance at Mobile, West Florida 2 Oct. 1764.

Durand, Peter. He and his son, Charles Durand, were endenized in England 6 Mar. 1685/6. They came to New York.

Durie, Josst. He took the oath of allegiance in Boswijck, Kings County, New York 26–30 Sep. 1687. He had been in the colony 12 years.

Durouzeaux, Daniel. He was born at St. Jean d'Angely, France, the son of Daniel Durouzeaux and Marye Souchard. His wife was Elizabeth Foucheraud. Their sons were Daniel Durouzeaux and Pierre Durouzeaux born in South Carolina. They were naturalized in South Carolina 10 Mar. 1696/7. He also appeared as Daniel Duraso. He was a shammy dresser.

Durot, George David. He was naturalized in New York 11 Sep. 1761.

Durr, Johannes Balthasar. He was naturalized in Maryland 7 Sep. 1768. He was a German.

Durr, Michael. He was naturalized in Pennsylvania 13–15 Apr. 1748. He was from Philadelphia.

Durst, Paul. He was naturalized in Pennsylvania 24 Sep. 1760. He was from Berks County.

DuSimitiere, Pierre Eugene. He was naturalized in New York 20 May 1769.

Duslar, Jacob. He was naturalized in New York 8 Mar. 1773.

Dusler, Andreas. He was naturalized in New York 11 Sep. 1761.

Dutarque, Louis. He was born in Picardie, France, the son of Mathieu Dutarque and Anne Foulon. He was naturalized in South Carolina 10 Mar. 1696/7. He was a weaver.

Dutartre, Pierre. He was the son of Daniel Dutartre and Anne Renault and was born in Chathaudun, Bause, France. His wife was Anne Poiteuin, a native of Duplesis Morne, Gaule, France, daughter of Anthoinee Poiteuin and Gabrielle Berou. They were naturalized in South Carolina 10 Mar. 1696/7. He was a weaver.

Dutens, Charles John. He was naturalized in New York 24 Nov. 1750.

Dutitree, Claudius. He was naturalized in Maryland 18 Oct. 1694.

Dutwyler, Felix. He was naturalized in Pennsylvania 11 Apr. 1763. He was from Springfield Township, Philadelphia County.

DuVoisin, John Henry. He was naturalized in Nova Scotia 10 July 1758.

DuVoor, Daniel. He took the oath of allegiance in Orange County, New York 26 Sep. 1687.

Duy, Christian. He was naturalized in Pennsylvania 11 Apr. 1761. He was from Philadelphia County.

Duyckinck, Evert. He was naturalized in New York 12 July 1715. He was a painter.

Duyckings, Evert. He took the oath to the King 21–26 Oct. 1664 after the conquest of New Netherland.

Dydelofzen, Claes. He took the oath to the King 21–26 Oct. 1664 after the conquest of New Netherland.

Dylander, Joannes. He was naturalized in Pennsylvania 19 May 1739. He was from Philadelphia County.

Dysher, Stephen. He was naturalized in Pennsylvania 24 Sep. 1760. He was from Berks County.

Eagle, Marcus. He was naturalized in Pennsylvania 10 Sep. 1761. He was from Lancaster County.

Early, Jacob. He was naturalized in Pennsylvania 10 Sep. 1761. He was from Berks County.

Easler, Christopher. He was naturalized in New Jersey 8 Oct. 1750.

Easter, Frederick. He was naturalized in Augusta County, Virginia 18 May 1762.

Easy, Godfrid. He was naturalized in New York 16 Feb. 1771.

Ebbert, Andrew. He was naturalized in Pennsylvania 10 Sep. 1761. He was from Berks County.

Ebbert, John. He was naturalized in New York 12 July 1715. He was a tailor.

Ebbinck, Jeronimus. He took the oath to the King 21–26 Oct. 1664 after the conquest of New Netherland.

Ebell, Peter. He took the oath to the King 21–26 Oct. 1664 after the conquest of New Netherland.

Eberhard, George. He was naturalized in Pennsylvania 10 Sep. 1761. He was from Philadelphia County.

Eberhard, Henry. He was naturalized in Pennsylvania 24 Sep. 1763. He was from Manchester Township, York County.

Eberhard, Paul. He was naturalized in Maryland 12 Sep. 1759.

Eberhardt, Nicholas Henry. He was naturalized in Pennsylvania 10–12 Apr. 1762. He was from Lancaster County.

Eberhart, Joseph. He was naturalized in Pennsylvania 29 Mar. 1735. He was from Bucks County.

Eberhart, Michael. He was naturalized in Pennsylvania 29 Mar. 1735. He was from Bucks County.

Eberley, George Christopher. He was naturalized in Pennsylvania 10 Sep. 1761. He was from Philadelphia County.

Ebersohl, Charles. He was naturalized in Pennsylvania 24–29 Sep. 1768. He was from Reading Township, Berks County.

Ebersoll, Christian. He was naturalized in Maryland 11 Sep. 1765. He was a German from Frederick County.

Ebert, Adam. He was naturalized in New York 6 Dec. 1746.

Ebert, Adam. He was naturalized in Maryland 15 Apr. 1761.

Ebert, Martin. He was naturalized in Pennsylvania 25 Sep. 1751. He was from York County.

Ebert, Michael. He was naturalized in Pennsylvania 25 Sep. 1751. He was from York County.

Eberth, John. He was naturalized in Pennsylvania 10 Sep. 1761. He was from Berks County.

Ebler, Johannes. He was naturalized in Pennsylvania 26 Sep. 1748. He was from Lancaster County.

Echard, Conrad. He was naturalized in Maryland 1742–1743.

Echlewick, Thomas. He was naturalized in Pennsylvania 29 Sep. 1709. He was from Philadelphia County.

Ecker, William. He was naturalized in New Jersey 20 Aug. 1755.

Eckhard, Henrick. He was naturalized in Pennsylvania 11 Apr. 1763. He was from Reading Township, Berks County.

Eckhardt, George Adam. He was naturalized in Maryland 14 Sep. 1768. He was a German.

Eckart, Adam. He was naturalized in Pennsylvania 10 Sep. 1762. He was from Philadelphia County.

Eckart, Jonathan. He was naturalized in New York 18 Oct. 1769. He was a trader from New York City.

Eckell, Jacob. He was naturalized in Pennsylvania 24 Sep. 1762. He was from Philadelphia County.

Ecker, Abraham. He was naturalized in New York 11 Sep. 1761.

Ecker, George. He was naturalized in New York 11 Sep. 1761.

Ecker, George. He was naturalized in New York 27 Jan. 1770.

Ecker, Jacob. He was naturalized in Pennsylvania 10–12 Apr. 1762. He was from Lancaster County.

Eckert, Adam. He was naturalized in New York 8–9 Sep. 1715. He was from Ulster County.

Eckert, John George. He was naturalized in New York 8–9 Sep. 1715. He was from Albany County.

Eckert, Philip. He was naturalized in New York 21 Oct. 1765. He was a carpenter from New York City.

Eckert, Philip. He was naturalized in Pennsylvania 10 Sep. 1761. He was from Lancaster County.

Eckert, Valentine. He was naturalized in Pennsylvania 10 Sep. 1761. He was from Berks County.

Eckhar, Nicholas. He was naturalized in New York 31 Jan. 1715/6. He was from Albany County.

Eckler, Augustus. He was naturalized in New York 11 Sep. 1761.

Eckler, Hendrick. He was naturalized in New York 11 Sep. 1761.

Ecklor, Jacob. He was naturalized in Maryland 15 Sep. 1762. He was from Baltimore County.

Ecklor, Ulrick. He was naturalized in Maryland 31 Aug. 1757.

Ecklor, Ulrick. He was naturalized in Maryland 15 Sep. 1762. He was from Baltimore County.

Eckman, Lawrens. He was naturalized in New York 3 July 1759.

Eckstein, Johannes. He was naturalized in Pennsylvania in 1730–31. He was from Philadelphia County.

Eckstine, Leonard. He was naturalized in Pennsylvania 11 Apr. 1761. He was from Philadelphia County.

Eder, Casper. He was naturalized in Maryland 15 Apr. 1761.

Edgar, John. He was naturalized in Maryland 14 May 1696. He lived in Somerset County.

Ederick, John. He was naturalized in Pennsylvania 10–12 Apr. 1762. He was from Philadelphia County.

Edich, Hans Michiel. He was naturalized in New York 14 Feb. 1715/6. He was from Albany County.

Edich, Hans Michiel, Jr. He was naturalized in New York 14 Feb. 1715/6. He was from Albany County.

Edleman, Philip. He was naturalized in Maryland 31 Aug. 1757.

Edrion, Christian. He was naturalized in Maryland 9 Sep. 1772. He was a German.

Edwin, John. He was naturalized in Pennsylvania 24–29 Sep. 1768. He was from Bethlehem Township, Northampton County.

Eell, Hermanus. He was naturalized in New York 3 July 1759.

Eenloos, Abram. He was naturalized in New Castle County, Delaware 21 Feb. 1682/3.

Eeman, Laurens. He was naturalized in New York 3 July 1759.

Eff, Christian. He was naturalized in Pennsylvania 11 Apr. 1761. He was from Lancaster County.

Ege, Martin. He was naturalized in Pennsylvania 10 Sep. 1761. He was from Berks County.

Ege, Michael. He was naturalized in Pennsylvania 10–14 Apr. 1747. He was from Philadelphia County.

Eggman, John. He was naturalized in Pennsylvania 10 Apr. 1753. He was from Lancaster County.

Egle, John. He was naturalized in Pennsylvania 10 Apr. 1759.

Egle, Martin. He was naturalized in New York 23 Oct. 1765. He was a carpenter from New York City.

Egly, Casper. He was naturalized in Pennsylvania 24 Sep. 1762. He was from Berks County.

Egold, George Adam. He was naturalized in Pennsylvania 24–25 Sep. 1764. He was from Hannover Township, Philadelphia County.

Ehhaldt, Matthew. He was naturalized in Maryland 11 May 1774. He was a German.

Ehl, Johannes. He was naturalized in New York 11 Sep. 1761.

Ehler, George. He was naturalized in Pennsylvania 24 Sep. 1762. He was from Lancaster County.

Ehlich, Hans Georg. He was naturalized in New York 8–9 Sep. 1715. He was from Ulster County.

Ehny, David. He was naturalized in New York 31 Dec. 1761.

Ehny, Joachim George. He was naturalized in New York 31 Dec. 1761.

Ehrard, Jacob. He was naturalized in Pennsylvania 11 Apr. 1763. He was from Northern Liberties Township, Philadelphia County.

Ehrenhart, Jacob. He was naturalized in Pennsylvania 10 Apr. 1753. He was from Northampton County.

Ehrenzeller, Jacob. He was naturalized in Pennsylvania 24 Sep. 1756.

Ehring, Christian. He was naturalized in New York 29 July 1772. He was a weaver from New York City.

Ehrman, Wilhelm. He was naturalized in Pennsylvania 10 Sep. 1761. He was from Berks County.

Eichely, Adam. He was naturalized in Pennsylvania 11 Apr. 1741. He was from Philadelphia County.

Eichold, Martin. He was naturalized in Pennsylvania 10 Sep. 1761. He was from Lancaster County.

Eicholtz, Jacob. He was naturalized in Pennsylvania 24 Sep. 1753. He was from Lancaster County.

Eichorn, Jacob. He was naturalized in New Jersey in 1761.

Eick, Domes. He was naturalized in New Jersey in 1750. He was from Hunterdon County.

Eick, Philip. He was naturalized in New Jersey in 1750. He was from Hunterdon County.

Eigenbrode, Peter. He was naturalized in New York 8 Mar. 1773.

Eigenbrood, Johannes. He was naturalized in New York 3 July 1759.

Eigenbroodt, Hannes. He was naturalized in New York 11 Sep. 1761.

Eigenter, Johannes. He was naturalized in Pennsylvania 10–14 Apr. 1747. He was from Bucks County.

Eigh, Jacob. He was naturalized in New Jersey 8 July 1730. He was born in Germany.

Eighelberger, Frederick. He was naturalized in Pennsylvania 19 May 1739. He was from Lancaster County.

Eighenbrod, Jost. He was naturalized in Maryland 11 Sep. 1760.

Eigster, John. He was naturalized in Pennsylvania 19 Mar. 1739. He was from Philadelphia County.

Eikler, Augustus. He was naturalized in New York 27 Jan. 1770.

Einsler, Henry. He was naturalized in Maryland 11 Apr. 1764. He was a German.

Eisenhard, George. He was naturalized in Pennsylvania 24–25 Sep. 1764. He was from York Township, York County.

Eisenhaver, Elizabeth. She was naturalized in Pennsylvania 11 Apr. 1752. She was from Lancaster County.

Eisenhaver, Martin. He was naturalized in Pennsylvania 11 Apr. 1752. He was from Lancaster County.

Eisenhaver, Peter. He was naturalized in Pennsylvania 11 Apr. 1752. He was from Lancaster County.

Eisenlord, John. He was naturalized in New York 20 Mar. 1762.

Eisenlord, John. He was naturalized in New York 8 Mar. 1773.

Eisinbiess, John George. He was naturalized in Pennsylvania 10 Sep. 1761. He was from Berks County.

Ekell, Henry. He was naturalized in Pennsylvania 11 Apr. 1761. He was from Bucks County.

Eker, George. He was naturalized in New York 27 Jan. 1770.

Ekert, Jacob. He was naturalized in Pennsylvania 24 Sep. 1760. He was from Berks County.

Elberschidt, Frederick. He was naturalized in Pennsylvania in 1735. He was from Chester County.

Elbert, Adam. He was naturalized in New York 6 Dec. 1746.

Elberschidt, Frederick. He was naturalized in Pennsylvania 29 Mar. 1735. He was from Lancaster County.

Elbertse, Elbert. He took the oath of allegiance in Flackland, Kings County, New York 26–30 Sep. 1687. He had been in the colony 50 years.

Elesen, Tunis. He was naturalized in New York 8–9 Sep. 1715. He was from Ulster County.

Elexson, John. He was naturalized in Maryland 19 Apr. 1671. He lived in Kent County and was Swedish.

Elias, David. He was naturalized in New York 6 July 1723.

Elich, Andris. He was naturalized in New York 8–9 Sep. 1715. He was from Ulster County.

Elich, Hans Georg. He was naturalized in New York 8–9 Sep. 1715. He was from Ulster County.

Elie, Martin. He was naturalized in Pennsylvania 24–25 Sep. 1764. He was from Lebanon Township, Lancaster County.

Elison, Tunis. He took the oath of naturalization in New York 1 Sep. 1687 in Ulster County.

Elizer, Isaac. He was naturalized in New York 23 July 1763. He was a Jew from Rhode Island and was formerly a merchant of New York City. He had applied but been rejected by the Rhode Island Superior Court in 1762.

Ell, Johan Jacob. He was naturalized in New York 14 Oct. 1732.

Eller, Jacob. He was naturalized in North Carolina 23 Mar. 1763. He was from Rowan County.

Ellick, John. He was naturalized in Pennsylvania 11 Apr. 1763. He was from Philadelphia County.

Ellinger, George. He was naturalized in Pennsylvania 24 Sep. 1762. He was from Lancaster County.

Elliott, Andrew. He was naturalized in Pennsylvania 11–12 Apr. 1744. He was from Lancaster County.

Ellis, Hero. He was naturalized in New York 14 Oct. 1732.

Ellmaker, Leonhart. He was naturalized in Pennsylvania 19 May 1739. He was from Lancaster County.

Elrington, Christina. She was widow of Francis Elrington. She was the daughter of Abraham and Sophia Roeters. She was naturalized in New Jersey 8 July 1730. She was born in Amsterdam, Holland.

Elshever, Ludwick. He was naturalized in New York 11 Sep. 1761.

Elting, John. He took the oath of naturalization in New York 1 Sep. 1687 in Ulster County.

Elvendorop, Coinradt. He took the oath of naturalization in New York 1 Sep. 1687 in Ulster County.

Ely, David. He was naturalized in Pennsylvania 10 Apr. 1754. He was from Berks County.

Ely, Jean. He was an Acadian and took the oath of allegiance in Apr. 1730.

Emann, George. He was naturalized in Pennsylvania 13–15 Apr. 1748. He was from Philadelphia County.

Emar, Jean. He was naturalized in New York in Oct. 1740. He was a yeoman from New York City.

Embig, Christopher. He was naturalized in Pennsylvania 10 Sep. 1761. He was from Lancaster County.

Emegin, John Earnest. He was naturalized in New York 13 Mar. 1715/6.

Emegin, Johannis. He was naturalized in New York 13 Mar. 1715/6. He was from Albany County.

Emerick, John Peter. He was naturalized in Pennsylvania 10 Apr. 1772. He was from Gwinedth Township, Philadelphia County.

Emery, Paul. He was naturalized in Jamaica 4 July 1690. He was a doctor of physick.

Emich, Niclas. He was naturalized in New York 8–9 Sep. 1715. He was from Ulster County.

Emig, John. He was naturalized in Pennsylvania 24 Sep. 1762. He was from York County.

Emmert, Eva Maria. She was naturalized in Pennsylvania 25 Sep. 1751. She was from Lancaster County.

Emmert, George. He was naturalized in Pennsylvania 25 Sep. 1751. He was from Lancaster County.

Emmert, Philip. He was naturalized in Pennsylvania 24 Sep. 1741. He was from Philadelphia County.

Emrich, Johanis. He was naturalized in New York 8–9 Sep. 1715. He was from Ulster County.

Enck, Jacob. He was naturalized in Pennsylvania 10 Sep. 1761. He was from Lancaster County.

End, Johannes Dewalt. He was naturalized in Pennsylvania 6 Feb. 1730/1. He was from Philadelphia County.

Endres, John. He was naturalized in Pennsylvania 11 Apr. 1761. He was from Lancaster County.

Endreas, Peter. He was naturalized in Pennsylvania 6 Feb. 1730/1. He was from Philadelphia County.

Endris, Mary Elizabeth. She was naturalized in Pennsylvania 24 Sep. 1762. She was from Philadelphia County.

Endrivett, John. He was endenized in New York 18 Apr. 1695. [He was probably John Androvette.]

Endter, John. He was naturalized in Jamaica 31 July 1738.

Engar, Jost. He was naturalized in Pennsylvania 11–13 Apr. 1743. He was from Chester County.

Engars, Jacob. He was naturalized in Pennsylvania 11–13 Apr. 1743. He was from Chester County.

Engars, Johannes. He was naturalized in Pennsylvania 11–13 Apr. 1743. He was from Chester County.

Engel, Andones. He was naturalized in Pennsylvania 25 Sep. 1758.

Engeland, Theophilus. He was naturalized in Pennsylvania 24 Sep. 1762. He was from Lancaster County.

Engelfried, Johann Wilhelm. He was naturalized in Pennsylvania 24–25 Sep. 1764. He was from Philadelphia.

Engell, Paul. He and his son, Jacob Engell, were naturalized in Pennsylvania 29 Sep. 1709. They were from Philadelphia County.

Enghert, Philip. He was naturalized in Pennsylvania 19 May 1739. He was from Philadelphia County.

England, Abraham. He was naturalized in Maryland 14 Sep. 1763. He was a German.

Engle, Charles. He was naturalized in Maryland 9 Sep. 1761. He was from Frederick County.

Engle, Christian. He was naturalized in Pennsylvania 10 Sep. 1761. He was from Philadelphia County.

Engle, Henrick. He was naturalized in Pennsylvania 10 Sep. 1761. He was from Philadelphia County.

Engle, Jacob. He was naturalized in New Jersey 8 July 1730. He was born in Germany.

Engle, Jacob. He was naturalized in Pennsylvania 11 Apr. 1761. He was from Philadelphia County.

Engle, Paul. He was naturalized in Pennsylvania 10 Apr. 1765. He was from Germantown, Philadelphia County.

Engle, Peter. He was naturalized in Pennsylvania 12 Apr. 1750. He was from Chester County.

Engle, William. He was naturalized in New Jersey 8 July 1730. He was born in Germany.

Englehard, George. He was naturalized in Pennsylvania 11 Apr. 1761. He was from Berks County.

Englehort, Lodowick. He was naturalized in Pennsylvania 11–13 Apr. 1743. He was from Philadelphia County.

Englehort, Nicholas. He was naturalized in Pennsylvania 11–13 Apr. 1743. He was from Philadelphia County.

Englibright, Martin. He was naturalized in Pennsylvania 24 Sep. 1762. He was from York County.

Engleman, Jacob. He was naturalized in New Jersey in 1750. He was from Hunterdon County. He also appeared as Jacob Engelmann.

Engleman, Ludovicus. He was naturalized in Maryland 15 Sep. 1762. He was from Baltimore County.

Engul, Peter. He was naturalized in Maryland 15 Apr. 1763. He was a German from Frederick County.

Enloe, Henry. He was naturalized in Maryland 6 June 1674. He was Dutch. He also appeared as Henry Inloes.

Enriques, Daniel Bueno. He was endenized in England 5 Sep. 1662. He was a Portuguese. He settled in Barbados and was a Jew.

Enriques, Mose Hengas. He was endenized in England 18 Apr. 1664. He was a merchant and a Jew. He settled in Barbados.

Ensminger, John Nicholas. He was naturalized in Pennsylvania 24 Sep. 1759.

Ensminger, Philip. He was naturalized in Pennsylvania 24 Sep. 1762. He was from Berks County.

Ent, Valentine. He was naturalized in New Jersey 20 Aug. 1755.

Enters, John. He was naturalized in New York 24 Apr. 1767. He was a farmer from Westchester County.

Entler, Philip. He was naturalized in Pennsylvania 10 Apr. 1760.

Entzminger, Peter. He was naturalized in Pennsylvania 29 Mar. 1735. He was from Chester County.

Epee, Louis Long. He was an Acadian who took the oath of allegiance in Apr. 1730.

Epler, Adam. He was naturalized in Pennsylvania 24 Sep. 1760. He was from Berks County.

Epler, David. He was naturalized in Pennsylvania 10 Apr. 1767. He was from Earl Township, Lancaster County.

Epler, Jacob. He was naturalized in Pennsylvania 11 Apr. 1761. He was from Berks County.

Epler, Valentine. He was naturalized in Pennsylvania 11 Apr. 1761. He was from Berks County.

Epright, Philip. He was naturalized in Pennsylvania 10 Apr. 1754. He was from Lancaster County.

Eppely, John George. He was naturalized in Pennsylvania 10 Apr. 1760.

Epply, Jacob. He was naturalized in New York 22 Apr. 1761. He was a carman from New York City.

Erb, Jacob. He was naturalized in Pennsylvania 10 & 23 Apr. 1764. He was from Heidelberg Township, Berks County.

Erb, Mary. She was naturalized in Pennsylvania 10 & 23 Apr. 1764. She was from Heidelberg Township, Berks County.

Erb, Peter. He was naturalized in Maryland 12 Sep. 1759.

Erb, Peter. He was naturalized in Maryland 13 Apr. 1763. He was a German from Frederick County.

Erben, Adam. He was naturalized in Pennsylvania 10 & 23 Apr. 1764. He was from Philadelphia.

Erdman, Andrew. He was naturalized in Pennsylvania 11 Apr. 1761. He was from Northampton County.

Erdman, Yost. He was naturalized in Pennsylvania 10 Apr. 1766. He was from Lower Milford Township, Bucks County.

Ergetsinger, Baltus. He was naturalized in New York 3 July 1759.

Erhard, Conrad. He was naturalized in Maryland 19 Oct. 1743.

Erhard, Daniel. He was naturalized in Pennsylvania 10 Sep. 1761. He was from Philadelphia County.

Erickson, Mathew. He was naturalized in Maryland 13 May 1682. He lived in Kent County.

Erishman, Melcor. He was naturalized in Pennsylvania 14 Feb. 1729/30. He was from Lancaster County.

Erlach, Baltzer. He was naturalized in Pennsylvania 10 Apr. 1758.

Ermel, Johannes. He was naturalized in Pennsylvania 10 Apr. 1770. He was from Paradise Township, York County.

Ermel, William. He was naturalized in Pennsylvania 11 Apr. 1761. He was from Berks County.

Ernhold, Martin. He was naturalized in Pennsylvania 11 Apr. 1761. He was from Berks County.

Ernest, Mathias. He was naturalized in New York 16 Dec. 1737.

Ernst, Balthaser. He was naturalized in Pennsylvania 24–25 Sep. 1764. He was from Cheltenham Township, Philadelphia County.

Ernst, Conrad. He was naturalized in Pennsylvania 11 Apr. 1761. He was from Berks County.

Ernst, Johannes. He was naturalized in Pennsylvania 10 Apr. 1760.

Erpff, Philip. He was naturalized in Pennsylvania 24 Sep. 1760. He was from Lancaster County.

Ertell, Valentine. He was naturalized in Pennsylvania 10–12 Apr. 1762. He was from York County.

Eshpaw, John. He was naturalized in Maryland 19 May 1756.

Esmitt, Nicholas. He was naturalized in Jamaica 20 Sep. 1675.

Espenan, Dominique. He was naturalized in Jamaica 4 July 1734.

Espinosa, Abraham. He was endenized in London 3 July 1671. He was a merchant in Jamaica.

Ester, Adam. He was naturalized in Maryland 11 Sep. 1765.

Esterly, George. He was naturalized in Pennsylvania 24 Sep. 1753. He was from Philadelphia County.

Estharn, Jacob. He was naturalized in New York 8–9 Sep. 1715. He was from Lancaster County.

Estleman, Benedict. He was naturalized in Pennsylvania 24 Sep. 1753. He was from Lancaster County.

Eswine, Jacob. He was naturalized in New York 31 Jan. 1715/6. He was from Albany County.

Etchberger, Dewalt. He was naturalized in Maryland 11 May 1774. He was a German.

Etelin, David. He was naturalized in Pennsylvania 24–25 Sep. 1764. He was from Paxton Township, Lancaster County.

Etsal, Samuel. He took the oath to the King 21–26 Oct. 1664 after the conquest of New Netherland.

Etshberger, Jacob. He was naturalized in Pennsylvania 19 May 1739. He was from Lancaster County.

Etter, Daniel. He was naturalized in Pennsylvania 11 Apr. 1749. He was from Philadelphia County.

Etter, Gerhart. He was naturalized in Pennsylvania 24 Sep. 1755. He was from Lancaster County.

Etter, John. He was naturalized in Pennsylvania 10 Apr. 1755. He was from Lancaster County.

Etter, Peter. He was naturalized in Pennsylvania 11 Apr. 1749. He was from Philadelphia County.

Etting, Elijah. He was naturalized in Pennsylvania in Sep.–Oct. 1765. He was a Jew.

Etz, Christian. He was naturalized in New York 20 Mar. 1762.

Evedin, Jno. He took the oath of naturalization in New York 1 Sep. 1687 in Ulster County.

Evelman, William. He was naturalized in New Jersey 23 Oct. 1751.

Evensidell, Jacob. He was naturalized in Pennsylvania 11–13 Apr. 1743. He was from Philadelphia County.

Everhard, Jacob. He was naturalized in Maryland 7 May 1767. He was a German.

Everhott, Christopher. He was naturalized in Maryland 21 Sep. 1762. He was a German.

Everli, Henry. He was naturalized in Pennsylvania 11 Apr. 1752. He was from Lancaster County.

Everlie, John. He was naturalized in Maryland 11 Apr. 1764. He was a German.

Everly, Adam. He was naturalized in Maryland 10 Apr. 1760. He was from Frederick County.

Everly, George. He was naturalized in Pennsylvania 10–12 Apr. 1762. He was from Lancaster County.

Everly, Jacob. He was naturalized in Pennsylvania 24 Sep. 1755.

Everly, Linnard. He was naturalized in Maryland 10 Apr. 1760. He was from Frederick County.

Everly, Peter. He was naturalized in Pennsylvania 24 Sep. 1755.

Everthert, Johanis. He was naturalized in New York 8–9 Sep. 1715. He was from Ulster County.

Evertsa, John. He took the oath of naturalization in New York 1 Sep. 1687 in Ulster County.

Evertsen, Hendrik. He was naturalized in New Castle County, Delaware 21 Feb. 1682/3.

Evertson, Nicholas. He was naturalized in New York 22 Nov. 1715. He was a mariner from New York City.

Evertzen, Dirck. He took the oath to the King 21–26 Oct. 1664 after the conquest of New Netherland.

Evey, Adam. He was naturalized in Pennsylvania 11 Apr. 1763. He was from Philadelphia.

Ewald, Charles. He was naturalized in Pennsylvania 11 Apr. 1751. He was from Philadelphia County.

Exline, Christopher. He was naturalized in Pennsylvania 26–27 Sep. 1743. He was from Philadelphia County.

Eydenuer, Johannes. He was naturalized in Maryland 21 Sep. 1764. He was a German.

Eyes, Nicholas. He was naturalized in Pennsylvania 10–11 Apr. 1745. He was from Philadelphia County.

Eygenaar, Peter. He was naturalized in New York 8–9 Sep. 1715. He was from Ulster County.

Eykeinier, Lawrence. He was naturalized in New Jersey in 1770.

Eyler, Jacob. He was naturalized in Pennsylvania 11 Apr. 1761. He was from Philadelphia County.

Eyler, John. He was naturalized in New Jersey in 1758. He also appeared as Johannes Euler. He had been a resident of West Jersey for 21 years.

Eynklan, John. He was naturalized in Maryland 9 Sep. 1761. He was from Frederick County.

Faass, Philip. He was naturalized in Pennsylvania 24 Sep. 1760. He was from Philadelphia.

Faber, Adam. He was naturalized in Pennsylvania 10 Sep. 1761. He was from Lancaster County.

Faber, Bernhard. He was naturalized in Pennsylvania 10 Sep. 1761. He was from Lancaster County. He was a Moravian.

Fach, George. He was naturalized in New York 20 Dec. 1763.

Fach, Henry. He was naturalized in New York 18 Oct. 1765. He was a shoemaker from New York City.

Fackeroth, Philip. He was naturalized in Pennsylvania 10 Apr. 1765. He was from Oxford Township, Philadelphia County.

Fackler, Jacob. He was naturalized in Pennsylvania 25 Sep. 1750. He was from York County.

Fagett, John. He was endenized in New York 13 May 1699.

Fagh, John. He was naturalized in New York 20 Apr. 1769. He was a cartman from New York City.

Faiger, Paul. He was naturalized in Pennsylvania 24–25 Sep. 1764. He was from Plymouth Township, Philadelphia County.

Fail, Lodewich. He was naturalized in New York 20 Mar. 1762.

Fairday, Adam. He was naturalized in New York 15 Nov. 1715. He was a mariner from New York City.

Fairley, David. He was naturalized in New York 3 July 1759.

Faish, John Jacob. He was naturalized in New Jersey in 1766.

Falcao, Jacob Lopez. He was naturalized in Jamaica 1 July 1755.

Falck, Arnoldt. He was naturalized in New York 8–9 Sep. 1715. He was from Ulster County.

Falck, Johanis. He was naturalized in New York 8–9 Sep. 1715. He was from Ulster County.

Falckenberg, Christian. He was naturalized in New Jersey in 1761. He also appeared as Christopf Fulkenbara.

Falckner, Justus. He was naturalized in New York 25 Oct. 1715. He was a Lutheran minister.

Falk, Nicholas. He was naturalized in New York 3 July 1759.

Falkenham, Samuel. He was naturalized in New York 3 July 1759.

Falker, Adam. He was naturalized in Pennsylvania 20 Apr. 1757.

Falker, Adam. He was naturalized in Pennsylvania 24 Sep. 1762. He was from Lancaster County.

Falkner, Daniel. He was naturalized in Pennsylvania 12 Feb. 1700. He was the son of Daniel Falkner and was born in Langenreinsdorf, Saxony.

Faltz, John. He was naturalized in Pennsylvania 11–12 Apr. 1744. He was from Lancaster County.

Fandy, Frederick. He was naturalized in Pennsylvania 11–13 Apr. 1743. He was from Germantown.

Fannerstick, Detrich. He was naturalized in Pennsylvania 11 Apr. 1761. He was from Lancaster County.

Farber, Philip. He was naturalized in Maryland 11 Sep. 1765. He was a German from Frederick County.

Fardel, John. He took the oath of allegiance at Port Royal, Nova Scotia 16 Aug. 1695.

Farey, John. He was naturalized in Virginia 12 May 1705.

Farlinger, John. He was naturalized in New York 27 Jan. 1770.

Farlow, John. He was naturalized in Jamaica 4 Mar. 1709.

Farmer, Christian. He was naturalized in Maryland 28 Sep. 1763. He was a German from Frederick County.

Farmer, Lewis. He was naturalized in Pennsylvania 11 Apr. 1771. He was from Philadelphia.

Farmer, Peter. He was naturalized in Maryland 11 Apr. 1764. He was a German.

Faro, David Gabay. He was naturalized in Jamaica 27 Nov. 1696. He was a merchant.

Faro, Moses Gabay. He was naturalized in Jamaica 13 Nov. 1696.

Faro, Solomon Gabay. He was endenized in London 29 June 1668. He had his certificate recorded in Jamaica 18 June 1672.

Farren, Henry. He was naturalized in Jamaica 20 Aug. 1695.

Farrow, Henry. He was naturalized in North Carolina 22 Sep. 1763. He was from Rowan County and a German.

Farsnaught, Conrad. He was naturalized in Pennsylvania 11 Apr. 1761. He was from Lancaster County.

Fast, Nicholas. He was naturalized in Maryland 29 Sep. 1762. He was a German from Frederick County.

Faub, Peter. He was naturalized in Maryland 15 Sep. 1762. He was from Baltimore County.

Faubel, Jacob. He was naturalized in Maryland 6 Sep. 1769. He was a German.

Faucks, Michael. He was naturalized in Pennsylvania 10 & 23 Apr. 1764. He was from Philadelphia.

Fauconier, Peter. He, his wife Magdalena Fauconier, son Lewis Fauconier, son Peter Fauconier, and son Isaac Fauconier were endenized in England 24 Mar. 1684/5. They came to New York.

Faugeres, Louis. He was naturalized in New York 20 May 1769. He was a physician from New York City.

Fauire, Daniel. He was naturalized in Virginia 12 May 1705.

Faul, Johannes. He was naturalized in Maryland 12 Sep. 1759. He lived in Baltimore, Maryland.

Faure, Peter. He was naturalized in Virginia 12 May 1705. He was born in France.

Faust, Abraham. He was naturalized in Pennsylvania 11 Apr. 1749. He was from Bucks County.

Faust, John. He was naturalized in Pennsylvania 11 Apr. 1761. He was from Berks County.

Faust, John. He was naturalized in Pennsylvania 24 Sep. 1763. He was from Upper Salford Township, Philadelphia County.

Faust, Philip. He was naturalized in Pennsylvania 11–13 Apr. 1743. He was from Philadelphia County.

Fauz, Jacob. He was naturalized in Maryland 18 Oct. 1743. He was from Cannawatke.

Faver, John. He was naturalized in Richmond County, Virginia 14 Nov. 1711. He was born in France.

Faviere, James. He and his wife, Charlotte Faviere, were naturalized in New York 25 Nov. 1727. He was a merchant from New York City.

Faviers, Charlotte Bouyer. She was naturalized in New York 27 Apr. 1742. She was from New York City.

Favre, Francois. He took the oath of allegiance at Mobile, West Florida 2 Oct. 1764.

Favre, Jean. He took the oath of allegiance at Mobile, West Florida 2 Oct. 1764.

Favre, Simon. He took the oath of allegiance at Mobile, West Florida 2 Oct. 1764.

Favre, Guillaume. He took the oath of allegiance at Mobile, West Florida 2 Oct. 1764.

Fay, Simon. He was naturalized in Maryland 7 May 1767. He was a German from Frederick, Maryland.

Fayssoux, Daniel. He was naturalized in South Carolina 17 Oct. 1741.

Fearday, Abram. He was naturalized in New York 15 Nov. 1715. He was a mariner from New York City.

Fearror, Leonard. He was naturalized in Maryland 20 May 1736. He was from Baltimore County and was born in Germany.

Feather, Bernard. He was naturalized in Pennsylvania 11 Apr. 1761. He was from Lancaster County.

Feather, Peter. He was naturalized in Pennsylvania 24 Sep. 1759.

Feavre, Mariane. She took the oath of allegiance at Mobile, West Florida 2 Oct. 1764.

Feazer, Jacob. He was naturalized in North Carolina 23 Mar. 1763. He was from Rowan County.

Feber, Issac. He, his wife Catherine Feber, and son Abraham Feber were endenized in London 25 Aug. 1708. They came to New York.

Fedder, Harman. He took the oath to the King 21–26 Oct. 1664 after the conquest of New Netherland.

Fedder, Henry. He was naturalized in Pennsylvania 11 Apr. 1761. He was from Lancaster County.

Feder, Johann. He was naturalized in New York 20 Mar. 1762.

Feder, Henrich. He was naturalized in Maryland 12 Sep. 1759.

Federfaaff, Balthasar. He was naturalized in Pennsylvania 11 Apr. 1763. He was from Manheim Township, Lancaster County.

Federolfe, Peter. He was naturalized in Pennsylvania 11–13 Apr. 1743. He was from Philadelphia County.

Feeck, Jacob. He was naturalized in New York 11 Oct. 1715. He was from Albany County.

Feeck, Johannis. He was naturalized in New York 11 Oct. 1715. He was from Albany County.

Feeck, Peter. He was naturalized in New York 11 Oct. 1715. He was from Albany County.

Feedlee, Michael. He was naturalized in Pennsylvania 10 Apr. 1765. He was from New Hannover Township, Philadelphia County.

Feegly, John. He was naturalized in Pennsylvania 11 Apr. 1761. He was from Lancaster County.

Fees, Henrich. He was naturalized in New York 8–9 Sep. 1715. He was from Ulster County.

Feeser, Peter. He was naturalized in Pennsylvania 10 Sep. 1761. He was from Lancaster County.

Feick, Daniel. He was naturalized in New York 16 Feb. 1771.

Feight, Casper. He was naturalized in Pennsylvania 25–27 Sep. 1740. He was from Philadelphia County.

Feinnauer, Andreas. He was naturalized in New York 20 Mar. 1762

Feisser, John. He was naturalized in Pennsylvania 11 Apr. 1761. He was from York County.

Feit, Ulrich. He was naturalized in Maryland 14 Apr. 1762. He was a German.

Feithorn, Michael. He was naturalized in Pennsylvania 24 Sep. 1760. He was from Berks County.

Feitt, Henrick. He was naturalized in Maryland 9 Sep. 1761.

Feix, Peter. He was naturalized in New York 3 July 1759.

Felinck, Peter. He was naturalized in New York 24 July 1724.

Felkner, Henry. He was naturalized in Frederick County, Virginia 14 Aug. 1767.

Fell, Simon. He took the oath to the King 21–26 Oct. 1664 after the conquest of New Netherland.

Fellman, Jacob. He was naturalized in Pennsylvania 11–13 Apr. 1743. He was from Philadelphia County.

Fellon, Peter. He was naturalized in Virginia 12 May 1705.

Felta, Johannes. He was naturalized in New York 31 Dec. 1768.

Felthausen, John George. He was naturalized in New Jersey 14 Dec. 1773. It was disallowed 1 Sep. 1773.

Felthuysen, Christopher. He was naturalized in New York 3 May 1755.

Felthuysen, John Georg. He was naturalized in New York 3 May 1755.

Feltman, John. He was naturalized in Pennsylvania 11 Apr. 1761. He was from Lancaster County.

Felton, Girronimus. He was naturalized in New York in 1740.

Fentermaker, Philip. He was naturalized in Pennsylvania 10 Apr. 1755. He was from Berks County.

Ferberg, Cornelius. He was naturalized in New Jersey 3 June 1763.

Ferdinand, Father. He was a Roman Catholic priest and took the oath of allegiance at Mobile, West Florida 2 Oct. 1764.

Ferdinando, Peter. He and his children, Winifred Ferdinando, Elizabeth Ferdinando, Mary Ferdinando, and Ann Ferdinando, were naturalized in Maryland 18 Oct. 1694. They were from Charles County.

Fereira, David Henriques. He was naturalized in Jamaica 11 Aug. 1752.

Ferie, John. He was naturalized in Pennsylvania 14 Feb. 1729/30. He was from Lancaster County.

Fernandes, Aron Dias. He was naturalized in Jamaica 11 Oct. 1732.

Fernandes, Aron Dias. He was naturalized in Jamaica 26 Feb. 1740/1. He was a Jew.

Fernandes, Benjamin Dias. He was naturalized in Jamaica 2 Nov. 1742.

Fernandes, Benjamin Dias. He was naturalized in Jamaica in Feb. 1748/9. He was a Jew.

Fernandes, Daniel Alves. He was naturalized in Jamaica 25 Aug. 1741. He was a Jew.

Fernandes, David. He was naturalized in Jamaica 29 Nov. 1743. He was a Jew.

Fernandes, Ester Dias. She was naturalized in Jamaica 28 Nov. 1749. She was a Jewess.

Fernandes, Isaac Dias. He was naturalized in Jamaica 26 May 1709.

Fernandes, Moses Dias. He was naturalized in Jamaica 26 May 1709.

Fernandes, Moses Dias. He was naturalized in Jamaica 28 Nov. 1750. He was a Jew.
Fernandez, Abigail. She was naturalized in Jamaica 26 Feb. 1744/5. She was a Jewess.
Fernandez, Solomon Dias. He was naturalized in Jamaica 28 Nov. 1737.
Fernando, Francis. He was naturalized in Jamaica 11 Apr. 1698.
Fernando, John. He was naturalized in Jamaica 20 Oct. 1725.
Fernstermaker, Christian. He was naturalized in Pennsylvania 10 Apr. 1759.
Ferrari, Francis. He was naturalized in Rhode Island in June 1751. He was born in Genoa, Italy. He lived in Newport and was a merchant.
Ferreira, Elias Alves. He was naturalized in Jamaica 26 Mar. 1729.
Ferrick, George. He was naturalized in Jamaica 25 May 1742.
Ferro, David Silva. He was naturalized in Jamaica 24 Dec. 1764.
Ferro, Jacob. He was naturalized in Jamaica 9 Nov. 1713.
Ferro, Jacob, Jr. He was naturalized in Jamaica 18 May 1725.
Ferro, Jacob, Jr. He was naturalized in New York in 1740. He was a Jewish merchant from New York City.
Ferro, Moses. He was naturalized in Jamaica 15 Nov. 1733.
Fersler, Michael. He was naturalized in Pennsylvania in Sep. 1740. He was from Bucks County.
Fertado, David. He was naturalized in Jamaica 10 Dec. 1706.
Fertre, Lewis du. He was naturalized in Virginia 12 May 1705.
Fesler, Felix. He was naturalized in Pennsylvania 25–27 Sep. 1740. He was from Philadelphia.
Fessler, Leonard. He was naturalized in Pennsylvania 10 Apr. 1753. He was from Lancaster County.
Fetter, Henry. He was naturalized in Pennsylvania 11 Apr. 1761. He was from Northampton County.
Fetter, Michael. He was naturalized in Pennsylvania 11 Apr. 1761. He was from Berks County.
Feurtado, Isaac. He was naturalized in Jamaica 24 June 1720.
Feuter, Lewis. He was naturalized in New York 24 Mar. 1772.
Fetzer, Frederick. He was naturalized in Pennsylvania 10–12 Apr. 1762. He was from Philadelphia County.
Fewert, Bartholomew. He was endenized in New York 17 June 1698.
Fickthorn, Andreas. He was naturalized in Pennsylvania 11 Apr. 1763. He was from Berks County.
Ficks, Lawrence. He was naturalized in Pennsylvania 10 Sep. 1761. He was from Reading Township, Berks County.
Fiegel, William. He was naturalized in New York 31 Dec. 1768.
Fiegenheim, Christopher. He was naturalized in New York 18 Oct. 1774. He was from New York City.
Fierre, Daniel. He, his wife Anne Maria Fierre, son Andrew Fierre, and son Johannes Fierre were endenized in London 25 Aug. 1708. They came to New York.
Fiere, Philip. He was naturalized in Pennsylvania 14 Feb. 1729/30. He was from Lancaster County.
Fierst, Martin. He was naturalized in Maryland 14 Sep. 1753.
Fiet, Ulrick. He was naturalized in Maryland 9 Sep. 1761.
Figel, William. He was naturalized in Pennsylvania 24 Sep. 1760. He was from Northampton County.
Figuier, Isaac. He was naturalized in Virginia 12 May 1705.
Filbert, Samuel. He was naturalized in Pennsylvania 24 Sep. 1755. He was from Berks County.
Filbert, Nicholas. He petitioned for denization in North Carolina in 170[?].
Filchmir, Philip. He was naturalized in Pennsylvania 25–26 Sep./4 Oct. 1749. He was from Lancaster County.
Filipzen, Frederick. He took the oath to the King 21–26 Oct. 1664 after the conquest of New Netherland.
Filler, Baltzer. He was naturalized in Pennsylvania 11 Apr. 1763. He was from Frederick Township, Philadelphia County.
Filman, Philip. He was naturalized in Pennsylvania 11 Apr. 1763. He was from Upper Salford Township, Philadelphia County.

Fine, Petter. He was naturalized in New Jersey in 1750. He was from Hunterdon County. He also appeared as Pitter Fein.

Finehoudt, Cornelis. He took the oath of naturalization in New York 1 Sep. 1687 in Ulster County.

Finger, Peter. He was naturalized in Maryland 10 Sep. 1762.

Fink, Alexander, Jr. He was naturalized in New York 18 Oct. 1765. He was a butcher from New York City.

Fink, Sebastian. He was naturalized in Pennsylvania 19 May 1739. He was from Lancaster County.

Fir, Joseph. He was naturalized in Maryland 15 Sep. 1762. He was from Frederick County.

Firestone, Nicholas. He was naturalized in Pennsylvania 11 Apr. 1763. He was from Paradise Township, York County.

Fishborn, Philip. He was naturalized in Pennsylvania 30 May 1772. He was from Tawney Town, Pipe Creek Hundred, Frederick County, Maryland.

Fischer, Georgius. He was naturalized in Maryland 15 Sep. 1762. He was from Baltimore County.

Fischer, Jacob. He was naturalized in Pennsylvania 24–25 Sep. 1764. He was from Cheltenham Township, Philadelphia County.

Fischer, Jacob. He was naturalized in Pennsylvania 11 Apr. 1763. He was from Reading Township, Berks County.

Fischer, Johannes. He and his wife, Maria Barbara Fischer, were endenized in London 25 Aug. 1708. They came to New York.

Fischer, John. He was naturalized in Maryland 15 Sep. 1762. He was from Baltimore County.

Fischer, John. He was naturalized in New York 21 Oct. 1765. He was a tanner from New York City.

Fischer, John. He was naturalized in New York 8 Mar. 1773.

Fischer, Leonhard. He was naturalized in New York 27 July 1774.

Fischer, Michael. He was naturalized in Maryland 15 Sep. 1762. He was from Baltimore County.

Fischer, Michael. He was naturalized in Pennsylvania 10 Sep. 1761. He was from Berks County.

Fishel, John. He was naturalized in Pennsylvania 10 Sep. 1761. He was from Lancaster County.

Fishell, Frederick. He was naturalized in Pennsylvania 11 Apr. 1763. He was from Codorus Township, York County.

Fishell, John. He was naturalized in Pennsylvania 11 Apr. 1761. He was from York County.

Fisher, Adam. He was naturalized in Maryland 23 Apr. 1772. He was a German.

Fisher, Adam. He was naturalized in Pennsylvania 25–27 Sep. 1740. He was from Philadelphia County.

Fisher, Andrew. He was naturalized in Pennsylvania 25–27 Sep. 1740. He was from Philadelphia County.

Fisher, Conrad. He was naturalized in Pennsylvania 11–13 Apr. 1743. He was from Philadelphia County.

Fisher, Frederick. He was naturalized in North Carolina 22 Sep. 1763. He was from Rowan County and a German.

Fisher, Herman. He was naturalized in Pennsylvania 19 May 1739. He was from Philadelphia County.

Fisher, Henry. He was naturalized in New Jersey in 1739. He was born in Germany.

Fisher, Johannes. He was naturalized in New Jersey 6 June 1751.

Fisher, John. He was naturalized in Pennsylvania 11 Apr. 1751. He was from Philadelphia County.

Fisher, John Henry. He was naturalized in Pennsylvania 11 Apr. 1763. He was from Frankford Township, Philadelphia County.

Fisher, John William. He was naturalized in Pennsylvania 25–26 Sep./4 Oct. 1749. He was from Lancaster County.

Fisher, Martin. He and his sons Jacob Fisher and Philip Fisher were naturalized in New Jersey 8 July 1730. They were born in Germany.

Fisher, Martin. He was naturalized in Pennsylvania 10 Apr. 1760.

Fisher, Peter. He was naturalized in Maryland 15 Apr. 1772. He was a German.

Fisher, Peter. He was naturalized in Pennsylvania 24 Sep. 1760. He was from Berks County.

Fisher, Pieter. He was naturalized in New Jersey 8 July 1730.

Fisher, Pieter. He was naturalized in New Jersey 31 July 1740. He was born in Germany.

Fisler, Durst. He was naturalized in Pennsylvania 24 Sep. 1759.

Fisser, Jacob. He was naturalized in Maryland 15 Sep. 1762. He was from Baltimore County.

Fitiar, Herman. He was naturalized in Pennsylvania 10 & 23 Apr. 1764. He was from Reading Township, York County.

Fitler, John George. He was naturalized in Pennsylvania 24 Sep. 1760. He was from Philadelphia County.

Fitler, Valentine. He was naturalized in Maryland 21 Sep. 1762. He was a German.

Fitzer, Peter. He was naturalized in Pennsylvania 11 Apr. 1761. He was from Berks County.

Fix, Adam. He was naturalized in New Jersey in 1766. He was born in Germany and had been in the colony ten years.

Flaake, Arendt. He was naturalized in New York 24 Nov. 1750.

Flack, Andrew. He was naturalized in New Jersey in 1774. He lived in Roxbury Township, Morris County and was born in Germany.

Flack, Matthais. He was naturalized in New Jersey in 1774. He lived in Roxbury Township, Morris County and was born in Germany. He had lived in the colony twenty-four years.

Flag, Paul. He was naturalized in New Jersey 8 July 1730. He was born in Germany.

Flamin, Cornelius. He was naturalized in New York 18 Oct. 1715. He was a baker from New York City.

Flanc, Jean. He was an Acadian who took the oath of allegiance in Apr. 1730.

Flander, Jacob. He was naturalized in New York 31 Dec. 1768.

Flander, Jacob. He was naturalized in New York 8 Mar. 1773.

Flandreau, James. He was naturalized in New York 27 Mar. 1716. He was a yeoman from New Rochelle.

Fleck, Conrad. He was naturalized in Pennsylvania 24 Sep. 1763. He was from Northern Liberties Township, Philadelphia County.

Fleck, George. He was naturalized in Maryland 17 July 1765. He was a German.

Fleese, Michael. He was naturalized in Pennsylvania 24 Sep. 1759.

Flender, Johannes. He was naturalized in Maryland 21 Sep. 1764. He was a German.

Flesher, Peter. He was naturalized in Augusta County, Virginia 22 Aug. 1770.

Fles, David DaSilva. He was naturalized in Jamaica 27 Nov. 1744. He was a Jew.

Flesher, Peter. He was naturalized in Augusta County, Virginia 22 Aug. 1770.

Fleshman, Peter. He was naturalized in Orange County, Virginia 28 Jan. 1742/3. He was a German.

Fleuriau, Daniel. He was endenized in New York 29 July 1686.

Fleuriau, Pierre. He was endenized in New York 29 July 1686.

Fleurison, Lewis. He was naturalized in Jamaica 10 Apr. 1694.

Fleury, Abraham. He was born at Tours, France, the son of Charles Fleury and Madeleine Soupzmain. His wife was Marianne Fleury, the widow of Jacques Dugue; she was born in Paris, France. His stepdaughter, Marianne Dugue, was born in South Carolina. They were naturalized *ca.* 1696.

Fleury, Isaac. He was born at Tours, France, the son of Charles Fleury and Medalaine Soubmain. He was naturalized in South Carolina *ca.* 1696.

Fliegel, Valentine. He was naturalized in Maryland 11 Apr. 1759.

Flick, Peter. He was naturalized in Pennsylvania 11 Apr. 1763. He was from Heidelberg Township, Berks County.

Flickinger, Ulrick. He was naturalized in Pennsylvania 11 Apr. 1761. He was from Northampton County.

Flood, Michael. He was naturalized in Maryland 11 Sep. 1765.

Floras, Michael. He was naturalized in Pennsylvania 10 Apr. 1755. He was from Northampton County.

Flores, Solomon. He was naturalized in Jamaica 15 Nov. 1733.

Flournois, Jacob. He was naturalized in Virginia 12 May 1705.

Flournoy, Francois. He was naturalized in Virginia 12 May 1705.

Flournoy, Jacques. He was naturalized in Virginia 12 May 1705.

Fluck, Jacob. He was naturalized in Maryland 10 Apr. 1760. He was from Frederick County.

Flunean, George. He was naturalized in New York 27 Jan. 1770.

Fluri, Abraham. He was naturalized in Pennsylvania 11–13 Apr. 1743. He was from Philadelphia County.

Focken, John. He took the oath of naturalization in New York 1 Sep. 1687 in Ulster County.

Focks, Jacob. He was naturalized in Pennsylvania 24 Sep. 1760. He was from Philadelphia.

Fockler, John. He was naturalized in Pennsylvania 10–12 Apr. 1762. He was from York County.

Foeshay, John Luca. He was naturalized in New York 24 Mar. 1772.

Foesig, Philip Jacob. He was naturalized in Pennsylvania 24 Sep. 1763. He was from Reading Township, Berks County.

Foex, Johan Willem. He was naturalized in New York 31 Jan. 1715/6. He was from Albany County.

Fogelson, George. He was naturalized in Maryland 15 Apr. 1771. He was a German.

Fogeraut, Marie. She was the widow of Moyse Brigaud and was born in LaTremblade, France. She was naturalized in South Carolina ca. 1696. She also appeared as Marie Fougerout.

Fogleman, George. He was naturalized in North Carolina 23 Mar. 1763. He was from Rowan County.

Fogleman, Malachi. He was naturalized in North Carolina 22 Sep. 1763. He was from Rowan County and a German.

Folemir, Michael. He was naturalized in Pennsylvania 10 Sep. 1761. He was from Berks County.

Folk, Nicholas. He was naturalized in New York 26 Oct. 1764. He was a chirurgeon from New York City.

Folk, Peter. He was naturalized in Pennsylvania 24 Sep. 1746. He was from Lancaster County.

Folkers, Lambertus. He was naturalized in Nova Scotia 10 July 1758.

Folland, Johan Phillip. He was naturalized in New York 8–9 Sep. 1715. He was from Ulster County.

Folmar, Jacob. He was naturalized in Pennsylvania 25 Sep. 1752. He was from Berks County.

Folmer, Johannes. He was naturalized in New York 26 Apr. 1773. He was from Rhinebeck.

Foltz, Matthias. He was naturalized in Pennsylvania 11 Apr. 1761. He was from Philadelphia County.

Folwyter, Henry. He was naturalized in Maryland 15 Apr. 1761.

Foncequa, Isaac DaSilva. He was naturalized in Jamaica 5 Nov. 1753.

Fonerd, Daniel. He was a native of Switzerland and sought naturalization in Maryland 2 Apr. 1735. He was an inhabitant of Anne Arundel County.

Fonjall, Peter. He was naturalized in Virginia 12 May 1705. He also appeared as Peter Fonyeilles.

Fontaine, Jacques. He took the oath of allegiance in Boswijck, Kings County, New York 26–30 Sep. 1687. He was a native of the colony.

Fontaine, Johannis. He took the oath of allegiance in Boswijck, Kings County, New York 26–30 Sep. 1687. He was a native of the colony.

Fontaine, Louis. He was an Acadian and took the oath to George II at Annapolis River, Nova Scotia in Dec. 1729.

Fontaine, Louis. He was an Acadian who took the oath of allegiance in Apr. 1730.

Fonvielle, John. He was naturalized in Virginia 12 May 1705.

Fookes, David. He was naturalized in Pennsylvania 24–25 Sep./5 Oct. 1767. He was from Reading Township, Berks County.

Fookes, Peter. He was naturalized in Pennsylvania 24–25 Sep./5 Oct. 1767. He was from Macungy Township, Northampton County.

Forbes, Alexander. He was naturalized in Maryland 19 Oct. 1695. He lived in Talbot County.

Ford, Lawrence. He was naturalized in Jamaica 2 Dec. 1712.

Foret, Alexandre. He was an Acadian and took the oath of allegiance in Apr. 1730.

Foret, Charles. He was an Acadian and took the oath of allegiance in Apr. 1730.

Foret, Jacques. He was an Acadian and took the oath of allegiance in Apr. 1730.

Foret, Jacques. He was an Acadian and took the oath of allegiance in Apr. 1730.

Foret, Jacques. He was an Acadian and took the oath of allegiance in Apr. 1730.

Foret, Jean. He was an Acadian and took the oath of allegiance in Apr. 1730.

Foret, Jean. He was an Acadian and took the oath of allegiance in Apr. 1730.

Foret, Jean Baptiste. He was an Acadian who took the oath of allegiance in Apr. 1730.

Foret, Joseph. He was an Acadian who took the oath of allegiance in Apr. 1730.

Foret, Michel. He was an Acadian who took the oath of allegiance in Apr. 1730.

Foret, Pierre. He was an Acadian and took the oath of allegiance in Apr. 1730.

Forett, François. He was an Acadian and took the oath to George II at Annapolis River, Nova Scotia in Dec. 1729.

Forett, Jacques. He was an Acadian and took the oath to George II at Annapolis River, Nova Scotia in Dec. 1729.

Forett, Mathieu. He was an Acadian and took the oath to George II at Annapolis River, Nova Scotia in Dec. 1729.

Forgue, Francis. He was naturalized in Connecticut in May 1774 so that his son, Francis Forgue who was born in Connecticut, could inherit his realty and that the said Francis Forgue, Sr. could have the said purchases confirmed. He lived in Fairfield. He was born in Toulouse, France.

Forian, Peter. He was naturalized in Lunenburg County, Virginia 1 Sep. 1746.

Former, Christian. He was naturalized in New York 3 Jan. 1715/6. He was from Albany County.

Forner, John. He was naturalized in New York 29 July 1773. He was from Albany County.

Forneret, Louis. He took the oath of allegiance at Mobile, West Florida 2 Oct. 1764.

Forney, Marcus. He was naturalized in Pennsylvania 10 Apr. 1753. He was from York County.

Forney, Nicholas. He was naturalized in Pennsylvania 29–30 May 1772. He was from Manheim Township, York County.

Forneyee, John. He was naturalized in New York 8 Mar. 1773.

Forquerand, John. He was naturalized in Virginia 17 May 1705.

Forrer, Johannes. He was naturalized in Pennsylvania 10 Apr. 1755. He was from Berks County.

Forrest, Anthony. He was naturalized in Pennsylvania 10 Apr. 1758.

Forsben, Hendrick Egbertsen. He expressed his desire to be naturalized in New Castle County, Delaware 21 Feb. 1682/3.

Forsberg, Nicholas. He was naturalized in Pennsylvania 10 & 23 Apr. 1764. He was from Philadelphia.

Forsman, Jacob. He was naturalized in New Jersey 31 July 1740. He was from Sweden.

Forster, Peter. He was naturalized in New York 27 Jan. 1770.

Fort, Andreas. He was naturalized in New York 16 Feb. 1771.

Fortine, Catherine. She was naturalized in Maryland 11 Sep. 1765. She was a German and lived in Frederick, Maryland.

Fortnee, Michael. He was naturalized in Pennsylvania 24 Sep. 1753. He was from Lancaster County.

Fortune, Lewis. He was naturalized in Jamaica 26 May 1742. He was a Jew.

Fousa, Jean Batiste. He was an Acadian who took the oath to the King at the Mines, Pisiquit 31 Oct. 1727.

Foss, Philip. He was naturalized in Maryland 13 Apr. 1763. He was a German.

Foster, Andrew. He was naturalized in Jamaica 11 Nov. 1718.

Foster, Jacob Christopher. He was naturalized in New York 6 Dec. 1746.

Fotler, Jacob. He was naturalized in Pennsylvania 24–25 Sep. 1764. He was from Heidelberg Township, Lancaster County.

Foub, Nicholas. He was naturalized in Maryland 29 Sep. 1762. He was a German from Frederick County.

Foulke, John Wilhelm. He was naturalized in Pennsylvania 24 Sep. 1762. He was from Berks County.

Fountain, John. He was naturalized in Virginia 17 Mar. 1692.

Fountaine, Nicholas. He was made a denizen in Maryland 13 July 1665. He was late of Virginia. He also appeared as Nicholas Fontaine. He was French and lived in Somerset County.

Fourestier, Charles. He was naturalized in New York 16 Aug. 1715. He was a yeoman from New Rochelle.

Fourrestier, Charles. He was endenized in New York 6 Feb. 1695/6.

Fourrestier, Theophile. He was endenized in New York 6 Feb. 1695/6.

Foushee, James. He was naturalized in Richmond County, Virginia 6 Feb. 1711. He was a natural-born subject of the King of France.

Foussier, Philip. He was endenized in London in Aug. 1669. He was from Barbados. He was born in Rochelle, France of Protestant parents.

Fout, Baldus. He and his children, Baldus Fout, Maria Fout, and Catherine Fout, were naturalized in Maryland 4 June 1740. He was from Prince George's County and was born in Germany.

Fout, Jacob. He and his children, Jacob Fout, Henry Fout, Baldus Fout, Eve Fout, Mary Fout, Margarett Fout, and Catherine Fout, were naturalized in Maryland 4 June 1740. He was from Prince George's County and was born in Germany.

Foutin, Ann Mary. She was naturalized in Maryland 15 Apr. 1761. She was a German from Frederick, Maryland.

Fowcate, Peter. He was naturalized in Maryland 17 Sep. 1681.

Fox, Conrad. He was naturalized in Pennsylvania 10 Apr. 1767. He was from Frederick County, Maryland.

Fox, Henry. He was naturalized in Pennsylvania 24–25 Sep. 1764. He was from Douglass Township, Philadelphia County.

Fox, Jacob. He was naturalized in Pennsylvania 10–12 Apr. 1762. He was from Berks County.

Fox, John Jacob. He was naturalized in Pennsylvania 11 Apr. 1749. He was from Philadelphia County.

Fox, John Peter. He was naturalized in New Jersey 20 Aug. 1755.

Fox, Leonard. He was naturalized in New Jersey 28 Apr. 1762.

Fox, Mathias. He was naturalized in Maryland 15 Apr. 1771. He was a German.

Fox, Peter. He was naturalized in New York 24 Mar. 1762.

Fox, William. He was naturalized in Pennsylvania 24–25 Sep. 1764. He was from Philadelphia.

Foy, Michael. He was naturalized in Maryland 17 July 1765. He was a German.

Frachsell, Peter. He was naturalized in Pennsylvania 10 Apr. 1742. He was from Bucks County.

Frachsell, Peter, Jr. He was naturalized in Pennsylvania 10 Apr. 1742. He was from Bucks County.

Fraeger, Johann Georg. He was naturalized in Maryland 10 Sep. 1760.

Frailey, Frederick. He was naturalized in Rowan County, North Carolina 24 Sep. 1766.

France, Arrie. He took the oath of naturalization in New York 1 Sep. 1687 in Ulster County.

France, Jacob. He was naturalized in New York 24 Mar. 1772.

France, Solomon. He was naturalized in Jamaica 2 Dec. 1717.

Francis, John. He was naturalized in Jamaica 13 Aug. 1729.

Francis, Nicholas. He was naturalized in Pennsylvania 24 Sep. 1759.

Francis, Peter. He was naturalized in Jamaica 24 July 1708.

Francis, Stephen. He was naturalized in Maryland 11 June 1697. He was Italian.

Francisco, Peter. He took the oath of allegiance in New Uijtrceht, Kings County, New York 26–30 Sep. 1687. He was a native of the colony.

Franciscus, Christopher. He was naturalized 14 Feb. 1729/30. He was from Lancaster County.

Franck, Conrad. He was naturalized in New York 16 Dec. 1737.

Franck, Frederick. He was naturalized in New York 3 July 1759.

Franck, Johanis. He was naturalized in New York 8–9 Sep. 1715. He was from Ulster County.

Francken, Henry Andrew. He was naturalized in Jamaica 2 Mar. 1758.

Francken, Henry Andrew. He was naturalized in New York 3 Feb. 1768.

Franckford, Abraham. He took the oath of naturalization in New York 1 Sep. 1687 in Ulster County.

Franckfurter, Nicholas. He was naturalized in Maryland 6 Sep. 1769. He was a German.

Franckleberger, John. He was naturalized in Pennsylvania 10 Apr. 1753. He was from York County.

Franco, Abraham. He was endenized in England 3 June 1699. He settled in Barbados and was a Jew.

Francois, Joseph. He was an Acadian and took the oath to the King at the Mines, Pisiquit, Nova Scotia 31 Oct. 1727.

Frank, Andries. He was naturalized in New York 20 Mar. 1762.

Frank, Christophel. He was naturalized in New York 20 Mar. 1762.

Frank, Frederick. He was naturalized in New York 11 Sep. 1761.

Frank, Henry. He was naturalized in Pennsylvania 24 Sep. 1763. He was from Berwick Township, Lancaster County.

Frank, Jacob. He was naturalized in Maryland in Apr. 1749. He was from Frederick County.

Frank, Jacob. He was naturalized in Pennsylvania 11 Apr. 1749. He was from Philadelphia County.

Frank, Jacob. He was naturalized in Pennsylvania 24–25 Sep. 1764. He was from Germantown, Philadelphia County.

Frank, John Adam. He was naturalized in New York 16 Feb. 1771.

Frank, John Bernard. He was naturalized in Pennsylvania 11 Apr. 1761. He was from Lancaster County.

Frank, Michael. He was naturalized in Maryland 15 Sep. 1762. He was from Frederick County.

Frank, Peter. He was naturalized in Maryland 25 Sep. 1772.

Frank, Philip Lawrence. He was naturalized in Maryland 25 Sep. 1772.

Frank, Stephanus. He was naturalized in New York 11 Sep. 1761.

Frank, William. He was naturalized in North Carolina 22 Sep. 1763. He was from Rowan County and a German.

Frankhauser, Michael. He was naturalized in Pennsylvania 11 Apr. 1763. He was from Brecknock Township, Berks County.

Frankhouser, Peter. He was naturalized in Pennsylvania 11 Apr. 1761. He was from Lancaster County.

Franklin, Christian. He was naturalized in New York 31 Dec. 1761.

Franks, H. B. He was naturalized in Pennsylvania 10 Apr. 1755. He was from York County. He was a Jew.

Franks, Moses Benjamin. He was naturalized in New York 18 Oct. 1748. He was a Jew from New York City.

Franse, Abraham. He was naturalized in Jamaica 30 Mar. 1709.

Fransen, Hendrick. He expressed his desire to be naturalized in New Castle County, Delaware 21 Feb. 1682/3.

Franssen, Joost. He took the oath of allegiance in Breucklijn, Kings County, New York 26–30 Sep. 1687. He had been in the colony 33 years.

Fransz, Thys. He took the oath of allegiance in Orange County, New York 26 Sep. 1687.

Frantz, Jacob. He was naturalized in Pennsylvania 11 Apr. 1763. He was from Philadelphia.

Fraunveller, John. He was naturalized in Pennsylvania 10–12 Apr. 1762. He was from Berks County.

Fravell, Henry. He was naturalized in Frederick County, Virginia 12 Aug. 1767.

Frazon, Samuel Joseph. He was endenized in England 9 Mar. 1693/4. He settled in Barbados.

Freas, Frederick. He was naturalized in New Jersey in 1750. He was from Hunterdon County.

Freas, Philib. He was naturalized in New Jersey in 1750. He was from Hunterdon County. [He could be identical with Philip Eick.]

Freck, Philip. He was naturalized in Maryland 11 Sep. 1765. He was a German from Frederick County.

Frederick, Andrew. He was naturalized in Pennsylvania 11 Apr. 1763. He was from York Township, York County.

Frederick, Andrew. He was naturalized in New York 17 Apr. 1760. He was a baker from New York City.

Frederick, George. He was naturalized in Pennsylvania 10 Apr. 1760.

Frederick, George. He was naturalized in Pennsylvania 11 Apr. 1761. He was from Philadelphia County.

Frederick, George. He was naturalized in Pennsylvania 24 Sep. 1763. He was from Earl Township, Lancaster County.

Frederick, John. He was naturalized in Pennsylvania 11–12 Apr. 1744. He was from Philadelphia County.

Frederick, John. He was naturalized in Pennsylvania 14 Feb. 1729/30. He was from Lancaster County.

Frederick, Michael. He was naturalized in Pennsylvania 24 Sep. 1763. He was from Douglas Township, Philadelphia County.

Frederick, Phillip. He was naturalized in New York 11 Sep. 1761.

Fredericks, Hans. He was naturalized in New York 11 Sep. 1761.

Fredericks, Jan. He took the oath of allegiance in Breucklijn, Kings County, New York 26–30 Sep. 1687. He had been in the colony 35 years.

Freed, Peter. He was naturalized in Pennsylvania 10 Apr. 1765. He was from York Township, York County.

Freeh, Jacob. He was naturalized in Pennsylvania 19 May 1739. He was from Philadelphia County.

Freeman, Catherine. She was naturalized in Jamaica 5 Jan. 1736/7. She was a free Negro.

Freeman, Henry. He was naturalized in Maryland 6 June 1674. He was Swedish.

Freeman, Prudence. She was naturalized in Jamaica 24 Jan. 1718/9. She was a free Negro woman.

Freeman, Valentine. He was naturalized in Pennsylvania 25 Sep. 1744. He was from Lancaster County.

Freemont, Phillip. He was naturalized in Jamaica 31 July 1729.

Frees, Frederick. He was naturalized in Pennsylvania 24 Sep. 1771. He was from Frederick County, Virginia.

Freest, Simon. He was naturalized in Pennsylvania 10 Sep. 1761. He was from Berks County.

Freich, Jacob. He was naturalized in Pennsylvania 24 Sep. 1770. He was from Nockamixon, Bucks County.

Freidenbergh, Charles. He was naturalized in New York 20 May 1769.

Freidrick, Peter. He was naturalized in New York 3 July 1759.

Frelick, Jacob. He was naturalized in Pennsylvania 24–25 Sep. 1764. He was from Lancaster Township, Lancaster County.

Frely, Leonard. He was naturalized in Pennsylvania 11 Apr. 1761. He was from Philadelphia County.

French, George. He was naturalized in Maryland 20 Oct. 1747.

French, John. He was naturalized in Pennsylvania 29–30 May 1772. He was from Colebrookdale Township, Berks County.

Frere, Hugo. He was naturalized in New York 8–9 Sep. 1715. He was from Ulster County.

Freri, Hiugo, Sr. He took the oath of naturalization in New York 1 Sep. 1687 in Ulster County.

Freri, Hiugo, Jr. He took the oath of naturalization in New York 1 Sep. 1687 in Ulster County.

Fretcher, John. He was naturalized in New York 8 Mar. 1773.

Frett, Martin. He was naturalized in Antigua 12 Dec. 1700.

Frett, Peter. He was naturalized in Pennsylvania 11 Apr. 1763. He was from Windsor Township, York County.

Fretz, Ernst. He was naturalized in New York 31 Dec. 1761.

Fretz, Jacob. He was naturalized in New York 31 Dec. 1761.

Frey, George. He was naturalized in Maryland 11 Apr. 1764. He was a German.

Frey, Jacob. He was naturalized in Pennsylvania 19 May 1739. He was from Philadelphia County.

Frey, John. He was naturalized in Pennsylvania in Sep. 1740. He was from Bucks County.

Freys, Frederrich. He was naturalized in New Jersey in 1750. He was from Hunterdon County. [He also appeared as Frederick Freas.]

Frick, Conrad. He was naturalized in Pennsylvania 25–26 Sep./4 Oct. 1749. He was from Philadelphia County.

Frick, Frederick William. He was naturalized in Pennsylvania 10–12 Apr. 1762. He was from Berks County.

Frick, Jacob. He was naturalized in Pennsylvania 24 Sep. 1762. He was from Bucks County.

Fried, Johannes. He was naturalized in Pennsylvania 6 Feb. 1730/1. He was from Philadelphia County.

Fried, Paul. He was naturalized in Pennsylvania 6 Feb. 1730/1. He was from Philadelphia County.

Friehout, Abraham. He was naturalized in New York 20 Dec. 1763.

Frierich, Johan Adam. He was naturalized in New York 8–9 Sep. 1715. He was from Ulster County.

Fries, Jacob. He was naturalized in New Jersey in 1757. He was born in Germany. He had been in the colony 19 years.

Fries, Jacob. He was naturalized in Pennsylvania 24 Sep. 1762. He was from Northampton County.

Fries, Jan. He took the oath to the King 21–26 Oct. 1664 after the conquest of New Netherland.

Fries, Johannes. He was naturalized in New Jersey in 1764. He was born in Germany and had been in New Jersey thirteen years.

Fries, John, Jr. He was naturalized in New Jersey in 1764.

Fries, Martin. He sought naturalization in New Jersey in the 18th century.

Fries, Peter. He was naturalized in Pennsylvania 24 Sep. 1762. He was from Northampton County.

Frietshy, Leonard. He was naturalized in Pennsylvania 11 Apr. 1763. He was from Lower Saucon Township, Northampton County.

Frilich, Stephen. He was naturalized in New York 8–9 Sep. 1715. He was from Ulster County.

Fringer, Nicholas. He was naturalized in Pennsylvania 11 Apr. 1761. He was from Lancaster County.

Fritz, Christopher. He was naturalized in New York 17 Oct. 1744. He was a farmer from Dutchess County.

Fritz, Elias. He was naturalized in New York 21 Apr. 1757. He was a yeoman from New York City.

Fritz, Friederich. He sought naturalization in New Jersey in the 18th century.

Fritz, Hendrick. He was naturalized in New York 3 May 1755.

Fritz, John. He was naturalized in Pennsylvania 11 Apr. 1771. He was from Douglass Township, Philadelphia County.

Fritz, John. He was naturalized in Pennsylvania 24–25 Sep. 1764. He was from Southwark Township, Philadelphia County.

Fritz, John Martin. He was naturalized in Pennsylvania 10 Sep. 1761. He was from Berks County.

Fritz, Melchior. He was naturalized in Pennsylvania 11 Apr. 1763. He was from Richmond Township, Berks County.

Friva, Frans. He was naturalized in New York 11 Sep. 1761.

Frois, Isaac. He was naturalized in Jamaica 6 Jan. 1731/2.

Froise, Jacob. He was naturalized in Jamaica 10 Mar. 1685/6.

Froistour, John. He was naturalized in Jamaica 2[? torn] Oct. 1738.

Frolick, Christian. He was naturalized in New York 21 Apr. 1763. He was a sugar baker from New York City.

Frollig, Henrich. He was naturalized in New York 8–9 Sep. 1715. He was from Ulster County.

Frollig, Vallindin. He was naturalized in New York 8–9 Sep. 1715. He was from Ulster County.

From, Frederick. He was naturalized in Pennsylvania 10 Apr. 1760.

Fromaget, Charles. He was born at Chatelerault, France, the son of Charles Fromaget and Marie LeNain. He was naturalized in South Carolina 10 Mar. 1696/7. He was a planter.

Fromar, Paul. He was naturalized in Frederick County, Virginia 4 Aug. 1747.

Frosch, Sebastian. He was naturalized in Maryland 11 Apr. 1764. He was a German.

Frosh, George. He was naturalized in Maryland 13 Apr. 1763. He was a German.

Froshaur, John. He was naturalized in Maryland 15 Apr. 1761.

Frushower, Jacob. He was naturalized in Maryland 24 Sep. 1765. He was a German.

Frutz, Jacob. He was naturalized in Pennsylvania 10 Sep. 1761. He was from Lancaster County.

Fry, Christian. He was naturalized in Pennsylvania 24–25 Sep. 1764. He was from Springfield Township, Berks County.

Fry, Christopher. He was naturalized in Pennsylvania 24 Sep. 1755. He was from Lancaster County.

Fry, Francis. He was naturalized in New York 16 Feb. 1771.

Fry, Francis. He was naturalized in New York 8 Mar. 1773.

Fry, Godfrey. He was naturalized in Pennsylvania 24 Sep. 1762. He was from York County.

Fry, Henry. He was naturalized in Maryland 18 Sep. 1765. He was a German.

Fry, Henry. He was naturalized in Pennsylvania 10–12 Apr. 1762. He was from Berks County.

Fry, Jacob. He was naturalized in Pennsylvania 10 Sep. 1761. He was from Lancaster County.

Fry, Jacob. He was naturalized in New York 24 Oct. 1757.

Fry, Jacob. He was naturalized in Pennsylvania 10–12 Apr. 1762. He was from Northampton County.

Fry, Jacob. He was naturalized in New York 20 Mar. 1762.

Fry, Jacob. He was naturalized in Pennsylvania 24 Sep. 1763. He was from Brecknock Township, Berks County.

Fry, John. He was naturalized in Pennsylvania 11 Apr. 1763. He was from Philadelphia.

Fry, Jurry. He was naturalized in New York 20 Mar. 1763.

Fry, Martin. He was naturalized in Pennsylvania 10 & 23 Apr. 1764. He was from Strasburg Township, York County.

Fry, Negro. He was naturalized in Pennsylvania 10 Apr. 1759.

Fry, Rudolph. He was naturalized in Pennsylvania 10 Sep. 1761. He was from Philadelphia County.

Fry, Valentine. He was naturalized in Pennsylvania 24 Sep. 1763. He was from Heidelberg Township, Berks County.

Fryday, John George. He was naturalized in New York 19 Jan. 1774. He was a schoolmaster from New York City.

Frye, Jacob. He was naturalized in Pennsylvania 11 Apr. 1741. He was from Philadelphia County.

Fryemoet, John Caspar. He was naturalized in New York 15 Oct. 1765. He was a clergyman.

Frymeyer, Michiel. He was naturalized in New York 13 Mar. 1715/6. He was from Albany County.

Fuckerodt, George. He was naturalized in Pennsylvania 20 & 23 Apr. 1764. He was from Oxford Township, Philadelphia County.

Fuckerodt, Jacob. He was naturalized in Pennsylvania 10 & 23 Apr. 1764. He was from Oxford Township, Philadelphia County.

Fucks, Andreas. He was naturalized in Pennsylvania 10–12 Apr. 1762. He was from Berks County.

Fucks, Conrad. He was naturalized in Pennsylvania 24 Sep. 1762. He was from Northampton County.

Fucks, John George. He was naturalized in Maryland 10 Sep. 1761.

Fuertado, Isaac. He was naturalized in Jamaica 25 Nov. 1740. He was a Jew.

Fuertado, Isaac Henriques. He was naturalized in Jamaica 29 Apr. 1745.

Fueter, Daniel Christian. He was naturalized in New York 3 July 1759. He was also naturalized 31 July 1765. He was a silversmith from New York City.

Fueter, Lewis. He was naturalized in New York 16 Feb. 1771. He was a silversmith from New York City.

Fuhrer, Johann. He was naturalized in New York 8–9 Sep. 1715. He was from Ulster County.

Furhre, Valedien. He was naturalized in New York 8–9 Sep. 1715. He was from Ulster County.

Fulbright, William. He was naturalized in Pennsylvania 24 Sep. 1762. He was from Northampton County.

Fulkemer, John Martin. He was naturalized in New Jersey 6 Dec. 1769.

Fullwider, Jacob. He was naturalized in North Carolina 22 Sep. 1763. He was from Rowan County and a German.

Fulwevez, Gerrit. He took the oath to the King 21–26 Oct. 1664 after the conquest of New Netherland.

Funck, Jacob. He was naturalized in New York 17 Oct. 1753. He was a baker from New York City.

Funk, Christopher. He was naturalized in Pennsylvania 6 Feb. 1730/1. He was from Philadelphia County.

Funk, Henry. He was naturalized in Maryland 10 Sep. 1762.

Funk, Henry. He was naturalized in Pennsylvania 14 Feb. 1729/30. He was from Lancaster County.

Funk, Jacob. He was naturalized in Pennsylvania 14 Feb. 1729/30. He was from Lancaster County.

Funk, John. He was naturalized in Pennsylvania 14 Feb. 1729/30. He was from Lancaster County.

Funk, Joseph. He was naturalized in Pennsylvania 10 Apr. 1765. He was from Northern Liberties Township, Philadelphia County.

Funk, Martin. He was naturalized in Pennsylvania 11 Apr. 1761. He was from Lancaster County.

Funk, Michael. He was naturalized in Maryland 11 Sep. 1760. He lived in Frederick County and was a German.

Funnell, Andrew. He was admitted into the colony of Massachusetts 1 Feb. 1691. He was French.

Funnell, Benjamin. He was admitted into the colony of Massachusetts 1 Feb. 1691. He was French.

Funnell, John. He was admitted into the colony of Massachusetts 1 Feb. 1691. He was French.

Furney, Adam. He and his children, Mark Furney, Nicholas Furney, Philip Furney, Charlott Furney, Mary Furney, and Clara Furney, were naturalized in Maryland 4 June 1738. He was from Baltimore County and was born in Germany.

Furre, John. He became a denizen in North Carolina 7 Oct. 1697. He was a native of France and came with his father, Peter Furre, to North Carolina when he was very young. His father was a Protestant and was compelled to flee from his country. His father was dead.

Furry, John. He was naturalized in Pennsylvania 25 Sep. 1750. He was from Lancaster County.

Furtado, David Mendez. He was naturalized in Jamaica 15 Mar. 1721/2.

Furtado, David Orobio. He was naturalized in Jamaica 27 Mar. 1738/9.

Furtado, Ester Henriques. She was naturalized in Jamaica 23 Feb. 1747/8. She was a Jewess.

Furtado, Isaac Henriques. He was naturalized in Jamaica 28 Nov. 1750. He was a Jew.

Furtado, Isaac Jesuron. He was naturalized in Jamaica 16 Mar. 1724.

Furtado, Ishac Aboab. He was endenized in England 10 Dec. 1695. He settled in Barbados and was a Jew. He also appeared as Isha Aboab.

Furtado, Jacob Mendes. He was naturalized in Jamaica 30 Dec. 1717.

Furtado, Judith Orobio. She was naturalized in Jamaica 27 Aug. 1745. She was a Jewess.

Furtado, Rachael Orobio. She was naturalized in Jamaica 31 May 1743. She was a Jewess.

Fux, George. He was naturalized in Maryland 13 Oct. 1756. He was German and a Mennonist.

Fuzbando, Michael. He was naturalized in Jamaica 1 June 1710.

Gaab, George Adam. He was naturalized in Pennsylvania 11 Apr. 1761. He was from Philadelphia County.

Gaag, Adam. He was naturalized in Maryland 10 Sep. 1760.

Gabaud, Stephen. He was naturalized in Jamaica 29 Apr. 1716. He was a surgeon.

Gabay, Abraham David. He was naturalized in Jamaica 2 Oct. 1678.

Gabay, Isaac. He was endenized in New York 15 June 1696.

Gabay, Jacob. He was naturalized in Jamaica 21 Feb. 1703.

Gabay, Samuel. He was naturalized in Jamaica 27 Jan. 1684/5.

Gabel, Peter. He was naturalized in Pennsylvania 24 Sep. 1763. He was from New Hannover Township, Philadelphia County.

Gabriel, Benjamin Rodriques. He was naturalized in Jamaica 26 Feb. 1740/1. He was a Jew.

Gabry, Timotheus. He took the oath to the King 21–26 Oct. 1664 after the conquest of New Netherland.

Gaby, Rachell. She was naturalized in Jamaica 29 Dec. 1696. She was a widow.

Gack, Philip. He was naturalized in Maryland 15 Apr. 1761.

Gaebel, Henry. He was naturalized in Pennsylvania 10 Sep. 1761. He was from Lancaster County.

Gaerber, John. He was naturalized in Pennsylvania 24 Sep. 1762. He was from Berks County.

Gafft, George. He was naturalized in Pennsylvania 11 Apr. 1761. He was from York County.

Gaillard, Joachin. He was the son of Jean Gaillard and Marie Gaillard, of Montpellier, Languedoc, France. His wife was Ester Gaillard, the daughter of Andre Paparel and Caterine Paparel, of Bouin, Forest, France. Their children were Jean Gaillard and Pierre Gaillard. They were naturalized in South Carolina ca. 1696.

Gaillard, Pierre. He was born at Cherneux, Poitou, France, the son of Pierre Gaillard and Jacquete Jolain. His wife was Elizabeth Leclair. Their daughter, Clermonde Gaillard, was born in South Carolina. Elizabeth Leclair's two children by her first husband, Jean Melet, were Elizabet Melet and Marthe Melet, and they were born in New York. They were naturalized in South Carolina 10 Mar. 1696/7. He was a clockmaker.

Gaitz, Baltzer. He was naturalized in Pennsylvania 24 Sep. 1762. He was from Lancaster County.

Galar, Adam. He was naturalized in Pennsylvania 29 Mar. 1735. He was from Philadelphia County.

Galerme, Jean Baptiste. He was an Acadian who took the oath of allegiance in Apr. 1730.

Gallais, John. He, his wife Mary Gallais, and children John Gallais, Paul Gallais, Sansom Gallais, Francis Gallais, Mary-Anna Gallais, and Judith Gallais were endenized in England 5 Mar. 1685/6. They came to New York.

Gallaudet, Pierre Elizee. He was naturalized in New York 17 June 1726.

Galler, Martin. He was naturalized in New York 3 May 1755.

Gallete, Jacob. He was naturalized in Pennsylvania 19 May 1739. He was from Philadelphia County.

Gallinger, Michael. He was naturalized in New York 3 July 1759.

Gallman, Jacob. He was naturalized in Maryland 13 Sep. 1758. He was from Alsace.

Gallopin, Jacques. He was born at Laigle, Normandie, France, the son of Simeon Gallopin and Louise Malherbe. He was naturalized in South Carolina 10 Mar. 1696/7. He was a saddler.

Galman, Henrich. He was naturalized in Maryland 27 Sep. 1771. He was a German.

Gam, Leonhart. He was naturalized in New Jersey in 1761. He had been in the colony thirty years. He was born in Germany.

Gamper, Henry. He was naturalized in Pennsylvania 24–25 Sep. 1764. He was from Blockley Township, Philadelphia County.

Gampert, Nicholas. He was naturalized in Pennsylvania 11 Apr. 1761. He was from Philadelphia County.

Gandon, James. He was naturalized in London on 1 Feb. 1710. He had his certificate recorded in Jamaica 14 May 1726. He was a Protestant.

Ganiar, Francis. He was naturalized in New York 27 Sep. 1715. He was a yeoman from New Rochelle.

Ganison, Egbrett. He was made a denizen in Maryland 2 Mar. 1664/5. He was of Petuxent.

Gans, Bernard. He was naturalized in New York 29 July 1761. He was a vintner from New York City.

Gans, Justus. He was naturalized in New Jersey 20 Aug. 1755.

Gansell, George. He was naturalized in Pennsylvania 11 Apr. 1761. He was from Berks County.

Gansepoel, David. He was naturalized in London 23 Jan. 1699. He was from the Leeward Islands. He had served as a captain of foot in Col. Holt's Regiment. He had left France nine years before to serve under Col. Fox.

Ganter, Peter. He was naturalized in Pennsylvania 10 Sep. 1761. He was from Lancaster County.

Gantreaux, Charles. He was an Acadian who took the oath of allegiance in Apr. 1730.

Gantreaux, Charles. He was an Acadian who took the oath of allegiance in Apr. 1730.

Gantreaux, Claude. He was an Acadian who took the oath of allegiance in Apr. 1730.

Gantreaux, Francois. He was an Acadian who took the oath of allegiance in Apr. 1730.

Gantz, Adam. He was naturalized in Maryland 12 Sep. 1759. He lived in Baltimore, Maryland.

Gantz, John. He was naturalized in Pennsylvania 24 Sep. 1762. He was from Philadelphia County.

Garber, Hans. He was naturalized in Pennsylvania 25 Sep. 1744. He was from Lancaster County.

Garber, Michael. He was naturalized in Pennsylvania 25 Sep. 1744. He was from Lancaster County.

Garceau, Daniel. He was an Acadian who took the oath at Annapolis in Dec. 1729.

Garceau, Daniel. He was an Acadian and took the oath to George II at Annapolis River, Nova Scotia in Dec. 1729.

Garceau, Joseph. He was an Acadian and took the oath to George II at Annapolis River, Nova Scotia in Dec. 1729.

Garceau, Joseph. He was an Acadian who took the oath of allegiance in Apr. 1730.

Garcia, Paul. He was naturalized in Jamaica 15 Dec. 1761.

Garçon, Piere. He was an Acadian and took the oath to George II at Annapolis River, Nova Scotia in the winter of 1730.

Garde, John. He was naturalized in New York 6 Dec. 1746.

Garder, Peter. He was naturalized in Maryland 1 May 1736. He was from Baltimore County and was born in Germany.

Gardiner, Henry. He was naturalized in North Carolina 22 Sep. 1763. He was from Rowan County and a German.

Gardner, Christian. He was naturalized in Maryland 3 Sep. 1765. He was a German.

Gardner, John. He was naturalized in Pennsylvania 24–25 Sep. 1764. He was from Germantown, Philadelphia County.

Gardner, Peter. He was naturalized in Pennsylvania 11–12 Apr. 1744. He was from Lancaster County.

Gardner, Peter. He was naturalized in New York 8 Mar. 1773.

Garieau, Daniel. He was an Acadian and took the oath to George II at Annapolis River, Nova Scotia in the winter of 1730.

Garieau, Joseph. He was an Acadian and took the oath to George II at Annapolis River, Nova Scotia in the winter of 1730.

Garland, Christopher. He was naturalized in Jamaica 12 Nov. 1767.

Garlof, Elias. He was naturalized in New York 11 Sep. 1761.

Garlogh, Adam. He was naturalized in New York 27 Jan. 1770.

Garner, Isaac. He was naturalized in New York 26 July 1715. He was a cordwainer. He also appeared as Isaac Garnier.

Garner, Jean. He was endenized in New York 23 Dec. 1695.

Garnier, Daniel. He was born at L'Isle de Re, France, the son of Daniel Garnier and Marie Chevallier. His wife was Elizabeth Fanton. Their children, born at L'Isle de Re, were Etienne Garnier, Rachel Garnier, Margueritte Garnier, and Anne Garnier. They were naturalized in South Carolina ca. 1696.

Garnier, Elizabeth. She was the widow of Daniel Horry and was the daughter of Daniel Garnier and Elizabeth Fanton. She was born at L'Isle de Re, France. Her children, Elizabeth Marye Horry, Lidie Horry, Marye Horry, were born in South Carolina. They were naturalized in South Carolina ca. 1696.

Garnier, Isaac. He was naturalized in New York 26 July 1715. He was a cordwainer.

Garr, Andrew. He was naturalized in Orange County, Virginia 28 Jan. 1742/3.

Garr, John Adam. He was naturalized in Orange County, Virginia 28 Jan. 1742/3.

Garr, Lawrance. He was naturalized in Orange County, Virginia 28 Jan. 1742/3.

Garreau, Jean. He was naturalized in New York 12 July 1715. He was a chirurgeon.

Garret, Isaac. He was naturalized in Virginia ca. 1704.

Garrets, Rutgertson. He was naturalized in Maryland 19 Apr. 1671. He lived in Baltimore County and was Dutch. He was from Amerfoord, Holland.

Garretson, Frederick. He was naturalized in Maryland 4 Apr. 1761. He lived in Frederick County.

Garrison, Isaac. He was naturalized 19 Mar. 1705/6. He was born in Montauban, France, son of Isaac Garrison and Catherine DeRomagnac. He came to New York.

Garrit, Nicholas. He was naturalized 16 June 1689. He was born at Rarenshing/Ravensting, Germany, son of Garret and Baring Garrit. He came to New York.

Garritson, ——. He took the oath to the King 21–26 Oct. 1664 after the conquest of New Netherland.

Garrott, Jacob. He was endenized in New York 17 Sep. 1685.

Garseau, Pierre. He was an Acadian who took the oath at Annapolis River in Dec. 1729.

Gartenhower, Jacob. He was naturalized in Maryland 16 Apr. 1761.

Gartner, David. He was naturalized in New York 15 Oct. 1765. He was a tailor from New York City.

Gascha, Peter. He was naturalized in Pennsylvania 10 Apr. 1765. He was from York Township, York County.

Gash, Conjuist. He was naturalized in Maryland 27 Oct. 1743.

Gash, Godfrey. He was naturalized in Maryland 27 Oct. 1743.

Gasner, John. He was naturalized in New York 29 July 1762. He was a glazier from New York City.

Gassell, Hubbard. He was naturalized in Pennsylvania 6 Feb. 1730/1. He was from Philadelphia County.

Gassman, Rudolph. He was naturalized in New York 20 Mar. 1762.

Gassner, Dominicus. He was naturalized in Pennsylvania 10–14 Apr. 1747. He was from Philadelphia County.

Gateau, Nicholas. He was naturalized in Pennsylvania in 1704. He was born in Paris, France, the son of Nicholas Gateau.

Gateau, Nicholas. He was naturalized in Pennsylvania in 1724. He was from France and was a Protestant.

Gates, John. He was naturalized in Pennsylvania 24 Sep. 1755. He was from Philadelphia County.

Gatler, Christopher. He was naturalized in Pennsylvania 10 Apr. 1754. He was from Philadelphia County.

Gatler, Martin. He was naturalized in Pennsylvania 10 Apr. 1754. He was from Philadelphia County.

Gaudet, Anth. He was an Acadian who took the oath of allegiance in Apr. 1730.

Gaudet, Augustin. He was an Acadian who took the oath of allegiance in Apr. 1730.
Gaudet, Bernard. He was an Acadian who took the oath at Annapolis in Dec. 1729.
Gaudet, Bernard. He was an Acadian who took the oath at Annapolis in Dec. 1729.
Gaudet, Claude. He was an Acadian who took the oath of allegiance in Apr. 1730.
Gaudet, Claude. He was an Acadian who took the oath of allegiance in Apr. 1730.
Gaudet, Denis. He was an Acadian who took the oath of allegiance in Apr. 1730.
Gaudet, Guillaume. He was an Acadian who took the oath of allegiance in Apr. 1730.
Gaudet, Jean. He was an Acadian who took the oath at Annapolis River in Dec. 1729.
Gaudet, Jean Baptiste. He was an Acadian who took the oath of allegiance at the Mines, Pisiquit, Nova Scotia 31 Oct. 1727.
Gaudet, Jean Baptiste. He was an Acadian who took the oath of allegiance in Apr. 1730.
Gaudet, Pierre. He was an Acadian who took the oath of allegiance at Annapolis River in Dec. 1729.
Gaudet, Pierre. He was an Acadian who took the oath of allegiance at Annapolis River in Dec. 1729.
Gaudet, Pierre. He was an Acadian who took the oath of allegiance in Apr. 1730.
Gaudet, Pierre. He was an Acadian who took the oath of allegiance in Apr. 1730.
Gaudineau, Giles. He and his daughters, Ellena Gaudineau and Susanna Gaudineau, were endenized in New York 26 Aug. 1696.
Gaudovin, Isaac. He was naturalized in Virginia 12 May 1705.
Gauff, Dieter. He was naturalized in Pennsylvania 29 Mar. 1735. He was from Bucks County.
Gaufres, John. He was naturalized in Pennsylvania 11 Apr. 1749. He was from Philadelphia County.
Gauger, George. He was naturalized in New Jersey in 1761.
Gaultier, Abraham. He was endenized in London 20 Feb. 1662/3. He was from Barbados.
Gaultier, John. He was endenized in England 2 Mar. 1681. He came to New York.
Gaultier, John. He was endenized in Maryland 26 Apr. 1768. He was born in France.
Gaultier, Daniel. He was naturalized in Jamaica 28 Feb. 1693/4.
Gautier, Charles. He was an Acadian and took the oath to the King at the Mines, Pisiquit, Nova Scotia 31 Oct. 1727.
Gautier, Francois. He was an Acadian and took the oath to the King at the Mines, Pisiquit, Nova Scotia 31 Oct. 1727.
Gautier, Jean Batiste. He was an Acadian and took the oath to the King at the Mines, Pisiquit, Nova Scotia 31 Oct. 1727.
Gautier, Nicolas. He was an Acadian and took the oath to George II at Annapolis River, Nova Scotia in Dec. 1729.
Gautier, Pierre. He was an Acadian and took the oath to the King at the Mines, Pisiquit, Nova Scotia 31 Oct. 1727.
Gautier, Zachariah. He was naturalized in Jamaica 21 Feb. 1681/2.
Gautreaux, Charles. He was an Acadian who took the oath of allegiance in Apr. 1730.
Gautreaux, Jean. He was an Acadian who took the oath of allegiance in Apr. 1730.
Gautrot, Charles. He was an Acadian who took the oath of allegiance 31 Oct. 1727.
Gautrot, Charles. He was an Acadian who took the oath of allegiance in Apr. 1730.
Gautrot, Claude. He was an Acadian who took the oath of allegiance in Apr. 1730.
Gautrot, Claude. He was an Acadian who took the oath of allegiance in Apr. 1730.
Gautrot, Jacques. He was an Acadian who took the oath of allegiance in Apr. 1730.
Gautrot, Jean. He was an Acadian who took the oath of allegiance in Apr. 1730.
Gautrot, Jean. He was an Acadian who took the oath of allegiance in Apr. 1730.
Gautrot, Pierre. He was an Acadian who took the oath of allegiance at the Mines, Pisiquit, Nova Scotia 31 Oct. 1727.
Gautrot, Pierre. He was an Acadian who took the oath of allegiance in Apr. 1730.
Gauvot, Jean Baptiste. He was an Acadian who took the oath of allegiance 31 Oct. 1727.
Gavy, Philip. He was naturalized in Pennsylvania 26–27 Sep. 1743. He was from Bucks County.
Gayman, Christian. He was naturalized in Pennsylvania 24 Sep 1762. He was from Berks County.
Gear, Andrew. He was naturalized in Pennsylvania 11 Apr. 1761. He was from Lancaster County.
Gear, Paul. He was naturalized in Pennsylvania 11 Apr. 1761. He was from Lancaster County.

Geari, Jacob. He was naturalized in Pennsylvania 26 Sep. 1748. He was from Philadelphia County.

Gebhard, Nicholas. He was naturalized in Pennsylvania 24–25 Sep. 1764. He was from Bethel Township, Berks County.

Gebhart, Andrew. He was naturalized in Maryland 11 Sep. 1765. He was a German from Frederick County.

Gebhart, Belsar. He was naturalized in Nova Scotia 15 Sep. 1758.

Gebhart, Mathias. He was naturalized in Maryland 15 Sep. 1762. He was from Baltimore County.

Gebhart, Peter. He was naturalized in Pennsylvania 25 Sep. 1750. He was from Lancaster County.

Gebler, Matthias. He was naturalized in Pennsylvania 24–25 Sep. 1764. He was from Passyunk Township, Philadelphia County.

Geeting, Henry. He was naturalized in Pennsylvania in Maryland 1 Oct. 1767. He was a German.

Geer, John. He was naturalized in Pennsylvania 10 Apr. 1760.

Geerhart, Frederick. He was naturalized in Pennsylvania 24 Sep. 1755. He was from Berks County.

Geerhart, Peter. He was naturalized in Pennsylvania 24 Sep. 1753. He was from Philadelphia County.

Geeser, George. He was naturalized in New Jersey 20 Aug. 1755.

Geetz, John. He was naturalized in Pennsylvania 24 Sep. 1763. He was from Philadelphia.

Geezy, Jacob. He was naturalized in Pennsylvania 24 Sep. 1766.

Gehler, Fredrick. He was naturalized in New York 20 Mar. 1762.

Gehring, Balthasar. He was naturalized in New Jersey in 1760. He also appeared as Balthasar Keering. He had been in the colony thirty-two years. He was born in Germany.

Geiger, Henry. He was naturalized in Pennsylvania 11 Apr. 1761. He was from Northampton County.

Geiger, John Frederick. He was naturalized in New York 3 July 1759.

Geiger, Paul. He was naturalized in Pennsylvania 10 Apr. 1767. He was from Robinson Township, Berks County.

Geiger, Peter. He was naturalized in New Jersey in 1772. He also appeared as Peter Kyer. He was born in Germany.

Geinert, John George. He was naturalized in Pennsylvania 24 Sep. 1762. He was from Northampton County.

Geiring, Andreas. He was naturalized in Pennsylvania 11 Apr. 1761. He was from Northampton County.

Geisberts, Andreas. He was naturalized in Pennsylvania 19 May 1739. He was from Philadelphia County.

Geisel, Paul. He was naturalized in Pennsylvania 10–14 Apr. 1747. He was from Philadelphia County.

Geisler, George. He was naturalized in Pennsylvania 24 Sep. 1759.

Geist, Christian. He was naturalized in Maryland 5 Aug. 1721. He lived in Annapolis and was Swedish. He also appeared as Christian Gist.

Geist, George. He was naturalized in Maryland 10 Apr. 1762. He was a German from Anne Arundel County.

Geldbagh, Johannes. He was naturalized in Pennsylvania 19 May 1739. He was from Philadelphia County.

Gelinger, Andrew. He was naturalized in Pennsylvania 10–12 Apr. 1762. He was from Lancaster County.

Gelon, Louis. He was endenized in New York 23 Dec. 1695.

Gemelin, Christian. He was naturalized in Pennsylvania 24 Sep. 1745. He was from Philadelphia County.

Gemelin, Mathias. He was naturalized in Pennsylvania 6 Feb. 1730/1. He was from Philadelphia County.

Gendron, Jean. He was born at Maran, d'Onis, France, the son of David Gendron and Caterine Gendron. He was naturalized in South Carolina ca. 1696.

Gendron, Phillipe. He was born at Maran, d'Onis, France, the son of David Gendron and Caterine Gendron. His wife was Magdelaine Gendron, the daughter of — Chardon of Tours, Tourenne, France. Their children were Jean Gendron, Magdelaine Gendron, Elizabeth Gendron, Mariane

Gendron, and Jeane Gendron all of whom were born in South Carolina. By her former deceased husband, Louis Pasaquereau, Magdelaine Gendron's children were—Pasaquereau, Pierre Pasaquereau, Isaac Pasaquereau, Charles Pasaquereau. The first three Pasaquereau children were born in Tours, France and the last was born in London, England. They were naturalized in South Carolina *ca.* 1696.

Genne, Elizabeth. She was naturalized in Northampton County, Virginia 17 Sep. 1756. She was born at St. Patrick and was the daughter of Elizabeth Hacke, wife of Theodore Hacke.

Gennevine, Leonard. He was naturalized in Pennsylvania 10 & 23 Apr. 1764. He was from Manheim Township, York County.

Genslin, Jacob. He was naturalized in Pennsylvania 11 Apr. 1761. He was from Philadelphia County.

Genter, John Heinrich. He was naturalized in New York 3 July 1759.

Gentz, Peter. He was naturalized in Maryland 10 Sep. 1760.

Gentzler, Conrad. He was naturalized in Pennsylvania 11 Apr. 1761. He was from York County.

Gentzler, Philip. He was naturalized in Pennsylvania 24 Sep. 1763. He was from York Township, York County.

George, John. He was naturalized in New York 31 July 1754. He was a farmer from Kakyat, Orange County.

George, Peter. He was naturalized in Jamaica 6 Dec. 1739.

George, Peter. He was naturalized in Pennsylvania 10 Apr. 1755. He was from Bucks County.

Georger, Feight. He was naturalized in Pennsylvania 11 Apr. 1741. He was from Philadelphia County.

Gephart, Philip. He was naturalized in Pennsylvania 24 Sep. 1755. He was from Berks County.

Gerard, Francois. He took the oath of allegiance at Mobile, West Florida 2 Oct. 1764.

Gerard, Peter. He was naturalized in Pennsylvania 24–25 Sep./5 Oct. 1767. He was from Upper Milford Township, Northampton County.

Gerbeau, Elias. He was naturalized in New York 23 Dec. 1765.

Gerbeau, Henry. He was naturalized in New York 20 Mar. 1762.

Gerber, Valentine. He was naturalized in Pennsylvania 24 Sep. 1755. He was from Lancaster County.

Gerbrants, Francis. He was endenized in London 24 June 1703. He came to New York.

Geret, George. He was naturalized in Pennsylvania 30 May 1769. He was from Tulpehocken Township, Berks County.

Gerhart, Adam. He was naturalized in Pennsylvania 11 Apr. 1761. He was from Berks County.

Gerhart, Jacob. He was naturalized in Pennsylvania 24 Sep. 1762. He was from Berks County.

Gerhart, Jacob. He was naturalized in New Jersey 8 July 1730. He was born in Germany.

Gerich, Hans Martin. He was naturalized in Pennsylvania 6 Feb. 1730/1. He was from Philadelphia County.

Gering, Pierre. He was an Acadian who took the oath of allegiance in Apr. 1730.

Gerlach, George. He was naturalized in Pennsylvania 24–25 Sep. 1764. He was from Lancaster Township, Lancaster County.

Gerlach, John. He was naturalized in Pennsylvania 24–25 Sep. 1764. He was from Philadelphia.

Gerlach, William. He was naturalized in New York 3 July 1759.

German, Adam. He was naturalized in Pennsylvania 10 Apr. 1765. He was from Earl Township, Lancaster County.

German, Elias. He was naturalized in Jamaica 24 Nov. 1716.

German, Jost. He was naturalized in New York 18 Oct. 1774. He was from Ulster County.

Gerner, Matthew. He was naturalized in Pennsylvania 10 Apr. 1765. He was from Earl Township, Lancaster County.

Gernhart, Henry. He was naturalized in Maryland 15 Sep. 1761.

Gernreich, Johan Peter. He was naturalized in New York 24 Oct. 1743. He was a yeoman from Dutchess County.

Gerock, John Sigfred. He was naturalized in Pennsylvania 10 Apr. 1765. He was from Lancaster Township, Lancaster County. He was a minister.

Gerome, Charles. He was naturalized in New York 20 Dec. 1763. He was a confectioner from New York City.

Gerretsen, Arien. He was naturalized in New York 8–9 Sep. 1715. He was from Ulster County.

Gerrits, Abram. He took the oath of allegiance in Orange County, New York 26 Sep. 1687.

Gerrits, Johannes. He took the oath of allegiance in Orange County, New York 26 Sep. 1687.

Gerritse, Cornelis Gerris. He took the oath of allegiance in New Uijtrceht, Kings County, New York 26–30 Sep. 1687.

Gerritse, Rem. He took the oath of allegiance in Gravens End, Kings County, New York 26–30 Sep. 1687. He was a native of the colony.

Gerritse, Stoffel. He took the oath of allegiance at New Uijtrecht, Kings County, New York 26–30 Sep. 1687.

Gerritsz, Hendrick. He took the oath of allegiance in Orange County, New York 26 Sep. 1687.

Gerritsz, Huybert. He took the oath of allegiance in Orange County, New York 26 Sep. 1687.

Gerritts, Cornelis. He took the oath of naturalization in New York 1 Sep. 1687 in Ulster County.

Gerrittsa, John. He took the oath of naturalization in New York 1 Sep. 1687 in Ulster County.

Gerrittsa, John. He took the oath of naturalization in New York 1 Sep. 1687 in Ulster County.

Gerritzen, Hendrik. He was naturalized in New Castle County, Delaware 21 Feb. 1682/3.

Gerritzen, Poul. He was naturalized in New Castle County, Delaware 21 Feb. 1682/3.

Gerrnant, George. He was naturalized in Pennsylvania 11 Apr. 1761. He was from Berks County.

Gerrotts, Cornelis. He took the oath of naturalization in New York 1 Sep. 1687 in Ulster County. He was from New Church.

Gerster, George. He was naturalized in Pennsylvania 10 Apr. 1765. He was from Oxford Township, Philadelphia County.

Gertzens, Geele. He was naturalized in Nova Scotia 5 July 1758.

Gerureau, Jacob. He was naturalized in New York 2 Aug. 1715. He was a currier from New York City.

Gerwaes, Thys. He took the oath of allegiance in Orange County, New York 26 Sep. 1687.

Geshwind, Eberhard. He was naturalized in Pennsylvania 11 Apr. 1761. He was from Berks County.

Gesler, Matthew. He was naturalized in Orange County, Virginia 15 Oct. 1745. He was a native of Wurttemberg. He had been in the colony seven years.

Gesseron, George Michael. He was naturalized in Maryland in Apr. 1749. He was from Frederick County.

Gessiner, Hendrick. He was naturalized in New York 10 Jan. 1715/6. He was a yeoman from Westchester County.

Geston Tanner, Christopher. He was naturalized in Maryland 19 Oct. 1743.

Getsedaner, Gabriel. He was naturalized in Maryland 14 Apr. 1761.

Gettier, Christopher. He was naturalized in Maryland 31 Aug. 1757.

Getting, Henry. He was naturalized in Maryland 1 Oct. 1767. He was a German.

Gevandon, Anthony. He was naturalized in Virginia 12 May 1705.

Geyer, Henry. He was naturalized in Pennsylvania 25 Sep. 1753. He was from Philadelphia County.

Geygar, Valentine. He was naturalized in Pennsylvania in Sep. 1740. He was from Philadelphia County.

Geyger, Frederick. He was naturalized in New York 11 Sep. 1761.

Gianane, Silvester. He was naturalized in Lunenburg County, Virginia 1 Sep. 1746.

Gibbs, Abraham. He was naturalized in Maryland 15 Apr. 1761.

Gickert, Jacob. He was naturalized in Pennsylvania 11 Apr. 1761. He was from Berks County.

Giddemen, Johannes. He and his son, Hendrick Giddeman, were naturalized in New Jersey 8 July 1730. They were born in Germany.

Gideon, Rowland. He was endenized in England in 30 July 1679 and settled in Boston, Massachusetts by 1674.

Gieger, Jacob. He was naturalized in Pennsylvania 10 Sep. 1761. He was from Philadelphia County.

Giekert, Henry. He was naturalized in Pennsylvania 10 Apr. 1760.

Giesselman, Michael. He was naturalized in Pennsylvania 11 Apr. 1761. He was from York County.

Giesert, Frederick. He was naturalized in Maryland 12 Sep. 1764. He was a German from Frederick County.

Giesy, David. He was naturalized in Pennsylvania 10 Apr. 1755. He was from Northampton County.

Giger, William. He was naturalized in Pennsylvania 24 Sep. 1760. He was from Philadelphia County.

Gignilliat, Jean Francois. He was born at Venay, Switzerland, the son of Abraham Gignilliat and Marye de Ville. His wife was Suzanne LeSerruier. Their children, Marye Elizabeth Gignilliat, Henry Gignilliat, Pierre Gignilliat, and Abraham Gignilliat, were born in South Carolina. They were naturalized in South Carolina *ca.* 1696.

Gilbert, Anthony. He was naturalized in Pennsylvania 25–27 Sep. 1740. He was from Philadelphia County.

Gilbert, Bernard. He was naturalized in Pennsylvania 24 Sep. 1760. He was from Philadelphia County.

Gilbert, Conrad. He was naturalized in Pennsylvania 24 Sep. 1760. He was from Philadelphia County.

Gilbert, George. He was naturalized in Pennsylvania 10 Sep. 1760. He was from Berks County.

Giles, Stephen. He was naturalized in Jamaica 22 Dec. 1708.

Gilligan, Manual Manasses. He was a natural-born English subject. He settled in St. Thomas and was naturalized a subject of the King of Denmark. He was naturalized 22 Mar. 1704.

Gillisz, John. He took the oath of allegiance in Orange County, New York 26 Sep. 1687.

Gilloroey, Piere. He took the oath of allegiance at Mobile, West Florida 2 Oct. 1764.

Gillot, Samuel. He was naturalized in New York 21 Oct. 1741. He was a merchant from Westchester County.

Gilman, John Adolph. He was naturalized in Pennsylvania 24–25 Sep. 1764. He was from Germantown. Philadelphia County.

Gilwicks, Frederick. He was naturalized in Pennsylvania 10 Apr. 1760.

Ginginger, Martin. He was naturalized in Pennsylvania 11 Apr. 1761. He was from Northampton County.

Girard, Abraham. He was naturalized in New York 19 July 1715. He was a sail-maker.

Girardeau, Jean. He was born at Tattemont, Poitou, France. He was the son of Pierre Girardeau and Catherine Lareine. He was naturalized in South Carolina *ca.* 1696.

Girardin, Jacob. He was naturalized in Pennsylvania 10 Apr. 1755. He was from Berks County.

Giroar, Alexandre. He was an Acadian and took the oath to George II at Annapolis River, Nova Scotia in Dec. 1729.

Giroar, Charles. He was an Acadian and took the oath to George II at Annapolis River, Nova Scotia in Dec. 1729.

Giroar, Claude. He was an Acadian and took the oath to George II at Annapolis River, Nova Scotia in Dec. 1729.

Giroar, Claude. He was an Acadian who took the oath of allegiance in Apr. 1730.

Giroar, Etienne. He was an Acadian who took the oath of allegiance in Apr. 1730.

Giroar, François. He was an Acadian and took the oath to George II at Annapolis River, Nova Scotia in Dec. 1729.

Giroar, Guillaume. He was an Acadian and took the oath to George II at Annapolis River, Nova Scotia in Dec. 1729.

Giroar, Honore. He was an Acadian who took the oath of allegiance in Apr. 1730.

Giroar, Jacques. He was an Acadian and took the oath to George II at Annapolis River, Nova Scotia in Dec. 1729.

Giroar, Jacques. He was an Acadian who took the oath of allegiance in Apr. 1730.

Giroar, Jermain. He was an Acadian who took the oath of allegiance in Apr. 1730.

Giroar, Jermain. He was an Acadian who took the oath of allegiance in Apr. 1730.

Giroar, Louis. He was an Acadian and took the oath to George II at Annapolis River, Nova Scotia in Dec. 1729.

Giroir, Jacques. He was an Acadian who took the oath of allegiance in Apr. 1730.

Girouer, Alexandre. He took the oath of allegiance at Port Royal, Nova Scotia 16 Aug. 1695.

Girouer, Jacob. He took the oath of allegiance at Port Royal, Nova Scotia 16 Aug. 1695.

Girrard, Pierre. He was born at Poitiers, France, the son of Pierre Girrard and Judith Fruschard. He was naturalized in South Carolina *ca.* 1696.

Gisborts, Gerrit. He took the oath of naturalization in New York 1 Sep. 1687 in Ulster County.

Giselbreecht, Gottfried. He was naturalized in New York 24 Apr. 1749. He was a physician from Dutchess County.

Gittinger, John. He was naturalized in Pennsylvania 10 Apr. 1760.

Gittleman, Henry. He was naturalized in Pennsylvania 10 Sep. 1761. He was from Philadelphia County.

Glaidy, John. He was naturalized in Pennsylvania 11 Apr. 1761. He was from York County.

Glanderff, Johannes. He was naturalized in New York 24 July 1724.

Glass, Fred. He was naturalized in Pennsylvania 11 Sep. 1761. He was from Lancaster County.

Glass, Phillip. He was naturalized in Frederick County, Virginia 5 May 1747.

Glassbenner, George. He was naturalized in Pennsylvania 24 Sep. 1762. He was from Lancaster County.

Glattsfelder, Casper. He was naturalized in Pennsylvania 11 Apr. 1763. He was from Codorus Township, York County.

Gleim, Jacob Christian. He was naturalized in Pennsylvania 11 Apr. 1761. He was from Philadelphia County.

Glegorie, Michell. He was naturalized in Jamaica 27 Nov. 1728.

Glinder, Conrad. He was naturalized in Pennsylvania 10 Sep. 1761. He was from Berks County.

Gloria, Peter. He was endenized in London 15 Apr. 1687. He had his certificate recorded in Jamaica 3 June 1721.

Glosser, Michael. He was naturalized in Pennsylvania 10 Sep. 1761. He was from Berks County.

Glockner, Casper. He was naturalized in Pennsylvania 24–25 Sep. 1764. He was from Passyunk Township, Philadelphia County.

Gloudisz, Johanes VanBeverhoudt. He was naturalized in New York 24 Nov. 1750.

Goats, George. He was naturalized in Maryland in Apr. 1749. He was from Frederick County.

Gobel, David. He was naturalized in New York 21 Oct. 1765. He was a baker from New York City.

Gobler, Jacob. He was naturalized in Pennsylvania 10–12 Apr. 1762. He was from Philadelphia County.

Goderus, Joost. He took the oath to the King 21–26 Oct. 1664 after the conquest of New Netherland.

Godet, Bernard. He took the oath of allegiance at Port Royal, Nova Scotia 16 Aug. 1695.

Godet, Bernard. He was an Acadian and took the oath to George II at Annapolis River, Nova Scotia in the winter of 1730.

Godet, Pierre. He took the oath of allegiance at Port Royal, Nova Scotia 16 Aug. 1695.

Godet, Pierre. He was an Acadian and took the oath to George II at the Mines, Pisiquit 31 Oct. 1727.

Godet, Theodore. He was naturalized in England 9 Sep. 1698. He settled in Bermuda.

Godett, Bernard. He was an Acadian and took the oath to George II at Annapolis River, Nova Scotia in the winter of 1730.

Godett, Jean. He was an Acadian and took the oath to George II at Annapolis River, Nova Scotia in the winter of 1730.

Godett, Piere. He was an Acadian and took the oath to George II at Annapolis River, Nova Scotia in the winter of 1730.

Godett, Piere. He was an Acadian and took the oath to George II at Annapolis River, Nova Scotia in the winter of 1730.

Godfredo, Leonardo. He was naturalized in Jamaica 17 May 1688.

Godfrey, John. He was naturalized in Jamaica 29 May 1741.

Godfrey, Peter. He was naturalized in Jamaica 10 Nov. 1700.

Godin, Pierre. He was endenized in New York 17 Sep. 1685.

Godineou, Gilles. He petitioned to be naturalized in New York 19 Aug. 1687.

Godschall, Nicholas. He was naturalized in Pennsylvania 24 Sep. 1763. He was from Greenwich Township, Berks County.

Godshall, Andrew. He was naturalized in Pennsylvania 11 Apr. 1749. He was from Philadelphia County.

Godson, Peter. He was endenized in Virginia 7 Nov. 1666. He was born in France.

Goebel, Maurits. He was naturalized in New York 3 July 1759.

Goeglets, Hendrick. He was naturalized in New Jersey 16 Dec. 1748. He was born in Switzerland.

Goehmung, Andreas. He was naturalized in Maryland 14 Sep. 1763. He was a German.

Goelet, Jacobus. He was naturalized in New York 27 Sep. 1715. He was a bricklayer from New York City.

Goerts, Hartman. He was naturalized in Maryland 10 Sep. 1760.

Goetling, Wilhelm. He was naturalized in Pennsylvania 24–25 Sep. 1764. He was from Philadelphia.

Goetschius, John Henry. He was naturalized in New York 19 Jan. 1748/9. He was a minister from Hackensack, New Jersey.

Goetschius, John Mauritzius. He was naturalized in New York 19 Jan. 1748/9. He was a chirurgeon from Hackensack, New Jersey.

Goll, Balthasar. He was naturalized in Pennsylvania 10 Apr. 1765. He was from York Township, York County.

Gohman, Michael. He was naturalized in Pennsylvania 14 Feb. 1729/30. He was from Lancaster County.

Goller, Jacob. He was naturalized in Maryland 15 Apr. 1761.

Golley, Peter. He was naturalized in Maryland 22 May 1695. He lived in Talbot County.

Gollman, Henrick. He was naturalized in Pennsylvania 24 Sep. 1741. He was from Philadelphia County.

Golneck, Constyn. He was naturalized in New York 11 Sep. 1761.

Gombauld, Daniel. He petitioned to be naturalized in New York 19 Aug. 1687.

Gombauld, Moise. He was naturalized in New York 29 Oct. 1730.

Gombauld, Moses. He was naturalized in New York 28 July 1741. He was a merchant from New York City.

Gomber, John. He was naturalized in Maryland 11 Apr. 1761.

Gomez, Abraham. He was endenized in Barbados 14 Dec. 1694.

Gomez, Daniel. He was endenized in London 29 Dec. 1714. He was from New York. His certificate was also recorded in Jamaica in 1724.

Gomez, Daniel. He was naturalized in New York in 1740. He was a Jewish merchant from New York City.

Gomez, David. He was endenized in London 29 Dec. 1714. He was a merchant from New York.

Gomez, David. He was naturalized in New York in 1740–41. He was a Jewish merchant from New York City. His certificate was also recorded in Jamaica in 1742.

Gomez, Ester. She was naturalized in Jamaica 29 Nov. 1703.

Gomez, Isaac. He was endenized in Barbados 14 Dec. 1695.

Gomez, Jacob. He was endenized in London 29 Dec. 1714. He was from New York. His certificate was also recorded in Jamaica in 1724.

Gomez, Ludovico. He was endenized in London 18 Apr. 1705. He was from New York.

Gomez, Mordecai. He was endenized in London 29 Dec. 1714. He was from New York. His certificate was also recorded in Jamaica in 1724.

Gomez, Mordecai. He was naturalized in New York 1740–41. He was a Jewish merchant from New York City.

Gomez, Moses. He was naturalized in Jamaica 4 Aug. 1725.

Gondy, Christian. He was naturalized in Pennsylvania 19 May 1739. He was from Philadelphia County.

Gonkle, John. He was naturalized in Pennsylvania 10 Apr. 1754. He was from Lancaster County.

Gonsales, Diego Lewes. He was naturalized in Jamaica 26 Apr. 1688. His alias was Isaac Nunes.

Gonsales, Isaack. He was naturalized in Jamaica 29 July 1690.

Gonsales, Rebecca. She was naturalized in Jamaica 28 Feb. 1703.

Gonzales, Hester Nunes. She was naturalized in Jamaica 24 Oct. 1718.

Gonzille, Jacque. He was an Acadian and took the oath to George II at Annapolis River, Nova Scotia in the winter of 1730.

Good, Christian. He was naturalized in Pennsylvania 24 Sep. 1760. He was from Lancaster County.

Good, George. He was naturalized in Pennsylvania 19 May 1739. He was from Philadelphia County.

Good, Lawrence. He was naturalized in Pennsylvania 10 Apr. 1755. He was from Northampton County.

Good, Michael. He was naturalized in Pennsylvania 19 May 1739. He was from Philadelphia County.

Good, Peter. He was naturalized in Pennsylvania 11–12 Apr. 1744. He was from Lancaster County.

Goodbardly, John. He was naturalized in New York 3 July 1759.

Goodbrode, William. He was naturalized in New York 8 Mar. 1773.

Goodhart, Frederick. He was naturalized in Pennsylvania 11 Apr. 1761. He was from Berks County.

Goodheart, Steffel. He was naturalized in North Carolina 11 Oct. 1754. He was from Rowan County.

Goodling, John Peter. He was naturalized in Pennsylvania 10–12 Apr. 1762. He was from York County.

Goodman, Christopher. He was naturalized in Pennsylvania 11 Apr. 1761. He was from Northampton County.

Goodman, Stephen. He was naturalized in Pennsylvania 11 Apr. 1763. He was from Lower Merrion Township, Philadelphia County.

Goodman, William. He was naturalized in Maryland 15 Apr. 1761.

Goodperlet, John. He was naturalized in New York 19 Apr. 1759. He was a tailor from New York City.

Gooldin, Samuel. He was naturalized in Pennsylvania 19 May 1739. He was from Philadelphia County.

Goos, Adam. He was naturalized in Pennsylvania 24 Sep. 1759.

Goot, Hans. He was naturalized in Pennsylvania 14 Feb. 1729/30. He was from Lancaster County.

Goot, Jacob. He was naturalized in Pennsylvania 14 Feb. 1729/30. He was from Lancaster County.

Goothouse, Henry. He was naturalized in Pennsylvania 25–27 Sep. 1740. He was from Lancaster County.

Gootz, Jacob. He was naturalized in Pennsylvania 10 Sep. 1761. He was from Berks County.

Gor, Michael. He was naturalized in Maryland 11 Apr. 1759.

Gore, Casper. He was naturalized in Pennsylvania 24 Sep. 1755. He was from Lancaster County.

Gorgaes, John. He was naturalized in Pennsylvania 29 Sep. 1709. He was from Philadelphia County.

Gori, John. He was naturalized in Virginia 12 May 1705.

Gori, Peter. He was naturalized in Virginia 12 May 1705.

Gorigher, Nicholas. He was naturalized in Pennsylvania 10 Sep. 1761. He was from Berks County.

Gorner, Johannes. He was naturalized in Pennsylvania 24 Sep. 1741. He was from Lancaster County.

Goserez, Jacob Mendez. He was naturalized in Jamaica 15 June 1675.

Goster, John Henry. He was naturalized in Pennsylvania 10 Sep. 1761. He was from Berks County.

Gotleck, John. He was naturalized in Pennsylvania 24 Sep. 1755. He was from Lancaster County.

Gotschall, Nicholas. He was naturalized in Pennsylvania 24 Sep. 1762. He was from Berks County.

Gottschik, George. He was naturalized in Pennsylvania 29 Sep. 1709. He was from Philadelphia County.

Gotshall, Christopher. He was naturalized in Pennsylvania 11 Apr. 1761. He was from Berks County.

Gotshall, Frederick. He was naturalized in Pennsylvania 19 May 1739. He was from Philadelphia County.

Gotshall, Herman. He was naturalized in Pennsylvania 25–27 Sep. 1740. He was from Philadelphia County.

Gottee, John. He and his wife, Margaret Gottee, were naturalized in Maryland 19 Apr. 1671. They lived in Dorchester County and were French.

Gottshall, Peter. He was naturalized in Pennsylvania 11 Apr. 1761. He was from Lancaster County.

Gouches, Michael. He was naturalized in Maryland 15 Sep. 1762. He was from Frederick County.

Goudin, Louis. He was naturalized in South Carolina 10 Mar. 1696/7. He was a planter.

Goukes, Reinier. He took the oath to the King 21–26 Oct. 1664 after the conquest of New Netherland.

Gouldin, Christian. He was naturalized in Pennsylvania in 1730–31. He was from Philadelphia County.

Gouldin, Samuel. He was naturalized in Pennsylvania in 1730–31. He was from Philadelphia County.

Gourdain, Louis. He was born at Concourt, Artois, France, the son of Valentin Gourdain and Marye Piedeuin. He was naturalized in South Carolina ca. 1696.

Gouscie, Louis. He was an Acadian and took the oath of allegiance in Apr. 1730.

Gouverneur, Abraham. He was naturalized in New York 19 July 1715.

Gouverneur, Isaac. He was naturalized in New York 19 July 1715. He was a merchant.

Gouverneur, Sarah. She was naturalized in New York 6 July 1723. She was the wife of Isaac Gouverneur.

Goutee, John. He was naturalized in Maryland 22 May 1695. He lived in Talbot County.

Goutee, Joseph. He and his sons, John Goutee and Joseph Goutee, were naturalized in Maryland 22 May 1695. They lived in Talbot County.

Gouzille, Jacques. He was an Acadian and took the oath of allegiance at Annapolis River in Dec. 1729.

Goval, Frederick. He was naturalized in Maryland 11 Sep. 1765.

Gower, Nicholas. He was naturalized in Pennsylvania 10 Sep. 1761. He was from Berks County.

Graaf, Hans. He was naturalized in Pennsylvania 14 Feb. 1729/30. He was from Lancaster County.

Graaf, Henry. He was naturalized in New Jersey 21 Oct. 1754.

Graaf, Jacob. He was naturalized in New York 3 July 1759.

Graaf, Jacob. He was naturalized in New York 16 Feb. 1771.

Graaf, Johannes Jacob. He was naturalized in New York 29 July 1752. He was a farmer from Kings County.

Graaf, Martyn. He was naturalized in Pennsylvania 14 Feb. 1729/30. He was from Lancaster County.

Graaff, Sebastian. He was naturalized in Pennsylvania 11 Apr. 1741. He was from Philadelphia County.

Grabeel, Joseph. He was naturalized in Maryland 21 Sep. 1764. He was a German.

Graber, Henry. He was naturalized in Pennsylvania 11 Apr. 1761. He was from Berks County.

Graber, Henry. He was naturalized in Pennsylvania 10–12 Apr. 1762. He was from Lancaster County.

Graber, Philip. He was naturalized in Pennsylvania 10–12 Apr. 1762. He was from Lancaster County.

Graebal, Joseph. He was naturalized in Maryland 11 Sep. 1765. He was a German from Frederick County.

Graebel, Henry. He was naturalized in Pennsylvania 10 Sep. 1761. He was from Lancaster County.

Graeff, Gerhard. He was naturalized in Pennsylvania 23 Nov. 1773. He was from Dover Township, York County.

Graeft, Johannes. He was naturalized in New York 31 Dec. 1761.

Graet, Johannis. He was naturalized in New York 14 Feb. 1715/6. He was from Albany County.

Graf, Christian. He was naturalized in New York 8 Mar. 1773.

Graff, George. He was naturalized in Pennsylvania 25 Sep. 1751. He was from Lancaster County.

Graff, Hans. He was naturalized in Pennsylvania 19 May 1739. He was from Lancaster County.

Graff, Jacob. He was naturalized in Pennsylvania 11–13 Apr. 1743. He was from Lancaster County.

Graff, Jacob, Jr. He was naturalized in Pennsylvania 11 Apr. 1761. He was from Philadelphia County.

Graff, Joseph. He was naturalized in Pennsylvania 29 Mar. 1735. He was from Philadelphia County.

Graff, Jacob. He was naturalized in Pennsylvania 10 Sep. 1761. He was from Lancaster County.

Graff, John. He was naturalized in Pennsylvania 24 Sep. 1755. He was from Philadelphia.

Graff, John. He was naturalized in Pennsylvania 10–12 Apr. 1762. He was from Lancaster County.

Graff, John George. He was naturalized in Pennsylvania 25 Sep. 1744. He was from Lancaster County.

Graff, Martyn. He was naturalized in Pennsylvania 14 Feb. 1729/30. He was from Lancaster County.

Graff, Sebastian. He was naturalized in Pennsylvania 19 May 1739. He was from Lancaster County.

Graff, William. He was naturalized in Pennsylvania 10 Sep. 1761. He was from Berks County.

Graffe, Christopher. He was naturalized in Pennsylvania 10 Apr. 1760.

Graffe, Jacob. He was naturalized in Pennsylvania 11–13 Apr. 1743. He was from Philadelphia County.

Graffe, John Casper. He was naturalized in Pennsylvania 10 Apr. 1760.

Graft, George. He was naturalized in Maryland 12 Sep. 1765. He was a German from Frederick County.

Grall, Isaac. He was naturalized in Pennsylvania 25–27 Sep. 1740. He was from Philadelphia County.

Grandy, George. He was naturalized in Jamaica 22 Nov. 1709.

Granadam, Francis. He was endenized in Maryland 22 June 1771. He was born in Germany.

Granger, Charles. He was an Acadian who took the oath of allegiance in Apr. 1730.

Granger, Charles. He was an Acadian who took the oath of allegiance in Apr. 1730.

Granger, Claude. He was an Acadian who took the oath of allegiance in Apr. 1730.

Granger, Claude. He was an Acadian who took the oath of allegiance in Apr. 1730.

Granger, Francois. He was an Acadian who took the oath of allegiance in Apr. 1730.

Granger, Joseph Jo. He was an Acadian and took the oath to the King at the Mines, Pisiquit, Nova Scotia 31 Oct. 1727.

Granger, Joseph. He was an Acadian who took the oath of allegiance in Apr. 1730.

Grange[r], Lorans. He took the oath of allegiance at Port Royal, Nova Scotia 16 Aug. 1695.

Granger, Lawrence. He was an Acadian and took the oath to George II at Annapolis River, Nova Scotia in Dec. 1729.

Granger, Piere. He was an Acadian and took the oath to George II at Annapolis River, Nova Scotia in Dec. 1729.

Granger, Pierre, Sr. He was an Acadian and took the oath to the King at the Mines, Pisiquit, Nova Scotia 31 Oct. 1727.

Granger, Pierre. He was an Acadian who took the oath of allegiance in Apr. 1730.

Granger, Rene. He was an Acadian and took the oath to the King at the Mines, Pisiquit, Nova Scotia 31 Oct. 1727.

Granger, Rene, Jr. He was an Acadian and took the oath to the King at the Mines, Pisiquit, Nova Scotia 31 Oct. 1727.

Granger, Rene. He was an Acadian who took the oath of allegiance in Apr. 1730.

Granger, Rene. He was an Acadian who took the oath of allegiance in Apr. 1730. [second of the name]

Grasset, Augustus. He and his wife Mary Grasset were endenized in England 8 May 1681/2. They came to New York

Grassold, Christian. He was naturalized in Pennsylvania 19 May 1739. He was from Philadelphia County.

Gratener, Henry. He was naturalized in Maryland 14 Sep. 1763. He was a German.

Grats, Barnard. He was naturalized in Pennsylvania 11 Apr. 1763. He was from Philadelphia. He was a Jew.

Gratt, Felta. He was naturalized in Maryland 20 Oct. 1747. He was a Quaker.

Gratz, Jacob. He was naturalized in Pennsylvania 10 Apr. 1760.

Gratz, Michael. He was naturalized in Pennsylvania 24 Sep. 1766. He was a Jew. He was from Philadelphia.

Gratz, Michael. He was naturalized in Pennsylvania 10 Sep. 1761. He was from Philadelphia County.

Grauss, George. He was naturalized in Pennsylvania 24 Sep. 1770. He was from Coventry Township, Chester County.

Graverat, Isaac. He was endenized in New York 9 Nov. 1670.

Graves, John. He was naturalized in North Carolina 23 Mar. 1763.

Grays, Lawrence. He was naturalized in Virginia 28 Jan. 1742/3. He was from Rowan County.

Grays, Lawrence. He was naturalized in Virginia 28 Jan. 1742/3. He was from Wurttemberg and had lived in the colony seven years.

Greanmore, William. He was naturalized in Pennsylvania 11–13 Apr. 1743. He was from Philadelphia County.

Greater, Jacob. He was naturalized in Pennsylvania 24 Sep. 1755. He was from Berks County.

Greder, Jacob. He was naturalized in Pennsylvania 11–13 Apr. 1743. He was from Philadelphia County.

Greeger, Lawrence. He was naturalized in Maryland in Apr. 1749. He was from Frederick County.

Green, George. He was naturalized in Jamaica 9 Aug. 1707.

Green, Gerard. He was naturalized in Maryland 24 Sep. 1765. He was a German.

Green, Henry. He was naturalized in Maryland 6 June 1674. He lived in Talbot County and was Dutch.

Greenea, Phillippe. He was naturalized in Jamaica 14 Nov. 1726.

Greening, Albert. He and his children were naturalized in Maryland 28 Feb. 1721/2. He lived in Anne Arundel County and was German.

Greenevald, Philip. He was naturalized in Maryland 25 Oct. 1756. He was German.

Greenwalt, John. He was naturalized in Pennsylvania 11 Apr. 1761. He was from Philadelphia County.

Greenwalt, Philip. He was naturalized in Pennsylvania 24 Sep. 1759.

Greeseman, John. He was naturalized in Pennsylvania 24–25 Sep./5 Oct. 1767. He was from Whitehall Township, Northampton County.

Gref, Adam. He was naturalized in Maryland 10 Sep. 1772.

Gregg, John Conrad. He was naturalized in Pennsylvania 24 Sep. 1770. He was from Newport, Newcastle County, [Delaware].

Greiff, Stephen. He was naturalized in Pennsylvania 19 May 1739. He was from Philadelphia County.

Greiner, Jacob. He was naturalized in Pennsylvania 24–25 Sep. 1764. He was from Philadelphia.

Grelot, Bartholomew. He took the oath of allegiance at Mobile, West Florida 2 Oct. 1764.

Grerard, Peter. He was naturalized in Pennsylvania 24–25 Sep./5 Oct. 1767. He was from Upper Milford Township, Northampton County.

Gress, Michael. He was naturalized in New York 29 July 1762. He was a saddler.

Gressman, Ludwig. He was naturalized in New York 3 July 1759.

Greter, Martin. He was naturalized in Pennsylvania 11–13 Apr. 1743. He was from Philadelphia County.

Grevenraat, Isaac. He took the oath to the King 21–26 Oct. 1664 after the conquest of New Netherland.

Greyshir, Michael. He was naturalized in Pennsylvania 24 Sep. 1762. He was from Berks County.

Griechach, Jacob. He was naturalized in New York 20 Mar. 1762.

Grienwald, Peter. He was naturalized in Pennsylvania 11 Apr. 1763. He was from Richmond Township, Berks County.

Griggs, Andrew. He was naturalized in Jamaica 5 Oct. 1700.

Grim, Andrew. He was naturalized in Maryland 14 Apr. 1762. He was a German from Frederick County.

Grim, Caspar. He was naturalized in New Jersey 28 Apr. 1762.

Grim, David. He was naturalized in New York 18 Apr. 1769. He was a vintner from New York City.

Grim, Jacob. He was naturalized in Pennsylvania 11 Apr. 1761. He was from Berks County.

Grim, Jacob. He was naturalized in New York 1 Aug. 1750. He was a felt-maker from New York City.

Grim, Peter. He was naturalized in New York 6 Dec. 1746.

Grim, Philip. He was naturalized in New York 6 Dec. 1746.

Grimm, Getty. He was naturalized in Pennsylvania 26–27 Sep. 1743. He was from Bucks County.

Grimm, Jacob. He was naturalized in Pennsylvania 24 Sep. 1762. He was from Northampton County.

Grimkee, Frederick. He was naturalized in South Carolina 8 Feb. 1742/3.

Grimkee, John Paul. He was naturalized in South Carolina 12 May 1748.

Grindler, Philip. He was naturalized in Maryland 11 Sep. 1765.

Gripe, John. He was naturalized in Jamaica 16 Jan. 1717/8.

Grivois, Joseph. He was an Acadian and took the oath of allegiance in Apr. 1730.

Gro, Michael. He was naturalized in Maryland 9 Sep. 1761.

Groal, Peter. He was naturalized in Maryland 15 Sep. 1762. He was from Frederick County.

Groce, John. He was naturalized in Pennsylvania 11 Apr. 1761. He was from Berks County.

Groen, Jacob Marius. He was naturalized in New York 12 July 1715. He was a silversmith.

Groes, Philippus. He was naturalized in Maryland 23 Sep. 1758.

Grof, John George. He was naturalized in Pennsylvania 11 Apr. 1752. He was from Lancaster County.

Groff, Andrew. He was naturalized in Pennsylvania 25 Sep. 1751. He was from Lancaster County.

Groff, George. He was naturalized in Pennsylvania 19 May 1739. He was from Lancaster County.

Groff, John. He was naturalized in Pennsylvania 24–25 Sep. 1764. He was from Plymouth Township, Philadelphia County.

Groh, Frederick. He was naturalized in Pennsylvania 24 Sep. 1763. He was from Lower Merrion Township, Philadelphia County.

Grohe, Christopher. He was naturalized in Maryland 15 Sep. 1762. He was from Baltimore County.

Gronce, Peter. He was naturalized in New York 27 Jan. 1770.

Gronain, John. He was naturalized in New York 22 June 1734.

Grooten, Lambert. He was endenized in Accomack County, Virginia 1 Apr. 1658. He was Dutch.

Groothouse, John. He was naturalized in Pennsylvania 25–27 Sep. 1740. He was from Philadelphia County.

Gros, Johan Daniel. He was naturalized in New York 8 Mar. 1773.

Grose, John. He was naturalized in Pennsylvania 25–26 Sep./4 Oct. 1749. He was from Philadelphia County.

Grosh, Philip. He was naturalized in Pennsylvania 16 May 1769. He was from Hempfield Township, Lancaster County.

Gross, Francis. He was naturalized in Maryland 10 Apr. 1770.

Gross, Michael. He was naturalized in Pennsylvania 24 Sep. 1753. He was from Lancaster County.

Gross, Philippus. He was naturalized in Maryland 23 Sep. 1758.

Gross, Valentine. He was naturalized in Pennsylvania 24 Sep. 1755. He was from Lancaster County.

Groth, Andreas Henry. He was naturalized in Pennsylvania in 4 Mar. 1763. He was from Denmark.

Grotzinger, George. He was naturalized in New York 29 Mar. 1762.

Groudain, John. He was naturalized in New York 22 June 1734.

Groundhart, John George. He was naturalized in New York 8 Mar. 1773.

Grouse, William. He was naturalized in Maryland 11 Sep. 1765.

Grout, John. He was naturalized in Pennsylvania 11 Apr. 1749. He was from Philadelphia County.

Grove, Abraham. He was naturalized in Pennsylvania 24–25 Sep. 1764. He was from Earl Township, Lancaster County. He was a Moravian.

Grove, Christian. He was naturalized in Pennsylvania 10–12 Apr. 1762. He was from Lancaster County.

Grove, Francis. He was naturalized in Pennsylvania 10 Sep. 1761. He was from York County.

Grove, Jacob. He was naturalized in Pennsylvania 10 Apr. 1760.

Grove, John. He was naturalized in Pennsylvania 11 Apr. 1761. He was from York County.

Growar, John. He was naturalized in Pennsylvania 24–25 Sep./5 Oct. 1767. He was from Lower Merion Township, Philadelphia County.

Groward, John. He was naturalized in Massachusetts 7 Dec. 1731.

Growl, Michael. He was naturalized in Pennsylvania 10 Sep. 1761. He was from Berks County.

Grubb, Conrad. He was naturalized in Pennsylvania 11–13 Apr. 1743. He was from Philadelphia County.

Grubb, Henry. He was naturalized in Pennsylvania 11–13 Apr. 1743. He was from Philadelphia County.

Grubber, Christian. He was naturalized in Pennsylvania 10 Apr. 1760.

Gruber, John. He was naturalized in Pennsylvania 10 Sep. 1761. He was from Chester County.

Gruber, Peter. He was naturalized in Pennsylvania in Sep. 1740. He was from Bucks County.

Grundick, John. He was naturalized in Maryland 8 Sep. 1772. He was a German.

Gryder, Martin. He was naturalized in Pennsylvania 24 Sep. 1762. He was from Kent County, Delaware.

Gubelius, Peter. He was naturalized in Pennsylvania 11 Apr. 1761. He was from Lancaster County.

Gubban, Lasse Andries. He expressed his desire to be naturalized in New Castle County, Delaware 21 Feb. 1682/3.

Guedes, Jacob Deleon. He was naturalized in Jamaica 12 Dec. 1710.

Guepin, John. He was naturalized in Jamaica 11 Sep. 1680.

Guerant, John. He was naturalized in Virginia 12 May 1705.

Guerard, Dr. Jacob. He was naturalized in South Carolina 10 Mar. 1696/7.

Guerard, John. He was naturalized in South Carolina 10 Mar. 1696/7. He was a weaver.

Guerard, Peter Jacob. He was naturalized in South Carolina 10 Mar. 1696/7. He was a goldsmith.

Guerin, Gasper. He and his heirs were made denizens in Maryland 2 Mar. 1664/5.

Guerin, Girard. He took the oath of allegiance at Port Royal, Nova Scotia 16 Aug. 1695.

Guerin, John. He was naturalized in Virginia 12 May 1705.

Guerin, Mathurin. He was born at St. Nazaire, Xaintonge, France, the son of Pierre Guerin and Jeanne Billebaud. Her name also appeared as Jeanne Bilbau. His wife was Marie Nicollas who also appeared as Marie Nicholas. She was born LaChaume, Poitou, France, the daughter of Andre Nicholas and Francoise Dunot. They were naturalized in South Carolina 10 Mar. 1696/7. He was a gardener. He also appeared as Matline Guerin.

Guerineau, John. He was naturalized in New York 20 Dec. 1763.

Guerpin, Marie. She petitioned to be naturalized in New York 19 Aug. 1687.

Guerri, Pierre. He was the son of Jacques Guerri and Anne Guerri of Seuvet, Poitou, France. His wife was Jeanne Broussard, the daughter of Louis Broussard and Judith Broussard, of the same place. Their first son, Francois Guerri, was born in Dublin, Ireland, and their children Jean Guerri, Pierre Guerri, Jean Jacques Guerri, and Jeane Elizabeth Guerri were born in South Carolina. They were naturalized in South Carolina ca. 1696.

Guerrian, Francois. He was the son of Pierre Guerrian and Janne Billelbeau and was born in St. Nazere, Saintonge, France. His wife was Anne Arrine. They were naturalized in South Carolina ca. 1696.

Guerrin, Estienne. He was naturalized in New York 16 Aug. 1715. He was a yeoman from New Rochelle.

Guibal, Jean. He was the son of Henry Guibal and Claude Guibal, of St. Andre de Val, Languedoc, France. His wife was Ester Guibal, the daughter of Jean LeCert and Marie LeCert of Rennes, Bretagne, France. They were naturalized in South Carolina ca. 1696.

Guibert, Joshua. He was naturalized in Maryland 15 Nov. 1678. He was born in Rheims, France.

Guicard, Samuel. He was naturalized in Maryland 15 Nov. 1712. He lived in Anne Arundel County.

Guichard, Hubert. He was endenized in London 10 Feb. 1727. He was a planter from St. Christopher.

Guideon, Abraham. He was endenized in England 19 Aug. 1688. He settled in Barbados and was a Jew.

Guideon, Rowland. He was endenized in England 19 Aug. 1688. He settled in Barbados and was a Jew.

Guiden, Sampson. He was endenized in England 19 Aug. 1688. He settled in Barbados and was a Jew.

Guidry, Claude. He took the oath of allegiance at Port Royal, Nova Scotia 16 Aug. 1695.

Guignard, Gabriel. He was naturalized in South Carolina 24 Oct. 1741.

Guil, John. He was naturalized in Virginia 12 May 1705. He also appeared as John Gill.

Guil, Joseph. He was naturalized in Virginia 12 May 1705.

Guil, Stephen. He was naturalized in Virginia 12 May 1705. He also appeared as Stephen Gill.

Guilbeau, Pierre. He was an Acadian who took the oath of Annapolis in Dec. 1729.

Guillbaud, Charles. He was an Acadian and took the oath to George II at Annapolis River, Nova Scotia in Dec. 1729.

Guillbaud, Charles. He was an Acadian and took the oath to George II at Annapolis River, Nova Scotia in Dec. 1729.

Guillebau, Pierre. He took the oath of allegiance at Port Royal, Nova Scotia 16 Aug. 1695.

Guillett, Charles. He was endenized in London 29 Sep. 1698. He came to New York.

Guillo, Piere. He was an Acadian and took the oath to George II at Annapolis River, Nova Scotia in the winter of 1730.

Guillon, Francois. He was naturalized in Jamaica 27 Oct. 1731.

Guillot, Rene. He was an Acadian who took the oath of allegiance in Apr. 1730.

Guimard, Peter. He was endenized in England 3 July 1701. He came to New York.

Guindan, Estienne. He took the oath to the King 21–26 Oct. 1664 after the conquest of New Netherland.

Guion, Abraham. He was endenized in New York in Oct. 1697. He was a French Protestant.

Guion, Lewis. He was naturalized in New York 6 Sep. 1715. He was a blacksmith from New Rochelle.

Guion, Louis. He was endenized in New York 6 Feb. 1695/6.

Guion, Louis. He was endenized in New York 6 Feb. 1695/6. He was the son of Louis Guion.

Guions, Lewis. He was naturalized in New York 16 Sep. 1715.

Guise, Peter. He was naturalized in Maryland 15 Apr. 1771. He was a German.

Guise, Willem. He was naturalized in New Jersey 8 July 1730. He was born in Germany.

Guishard, Francis. He was naturalized in South Carolina 20 Jan. 1741.

Guitmett, Stephen. He was naturalized in Jamaica 16 Sep. 1707.

Gulch, Melchior. He, his wife Anne Catherine Gulch, son Heinrich Gulch, and daughter Magdalena Gulch were endenized in London 25 Aug. 1708. Magdalena Gulch also appeared as Margaret Gulch. They came to New York.

Gulick, Jochem. He took the oath of allegiance in Gravens End, Kings County, New York 26–30 Sep. 1687. He had been in the colony 34 years.

Gull, John. He was naturalized in Pennsylvania 25–27 Sep. 1740. He was from Philadelphia County.

Gummell, Martinus. He was naturalized in Maryland 11 Apr. 1759.

Gump, George. He was naturalized in Maryland 10 Apr. 1746. He lived in Prince George's County.

Gunckel, John. He was naturalized in Pennsylvania 10 Sep. 1761. He was from Berks County.

Gunter, Johan Frederick. He was naturalized in New York 12 July 1729.

Gurner, Peter. He was naturalized in Frederick County, Virginia 4 Aug. 1747.

Gurhart, Rudolph. He was naturalized in Pennsylvania 11 Apr. 1761. He was from Berks County.

Guteres, Jacob Mendez, Jr. He was naturalized in Jamaica 20 Oct. 1699.

Guteres, Leah Mendez. She was naturalized in Jamaica 2 Jan. 1701/2.

Guteres, Moses. He was naturalized in Jamaica 28 Dec. 1700.

Guteyahr, John Christian. He was naturalized in Pennsylvania 10 Sep. 1761. He was from Lancaster County.

Gutierez, Isaque Mendez. He sought to be a denizen 30 Aug. 1692. He was from Jamaica and a Jew.

Gutierez, Sarah Mendez. She was naturalized in Jamaica 3 Nov. 1716. She was wife of Jacob Mendez Gutierez.

Gutteres, Aaron de Mattos. He was endenized in London 15 Dec. 1732. He was from Barbados.

Gutteres, Jacob Mendes. He was naturalized in Jamaica 6 Jan. 1670.

Gutteres, Jacob Mendes, Jr. He was naturalized in Jamaica 29 Mar. 1695.

Gutteres, Jacob Mendes. He was naturalized in Jamaica 25 Nov. 1740. He was a Jew.

Gutteres, Lues Dias. He was endenized in England 12 July 1661. He also appeared as Luodivus Dios Gutieres. He was a Jew.

Gutterez, Gabriel. He was naturalized in Jamaica 4 Dec. 1704.

Guyer, George. He was naturalized in Pennsylvania 10 Sep. 1761. He was from Lancaster County.

Guyger, Jesse. He was naturalized in Pennsylvania 24–25 Sep. 1764. He was from Merrion Township, Philadelphia County.

Gyer, Casper. He was naturalized in Pennsylvania 24–25 Sep. 1764. He was from Philadelphia.
Gyer, Paul. He was naturalized in Pennsylvania 24 Sep. 1762. He was from York County.
Gyl, Rachell Henriques. She was naturalized in Jamaica 8 June 1696. She was a widow.
Gyselbreght, Godfreyd. He was naturalized in New York 3 May 1755.
Gyger, Christian. He was naturalized in Pennsylvania 10 Sep. 1761. He was from Lancaster County.
Gyser, Christopher. He was naturalized in Maryland 24 Sep. 1762. He was a German from Frederick County.
Gyser, Christopher. He was naturalized in Pennsylvania 11 Apr. 1763. He was from Marlborough Township, Philadelphia County.
Gysert, Melchior. He was naturalized in Pennsylvania 24–25 Sep. 1764. He was from Paxton Township, Lancaster County.
Gysinger, John. He was naturalized in Maryland 24 Sep. 1765. He was a German.
Haag, Andrew. He was naturalized in New Jersey in 1762. He was born in Germany. He had lived in New Jersey eight years.
Haag, Andrew. He was naturalized in New Jersey in 1771. He was born in Germany. He also appeared as Andrew High. He resided in Hopewell, Cumberland County.
Haaghort, Geradus. He was naturalized in New York 24 Oct. 1753. He was a clerk from Essex County, New Jersey.
Haan, George. He was naturalized in Maryland 14 Sep. 1763. He was a German from Frederick County.
Haan, Henry. He was naturalized in New York 8 Mar. 1773.
Haan, Philip. He was naturalized in Pennsylvania 19 May 1739. He was from Philadelphia County.
Haas, Adam. He was naturalized in Pennsylvania 24–25 Sep. 1764. He was from Germantown Township, Philadelphia County.
Haas, Hans Jury. He was naturalized in New York 13 Dec. 1737.
Haas, John. He was naturalized in New Jersey in 1768.
Haas, John Hartman. He was naturalized in Pennsylvania 10 & 23 Apr. 1764. He was from Providence Township, Philadelphia County.
Haas, John Philip de. He was naturalized in Pennsylvania 10 & 23 Sep. 1764. He was from Philadelphia.
Haas, Peter. He was naturalized in Pennsylvania 24 Sep. 1759.
Habener, Andrew. He was naturalized in New York 29 July 1762. He was a cordwainer from New York City.
Haber, Zacharias. He was naturalized in New York 22 June 1734.
Haberling, Johannes. He was naturalized in Pennsylvania 24 Sep. 1746. He was from Lancaster County.
Haberman, Hendrick. He was naturalized in New York 11 Sep. 1761.
Haberman, Jacob. He was naturalized in New York 11 Sep. 1761.
Habersacker, John. He was naturalized in Pennsylvania 11 Apr. 1761. He was from Berks County.
Haberte, John. He was naturalized in Maryland 11 Apr. 1759.
Hache, Michel. He was an Acadian and took the oath of allegiance in Apr. 1730.
Hack, Jacob. He sought naturalization in New Jersey in the 18th century.
Hacke, George. He was endenized in Northampton County, Virginia 28 Mar. 1653. He was a native of Cologne, Germany.
Hacke, George. He was naturalized in Northampton County, Virginia 1 Apr. 1658. He was a Dutchman.
Hacke, Theodore. He and his wife, Elizabeth Hacke, were naturalized in Northampton County, Virginia 17 Sep. 1656.
Hackenmiller, John Albright. He was naturalized in Pennsylvania 24 Sep. 1759.
Hacker, George. He was naturalized in Pennsylvania 24 Sep. 1760. He was from Lancaster County.
Hacker, Jacob. He was naturalized in Pennsylvania 24 Sep. 1762. He was from Lancaster County.
Hackerschmid, Conrad. He was naturalized in Maryland 9 Sep. 1761.
Hackner, Wolfgang. He was naturalized in Pennsylvania 11 Apr. 1761. He was from Berks County.

Hadler, Sebastian. He was naturalized in Maryland 9 Sep. 1761. He was from Anne Arundel County.

Hadn, Ludwick. He was naturalized in New Jersey 8 Dec. 1744.

Haecks, Simon. He took the oath of allegiance in Boswijck, Kings County, New York 26–30 Sep. 1687. He had been in the colony 16 years.

Haeffner, Henry. He was naturalized in Pennsylvania 11 Apr. 1763. He was from Richmond Township, Berks County.

Haelaret, Theodore. He was naturalized in Jamaica 21 Feb. 1681/2.

Haemerbergh, Rosloff. He was naturalized in Jamaica 27 Mar. 1760.

Haesbrock, Abraham. He took the oath of naturalization in New York 1 Sep. 1687 in Ulster County. He was styled lieutenant.

Haesbrock, John. He took the oath of naturalization in New York 1 Sep. 1687 in Ulster County.

Haffaa, Melchior. He was naturalized in Pennsylvania 24 Sep. 1760. He was from Berks County.

Hafflefinger, Jacob. He was naturalized in Pennsylvania 11–13 Apr. 1743. He was from Philadelphia County.

Haffner, George. He was naturalized in Pennsylvania 11 Apr. 1761. He was from Berks County.

Hafften, Jacob Hend. He took the oath of allegiance in Flackbush, Kings County, New York 26–30 Sep. 1687. He had been in the colony 23 years.

Hafner, Frederick. He was naturalized in Maryland in Apr. 1749. He was from Frederick County.

Hafner, Frederick. He was naturalized in Maryland 14 Apr. 1761.

Hafner, John George. He was naturalized in Pennsylvania 10 Sep. 1761. He was from Philadelphia County.

Hafner, John Michael. He was naturalized in Maryland in Apr. 1749. He was from Frederick County.

Hag, Adam. He was naturalized in New Jersey 20 Aug. 1755.

Hagar, David. He was naturalized in Maryland 21 Sep. 1764. He was a German.

Hagar, John. He was naturalized in Maryland 14 Sep. 1763. He was a German.

Hagebuck, Andrew. He was naturalized in Pennsylvania 10–12 Apr. 1762. He was from Berks County.

Hagelsieb, Carl Lewis. He was naturalized in Nova Scotia 6 July 1758.

Hageman, Ulrich. He was naturalized in Pennsylvania 25 Feb.1725/26. He was born in Germany.

Hagenburger, Herbert. He was naturalized in New Jersey in 1750. He also appeared as Herbert Hacheburger.

Hagener, Jeremias Janssen. He took the oath to the King 21–26 Oct. 1664 after the conquest of New Netherland.

Hagener, Valentine. He was naturalized in Pennsylvania 11 Apr. 1763. He was from Philadelphia.

Hagedorn, Christopel. He was naturalized in New York 22 Nov. 1715. He was from Albany County.

Hagedorn, Willem. He was naturalized in New York 14 Feb. 1715/6. He was from Albany County.

Hager, Hendrick. He was naturalized in New York 8 Mar. 1773.

Hager, John Frederick. He was naturalized in New York 4 Oct. 1715. He was a minister from Palatine.

Hagerman, Christopher. He was naturalized in New York 11 Sep. 1761.

Hagey, John. He was naturalized in Pennsylvania 19 May 1739. He was from Lancaster County.

Hagi, Johannes. He was naturalized in New Jersey in 1759. He also appeared as John Hager and John Hage. He was born in Germany.

Hagmayer, Conrode. He was naturalized in Maryland 11 Apr. 1753.

Hagner, John. He was naturalized in Pennsylvania 24 Nov. 1769. He was from Manchester Township, York County.

Hagner, John Frederick. He was naturalized in Pennsylvania 11 Apr. 1761. He was from Philadelphia County.

Hahn, Coenraad. He was naturalized in New York 11 Sep. 1761.

Hahn, John. He was naturalized in Maryland 14 Sep. 1763. He was a German from Frederick County.

Hahn, Lodowich. He was naturalized in Maryland 12 Apr. 1758.

Hahn, Michael. He was naturalized in Maryland 12 Sep. 1759.

Hail, Thomas. He was naturalized in Pennsylvania 11 Apr. 1749. He was from Philadelphia County.

Hailenmann, Mattheus. He was naturalized in New York 3 July 1759.

Haim, Joseph. He was naturalized in Jamaica 10 July 1744.

Haimsell, Stophel. He was naturalized in Pennsylvania 10 Apr. 1759.

Hain, John. He was endenized in England 14 Oct. 1681. He came to New England.

Haine, Nicholas. He was naturalized in Pennsylvania 11 Apr. 1763. He was from Cocalico Township, Lancaster County.

Haine, Peter. He was naturalized in New York 20 Mar. 1762.

Haines, Marcus. He was naturalized in Pennsylvania 24 Sep. 1762. He was from York County.

Hains, William. He was naturalized in Pennsylvania 10 Apr. 1760.

Hainz, John. He was naturalized in Maryland 15 Sep. 1762. He was from Frederick County.

Hak, Anna. She and her children, George Hak and Peter Hak, were naturalized in Maryland 1 May 1666. She was born in Amsterdam, Holland and her children in Accomack County, Virginia. They also appeared as Anna Hack, George Hack, and Peter Hack.

Haldeman, Nicholas. He was naturalized in Pennsylvania 11–13 Apr. 1743. He was from Philadelphia County.

Haldeman, Nicholas, Jr. He was naturalized in Pennsylvania 11–13 Apr. 1743. He was from Philadelphia County.

Halderman, Christian. He was naturalized in Pennsylvania 11–13 Apr. 1743. He was from Philadelphia County.

Haldiman, Peter. He was naturalized in Maryland in Dec. 1769.

Hall, John. He was naturalized in Jamaica 19 Sep. 1760.

Hall, Philip. He was naturalized in Pennsylvania 24 Sep. 1763. He was from Philadelphia.

Hall, Thomas. He took the oath to the King 21–26 Oct. 1664 after the conquest of New Netherland.

Hall, Thomas. He was naturalized in New Jersey 20 Aug. 1755.

Hallem, Michael. He was naturalized in Pennsylvania 22 May 1769. He was from Antrim Township, Cumberland County.

Haller, Zacharias. He was naturalized in Pennsylvania 10 Apr. 1770. He was from Lindon Township, Northampton County.

Halling, Michael Jansen. He was naturalized in Pennsylvania 19 May 1739. He was from Philadelphia County.

Hallman, John. He was naturalized in Pennsylvania 11–13 Apr. 1743. He was from Philadelphia County.

Halstead, Elizabeth. She was naturalized in Jamaica 27 Jan. 1719/20.

Halstead, Mary. She was naturalized in Jamaica 1 Mar. 1696. She was the wife of Lawrence Halstead.

Halth, John. He was naturalized in New York 16 Feb. 1771.

Ham, Casper. He was naturalized in New York 14 Feb. 1715/6. He was from Albany County.

Ham, Coenraet. He was naturalized in New York 17 Jan. 1715/6. He was from Albany County.

Ham, John. He took the oath of allegiance at Mobile, West Florida 2 Oct. 1764.

Ham, Peter. He was naturalized in New York 28 Feb. 1715/6. He was from Albany County.

Haman, Philip. He was naturalized in Maryland 11 Sep. 1765.

Hambell, Jacob. He was naturalized in North Carolina 22 Sep. 1763. He was from Rowan County and a German.

Hambough, Johan Willem. He was naturalized in New York 17 Jan. 1715/6. He was from Albany County.

Hambright, Adam. He was naturalized in Pennsylvania 10 Apr. 1760.

Hamego, Aaron. He was naturalized in Jamaica 13 May 1685.

Hamel, Estienne. He petitioned to be naturalized in New York 19 Aug. 1687.

Hamel, Estienne. He was an Acadian and took the oath of allegiance in Apr. 1730.

Hamell, Estienne. He was an Acadian who took the oath of allegiance to the King at the Mines, Pisiquit 31 Oct. 1727.

Hamesago, Moses. He was endenized in Feb. 1663 in Barbados. He was a native of Spain.

Hamilton, Col. Walter. He was naturalized in Nevis 11 Mar. 1703. He was born of English parents.

Hamine, Valentine. He was naturalized in Pennsylvania 24 Sep. 1763. He was from Paradise Township, York County.

Hamme, Valentine. He was naturalized in Pennsylvania 24 Sep. 1763. He was from Paradise Township, York County.

Hammer, Andrew. He was naturalized in Pennsylvania 10 Apr. 1765. He was from Brecknock Township, Lancaster County.

Hammer, Francis. He was naturalized in Maryland 11 Sep. 1765. He was a German from Frederick County.

Hammer, George. He was naturalized in Augusta County, Virginia 18 May 1762.

Hammer, Michael. He was naturalized in New Jersey 7 Apr. 1761.

Hammersmith, Philip. He was naturalized in Pennsylvania 10 Apr. 1767. He was from Douglass Township, Philadelphia County.

Hammond, Andrew. He was naturalized in Maryland 9 Sep. 1761. He was from Anne Arundel County.

Hammond, John. He was naturalized in Maryland 9 Sep. 1761. He was from Anne Arundel County.

Hammond, John George. He was naturalized in Maryland 9 Sep. 1761. He was from Anne Arundel County.

Hammond, Mathew. He was naturalized in Maryland 9 Sep. 1761. He was from Anne Arundel County.

Hammond, Peter. He was naturalized in Maryland 29 Nov. 1774. He was a German.

Hamon, Jacob. He was naturalized in North Carolina 22 Mar. 1764. He was from Rowan County and a German.

Hamond, John. He was naturalized in Maryland 15 Sep. 1762. He was from Frederick County.

Hampher, John. He was naturalized in Pennsylvania 14 Feb. 1729/30. He was from Lancaster County.

Hamshaw, Anthony. He was naturalized in Pennsylvania 11 Apr. 1761. He was from Berks County.

Han, Jacob. He was naturalized in Maryland 17 Sep. 1764. He was a German.

Han, William. He was naturalized in New Jersey 8 July 1730. He was born in Germany.

Hancen, Anthony. He was naturalized in Sussex County, Delaware 28 Apr. 1683. His alias was Anthony Haverla.

Hanchier, Peter. He was naturalized in Frederick County, Virginia 7 Aug. 1770.

Hanely, John Sigismund. He was naturalized in Pennsylvania 25–26 Sep./4 Oct. 1749. He was from Lancaster County.

Handshuh, John Frederick. He was naturalized in Pennsylvania 24 Sep. 1760. He was from Philadelphia County.

Handwerk, John Nicholas. He was naturalized in Pennsylvania 24 Sep. 1760. He was from Northampton County.

Haneline, John. He was naturalized in North Carolina 26 Sep. 1767. He was from Rowan County. He also appeared as John Hainline.

Haninger, Michael. He was naturalized in Pennsylvania 26–27 Sep. 1743. He was from Philadelphia County.

Hank, Jacobus. He was naturalized in Maryland 15 Sep. 1762.

Hanley, Stophel. He was naturalized in Pennsylvania 10 Apr. 1759.

Hanly, Christopher. He was naturalized in Pennsylvania 10 Apr. 1766. He was from Earl Township, Lancaster County.

Hann, Hendrick. He was naturalized in New York 17 Jan. 1770.

Hanniberger, John. He was naturalized in Pennsylvania 26–27 Sep. 1743. He was from Lancaster County.

Hannithar, Simon. He was naturalized in Jamaica 12 Oct. 1699.

Hans, Henrick. He was naturalized in Pennsylvania in Sep. 1740. He was from Philadelphia County.

Hans, Hieronimus. He was naturalized in Pennsylvania in Sep. 1740. He was from Philadelphia County.

Hansberger, Ulrick. He was naturalized in Pennsylvania 10 Apr. 1759.

Hanse, Henry. He was naturalized in Pennsylvania 11 Apr. 1761. He was from Lancaster County.

Hanse, Jacob. He was naturalized in Pennsylvania 20 Sep. 1766. He was a mariner and a German.

Hanses, Josiah James. He was naturalized in Jamaica 11 Nov. 1703. He was a minor and was born on the high seas of English parents in an English bottom.

Hansith, Bernard Michael. He was naturalized in Maryland 24 Sep. 1753.

Hanson, Godfried. He was naturalized in New York 28 Feb. 1715/6. He was a rope-maker from Rye.

Hanson, Nicholas. He was naturalized in Jamaica 23 Feb. 1704/5.

Hanssen, Gerrit. He took the oath of allegiance in Flackland, Kings County, New York 26–30 Sep. 1687. He was a native of the colony.

Hanssen, Joris. He took the oath of allegiance in Breucklijn, Kings County, New York 26–30 Sep. 1687. He was a native of the colony.

Hanssen, Machiel. He took the oath of allegiance in Breucklijn, Kings County, New York 26–30 Sep. 1687. He was a native of the colony.

Hanssen, Simon. He took the oath of allegiance in Flackbush, Kings County, New York 26–30 Sep. 1687. He had been in the colony 48 years.

Hansun, Hans. He was naturalized in Maryland 20 Oct. 1671. He was born in Delaware Bay of Swedish parents. He also appeared as Hans Hanson.

Hanswurth, Michael. He was naturalized in New York 3 July 1759.

Hapach, Jost. He was naturalized in New Jersey in 1750. He also appeared as Jost George Habach. He was from Hunterdon County.

Harberdinck, Johannes. He was naturalized in New York 15 Nov. 1715. He was a shoemaker from New York City.

Harbine, Peter. He was naturalized in Pennsylvania 11 Apr. 1761. He was from Berks County.

Hardenbergh, Johanis. He was naturalized in New York 8–9 Sep. 1715. He was from Ulster County.

Hardenbroeck, Abell. He took the oath to the King 21–26 Oct. 1664 after the conquest of New Netherland.

Hardenbroeck, Johannes. He took the oath to the King 21–26 Oct. 1664 after the conquest of New Netherland.

Hardlis, George. He was naturalized in Maryland 11 Sep. 1765.

Hare, Abraham. He was naturalized in Pennsylvania 14 Feb. 1729/30. He was from Lancaster County.

Harff, Johannes Balthaser. He was naturalized in New Jersey 6 Dec. 1769.

Hargarater, John. He was naturalized in Pennsylvania 24 Sep. 1755. He was from Berks County.

Hargate, Peter. He was naturalized in Maryland 24 Sep. 1762. He was a German from Frederick County.

Hariem, Tobias. He was naturalized in Maryland 7 May 1767. He was a German from Frederick County.

Hariman, Joseph. He was naturalized in Maryland 24 Sep. 1753.

Harlacher, Godfried. He was naturalized in Pennsylvania 10–14 Apr. 1747. He was from Philadelphia County.

Harman, Jacob. He was naturalized in Augusta County, Virginia 16 Aug. 1758.

Harman, John. He was naturalized in Frederick County, Virginia 5 May 1747.

Harman, Marricks. He was naturalized in Maryland 11 Sep. 1765.

Harman, William. He was naturalized in Pennsylvania 2 Feb. 1765. He was a baker from Philadelphia. He came into the province as an infant from Germany.

Harmansa, Thomas. He took the oath of naturalization in New York 13 June 1687.

Harmany, Nicholas. He was naturalized in Pennsylvania 11–13 Apr. 1743. He was from Philadelphia County.

Harmenson, Thomas. He was naturalized in Northampton County, Virginia Sep. 1673 and 8 June 1680.

Harmenssen, Jan. He took the oath of allegiance in Kings County, New York 26–30 Sep. 1687. He was from Amesfoort. He had been in the colony 29 years.

Harmer, Gothofrid. He was made a denizen in Maryland 29 July 1661. He was Swedish and was late of New Amstel.

Harmony, Lodowick. He was naturalized in Pennsylvania 25–27 Sep. 1740. He was from Philadelphia County.

Harnest, Jacob. He was naturalized in Pennsylvania 26–27 Sep. 1743. He was from Lancaster County.

Harnick, Peter. He took the oath of allegiance in Orange County, New York 26 Sep. 1687.

Harnish, Samuel. He was naturalized in Pennsylvania 24 Sep. 1766.

Harnist, Martin. He was naturalized in Pennsylvania 14 Feb. 1729/30. He was from Lancaster County.

Harout, Peter. He was a native of France and lived in Charles County, Maryland. He was naturalized in Maryland 18 Oct. 1742. He also appeared as Peter Harrant.

Harpain, James. He sought naturalization in New York 12 Nov. 1748.

Harper, Jacob. He was naturalized in Augusta County, Virginia 16 Oct. 1765.

Harralson, Paul. He was naturalized in Virginia 23 Mar. 1703.

Harramansa, Thomas. He was naturalized in New York 1 Sep. 1687 in Ulster County.

Harriott, David. He was naturalized in Maryland 1742–1743.

Harris, Sarah. She was naturalized in Jamaica 5 Mar. 1722.

Harrison, Erasmus. He was endenized in New York 22 June 1686.

Harrison, Paul. He was naturalized in North Carolina 22 Sep. 1763. He was from Rowan County and a German.

Harry, Martin. He was naturalized in Pennsylvania 24 Sep. 1763. He was from Rowan County and a German.

Harsh, Frederick. He was naturalized in Maryland 16 Sep. 1762. He was a German from Frederick County.

Hart, Abraham. He was naturalized in Jamaica 4 Apr. 1706.

Hart, Casper. He was endenized in New York 22 June 1686.

Hart, Conrad. He was naturalized in Pennsylvania 10 Sep. 1761. He was from Berks County.

Hart, Levy. He was naturalized in New York 27 Oct. 1763. He was a Jewish merchant.

Hart, Mary. She was naturalized in Pennsylvania 10 & 23 Apr. 1764. She was from Easton Township, Northampton County. She was a Jewess.

Hart, Myer. He was naturalized in Pennsylvania 10–23 Sep. 1764. He was a Jew. He was from Easton Township, Northampton County.

Hart, Solomon. He was naturalized in New York 27 Apr. 1741. He was a Jew.

Hartel, Hannis. He was naturalized in New York 27 Jan. 1770.

Harter, Henry. He was naturalized in New Jersey 20 Aug. 1755.

Hartestein, Michael. He was naturalized in New York 15 Oct. 1765. He was a laborer from New York City.

Hartline, Leonhart. He was naturalized in Pennsylvania 19 May 1739. He was from Philadelphia County.

Hartman, Adam. He was naturalized in New York 8 Mar. 1773.

Hartman, Christian. He was naturalized in New York 23 Aug. 1715. He was a joiner from New York City.

Hartman, Christian. He was naturalized in Pennsylvania 11 Apr. 1761. He was from Lancaster County.

Hartman, Felters. He was naturalized in Maryland 26 Apr. 1750.

Hartman, George. He was naturalized in Maryland 17 Sep. 1751.

Hartman, George. He was naturalized in Pennsylvania 10 Apr. 1760.

Hartman, Jacob. He was naturalized in Pennsylvania 10 May 1739. He was from Lancaster County.

Hartman, John. He was naturalized in New Jersey 6 Dec. 1769.

Hartman, John. He was naturalized in Pennsylvania 11–12 Apr. 1744. He was from Philadelphia County.

Hartman, Lewis. He was naturalized in Jamaica 18 July 1715.

Hartman, Margaret. She was naturalized in Maryland 11 Sep. 1765. She was a German and lived in Frederick, Maryland.

Hartman, Matthias. He was naturalized in Pennsylvania 24 Nov. 1769. He was from Dover Township, York County.

Hartman, Theophilus. He was naturalized in Pennsylvania 19 May 1739. He was from Lancaster County.

Hartman, Theophilus, Jr. He was naturalized in Pennsylvania 19 May 1739. He was from Lancaster County.

Hartman, Ulrick. He was naturalized in Pennsylvania 11 Apr. 1761. He was from Philadelphia County.

Hartner, John. He was naturalized in Maryland 11 Sep. 1765. He was a German from Frederick County.

Hartramff, Melchoir. He was naturalized in Pennsylvania 26 Sep. 1748. He was from Philadelphia County.

Hartrampff, Abraham. He was naturalized in Pennsylvania 24 Sep. 1745. He was from Philadelphia County.

Harts, John. He was naturalized in Maryland 13 Sep. 1758.

Hartsell, George. He was naturalized in Pennsylvania in Sep. 1740. He was from Bucks County.

Hartsle, George Henry. He was naturalized in Maryland in Sep. 1740. He was from Bucks County.

Hartsman, Mathias Ulrich. He was naturalized in Maryland 12 Sep. 1753.

Hartwake, George. He was naturalized in Maryland 10 Sep. 1762.

Hartway, Feiters. He was naturalized in Maryland 26 Apr. 1750.

Hartwick, John Christopher. He was naturalized in Pennsylvania 24 Sep. 1754. He was from Philadelphia County.

Harvey, Gideon. He was naturalized in Northumberland County, Virginia 17 Sep. 1656. He was a native of the Hague, Holland and was the son of John and Elizabeth Harvey of Westminster, Middlesex, England.

Harvey, Thomas. He and his children were naturalized in Maryland 3 June 1715. He lived in Calvert County and was French.

Harvick, Nicholas. He was naturalized in Pennsylvania 24 Sep. 1766.

Hasbrouck, Abraham. He was naturalized in New York 8–9 Sep. 1715. He was from Ulster County.

Haselbecher, John Philip. He was naturalized in Pennsylvania 10 Apr. 1769. He was from Douglass Township, Berks County.

Hasenclever, Francis Caspar. He was naturalized in Pennsylvania 26 Feb. 1773. He was from Philadelphia and was a merchant.

Hasis, Georg. He was naturalized in New York 3 July 1759.

Hassart, Arent. He was naturalized in Pennsylvania 1725–26. He was born in Germany.

Hassel, Christian. He was naturalized in New Jersey 8 July 1730. He was born in Germany.

Hassel, Elias. He was naturalized in Pennsylvania in Sep. 1740. He was from Bucks County.

Hassen, Christian. He was naturalized in New Jersey 20 Aug. 1755.

Hassert, Arent. He was naturalized in Pennsylvania 25 Feb. 1725/6.

Hassert, Arent. He was naturalized in Pennsylvania 25 Sep. 1740. He was from Philadelphia.

Hassinger, Herman. He was naturalized in Pennsylvania 11 Apr. 1761. He was from Berks County.

Hastadder, John. He was naturalized in Pennsylvania 11–12 Apr. 1744. He was from Lancaster County.

Hastadder, Oswald. He was naturalized in Pennsylvania 11–12 Apr. 1744. He was from Lancaster County.

Hatier, John. He was endenized in New York 30 May 1695.

Hatt, Conrad. He was naturalized in Nova Scotia 5 July 1758.

Hauck, Jacob. He was naturalized in Pennsylvania 13–15 Apr. 1748. He was from Bucks County.

Hauer, Nicholas. He was naturalized in Pennsylvania 24–25 Sep. 1764. He was from Lancaster Township, Lancaster County.

Hauk, Jacob. He was naturalized in Maryland 11 Apr. 1764. He was a German.

Hauk, Michael. He was naturalized in Pennsylvania 25 Sep. 1750. He was from Philadelphia County.

Hauk, Tobias. He was naturalized in New Jersey in 1751. He was from Somerset County.

Hauk, Stephen. He was naturalized in Pennsylvania 24 Sep. 1762. He was from Berks County.

Hauke, William. He was naturalized in Pennsylvania 19 May 1739. He was from Philadelphia County.

Hauker, William. He was naturalized in Pennsylvania 11 Apr. 1752. He was from Lancaster County.

Haumaid, Jean. He was naturalized in New York 8 Mar. 1773.

Haun, Henry. He was naturalized in Pennsylvania 25 Sep. 1758.

Haupt, Bastian. He was naturalized in Pennsylvania 25 Sep. 1750. He was from Philadelphia County.

Haus, Balthazar. He was naturalized in Pennsylvania 11–13 Apr. 1743. He was from Bucks County.

Haus, John. He was naturalized in Maryland 23 Apr. 1772. He was a German.

Haus, Peter. He was naturalized in Pennsylvania 10 Apr. 1760.

Hauser, Abraham. He was naturalized in Pennsylvania 11 Apr. 1761. He was from Philadelphia County.

Hauser, Casper. He was naturalized in Maryland 12 Sep. 1763. He was a German.

Hauser, Joseph. He was naturalized in New York 20 Dec. 1763.

Haushaller, John Adam. He was naturalized in Pennsylvania 10 Sep. 1761. He was from Berks County.

Hausz, Johannus. He was naturalized in New York 27 July 1721.

Haut, John George. He was naturalized in Maryland 16 Apr. 1761.

Hautbois, Pierre. He was an Acadian and took the oath to George II at Annapolis River, Nova Scotia in the winter of 1730.

Hautbois, Pierre. He was an Acadian and took the oath of allegiance in Apr. 1730.

Hautz, Philip. He was naturalized in Pennsylvania 25 Sep. 1751. He was from Lancaster County.

Hautz, Philip Lawrence. He was naturalized in Pennsylvania 25 Sep. 1751. He was from Lancaster County.

Havener, Ludwick. He was naturalized in Augusta County, Virginia 18 May 1762.

Havener, Nicholas. He was naturalized in Pennsylvania 25 Sep. 1750. He was from Lancaster County.

Havenor, Nicholas. He was naturalized in Augusta County, Virginia 28 May 1762.

Haver, Christiaen. He was naturalized in New York 17 Jan. 1715/6. He was from Albany County.

Hawk, Andrew. He was naturalized in Pennsylvania 11–13 Apr. 1743. He was from Philadelphia County.

Hawker, Adam. He was naturalized in Pennsylvania 10–12 Apr. 1762. He was from Lancaster County.

Hawse, Symon. He was naturalized in New York 27 Apr. 1716. He was from Albany County.

Hay, Charles. He was naturalized in Pennsylvania 11 Apr. 1763. He was from Bristol Township, Philadelphia County.

Hay, David. He was naturalized in New York in 1740–41. He was a Jew.

Hay, Judah. He was naturalized in New York in 1740–41. He was a Jewish merchant.

Hay, Melchior. He was naturalized in Pennsylvania 10–12 Apr. 1762. He was from Northampton County.

Haymaker, Adam. He was naturalized in Frederick County, Virginia 3 Oct. 1765.

Hayn, Frederick. He was naturalized in New Jersey in 1768.

Hayne, John Christopher. He was naturalized in Pennsylvania 11 Apr. 1761. He was from Lancaster County.

Hays, David. He was naturalized in New York 12 June 1729.

Hays, Isaac. He was naturalized in New York 26 Apr. 1748. He was a tallow chandler from New York City. He was a Jew.

Hays, Jacob. He was naturalized in New York 6 July 1723.

Hays, Judah. He was naturalized in New York 12 July 1729.

Hayser, John Ernst. He was naturalized in Pennsylvania 10 & 23 Apr. 1764. He was from Philadelphia.

Hayworth, Richard. He was naturalized in Frederick County, Virginia 3 June 1765.

Hazerman, Christopher. He was naturalized in New York 11 Sep. 1761.

Hazlebach, Nicholas. He was naturalized in Pennsylvania 10 & 23 Apr. 1764. He was from Germantown, Philadelphia County.

Headerick, George. He was naturalized in Pennsylvania 10 Apr. 1755. He was from Lancaster County.

Heagy, Jacob. He was naturalized in Pennsylvania 10–11 Apr. 1745. He was from Lancaster County.

Heanes, Johannes. He was naturalized in Pennsylvania 11–13 Apr. 1743. He was from Philadelphia County.

Hearing, Henry. He was naturalized in New York 31 Dec. 1768.

Heartman, Joseph. He was naturalized in Maryland 11 Apr. 1764. He was a German.

Heath, William. He was naturalized in Jamaica in Sep. 1690.

Heauke, Jacob. He was naturalized in Pennsylvania 10 Apr. 1757.

Heavely, Adam. He was naturalized in Pennsylvania 10 Apr. 1755. He was from Northampton County.

Heavenor, Melchoir. He was naturalized in Pennsylvania 25 Sep. 1750. He was from Philadelphia County.

Hebener, Christopher. He was naturalized in Pennsylvania 10 Apr. 1755. He was from Philadelphia County.

Heberlin, Andrew. He was naturalized in Maryland 13 May 1774. He was a German from Frederick County.

Hebert, Alexandre. He was an Acadian and took the oath at Annapolis River in Dec. 1729.

Hebert, Antoine. He was an Acadian and took the oath at Annapolis River in Dec. 1729.

Hebert, August. He was an Acadian and took the oath of allegiance in Apr. 1730.

Hebert, Augustin. He was an Acadian who took the oath to the King at the Mines, Pisiquit, Nova Scotia 31 Oct. 1727.

Hebert, Emanuel. He took the oath of allegiance at Port Royal, Nova Scotia 16 Aug. 1695.

Hebert, Germain. He was an Acadian and took the oath to the King at the Mines, Pisiquit, Nova Scotia 31 Oct. 1727.

Hebert, Guillaume. He was an Acadian and took the oath to the King at the Mines, Pisiquit, Nova Scotia 31 Oct. 1727.

Hebert, Jacques. He was an Acadian and took the oath to the King at the Mines, Pisiquit, Nova Scotia 31 Oct. 1727.

Hebert, Louis. He was an Acadian and took the oath at Annapolis River in Dec. 1729.

Hebert, Michel. He was an Acadian and took the oath of allegiance in Apr. 1730.

Hebert, Pierre. He was an Acadian who took the oath of allegiance at the Mines, Pisiquit, Nova Scotia 31 Oct. 1727.

Hebert, Pierre. He was an Acadian who took the oath of allegiance at Annapolis River in Dec. 1729.

Hebert, Pierre. He was an Acadian and took the oath of allegiance in Apr. 1730.

Hebert, Rene. He was an Acadian and took the oath to the King at the Mines, Pisiquit, Nova Scotia 31 Oct. 1727.

Hecht, Frederick William. He was naturalized in New York 1 Aug. 1766. He was from New York City.

Heck, Jacob. He was naturalized in Pennsylvania 11 Apr. 1761. He was from Berks County.

Heck, Jacob. He was naturalized in Pennsylvania 24 Sep. 1762. He was from York County.

Heck, John Jost. He was naturalized in Pennsylvania 11 Apr. 1741. He was from Lancaster County.

Heckeler, Rudolph. He was naturalized in Pennsylvania 10 Apr. 1753. He was from Berks County.

Heckendon, Jacob. He was naturalized in Maryland 15 Apr. 1761.

Heddings, Lawrence. He had a certificate of naturalization which he registered in New York City 13 Dec. 1700.

Heder, Henrik. He was naturalized in New York 7 Aug. 1744. He was a carman from New York City.

Heder, Henry. He sought naturalization in New York 3 Nov. 1739.

Hedrick, William. He was naturalized in Pennsylvania 11 Apr. 1761. He was from Berks County.

Hedrick, Yost. He was naturalized in Pennsylvania 11 Apr. 1761. He was from Berks County.

Heebner, John Christopher. He was naturalized in Pennsylvania 25–26 Sep./4 Oct. 1749. He was from Philadelphia County.

Heekendorn, John. He was naturalized in Pennsylvania 10 Sep. 1761. He was from York County.

Heekendorn, Martin. He was naturalized in Pennsylvania 24 Sep. 1759.

Heemer, Juryh Herck. He was naturalized in New York 11 Oct. 1715. He was from Albany County.

Heen, Peter. He was naturalized in New York 20 Mar. 1762.

Heerback, John George. He was naturalized in Maryland 9 Sep. 1761. He was a farmer and joiner from Frederick County.

Heerbenk, John. He was naturalized in New York 20 Apr. 1769. He was a tanner from New York City.

Heerin, Mary. She was naturalized in Maryland 10 Apr. 1771. She was a German.

Heermans, Jan. He was naturalized in New York 8–9 Sep. 1715. He was from Albany County.

Heese, Frederick. He was naturalized in Pennsylvania 24 Sep. 1762. He was from Berks County.

Hefflefinger, Collee. He was naturalized in Pennsylvania 11–13 Apr. 1743. He was from Philadelphia County.

Hefflefinger, Henry. He was naturalized in Pennsylvania 11–13 Apr. 1743. He was from Philadelphia County.

Heffley, Peter. He was naturalized in Pennsylvania 11 Apr. 1761. He was from Lancaster County.

Hefflin, Charles. He was naturalized in Pennsylvania 24 Sep. 1760. He was from Berks County.

Heffner, John. He was naturalized in Maryland 29 Sep. 1764. He was a German from Frederick County.

Hefft, George. He was naturalized in Pennsylvania 10 Sep. 1761. He was from Lancaster County.

Hefner, Michael. He was naturalized in Maryland 10 Sep. 1762.

Hegeman, Abram. He took the oath of allegiance in Flackbush, Kings County, New York 26–30 Sep. 1687. He was a native of the colony.

Hegeman, Hendrickus. He took the oath of allegiance in Flackbush, Kings County, New York 26–30 Sep. 1687. He had been in the colony 36 years.

Hegeman, Isaack. He took the oath of allegiance in Flackbush, Kings County, New York 26–30 Sep. 1687. He was a native of the colony.

Hegeman, Joseph. He took the oath of allegiance in Flackbush, Kings County, New York 26–30 Sep. 1687. He had been in the colony 37 years.

Hegeman, Jacobus. He took the oath of allegiance in Flackbush, Kings County, New York 26–30 Sep. 1687. He had been in the colony 36 years.

Heger, Hendrick. He was naturalized in New York 3 May 1755.

Hehart, John. He was naturalized in Pennsylvania 11 Apr. 1761. He was from Berks County.

Hei, Charles. He was naturalized in Pennsylvania 10 & 23 Apr. 1764. He was from Tulpehocken Township, Berks County.

Heidler, Jacob. He was naturalized in Pennsylvania 10 Sep. 1761. He was from Berks County.

Heidley, Leonard. He was naturalized in Pennsylvania 24–25 Sep./5 Oct. 1767. He was from Lower Merion Township, Philadelphia County.

Heidrick, Abraham. He was naturalized in Pennsylvania 11–13 Apr. 1743. He was from Philadelphia County.

Heidrig, George. He was naturalized in Pennsylvania 11–13 Apr. 1743. He was from Philadelphia County.

Heidsher, Nicholas. He was naturalized in Pennsylvania 10 Sep. 1761. He was from Berks County.

Heigle, Michael. He was naturalized in New York 16 Feb. 1771.

Heilig, Hendrick. He was naturalized in Pennsylvania 11 Apr. 1749. He was from Philadelphia County.

Heilman, George Adam. He was naturalized in Pennsylvania 10 Sep. 1761. He was from Chester County.

Heilman, Henry. He was naturalized in Pennsylvania 24 Sep. 1746. He was from Philadelphia County.

Heinerigh, Koenraet. He was naturalized in New Jersey 8 July 1730. He was born in Germany.

Heim, David. He was naturalized in Pennsylvania 24–25 Sep. 1764. He was from Northern Liberties Township, Philadelphia County.

Heims, Andrew. He was naturalized in Pennsylvania 24 Sep. 1763. He was from Philadelphia.

Heims, Peter. He was naturalized in Pennsylvania 10 Apr. 1765. He was from Philadelphia.

Heiner, Johannis. He was naturalized in New York 3 Jan. 1715/6. He was from Albany County.

Heinse, Jacob. He took the oath to the King 21–26 Oct. 1664 after the conquest of New Netherland.

Heintz, Andreas. He was naturalized in New York 8 Mar. 1773.

Heintz, Anthony. He was naturalized in Pennsylvania 11–13 Apr. 1743. He was from Bucks County.

Heintz, Michael. He was naturalized in Pennsylvania 11–13 Apr. 1743. He was from Philadelphia County.

Heintz, Michael, Jr. He was naturalized in Pennsylvania 11–13 Apr. 1743. He was from Philadelphia County.

Heise, Adam. He was naturalized in Pennsylvania 11 Apr. 1763. He was from Northern Liberties Township, Philadelphia County.

Heiser, John. He was naturalized in Pennsylvania 25–27 Sep. 1740. He was from Philadelphia County.

Heiser, William. He was naturalized in Maryland 10 Sep. 1772.

Heisler, George. He was naturalized in Pennsylvania 10 Apr. 1755. He was from Philadelphia County.

Heisler, Jacob. He was naturalized in Pennsylvania 24 Sep. 1770. He was from Gwinedth Township, Philadelphia County.

Heiss, Matthias. He was naturalized in Pennsylvania 24–25 Sep. 1764. He was from Cheltenham Township, Philadelphia County.

Heist, George. He was naturalized in Pennsylvania 10 Sep. 1761. He was from Berks County.

Heist, Henry. He was naturalized in Pennsylvania 10 Sep. 1761. He was from Philadelphia County.

Heist, John Nicholas. He was naturalized in Pennsylvania 10 Apr. 1757.

Heist, John Philip. He was naturalized in Pennsylvania 24 Sep. 1755.

Heit, Andrew. He was naturalized in Pennsylvania 12 Apr. 1750. He was from Chester County.

Heitz, Jacob. He was naturalized in New York 29 July 1761. He was a carman from New York City.

Heiz, Anna Dorothea. She was naturalized in Pennsylvania 11 Apr. 1749. She was from Bucks County.

Hekman, Conrad. He was naturalized in Maryland 11 Sep. 1760.

Held, John Dethrick. He was naturalized in Pennsylvania 25–26 Sep./4 Oct. 1749. He was from Philadelphia County.

Hellaert, Jacob. He was naturalized in Jamaica 29 Nov. 1692.

Heller, Christian. He was naturalized in Pennsylvania 10 Apr. 1755. He was from Northampton County.

Heller, Daniel. He was naturalized in Pennsylvania 11 Apr. 1763. He was from Lower Saucon Township, Northampton County.

Heller, Ludwick. He was naturalized in Pennsylvania 11 Apr. 1763. He was from Lower Saucon Township, Northampton County.

Heller, Simon. He was naturalized in Pennsylvania 11 Apr. 1763. He was from Lower Saucon Township, Northampton County.

Hellibrandts, Petter. He took the oath of naturalization in New York 1 Sep. 1687 in Ulster County.

Helm, Adam. He was naturalized in Pennsylvania 24 Sep. 1762. He was from Philadelphia County.

Helm, George. He was naturalized in Frederick County, Virginia 2 Oct. 1765.

Helm, Jacob. He was naturalized in Pennsylvania 10 & 23 Apr. 1764. He was from Providence Township, Philadelphia County.

Helm, Symon. He was naturalized in New York 8–9 Sep. 1715. He was from Ulster County.

Helmer, Leendert. He was naturalized in New York 11 Oct. 1715. He was from Albany County.

Helmer, Philips. He was naturalized in New York 11 Oct. 1715. He was from Albany County.

Helms, Emus. He was naturalized in New York 4 Aug. 1746. He was a mariner from New York City.

Helms, Michael. He was naturalized in New York 8–9 Sep. 1715. He was from Ulster County.

Helsel, Simbright. He was naturalized in Pennsylvania 11 Apr. 1763. He was from Langenhose, Frederick County, Maryland.

Helsel, Tobias. He was naturalized in Pennsylvania 10 Sep. 1761. He was from York County.

Helsenstine, Nicholas. He was naturalized in Maryland 11 Sep. 1765. He was a German from Frederick County.

Helwig, Frederick. He was naturalized in Pennsylvania 10 Apr. 1755. He was from Berks County.

Helzell, Philip. He was naturalized in Pennsylvania 24 Sep. 1763. He was from Philadelphia.

Hembell, William. He was naturalized in Pennsylvania 21 Mar. 1772. He was born in Gelnhausen, Hesse-Cassel. His naturalization was annulled 19 May 1773. He was a tailor from Philadelphia..

Hemicker, Michael. He was naturalized in Pennsylvania 13 May 1771. He was from York, York County.

Hemstone, Mathias. He was naturalized in Maryland 8 Sep. 1761. He was from Frederick County.

Hencke, Christian. He was naturalized in New York 8–9 Sep. 1715. He was from Ulster County.

Hend, John. He was naturalized in Maryland 19 Oct. 1743.

Henderer, Jacob. He was naturalized in New York 23 Apr. 1765. He was a cordwainer from Albany County.

Henderson, Henry. He was naturalized in Maryland 6 June 1674. He was Swedish.

Hendrick, Baltazar. He was naturalized in Pennsylvania 11–13 Apr. 1743. He was from Germantown.

Hendrick, David. He was naturalized in Jamaica 12 June 1746.

Hendrick, Francis. He was naturalized in North Carolina in May 1697. He had previously been naturalized but lost his papers so he had to reapply.

Hendrick, Godfred. He was naturalized in New York 16 Dec. 1737.

Hendricks, Agbert. He took the oath of naturalization in New York 1 Sep. 1687 in Ulster County.

Hendricks, Brown. He took the oath of naturalization in New York 1 Sep. 1687 in Ulster County.

Hendricks, Dirrick. He took the oath of naturalization in New York 1 Sep. 1687 in Ulster County.

Hendricks, Ephraim. He took the oath of allegiance in Breucklijn, Kings County, New York 26–30 Sep. 1687. He had been in the colony 33 years.

Hendricks, Harrama. He took the oath of naturalization in New York 1 Sep. 1687 in Ulster County.

Hendricks, Hendrick. He took the oath of naturalization in New York 1 Sep. 1687 in Ulster County.

Hendricks, Jochijam. He took the oath of naturalization in New York 1 Sep. 1687 in Ulster County.

Hendricks, John. He took the oath of naturalization in New York 1 Sep. 1687 in Ulster County.

Hendricks, Leonard. He was naturalized in Pennsylvania 11–13 Apr. 1743. He was from Philadelphia County.

Hendricks, Paul. He was naturalized in Pennsylvania 11–13 Apr. 1743. He was from Philadelphia County.

Hendricks, Roloff. He took the oath of naturalization in New York 1 Sep. 1687 in Ulster County.

Hendricks, William. He and his sons, Hendrick Hendricks and Lawrence Hendricks, were naturalized in Pennsylvania 29 Sep. 1709. They were from Philadelphia County.

Hendrickse, Albert. He took the oath of allegiance in Boswijck, Kings County, New York, 26–30 Sep. 1687. He had been in the colony 25 years.

Hendrickse, Willem. He took the oath of allegiance in Flackbush, Kings County, New York 26–30 Sep. 1687. He was a native of the colony.

Hendrickson, Bartholomew. He was endenized in Maryland 29 July 1661. He was Swedish and was late of New Amstell.

Hendrickson, Evert. He expressed his desire to be naturalized in New Castle County, Delaware 21 Feb. 1682/3.

Hendrickson, Hendrick. He was endenized in Maryland 29 July 1661. He was Swedish and was late of New Amstell.

Hendrickson, John. He and his children, Hannah Hendrickson, John Hendrickson, Margaret Hendrickson, Martha Hendrickson, Mary Hendrickson, Mildred Hendrickson, Rachel Hendrickson, Rebecca Hendrickson, Ruth Hendrickson, and Samuel Hendrickson, were naturalized in Maryland 16 June 1730. They lived in Kent County. He was a native of Rotterdam, Holland.

Hendrickzen, Frederic. He took the oath to the King 21–26 Oct. 1664 after the conquest of New Netherland.

Hendrickzen, Gerrit. He took the oath to the King 21–26 Oct. 1664 after the conquest of New Netherland. He was from Amsterdam.

Hendrickzen, Hendrick. He took the oath to the King 21–26 Oct. 1664 after the conquest of New Netherland. He was from Ireland.

Hendrickzen, Hubert. He took the oath to the King 21–26 Oct. 1664 after the conquest of New Netherland. He was from Ceulen [i.e. Cologne].

Hendriksen, Jan. He expressed his desire to be naturalized in New Castle County, Delaware 21 Feb. 1682/3.

Heninger, Conrad. He was naturalized in Pennsylvania 11–13 Apr. 1743. He was from Philadelphia County.

Henkey, Henry. He was naturalized in Pennsylvania 11 Apr. 1763. He was from Springfield Township, Philadelphia County.

Hennakin, Roelof. He was naturalized in Jamaica 29 Nov. 1692.

Hennegar, Michael. He was naturalized in New York 20 May 1769. He was from New York City.

Henninger, Adam. He was naturalized in New York 27 July 1744. He was from New York City.

Henninger, Christopher. He was naturalized in New York 27 July 1744. He was from New York City.

Henning, Hieronimus. He was naturalized in Pennsylvania 24 Sep. 1759.

Henning, Jacob. He was naturalized in Pennsylvania 24 Sep. 1762. He was from Lancaster County.

Henriau, Daniel. He petitioned to be naturalized in New York 19 Aug. 1687.

Henriau, Pierre. He petitioned to be naturalized in New York 19 Aug. 1687.

Henrich, Lourens. He was naturalized in New York 8–9 Sep. 1715. He was from Ulster County.

Henrick, Jacob. He was naturalized in Pennsylvania 24 Sep. 1762. He was from York County.

Henricus, David DeSilva. He was naturalized in Jamaica 13 May 1740.

Henriques, Abraham Baruch. He was endenized in England 16 Dec. 1687. He settled in Barbados and was a Jew.

Henriques, Abraham Gomez. He was endenized in England 11 Aug. 1668. He settled in Barbados and was a Jew.

Henriques, Abraham Lopez. He was naturalized in Jamaica 26 May 1741. He was a Jew.

Henriques, Benjamin. He was naturalized in Jamaica 15 Jan. 1685/6.

Henriques, Bonvenida Gabay. He was naturalized in Jamaica 20 Mar. 1716.

Henriques, Daniel Bueno. He was endenized in Barbados 24 July 1661. He was a native of Seville, Spain. He was a Jew and a merchant.

Henriques, Daniel Bueno. He was endenized in Barbados in 1677.

Henriques, Daniel Bueno. He was naturalized in Jamaica 18 Jan. 1694/5.

Henriques, David. He was naturalized in Jamaica 25 Sep. 1699.

Henriques, David Gomez. He was endenized in London 29 June 1668. He had his certificate recorded in Jamaica 18 June 1672.

Henriques, David Lopez. He was naturalized in Jamaica ca. 1722. [His name appears in the index, but the entry for him is missing.]

Henriques, David Lopez. He was naturalized in Jamaica 31 Dec. 1729.

Henriques, Isaac Gutieres. He was naturalized in Jamaica 28 May 1728.

Henriques, Isaac Jesurum. He was naturalized in Jamaica 24 Apr. 1728.

Henriques, Isaac Nunes. He was naturalized in New York 23 Oct. 1741. He was a Jew.

Henriques, Isaac DaSilva. He was naturalized in Jamaica 26 Feb. 1740/1. He was a Jew.

Henriques, Jacob DeSusa. He was naturalized in Jamaica 22 Aug. 1715.

Henriques, Jacob Gabay. He was naturalized in Jamaica 5 Sep. 1751.

Henriques, Jacob Gutteres. He was naturalized in Jamaica 26 Feb. 1740/1. He was a Jew.

Henriques, Jacob Lopes. He was naturalized in Jamaica 30 Aug. 1743. He was a Jew.

Henriques, Jacob Nunes. He was naturalized in Jamaica 26 Feb. 1744/5. He was a Jew.

Henriques, Joseph Bueno. He was endenized in England 9 Mar. 1693/4. He settled in Barbados.

Henriques, Rachael. She was naturalized in Jamaica 31 May 1743. She was a Jewess.

Henriques, Rebecka Gutteres. She was naturalized in Jamaica 26 Apr. 1733.

Henriques, Manoel. He was endenized in England 25 Feb. 1687/8. He was a merchant in London and was going to reside in one of his Majesty's plantations in America to promote trade. He had lived in London for several years.

Henriques, Moses Lopes. He was naturalized in Jamaica 25 Nov. 1740. He was a Jew.

Henriques, Moses Nunes. He was naturalized in Jamaica 27 Aug. 1745. He was a Jew.

Henriques, Rachel. She was naturalized in Jamaica 27 Aug. 1745. She was a Jewess.

Henriques, Rachel Lopes. She was naturalized in Jamaica 28 Feb. 1743/4. She was a Jewess.

Henriques, Sarah Lopez. She was naturalized in Jamaica 28 Feb. 1743/4. She was a Jewess.

Henriquez, Isaac. He was endenized in England 2 Oct. 1662. He settled in Barbados. He was a Jew.

Henry, Francis. He was naturalized in Sussex County, Delaware 28 Apr. 1683.

Henry, J. B. He was an Acadian and took the oath of allegiance in Apr. 1730.

Henry, Jean. He was an Acadian and took the oath of allegiance in Apr. 1730.

Henry, Jean, Jr. He was an Acadian and took the oath of allegiance in Apr. 1730.

Henry, Joseph. He was an Acadian and took the oath of allegiance in Apr. 1730.

Henry, Martin. He was an Acadian and took the oath of allegiance in Apr. 1730.

Henry, Peter. He was naturalized in New Jersey in 1762. He was born in Germany. He also appeared as Peter Henrich. He had been in the colony seven and a half years. He was from Cumberland County.

Henry, Pierre. He was an Acadian and took the oath of allegiance in Apr. 1730.

Hentzell, Michael. He was naturalized in Pennsylvania 11 Apr. 1761. He was from Berks County.

Henzel, Philip. He was naturalized in Pennsylvania 10–12 Apr. 1762. He was from Berks County.

Heppenheimer, Andrew. He was naturalized in Maryland 12 Sep. 1759.

Heraud, Jean. He was born at Oleron, France. He was naturalized in South Carolina *ca.* 1696.

Herbein, Jonathan. He was naturalized in Pennsylvania 6 Feb. 1730/1. He was from Philadelphia County.

Herbergs, John. He was naturalized in New Jersey 20 June 1765.

Herbergs, John. He was naturalized in Pennsylvania 20 Sep. 1766. He was a German.

Herbert, Andrew. He was naturalized in Virginia 7 Nov. 1666. He was a Dutchman.

Herbert, John. He was naturalized in New York 23 Oct. 1765. He was a butcher from New York City.

Herbogh, Jacob. He was naturalized in Maryland 15 Sep. 1762. He was a German from Frederick County.

Herbogh, Ludvik. He was naturalized in Maryland 10 Apr. 1760. He was from Frederick County.

Herckhemer, Hans Jury. He was naturalized in New York 31 Jan. 1715/6. He was from Albany County.

Herder, Lowrence. He was naturalized in New York 28 Feb. 1715/6. He was from Albany County.

Herder, Michel. He was naturalized in New York 17 Jan. 1715/6. He was from Albany County.

Hereinger, Nicholas. He was naturalized in New York 29 Oct. 1730.

Hergelrat, Valentine. He was naturalized in Pennsylvania 19 May 1739. He was from Lancaster County.

Herger, Gottlieb. He was naturalized in Pennsylvania 29 Mar. 1739. He was from Philadelphia County.

Herger, Michael. He was naturalized in Pennsylvania 19 Mar. 1739. He was from Philadelphia County.

Herhardt, Symon. He was naturalized in New York 3 Jan. 1715/6. He was from Albany County.

Herhold, George. He was naturalized in Pennsylvania 10 & 23 Apr. 1764. He was from Heidelberg Township, Berks County.

Hering, John Andrew. He was naturalized in New York 25 Oct. 1748. He was a weaver from New York City.

Hering, Karel. He was naturalized in New York 3 May 1755.

Herley, Rudolph. He was naturalized in New Jersey 8 July 1730. He was born in Germany.

Herman, Augustine. He was made a denizen in Maryland 14 Jan. 1660. He had previously lived in Manhattan, New York.

Herman, Augustine. He and his children, Anna Herman, Casparus Herman, Ephraim Herman, Francina Herman, Georgius Herman, Judith Herman, and Margarita Herman, were naturalized in Maryland 1 May 1666. He was born in Prague, Bohemia.

Herman, Casper. He expressed his desire to be naturalized in New Castle County, Delaware 21 Feb. 1682/3.

Herman, Christian. He was naturalized in Pennsylvania 14 Feb. 1729/30. He was from Lancaster County.

Herman, Daniel. He was naturalized in Pennsylvania 14 Feb. 1729/30. He was from Lancaster County.

Herman, Ephraim. He expressed his desire to be naturalized in New Castle County, Delaware 21 Feb. 1682/3.

Herman, George. He was naturalized in Maryland 14 Sep. 1763. He was a German from Frederick County.

Herman, Jacob. He was naturalized in Maryland 11 Sep. 1765.

Herman, Jacob. He was naturalized in Pennsylvania 6 Feb. 1730/1. He was from Philadelphia County.

Herman, John. He was naturalized in Maryland 15 Apr. 1772. He was a German.

Herman, Leonard. He was naturalized in Pennsylvania 11–12 Apr. 1744. He was from Philadelphia County.

Herman, Michael. He was naturalized in Maryland 7 May 1767. He was a German from Frederick County.

Hermel, Abraham. He took the oath to the King 21–26 Oct. 1664 after the conquest of New Netherland.

Hermell, Henrick. He was naturalized in Pennsylvania 25–27 Sep. 1740. He was from Philadelphia County.

Hermensen, Jan. He was naturalized in New Castle County, Delaware 21 Feb. 1682/3.

Hermicke, John Nicholas. He was naturalized in Pennsylvania 24 Sep. 1759.

Hermzen, Pieter. He took the oath to the King 21–26 Oct. 1664 after the conquest of New Netherland.

Herner, Frederick. He was naturalized in Pennsylvania 24 Sep. 1762. He was from Berks County.

Herner, Nicholas. He was naturalized in Pennsylvania 10 Apr. 1760.

Herniess, John George. He was naturalized in Pennsylvania 10–12 Apr. 1762. He was from Philadelphia County.

Heron, Francis. He was naturalized in Jamaica 30 Aug. 1743.

Heroy, Charles. He was naturalized in New York 21 Jan. 1752. He was a weaver from Westchester County.

Heroy, James. He was naturalized in New York 21 Jan. 1752. He was a cartman from New York City.

Herpain, James. He was naturalized in New York 22 Nov. 1750.

Herple, Peter. He was naturalized in Pennsylvania 11 Apr. 1761. He was from Berks County.

Herr, Peter. He was naturalized in Pennsylvania 11 Apr. 1761. He was from Northampton County.

Herrbenk, John. He was naturalized in New York 20 Apr. 1769. He was a tanner from New York City.

Herrenbecker, Joseph. He sought naturalization in New Jersey in the 18th century.

Herring, Henry. He was naturalized in New York 8 Mar. 1773.

Herring, Ludwick. He was naturalized in Pennsylvania 24 Sep. 1760. He was from Philadelphia County.

Herriot, Andreas. He was naturalized in Maryland 18 Oct. 1743. He was from Cannawatke.

Hersher, Lawrence. He was naturalized in Pennsylvania 24 Sep. 1762. He was from York County.

Hershman, Mathias. He was naturalized in Maryland 3 Sep. 1765. He was a German from Frederick County.

Hersman, Henry. He was naturalized in Maryland 18 Sep. 1765. He was a German.

Hertel, Jacob. He was naturalized in New Jersey in 1766.

Hertsog, Frederick. He was naturalized in Pennsylvania 25 Sep. 1752. He was from Philadelphia.

Hertte, Peter. He was naturalized in New York 8–9 Sep. 1715. He was from Ulster County.

Hertz, Andrew. He was naturalized in Pennsylvania 11 Apr. 1761. He was from Northampton County.

Hertz, Casparus. He was naturalized in New York 17 Apr. 1746. He was a cartman from New York City.

Hertz, Jacob. He was naturalized in New York 29 July 1761. He was a carman from New York City.

Hertzog, William. He was naturalized in New Jersey in 1765. He was born in Germany. He resided in Detford Township, Gloucester County. He had been in the colony fourteen years.

Herwagen, Phillip. He was naturalized in New York 11 Sep. 1761.

Hes, Johannis. He was naturalized in New York 17 Jan. 1715/6. He was from Albany County.

Hes, Niccolas. He was naturalized in New York 17 Jan. 1715/6. He was from Albany County.

Hesfer, William. He was naturalized in Pennsylvania 24 Sep. 1762. He was from Berks County.

Hess, Balthasar. He was naturalized in New Jersey in 1768. He was born in Germany.

Hess, Johan. He was naturalized in Pennsylvania 11 Apr. 1763. He was from Tolpohocken Township, Berks County.

Hess, Johan. He was naturalized in New York 3 May 1755.

Hess, John. He was naturalized in New York 21 Apr. 1762. He was a tallow chandler in New York City.

Hess, John. He was naturalized in Pennsylvania 14 Feb. 1729/30. He was from Lancaster County.

Hess, Lewis. He was naturalized in Pennsylvania 24–25 Sep. 1764. He was from Philadelphia.

Hess, Michael. He was naturalized in Pennsylvania 24 Sep. 1753. He was from Lancaster County.

Hess, Nicholas. He was naturalized in Pennsylvania 11 Apr. 1761. He was from Philadelphia County.

Hess, Ulrick. He was naturalized in Pennsylvania 10 & 23 Apr. 1764. He was from Strasburg Township, York County.

Hesselius, Gustavus. He and his daughter, Mary Hesselius, were naturalized in Maryland 5 Aug. 1721. He lived in Prince George's County and was a limner. He was Swedish.

Hesselius, Gustavus. He was naturalized in Pennsylvania in Sep. 1740. He was from Philadelphia.

Hessler, Michael. He was naturalized in Pennsylvania 10 Sep. 1761. He was from Berks County.

Hesz, Hendrick. He was naturalized in New York 11 Sep. 1761.

Hettlestein, Jacob. He was naturalized in Pennsylvania 6 Feb. 1730/1. He was from Philadelphia County. His name also appeared as Jacob Hottlestein.

Hetzell, Michael. He was naturalized in Pennsylvania 24–25 Sep. 1764. He was from Northern Liberties Township, Philadelphia County.

Heuster, Francis. He was naturalized in Maryland 9 Sep. 1761. He was from Baltimore County.

Hewit, Hendriet. He took the oath of allegiance at Mobile, West Florida 2 Oct. 1764.

Hewit, Piere. He took the oath of allegiance at Mobile, West Florida 2 Oct. 1764.

Hewreissen, Bernhard. He was naturalized in Pennsylvania 11 Apr. 1761. He was from York County.

Heybertsin, Lambert. He took the oath of naturalization in New York 1 Sep. 1687 in Ulster County.

Heybey, Peter. He was naturalized in Pennsylvania 11–13 Apr. 1743. He was from Philadelphia County.

Heydorn, Hendrick. He was naturalized in New York 17 Jan. 1715/6. He was from Albany County.

Heyell, John George. He was naturalized in Maryland 19 Oct. 1743. He was from Manaquice.

Heyer, Dietrick. He was naturalized in New York 19 Apr. 1769. He was a sugar boiler from New York City.

Heyer, Leonhart. He was naturalized in Pennsylvania 19 May 1739. He was from Lancaster County.

Heyler, Johannes. He was naturalized in New Jersey 3 June 1763.

Heyman, Moses. He was naturalized in Pennsylvania 10–14 Apr. 1747. He was from Philadelphia County. He was a Jew.

Heymberger, George Thomas. He was naturalized in Pennsylvania 10–12 Apr. 1762. He was from Philadelphia County.

Heyn, Johannis Jury. He was naturalized in New York 3 Jan. 1715/6. He was from Albany County.

Heyney, Conrad. He was naturalized in New York 31 Dec. 1768.

Heyney, Frederick. He was naturalized in New York 31 Dec. 1768.

Heyns, William. He was naturalized in New York 11 Sep. 1761.

Heyntie, Michial. He was naturalized in New York 17 Jan. 1715/6. He was from Albany County.

Heypt, Philips. He was naturalized in New York 17 Jan. 1715/6. He was from Albany County.

Heyser, Hans Pieter. He was naturalized in New York 22 Nov. 1722. He was from Albany County.

Heyser, Hendrick. He was naturalized in New York 3 July 1759.

Heyser, Valentine. He was naturalized in Pennsylvania in 1739. He was from Philadelphia County.

Heyter, John Michael. He was naturalized in Pennsylvania 25 Sep. 1744. He was from Philadelphia County.

Hibbert, Alexandre. He was an Acadian and took the oath to George II at Annapolis River, Nova Scotia in the winter of 1730.
Hibbert, Alexandre. He was an Acadian and took the oath to George II at Annapolis River, Nova Scotia in the winter of 1730.
Hibbert, Alexandre. He was an Acadian and took the oath of allegiance in Apr. 1730.
Hibbert, Antoine. He was an Acadian and took the oath to George II at Annapolis River, Nova Scotia in the winter of 1730.
Hibbert, Baptiste. He was an Acadian and took the oath of allegiance in Apr. 1730.
Hibbert, Charles. He was an Acadian and took the oath of allegiance in Apr. 1730.
Hibbert, Francois. He was an Acadian and took the oath of allegiance in Apr. 1730.
Hibbert, Jacques. He was an Acadian and took the oath of allegiance in Apr. 1730.
Hibbert, Jean. He was an Acadian and took the oath of allegiance in Apr. 1730.
Hibbert, Jean Denis. He was an Acadian and took the oath of allegiance in Apr. 1730.
Hibbert, Joseph. He was an Acadian and took the oath of allegiance in Apr. 1730.
Hibbert, Joseph. He was an Acadian and took the oath of allegiance in Apr. 1730.
Hibbert, Louis. He was an Acadian and took the oath to George II at Annapolis River, Nova Scotia in the winter of 1730.
Hibbert, Louis. He was an Acadian and took the oath of allegiance in Apr. 1730.
Hibbert, Piere. He was an Acadian and took the oath to George II at Annapolis River, Nova Scotia in the winter of 1730.
Hibbert, Pierre. He was an Acadian and took the oath of allegiance in Apr. 1730.
Hibbert, Pierre. He was an Acadian and took the oath of allegiance in Apr. 1730.
Hibbert, Pierre. He was an Acadian and took the oath of allegiance in Apr. 1730.
Hibbert, Pierre, Jr. He was an Acadian and took the oath of allegiance in Apr. 1730.
Hibner, Christopher. He was naturalized in Pennsylvania 24 Sep. 1745. He was from Philadelphia County.
Hibner, David. He was naturalized in Pennsylvania 24 Sep. 1745. He was from Philadelphia County.
Hibner, Ludwick. He was naturalized in Pennsylvania 24 Sep. 1766. He was from Bethlehem, Northampton County.
Hibsham, Gerrharat. He was naturalized in Pennsylvania 10 Apr. 1760.
Hickerel, Herman. He was naturalized in Maryland 11 Sep. 1765.
Hickleman, Michael. He was naturalized in Maryland 11 Apr. 1764. He was a German.
Hickman, Adam. He was naturalized in Pennsylvania 11 Apr. 1761. He was from Berks County.
Hickman, Cronomus. He was naturalized in Pennsylvania 11–12 Apr. 1744. He was from Lancaster County.
Hickman, John. He was naturalized in Pennsylvania 10 Sep. 1761. He was from Lancaster County.
Hickner, Hans George. He was naturalized in Pennsylvania 19 May 1739. He was from Philadelphia County.
Hiem, John. He was naturalized in Pennsylvania 24 Sep. 1762. He was from Berks County.
Hienkle, Christopher. He was naturalized in Pennsylvania 24 Sep. 1760. He was from Philadelphia County.
Hierlogh, Carel. He was naturalized in New Jersey 8 July 1730. He was born in Germany.
Highberger, Andrew. He was naturalized in Pennsylvania 11 Apr. 1763. He was from Springfield Township, Philadelphia County.
Highmager, Christopher. He was naturalized in Pennsylvania 25 Sep. 1747. He was from Bucks County.
Higner, Mathias. He was naturalized in Pennsylvania 26–27 Sep. 1743. He was from Philadelphia County.
Hilbert, Charles. He was an Acadian and took the oath of allegiance in Apr. 1730.
Hilbert, Charles. He was an Acadian and took the oath of allegiance in Apr. 1730. He was the son of Jacques Hilbert.
Hilbert, Charles. He was an Acadian and took the oath of allegiance in Apr. 1730.
Hilbert, Emmanuel. He was an Acadian and took the oath of allegiance in Apr. 1730.
Hilbert, Etienne. He was an Acadian and took the oath of allegiance in Apr. 1730.

Hilbert, Francois. He was an Acadian and took the oath of allegiance in Apr. 1730.
Hilbert, Guillaume. He was an Acadian and took the oath of allegiance in Apr. 1730.
Hilbert, Jacques. He was an Acadian and took the oath of allegiance in Apr. 1730.
Hilbert, Jean. He was an Acadian and took the oath of allegiance in Apr. 1730.
Hilbert, Jean. He was an Acadian and took the oath of allegiance in Apr. 1730.
Hilbert, Jean. He was an Acadian and took the oath of allegiance in Apr. 1730.
Hilbert, Jean. He was an Acadian and took the oath of allegiance in Apr. 1730.
Hilbert, Jean. He was an Acadian and took the oath of allegiance in Apr. 1730.
Hilbert, Jermain. He was an Acadian and took the oath of allegiance in Apr. 1730.
Hilbert, Joseph. He was an Acadian and took the oath of allegiance in Apr. 1730.
Hilbert, Paul. He was an Acadian and took the oath of allegiance in Apr. 1730.
Hilbert, Pierre. He was an Acadian and took the oath of allegiance in Apr. 1730.
Hilbert, Pierre. He was an Acadian and took the oath of allegiance in Apr. 1730.
Hilbert, Pierre. He was an Acadian and took the oath of allegiance in Apr. 1730.
Hilbert, Rene. He was an Acadian and took the oath of allegiance in Apr. 1730.
Hildebrand, Jacob. He was naturalized in Pennsylvania 24–25 Sep. 1764. He was from Lancaster Township, Lancaster County.
Hildebrand, John. He was naturalized in Maryland 24 Sep. 1762. He was a German from Frederick County.
Hildenbrandt, Wendell. He was naturalized in New York 20 Mar. 1762.
Hilderbrand, Heronemas. He was naturalized in Maryland 7 May 1767. He was a German.
Hildebridle, Martin. He was naturalized in Pennsylvania 11–13 Apr. 1743. He was from Philadelphia County.
Hildner, Wilhelm. He was naturalized in Pennsylvania 24–25 Sep. 1764. He was from Whitemarsh Township, Philadelphia County.
Hilig, George. He was naturalized in Pennsylvania 11–13 Apr. 1743. He was from Philadelphia County.
Hill, Adam. He was naturalized in Pennsylvania 26–27 Sep. 1743. He was from Philadelphia County.
Hill, Christian. He was naturalized in New York 8 Mar. 1773.
Hill, Gotliff. He was naturalized in Pennsylvania 26–27 Sep. 1743. He was from Lancaster County.
Hill, Jacob. He was naturalized in Pennsylvania 29 Mar. 1739. He was from Philadelphia.
Hill, Jacob. He was naturalized in New Jersey in 1759.
Hill, John. He was naturalized in New York 20 Apr. 1769. He was a laborer in New York City.
Hill, John. He was naturalized in New York 20 May 1769.
Hill, Peter. He was naturalized in New Jersey in 1759.
Hill, Peter. He was naturalized in Maryland 24 Sep. 1765. He was a German.
Hillecas, Fredrick. He was naturalized in New York 20 Dec. 1763.
Hillegas, John Adam. He was naturalized in Pennsylvania 10 & 23 Apr. 1764. He was from Upper Hannover Township, Philadelphia County.
Hillegas, John Pieter. He was naturalized in New York 3 July 1759.
Hillegas, Michael. He was naturalized in Pennsylvania 11 Apr. 1749. He was from Philadelphia County.
Hillegas, Peter. He was naturalized in Pennsylvania 29 Mar. 1735. He was from Philadelphia.
Hillengas, Frederick. He was naturalized in Pennsylvania 19 May 1739. He was from Philadelphia County.
Hilligart, William. He was naturalized in Pennsylvania 5 Mar. 1725/6. He was born in Germany.
Hilman, Antonius. He was naturalized in Pennsylvania 6 Feb. 1730/1. He was from Philadelphia County.
Hillman, Henry. He was naturalized in New York 22 Jan. 1772. He was from New York City.
Hilschiner, Michel. He was naturalized in New York 20 Mar. 1762.
Hiltzheimer, Jacob. He was naturalized in Pennsylvania 10–12 Apr. 1762. He was from Philadelphia County.
Himalbarger, Valentine. He was naturalized in Pennsylvania 11 Apr. 1761. He was from Berks County.

Himns, George. He was naturalized in New Jersey 7 Dec. 1763.

Hinckel, Casper. He was naturalized in Pennsylvania 10–12 Apr. 1762. He was from Berks County.

Hinckel, George. He was naturalized in Maryland 1 Oct. 1767. He was a German from Frederick County.

Hinckel, George Henry. He was naturalized in Maryland 7 May 1767. He was a German from Frederick County.

Hinckle, Jacob. He was naturalized in Maryland 1 Oct. 1767. He was a German from Frederick County.

Hiner, Graft. He was naturalized in Pennsylvania 24 Sep. 1755. He was from Berks County.

Hinkel, Anthony. He was naturalized in Pennsylvania 19 May 1739. He was from Philadelphia County.

Hinnelin, Matthias. He was naturalized in Pennsylvania 10 Sep. 1761. He was from Berks County.

Hinnen, John. He was naturalized in New Jersey in 1762. He was born in Sweden. He also appeared as Hans Hinnen. He was from Cumberland County.

Hinnige, Ludowick. He was naturalized in Pennsylvania 19 May 1739. He was from Philadelphia County.

Hinterlicter, Casper. He was naturalized in Pennsylvania 11 Apr. 1763. He was from Marlborough Township, Philadelphia County.

Hinterlicter, Mattheus. He was naturalized in Pennsylvania 11 Apr. 1763. He was from Marlborough Township, Philadelphia County.

Hinton, Adam. He was naturalized in Pennsylvania 10–14 Apr. 1747. He was from Philadelphia County.

Hip, George. He was naturalized in New York 3 July 1759.

Hip, Stephen. He was naturalized in New York 3 July 1759.

Hirsh, Conrad. He was naturalized in Maryland 13 Apr. 1763. He was a German.

Hirsh, Michael. He was naturalized in Pennsylvania 24–25 Sep./5 Oct. 1767. He was from Lebanon Township, Lancaster County.

Hirt, John. He was naturalized in Pennsylvania 10 Apr. 1765. He was from Whitemarsh Township, Philadelphia County.

Hiskle, Christopher. He was naturalized in Frederick County, Virginia 4 Aug. 1768.

Hiss, John. He was naturalized in Pennsylvania 10 Apr. 1755. He was from Berks County.

Hister, Daniel. He was naturalized in Pennsylvania 11 Apr. 1749. He was from Philadelphia County.

Hister, Joseph. He was naturalized in Pennsylvania 10 Apr. 1758.

Hite, Alexander. He was naturalized in Frederick County, Virginia 5 Sep. 1769.

Hite, Jacob. He was naturalized in Frederick County, Virginia 5 Sep. 1769.

Hitfelfinger, Martin. He was naturalized in Pennsylvania 11 Apr. 1761. He was from Lancaster County.

Hitner, George, Jr. He was naturalized in Pennsylvania in 2 Feb. 1765. He was a saddler from Philadelphia and came into the province from Germany as an infant.

Hittle, Peter. He was naturalized in Pennsylvania 10 Apr. 1755. He was from Northampton County.

Hivener, Adam. He was naturalized in Maryland 15 Apr. 1767. He was a German.

Hivener, George. He was naturalized in Maryland 15 Apr. 1767. He was a German.

Hobre, Andrew. He was naturalized in Maryland 20 Oct. 1747.

Hoch, Hans. He was naturalized in Pennsylvania 6 Feb. 1730/1. He was from Philadelphia County.

Hoch, Jacob. He was naturalized in Pennsylvania 6 Feb. 1730/1. He was from Philadelphia County.

Hoch, Melchor. He was naturalized in Pennsylvania 6 Feb. 1730/1. He was from Philadelphia County.

Hoch, Samuel. He was naturalized in Pennsylvania 6 Feb. 1730/1. He was from Philadelphia County.

Hochel, Justice. He was naturalized in Maryland 10 Apr. 1762. He was a German from Anne Arundel County.

Hochstrasser, Jacob. He was naturalized in New York 16 Feb. 1771.

Hock, Hans Hendrick. He was naturalized in New York 17 Jan. 1715/6. He was from Albany County.

Hock, Johan. He was naturalized in Pennsylvania 19 May 1739. He was from Lancaster County.

Hockgenung, Leonard. He was naturalized in Pennsylvania 11 Apr. 1761. He was from Berks County.

Hodell, George. He was naturalized in Frederick County, Virginia 2 June 1767.

Hodler, Peter. He was naturalized in New York 24 Mar. 1772.

Hoefer, David. He was naturalized in New York 22 Nov. 1715. He was from Albany County.

Hoeflich, Carl. He was naturalized in New York 20 Mar. 1762.

Hoerer, Henry. He was naturalized in Pennsylvania 24 Sep. 1759.

Hoertse, Jacob. He was naturalized in New York 29 July 1762. He was a mason from New York City.

Hoeshield, Adam. He was naturalized in New Jersey 8 Dec. 1744.

Hoff, Adam. He was naturalized in Pennsylvania 24 Sep. 1762. He was from York County.

Hoff, Valentine. He was naturalized in Pennsylvania 11 Apr. 1761. He was from Berks County.

Hoffeman, Marten. He took the oath of naturalization in New York 1 Sep. 1687 in Ulster County.

Hoffer, George. He was naturalized in Pennsylvania 10 Sep. 1761. He was from Lancaster County.

Hoffer, Matthias. He was naturalized in Pennsylvania 11 Apr. 1761. He was from Lancaster County.

Hoffert, Christian. He was naturalized in Pennsylvania 11 Apr. 1761. He was from Philadelphia County.

Hoffgoet, Hans Jury. He was naturalized in New York 3 May 1755.

Hoffman, Adam. He was naturalized in Maryland 11 Sep. 1765.

Hoffman, Adam. He was naturalized in Pennsylvania 11 Apr. 1763. He was from North Wales Township, Philadelphia County.

Hoffman, Andreas. He was naturalized in Pennsylvania 11–13 Apr. 1743. He was from Chester County.

Hoffman, Carl. He was naturalized in New York 3 July 1759.

Hoffman, Christian. He was naturalized in Pennsylvania 11 Apr. 1761. He was from Berks County.

Hoffman, Christopher. He was naturalized in Pennsylvania 25–26 Sep./4 Oct. 1749. He was from Philadelphia County.

Hoffman, Daniel. He was naturalized in Pennsylvania 11 Apr. 1763. He was from Reading Township, Berks County.

Hoffman, Francis. He was naturalized in Maryland 29 Nov. 1774. He was a German.

Hoffman, Frederick. He was naturalized in Pennsylvania 24–25 Sep. 1764. He was from Tulpehocken Township, Berks County.

Hoffman, George. He was naturalized in Maryland 17 Sep. 1764. He was a German.

Hoffman, George. He was naturalized in Pennsylvania 24 Sep. 1745. He was from Philadelphia County.

Hoffman, George. He was naturalized in Pennsylvania 25 Sep. 1751. He was from Bucks County.

Hoffman, George. He was naturalized in Pennsylvania 10 Apr. 1754. He was from Philadelphia County.

Hoffman, George. He was naturalized in Pennsylvania 10 Sep. 1761. He was from Berks County.

Hoffman, Henry. He was naturalized in New Jersey 20 Aug. 1755.

Hoffman, Henry. He was naturalized in Maryland 11 Sep. 1765.

Hoffman, Henry. He was naturalized in Pennsylvania 24–25 Sep. 1764. He was from Chestnut Hill Township, Philadelphia County.

Hoffman, Jacob. He was naturalized in Pennsylvania in Sep. 1740. He was from Philadelphia County.

Hoffman, Jacob. He was naturalized in Pennsylvania 10–14 Apr. 1747. He was from Lancaster County.

Hoffman, Johannes. He was naturalized in New Jersey 8 Dec. 1744.

Hoffman, Johannes. He was naturalized in Pennsylvania 11 Apr. 1761. He was from Berks County.

Hoffman, John. He was naturalized in Maryland 16 Sep. 1751.

Hoffman, John. He was naturalized in Pennsylvania 24 Sep. 1763. He was from Lancaster Township, Lancaster County.

Hoffman, John George. He was naturalized in Pennsylvania 25–27 Sep. 1740. He was from Philadelphia County.

Hoffman, John William. He was naturalized in Pennsylvania 10 Apr. 1760.

Hoffman, Jury. He was naturalized in New York 3 July 1759.

Hoffman, Michael. He was naturalized in New York 3 May 1755.

Hoffman, Michael. He was naturalized in New York 3 July 1759.

Hoffman, Michael. He was naturalized in Pennsylvania 24 Sep. 1757.

Hoffman, Nicholas. He was naturalized in Pennsylvania 10 & 23 Apr. 1764. He was from Dover Township, York County.

Hoffman, Peter. He was naturalized in New Jersey 21 Oct. 1754.

Hoffman, Peter. He was naturalized in Maryland 11 Sep. 1765.

Hoffman, Philip. He was naturalized in New York 20 Mar. 1762.

Hoffman, Philip. He was naturalized in Pennsylvania 10–12 Apr. 1762. He was from Lancaster County.

Hoffman, Valentine. He was naturalized in Pennsylvania 11 Apr. 1761. He was from Berks County.

Hoffman, Valentine. He was naturalized in Pennsylvania 11 Apr. 1761. He was from Lancaster County.

Hoffman, William. He was naturalized in New Jersey 21 Oct. 1754.

Hoffman, Yost. He was naturalized in Pennsylvania 11 Apr. 1761. He was from Lancaster County.

Hoffsteder, Christian. He was naturalized in New York 8 Mar. 1773.

Hofman, Burchard. He was naturalized in Pennsylvania 26–27 Sep. 1743. He was from Philadelphia County.

Hofman, Coenrat. He was naturalized in New York 8–9 Sep. 1715. He was from Ulster County.

Hofman, Hendrick. He was naturalized in New York 8–9 Sep. 1715. He was from Ulster County.

Hofman, Jacob. He was naturalized in Pennsylvania 25 Sep. 1744. He was from Philadelphia County.

Hofman, Leonard. He was naturalized in Maryland 16 Apr. 1761.

Hofman, Michael. He was naturalized in Pennsylvania 24 Sep. 1760. He was from Philadelphia County.

Hofses, Johannes. He was naturalized in New Jersey 6 Dec. 1769.

Hoft, Adam. He was naturalized in New York 31 Jan. 1715/6. He was from Albany County.

Hoft, Andries. He was naturalized in New York 31 Jan. 1715/6. He was from Albany County.

Hogermoed, Mathias Adam. He was naturalized in Pennsylvania 6 Feb. 1730/1. He was from Philadelphia County.

Hogetilen, John Williamson. He took the oath of naturalization in New York 1 Sep. 1687 in Ulster County.

Hoggabugh, Jacob. He was naturalized in Pennsylvania 10 Sep. 1761. He was from Berks County.

Hoggberr, Michael. He was naturalized in Pennsylvania 24–25 Sep. 1764. He was from Upper Hannover Township, Philadelphia County.

Hogman, Jacob. He was naturalized in Pennsylvania 11–13 Apr. 1743. He was from Philadelphia County.

Hohl, George. He was naturalized in Nova Scotia 15 Sep. 1758.

Hoin, Godfrey. He was naturalized in New York 24 Nov. 1750.

Hoining, Conradt. He was naturalized in New York 8 Mar. 1773.

Holder, Nicholas, Sr. He was naturalized in Pennsylvania 11 Apr. 1761. He was from Berks County.

Holder, Nicholas, Jr. He was naturalized in Pennsylvania 11 Apr. 1761. He was from Berks County.

Holland, John Francis. He was naturalized in Maryland 15 Apr. 1707. He lived in Baltimore County. He was German.

Hollenbaik, George. He was naturalized in Pennsylvania 6 Feb. 1730/1. He was from Philadelphia County.

Holler, George. He was naturalized in Pennsylvania 11 Apr. 1761. He was from York County.

Hollebush, Christian. He was naturalized in Pennsylvania 24–25 Sep. 1764. He was from Frederic Township, Philadelphia County.

Hollebush, Peter. He was naturalized in Pennsylvania 24–25 Sep. 1764. He was from Frederic Township, Philadelphia County.

Hollinger, Christian. He was naturalized in Pennsylvania 24 Sep. 1760. He was from Lancaster County.

Hollinger, Jacob. He was naturalized in Pennsylvania 21 Nov. 1770. He was from Lancaster, Lancaster County.

Hollingsmith, Conrad. He was naturalized in Maryland in Apr. 1749. He was from Frederick County.

Holsaaert, Anthony. He was naturalized in New York 28 Feb. 1715/6. He was a shoemaker from New Utrecht.

Holsbaun, Andreas. He was naturalized in Pennsylvania 11 Apr. 1761. He was from Lancaster County.

Holst, Barent. He took the oath to the King 21–26 Oct. 1664 after the conquest of New Netherland.

Holst, Nicholas. He was naturalized in Jamaica 5 May 1720.

Holstein, Eva Barbara. She was naturalized in Pennsylvania 25 Sep. 1751. She was from Lancaster County.

Holtz, Benedict. He was naturalized in Maryland 14 Apr. 1761.

Holtz, Jacob. He was naturalized in Maryland 11 Sep. 1765.

Holtz, Jacob. He was naturalized in Maryland 16 Sep. 1773. He was a German.

Holtzapfel, Erasmus. He was naturalized in Pennsylvania 24 Sep. 1763. He was from Manchester Township, York County.

Holtzclaw, Jacob. He was naturalized in Spotsylvania County, Virginia 11 July 1722. He was a native of Nassau, Siegen, Germany.

Holtzetter, Peter. He was naturalized in Pennsylvania 25 Sep. 1747. He was from Philadelphia County.

Holtzhousen, Casper. He was naturalized in Pennsylvania 26 Sep. 1748. He was from Bucks County.

Holtzman, Henry. He was naturalized in Pennsylvania 24–25 Sep. 1764. He was from Tulpehocken Township, Berks County.

Holzafret, William. He was naturalized in New York 16 Dec. 1737.

Holzapel, William. He was naturalized in New York 16 Dec. 1737.

Holzendorf, Frederick. He was naturalized in South Carolina 12 May 1748.

Holzman, Frederick. He was naturalized in Maryland 28 Sep. 1762. He was a German from Frederick County.

Homan, Peter. He was naturalized in New York 11 Sep. 1761.

Homer, Adam. He was naturalized in New Jersey 8 July 1730. He was born in Germany.

Homer, Christian. He was naturalized in Pennsylvania 10 Apr. 1759.

Homer, Herbert. He was naturalized in New Jersey 8 July 1730. He was born in Germany.

Hommel, Harmanus. He was naturalized in New York 8–9 Sep. 1715. He was from Ulster County.

Honake, Rudolph. He was naturalized in Pennsylvania 24 Sep. 1755. He was from Rockhill Township, Bucks County.

Hone, Gasper. He was naturalized in Maryland 11 Sep. 1765.

Honerkin, Jacob. He was naturalized in Maryland 15 Apr. 1761.

Honetta, Andrew. He was naturalized in Pennsylvania 11 Apr. 1761. He was from Philadelphia County.

Honey, George. He was naturalized in Maryland 14 Sep. 1753.

Honig, George. He was naturalized in Pennsylvania 11 Apr. 1761. He was from Lancaster County.

Honnold, Georg. He was naturalized in New Jersey in 1772. He was born in Germany and resided in New Town, Gloucester County. He had been in the colony twenty years.

Honshire, John. He was naturalized in Pennsylvania 24 Sep. 1762. He was from Lancaster County.

Hoober, Christian. He was naturalized in Pennsylvania 10 Apr. 1753. He was from Lancaster County.

Hoober, Henry. He was naturalized in Pennsylvania 10 Apr. 1765. He was from Lower Milford Township, Bucks County.

Hoobler, Abraham. He was naturalized in Pennsylvania 24 Sep. 1753. He was from Lancaster County.

Hoobler, John. He was naturalized in Pennsylvania 24 Sep. 1763. He was from Blanfield Township, Northampton County.

Hoobley, Michael. He was naturalized in Pennsylvania 10 Apr. 1753. He was from Lancaster County.

Hoodt, Caspar. He was naturalized in Pennsylvania 29 Sep. 1709. He was from Philadelphia County. He was born in Helmarshausen, Hesse, the son of Mathias Hoodt. He was also naturalized 25 July 1701.

Hooffman, Michael. He was naturalized in Pennsylvania 11–13 Apr. 1743. He was from Bucks County.

Hoofman, John. He was naturalized in Maryland 14 Sep. 1751.

Hoofman, Peter. He was naturalized in Maryland 27 Sep. 1746.

Hoofman, Philip. He was naturalized in Frederick County, Virginia 3 June 1767.

Hoofnaigle, John. He was naturalized in Pennsylvania 10–12 Apr. 1762. He was from Lancaster County.

Hoofney, George. He was naturalized in Pennsylvania 10–12 Apr. 1762. He was from Lancaster County.

Hooghe, William. He was naturalized in Maryland 11 Sep. 1765. He was a German.

Hoogheland, Christoffle. He took the oath to the King 21–26 Oct. 1664 after the conquest of New Netherland.

Hooglant, Dirck Jan. He took the oath of allegiance in Flackbush, Kings County, New York 26–30 Sep. 1687. He had been in the colony 30 years.

Hooglant, Jan Dircks. He took the oath of allegiance in Flackbush, Kings County, New York 26–30 Sep. 1687. He was a native of the colony.

Hooglant, Willem Dircks. He took the oath of allegiance in Flackbush, Kings County, New York 26–30 Sep. 1687. He was a native of the colony.

Hoogstraser, Paul. He was naturalized in New York 11 Sep. 1761.

Hoogtilin, William. He took the oath of naturalization in New York 1 Sep. 1687 in Ulster County.

Hook, Jacob. He was naturalized in Maryland 7 Sep. 1769. He was a German.

Hook, Joseph. He was naturalized in Maryland 7 Sep. 1769. He was a German.

Hook, Rudolph. He was naturalized in Maryland 7 Sep. 1768.

Hookart, Jacob. He was naturalized in Pennsylvania 24 Sep. 1759.

Hool, Andreas. He was naturalized in Maryland 14 Apr. 1762. He was a German.

Hoolf, Jacob. He was naturalized in Maryland 19 May 1756.

Hoopman, Jacob. He was naturalized in Maryland 14 Apr. 1762. He was a German.

Hoorenbeek, Loudewyck. He was naturalized in New York 8–9 Sep. 1715. He was from Ulster County.

Hoove, Frederick. He was naturalized in Pennsylvania 10 Sep. 1761. He was from Berks County.

Hoover, Andrew. He was naturalized in Pennsylvania 10 Sep. 1761. He was from Frederick, Maryland.

Hoover, Christian. He was naturalized in Pennsylvania 26–27 Sep. 1743. He was from Lancaster County.

Hoover, Henrick. He was naturalized in Pennsylvania 24 Sep. 1741. He was from Philadelphia County.

Hoover, Jacob. He was naturalized in Pennsylvania 26–27 Sep. 1743. He was from Lancaster County.

Hoover, Leonhard. He was naturalized in Maryland 15 Sep. 1762. He was from Frederick County.

Hoover, Ulrick. He was naturalized in Pennsylvania 26–27 Sep. 1743. He was from Lancaster County.

Hopff, John. He was naturalized in Pennsylvania 17 May 1771. He was from Tulpehocken Township, Berks County.

Hopper, Cornelius. He was naturalized in Maryland 11 Sep. 1765.

Hoppiker, Hans. He was naturalized in Pennsylvania 24 Sep. 1762. He was from Lancaster County.

Horch, Elias. He was naturalized in Maryland 31 Aug. 1757.

Horch, Johannes Elias. He was naturalized in Maryland 11 Apr. 1759.

Horlacher, Michael. He was naturalized in Pennsylvania 11 Apr. 1761. He was from Bucks County.

Horn, Andrew. He was naturalized in Pennsylvania 10 & 23 Apr. 1764. He was from Warwick Township, Lancaster County.

Horn, Hieronimus. He was naturalized in New Jersey 8 July 1730. He was born in Germany.

Hornbergher, Bartholomeus. He was naturalized in Pennsylvania in Sep. 1740. He was from Bucks County.

Horne, George. He was naturalized in Pennsylvania 24 Sep. 1746. He was from Philadelphia County.

Hornecker, John. He was naturalized in Pennsylvania 10 Apr. 1765. He was from Rockland Township, Bucks County.

Hornefer, Henrich. He was naturalized in New York 21 Oct. 1765. He was a baker from New York City.

Horning, Nicolas. He was naturalized in New York 11 Oct. 1715. He was from Albany County.

Horry, Ellye. He was born at Charenton, France, the son of Jean Horry and Madelaine DuFrene. He was naturalized in South Carolina ca. 1696.

Horry, Suzanne. She was born at Neu Chatell, Switzerland and was the widow of Jacques Varin. She was the daughter of Samuel Horry and Jeanne Dubois. Her children, born in South Carolina, were Suzanne Horry and Jacob Horry. They were naturalized in South Carolina ca. 1696.

Horse, Peter. He was naturalized in Augusta County, Virginia 17 Aug. 1757.

Horsfield, John Adam. He was naturalized in Pennsylvania 10 & 23 Apr. 1764. He was from Bethlehem Township, Northampton County.

Horst, George Ludowick. He was naturalized in Pennsylvania 19 May 1739. He was from Lancaster County.

Horteg, Johannes. He was naturalized in New York 31 Dec. 1768.

Hortements, Pr. Claude. He was an Acadian and took the oath of allegiance in Apr. 1730.

Hortigh, John. He was naturalized in New York 8 Mar. 1773.

Hortile, Adam. He was naturalized in New York 8–9 Sep. 1715. He was from Ulster County.

Hosman, Herman. He was naturalized in New York 8–9 Sep. 1715. He was from Ulster County.

Hosman, Johan Lowerns. He was naturalized in New York 8–9 Sep. 1715. He was from Ulster County.

Hosman, John Christian. He was naturalized in New York 8–9 Sep. 1715. He was from Ulster County.

Hoss, Jacob. He was naturalized in Maryland 5 May 1768. He was a German from Frederick County.

Hoss, Philip. He was naturalized in Pennsylvania 10–12 Apr. 1762. He was from Lancaster County.

Hossler, Jacob. He was naturalized in Maryland 5 May 1768. He was a German from Frederick County.

Hoster, Wilhelm. He was naturalized in Pennsylvania 11 Apr. 1763. He was from Heidelberg Township, Lancaster County.

Hott, George. He was naturalized in Pennsylvania 10 Sep. 1761. He was from Lancaster County.

Hottenstyn, Jacob. He was naturalized in Pennsylvania 10 Sep. 1761. He was from Lancaster County.

Houbman, Jacob. He was naturalized in Maryland 9 Sep. 1761.

Houck, Jury. He was naturalized in New York 17 Jan. 1715/6. He was from Albany County.

Hough, George. He was naturalized in New York 16 Feb. 1771.

Hough, George. He was naturalized in Pennsylvania 11–12 Apr. 1744. He was from Lancaster County.

Hough, Jacob. He was naturalized in Pennsylvania 11–12 Apr. 1744. He was from Lancaster County.

Hough, Philip. He was naturalized in Pennsylvania 11–13 Apr. 1743. He was from Philadelphia County.

Hough, Samuel. He was naturalized in Pennsylvania 11–12 Apr. 1744. He was from Lancaster County.

Houghstrasser, Jacob. He was naturalized in New York 16 Feb. 1771.

Houk, Jacob. He was naturalized in Pennsylvania 24–25 Sep. 1764. He was from Frederic Township, Philadelphia County.

Houpman, Henry. He was naturalized in Maryland 15 Apr. 1772. He was a German.

Hous, Rynier. He was naturalized in New York 10 Jan. 1715/6. He was a yeoman from Phillipsburgh.

House, John. He was naturalized in Maryland 17 May 1743. He was a German.

House, William. He was naturalized in Maryland 7 May 1767. He was a German from Frederick County.

Householder, George. He was naturalized in Pennsylvania 24 Sep. 1762. He was from Lancaster County.

Householder, Lawrence. He was naturalized in Pennsylvania 24 Sep. 1760. He was from Lancaster County.

Houser, Henry. He was naturalized in Jamaica 10 June 1675.

Houser, Jacob. He was naturalized in Pennsylvania 24–25 Sep. 1764. He was from Earl Township, Lancaster County. He was a Moravian.

Houser, Woolrick. He was naturalized in Pennsylvania 14 Feb. 1729/30. He was from Lancaster County.

Houselt, Jacob. He was naturalized in New Jersey 8 July 1730. He was born in Germany.

Houshilt, Matthias. He was naturalized in New Jersey 8 Dec. 1744.

Housilt, Johan. He was naturalized in New Jersey 8 July 1730. He was born in Germany.

Housman, Frederick. He was naturalized in Pennsylvania 13 May 1771. He was from York, York County.

Housman, Jacob. He was naturalized in North Carolina 22 Sep. 1764. He was from Rowan County and was a German.

Housom, John. He was naturalized in Pennsylvania 10–14 Apr. 1747. He was from Lancaster County.

Hout, George. He was naturalized in Maryland 15 Apr. 1761.

Houtschilt, Ernest. He was naturalized in New York 25 Nov. 1751.

Houtvat, Adrian. He was naturalized in New York 24 Nov. 1750.

Houver, John Woolrick. He was naturalized in Pennsylvania 14 Feb. 1729/30. He was from Lancaster County.

Houy, Daniel. He was naturalized in Pennsylvania 25 Sep. 1751. He was from Lancaster County.

Houys, Christian. He was naturalized in New York 11 Oct. 1715. He was from Albany County.

Houze, John. He was naturalized in New Jersey 20 June 1765.

Hover, John. He was naturalized in Pennsylvania 11 Apr. 1761. He was from Lancaster County.

Hover, Michael. He was naturalized in Augusta County, Virginia 17 Aug. 1773.

Hover, Nicholas. He was naturalized in Maryland 11 Sep. 1765.

Hover, Sebastian. He was naturalized in Augusta County, Virginia 18 May 1762.

Hover, Vandal. He was naturalized in Maryland 11 Sep. 1765.

Hoversticht, Michael. He was naturalized in Pennsylvania 11 Apr. 1751. He was from Lancaster County.

Hoverstick, Adam. He was naturalized in Augusta County, Virginia 16 Mar. 1774.

Howell, Johanna. She was naturalized in Jamaica 21 Sep. 1716. She was the wife of Samuel Howell.

Hower, Michael. He was naturalized in Maryland 26 Sep. 1765. He was a German.

Howg, Peter. He was naturalized in Pennsylvania 11 Apr. 1761. He was from Philadelphia County.

Howrieau, Daniel. He was endenized in New York 19 July 1686. He was a brother of Pierre Howrieau.

Howrieau, Pierre. He was endenized in New York 19 July 1686. He was a brother of Daniel Howrieau.

Hows, George. He was naturalized in Pennsylvania 25–27 Sep. 1740. He was from Philadelphia County.

Howser, John. He was naturalized in Pennsylvania 14 Feb. 1729/30. He was from Lancaster County.

Hoy, John. He was naturalized in Pennsylvania 10 Apr. 1760.

Hoyer, Erich Christian. He was naturalized in New York 29 July 1746. He was a schoolmaster from New York City.

Hoyer, Matthew. He was naturalized in New York 28 Oct. 1760. He was a baker from New York City.

Hoyl, Andrew. He was naturalized in Maryland 20 Sep. 1765. He was a German.

Hoyl, Wendal. He was naturalized in Pennsylvania 10 Sep. 1761. He was from Lancaster County.

Hoyle, George. He was naturalized in Pennsylvania 24 Sep. 1760. He was from Lancaster County.

Hoyle, Jacob. He was naturalized in Pennsylvania 24 Sep. 1760. He was from Lancaster County.

Hubbach, Anthony. He was naturalized in New Jersey 8 July 1730. He was born in Germany.

Hubbley, Bernard. He was naturalized in Pennsylvania 26–27 Sep. 1743. He was from Lancaster County.

Hubener, John, Jr. He was naturalized in Pennsylvania 11–13 Apr. 1743. He was from Philadelphia County.

Huber, Adam. He was naturalized in Maryland 12 Sep. 1764. He was a German from Frederick County.

Huber, Adam. He was naturalized in Maryland 11 Sep. 1765. He was a German from Frederick County.

Huber, Casper. He was naturalized in New York 3 July 1759.

Huber, Daniel. He was naturalized in Pennsylvania 11 Apr. 1761. He was from Lancaster County.

Huber, Hans Jacob. He was naturalized in New York 23 Apr. 1747. He was a yeoman from New York City.

Huber, Henry. He was naturalized in Pennsylvania 11 Apr. 1761. He was from Bucks County.

Huber, Jacob. He was naturalized in Pennsylvania 25–27 Sep. 1740. He was from Lancaster County.

Huber, Jacob. He was naturalized in Pennsylvania 10 & 23 Apr. 1764. He was from Rockhill Township, Bucks County.

Huber, John. He was naturalized in Pennsylvania 11 Apr. 1749. He was from Bucks County.

Huber, John. He was naturalized in Pennsylvania 10 Sep. 1761. He was from Lancaster County.

Huber, John. He was naturalized in Pennsylvania 10–12 April 1762. He was from York County.

Huber, Michael. He was naturalized in Pennsylvania 30 May 1772. He was from Coset's Run, Frederick County, Maryland.

Huber, Nicholas. He was naturalized in Pennsylvania 11 Apr. 1761. He was from Lancaster County.

Huber, Peter. He was naturalized in Pennsylvania 11 Apr. 1761. He was from Lancaster County.

Huber, Peter. He was naturalized in Maryland 11 Sep. 1765. He was a German from Frederick County.

Huber, Rudolph. He was naturalized in Pennsylvania 10 Apr. 1765. He was from Philadelphia.

Huber, Ulrich. He was naturalized in Maryland 11 Sep. 1765. He was a German.

Hubertson, Hubert. He and his son, Jacob Hubertson, were endenized in London 25 Aug. 1708. They came to New York.

Hubler, Jacob. He was naturalized in Pennsylvania 11 Apr. 1761. He was from Berks County.

Hubley, Frederick. He was naturalized in Pennsylvania 24–25 Sep. 1764. He was from Lancaster Township, Lancaster County.

Hubner, Georg. He was naturalized in New York 3 July 1759.

Hubner, George. He was naturalized in Pennsylvania 19 May 1739. He was from Philadelphia County.

Hubner, Hans. He was naturalized in Pennsylvania 11–13 Apr. 1743. He was from Philadelphia County.

Hubner, Henry. He was naturalized in New York 3 July 1759.

Huebner, Adam. He was naturalized in Maryland 11 Apr. 1764. He was from Frederick County.

Huebner, Michael. He was naturalized in Maryland 11 Apr. 1764. He was a German from Frederick County.

Huesung, John George. He was naturalized in Pennsylvania 24 Sep. 1763. He was from Brecknock Township, Berks County.

Huett, Peter. He was naturalized in Pennsylvania 10 Apr. 1766. He was from Exeter Township, Berks County.

Huey, Adam. He was naturalized in Pennsylvania 11 Apr. 1761. He was from Northampton County.

Hufferner, Melechior. He was naturalized in Maryland 29 Sep. 1764. He was a German.

Huffman, Casper. He was naturalized in Maryland 16 Sep. 1773. He was a German.

Huffman, George. He was naturalized in Maryland 11 Sep. 1760.

Huffnagle, Arnold. He was naturalized in Pennsylvania 6 Feb. 1730/1. He was from Philadelphia County.

Hufford, Melcor. He was naturalized in Pennsylvania 14 Feb. 1729/30. He was from Lancaster County.

Huger, Daniel. He was endenized in England 8 Mar. 1681/2. He came to New York.

Huges, Jacob. He took the oath to the King 21–26 Oct. 1664 after the conquest of New Netherland.

Hugon, Francois. He was an Acadian and took the oath of allegiance in Apr. 1730

Hugur, Daniel. He was born in London, England and was the son of Jean Huger and Anne Rassin. His wife was Margueritte Perdriau. Their children were Margueritte Huger born in Rochelle, France, Daniel Huger, and Madeleine Huger. The latter two were born in South Carolina. They were naturalized in South Carolina *ca.* 1696.

Huhl, Marcus. He was naturalized in Pennsylvania 6 Feb. 1730/1. He was from Philadelphia.

Huiand, John. He was naturalized in Pennsylvania 11 Apr. 1761. He was from Berks County.

Huijcken, Willem. He took the oath of allegiance in Breucklijn, Kings County, New York 26–30 Sep. 1687. He had been in the colony 24 years.

Huisman, Abraham. He was naturalized in New York 22 June 1734.

Huke, Ludwick. He was naturalized in Pennsylvania 24 Sep. 1762. He was from Bucks County.

Hullman, Adam. He was naturalized in Pennsylvania 10 Sep. 1761. He was from Lancaster County.

Hulsekamp, Gerard. He was naturalized in Pennsylvania 10 Apr. 1772. He was from Philadelphia.

Hulster, Leonard. He was naturalized in Pennsylvania 25 Sep. 1744. He was from Lancaster County.

Humber, Jacob. He was naturalized in Maryland 3 May 1768. He was a German.

Humbert, William. He was naturalized in Maryland 24 Sep. 1762. He was a German from Frederick County.

Humble, Martin. He was naturalized in Pennsylvania in Sep. 1740. He was from Philadelphia County.

Humble, Uriah, Jr. He was naturalized in Pennsylvania in Sep. 1740. He was from Bucks County.

Humer, Jacob. He was naturalized in Maryland 13 Apr. 1763. He was a German.

Hummel, Elias. He was naturalized in Pennsylvania 10 Apr. 1760.

Hummel, Frederick. He was naturalized in Pennsylvania 24 Sep. 1762. He was from Lancaster County.

Hummel, John. He was naturalized in Maryland 11 Sep. 1765. He was a German and lived in Frederick, Maryland.

Hunemaker, Jacob. He was naturalized in Maryland 11 Apr. 1764. He was a German.

Hungate, Simon. He was naturalized in Virginia 12 May 1705.

Hungazel, Samuel. He was naturalized in Virginia 12 May 1705.

Hunsucker, Valentine. He was naturalized in Pennsylvania 6 Feb. 1730/1. He was from Philadelphia County.

Hunter, Adam. He was naturalized in Frederick County, Virginia 12 Nov. 1751.

Hunter, Anthony. He was naturalized in Pennsylvania 25–27 Sep. 1740. He was from Philadelphia County.

Hunter, Charles. He was naturalized in Pennsylvania 11 Apr. 1741. He was from Philadelphia County.

Hunter, Isaac. He was naturalized in Pennsylvania 25–27 Sep. 1740. He was from Philadelphia County.

Hunter, John. He was naturalized in Pennsylvania 25–27 Sep. 1740. He was from Philadelphia County.

Huntsberger, Jacob. He was naturalized in Pennsylvania 11–13 Apr. 1743. He was from Philadelphia County.

Huntz, Devalt. He was naturalized in Maryland 9 Sep. 1761.

Huntziger, Johannes. He was naturalized in New York 25 Apr. 1743. He was a blacksmith from Dutchess County.

Hupp, Augustus. He was naturalized in Maryland 11 Sep. 1765. He was a German from Frederick County.

Huppell, Joseph. He was naturalized in New Jersey 3 June 1763.

Hurback, John. He was naturalized in Pennsylvania 24 Sep. 1762. He was from York County.

Hurlieman, Faelix. He was naturalized in Pennsylvania 24 Sep. 1760. He was from Philadelphia County.

Hurtzell, Ulrick. He was naturalized in Pennsylvania 24 Sep. 1763. He was from Upper Salford Township, Philadelphia County.

Hush, Valentine. He was naturalized in Maryland 14 Sep. 1763. He was a German.

Hushaa, Dewald. He was naturalized in Pennsylvania 24–25 Sep./5 Oct. 1767. He was from Brecknock Township, Lancaster County.

Husk, Ludowick. He was naturalized in New Jersey in 1769. He was born in Germany.

Huson, Christopher. He was naturalized in New Jersey 28 Apr. 1762.

Hutchinson, William. He was naturalized in Jamaica 25 May 1700.

Huth, Jacob. He was naturalized in New York 3 July 1759.

Huy, David. He was naturalized in New York 1740–41. He was a Jew.

Huybertsen, Dirk. He expressed his desire to be naturalized in New Castle County, Delaware 21 Feb. 1682/3.

Huyblingh, Coenraad. He was naturalized in Jamaica 4 June 1754.

Huzel, John George. He was naturalized in Maryland 19 Oct. 1743. He was from Manaquice.

Hyer, Johan Frederick. He was naturalized in New York 28 July 1773. He was an organ builder.

Hyle, John. He was naturalized in Maryland 13 Apr. 1763. He was a German from Frederick County.

Hynicky, Adam. He was naturalized in Pennsylvania 24–25 Sep./5 Oct. 1767. He was from York Township, York County.

Hymer, Gabriel. He was naturalized in New Jersey 3 June 1763.

Hyner, Nicholas. He was naturalized in Maryland 14 Oct. 1774. He was a German from Baltimore County.

Hysing, Jacob. He was naturalized in Maryland 3 Sep. 1765. He was a German from Frederick County.

Hysler, Nicholas. He was naturalized in Maryland 11 Sep. 1765.

Hyssley, Conrad. He was naturalized in Pennsylvania 10 Apr. 1760.

Hysson, Paulser. He was naturalized in Maryland 9 Sep. 1761. He was from Frederick County.

Hyster, Peter. He was naturalized in Pennsylvania 24 Sep. 1755. He was from Philadelphia County.

Iacay, Baptiste. He was an Acadian and took the oath to George II at Annapolis River, Nova Scotia in the winter of 1730.

Ibach, Jacob. He was naturalized in Maryland 9 Apr. 1760. He lived in Baltimore County.

Icks, Nicholas. He was naturalized in Pennsylvania 11 Apr. 1749. He was from Philadelphia County.

Icleberger, Martin. He was naturalized in Pennsylvania 10 Apr. 1760.

Iden, John. He was naturalized in Pennsylvania 29 Mar. 1739. He was from Philadelphia.

Idlesberry, Francis. He was endenized in Maryland 12 Feb. 1773. He was born in Germany.

Igenor, Jacob. He was naturalized in North Carolina 19 Oct. 1753. He was from Rowan County.

Iglefritz, George. He was naturalized in Pennsylvania 11 Apr. 1761. He was from York County.

Ikken, Catharine. She was naturalized in Pennsylvania 11 Apr. 1771. She was from Upper Milford Township, Northampton County.

Iler, Adolph. He was naturalized in Frederick County, Virginia 1 Nov. 1768.

Ilgner, Christian. He was naturalized in Pennsylvania 23 Nov. 1771. He was from Lancaster, Lancaster County.

Imbert, Andrew. He was naturalized in Maryland 18 Oct. 1694.

Imbert, John. He was naturalized in Virginia 12 May 1705.

Imbler, Lodowick. He was naturalized in Pennsylvania 24 Sep. 1759.

Imel, John. He was naturalized in Pennsylvania 25 Sep. 1751. He was from Lancaster County.

Imhoff, Everet. He and his sons, Gerhard Imhoff, Herman Imhoff, and Peter Imhoff, were naturalized in Pennsylvania 29 Sep. 1709. They were from Philadelphia. They also appeared as Everet Imhoffee, Gerhard Imhoffee, Herman Imhoffee, and Peter Imhoffee.

Immel, Henry Michael. He was naturalized in Pennsylvania 19 May 1739. He was from Lancaster County.

Immel, John. He was naturalized in New Jersey 20 Aug. 1755.

Immel, Leonard. He was naturalized in Pennsylvania 10 Sep. 1761. He was from York County.

Immoberstake, Abraham. He was naturalized in Pennsylvania 24 Sep. 1759.

Inbert, Andrew. He promised allegiance to the King and obedience to William Penn in Pennsylvania 10 Sep. 1683.

Ingel, Melcher. He was naturalized in Pennsylvania 26–27 Sep. 1743. He was from Lancaster County.

Ingle, George. He was naturalized in North Carolina 23 Mar. 1763. He was from Rowan County.

Inkel, Henry. He was naturalized in Pennsylvania 24–25 Sep./5 Oct. 1767. He was from Frederick County, Maryland.

Ipa, Casper. He was naturalized in Pennsylvania 11 Apr. 1761. He was from Lancaster County.

Irick, John. He was naturalized in New Jersey in 1770.

Irish, Francis. He was naturalized in Maryland 10 Sep. 1760. He also appeared as Francis Frish.

Isaac, Jacob. He was naturalized in Pennsylvania 10 Apr. 1758.

Isaackzen, Arent. He took the oath to the King 21–26 Oct. 1664 after the conquest of New Netherland.

Isaackzen, Denys. He took the oath to the King 21–26 Oct. 1664 after the conquest of New Netherland.

Isaacs, Aaron. He was naturalized in New York 20 Oct. 1764.

Isaacs, Abraham. He was naturalized in New York in 1740–41. He was a Jewish merchant from New York City.

Isaacs, Samuel. He was naturalized in New York 27 Jan. 1770.

Isagar, Jonathan. He was naturalized in Maryland 20 Oct. 1747. He was also known as Jonathan Hagar.

Iseberger, Gabriel. He was naturalized in Pennsylvania 11–13 Apr. 1743. He was from Philadelphia County.

Isenhart, Christopher. He was naturalized in New York 20 Mar. 1762.

Ish, Peter. He was naturalized in Pennsylvania 24 Sep. 1763. He was from Lancaster Township, Lancaster County.

Isler, Martin. He was naturalized in Nova Scotia 5 July 1758.

Israel, David. He was endenized in England 27 Dec. 1662. He lived in Barbados and was a Jew.

Israel, Henriq'. He was naturalized in Jamaica 26 Feb. 1740/1. He was a Jew.

Israel, Jacob. He took the oath to the King 21–26 Oct. 1664 after the conquest of New Netherland.

Israel, Jacob. He was naturalized in Jamaica 18 Jan. 1736/7.

Israel, Joseph. He was naturalized in Jamaica 13 Feb. 1692/3.

Israel, Michael. He was naturalized in Pennsylvania 25 Sep. 1752. He was from Philadelphia. He was a Jew. His name also appears as Midrach Israel.

Israello, Angel. He was naturalized in Maryland 17 Sep. 1751.

Isseley, Malachi. He was naturalized in North Carolina 22 Sep. 1763. He was from Rowan County and a German.

Issler, Loadowick. He was naturalized in North Carolina 22 Sep. 1764. He was from Rowan County and a German.

Ivy, Mary. She was naturalized in Jamaica 21 Apr. 1692. She was the wife of George Ivy.

Izenhart, Andreas. He was naturalized in Pennsylvania 11 Apr. 1761. He was from Northampton County.

Jaboien, Nicholaus. He was naturalized in New York 17 June 1726.

Jackis, Frederick. He was naturalized in Pennsylvania 11 Apr. 1761. He was from Berks County.

Jackle, Jeremiah. He was naturalized in Pennsylvania 25 Sep. 1751. He was from Philadelphia County.

Jacky, John George. He was naturalized in Frederick County, Virginia 4 Aug. 1747.

Jacob, Francisus. He was naturalized in Maryland 29 Sep. 1764. He was a German.

Jacob, Barentz. He was naturalized in Pennsylvania in Sep.–Oct. 1765. He was a Jew.

Jacob, John. He was naturalized in Pennsylvania 13 May 1768. He was from Bern Township, Berks County.

Jacob, Martin. He was naturalized in Maryland 11 Sep. 1765. He was a German from Frederick County.

Jacob, Nicholas. He was naturalized in Pennsylvania 10 & 23 Apr. 1764. He was from Philadelphia.

Jacobi, Christopher. He was naturalized in New York 15 Jan. 1750/1. He was a stocking weaver from Germantown, Pennsylvania.

Jacobi, Diederick. He was naturalized in Jamaica 7 May 1741.

Jacobi, Ulrigh. He was naturalized in New York 17 Jan. 1715/6. He was from Albany County.

Jacobs, Adam. He was naturalized in Pennsylvania 11 Sep. 1761. He was from Lancaster County.

Jacobs, Amsel. He was naturalized in Jamaica 26 July 1750.

Jacobs, Arrent. He took the oath of naturalization in New York 1 Sep. 1687 in Ulster County.

Jacobs, Barrant. He took the oath of naturalization in New York 1 Sep. 1687 in Ulster County.

Jacobs, Crains. He took the oath to the King 21–26 Oct. 1664 after the conquest of New Netherland.

Jacobs, David. He was naturalized in New York 20 Mar. 1762.

Jacobs, Leury. He took the oath of naturalization in New York 1 Sep. 1687 in Ulster County.

Jacobs, Petter. He took the oath of naturalization in New York 1 Sep. 1687 in Ulster County.

Jacobs, Philip. He was naturalized in New York 22 Apr. 1774.

Jacobs, Tunis. He took the oath of naturalization in New York 1 Sep. 1687 in Ulster County.

Jacobs, William. He took the oath of naturalization in New York 1 Sep. 1687 in Ulster County.

Jacobse, Cornelis. He was naturalized in New York 7 June 1684. He was from New York City.

Jacobse, Pieter. He was naturalized in New York 27 Sep. 1715. He was a bricklayer from New York City.

Jacobsen, Christopher. He was naturalized in New York 3 May 1755.

Jacobson, Goody. He was naturalized in Jamaica 17 Feb. 1724/5. He was a butcher.

Jacobson, Jacob. He was endenized in Maryland 29 July 1661. He was Swedish and late of New Amstel.

Jacobson, Jeffrey. He was naturalized in Maryland 6 June 1674. He was Swedish.

Jacobson, Nicholas. He was naturalized in Jamaica 25 Sep. 1701.

Jacobson, Peter. He was endenized in Maryland 29 July 1661. He was Swedish and late of New Amstel.

Jacqueri, Daniel. He took the oath of allegiance at Mobile, West Florida 2 Oct. 1764.

Jacques, Baptiste. He was an Acadian who took the oath of allegiance at Annapolis River in Dec. 1729.

Jacques, Jacqueline. She applied for naturalization 24 Apr. 1704 in Virginia.

Jacquet, Jan, Jr. He expressed his desire to be naturalized in New Castle County, Delaware 21 Feb. 1682/3.

Jacquet, Jean Paul. He was naturalized in New Castle County, Delaware 21 Feb. 1682/3.

Jacquet, Pieter. He was naturalized in New Castle County, Delaware 21 Feb. 1682/3.

Jager, Andreas. He was naturalized in Pennsylvania 19 May 1739. He was from Philadelphia County.

Jager, Anthony. He was naturalized in Pennsylvania 19 May 1739. He was from Philadelphia County.

Jager, George. He was naturalized in Pennsylvania 6 Feb. 1730/1. He was from Philadelphia County.

Jager, Nicholas. He was naturalized in Pennsylvania 19 May 1739. He was from Philadelphia County.

Jago, Moses Hamos. He was endenized in England 20 Feb. 1662/3. He settled in Barbados and was a Jew. He also appeared as Moses Hamos Gago.

Jamain, Elias. He was endenized in London 11 Mar. 1699/1700. He came to New York.

Jamain, Judith. She was naturalized in New York 6 Mar. 1715/6. She was a spinster from New York City.

Janse, Hendrick. He took the oath of allegiance in Flackbush, Kings County, New York 26–30 Sep. 1687. He was a native of the colony.

Janse, Jacob. He took the oath of allegiance in Boswijck, Kings County, New York 26–30 Sep. 1687. He was a native of the colony.

Janse, Jan. He took the oath of allegiance in Boswijck, Kings County, New York 26–30 Sep. 1687. He had been in the colony 36 years.

Janse, Joseph. He was naturalized in New York 6 Dec. 1715. He was from Albany County.

Janse, Lambert. He took the oath of allegiance in New Uijtrceht, Kings County, New York 26–30 Sep. 1687. He had been in the colony 22 years.

Janse, Laurens. He took the oath of allegiance in New Uijtrceht, Kings County, New York 26–30 Sep. 1687. He was a native of the colony.

Janse, Peter Guil. He took the oath of allegiance in Flackbush, Kings County, New York 26–30 Sep. 1687. He had been in the colony 45 years.

Janse, Willem Guil. He took the oath of allegiance in Flackbush, Kings County, New York 26–30 Sep. 1687. He had been in the colony 47 years.

Jansen, Claus. He and his sons, John Jansen and William Jansen, were naturalized in Pennsylvania 29 Sep. 1709. They were from Philadelphia County.

Jansen, Cunrad. He was naturalized in Pennsylvania 29 Sep. 1709. He was from Philadelphia County.

Jansen, Dirk, Jr. He was naturalized in Pennsylvania 29 Sep. 1709. He was from Philadelphia County.

Jansen, Harmen. He expressed his desire to be naturalized in New Castle County, Delaware 21 Feb. 1682/3.

Jansen, John Bernard. He was naturalized in Nova Scotia 4 July 1758.

Jansen, Lambert. He took the oath of allegiance in Flackbush, Kings County, New York 26–30 Sep. 1687. He was a native of the colony.

Jansen, Peter. He was naturalized in Pennsylvania 29 Sep. 1709. He was from Philadelphia County.

Jansen, Sybrant. He expressed his desire to be naturalized in New Castle County, Delaware 21 Feb. 1682/3.

Jansin, Jost. He took the oath of naturalization in New York 1 Sep. 1687 in Ulster County.

Janssen, Barent. He took the oath of allegiance in Flackbush, Kings County, New York 26–30 Sep. 1687. He was a native of the colony.

Janssen, Casper. He took the oath of allegiance in Breucklijn, Kings County, New York 26–30 Sep. 1687. He was a native of the colony.

Janssen, Hans. He took the oath of allegiance in Flackland, Kings County, New York 26–30 Sep. 1687. He had been in the colony 47 years.

Janssen, Joost. He was naturalized in New York 3 May 1755.

Janssen, Swaen. He took the oath of allegiance in New Uijtrceht, Kings County, New York 26–30 Sep. 1687. He had been in the colony 33 years.

Janvier, Thomas. He was endenized in Pennsylvania 21 Feb. 1694/5. He was from France. He was a carpenter.

Janze, Daniel. He was naturalized in New York 17 Jan. 1715/6. He was from Albany County.

Janze, Evert. He was naturalized in New York 22 Nov. 1715. He was from Albany County.

Janzen, Abraham. He took the oath to the King 21–26 Oct. 1664 after the conquest of New Netherland.

Janzen, Claes. He took the oath to the King 21–26 Oct. 1664 after the conquest of New Netherland.

Janzen, Claes. He took the oath to the King 21–26 Oct. 1664 after the conquest of New Netherland. He was from Langendick.

Janzen, Cornelis. He took the oath to the King 21–26 Oct. 1664 after the conquest of New Netherland. He was from Hoorn.

Janzen, Cors. He took the oath to the King 21–26 Oct. 1664 after the conquest of New Netherland.

Janzen, Frans. He took the oath to the King 21–26 Oct. 1664 after the conquest of New Netherland. He was from Hooghten.

Janzen, Galma Sibrant. He took the oath to the King 21–26 Oct. 1664 after the conquest of New Netherland.

Janzen, Hendrick. He took the oath to the King 21–26 Oct. 1664 after the conquest of New Netherland. He was a baker.

Janzen, Jan. He took the oath to the King 21–26 Oct. 1664 after the conquest of New Netherland. He was from Brestee.

Janzen, Jan. He took the oath to the King 21–26 Oct. 1664 after the conquest of New Netherland. He was from Langedick.

Janzen, Jurien. He took the oath to the King 21–26 Oct. 1664 after the conquest of New Netherland.

Janzen, Pieter. He took the oath to the King 21–26 Oct. 1664 after the conquest of New Netherland.

Janzen, Pieter. He took the oath to the King 21–26 Oct. 1664 after the conquest of New Netherland. He was of the Long Street.

Janzen, Roeloff. He took the oath to the King 21–26 Oct. 1664 after the conquest of New Netherland. He was from Meppelen.

Janzen, Sick. He took the oath to the King 21–26 Oct. 1664 after the conquest of New Netherland.

Jarboe, John. He was made a denizen in Maryland 30 July 1661. He was Dutch and was late of New Amstel.

Jarboe, John. He was naturalized in Maryland 1 May 1666. He was also known as John Parks and was of Dijon, France.

Jareau, Baptiste. He was an Acadian and took the oath of allegiance in Apr. 1730.

Jarger, Hans George. He was naturalized in Pennsylvania 19 May 1739. He was from Philadelphia County.

Jarger, Peter. He was naturalized in Pennsylvania 19 May 1739. He was from Philadelphia County.

Javert, John. He was naturalized in Pennsylvania 29 Sep. 1709. He was from Philadelphia County. He also appeared as John Jawert. As Johannes Jawert, he was naturalized in Pennsylvania 12 Feb. 1700/1, the son of Balthazar Jawert.

Jay, August. He took the oath of naturalization in New York 1 Sep. 1687 in Ulster County.

Jeem, John. He was naturalized in Maryland 10 Apr. 1762. He was a German from Anne Arundel County.

Jefback, Johan Coenraet. He was naturalized in New York 31 Jan. 1715/6. He was from Albany County.

Jegee, Rene dit Desroziers. He was an Acadian who took the oath of allegiance to the King at the Mines, Pisiquit 31 Oct. 1727.

Jegou, Peter. He expressed his desire to be naturalized in New Castle County, Delaware 21 Feb. 1682/3.

Jenda, Baruh. He was naturalized in Jamaica 18 May 1709.

Jenigo, Morris. He was naturalized in Jamaica 24 Feb. 1685/6.

Jennings, Bonella. She was naturalized in Jamaica 1 Mar. 1696.

Jenticou, Ernest Lewis. He was naturalized in Jamaica 29 Apr. 1742.

Jessen, Detlib. He was naturalized in Nova Scotia 5 July 1758.

Jesserson, Michael. He was naturalized in Maryland 15 Apr. 1761.

Joanny, John. He was naturalized in Virginia 12 May 1705. He was born in France.

Job, John Nicholas. He was naturalized in Pennsylvania 10 Apr. 1760.

Jockem, Andrew. He was naturalized in Maryland 17 July 1765. He was a German.

Joder, Joest. He was naturalized in Pennsylvania 6 Feb. 1730/1. He was from Philadelphia County.

Joder, John. He was naturalized in Pennsylvania 6 Feb. 1730/1. He was from Philadelphia County.

Joder, John, Jr. He was naturalized in Pennsylvania 6 Feb. 1730/1. He was from Philadelphia County.

Joder, John. He was naturalized in Pennsylvania 29 Mar. 1735. He was from Bucks County.

Joder, John, Jr. He was naturalized in Pennsylvania 29 Mar. 1735. He was from Bucks County.

Jogkimzen, Andries. He took the oath to the King 21–26 Oct. 1664 after the conquest of New Netherland.

Johnson, Adam. He was charged in Sussex Co., Del. court on 21 July 1687 of not being a denizen. John Millington testified in his behalf. He exercised the trade of a merchant and factor. The jury found in his favor that he had cleared his sloop at New York and entered the port of Lewes, Delaware.

Johnson, Albort. He was naturalized in Maryland 13 May 1682. He was from Talbot County.

Johnson, Barnard. He was naturalized in Maryland 19 Apr. 1671. He was from Calvert County and was Dutch. He was a cooper.

Johnson, Christopher. He was naturalized in New York 20 Apr. 1768. He was a tavern keeper from New York City.

Johnson, Cornelis. He was naturalized in Sussex County, Delaware 28 Apr. 1683.

Johnson, Cornelius. He was naturalized in Maryland 6 June 1674 and was born in Fiacina, Holland.

Johnson, Cornelius. He was endenized in London in 1688. He had his certificate recorded in Barbados 14 Aug. 1693.

Johnson, Cornelius. He was naturalized in Jamaica 28 Feb. 1721/2.

Johnson, Garratt. He was naturalized in Virginia in Feb. 1676/7.

Johnson, Gerritt. He took the oath of naturalization in New York 1 Sep. 1687 in Ulster County.

Johnson, Hendrick. He was made a denizen in Maryland 26 Feb. 1668. He was late of Amsterdam.

Johnson, Hendrick. He took the oath of naturalization in New York 1 Sep. 1687 in Ulster County.

Johnson, Jacob. He was naturalized in Virginia Apr. 1679.

Johnson, Jacob. He was naturalized in Maryland 13 May 1682. He lived in Talbot County.

Johnson, John. He was naturalized in Maryland 6 June 1674. He lived in Talbot County and was Dutch.

Johnson, John. He was endenized in Virginia 13 Mar. 1659/60. He was a Dutchman and a millwright.

Johnson, Paul. He was naturalized in New Jersey in 1757. He also appeared as Paul Janson. He was from Germany. He had been in the colony 13 years.

Johnson, Lawrence. He was naturalized in Jamaica 13 Feb. 1693/4.

Johnson, Paule. He was made a denizen in Maryland 29 July 1661. He was Swedish and was late of New Amstel.

Johnson, Paulus. He was endenized in New York 22 June 1686.

Johnson, Peter. He was naturalized in Maryland 8 May 1669. He was Swedish.

Johnson, Peter. He was naturalized in New Jersey in 1757. He also appeared as Peter Janson. He was from Germany. He had lived in Pennsylvania eleven years and two years in New Jersey.

Johnson, Petter. He took the oath of naturalization in New York 1 Sep. 1687 in Ulster County.

Johnson, Roulof. He took the oath of naturalization in New York 1 Sep. 1687 in Ulster County.

Johnson, Theodore. He was naturalized in South Carolina on or about 2 Mar. 1699/1700.

Johnson, Thomas. He took the oath of naturalization in New York 1 Sep. 1687 in Ulster County.

Johnston, John. He was naturalized in Pennsylvania 25 Sep. 1744. He was from Lancaster County.

Johnston, Simon. He was naturalized in Maryland 6 Nov. 1685.

Johonnott, Daniel. He was naturalized in Massachusetts 12 Apr. 1731.

Joley, Peire. He took the oath of allegiance at Mobile, West Florida 2 Oct. 1764.

Jolyne, Andrew. He was endenized in New York 6 Aug. 1686. He also appeared as Andrew Jolain.

Jonas, Jacob. He was naturalized in Jamaica 2 Oct. 1771.

Jonas, Simon. He was naturalized in North Carolina 26 Mar. 1767. He was from Rowan County.

Joner, Jonens. He was naturalized in Pennsylvania 24 Sep. 1745. He was from Lancaster County.

Jong, Hendrick. He was naturalized in New York 3 Jan. 1715/6. He was from Albany County.

Jong Bloet, Johanes. He was naturalized in New York 8 Nov. 1735.

Joon, Jochem. He was naturalized in Maryland 12 Sep. 1759.

Joorisen, Jacob. He took the oath of allegiance in Breucklijn, Kings County, New York 26–30 Sep. 1687. He was a native of the colony.

Joorissen, Harmen. He took the oath of allegiance in Breucklijn, Kings County, New York 26–30 Sep. 1687. He was a native of the colony.

Joosten, Caspar. He took the oath of allegiance in Orange County, New York 26 Sep. 1687.

Joosten, Jacob. He took the oath to the King 21–26 Oct. 1664 after the conquest of New Netherland.

Joosten, Jan. He took the oath to the King 21–26 Oct. 1664 after the conquest of New Netherland.

Joran, Jacob. He was naturalized in New York 8 Mar. 1773.

Jordan, Caspar, Jr. He was naturalized in New York 11 Sep. 1761.

Jordan, John. He was naturalized in Pennsylvania 24–25 Sep. 1764. He was from Oley Township, Berks County.

Jordan, Stephen. He was naturalized in New York 20 Mar. 1762.

Jordon, Hannes, Jr. He was naturalized in New York 11 Sep. 1761.

Jores, Rutt. He took the oath of naturalization in New York 1 Sep. 1687 in Ulster County.

Jorrigg, Abraham. He was naturalized in Pennsylvania 24 Sep. 1762. He was from Lancaster County.

Joseph, George Henry. He was naturalized in Pennsylvania 11 Apr. 1761. He was from Bucks County.

Josephson, Manuel. He sought naturalization in New York 27 Nov. 1756.

Josephson, Myer. He was naturalized in Pennsylvania 11 Apr. 1763. He was from Reading Township, Berks County. He was a Jew.

Jost, John George. He was naturalized in Nova Scotia 15 Sep. 1758.

Josten, John. He took the oath of naturalization in New York 1 Sep. 1687 in Ulster County.

Jouch, John. He was naturalized in New York 18 Oct. 1768. He was a shingle shaver from New York City.

Jouet, Daniel. He was born at L'Isle de Re, France, the son of Daniel Jouet and Elizabeth Jouet. His wife was Marie Courcier, daughter of Jean Coursier and Anne Perrotau. Their children were Daniel Jouet born in L'Isle de Re, France, Pierre Jouet born in France, Marie Jouet born at Plymouth, Massachusetts, Elizabeth Jouet, and Annie Jouet. The latter two were born in New York. They were naturalized in South Carolina 10 Mar. 1696/7. He was a sailmaker.

Jouneau, Abraham. He was endenized in England 11 Mar. 1699/1700. He came to New York.

Jouneau, Pierre. He petitioned for naturalization in New York 19 Aug. 1687.

Jourdain, Jean. He was naturalized in Maryland 8 May 1669. He was born in Rouen, France.

Jourdean, John. He was made a denizen in Maryland 17 July 1667.

Juda, Weinbert. He was naturalized in Maryland 15 Sep. 1762. He was from Frederick County.

Judah, Baruch. He was naturalized in New York 10 Jan. 1715/6. He was a merchant from New York City.

Judith, Jacob. He was naturalized in Maryland 1 Oct. 1767. He was a German.

Judy, John. He was naturalized in Maryland 16 Sep. 1762. He was a German from Frederick County.

Judy, Philip. He was naturalized in Maryland 27 Apr. 1763. He was a German from Frederick County.

Juin, Lewis. He was naturalized in South Carolina 10 Mar. 1696/7. He was a planter.

Juin, Reni. He was naturalized in South Carolina 10 Mar. 1696/7. He was a planter.

Juing, George. He was born at Cherneux, Poitou, France, the son of Rene Juing and Judith Pie. His wife was Suzanne LeRiche born in London, England. Their son, Jean Juing, was born in South Carolina. They were naturalized in South Carolina 10 Mar. 1696/7. He was a planter. He also appeared as George Juin.

Julian, Charle. He was naturalized in New York 6 Dec. 1746.

Julius, Julius. He was naturalized in Pennsylvania 11–13 Apr. 1743. He was from Philadelphia County.

Junck, Johan Mattheis. He was naturalized in New York 8–9 Sep. 1715. He was from Ulster County.

Jung, Abraham. He was naturalized in New York 22 Jan. 1772. He was a gardener from New York City.

Jung, Andreas. He was naturalized in Nova Scotia 5 July 1758.

Jung, Jacob. He was naturalized in Maryland 11 May 1774. He was a German.

Jung, Johannes. He was naturalized in Maryland 9 Sep. 1761.

Jung, Johannes. He was naturalized in Nova Scotia 5 July 1758.

Jung, Mattheas. He was naturalized in Pennsylvania 19 May 1739. He was from Lancaster County.

Junghen, Herman. He was naturalized in Pennsylvania 11–13 Apr. 1743. He was from Philadelphia County.

Juny, Peter. He was naturalized in New York 20 Mar. 1762.

Juriaense, Barent. He took the oath of allegiance in Gravens End, Kings County, New York 26–30 Sep. 1687. He had been in the colony 29 years.

Jurianse, Johanes. He was naturalized in New York 6 Dec. 1746.

Jurianzen, Lantsman Arent. He took the oath to the King 21–26 Oct. 1664 after the conquest of New Netherland.

Jury, Hans. He was naturalized in New York 11 Sep. 1761.

Justus, George. He was naturalized in Pennsylvania 24–25 Sep. 1764. He was from Philadelphia.

K—rick, Conrad. He was naturalized in New Jersey in 1759.

Kaalsitt, Mattys. He was naturalized in New Jersey 8 July 1730. He was born in Germany.

Kabel, Peter. He was naturalized in Pennsylvania 10 Apr. 1767. He was from Marlborough Township, Philadelphia County.

Kachel, Andreas. He was naturalized in Pennsylvania 19 Nov. 1770. He was from Cumru, Berks County.

Kachlin, Charles. He was naturalized in Pennsylvania 10 Sep. 1761. He was from Bucks County.

Kaes, Johan Philip. He was naturalized in New Jersey 8 July 1730. He was born in Germany.

Kaes, Willem. He was naturalized in New Jersey 8 July 1730. He was born in Germany.

Kaforth, Gerhard. He was naturalized in Pennsylvania 11 Apr. 1761. He was from Lancaster County.

Kagy, Jacob. He was naturalized in Pennsylvania 10 Apr. 1760.

Kahmer, Rinehart. He was naturalized in Pennsylvania 24–25 Sep. 1764. He was from Philadelphia.

Kaile, David. He was naturalized in New Jersey in 1751. He was born in the Palatinate and had been in the colony 22 years.

Kaine, John. He was naturalized in New York 31 Dec. 1768.

Kaiser, Jacob. He was naturalized in Pennsylvania 10 & 23 Apr. 1764. He was from Philadelphia.

Kalb, Michael. He was naturalized in Pennsylvania 11–13 Apr. 1743. He was from Philadelphia County.

Kalder, Martin. He was naturalized in Pennsylvania 10–11 Apr. 1746. He was from Lancaster County.

Kalkgleeser, Emmanuel. He was naturalized in Pennsylvania 11–13 Apr. 1743. He was from Germantown.

Kalkgleeser, Jacob. He was naturalized in Pennsylvania 11–13 Apr. 1743. He was from Germantown.

Kaller, Valentine. He was naturalized in Pennsylvania 10 Sep. 1761. He was from Lancaster County.

Kam, George Michael. He was naturalized in Pennsylvania 10 Apr. 1760.

Kamerer, Ludwig. He was naturalized in Maryland 21 Sep. 1764. He was a German from Frederick County.

Kammerer, Frederick. He was naturalized in Pennsylvania 11 Apr. 1763. He was from Macungy Township, Northampton County.

Kamminga, Hendrick Janse. He took the oath of allegiance in New Uijtrceht, Kings County, New York 26–30 Sep. 1687. He was a native of the colony.

Kamp, David. He was naturalized in Pennsylvania 11 Apr. 1763. He was from Richmond Township, Berks County.

Kangweer, Jacob. He was naturalized in Pennsylvania 29 Mar. 1735. He was from Bucks County.

Kank, Johannes. He was naturalized in New Jersey 21 Oct. 1754.

Kann, John. He was naturalized in Pennsylvania 24 Sep. 1762. He was from Lancaster County.

Kapp, Eva Margaretta. She was naturalized in Pennsylvania 25 Sep. 1751. She was from Lancaster County.

Kapp, Martin. He was naturalized in Pennsylvania 25 Sep. 1751. He was from Lancaster County.

Kappa, Peter. He was naturalized in Pennsylvania 10 Apr. 1766. He was from Hunterdon County, New Jersey.

Kapple, Hans George. He was naturalized in Pennsylvania 24 Sep. 1741. He was from Philadelphia County.

Kapouche, Jacob. He was naturalized in New York 8–9 Sep. 1715. He was from Ulster County.

Karcher, Maratin. He was naturalized in Pennsylvania 10 Apr. 1759.

Karcher, Michael. He was naturalized in Pennsylvania 25 Sep. 1758.

Kare, Christian. He was naturalized in Pennsylvania 20 May 1769. He was from Manheim Township, York County.

Karel, Jurry. He was naturalized in New York 24 Mar. 1772.

Karger, Philip. He was naturalized in New York 3 May 1755.

Karl, Michael. He was naturalized in Pennsylvania 10 Apr. 1760.

Karn, George Jacob. He was naturalized in Pennsylvania 10 Apr. 1755. He was from Northampton County.

Karne, John. He was naturalized in New York 27 Jan. 1770.

Karsner, George. He was naturalized in Maryland 11 Sep. 1765.

Karst, Jacob. He was naturalized in Pennsylvania 11–13 Apr. 1743. He was from Philadelphia.

Kasdrop, Jacob. He was naturalized in Pennsylvania 6 Feb. 1730/1. He was from Philadelphia.

Kase, Johannes. He was naturalized in New Jersey 21 Oct. 1754.

Kase, Matthias. He was naturalized in New Jersey 21 Oct. 1754.

Kass, George. He was naturalized in New York 3 July 1759. He was from Albany County.

Kassle, Johannes. He was naturalized in Pennsylvania 11–13 Apr. 1743. He was from Philadelphia County.

Kassle, Julius. He was naturalized in Pennsylvania 11–13 Apr. 1743. He was from Philadelphia County.

Kassler, Barnard. He was naturalized in Maryland 18 July 1759.

Kast, George. He was naturalized in Pennsylvania 25 Sep. 1758.

Kast, Hans Jury. He was naturalized in New York 11 Oct. 1715. He was from Albany County.

Kastner, Johannes. He was naturalized in Pennsylvania 11 Apr. 1741. He was from Lancaster County.

Kat, Claes Cornelissen. He took the oath of allegiance in Boswijck, Kings County, New York 26–30 Sep. 1687. He had been in the colony 25 years.

Katterman, Jacob. He was naturalized in Pennsylvania 25 Sep. 1751. He was from Lancaster County.

Katts, George. He was naturalized in New Jersey in 1761. He had been in the colony twenty-one years. He was born in Germany.

Katz, John Henry. He was naturalized in Pennsylvania 10 Apr. 1760.

Katz, Michael. He was naturalized in New Jersey in 1761. He had been in the colony twenty-one years. He was born in Germany. He was of Salem County.

Kauble, Michael. He was naturalized in Pennsylvania 25 Sep. 1758.

Kaufman, Catharine. She was naturalized in Pennsylvania 10 Apr. 1759.

Kauk, George. He was naturalized in New Jersey in 1759.

Kaul, Christian. He was naturalized in New Jersey 21 Oct. 1754.

Kaul, Christian. He was naturalized in New Jersey 20 Aug. 1755.

Kaulbach, Martin. He was naturalized in Nova Scotia 5 July 1758.

Kaust, Martin. He was naturalized in Pennsylvania 25 Sep. 1758.

Kautz, George. He was naturalized in New Jersey in 1771. He also appeared as George Coutz. He resided in Upper Alvis Creek Township, Salem County. He was born in Germany.

Kauzer, Adam. He was naturalized in New York 20 Mar. 1762.

Kayman, Benedict. He was naturalized in Pennsylvania 10 Apr. 1759.

Kayser, Sebastian. He was naturalized in Pennsylvania 24 Sep. 1762. He was from Northampton County.

Kayser, Valentine. He was naturalized in Pennsylvania 10–12 Apr. 1762. He was from Berks County.

Keaner, Abraham. He was naturalized in North Carolina 26 Mar. 1767. He was from Rowan County.

Kearman, Mark. He was naturalized in New Jersey in 1771. He resided in Upper Alvis Township, Salem County.

Kearn, Leonard. He was naturalized in North Carolina 22 Sep. 1763. He was from Rowan County and a German.

Kearsner, Conrad. He was naturalized in Pennsylvania 10 Apr. 1753. He was from Berks County.

Kebner, Benedict. He was naturalized in Pennsylvania 10 & 23 Apr. 1764. He was from Bern Township, Berks County.

Keechline, Peter. He was naturalized in Pennsylvania 10 Apr. 1759.

Keefaber, Conrad. He was naturalized in Pennsylvania 10 & 23 Apr. 1764. He was from Manheim Township, York County.

Keefer, Abraham. He was naturalized in Pennsylvania 11 Apr. 1761. He was from Berks County.

Keefer, George. He was naturalized in Pennsylvania 24–25 Sep. 1764. He was from Philadelphia.

Keefer, Jacob. He was naturalized in Pennsylvania in Sep. 1740. He was from Bucks County.

Keefer, Valentine. He was naturalized in Pennsylvania 19 May 1739. He was from Philadelphia County.

Keehmle, Conrad. He was naturalized in Pennsylvania 11 Apr. 1751. He was from Philadelphia County.

Keeler, Frederick. He was naturalized in Pennsylvania 24 Sep. 1763. He was from Worcester Township, Philadelphia County.

Keeler, George. He was naturalized in Maryland 11 Sep. 1765. He was a German from Frederick County.

Keeler, Valentine. He was naturalized in Pennsylvania 25–27 Sep. 1740. He was from Philadelphia County.

Keeler, Valentine. He was naturalized in Pennsylvania 25–27 Sep. 1740. He was from Philadelphia County.

Keemer, George. He was naturalized in Pennsylvania 11 Apr. 1761. He was from Philadelphia County.

Keemer, Wendal. He was naturalized in Pennsylvania 10 Sep. 1761. He was from Philadelphia County.

Keen, George. He was naturalized in Pennsylvania 24 Sep. 1762. He was from Northampton County.

Keen, John William. He was naturalized in Pennsylvania 24 Sep. 1762. He was from Northampton County.

Keene, Jacob. He was naturalized in Pennsylvania 24 Sep. 1755. He was from Berks County.

Keener, Adam. He was naturalized in Pennsylvania 11 Apr. 1761. He was from Lancaster County.

Keener, Gasper. He was naturalized in North Carolina 11 Oct. 1754. He was from Rowan County.

Keener, Melchor. He was naturalized in Maryland 10 Sep. 1762.

Keentzey, Jacob. He was naturalized in Pennsylvania 10 Sep. 1761. He was from Lancaster County.

Keer, Conrad. He was naturalized in Pennsylvania 29 Mar. 1735. He was from Philadelphia County.

Keerren, Jacob. He took the oath to the King 21–26 Oct. 1664 after the conquest of New Netherland.

Keeton, John. He was naturalized in Virginia Apr. 1679. He was from Nansemond County.

Keever, John. He was naturalized in Pennsylvania 10 Sep. 1761. He was from Hunterdon County, New Jersey.

Kehaughan, Elizabeth. She was naturalized in Jamaica 18 Jan. 1708.

Kehl, John. He was naturalized in Pennsylvania 24 Sep. 1762. He was from Berks County.

Kehl, John George. He was naturalized in Pennsylvania 11 Apr. 1751. He was from Lancaster County.

Kehler, John. He was naturalized in Pennsylvania 24–25 Sep. 1764. He was from Lancaster Township, Lancaster County.

Kehnly, Lawrence. He was naturalized in Pennsylvania 11 Apr. 1761. He was from Northampton County.

Keibler, George. He was naturalized in Maryland 16 Sep. 1773. He was a German.

Keider, John. He was naturalized in Pennsylvania 10–11 Apr. 1746. He was from Philadelphia County.

Keifer, Frederick. He was naturalized in Maryland 3 Sep. 1765. He was a German from Sharpsburgh, Maryland.

Keiffer, George. He was naturalized in Maryland 3 Sept. 1765. He was a German.

Keifsneider, Conrad. He was naturalized in Pennsylvania 24 Sep. 1762. He was from Berks County.

Keilman, Philip. He was naturalized in New York 3 July 1759.

Keiner, Peter. He was naturalized in Maryland 15 Apr. 1773. He was a German.

Keilwein, Philip. He was naturalized in Pennsylvania 6 Feb. 1730/1. He was from Philadelphia County.

Keiser, Christopher. He was naturalized in Pennsylvania 11 Apr. 1761. He was from Berks County.

Keiser, Michael. He was naturalized in Pennsylvania 11 Apr. 1761. He was from Berks County.

Keisinger, Philip. He was naturalized in Pennsylvania 6 Feb. 1730/1. He was from Bucks County.

Keisner, Martin. He was naturalized in Maryland 20 Oct. 1747.

Keitzmiller, Jacob. He was naturalized in Pennsylvania 11–13 Apr. 1743. He was from Lancaster County.

Kekrigh, Frederick. He was naturalized in New York 3 July 1759.

Kelchner, Mathias. He was naturalized in Pennsylvania 10 Apr. 1760.

Kelder, Hans. He was naturalized in New York 8–9 Sep. 1715. He was from Ulster County.

Kelderman, Herman. He was naturalized in Virginia Oct. 1673.

Keler, Mathias. He was naturalized in Pennsylvania 24 Sep. 1755. He was from Philadelphia County.

Kelkner, George. He was naturalized in Pennsylvania 11–13 Apr. 1743. He was from Philadelphia County.

Kelkner, Michael. He was naturalized in Pennsylvania 11–13 Apr. 1743. He was from Philadelphia County.

Kelkner, Michael. He was naturalized in Pennsylvania 24 Sep. 1760. He was from Berks County.

Kell, John William. He was naturalized in Pennsylvania 24 Sep. 1762. He was from Northampton County.

Kellar, John, Jr. He was naturalized in New York 8 Mar. 1773.

Keller, Abraham. He was naturalized in Maryland 26 Sep. 1765. He was a German.

Keller, Andreas. He was naturalized in New York 11 Sep. 1761.

Keller, Charles. He was naturalized in Pennsylvania 19 May 1739. He was from Lancaster County.

Keller, Conrad. He was naturalized in Pennsylvania 24 Sep. 1760. He was from Berks County.

Keller, Conrad. He was naturalized in Pennsylvania 11 Apr. 1761. He was from Berks County.

Keller, Conrade. He and his children, Matthias Keller, Gasparus Keller, Susanna Keller, and Barbara Keller, were naturalized in Maryland 3 May 1740. He was from Prince George's County and was born in Germany.

Keller, Corneret. He took the oath of allegiance at Mobile, West Florida 2 Oct. 1764.

Keller, Felix. He was naturalized in New York 3 July 1759.

Keller, George. He was naturalized in Frederick County, Virginia 4 Aug. 1747.

Keller, George. He was naturalized in Pennsylvania 11 Apr. 1761. He was from Lancaster County.

Keller, Henry. He was naturalized in New York 3 July 1759.

Keller, Henry. He was naturalized in Pennsylvania 25 Sep. 1751. He was from Bucks County.

Keller, Hans. He was naturalized in Pennsylvania 11 Apr. 1761. He was from Berks County.

Keller, Jacob. He was naturalized in Maryland 4 Apr. 1761.

Keller, Jacob. He was naturalized in Maryland 7 May 1767. He was a German.

Keller, Jacob. He was naturalized in Pennsylvania 11–13 Apr. 1743. He was from Lancaster County.

Keller, Jacob. He was naturalized in Pennsylvania 11 Apr. 1761. He was from Lancaster County.

Keller, Jacob. He was naturalized in New York 3 July 1759.

Keller, John. He was naturalized in Maryland 26 Sep. 1765. He was a German.

Keller, John. He was naturalized in Pennsylvania 6 Feb. 1730/1. He was from Philadelphia.

Keller, John. He was naturalized in Maryland 7 May 1767. He was a German.

Keller, John. He was naturalized in Pennsylvania 24 Sep. 1760. He was from Northampton County.

Keller, Michael. He was naturalized in Pennsylvania 11 Apr. 1749. He was from Bucks County.

Keller, Nicholas. He was naturalized in Pennsylvania 18–20 May 1772. He was from Coventry, Berks County.

Keller, Nicholas. He was naturalized in New York 8 Mar. 1773.

Keller, Philip. He was naturalized in Maryland 7 May 1767.

Keller, Rudolph. He was naturalized in Maryland in Apr. 1749. He was from Frederick County.

Keller, Rudolph. He was naturalized in New York 3 July 1759.

Keller, Rudulph. He was naturalized in Maryland 11 Sep. 1765.

Keller, Sebastian. He was naturalized in Pennsylvania 24 Sep. 1760. He was from Lancaster County.

Kellerman, Jacob. He was naturalized in Jamaica 1 Oct. 1762.

Kellor, George. He was naturalized in Frederick County, Virginia 3 June 1767.

Kelm, Maria Ursula. She was naturalized in Pennsylvania 11 Apr. 1751. She was from Lancaster County.

Kelmer, Jurich. He was naturalized in New York 17 Jan. 1715/6. He was from Albany County.

Kelsor, Andrew. He was naturalized in Maryland 29 Nov. 1774. He was a German.

Kelthsh, Johannes. He was naturalized in New York 8 Mar. 1773.

Kemmanne, Caspel Englebert. He was naturalized in New York 24 Nov. 1755.

Kemmell, George. He was naturalized in Pennsylvania 24–25 Sep. 1764. He was from Lancaster Township, Lancaster County.

Kemp, Christian. He was naturalized in Maryland 27 Sep. 1746.

Kemp, Conrad. He was naturalized in Maryland 17 May 1743. He was a German.

Kemp, Dewald. He was naturalized in Pennsylvania 11–13 Apr. 1743. He was from Philadelphia County.

Kemp, Frederick. He was naturalized in Maryland 16 Sep. 1751.

Kemp, Gilbert. He was naturalized in Maryland 27 Sep. 1746.

Kemp, Jacob. He was naturalized in Pennsylvania 29 Mar. 1735. He was from Philadelphia.

Kemp, Nicholas. He was naturalized in Maryland 15 Sep. 1762. He was from Frederick County.

Kemp, Thomas. He was naturalized in New York 31 Dec. 1768. He was a yeoman from Westchester County.

Kemper, Jacob. He was naturalized in New Jersey 8 June 1751.

Kemper, John. He was naturalized in New Jersey 20 Aug. 1755.

Kendall, Mary. She was naturalized in Jamaica 26 Sep. 1707.

Kenbold, Jacob. He was naturalized in Maryland 6 Sep. 1769. He was a German.

Kendel, Catharina. She was naturalized in Pennsylvania 11 Apr. 1763. She was from Berks County.

Kenckele, Frederick. He was naturalized in Maryland 13 Sep. 1764. He was a German from Frederick, Maryland.

Kendick, George. He was naturalized in Pennsylvania 14 Feb. 1729/30. He was from Lancaster County.

Kendrick, Henry. He was naturalized in Pennsylvania 26–27 Sep. 1743. He was from Lancaster County.

Kenig, Godfried. He was naturalized in Pennsylvania 24 Sep. 1724. He was from York County.

Kenig, Jacob Philip. He was naturalized in Pennsylvania 24 Sep. 1724. He was from York County.

Kentner, George. He was naturalized in Augusta County, Virginia 19 Aug. 1772.

Kentner, Michael. He was naturalized in Augusta County, Virginia 19 Aug. 1772.

Kentz, George. He was naturalized in Pennsylvania 10 Apr. 1757.

Kephart, Peter. He was naturalized in Maryland 1 Oct. 1767. He was a German.

Kepler, Andreas. He was naturalized in Pennsylvania 19 May 1739. He was from Philadelphia County.

Kepler, Hans Bernhard. He was naturalized in Pennsylvania in Sep. 1740. He was from Philadelphia County.

Kepler, John George. He was naturalized in Pennsylvania in Sep. 1740. He was from Philadelphia County.

Keplinger, John. He was naturalized in Frederick County, Virginia 2 Mar. 1768.

Keplinger, Leonard. He was naturalized in Pennsylvania 10 Apr. 1766. He was from Cumry Township, Berks County.

Kepotz, Daniel. He was naturalized in Pennsylvania 24 Sep. 1753. He was from Lancaster County.

Kepple, Henry. He was naturalized in Pennsylvania 11 Apr. 1761. He was from Philadelphia County.

Kerbs, Hugo Ernestus. He took the oath of allegiance at Mobile, West Florida 2 Oct. 1764.

Kerger, David. He was naturalized in Pennsylvania 10–11 Apr. 1745. He was from Philadelphia County.

Kerger, Heinrick. He was naturalized in New York 31 Dec. 1761.

Kerker, Philip. He was naturalized in Pennsylvania 11 Apr. 1751. He was from Philadelphia County.

Kerma, Henry. He was naturalized in North Carolina 22 Sep. 1764. He was from Rowan County and a German.

Kermer, Michael, Jr. He was naturalized in New York 8 Mar. 1773.

Kern, Abraham. He was naturalized in Pennsylvania 10 Sep. 1761. He was from Lancaster County.

Kern, Baltlzer. He was naturalized in New York 31 Dec. 1768.

Kern, Christian. He was naturalized in Pennsylvania 10 Apr. 1755. He was from Bucks County.

Kern, Christoph. He was naturalized in New Jersey in 1759.

Kern, Hans. He was naturalized in New York 11 Sep. 1761.

Kern, Jacob. He was naturalized in New York 20 Mar. 1762.

Kern, Jacob. He was naturalized in Pennsylvania 10 Apr. 1754. He was from Berks County.

Kern, Frederick. He was naturalized in Pennsylvania 11 Apr. 1761. He was from Northampton County.

Kern, George. He was naturalized in Pennsylvania 10–14 Apr. 1747. He was from Philadelphia County.

Kern, Jacob. He was naturalized in Pennsylvania 10 Apr. 1754. He was from Berks County.

Kern, Jacob. He was naturalized in Pennsylvania 11 Apr. 1763. He was from York Township, York County.

Kern, John Simon. He was naturalized in Maryland in Apr. 1749. He was from Frederick County.

Kern, Mathias. He was naturalized in Pennsylvania 10 Apr. 1760.

Kern, Matthew. He was naturalized in Pennsylvania 24–25 Sep. 1764. He was from Cushehoppen Township, Philadelphia County.

Kern, Nicholas. He was naturalized in Pennsylvania 10 Apr. 1742. He was from Bucks County.

Kerner, Andries. He was naturalized in New York 8–9 Sep. 1715. He was from Ulster County.

Kerner, Andries Lodewyck. He was naturalized in New York 8–9 Sep. 1715. He was from Ulster County.

Kerner, Nicholas. He was naturalized in New York 8–9 Sep. 1715. He was from Ulster County.

Kernise, Michael. He was naturalized in Pennsylvania 10 Apr. 1760.

Kernwaner, George. He was naturalized in New York 11 Sep. 1761.

Kerper, Julius. He was naturalized in Pennsylvania 11 Apr. 1761. He was from Berks County.

Kersberger, Jacob. He was naturalized in Pennsylvania 29 Mar. 1735. He was from Chester County.

Kersener, Martin. He was naturalized in Pennsylvania 11 Apr. 1761. He was from Berks County.

Kershner, George. He was naturalized in Pennsylvania 11 Apr. 1761. He was from Northampton County.

Kersten, John Henry. He was naturalized in Pennsylvania 29 Sep. 1709. He was from Philadelphia County.

Kes, Bastiyan. He was naturalized in New Jersey 8 Dec. 1744.

Kesler, George. He was naturalized in New Jersey 7 Dec. 1763.

Kesler, Leonard. He was naturalized in Pennsylvania 11 Apr. 1763. He was from Philadelphia.

Kesmer, Michael, Jr. He was naturalized in New York 16 Feb. 1771.

Kesselaer, David. He was naturalized in New York 17 Jan. 1715/6. He was from Albany County.

Kessleberry, Henry. He was naturalized in Pennsylvania 29 Sep. 1709. He was from Philadelphia County.

Kessler, Johannis. He was naturalized in New York 3 Jan. 1715/6. He was from Albany County.

Kessinger, Mathias. He was naturalized in Maryland 11 Sep. 1765. He was a German from Frederick County.

Kessler, Jacob. He was naturalized in Maryland 12 Sep. 1759.

Kettel, Henrich. He was naturalized in New York 8–9 Sep. 1715. He was from Ulster County.

Kettel, Nicolas. He was naturalized in New York 8–9 Sep. 1715. He was from Ulster County.

Kettleman, Christopher. He was naturalized in Maryland 4 Sep. 1765. He was a German from Frederick County.

Kettleman, John. He was naturalized in New York 24 Nov. 1750.

Kettner, George Michael. He was naturalized in Pennsylvania 13 May 1768. He was from Tolpohocken Township, Berks County.

Keuninck, Albert. He took the oath to the King 21–26 Oct. 1664 after the conquest of New Netherland.

Kever, Jacob. He was naturalized in Maryland 16 Apr. 1773. He was a German.

Kevett, Peter. He was naturalized in North Carolina 22 Sep. 1763. He was from Rowan County and a German.

Keys, George. He was naturalized in Maryland 16 Apr. 1767. He was a German from Baltimore County.

Keysele, Frederick. He was naturalized in Pennsylvania 24 Sep. 1755. He was from Lancaster County.

Keyser, Dirk. He and his son, Peter Keyser, were naturalized in Pennsylvania 29 Sep. 1709. They were from Philadelphia County.

Keyser, George Michael. He was naturalized in New York 21 Jan. 1761. He was a laborer from New York City.

Keyser, Hieronimus. He was naturalized in New Jersey 8 July 1730. He was born in Germany.

Keyser, Johannis. He was naturalized in New York 11 Oct. 1715. He was from Albany County.

Keyser, Nicholas. He was naturalized in Pennsylvania 29 Mar. 1735. He was from Philadelphia County.

Keyseryck, Bastiaen. He was naturalized in New York 3 July 1759.

Keysler, Jacob. He was naturalized in Maryland 14 Sep. 1770. He was a German.

Kibler, Michael. He was naturalized in Maryland 14 Apr. 1762. He was a German from Frederick County.

Kickeline, Andreas. He was naturalized in Pennsylvania 24 Sep. 1760. He was from Bucks County.

Kidweller, Rudolph. He was naturalized in Pennsylvania 11 Apr. 1761. He was from Bucks County.

Kieber, Jacob. He was naturalized in Pennsylvania 25 Sep. 1769. He was from Worcester Township, Philadelphia County.

Kiefer, Christian. He was naturalized in Maryland 11 Apr. 1764. He was a German from Frederick County.

Kiefer, Ludwick. He was naturalized in Pennsylvania 10 Apr. 1765. He was from Codorus Township, York County.

Kieffer, Bartel. He was naturalized in Maryland 15 Apr. 1767. He was a German.

Kiehmly, George. He was naturalized in Pennsylvania 24–25 Sep. 1764. He was from Philadelphia.

Kiem, John. He was naturalized in Pennsylvania 11–13 Apr. 1743. He was from Philadelphia County.

Kiemil, Jacob. He was naturalized in Pennsylvania 11 Sep. 1761. He was from Northampton County.

Kierman, Fredrick. He was naturalized in New York 22 Nov. 1715. He was from Albany County.

Kiers, Edward William. He was naturalized in New York 25 July 1769.

Kierson, Jan. He took the oath of allegiance in New Uijtrceht, Kings County, New York 26–30 Sep. 1687. He had been in the colony 38 years.

Kierstede, Hans. He took the oath to the King 21–26 Oct. 1664 after the conquest of New Netherland.

Kiesling, George. He was naturalized in Pennsylvania 10 Apr. 1766. He was from Bern Township, Berks County.

Kiesling, Jacob. He was naturalized in Pennsylvania 10 Apr. 1766. He was from Bern Township, Berks County.

Kiesslar, Pieter. He was naturalized in New York 8–9 Sep. 1715. He was from Ulster County.

Kifaber, Philip. He was naturalized in Maryland 10 Apr. 1760.

Kik, Henry. He was naturalized in Pennsylvania 10 Apr. 1760.

Kilbrunn, Lawrence. He was naturalized in New York 20 Apr. 1768. He was a merchant from New York City.

Kile, Adam. He was naturalized in Maryland 10 Apr. 1760. He was from Frederick County.

Kileman, Philip. He was naturalized in New York 16 Feb. 1771.

Kilin, William. He was naturalized in New Jersey 20 Aug. 1755. He also appeared as William Kelin.

Killhoffer, Benjamin. He was naturalized in New Jersey in 1765. He was born in Sweden. He lived in Salem County. He had been in the colony fifteen years.

Killis, John. He was naturalized in Pennsylvania 24 Sep. 1760. He was from Philadelphia County.

Kilm, Conrad. His family included his wife Anna Maria Kilm, and son John Kilm. He was a cooper from Annapolis, Maryland. He sought naturalization 7 Aug. 1729. The upper house approved the bill but the lower house did not. He also appeared as Conrad Kilin.

Kilman, Nicholas. He was naturalized in New York 2 Aug. 1763. He was an innholder from New York City.

Kiltz, Adam. He was naturalized in New York 29 Mar. 1762.

Kiltz, Johan Nekel. He was naturalized in New York 20 Mar. 1762.

Kiltz, Johannis. He was naturalized in New York 20 Mar. 1762.

Kiltz, Peter. He was naturalized in New York 20 Mar. 1762.

Kime, Phillip. He was naturalized in North Carolina 22 Sep. 1763. He was from Rowan County and a German.

Kime, Valentine. He was naturalized in Pennsylvania 10 Apr. 1765. He was from Maiden Creek Township, Berks County.

Kince, Philip. He was German and was naturalized in Maryland 10 Oct. 1742.

Kind, Martin. He was naturalized in Pennsylvania 10 Apr. 1760.

Kindick, George. He was naturalized in Pennsylvania 14 Feb. 1729/30. He was from Lancaster County.

Kindig, John. He was naturalized in Pennsylvania 11–13 Apr. 1743. He was from Lancaster County.

Kindig, Martin. He was naturalized in Pennsylvania 11–13 Apr. 1743. He was from Lancaster County.

King, Abraham. He was naturalized in Maryland 29 Sep. 1762. He was a German from Frederick County.

King, Jacob. He was naturalized in Pennsylvania 10 Apr. 1765. He was from Lynn Township, Northampton County.

King, James. He was naturalized in Frederick County, Virginia 3 June 1766.

King, Johann Marcus. He was naturalized in New York 8 Nov. 1715. He was a printer from New York City.

King, John. He was naturalized in Pennsylvania 11 Apr. 1761. He was from Philadelphia County.

King, John Nicholas. He was naturalized in Pennsylvania 10–12 Apr. 1762. He was from York County.

King, Michael. He was naturalized in New Jersey 20 Aug. 1755.

King, Michael. He was naturalized in North Carolina 22 Sep. 1763. He was from Rowan County and a German.

King, Peter. He was naturalized in Pennsylvania 24 Sep. 1770. He was from Hatfield Township, Philadelphia County.

King, Simeon. He was naturalized in Pennsylvania 14 Feb. 1729/30. He was from Lancaster County.

Kingfield, Wendel. He was naturalized in Pennsylvania 24–25 Sep. 1764. He was from Lower Merrion Township, Philadelphia County.

Kingrick, Peter. He was naturalized in Pennsylvania 24 Sep. 1762. He was from Lancaster County.

Kingry, John. He was naturalized in Pennsylvania 26–27 Sep. 1743. He was from Lancaster County.

Kinkee, Herman. He and his children were naturalized in Maryland 22 Apr. 1720. He lived in Cecil County and was Dutch.

Kinking, Abraham. He was naturalized in Pennsylvania 6 Feb. 1730/1. He was from Philadelphia.

Kinkner, John George. He was naturalized in Pennsylvania 29 Mar. 1735. He was from Bucks County.

Kinser, Jacob. He was naturalized in Pennsylvania 24 Sep. 1762. He was from Lancaster County.

Kinsey, Christian. He was naturalized in Pennsylvania 11 Apr. 1761. He was from Berks County.

Kintrin, Christian. He was naturalized in Pennsylvania 11–13 Apr. 1743. He was from Philadelphia County.

Kintzer, Nicholas. He was naturalized in Pennsylvania 10 Apr. 1760.

Kintzing, Abraham. He was naturalized in Pennsylvania 25–27 Sep. 1740. He was from Philadelphia.

Kinzmiller, Martin. He was naturalized in Maryland 18 Oct. 1743. He was from Cannawatke. He also appeared as Martin Kijsmuller.

Kiphaven, John. He was naturalized in Sussex County, Delaware 28 Apr. 1683.

Kipp, Hendrick. He took the oath to the King 21–26 Oct. 1664 after the conquest of New Netherland. He was styled "d'oude" for senior.

Kipp, Isaac. He took the oath to the King 21–26 Oct. 1664 after the conquest of New Netherland.

Kipp, Jacob. He took the oath to the King 21–26 Oct. 1664 after the conquest of New Netherland.

Kipper, Jacob. He was naturalized in New Jersey in 1761.

Kipper, John. He was naturalized in New Jersey in 1757. He was born in Germany. He had been in the colony 16 years.

Kipports, Jacob. He was naturalized in Maryland 13 Sep. 1758.

Kirch, George. He was naturalized in Maryland 17 Apr. 1772.

Kirchner, Jasper. He was naturalized in Maryland 17 July 1765. He was a German.

Kirke, John. He was naturalized in Northumberland County, Virginia 17 Sep. 1656. He was born in Normandy, France, son of Jarvice Kirke, who was born in Derbyshire, England.

Kirke, Mary. She was naturalized in Northumberland County, Virginia 17 Sep. 1656. She was born in Normandy, France, daughter of Jarvice Kirke, who was born in Derbyshire, England. She was the wife of John West.

Kirker, Godfried. He was naturalized in Pennsylvania 11 Apr. 1763. He was from Heidelberg Township, Berks County.

Kis, Frederick. He was naturalized in Maryland 20 Sep. 1760.

Kirman, Michael. He was naturalized in Pennsylvania 11 Apr. 1763. He was from Northern Liberties Township, Philadelphia County.

Kirsten, Rosind. He was naturalized in Pennsylvania 10–12 Apr. 1762. He was from Berks County.

Kirtz, Henry. He was naturalized in Pennsylvania 10 Apr. 1765. He was from Philadelphia.

Kiselar, Paulus. He was naturalized in New York 23 Oct. 1770. He was a farmer from Orange County.

Kishtler, George. He was naturalized in Pennsylvania 10–12 Apr. 1762. He was from Berks County.

Kisle, Lenard. He was naturalized in Maryland 11 Sep. 1765. He lived in Hydleburg Township, York County, [Pennsylvania].

Kisler, Abraham. He was naturalized in Pennsylvania 10 Apr. 1765. He was from Heidelberg Township, Berks County.

Kissinger, Michael. He was naturalized in Pennsylvania 24–25 Sep. 1764. He was from Cocalico Township, Lancaster County.

Kistler, John. He was naturalized in Pennsylvania 10 Sep. 1761. He was from Berks County.

Kitchin, Justus Englehard. He was naturalized in Maryland 17 Dec. 1708. He was German and was a painter. [He was actually Justus Englehard Kuehn.]

Kitner, Henry. He was naturalized in Pennsylvania 10 Sep. 1761. He was from Berks County.

Kitteman, Johan. He was naturalized in New York 3 May 1755.

Kittering, John Adam. He was naturalized in Pennsylvania 11 Apr. 1761. He was from Lancaster County.

Kittler, Adam. He was naturalized in Pennsylvania in Sep. 1740. He was from Philadelphia County.

Kitts, Hans. He was naturalized in New York 11 Sep. 1761.

Kitts, Jacob. He was naturalized in New York 11 Sep. 1761.

Kitz, Jacob. He was naturalized in Pennsylvania 24 Sep. 1760. He was from Lancaster County.

Klabsattle, Michael. He was naturalized in Maryland 11 Sep. 1765. He lived in Mt. Pleasant Township, York County, Pennsylvania.

Klamter, Adam. He was naturalized in Pennsylvania 29 Mar. 1735. He was from Philadelphia.

Klankerwick, William. He was naturalized in Maryland 16 Sep. 1762. He was from Frederick County. He was a German.

Kleber, Baltazar. He was naturalized in Pennsylvania 24 Sep. 1763. He was from Reading Township, Berks County.

Klebsatel, Andreas. He was naturalized in New York 16 Dec. 1737.

Klee, Nicholas. He was naturalized in Pennsylvania 11 Apr. 1761. He was from Berks County.

Kleim, Johan. He was naturalized in Pennsylvania 19 May 1739. He was from Philadelphia County.

Klein, Frederick. He was naturalized in Maryland 12 Sep. 1764. He was a German.

Klein, Frederick. He was naturalized in New York 3 July 1759.

Klein, George. He was naturalized in New York 21 Oct. 1765. He was a baker from New York City.

Klein, Henrick. He was naturalized in Pennsylvania 24 Sep. 1741. He was from Philadelphia County.

Klein, Hieronimus. He was naturalized in New York 8–9 Sep. 1715. He was from Ulster County.

Klein, Jacob. He was naturalized in New Jersey in 1759.

Klein, Johan Jacob. He was naturalized in New York 8–9 Sep. 1715. He was from Ulster County.

Klein, John. He was naturalized in New York 21 Oct. 1765. He was a nailsmith from New York City.

Klein, John Isaac. He was naturalized in Pennsylvania 6 Feb. 1730/1. He was from Philadelphia County.

Klein, Lodowig. He was naturalized in New Jersey in 1773. He resided in Greenwich Township, Sussex County. He also appeared as Lodowick Cline.

Klein, Michael. He was naturalized in Pennsylvania 19 May 1739. He was from Philadelphia County.

Klein, Michael. He was naturalized in Pennsylvania 10 Apr. 1760.

Kleinhoff, Caspar. He was naturalized in Pennsylvania 29 Sep. 1709. He was from Philadelphia County. He was naturalized 18 May 1704. He was a native of [?] Rattingen in the Electorate of the Palatinate, the son of John Kleinhoff.

Klemmer, Jacob. He was naturalized in Pennsylvania 6 Feb. 1730/1. He was from Bucks County.

Klepinger, George. He was naturalized in Pennsylvania 11 Apr. 1751. He was from Philadelphia County.

Kleyn, Adam. He was naturalized in New York 31 Jan. 1715/6. He was from Albany County.

Kleyn, Johannes. He sought naturalization in New York 27 Nov. 1756.

Kleyn, Pieter. He was naturalized in New York 3 May 1755.

Kleyne, Michael. He was naturalized in New York 8 Mar. 1773.

Kleynman, Thomas. He was naturalized in New York 3 Feb. 1768.

Klien, Henry. He was naturalized in Pennsylvania 10 Sep. 1761. He was from Philadelphia County.

Klien, Phillip Heinrich. He was naturalized in New York 3 July 1759.

Kliest, Daniel. He was naturalized in Pennsylvania 10 & 23 Apr. 1764. He was from Bethlehem Township, Northampton County.

Klimmer, Christian. He was naturalized in Pennsylvania 29 Mar. 1735. He was from Bucks County.

Klinck, Jacob. He was naturalized in New York 28 Apr. 1765. He was carman in New York City.

Klinck, John. He was naturalized in New York 15 Oct. 1765. He was a carman from New York City.

Klinckenberg, Wellem. He took the oath of allegiance in New Uijtrceht, Kings County, New York 26–30 Sep. 1687. He was a native of the colony.

Kline, George. He was naturalized in Pennsylvania 19 May 1739. He was from Philadelphia County.

Kline, Godfried. He was naturalized in Pennsylvania 10 Apr. 1765. He was from Lancaster Township, Lancaster County.

Kline, John. He was naturalized in Pennsylvania 24 Sep. 1762. He was from Berks County.

Kline, John. He was naturalized in New York 15 Oct. 1765. He was a baker from New York City.

Klinger, Alexander. He was naturalized in Pennsylvania 10 Sep. 1761. He was from Berks County.

Klinger, John Peter. He was naturalized in Pennsylvania 10 Sep. 1761. He was from Berks County.

Klinger, John Philip. He was naturalized in Pennsylvania 10 Sep. 1761. He was from Berks County.

Klingman, Peter. He was naturalized in Pennsylvania 24 Sep. 1762. He was from Berks County.

Kliss, Erhard. He was naturalized in Pennsylvania 11 Apr. 1768. He was from Earl Township, Lancaster County.

Klock, Hendrick. He was naturalized in New York 11 Oct. 1715. He was from Albany County.

Klock, Pelegrom. He took the oath of allegiance in Boswijck, Kings County, New York 26–30 Sep. 1687. He had been in the colony 31 years.

Klug, Charles. He was naturalized in Pennsylvania 24–25 Sep. 1764. He was from Lancaster County.

Klumberg, Philip. He was naturalized in Pennsylvania 24–25 Sep. 1764. He was from Philadelphia.

Klumpges, Paul. He and his son, John Klumpges, were naturalized in Pennsylvania 29 Sep. 1709. He was from Philadelphia County.

Klyn, Coenradt. He was naturalized in New York 31 Dec. 1768.

Klyn, Jacob. He was naturalized in New York 31 Dec. 1768.

Klyn, Jacob, Jr. He was naturalized in New York 31 Dec. 1768.

Klyn, Johannis. He was naturalized in New York 8–9 Sep. 1715. He was from Ulster County.

Klyn, Johannis Peter. He was naturalized in New York 17 Oct. 1744. He was a farmer from Dutchess County.

Klyne, Johannes. He was naturalized in New York 31 Dec. 1761.

Knabelt, Philip. He was naturalized in Maryland in Apr. 1749.

Knab, Michael. He was naturalized in Pennsylvania 10 Apr. 1755. He was from Berks County.

Knabelt, Philip. He was naturalized in Maryland in Apr. 1749. He was from Frederick County.

Knafe, Jacob, Jr. He was naturalized in New York 11 Sep. 1761.

Knafe, John. He was naturalized in New York 11 Sep. 1761.

Knagy, John. He was naturalized in Pennsylvania 11 Apr. 1761. He was from Lancaster County.

Knairr, George. He was naturalized in Pennsylvania 24–25 Sep. 1764. He was from Philadelphia.

Knapp, Frederick. He was naturalized in Pennsylvania 11 Apr. 1763. He was from Springfield Township, Philadelphia County.

Knappenberger, Michael. He was naturalized in Pennsylvania 19 May 1739. He was from Philadelphia County.

Knastrig, John. He was naturalized in Maryland 1 Oct. 1767. He was a German.

Knaufe, Henrick. He was naturalized in Maryland 11 Sep. 1765.

Knaus, Ludowick. He was naturalized in Pennsylvania 19 May 1739. He was from Philadelphia County.

Knauss, John. He was naturalized in Pennsylvania 10 Apr. 1753. He was from Northampton County.

Knauss, Sebastian Henry. He was naturalized in Pennsylvania 10 Apr. 1753. He was from Northampton County.

Knaut, John Phillip. He was naturalized in Nova Scotia 11 Sep. 1758.

Knave, Jaed. He was naturalized in Maryland 19 Oct. 1743. He was a Quaker.

Knebbell, Stophel. He was naturalized in Pennsylvania 24–25 Sep./5 Oct. 1767. He was from Bethel Township, Berks County.

Knecht, Mattys. He was naturalized in New York 1 Aug. 1750. He was a mason from New York City.

Kneegher, Michael. He was naturalized in Maryland 12 Sep. 1759. He lived in Frederick County.

Knepley, Melcher. He was naturalized in Pennsylvania 11 Apr. 1761. He was from Northampton County.

Kneskern, Peter. He was naturalized in New York 11 Oct. 1715. He was from Albany County.

Knight, John Conrad. He was naturalized in Pennsylvania 10 & 23 Apr. 1764. He was from Conawawga Township, York County.

Knight, Peter. He was naturalized in Pennsylvania 24 Sep. 1757.

Knobb, Peter. He was naturalized in Pennsylvania 10 Sep. 1761. He was from Berks County.

Knobel, Philip. He was naturalized in Maryland 17 Sep. 1764. He was a German.

Knock, William John. He was naturalized in Jamaica 21 July 1760.

Knodel, Michael. He was naturalized in Nova Scotia 10 July 1758.

Knoertzer, Balthazar. He was naturalized in Pennsylvania 25 Sep. 1751. He was from York County.

Knoesvelt, Bay. He took the oath to the King 21–26 Oct. 1664 after the conquest of New Netherland.

Knop, Peter. He was naturalized in Pennsylvania 24 Sep. 1755. He was from Berks County.

Knopp, Lenard. He was naturalized in Pennsylvania 25–27 Sep. 1740. He was from Philadelphia County.

Knoll, Michael. He was naturalized in Pennsylvania 11–13 Apr. 1743. He was from Philadelphia County.

Knopple, Peter. He was naturalized in Pennsylvania 26–27 Sep. 1743. He was from Lancaster County.

Knorr, Peter. He was naturalized in Pennsylvania 10 Sep. 1761. He was from Berks County.

Knott, Peter. He was naturalized in New Jersey 16 Aug. 1733. He lived in Monmouth County.

Knous, Godfrey. He was naturalized in Pennsylvania 10 Apr. 1755. He was from Northampton County.

Knower, Christopher. He was naturalized in Pennsylvania 24–25 Sep. 1764. He was from East Nantmele Township, Chester County.

Knurenshield, Christopher. He was naturalized in Pennsylvania 10 Sep. 1761. He was from Lancaster County.

Koal, Georg Wilhelm. He was naturalized in New York 8–9 Sep. 1715. He was from Ulster County.

Kober, Paul. He was naturalized in Pennsylvania 11 Apr. 1761. He was from Philadelphia County.

Koberstein, Georg. He was naturalized in Maryland 7 Sep. 1768. He was a German.

Koch, Adam. He was naturalized in Pennsylvania 10 Sep. 1761. He was from Cumberland County.

Koch, Anton. He was naturalized in Nova Scotia 5 July 1758.

Koch, Catharine. She was naturalized in Pennsylvania 10 Apr. 1758.

Koch, Hanborn. He was naturalized in New Jersey 21 Oct. 1754.

Koch, Hendrick. He was naturalized in New Jersey 21 Oct. 1754.

Koch, Johannes Casparus. He, his wife, Katherine Koch, and sons Joseph Koch, Anthony Koch, and Jacobus Koch, were naturalized in New Jersey 31 July 1740. They were from Germany.

Koch, William. He was naturalized in Pennsylvania 10 Apr. 1760.

Kochertal, Rev. Joshua De. He, his wife Sibylle Charlotte De Kochertal, daughter Benigna De Kochertal, son Christian Joshua De Kochertal, and daughter Susanne Sibylle De Kochertal were endenized in London 25 Aug. 1708. They came to New York.

Kochler, Albright. He was naturalized in Pennsylvania 10 Sep. 1761. He was from Lancaster County.

Kock, Albertus. He was naturalized in New York 31 Dec. 1761.

Kock, Casparus. He was naturalized in New York 31 Dec. 1761.

Kock, Jan Jelezen. He took the oath to the King 21–26 Oct. 1664 after the conquest of New Netherland.

Kock, Jans Joost. He was naturalized in New York 3 July 1759.

Kock, Johannes. He was naturalized in Pennsylvania 10 Sep. 1761. He was from Berks County.

Kock, John Michael. He was naturalized in Pennsylvania 24 Sep. 1762. He was from Northampton County.

Kock, Michael. He was naturalized in Pennsylvania 10 Sep. 1761. He was from Berks County.

Kock, Peter. He was naturalized in Pennsylvania in Sep. 1740. He was from Philadelphia.

Kock, Rudolph. He was naturalized in New York 31 Dec. 1761.

Kockanon, Jacob. He was naturalized in Pennsylvania 10 Sep. 1761. He was from Lancaster County.

Kocken, Johannes. He was naturalized in Pennsylvania 6 Feb. 1730/1. He was from Philadelphia County.

Kockenbach, Henry. He was naturalized in Pennsylvania 24 Sep. 1762. He was from Northampton County.

Kockendoffer, George Peter. He was naturalized in Pennsylvania 11 Apr. 1763. He was from Philadelphia.

Kocker, George. He was naturalized in Pennsylvania 10–14 Apr. 1747. He was from Philadelphia County.

Kocknower, Jacob. He was naturalized in Pennsylvania 10 Sep. 1761. He was from Lancaster County.

Kockuyt, Joost. He took the oath of allegiance in Boswijck, Kings County, New York 26–30 Sep. 1687. He had been in the colony 27 years.

Koeck, Laurens. He took the oath of allegiance in Boswijck, Kings County, New York 26–30 Sep. 1687. He had been in the colony 26 years.

Koeffer, Baltus. He was naturalized in New York 8–9 Sep. 1715. He was from Ulster County.

Koeffor, Wilhelm. He was naturalized in New York 8–9 Sep. 1715. He was from Ulster County.

Koehler, Peter. He was naturalized in Pennsylvania 22 Nov. 1769. He was from Lancaster, Lancaster County.

Koenig, Henry Anthony. He was naturalized in Pennsylvania 24 Sep. 1762. He was from Berks County.

Koffman, Samuel. He was naturalized in Pennsylvania 10 & 23 Apr. 1764. He was from Lower Milford Township, Bucks County.

Koghnot, John Everhardt. He was naturalized in New York 11 Sep. 1761.

Koghnot, John Everhardt, Jr. He was naturalized in New York 11 Sep. 1761.

Kohl, Adam. He was naturalized in Nova Scotia 15 Sep. 1758.

Kohl, Frederick. He was naturalized in Nova Scotia 15 Sep. 1758.

Kohl, Philip. He was naturalized in Pennsylvania 24 Sep. 1762. He was from Berks County.

Kohler, George. He was naturalized in Maryland 12 Sep. 1764. He was a German from Frederick County.

Kohler, Jacob. He was naturalized in Pennsylvania 10 Apr. 1760.

Kohler, John Rudolph. He was naturalized in Pennsylvania 24–25 Sep. 1764. He was from Northern Liberties Township, Philadelphia County.

Kohler, Jonas. He was naturalized in Pennsylvania 11 Apr. 1751. He was from Philadelphia County.

Kohn, Adam. He was naturalized in Pennsylvania 24 Sep. 1762. He was from York County.

Koke, John. He was naturalized in Pennsylvania 25 Sep. 1769. He was from Maiden Creek Township, Berks County.

Koker, Peter. He was naturalized in Pennsylvania 10 Apr. 1760.

Kokert, Daniel. He was naturalized in Pennsylvania 10 Apr. 1754. He was from Northampton County.

Kolb, Conrath. He was naturalized in Pennsylvania 19 May 1739. He was from Philadelphia County.

Kolb, Dielman. He was naturalized in Pennsylvania 6 Feb. 1730/1. He was from Philadelphia County.

Kolb, Jacob. He was naturalized in Pennsylvania 6 Feb. 1730/1. He was from Philadelphia County.

Kolb, Martin. He was naturalized in Pennsylvania 6 Feb. 1730/1. He was from Philadelphia County.

Kolb, Michael. He was naturalized in Maryland 11 Sep. 1765. He was a German from Frederick, Maryland.

Kole, Michael. He was naturalized in New York 20 Mar. 1762.

Kole, Paul. He was naturalized in New Jersey 8 July 1730. He was born in Germany.

Kole, Philip. He was naturalized in New York 31 Dec. 1768.

Koll, George Michael. He was naturalized in Pennsylvania 10 Sep. 1761. He was from Philadelphia County.

Kolsinger, Bernard. He was naturalized in Pennsylvania 11 Apr. 1751. He was from York County.

Konig, Michael. He was naturalized in New York 20 Mar. 1764.

Koogher, Johan Peter. He was naturalized in Pennsylvania 11–13 Apr. 1743. He was from Lancaster County.

Kook, John George. He was naturalized in New York 6 Dec. 1746.

Kookert, Adam. He was naturalized in Pennsylvania 24 Sep. 1759.

Kool, Barrent Jacobzen. He took the oath to the King 21–26 Oct. 1664 after the conquest of New Netherland.

Kool, Johannes. He was naturalized in New York 23 Oct. 1747. He was a cordwainer from New York City.

Kool, Jacob Sable. He was naturalized in Pennsylvania 11–13 Apr. 1743. He was from Bucks County.

Koon, Henry. He was naturalized in Pennsylvania 10 Apr. 1753. He was from York County.

Koon, John. He was naturalized in Maryland 15 Apr. 1772. He was a German.

Koose, Frederick. He was naturalized in New York 27 Jan. 1770.

Kop, Jacob. He was naturalized in New York 11 Oct. 1715. He was from Albany County.

Koplin, Christian. He was naturalized in Pennsylvania 11 Apr. 1751. He was from Philadelphia County.

Koplin, Matthias. He was naturalized in Pennsylvania 19 May 1739. He was from Philadelphia County.

Kopp, Jacob. He was naturalized in Pennsylvania 11 Apr. 1761. He was from Philadelphia County.

Kopp, Jacob. He was naturalized in Pennsylvania 24 Sep. 1762. He was from Philadelphia County.

Kopp, Michael. He was naturalized in New York 21 Oct. 1765. He was a cooper from New York City.

Koppenheffer, Michael. He was naturalized in Pennsylvania 19 May 1739. He was from Lancaster County.

Koppenheffer, Thomas. He was naturalized in Pennsylvania 19 May 1739. He was from Lancaster County.

Korner, Gaspard. He was naturalized in Virginia 12 May 1705.

Korneu, John. He was naturalized in Virginia 27 Jan. 1770.

Korning, Nicholas. He was naturalized in New York 11 Oct. 1715. He was from Albany.

Korr, Jacob. He was naturalized in Pennsylvania 10–12 Apr. 1762. He was from Philadelphia County.

Kortreght, Hendrick. He was naturalized in New York 8–9 Sep. 1715. He was from Ulster County.

Kosser, John. He was naturalized in Pennsylvania 24–25 Sep. 1764. He was from Northern Liberties Township, Philadelphia County.

Kost, Francis. He was naturalized in Maryland 13 Apr. 1761.

Koster, Joannes. He was naturalized in Pennsylvania 15 May 1706.

Kother, Conrad. He was naturalized in Pennsylvania 10 & 23 Apr. 1764. He was from Hilltown Township, Bucks County.

Kouffman, David. He was naturalized in Pennsylvania 6 Feb. 1730/1. He was from Philadelphia County.

Kough, George. He was naturalized in New York 8 Mar. 1773.

Kough, Jacob. He was naturalized in Pennsylvania 11–13 Apr. 1743. He was from Philadelphia County.

Kough, John. He was naturalized in New York 8 Mar. 1773.

Kough, Jost. He was naturalized in New York 8 Mar. 1773.

Kough, Matthias. He was naturalized in New York 27 Jan. 1770.

Kountzer, Bernard. He was naturalized in Pennsylvania 24 Sep. 1753. He was from Philadelphia County.

Kous, John Thys. He was naturalized in New York 15 Oct. 1765. He was a farmer from Dutchess County.

Kouse, Philip. He was naturalized in Pennsylvania 24–25 Sep. 1764. He was from Oley Township, Philadelphia County.

Kow, Michael Christopher. He was naturalized in New York 8 Nov. 1735.

Kowsman, Adam. He was naturalized in Pennsylvania 10 Sep. 1761. He was from Philadelphia County.

Kraemer, Peter. He was naturalized in Maryland 12 Sep. 1759.

Kraaff, Henry. He was naturalized in Pennsylvania 24–25 Sep. 1764. He was from Tulpehocken Township, Berks County.

Kraan, Ludwick. He was naturalized in New York 11 Sep. 1761.

Kraeuter, John. He was naturalized in Virginia 11 Apr. 1759.

Kramer, Helfry. He was naturalized in Maryland 26 Sep. 1765. He was a German.

Kramer, Henrich. He was naturalized in Maryland 13 Sep. 1768. He was a German.

Kramer, Jacob. He was naturalized in Maryland 15 Sep. 1762. He was from Frederick County.

Kramer, Jan. He was naturalized in New York 12 July 1715.

Kramer, John. He was naturalized in Pennsylvania 10–12 Apr. 1762. He was from Lancaster County.

Kramer, Philip. He was naturalized in Pennsylvania 10 Apr. 1766. He was from Reading Township, Berks County.

Kranenger, Daniel. He was naturalized in Pennsylvania 24 Sep. 1754. He was from Philadelphia County.

Kraps, Henry. He was naturalized in Pennsylvania 11–13 Apr. 1743. He was from Philadelphia County.

Kraps, Michael. He was naturalized in Pennsylvania 11–13 Apr. 1743. He was from Philadelphia County.

Kraps, Simon. He was naturalized in Pennsylvania 11–13 Apr. 1743. He was from Philadelphia County.

Kratz, Valentine. He was naturalized in Pennsylvania 11–13 Apr. 1743. He was from Philadelphia County.

Kratzer, Leonard. He was naturalized in New York 8 Mar. 1773.

Kraus, Jacob. He was naturalized in Pennsylvania 24 Sep. 1741. He was from Philadelphia County.

Kraus, Michael. He was naturalized in Pennsylvania 24 Sep. 1760. He was from Berks County.

Kraus, Michael. He was naturalized in Pennsylvania 19 May 1739. He was from Philadelphia County.

Krause, Christopher. He was naturalized in Pennsylvania 13–15 Apr. 1748. He was from Philadelphia County.

Krause, John Henry. He was naturalized in Pennsylvania 10 Sep. 1761. He was from Philadelphia County.

Krauskop, Ludewyk. He was naturalized in New York 20 Apr. 1769. He was a farmer from outside of New York City.

Krauss, Henry. He was naturalized in Pennsylvania 24 Sep. 1762. He was from Philadelphia County.

Kraver, Andreas. He was naturalized in Pennsylvania 29 Mar. 1735. He was from Philadelphia County.

Krazinger, George. He was naturalized in Maryland 4 Sep. 1765. He was a German from Sharpesburgh, Maryland.

Kreber, Anthony. He was naturalized in Pennsylvania 10–12 Apr. 1762. He was from York County.

Kreebel, George. He was naturalized in Pennsylvania 10 Apr. 1755. He was from Philadelphia County.

Kreemer, Adam. He was naturalized in Pennsylvania 18 Nov. 1768. He was from Warrington Township, York County.

Kreemer, Frederick. He was naturalized in Pennsylvania 10 Sep. 1761. He was from Berks County.

Kreemer, George. He was naturalized in Pennsylvania 11 Apr. 1763. He was from Greenwick Township, Berks County.

Kreestman, Daniel. He was naturalized in Pennsylvania 19 May 1739. He was from Philadelphia County.

Kreicher, Bastian. He was naturalized in Pennsylvania 10–12 Apr. 1762. He was from Berks County.

Kreicher, Forst. He was naturalized in Pennsylvania 10–12 Apr. 1762. He was from Berks County.

Kreiger, Lorenz. He was naturalized in Maryland 9 Sep. 1761. He was from Frederick County and a farmer.

Kreiner, Dieterich. He was naturalized in Pennsylvania 6 Feb. 1730/1. He was from Philadelphia County.

Kreisser, Stophel. He was naturalized in Pennsylvania 22–24 Nov. 1773. He was from York, York County.

Kreitzer, Peter. He was naturalized in Pennsylvania 24–25 Sep. 1764. He was from Tulpehocken Township, Berks County.

Krehl, Michael. He was naturalized in Pennsylvania 21 Nov. 1770. He was from Bethel Township, Lancaster County.

Kremler, Henry. He was naturalized in Pennsylvania 11 Apr. 1763. He was from Reading Township, Berks County.

Kremling, John. He sought naturalization in New Jersey in the 18th century.

Krems, Johannis. He was naturalized in New York 28 Feb. 1715/6. He was from Albany County.

Kress, Charles. He was naturalized in Pennsylvania 11–13 Apr. 1743. He was from Philadelphia County.

Kress, Henry. He was naturalized in Pennsylvania 11 Apr. 1763. He was from Germantown, Philadelphia County.

Kressman, Johann Nicholas. He was naturalized in Pennsylvania 6 Feb. 1730/1. He was from Philadelphia County.

Kreyer, Henry. He was naturalized in Pennsylvania 24–25 Sep. 1764. He was from Abington Township, Philadelphia County.

Krey, John. He and his son, William Krey, were naturalized in Pennsylvania 29 Sep. 1709. They were from Philadelphia County. They also appeared as John Frey and William Frey.

Kribeld, Christopher. He was naturalized in Pennsylvania 10–11 Apr. 1745. He was from Philadelphia County.

Kribell, Caspar. He was naturalized in Pennsylvania 11–13 Apr. 1743. He was from Philadelphia County.

Kribell, George. He was naturalized in Pennsylvania 11–13 Apr. 1743. He was from Philadelphia County.

Krider, Michael. He was naturalized in Pennsylvania 11–13 Apr. 1743. He was from Philadelphia County.

Krierchbaum, Adam. He was naturalized in Pennsylvania 24–25 Sep. 1764. He was from Tulpehocken Township, Berks County.

Kriesinger, Godlieb. He was naturalized in Pennsylvania 24–25 Sep. 1764. He was from Germantown Township, Philadelphia County.

Krill, Adam. He was naturalized in Pennsylvania 10 Sep. 1763. He was from Lancaster County.

Krim, Alexander. He was naturalized in Maryland 3 Sep. 1765. He was a German.

Kripner, Paulus. He was naturalized in Pennsylvania 29 Mar. 1735. He was from Philadelphia.

Krips, Henry. He was naturalized in Pennsylvania 10–12 Apr. 1762. He was from Philadelphia County.

Krise, Stephen. He was naturalized in Maryland 11 Sep. 1765. He was a resident of Germany Township, York County, Pennsylvania and was a German.

Kroft, Nicholas. He was naturalized in Pennsylvania 10–14 Apr. 1747. He was from Philadelphia County.

Krom, Gysbert. He was naturalized in New York 8–9 Sep. 1715. He was from Ulster County.

Krop, Jacob. He was naturalized in Pennsylvania 11–13 Apr. 1743. He was from Philadelphia County.

Krots, Johannis. He was naturalized in New York 3 Feb. 1768.

Kroush, Jacob. He was naturalized in New York 14 Feb. 1715/6. He was from Albany County.

Krowser, Sebastian. He was naturalized in Pennsylvania 10 Sep. 1761. He was from Berks County.

Krowt, Peter. He was naturalized in Pennsylvania 24 Sep. 1763. He was from Worcester Township, Philadelphia County.

Krowter, Jacob. He was naturalized in Pennsylvania 10–12 Apr. 1762. He was from Lancaster County.

Krug, Valentine. He was naturalized in Pennsylvania 24 Sep. 1753. He was from Lancaster County.

Kruger, Casper. He was naturalized in Maryland 15 Apr. 1761.

Kruger, Peter. He was naturalized in Pennsylvania 11 Apr. 1763. He was from Tulpehocken Township, Berks County.

Krup, Andrew. He was naturalized in Maryland 16 Sep. 1773. He was a German.

Kryder, Abraham. He was naturalized in Pennsylvania 24–25 Sep. 1764. He was from Allentown Township, Northampton County.

Kryder, Martin. He was naturalized in Pennsylvania 10–12 Apr. 1762. He was from Philadelphia County.

Krype, Jacob. He was naturalized in Maryland 21 Sep. 1762. He was a German.

Kugler, John George. He was naturalized in Pennsylvania 10–12 Apr. 1762. He was from Philadelphia County.

Kugler, Mattheus. He was naturalized in New York 20 Mar. 1762.

Kuhl, Frederick. He was naturalized in Pennsylvania in 4 Mar. 1763. He was from Denmark.

Kuhl, Jacob. He was naturalized in Pennsylvania 11 Apr. 1761. He was from Berks County.

Kuhn, Adam Simon. He was naturalized in Pennsylvania 11–12 Apr. 1744. He was from Lancaster County.

Kuhn, Frederick. He was naturalized in Pennsylvania 10 & 23 Apr. 1764. He was from York Township, York County.

Kuhn, Jacob. He was naturalized in Nova Scotia 15 Sep. 1758.

Kuhn, John. He was naturalized in Pennsylvania 11 Apr. 1763. He was from Philadelphia.

Kuhns, John. He was naturalized in Nova Scotia 10 July 1758.

Kuhns, Michael. He was naturalized in Pennsylvania 10 Apr. 1760.

Kuhrr, Thomas. He was naturalized in Pennsylvania 10 Sep. 1761. He was from Berks County.

Kule, Christian. He was naturalized in New Jersey 21 Oct. 1754.

Kull, Koenraet. He was naturalized in New Jersey 8 July 1730. He was born in Germany.

Kulp, Matthias. He was naturalized in Pennsylvania 24 Sep. 1762. He was from Berks County.

Kults, Conradt. He was naturalized in New York 24 Nov. 1750.

Kume, Adriaen. He took the oath of allegiance in Flackland, Kings County, New York 26–30 Sep. 1687. He had been in the colony 26 years.

Kunders, Denis. He and his sons, Cunrad Cunrads, Matthias Cunrads, and John Cunrads, were naturalized in Pennsylvania 29 Sep. 1709. They were from Philadelphia County.

Kuneman, Hendred. He sought naturalization in New Jersey in the 18th century.

Kuns, Jacob. He was naturalized in Pennsylvania 11 Apr. 1763. He was from Springfield Township, Philadelphia County.

Kunts, Hans Jacob. He was naturalized in Pennsylvania 26–27 Sep. 1743. He was from Lancaster County.

Kuntz, Francis. He was naturalized in Pennsylvania 24 Sep. 1762. He was from Lancaster County.

Kuntz, Henry. He was naturalized in Maryland 11 Sep. 1765.

Kuntz, Jacob. He was naturalized in Pennsylvania 10 Apr. 1765. He was from Germany Township, York County.

Kuntz, Jacob. He was naturalized in Pennsylvania 10–12 Apr. 1762. He was from Berks County.

Kuntz, Michael. He was naturalized in Pennsylvania 11–13 Apr. 1743. He was from Philadelphia County.

Kuntz, Peter. He was naturalized in Maryland 14 Sep. 1763. He was a German.

Kuntz, William. He was naturalized in Maryland 29 Sep. 1764. He was a German.

Kupeius, William. He was naturalized in Jamaica 1 [torn] 1691.

Kurts, Arnst. He was naturalized in Pennsylvania 24 Sep. 1754. He was from Philadelphia County.

Kurts, Johannes. He was naturalized in New York 24 Oct. 1741. He was a shoemaker from Albany County.

Kurtz, Abraham. He was naturalized in Pennsylvania 10 Sep. 1761. He was from Lancaster County.

Kurtz, Arnold. He was naturalized in Pennsylvania 24 Sep. 1763. He was from Limerick Township, Philadelphia County.

Kurtz, Jacob. He was naturalized in Pennsylvania 13 May 1768. He was from Cumru Township, Berks County.

Kurtz, Johannes. He was naturalized in Pennsylvania 11 Apr. 1763. He was from Berks County.

Kurtz, Johan Christopher. He was naturalized in New York 8–9 Sep. 1715. He was from Ulster County.

Kurtz, John Nicholas. He was naturalized in Pennsylvania 24 Sep. 1760. He was from Philadelphia County.

Kurtz, Peter. He was naturalized in New Jersey 20 June 1765.

Kurtz, Michael. He was naturalized in Pennsylvania 24 Sep. 1763. He was from New Hannover Township, Philadelphia County.

Kurtz, William. He was naturalized in Pennsylvania 24–25 Sep./5 Oct. 1767. He was from Earl Township, Lancaster County.

Kuster, Hermanus. He was naturalized in Pennsylvania 6 Feb. 1730/1. He was from Philadelphia County.

Kuster, John. He was naturalized in Pennsylvania 11 Apr. 1761. He was from Lancaster County.

Kuster, John. He was naturalized in Pennsylvania 10 Sep. 1761. He was from Lancaster County.

Kustor, Conrad. He was naturalized in Pennsylvania 29 Mar. 1735. He was from Philadelphia County.

Kutch, Jacob. He was naturalized in Pennsylvania 24–25 Sep. 1764. He was from Passyunk Township, Philadelphia County.

Kuth, Samuel. He was naturalized in Pennsylvania 11 Apr. 1761. He was from Berks County.

Kutz, George. He was naturalized in Pennsylvania 10 Sep. 1761. He was from Berks County.

Kuyper, Cornelius. He was naturalized in New York 29 July 1761. He was a house painter from New York City.

Kyer, Peter. He was naturalized in New Jersey in 1771. He resided in Woolwich Township, Gloucester County. He had lived in the colony six or seven years.

Kyle, Gabriel. He was naturalized in Augusta County, Virginia 18 May 1762.

Kyme, Johannes. He was naturalized in Pennsylvania 11–13 Apr. 1743. He was from Philadelphia County.

Kynlander, Bernhard. He was naturalized in New York 21 Apr. 1750. He was a tanner from Westchester County.

Kyper, Michael. He was naturalized in Pennsylvania 10 Apr. 1755. He was from Northampton County.

Labaer, William. He was naturalized in Pennsylvania 11 Apr. 1749. He was from Bucks County.

Labar, Philip. He was naturalized in Pennsylvania 19 May 1739. He was from Philadelphia County.

Labat, Ignace. He was naturalized in New York 16 Feb. 1771.

LaCampaigne, William Peter. He was naturalized in Jamaica 13 Nov. 1731.

Lacaze, James. He was naturalized in Virginia 12 May 1705.

Laconta, Moses. He took the oath of naturalization in New York 1 Sep. 1687 in Ulster County.

Lacounte, Anthony. He and his siblings, Hester Lacounte, John Lacounte, Moses Lacounte, Phillip Lacounte, and Katherine Lacounte, were naturalized in Maryland 6 June 1674. They were the children of Anthony Lacounte of Picardie, France. They were born in Maryland. *Vide* also LeCompte.

Lacourt, Anthonye. He was naturalized in Jamaica 26 Feb. 1750/1.

LaCroix, Nicolas. He was an Acadian and took the oath of allegiance in Apr. 1730.

Lacroix, William. He was naturalized in New York 3 July 1766.

Lacrum, William. He was naturalized in Jamaica 16 May 1751.

Ladesma, Abraham. He was naturalized in Jamaica 30 May 1722.

Ladesma, David Carvallo. He was naturalized in Jamaica 21 May 1708.

Ladesma, Moses. He was naturalized in Jamaica 23 Feb. 1742/3. He was a Jew.

Ladner, Andreas. He was naturalized in New York 22 Apr. 1761. He was a baker from New York City.

Ladshower, Francis. He was naturalized in Pennsylvania 11–13 Apr. 1743. He was from Philadelphia County.

Laenen, Gijsbert Thysen. He took the oath of allegiance in New Uijtrceht, Kings County, New York 26–30 Sep.1687. He had been in the colony 24 years.

Laenen, Theunis Janse Van Pelt. He took the oath of allegiance in New Uijtrceht, Kings County, New York 26–30 Sep. 1687. He had been in the colony 24 years.

Laenen, Jacob Thijssen. He took the oath of allegiance in New Uijtrceht, Kings County, New York 26–30 Sep. 1687. He was a native of the colony.

Laenen, Jan Thijssen. He took the oath of allegiance in New Uijtrceht, Kings County, New York 26–30 Sep. 1687. He was a native of the colony.

Laersen, Poul. He expressed his desire to be naturalized in New Castle County, Delaware 21 Feb. 1682/3.

Laeser, John Christian. He was naturalized in Pennsylvania 10–12 Apr. 1762. He was from Philadelphia County.

Laeter, Malachi. He was naturalized in Maryland 4 Apr. 1761. He lived in Frederick County.

LaFebre, Isaack. He took the oath of allegiance in Boswijck, Kings County, New York 26–30 Sep. 1687. He had been in the colony 4 years.

Laffever, Andries. He took the oath of naturalization in New York 1 Sep. 1687 in Ulster County.

Laffever, Symon. He took the oath of naturalization in New York 1 Sep. 1687 in Ulster County.

LaFite, Isaac. He was naturalized in Virginia 12 May 1705.

Laflower, Michael. He was naturalized in Jamaica 9 Feb. 1684/5.

Lafon, Jean. He took the oath of allegiance at Mobile, West Florida 2 Oct. 1764.

Lafon, Pierre Victor. He was naturalized in Rhode Island 9 June 1767. He was a merchant from Newport.

LaForge, Adriaen. He took the oath of allegiance in Boswijck, Kings County, New York 26–30 Sep. 1687. He had been in the colony 15 years.

LaForie, Rene Massomeau. He was naturalized in Virginia 12 May 1705.

Lafort, Marias. He was endenized in New York 27 Mar. 1695.

Lafoy, Pierre Victor. He was naturalized in Rhode Island 9 June 1767. He lived in Newport and was a merchant.

Lagautrais, Harpain, Sr. He took the oath of allegiance at Mobile, West Florida 2 Oct. 1764.

Lagautrais, Harpain, Jr. He took the oath of allegiance at Mobile, West Florida 2 Oct. 1764.

Lagear, Pierre. He was naturalized in New York 3 July 1759.

Lagille, George. He was naturalized in North Carolina 24 Sep. 1766. He was from Rowan County. He also appeared as George Logall.

Lagrand, James. He was naturalized in Virginia 12 May 1705.

Laguna, Abraham. He was naturalized in Jamaica 26 Feb. 1740/1. He was a Jew.

Laguna, Abraham Lopes. He was naturalized in Jamaica 19 June 1707.

Laguna, Daniel. He was naturalized in Jamaica 28 Apr. 1693.

Laguna, Esther. He was naturalized in Jamaica 6 Feb. 1743/4.

Laguna, Isaac Lopes. He was naturalized in Jamaica 14 Nov. 1721.

Laguna, Isaac Lopez. He was naturalized in Jamaica 13 July 1726.

Laguna, Jacob, Jr. He was naturalized in Jamaica 31 May 1743. He was a Jew.

Laguna, Rebecca. She was naturalized in Jamaica 28 Feb. 1743/4. She was a Jewess.

Laguna, Sarah Lopez. She was naturalized in Jamaica 23 Sep. 1725.

Laguna, Yshae. He was naturalized in Jamaica 29 Aug. 1708.

Lahn, John. He was naturalized in Pennsylvania 24–25 Sep. 1764. He was from Heidelberg Township, Lancaster County.

Laib, John George. He was naturalized in Pennsylvania 11 Apr. 1761. He was from Philadelphia County.

Laibell, Simon. He was naturalized in Pennsylvania 24 Sep. 1762. He was from Lancaster County.

LaLande, Pre. He was an Acadian and took the oath of allegiance in Apr. 1730.

Lalor, Conrod. He was naturalized in North Carolina 22 Sep. 1764. He was from Rowan County and a German.

Lamara, Aaron. He was naturalized in Jamaica 14 Dec. 1736.

Lamara, Aaron. He was naturalized in Jamaica 25 Nov. 1741. He was a Jew.

Lamara, Moses. He was naturalized in Jamaica 14 Dec. 1736.

Lamb, Conrad. He was naturalized in Maryland 12 Apr. 1771. He was a German.

Lamb, Peter. He was naturalized in Pennsylvania 11 Apr. 1761. He was from Berks County.

Lamberd, George. He was naturalized in Maryland 11 Sep. 1765.

Lamberse, Hendrick. He took the oath of allegiance in Breucklijn, Kings County, New York 26–30 Sep. 1687. He was a native of the colony.

Lamberse, Thomas. He took the oath of allegiance in Breucklijn, Kings County, New York 26–30 Sep. 1687. He had been in the colony 36 years.

Lambert, Balser. He was naturalized in Maryland 7 Sep. 1768. He was a German.

Lambert, Christopher. He was naturalized in Frederick County, Virginia 4 Aug. 1768.

Lambert, John. He was naturalized in Pennsylvania 18 Nov. 1768.

Lambert, Mathias. He was naturalized in Pennsylvania 13–15 Apr. 1748. He was from Lancaster County.

Lambertsa, Heybert. He took the oath of naturalization in New York 1 Sep. 1687 in Ulster County.

Lambertsin, Cornelis. He took the oath of naturalization in New York 1 Sep. 1687 in Ulster County.

Lambertsen, Huybert. He was naturalized in New York 8–9 Sep. 1715. He was from Ulster County.

Lambright, Anthony. He was naturalized in Pennsylvania 11 Apr. 1761. He was from Berks County.

Lame, John. He was naturalized in New Jersey 6 Dec. 1769.

Lame, Peter. He was naturalized in New Jersey 6 Dec. 1769.

Lamee, John. He and his children were naturalized in Maryland 15 Nov. 1712. He was from Dorchester County and was a weaver. He was Dutch.

Lamego, Rachell. She was naturalized in Jamaica 3 May 1703.

Lametra, Francis. He was naturalized in Jamaica in 1714.

Lamiater, Abraham. He took the oath of naturalization in New York 1 Sep. 1687 in Ulster County.

Lamiater, Jacob. He took the oath of naturalization in New York 1 Sep. 1687 in Ulster County.

Lamirre, Pierre. He was an Acadian and took the oath of allegiance in Apr. 1730.

Lammert, John. He was naturalized in New York 8–9 Sep. 1715. He was from Ulster County.

Lammerts, Adriaen. He took the oath of allegiance in Orange County, New York 26 Sep. 1687.

Lamon, John. He and his children, John Lamon, George Lamon, Louisa Lamon, Leonora Lamon, Catherine Lamon, and Margarett Lamon, were naturalized in Maryland 4 June 1738. He was from Baltimore County and was born in Germany.

Lamore, Peter. He was made a denizen in Maryland 14 Sep. 1663. He was French.

Lamore, Thomas. He was made a denizen in Maryland 14 Sep. 1663. He was French.

Lamotte, Alexander. He was naturalized in Jamaica 22 Apr. 1706.

Lamparder, John. He was naturalized in Pennsylvania 11 Apr. 1763. He was from Northern Liberties Township, Philadelphia County.

Lamparter, Joshua. He was naturalized in Pennsylvania 10 Apr. 1765. He was from Philadelphia.

Lamplin, Jacob. He was naturalized in New York 18 Oct. 1774. He was from New York City.

Lancisco, Henry. He was naturalized in Augusta County, Virginia 22 Mar. 1753.

Lanciscus, Jacob. He was naturalized in Pennsylvania 11 Apr. 1761. He was from Berks County.

Landas, Felix, Jr. He was naturalized in Pennsylvania 14 Feb. 1729/30. He was from Lancaster County.

Landaver, Johannes. He was naturalized in Pennsylvania 4 Mar. 1763. He was from the Duchy of Wurttemberg.

Landenberger, Matthew. He was naturalized in Pennsylvania 11 Apr. 1763. He was from Philadelphia.

Landes, Jacob, Jr. He was naturalized in Pennsylvania 11–13 Apr. 1743. He was from Philadelphia County.

Landes, Jacob. He was naturalized in Pennsylvania 11–13 Apr. 1743. He was from Philadelphia County.

Landgraff, Nicholas. He was naturalized in Jamaica 27 Mar. 1737.

Landis, Henry. He was naturalized in New Jersey 20 Aug. 1755.

Landre, Charles. He was an Acadian and took the oath to George II at Annapolis River, Nova Scotia in Dec. 1729.

Landri, Pierre. He was an Acadian and took the oath to George II at Annapolis River, Nova Scotia in Dec. 1729.

Landrie, Jean. He was an Acadian and took the oath to George II at Annapolis River, Nova Scotia in Dec. 1729.

Landrier, Claude. He was an Acadian and took the oath to George II at Annapolis River, Nova Scotia in Dec. 1729.

Landrier, John Batist. He was an Acadian and took the oath to George II at Annapolis River, Nova Scotia in Dec. 1729.

Landrin, Guilleaume. He was endenized in New York 6 Feb. 1695/6.

Landry, Abraham. He was an Acadian and took the oath to the King at the Mines, Pisiquit, Nova Scotia 31 Oct. 1727.

Landry, Abraham [second of the name]. He was an Acadian and took the oath to the King at the Mines, Pisiquit, Nova Scotia 31 Oct. 1727.

Landry, Abraham. He was an Acadian and took the oath of allegiance in Apr. 1730. He was the son of Germain Landry.

Landry, Abraham. He was an Acadian and took the oath of allegiance in Apr. 1730. He was the son of Germain Landry.

Landry, Abraham. He was an Acadian and took the oath of allegiance in Apr. 1730.

Landry, Abraham. He was an Acadian and took the oath of allegiance in Apr. 1730.

Landry, Alexandre. He was an Acadian and took the oath of allegiance in Apr. 1730.

Landry, Alexandre. He was an Acadian and took the oath of allegiance in Apr. 1730.

Landry, Antoine. He was an Acadian and took the oath to the King at the Mines, Pisiquit, Nova Scotia 31 Oct. 1727.

Landry, Antoine. He was an Acadian and took the oath of allegiance in Apr. 1730.

Landry, Baptiste. He was an Acadian and took the oath of allegiance in Apr. 1730.

Landry, Baptiste. He was an Acadian and took the oath of allegiance in Apr. 1730.

Landry, Benjamin. He was an Acadian and took the oath to the King at the Mines, Pisiquit, Nova Scotia 31 Oct. 1727.

Landry, Benjamin. He was an Acadian and took the oath of allegiance in Apr. 1730.

Landry, Charles. He was an Acadian and took the oath to the King at the Mines, Pisiquit, Nova Scotia 31 Oct. 1727.

Landry, Charles. He was an Acadian and took the oath of allegiance in Apr. 1730.

Landry, Charles. He was an Acadian and took the oath of allegiance in Apr. 1730.

Landry, Claude. He took the oath of allegiance at Port Royal, Nova Scotia 16 Aug. 1695.

Landry, Claude. He was an Acadian and took the oath to George II at Annapolis River, Nova Scotia in Dec. 1729.

Landry, Claude. He was an Acadian and took the oath to George II at Annapolis River, Nova Scotia in Dec. 1729.

Landry, Claude. He was an Acadian and took the oath to the King at the Mines, Pisiquit, Nova Scotia 31 Oct. 1727.

Landry, Claude, Sr. He was an Acadian and took the oath of allegiance in Apr. 1730.

Landry, Claude. He was an Acadian and took the oath of allegiance in Apr. 1730.

Landry, Francois. He was an Acadian and took the oath to the King at the Mines, Pisiquit, Nova Scotia 31 Oct. 1727.

Landry, Francois. He was an Acadian and took the oath of allegiance in Apr. 1730.

Landry, Francois. He was an Acadian and took the oath of allegiance in Apr. 1730.

Landry, Germain. He was an Acadian and took the oath to the King at the Mines, Pisiquit, Nova Scotia 31 Oct. 1727.

Landry, Germain. He was an Acadian and took the oath to the King at the Mines, Pisiquit, Nova Scotia 31 Oct. 1727.

Landry, Germain, Sr. He was an Acadian and took the oath of allegiance in Apr. 1730.

Landry, Jean. He was an Acadian and took the oath to the King at the Mines, Pisiquit, Nova Scotia 31 Oct. 1727.

Landry, Jean. He took the oath of allegiance to the King at Annapolis River in Dec. 1729.

Landry, Jean. He was an Acadian and took the oath of allegiance in Apr. 1730.

Landry, Jean. He was an Acadian and took the oath of allegiance in Apr. 1730.

Landry, Jean. He was an Acadian and took the oath of allegiance in Apr. 1730.

Landry, Jean Baptiste. He was an Acadian and took the oath of allegiance at the Mines, Pisiquit, Nova Scotia 31 Oct. 1727.

Landry, Jean Baptiste. He was an Acadian and took the oath of allegiance in Apr. 1730.

Landry, Jermain. He was an Acadian and took the oath of allegiance in Apr. 1730. [His forename was Germain.]

Landry, Jermain. He was an Acadian and took the oath of allegiance in Apr. 1730.

Landry, Joseph. He was an Acadian and took the oath of allegiance 31 Oct. 1727.

Landry, Joseph. He was an Acadian and took the oath to George II at Annapolis River, Nova Scotia in Dec, 1729.

Landry, Joseph. He was an Acadian and took the oath of allegiance in Apr. 1730.

Landry, Joseph. He was an Acadian and took the oath of allegiance in Apr. 1730.

Landry, Joseph. He was an Acadian and took the oath of allegiance in Apr. 1730.

Landry, Joseph. He was an Acadian and took the oath of allegiance in Apr. 1730.

Landry, Joseph. He was an Acadian and took the oath of allegiance in Apr. 1730.

Landry, Joseph. He was an Acadian and took the oath of allegiance in Apr. 1730.

Landry, Joseph. He was an Acadian and took the oath to the King at the Mines, Pisiquit, Nova Scotia 31 Oct. 1727.

Landry, Paul. He was an Acadian and took the oath of allegiance in Apr. 1730.

Landry, Paul. He was an Acadian and took the oath of allegiance in Apr. 1730.

Landry, Pierre. He took the oath of allegiance at Port Royal, Nova Scotia 16 Aug. 1695.

Landry, Pierre. He was an Acadian and took the oath to the King at the Mines, Pisiquit, Nova Scotia 31 Oct. 1727.

Landry, Pierre. He was an Acadian and took the oath to the King at the Mines, Pisiquit, Nova Scotia 31 Oct. 1727.

Landry, Pierre. He was an Acadian and took the oath to the King at the Mines, Pisiquit, Nova Scotia 31 Oct. 1727.

Landry, Pierre. He was an Acadian and took the oath to the King at the Mines, Pisiquit, Nova Scotia 31 Oct. 1727.

Landry, Pierre. He was an Acadian and took the oath to the King at the Mines, Pisiquit, Nova Scotia 31 Oct. 1727.

Landry, Pierre. He was an Acadian and took the oath of allegiance to the King at Annapolis River in Dec. 1729.

Landry, Pierre. He was an Acadian and took the oath of allegiance in Apr. 1730.

Landry, Pierre. He was an Acadian and took the oath of allegiance in Apr. 1730.

Landry, Pierre. He was an Acadian and took the oath of allegiance in Apr. 1730.

Landry, Pierre. He was an Acadian and took the oath of allegiance in Apr. 1730.

Landry, Pierre. He was an Acadian and took the oath of allegiance in Apr. 1730.

Landry, Pierre. He was an Acadian and took the oath of allegiance in Apr. 1730.

Landry, Rene. He was an Acadian and took the oath to the King at Mines, Pisiquit, Nova Scotia 31 Oct. 1727.

Landry, Rene. He was an Acadian and took the oath to the King at Mines, Pisiquit, Nova Scotia 31 Oct. 1727.

Landry, Rene. He was an Acadian and took the oath to the King at Mines, Pisiquit, Nova Scotia 31 Oct. 1727.

Landry, Rene. He was an Acadian and took the oath of allegiance in Apr. 1730.

Landry, Rene. He was an Acadian and took the oath of allegiance in Apr. 1730.

Landry, Rene. He was an Acadian and took the oath of allegiance in Apr. 1730.

Landtes, Jacob. He was naturalized in Pennsylvania 11–13 Apr. 1743. He was from Philadelphia County.

Lane, Cornelius. He was naturalized in Pennsylvania 11 Apr. 1752. He was from Lancaster County.

Lane, Henry. He was naturalized in Pennsylvania 24 Sep. 1754. He was from Lancaster County.

Lane, Peter. He was naturalized in Pennsylvania 11 Apr. 1752. He was from Lancaster County.

Laney, Titus. He was German and was naturalized in Maryland 15 Oct. 1742.

Lang, Christiaen. He was naturalized in New York 17 Jan. 1715/6. He was from Albany County.

Lang, Henry. He was naturalized in Jamaica 4 May 1736.

Langenecker, Daniel. He was naturalized in Pennsylvania 6 Feb. 1730/1. He was from Philadelphia County.

Langenecker, Johannes. He was naturalized in Pennsylvania 6 Feb. 1730/1. He was from Philadelphia County.

Langer, Abraham. He was naturalized in New York 17 Jan. 1715/6. He was from Albany County.

Langerbeen, Phillipus. He requested that his name be added to a naturalization bill in New York 10 Sep. 1731.

Langlade, Daniel. He was naturalized in Virginia 12 May 1705.

Langnier, Francis. He was naturalized in Jamaica 3 Oct. 1684.

Langs, Jacob. He was naturalized in New Jersey in 1759.

Lannius, Jacob. He was naturalized in Pennsylvania 11 Apr. 1761. He was from York County.

Lannon, Charles. He was an Acadian and took the oath to George II at Annapolis River, Nova Scotia in the winter of 1730.

Lannon, Joseph. He was an Acadian and took the oath to George II at Annapolis River, Nova Scotia in the winter of 1730.

Lannon, Pierre. He was an Acadian and took the oath of allegiance in Apr. 1730. He also appeared as Pierre Lannou.

Lanone, Pierre. He was an Acadian and took the oath to George II at Annapolis River, Nova Scotia in the winter of 1730.

LaNorr, Isaac. He was endenized in New York 14 May 1696.

Lanoue, Pierre. He took the oath of allegiance at Port Royal, Nova Scotia 16 Aug. 1695.

Lanoue, Pierre. He was an Acadian who took the oath of allegiance at Annapolis River in Dec. 1729.

Lansingh, Jan. He was naturalized in New York 11 Oct. 1715. He was from Albany County.

Lanson, Piere. He took the oath of allegiance at Mobile, West Florida 2 Oct. 1764.

Lantz, Andrew. He was naturalized in Pennsylvania 10 Apr. 1765. He was from Harlem Township, York County.

Lantz, Nicholas. He was naturalized in Pennsylvania 10 Apr. 1766. He was from Williams Township, Northampton County.

Lantze, John. He was naturalized in Frederick County, Virginia 2 Oct. 1765.

Lap, Ruthol. He was naturalized in Pennsylvania 25 Sep. 1750. He was naturalized in Pennsylvania 25 Sep.1750.

Lapierre, Charles. He was naturalized in Virginia 12 May 1705.

LaPierre, Francois. He was an Acadian and took the oath of allegiance in Apr. 1730.

Larch, Crattius. He was naturalized in Pennsylvania 11 Apr. 1761. He was from Northampton County.

Lardan, Jacques. He was born at Dieppe, France, the son of Jacques Lardan and Marie Poulart. His wife was Marthe Moreau. Their son was Jacques Lardan born in South Carolina. They were naturalized in South Carolina 10 Mar. 1696/7. He also appeared as James Lardant. He was a joiner.

Lardas, Angelica. She took the oath of allegiance at Mobile, West Florida 2 Oct. 1764.

Lardnare, Baptist Christian. He took the oath of allegiance at Mobile, West Florida 2 Oct. 1764.

Lardnare, Louis Charles. He took the oath of allegiance at Mobile, West Florida 2 Oct. 1764.

Lardnare, Nicholas. He took the oath of allegiance at Mobile, West Florida 2 Oct. 1764.

Larew, Abraham. He took the oath of naturalization in New York 1 Sep. 1687 in Ulster County.

LaRouse, Peter. He was naturalized in London 13 May 1664. He was from Barbados. He was a doctor in physick and was born in Montaben, Acquitaine, France.

Larow, George. He was naturalized in Pennsylvania 25 Sep. 1751. He was from Chester County.

Larow, Jonas. He was naturalized in Pennsylvania 25 Sep. 1751. He was from Lancaster County.

Larson, Abram. He was naturalized in Jamaica 11 Aug. 1709.

Lary, Caspar. He was naturalized in Nova Scotia 5 July 1758.

LaSalle, Pierre. He was born at Bordeaux, France, the son of Charles LaSalle and Susanne Hugla. His wife was Elizabeth Messett. Their children, born in South Carolina, were Pierre LaSalle and Elizabeth LaSalle. They were naturalized in South Carolina ca. 1696.

Lash, Daniel. He was naturalized in New York 3 July 1759.

Lashee, Abraham. He was naturalized in New Jersey 20 Aug. 1755.

Lasher, Charles. He was naturalized in New York 16 Dec. 1737.

Lashier, Johannes. He was naturalized in New York 17 June 1726.

Lasler, Martin. He was naturalized in New York 16 Feb. 1771.

Laterman, Frederick. He was naturalized in Maryland 20 May 1774.

LaTourrette, Jean. He was endenized 2 Oct. 1695 in New York.

Lattenburgher, Valentine. He was naturalized in Maryland 9 Sep. 1761.

Lau, Philip. He was naturalized in Pennsylvania 24 Sep. 1763. He was from Manchester Township, York County.

Laub, Michael. He was naturalized in Pennsylvania 10 Sep. 1761. He was from Berks County.
Laubersweiler, Bernard. He was naturalized in Pennsylvania 11 Apr. 1751. He was from Philadelphia County.
Laubinger, George Michael. He was naturalized in Frederick County, Virginia 4 Sep. 1765.
Laucks, Peter. He was naturalized in Pennsylvania 25 Sep. 1743. He was from Lancaster County.
Laudenbough, Conrad. He was naturalized in Pennsylvania 11 Apr. 1763. He was from York Township, York County.
Laudermeligh, Wilder. He was naturalized in Pennsylvania 11 Apr. 1761. He was from Lancaster County.
Laugbaugh, Christian. He was naturalized in Pennsylvania 24 Sep. 1759.
Laughton, Sampson. He was naturalized in Jamaica 17 Oct. 1751. He was also known as Samuel Laughton. He was a free Negro.
Lauman, Ludwick. He was naturalized in Pennsylvania 24 Sep. 1753. He was from Lancaster County.
Laumeister, Wendall. He was naturalized in Pennsylvania 10–12 Apr. 1762. He was from York County.
Laurans, John. He and his wife, Mary Laurans, were endenized in London 24 June 1705. They came to New York.
Laurens, Jan. He took the oath to the King 21–26 Oct. 1664 after the conquest of New Netherland.
Laurens, Thomas. He took the oath to the King 21–26 Oct. 1664 after the conquest of New Netherland.
Laurer, Gotfrid. He was naturalized in Maryland 13 Apr. 1763. He was a German from Frederick County.
Laurier, Harmen. He expressed his desire to be naturalized in New Castle County, Delaware 21 Feb. 1682/3.
Lautenschlaeger, Philip. He was naturalized in Maryland 12 Sep. 1759.
Lauterman, John. He was naturalized in New Jersey in 1768.
Lautman, Johann Georg. He was naturalized in Maryland 10 Sep. 1760.
Lautman, Peter. He was naturalized in New York 17 Jan. 1715/6. He was from Albany County.
LaVaustre, Francois. He was Acadian who took the oath of allegiance to the King 31 Oct. 1727.
Laux, Johannes. He was naturalized in New Jersey 8 July 1730. He was born in Germany.
Lauzun, John Daniel. He was naturalized in Jamaica 1 May 1757.
LaVache, Francois. He was an Acadian and took the oath to George II at the Mines, Pisiquit 31 Oct. 1727.
LaVache, Francois. He was an Acadian and took the oath of allegiance in Apr. 1731.
Laverne, Jacques. He was an Acadian and took the oath to George II at Annapolis River, Nova Scotia in Dec. 1729. He also appeared as Jacques Lavergne.
Laviele, John. He was naturalized in Maryland 22 Apr. 1720. He lived in Charles County and was French.
Lavigne, Estienne. He was endenized in New York 6 Feb. 1695/6.
Lavou, Joseph. He was naturalized in Jamaica 26 May 1742.
Law, David. He was naturalized in Pennsylvania 11 Apr. 1761. He was from Orange County, North Carolina.
Law, Mungo. He took the oath of allegiance at Mobile, West Florida 2 Oct. 1764.
Lawer, Johan Mathias. He was naturalized in New York 1 Nov. 1715. He was the son of Johan Peter Lawer.
Lawer, Johan Peter. He was naturalized in New York 1 Nov. 1715. He was a yeoman from Dutchess County.
Lawfer, Lawrence. He was naturalized in Pennsylvania 24 Sep. 1741. He was from Philadelphia County.
Lawrence, Christopher. He was naturalized in New York 6 July 1723.
Lawrence, Martha. She was naturalized in Northampton County, Virginia 17 Sep. 1656. She was born in Arnham, the Netherlands, daughter of Henry and Amy Lawrence.
Lawrence, Theodora. She was naturalized in Northampton County, Virginia 17 Sep. 1656. She was born in Viana, the Netherlands, daughter of Henry and Amy Lawrence.
Lawrence, William. He was naturalized in Northampton County, Virginia 17 Sep. 1656. He was born in Delph, the Netherlands, son of Henry and Amy Lawrence.

Lawrence, William. He was naturalized in New York 25 Oct. 1742. He was a gardener from New York City.

Lawrenzen, Arien. He took the oath to the King 21–26 Oct. 1664 after the conquest of New Netherland.

Laws, Hannah. She was naturalized in Jamaica 15 July 1743.

Lay, Joseph. He was naturalized in Nova Scotia 5 July 1758.

Lay, Ludwick. He was naturalized in Pennsylvania 24 Sep. 1762. He was from Lancaster County.

Lay, Michael. He was naturalized in Nova Scotia 5 July 1758.

Laydick, Philip. He was naturalized in New York 3 July 1759.

Lazares, Elias. He was naturalized in Jamaica 27 Aug. 1745. He was a Jew.

Lazarus, Solomon. He was naturalized in Jamaica 17 Nov. 1763.

Lazear, Joseph. He and his children, Deborah Lazear, Elizabeth Lazear, John Lazear, Joseph Lazear, Mary Lazear, and Thomas Lazear, were naturalized in Maryland 5 Aug. 1721. He lived in Prince George's County and was German. The children were born in Maryland.

Lazer, Hellebrant. He took the oath of naturalization in New York 1 Sep. 1687 in Ulster County.

Lazier, Claes. He took the oath of naturalization in New York 1 Sep. 1687 in Ulster County.

Lazier, John. He took the oath of naturalization in New York 1 Sep. 1687 in Ulster County.

Lazyrus, Henry. He was naturalized in Maryland 25 Sep. 1753. He was a Jew.

Leaderman, Michael. He was naturalized in Maryland 14 Apr. 1760. He was German.

Leahman, Jacob. He was naturalized in Maryland 28 Sep. 1762. He was a German from Maryland.

Leamen, Peter. He was naturalized in Pennsylvania 14 Feb. 1729/30. He was from Lancaster County. He also appeared as Peter Leamon.

Leamon, Christian. He was naturalized in Pennsylvania 11 Apr. 1741. He was from Philadelphia County.

Leaphart, Henry. He was naturalized in Maryland 1 May 1736. He was from Baltimore County and was born in Germany.

Learrin, Andrew. He promised allegiance to the King and obedience to William Penn in Pennsylvania 10 Sep. 1683.

Lease, Frederick. He was naturalized in Pennsylvania 10–12 Apr. 1762. He was from Berks County.

Lease, Henry. He was naturalized in Pennsylvania 10–12 Apr. 1762. He was from Berks County.

Leash, Peter. He was naturalized in Pennsylvania 10 Apr. 1765. He was from Passyunk Township, Philadelphia County.

Leatherman, Henry. He was naturalized in Maryland 27 Apr. 1772. He was a German.

LeBas, Jacques. He was born at Can, France, the son of Jean LeBas and Anne Samborne. His son, Pierre LeBas, was also born at Can, France and his mother was Catherine Varing. The father and son were naturalized in South Carolina ca. 1696.

Lebart, Henry. He was naturalized in Pennsylvania 26–27 Sep. 1743. He was from Lancaster County.

Lebelly, Michael. He was naturalized in Maryland 20 Sep. 1765. He was a German.

Lebengut, Peter. He was naturalized in Pennsylvania 24 Sep. 1762. He was from Berks County.

Leber, Coenraad. He was naturalized in New York 11 Sep. 1761.

Leberger, Adam. He was naturalized in Pennsylvania 25–27 Sep. 1740. He was from Philadelphia County.

Lebert, Jean. He was born at Redon, Bretagne, France, the son of Pierre Lebert and Jeanne Guernier. He was naturalized in South Carolina 10 Mar. 1696/7. He was a merchant.

Lebert, Jean. He was an Acadian and took the oath of allegiance in Apr. 1730.

Leblalane, Josep. He was an Acadian and took the oath to George II at Annapolis River, Nova Scotia in the winter of 1730.

Leblanc, Andre. He was an Acadian and took the oath to the King at the Mines, Pisiquit, Nova Scotia 31 Oct. 1727.

LeBlanc, Andrew. He was an Acadian and took the oath of allegiance in Apr. 1731.

Leblanc, Antoine. He was an Acadian and took the oath to the King at the Mines, Pisiquit, Nova Scotia 31 Oct. 1727.

Leblanc, Antoine. He was an Acadian and took the oath to the King at the Mines, Pisiquit, Nova Scotia 31 Oct. 1727.

LeBlanc, Antonine. He was an Acadian and took the oath of allegiance in Apr. 1730.

LeBlanc, Antonine. He was an Acadian and took the oath of allegiance in Apr. 1730.

LeBlanc, Baptiste. He was an Acadian and took the oath of allegiance in Apr. 1730. He appeared as Rene LeBlanc on another list.

LeBlanc, Bernard. He was an Acadian and took the oath of allegiance 31 Oct. 1727.

LeBlanc, Bernard. He was an Acadian and took the oath of allegiance in Apr. 1730.

LeBlanc, Charles. He was an Acadian who took the oath of allegiance at the Mines, Pisiquit, Nova Scotia 31 Oct. 1727. He was the son of Jean LeBlanc.

LeBlanc, Charles. He was an Acadian and took the oath of allegiance in Apr. 1730.

LeBlanc, Charles. He was an Acadian and took the oath of allegiance in Apr. 1730.

LeBlanc, Claude. He was an Acadian who the oath to the King at the Mines, Pisiquit, Nova Scotia 31 Oct. 1727.

LeBlanc, Claude. He was an Acadian and took the oath of allegiance in Apr. 1730.

LeBlanc, Claude. He was an Acadian and took the oath of allegiance in Apr. 1730.

LeBlanc, Claude. He was an Acadian and took the oath of allegiance in Apr. 1730.

LeBlanc, Daniel. He took the oath of allegiance at Port Royal, Nova Scotia 16 Aug. 1695.

Leblanc, Francois. He was an Acadian and took the oath to the King at the Mines, Pisiquit, Nova Scotia 31 Oct. 1727.

Leblanc, Francois. He was an Acadian and took the oath to the King at the Mines, Pisiquit, Nova Scotia 31 Oct. 1727.

Leblanc, Francois. He was an Acadian and took the oath to the King at the Mines, Pisiquit, Nova Scotia 31 Oct. 1727.

Leblanc, Francois [son of Antoine Leblanc]. He was an Acadian and took the oath to the King at the Mines, Pisiquit, Nova Scotia 31 Oct. 1727.

LeBlanc, Francois. He was an Acadian and took the oath of allegiance in Apr. 1730.

LeBlanc, Francois. He was an Acadian and took the oath of allegiance in Apr. 1730.

LeBlanc, Francois. He was an Acadian and took the oath of allegiance in Apr. 1730.

LeBlanc, Francois. He was an Acadian and took the oath of allegiance in Apr. 1730.

LeBlanc, Honore. He was an Acadian and took the oath of allegiance in Apr. 1730.

Leblanc, Jacques. He was an Acadian and took the oath to the King at the Mines, Pisiquit, Nova Scotia 31 Oct. 1727.

Leblanc, Jacques. He was an Acadian and took the oath to the King at the Mines, Pisiquit, Nova Scotia 31 Oct. 1727.

Leblanc, Jacques. He was an Acadian and took the oath to the King at the Mines, Pisiquit, Nova Scotia 31 Oct. 1727.

LeBlanc, Jacques. He was an Acadian and took the oath of allegiance in Apr. 1730.

LeBlanc, Ja[c]ques. He was an Acadian and took the oath of allegiance in Apr. 1730.

LeBlanc, Jacques. He was an Acadian and took the oath of allegiance in Apr. 1730.

LeBlanc, Ja[c]ques. He was an Acadian and took the oath of allegiance in Apr. 1730.

Leblanc, Jean. He was an Acadian and took the oath to the King at the Mines, Pisiquit, Nova Scotia 31 Oct. 1727.

Leblanc, Jean. He was an Acadian and took the oath to the King at the Mines, Pisiquit, Nova Scotia 31 Oct. 1727.

Leblanc, Jean, Sr. He was an Acadian and took the oath to the King at the Mines, Pisiquit, Nova Scotia 31 Oct. 1727.

LeBlanc, Jean. He was an Acadian and took the oath of allegiance in Apr. 1730.

LeBlanc, Jean, Sr. He was an Acadian and took the oath of allegiance in Apr. 1730.

LeBlanc, Jean. He was an Acadian and took the oath of allegiance in Apr. 1730.

LeBlanc, Jean. He was an Acadian and took the oath of allegiance in Apr. 1730.

LeBlanc, Jean. He was an Acadian and took the oath of allegiance in Apr. 1730.

LeBlanc, Jean. He was an Acadian and took the oath of allegiance in Apr. 1730. He was the son of Andre LeBlanc.

Leblanc, Jean Simon. He was an Acadian and took the oath to George II at Annapolis River, Nova Scotia in Dec. 1729.

LeBlanc, Joseph. He was an Acadian who took the oath to the King at the Mines, Pisiquit, Nova Scotia 31 Oct. 1727.

LeBlanc, Joseph. He was an Acadian who took the oath of allegiance to the King in Dec. 1729.

LeBlanc, Joseph. He was an Acadian and took the oath of allegiance in Apr. 1730.
LeBlanc, Joseph. He was an Acadian and took the oath of allegiance in Apr. 1730.
LeBlanc, Joseph. He was an Acadian and took the oath of allegiance in Apr. 1730.
LeBlanc, Joseph. He was an Acadian and took the oath of allegiance in Apr. 1730. He was a son of Andre LeBlanc.
LeBlanc, Paul. He was an Acadian and took the oath of allegiance in Apr. 1730.
LeBlanc, Paul. He was an Acadian and took the oath of allegiance in Apr. 1730.
LeBlanc, Paul. He was an Acadian and took the oath of allegiance in Apr. 1730.
Leblanc, Pierre. He was an Acadian and took the oath to the King at the Mines, Pisiquit, Nova Scotia 31 Oct. 1727.
Leblanc, Pierre. He was an Acadian and took the oath to the King at the Mines, Pisiquit, Nova Scotia 31 Oct. 1727.
Leblanc, Pierre [son of Jacques Leblanc]. He was an Acadian and took the oath to the King at the Mines, Pisiquit, Nova Scotia 31 Oct. 1727.
Leblanc, Pierre [son of Jean Leblanc, Sr.]. He was an Acadian and took the oath to the King at the Mines, Pisiquit, Nova Scotia 31 Oct. 1727.
LeBlanc, Pierre. He was an Acadian and took the oath of allegiance in Apr. 1730.
LeBlanc, Pierre. He was an Acadian and took the oath of allegiance in Apr. 1730. He was the son of Jean LeBlanc.
LeBlanc, Pierre. He was an Acadian and took the oath of allegiance in Apr. 1730.
LeBlanc, Pierre. He was an Acadian and took the oath of allegiance in Apr. 1730.
LeBlanc, Pierre. He was an Acadian and took the oath of allegiance in Apr. 1730.
LeBlanc, Pierre. He was an Acadian and took the oath of allegiance in Apr. 1730. He was the son of Andre LeBlanc.
Leblanc, R. He was an Acadian and took the oath to the King at the Mines, Pisiquit, Nova Scotia 31 Oct. 1727.
Leblanc, Rene. He was an Acadian and took the oath to the King at the Mines, Pisiquit, Nova Scotia 31 Oct. 1727.
Leblanc, Rene [son of Jacques Leblanc]. He was an Acadian and took the oath to the King at the Mines, Pisiquit, Nova Scotia 31 Oct. 1727.
LeBlanc, Rene. He was an Acadian and took the oath of allegiance in Apr. 1730.
LeBlanc, Rene. He was an Acadian and took the oath of allegiance in Apr. 1730.
LeBorgne, Emanuel. He took the oath of allegiance at Port Royal, Nova Scotia 16 Aug. 1695.
LeBove, Charles. He was an Acadian and took the oath of allegiance in Apr. 1730.
LeBove, Francois. He was an Acadian and took the oath of allegiance in Apr. 1730.
LeBove, Jean. He was an Acadian and took the oath of allegiance in Apr. 1730.
LeBove, Louis. He was an Acadian and took the oath of allegiance in Apr. 1730.
LeBoyteux, Gabriel. He was endenized in London 16 Dec. 1687. He came to New York.
Lebrieur, Jean Piere. He was naturalized in New York 6 Dec. 1746.
LeBrun, Charles. He was an Acadian and took the oath of allegiance in Apr. 1730.
LeBrun, Claude. He took the oath of allegiance at Mobile, West Florida 2 Oct. 1764.
LeChevalier, Jean. He was endenized in New York 2 Oct. 1695.
LeChevalier, Pierre. He was born at St. Lo, Normandie, France and was the son of Rolland LeChevallier and Ester Dallain. His wife was Madelainne Garillion who was born in Grenoble, France, daughter of Israel Garillion and Susanne Saunier. They were naturalized in South Carolina ca. 1696.
Lechner, George. He was naturalized in Pennsylvania 25 Sep. 1751. He was from Lancaster County.
Lechner, John George. He was naturalized in Pennsylvania 25 Sep. 1751. He was from Lancaster County.
Leckhard, Barnhard. He was naturalized in Maryland 11 Sep. 1765. He was a German from Frederick County.
LeCompte, Antoine. He, his wife, and children were made denizens in Maryland 2 Mar. 1664/5. Vide also Lacounte.
LeConte, Francis. He was endenized in New York 17 Apr. 1695.
LeConte, John. He was endenized in New York 29 July 1686.
Lecont, Moyse. He was naturalized in New York 8–9 Sep. 1715. He was from Ulster County.

Leddraugh, Andreas. He was naturalized in Pennsylvania 11–13 Apr. 1743. He was from Philadelphia County.

Leddraugh, Johannes. He was naturalized in Pennsylvania 11–13 Apr. 1743. He was from Philadelphia County.

Lederer, John. He was naturalized in Maryland 19 Apr. 1671. He lived in Calvert County and was German.

Lederman, Peter. He was naturalized in Pennsylvania 24 Sep. 1762. He was from Lancaster County.

Ledwick, John. He was naturalized in Jamaica 11 Apr. 1691.

Leeghte, John. He was naturalized in Pennsylvania 14 Feb. 1729/30. He was from Lancaster County.

Leek, Johannis. He was naturalized in New York 17 Jan. 1715/6. He was from Albany County.

Leeman, Christian. He was naturalized in Pennsylvania 19 May 1739. He was from Lancaster County.

Leeman, Martin. He sought naturalization in New Jersey in the 18th century.

Leer, Fredrick Willem. He was naturalized in New York 31 Jan. 1715/6. He was from Albany County.

LeEstap, Frederick. He took the oath of allegiance at Mobile, West Florida 2 Oct. 1764.

LeFebure, Isaac. He was naturalized in Virginia 12 May 1705.

LeFlau, Jean Baptist. He took the oath of allegiance at Mobile, West Florida 2 Oct. 1764.

Lefubres, Lewis. He petitioned for naturalization in North Carolina 8 Feb. 1739/40.

Legare, Francis. He and his two sons were admitted into the colony of Massachusetts 1 Feb. 1691. They were French.

LeGendre, Daniel. He was the son of Jacques and Maurice LeGendre of Rouen, Normandie, France. He was naturalized in South Carolina ca. 1696.

Leger, Jacques. He took the oath of allegiance at Port Royal, Nova Scotia 16 Aug. 1695.

Leger, Jacques. He was an Acadian and took the oath to George II at Annapolis River, Nova Scotia in the winter of 1730.

Leger, Jacques. He was an Acadian and took the oath of allegiance in Apr. 1730.

Leger, Jean. He was an Acadian and took the oath to George II at Annapolis River, Nova Scotia in Dec. 1729.

Leger, Jean. He was an Acadian and took the oath of allegiance in Apr. 1730.

LeGrand, Isaac. He was the son of Jean LeGrand Sr. d'Anvuile and Marie LeGrand, native of Caen, Normandie, France. His wife, Elizabeth LeGrand, was the daughter of Jean Dieu and Judith Dieu of Caen, Normandie, France. Their son, Isaac LeGrand, was born in Caen and their daughter, Elizabeth LeGrand, was born in South Carolina. They were naturalized in South Carolina ca. 1696.

LeGrand, John Rodolph. He was naturalized in South Carolina 14 Oct. 1744.

LeGrand, Pierre. He was endenized in New York 12 Apr. 1685.

Lehman, Christian. He was naturalized in Pennsylvania 11–13 Apr. 1743. He was from Germantown.

Lehman, John. He was naturalized in Pennsylvania 11–13 Apr. 1743. He was from Germantown.

Lehman, John Christopher. He was naturalized in Pennsylvania 11 Apr. 1763. He was from Reading Township, Berks County.

Lehman, Lubwick. He was naturalized in Pennsylvania 28 Nov. 1769. He was from Frederick Township, Philadelphia County.

Lehmenn, Johannes. He was naturalized in Pennsylvania 13–15 Apr. 1748. He was from Philadelphia County.

Lehnherr, Jacob. He was naturalized in Pennsylvania 10 Sep. 1761. He was from Lancaster County.

Lehr, Godfried. He was naturalized in Pennsylvania 24–25 Sep. 1764. He was from Passyunk Township, Philadelphia County.

Leibengut, Adam. He was naturalized in Pennsylvania 24 Sep. 1762. He was from Philadelphia County.

Leiberger, John. He was naturalized in Pennsylvania 19 May 1739. He was from Lancaster County.

Leidbach, Godfried. He was naturalized in New York 3 July 1759.

Leidick, George. He was naturalized in Pennsylvania 25 Sep. 1751. He was from Philadelphia County.

Leighner, Leonard. He was naturalized in Pennsylvania 10 Apr. 1760.

Leighte, John. He was naturalized in Pennsylvania 14 Feb. 1729/30. He was from Lancaster County.

Leikteter, Conrad. He was naturalized in Maryland 9 Sep. 1761. He was from Frederick County.

Leimbacker, Henry. He was naturalized in Pennsylvania 10 Apr. 1770. He was from Northampton, Bucks County.

Leinau, Andrew Erdman. He was naturalized in Pennsylvania 11 Apr. 1763. He was from Philadelphia.

Leinberger, Andreas. He was naturalized in Maryland 14 Apr. 1762. He was a German.

Leinhart, Michael. He was naturalized in New York 24 Mar. 1772.

Leinweeber, Henry. He was naturalized in Pennsylvania 24 Sep. 1762. He was from Lancaster County.

Leiser, Albrist. He was naturalized in Nova Scotia 15 Sep. 1758. [His forename might have been Albrecht.]

Leiser, Mathias. He was naturalized in Maryland 11 Sep. 1765. He was a German from Frederick County. He was also known as Henry Leiser.

Leisher, Nicholas, Jr. He was naturalized in Pennsylvania 29 Mar. 1735. He was from Philadelphia County.

Leisler, Jacob. He took the oath to the King 21–26 Oct. 1664 after the conquest of New Netherland.

Leitzing, Peter. He was endenized in Maryland 26 Apr. 1768. He was born in Germany.

LeJeune, Joseph. He was an Acadian and took the oath of allegiance in Apr. 1730.

Lejeune, Paul. He was an Acadian the took the oath to the King at the Mines, Pisiquit, Nova Scotia 31 Oct. 1727.

LeJeune, Paul. He was an Acadian and took the oath of allegiance in Apr. 1730.

LeJeune, Paul. He was an Acadian and took the oath of allegiance in Apr. 1730.

LeJeune, Pierre. He was an Acadian and took the oath of allegiance in Apr. 1730.

LeLande, Pierre. He was an Acadian and took the oath of allegiance in Apr. 1730.

Llemaire, John. He was naturalized in Maryland 6 June 1674. He was born in Anjou, France.

Leman, Cleman. He was naturalized in New York 8–9 Sep. 1715. He was from Ulster County.

Leman, Jacob. He was naturalized in Pennsylvania in 1735. He was from Chester County.

Leman, Wilhelm. He was naturalized in New York 8–9 Sep. 1715. He was from Ulster County.

Leman, Jacob. He was naturalized in Pennsylvania 29 Mar. 1735. He was from Lancaster County.

Leman, Peter. He was naturalized in Pennsylvania 26–27 Sep. 1743. He was from Lancaster County.

LeMare, Francis. He became a denizen in North Carolina 7 Oct. 1697. He was a native of France and a Protestant who because of his religion was compelled to flee from his country.

Lembert, Daniel. He was naturalized in New York 16 Aug. 1715. He was a yeoman from New Rochelle.

LeMercier, Andrew. He was naturalized in Massachusetts 12 Apr. 1731.

LeMire, Pierre. He was an Acadian who took the oath to the King at the Mines, Pisiquit 31 Oct. 1727.

Lemly, John. He was born in Frederick County, Virginia 4 Aug. 1768.

Lemmens, Hendrick. He expressed his desire to be naturalized in New Castle County, Delaware 21 Feb. 1682/3.

LeMoine, Jacobus. He was endenized in England 8 Mar. 1681/2 He came to South Carolina.

Lenard, Volentine. He was naturalized in North Carolina 23 Mar. 1763. He was from Rowan County. He also appeared as Volentine Lentz.

Lenck, Adam. He was naturalized in Maryland 15 Apr. 1761.

Lende, Ernst Ludewig. He was naturalized in New York 11 Sep. 1761.

Lengevelder, Coenraadt. He was naturalized in New York 3 July 1759.

Lening, Christopher. He was naturalized in New York 11 Sep. 1761.

Lenoir, Isaac. He was naturalized in Jamaica 13 Aug. 1690.

Lenson, John. He was naturalized in Pennsylvania 29 Sep. 1709. He was from Philadelphia County.

Lent, Peter. He was naturalized in Pennsylvania 10–12 Apr. 1762. He was from York County.

Lentz, Frederick Sigismund. He was naturalized in New York 18 Oct. 1763. He was from New York City.

LeNud, Nicholas. He was the son of Nicholas and Marie LeNud, of Dieppe, Normandie, France. He was naturalized in South Carolina *ca.* 1696.

Leonard, George. He was naturalized in New York 11 Sep. 1761. He was a butcher from New York City.

Leonard, Joseph. He was naturalized in Jamaica 18 Dec. 1706.

Leonhard, Wilhelm. He was naturalized in New York 21 Oct. 1765. He was a baker from New York City.

Leoperd, John. He was naturalized in North Carolina 22 Sep. 1763. He was from Rowan County and a German.

Leopold, George Adam. He was naturalized in Pennsylvania 11 Apr. 1763. He was from Philadelphia.

Leopold, Charles. He was naturalized in Pennsylvania 11 Apr. 1771. He was from Whitemarsh Township, Philadelphia County.

Leoron, Baptist. He was an Acadian and took the oath to George II at Annapolis River, Nova Scotia in the winter of 1730.

Leoron, Jacques. He was an Acadian and took the oath to George II at Annapolis River, Nova Scotia in the winter of 1730.

Leppy, Henry. He was naturalized in Pennsylvania 24–25 Sep. 1764. He was from Passyunk Township, Philadelphia County.

Leprince, Antoine. He was an Acadian and took the oath to the King at the Mines, Pisiquit, Nova Scotia 31 Oct. 1727.

LePrince, Antonie. He was an Acadian and took the oath of allegiance in Apr. 1730.

Leprince, Jean. He was an Acadian and took the oath to George II at Annapolis River, Nova Scotia in Dec. 1729.

LeQuie, Jean. He took the oath of allegiance in Boswijck, Kings County, New York 26–30 Sep. 1687. He had been in the colony 30 years.

Lerck, Christopher. He was naturalized in Pennsylvania 10 Apr. 1767. He was from Heidelberg Township, Berks County.

Lerets, Antony. He was naturalized in Pennsylvania 24 Sep. 1757.

Lerk, Caspar. He was naturalized in Pennsylvania 11 Apr. 1761. He was from Berks County.

LeRoux, John. He was endenized in London 20 Mar. 2 James II. He came to New York.

Lerow, Jonas. He was naturalized in Pennsylvania 14 Feb. 1729/30. He was from Lancaster County.

LeRoy, Adam. He was naturalized in Pennsylvania 10–12 Apr. 1762. He was from Lancaster County.

Le'Roy, Abraham. He was naturalized in Pennsylvania 24 Sep. 1763. He was from Lancaster Township, Lancaster County.

LeRoy, Jacob. He was naturalized in New York 3 May 1755.

LeRoy, Jean. He was an Acadian and took the oath of allegiance in Apr. 1730.

Le'Roy, John Peter. He was naturalized in Pennsylvania 24 Sep. 1763. He was from Lancaster Township, Lancaster County.

LeRoy, Pierre. He was naturalized in Rhode Island 16 June 1673. He had previously lived in the French West Indies. He lived in Newport.

Lerver, Tobias. He was naturalized in New York 20 Apr. 1763. He was a husbandman from Orange County.

Lescher, Nicholas. He was naturalized in Pennsylvania 6 Feb. 1730/1. He was from Philadelphia County.

Leseber, Johannes. He was naturalized in Pennsylvania 6 Feb. 1730/1. He was from Philadelphia County.

LeSerurier, James. He was endenized in England 16 June 1685. He was naturalized in South Carolina 2 Mar. 1699/1700. He was the son of James LeSerurier by Elizabeth Leger, his wife, and was born at Quentin, France.

LeSerurier, Jacques. He and his wife, Elizabeth Leger, were naturalized *ca.* 1696 in South Carolina. He was born at St. Quantin, Picardie, France and was the son of Pierre LeSerurier and

Marie LeComte. His wife was born in the same place and was the daughter of Jacques LeGer and Elizabeth Bossu.

Lesh, George. He was naturalized in Pennsylvania 24 Sep. 1755. He was from Lancaster County.

Lesher, George. He was naturalized in Pennsylvania 24–25 Sep. 1764. He was from Passyunk Township, Philadelphia County. [His name seemingly was incorrectly recorded as Lesher George.]

Lesher, John. He was naturalized in Pennsylvania 11–13 Apr. 1743. He was from Philadelphia County.

Lesher, Nicholas. He was naturalized in Pennsylvania in 1730–31. He was from Philadelphia County.

Lesher, Nicholas. He was naturalized in Pennsylvania 11 Apr. 1761. He was from Lancaster County.

Leshier, Henry. He was naturalized in Pennsylvania 24 Sep. 1757.

Lespinasse, James. He was naturalized in Jamaica 15 Mar. 1681.

Lesser, Frederick. He was naturalized in Pennsylvania 24 Sep. 1757. He was from Cocalico Township, Lancaster County.

Lessly, Benjamin. He was naturalized in Pennsylvania 10 & 23 Apr. 1764. He was from Brecknock Township, Lancaster County.

LeSueur, Abraham. He was born at Harfleur, Normandie, France, the son of Isaac Lesureru and Marye Senee. His wife was Catherine Poinsett. They were naturalized in South Carolina ca. 1696.

Letrer, Johan. He was naturalized in New York 11 Sep. 1761.

Letter, John. He was naturalized in Maryland 29 Sep. 1764. He was a German from Frederick County.

Letterman, Martin. He was naturalized in Pennsylvania 24 Sep. 1757.

Leunizen, Jacob. He took the oath of 21–26 Oct. 1664 after the conquest of New Netherland.

Leue, Henry. He was naturalized in Jamaica 31 Oct. 1732.

Leuz, John. He was naturalized in New York 8 Mar. 1773.

Levan, Bastian. He was naturalized in Pennsylvania 24 Sep. 1759.

Levan, Catherine. She was naturalized in Pennsylvania 10 Sep. 1761. She was from Berks County. She was the former Catherine Quimore.

Levan, Jacob. He was naturalized in Pennsylvania 11–13 Apr. 1742. He was from Philadelphia County.

Levand, Abraham. He was naturalized in Pennsylvania 6 Feb. 1730/1. He was from Philadelphia County.

Levand, Isaac. He was naturalized in Pennsylvania 6 Feb. 1730/1. He was from Philadelphia County.

Leveitzig, Bernard. He was naturalized in Pennsylvania 24 Sep. 1762. He was from Berks County.

Levely, William. He was naturalized in Maryland 10 Sep. 1760.

Levi, Asser. He took the oath to the King 21–26 Oct. 1664 after the conquest of New Netherland.

Levi, Moses. He was endenized in New York 30 May 1695.

Levick, John. He was naturalized in Pennsylvania in Sep. 1740. He was from Bucks County.

Levien, Gotchal. He was naturalized in Jamaica 28 June 1766.

LeVillam, John. He was naturalized in Virginia 12 May 1705.

Levine, Jean Baptist. He took the oath of allegiance at Mobile, West Florida 2 Oct. 1764.

Levingbecker, Johann Philip. He was naturalized in New York 24 July 1724.

Levron, Baptiste. He was an Acadian and took the oath of allegiance to the King in Dec. 1729.

Levron, Baptiste. He was an Acadian and took the oath of allegiance in Apr. 1730.

Levron, Jacques. He was an Acadian and took the oath of allegiance to the King in Dec. 1729.

Levron, Jacques. He was an Acadian and took the oath of allegiance in Apr. 1730.

Levron, Joseph. He was an Acadian and took the oath of allegiance in Apr. 1730.

Levy, Abraham. He was naturalized in Jamaica 10 Jan. 1707/8.

Levy, Asser. He was endenized in New York 21 Mar. 1664/5.

Levy, Gershom Moses. He sought naturalization in New York 27 Nov. 1756.

Levy, Haeman. He was naturalized in New York 24 Nov. 1750.

Levy, Henry. He was naturalized in Jamaica 28 Feb. 1742/3. He was a Jew.

Levy, Isaac. He was naturalized in Pennsylvania 11 Apr. 1763. He was from Philadelphia. He was a Jew.

Levy, Isaac. He was naturalized in New York in 1740–41. He was a Jewish merchant from New York City.

Levy, Moses. He was naturalized in New York 19 Apr. 1743. He was a Jewish merchant from New York City.

Levy, Moses. He was naturalized in Jamaica 31 May 1743. He was a Jew.

Levy, Myer. He sought naturalization in New York 27 Nov. 1756.

Levy, Samuel. He was naturalized in New York in 1740–41. He was a Jewish merchant from New York City.

Lewan, Daniel. He was naturalized in Pennsylvania 11–13 Apr.1743. He was from Philadelphia County.

Lewegood, Jacob. He was naturalized in Pennsylvania 11 Apr. 1763. He was from Tolpohocken Township, Berks County.

Lewis, Fielding. He was naturalized in Frederick County, Virginia 7 Aug. 1770.

Lewis, Jacob. He was naturalized in Pennsylvania 11 Apr. 1761. He was from Northampton County.

Lewis, John. He was naturalized in Jamaica 21 Mar. 1684.

Lewis, John. He was naturalized in New Jersey 30 Nov. 1723. He lived in Hunterdon County. He was born in Portugal.

Lewis, John. He was naturalized in New York 18 Jan. 1748. He was a mariner from New York City.

Ley, Christopher. He was naturalized in Pennsylvania 19 May 1739. He was from Lancaster County.

Ley, Felix. He was naturalized in Pennsylvania 10 & 23 Apr. 1764. He was from Rockhill Township, Bucks County.

Leyderbach, Godfrey. He was naturalized in New York 11 Sep. 1761.

Leydig, Jost. He was naturalized in Maryland 15 Apr. 1772.

Leymeister, Wilhelm. He was naturalized in Pennsylvania 11 Apr. 1761. He was from Berks County.

Leynsen, Joost. He was naturalized in New York 26 July 1715. He was a baker.

Leypold, John. He was naturalized in Maryland 14 Sep. 1770. He was a German.

L'Hommedieu, Benjamin. He petitioned for naturalization in New York 19 Aug. 1687.

L'Hommedieu, Jean. He petitioned for naturalization in New York 19 Aug. 1687.

Lhommedieu, Pietter. He took the oath of naturalization in New York 1 Sep. 1687 in Ulster County.

Libby, Conrod. He was naturalized in Maryland 12 Sep. 1759.

Libkep, Solomon. He was naturalized in Pennsylvania 25–26 Sep./4 Oct. 1749. He was from Bucks County.

Libough, John. He was naturalized in Pennsylvania 19 May 1739. He was from Lancaster County.

Liboschain, Marie Johanna. She was endenized in London 25 Aug. 1708. She came to New York.

Liboschain, Susanna. She was endenized in London 25 Aug. 1708. She came to New York.

Librook, Jacob. He was naturalized in Pennsylvania 11 Apr. 1761. He was from Berks County.

Lichtel, Anthony. He was naturalized in Pennsylvania 10 Apr. 1765. He was from Upper Salford Township, Philadelphia County.

Lictich, Peter. He was naturalized in Maryland 12 Sep. 1759.

Lidert, Jacob. He was naturalized in Pennsylvania 10 Sep. 1761. He was from Lancaster County.

Liebenstein, Felix. He was naturalized in Nova Scotia 6 July 1758.

Liebhardts, Tobias. He was naturalized in New York 11 Sep. 1761.

Liebegut, Jacob. He was naturalized in Pennsylvania 11 Apr. 1761. He was from Philadelphia County.

Liechtinwallner, John. He was naturalized in Pennsylvania 26–27 Sep. 1743. He was from Bucks County.

Lienback, Frederick. He was naturalized in Pennsylvania 24 Sep. 1760. He was from Berks County.

Lienback, Henry. He was naturalized in Pennsylvania 24 Sep. 1760. He was from Berks County.

Lienback, John. He was naturalized in Pennsylvania 24 Sep. 1760. He was from Berks County.

Liepe, Hans Caspar. He was naturalized in New York 31 Jan. 1715/6. He was from Albany County.

Lier, Valentine. He was naturalized in Pennsylvania 10–14 Apr. 1747. He was from Lancaster County.

Lieslaer, Martin. He was naturalized in New York 3 July 1759.

Liess, Peter. He was naturalized in Pennsylvania 11 Apr. 1763. He was from Tolpohocken Township, Berks County.

Liester, Philip. He was naturalized in Pennsylvania 11 Apr. 1763. He was from Rockland Township, Bucks County.

Liewenstien, George. He was naturalized in Pennsylvania 24 Sep. 1763. He was from Manchester Township, York County.

Light, John. He was naturalized in Pennsylvania 24–25 Sep. 1764. He was from Pilegrove, Salem County, New Jersey.

Light, John Jacob. He was naturalized in Pennsylvania 14 Feb. 1729/30. He was from Lancaster County.

Lighthert, Johan Barent. He was naturalized in New York 8–9 Sep. 1715. He was from Ulster County.

Limbach, Frederick. He was naturalized in Pennsylvania 24–25 Sep./5 Oct. 1767. He was from Upper Milford Township, Northampton County.

Lindenberger, George Ernst. He was naturalized in Pennsylvania 10–12 Apr. 1762. He was from Philadelphia County.

Lindenmuth, Ludwick. He was naturalized in Pennsylvania 16 May 1769. He was from Donegal Township, Lancaster County.

Linder, Benjamin. He was naturalized in New York 11 Sep. 1761. He was a practitioner in physic from New York City.

Linder, George. He was naturalized in New York 20 Apr. 1774.

Linder, Simon. He was naturalized in Frederick County, Virginia 2 Aug. 1769.

Line, John. He was naturalized in Pennsylvania 14 Feb. 1729/30. He was from Lancaster County.

Lingel, Paul. He was naturalized in Pennsylvania 10–12 Apr. 1762. He was from Berks County.

Lingenfelder, George. He was naturalized in Maryland 11 Sep. 1765.

Lingenfelter, Abraham. He was naturalized in Maryland 26 Mar. 1758. He lived in Frederick, Maryland.

Lingenfelter, George. He was naturalized in Maryland 15 Apr. 1761.

Lingenfelter, Johannes. He was naturalized in Maryland 13 Sep. 1758.

Lingenfelter, John. He was naturalized in Pennsylvania 11–13 Apr. 1743. He was from Lancaster County.

Lingenfelter, Valentine. He was naturalized in Maryland 4 Sep. 1765. He was a German from Frederick, Maryland.

Lingenfelter, Valentine. He was naturalized in Maryland 15 Apr. 1767. He was a German.

Lingenfelther, Bernard. He was naturalized in Maryland 15 Sep. 1762. He was from Frederick County.

Lingle, Lawrence. He was naturalized in North Carolina 22 Sep. 1763. He was from Rowan County and a German.

Linhear, Philip. He was naturalized in Pennsylvania 24 Sep. 1755. He was from Lancaster County.

Link, Andrew. He was naturalized in Maryland 14 Apr. 1760. He was a German.

Link, Jacob. He was naturalized in New Jersey in 1759. He was a Quaker.

Link, Mathias. He was naturalized in New York 3 July 1759.

Link, Willem. He was naturalized in New York 14 Feb. 1715/6. He was from Albany County.

Linker, George. He was naturalized in North Carolina 23 Mar. 1765. He was from Rowan County.

Linn, Adam. He was naturalized in Pennsylvania 25–26 Sep./4 Oct. 1749. He was from York County.

Linton, Francis. He was naturalized in Jamaica 31 May 1743.

Lintz, George. He was naturalized in Pennsylvania 24 Sep. 1755.

Lisboa, Samuel Mendes. He was naturalized in Jamaica 9 Nov. 1713.

Lisenbekler, Paul. He was naturalized in Pennsylvania 11 Apr. 1741. He was from Philadelphia County.

Liser, John. He was naturalized in Pennsylvania 24 Sep. 1760. He was from Lancaster County.
Liser, Jost. He was naturalized in Maryland 7 May 1767. He was a German.
Lish, Adam. He was naturalized in Pennsylvania 10 Apr. 1755. He was from Berks County.
Lisher, John. He was naturalized in Pennsylvania 10 Sep. 1761. He was from Northampton County.
Lishman, Henry. He was naturalized in New Jersey 6 Dec. 1769.
Lissenman, Hans. He was naturalized in New York 16 Dec. 1737.
Lister, Jost. He was naturalized in Maryland 7 May 1767. He was a German.
Littich, Peter. He was naturalized in Maryland 9 Apr. 1760. He lived in Baltimore, Maryland.
Littig, Philip. He was naturalized in Maryland 14 Apr. 1762. He was a German.
Little, Daniel. He was naturalized in North Carolina 19 Sep. 1753. He was from Rowan County.
Little, Gasper. He was naturalized in Maryland 16 Sep. 1765. He was a German.
Little, Peter. He was naturalized in Pennsylvania 24 Sep. 1760. He was from York County.
Littlejohn, Jno. George. He was naturalized in Pennsylvania 25–27 Sep. 1740. He was from Bucks County.
Littler, Henry. He was naturalized in Maryland 16 Sep. 1765. He was a German.
Livers, Arnold. He was naturalized in Maryland 3 May 1704. He was Dutch. He was a tailor.
Livreau, Moses. He was naturalized in Virginia 12 May 1705.
Loar, Herman. He was naturalized in Maryland 15 Sep. 1762.
Loakes, Nicolas. He was naturalized in New York 8–9 Sep. 1715. He was from Ulster County.
Loaks, Peter. He was naturalized in New York 8–9 Sep. 1715. He was from Ulster County.
Lob, Jacob. He was naturalized in Maryland 13 Apr. 1761.
Lob, John. He was naturalized in Pennsylvania 25 Sep. 1747. He was from Bucks County.
Loback, Peter. He was naturalized in Pennsylvania 25 Sep. 1744. He was from Philadelphia County.
Lobatto, Abraham Cohen. He was endenized in Barbados 2 Aug. 1661.
Lober, Peter. He was naturalized in Pennsylvania 11 Apr. 1771. He was from Colebrookdale Township, Berks County.
Lochman, Jacob. He was naturalized in Maryland. He was from Baltimore County and was born in Germany.
Lock, John. He was naturalized in Jamaica 24 May 1689.
Lodowick, David. He was naturalized in Pennsylvania 25 Sep. 1744. He was from Philadelphia County.
Lodwich, Johan Pieter. He was naturalized in New York 28 Feb. 1715/6. He was from Albany County.
Lodwick, Hendrick. He was naturalized in New York 17 Jan. 1715/6. He was from Albany County.
Lodwick, Michael. He was naturalized in Pennsylvania 24 Sep. 1759.
Lodz, Reynold. He was naturalized in New York 15 Oct. 1765. He was a gardener and French Protestant from Oyster Bay, Queens County. He also appeared as Reynold Low.
Loecksteen, Jurie. He was naturalized in New York 8–9 Sep. 1715. He was from Ulster County.
Loewe, George Adam. He was naturalized in Maryland 13 Apr. 1763. He was a German.
Lofland, Adrian. He was naturalized in New York 12 June 1689. He was the son of Henry and Adriana Lofland. He was born in Rotterdam, Holland.
Lohnes, Johannes. He was naturalized in Nova Scotia 5 July 1758.
Lohrens, Francis Peter. He was naturalized in Pennsylvania 24–25 Sep. 1764. He was from Lancaster Township, Lancaster County.
Loist, Christopher. He was naturalized in Pennsylvania 10–14 Apr. 1747. He was from Philadelphia County.
Lombardy, Peter. He was naturalized in New York 23 Dec. 1765.
Loney, Titus. He was naturalized in Maryland in 1742–43.
Long, Adam. He was naturalized in Maryland 11 Sep. 1765. He was a German from Frederick County.
Long, Christian. He was naturalized in Pennsylvania 19 May 1739. He was from Lancaster County.
Long, Elias. He was naturalized in Pennsylvania 24 Sep. 1741. He was from Philadelphia County.

Long, Joseph. He was naturalized in Pennsylvania 24 Sep. 1763. He was from Lancaster Township, Lancaster County.

Long, Martin. He was naturalized in Pennsylvania 24 Sep. 1762. He was from Berks County.

Long, Michael. He was naturalized in Pennsylvania 10–12 Apr. 1762. He was from York County.

Long, Nicholas. He was naturalized in Pennsylvania 11 Apr. 1761. He was from Berks County.

Long, Nicholas. He was naturalized in Pennsylvania 24 May 1771. He was from Lancaster, Lancaster County.

Long, William. He was naturalized in Pennsylvania 10 & 23 Apr. 1764. He was from New Providence Township, Philadelphia County.

Longanickar, David. He was naturalized in Pennsylvania 14 Feb. 1729/30. He was from Lancaster County.

Longemare, —. He was a minister. He was naturalized in South Carolina ca. 1696.

Longenacre, Jacob. He was naturalized in Pennsylvania 11 Apr. 1763. He was from Coventry Township, Chester County.

Longenacre, Susannah. She was naturalized in Pennsylvania 11 Apr. 1763. She was from Coventry Township, Chester County.

Longo, Antony. He was naturalized in Jamaica 26 Sep. 1690. He also appeared as Antony Congo. He was a Spanish Negro.

Lons, George. He was naturalized in Maryland 11 Sep. 1765.

Loon, David. He was naturalized in New York 16 Dec. 1737.

Lookerman, Govert. He was endenized prior to 19 Dec. 1664.

Lookerman, Jacob. He was naturalized in Maryland 15 Nov. 1678. He was born in New York when it was under Dutch control.

Lookermans, Govert. He took the oath to the King 21–26 Oct. 1664 after the conquest of New Netherland.

Looss, Jacob. He was naturalized in Pennsylvania 24 Sep. 1763. He was from Windsor Township, Berks County.

Looten, Jacob. He was naturalized in Maryland 13 May 1682. He lived in St. Mary's County.

Lopald, Matthias. He was naturalized in Pennsylvania 11 Apr. 1761. He was from Philadelphia County.

Lopes, Jacob. He was naturalized in Jamaica 5 Apr. 1693.

Lopes, Moses. He took his oath in London. He was born in Lisbon, Portugal. He had his certificate recorded in Jamaica 18 Mar. 1726/7.

Lopes, Mosi, Jr. He was endenized in London 30 June 1725. He was from Barbados.

Lopes, Rachall Rodriques. She was naturalized in Jamaica 18 Feb. 1723/4. She was the wife of Mordekay Rodriques Lopes. He was a shopkeeper.

Lopez, Aaron. He was naturalized in Massachusetts 15 Oct. 1762. He was a Jew. He lived in Swansey, Bristol Co., Mass. and had formerly lived at Newport, R.I. from 13 Oct. 1752 to 20 Sep. 1762. He had applied but been rejected by the Rhode Island Superior Court in 1762.

Lopez, Abigail. She was naturalized in Jamaica 28 Nov. 1750. She was a Jewess.

Lopez, Andrew. He was naturalized in Jamaica 26 Feb. 1703. He was a Jew.

Lopez, David. He was endenized in England 25 Oct. 1667. He settled in Barbados and was a Jew.

Lopez, David Preiria. He was naturalized in Jamaica 17 Oct. 1734.

Lopez, Manuel. He took the oath of allegiance at Mobile, West Florida 2 Oct. 1764.

Lopez, Moses, Jr. He was endenized 14 Apr. 1725. He was from Barbados.

Lopez, Moses. He was naturalized in Jamaica 19 May 1725.

Lopez, Moses. He was naturalized in New York in 1740–41. He was a Jew.

Lopez, Rebecca. She was naturalized in Jamaica 11 Feb. 1741/2.

Lopp, Hannis. He was naturalized in North Carolina 22 Sep. 1763. He was from Rowan County and a German.

L'Or, Alexandre. He was an Acadian and took the oath to George II at Annapolis River, Nova Scotia in Dec. 1729.

L'or, Charles. He was an Acadian and took the oath to George II at Annapolis River, Nova Scotia in Dec. 1729.

L'or, Jacques. He was an Acadian and took the oath to George II at Annapolis River, Nova Scotia in Dec. 1729.

L'Or, Jacques. He was an Acadian and took the oath of allegiance in Apr. 1730.

Lor, Jacques. He took the oath of allegiance at Port Royal, Nova Scotia 16 Aug. 1695.

Lor, Jean. He was an Acadian and took the oath to George II at Annapolis River, Nova Scotia in Dec. 1729.

Lor, Jullien. He took the oath of allegiance at Port Royal, Nova Scotia 16 Aug. 1695.

L'or, Pierre. He was an Acadian and took the oath to George II at Annapolis River, Nova Scotia in Dec. 1729.

Lorange, John. He was naturalized in Virginia 12 May 1705.

Lorats, Henry. He was naturalized in Pennsylvania 24 Sep. 1755. He was from Philadelphia County.

Lorentz, John Peter. He was naturalized in New York 22 Oct. 1768. He was a yeoman from Dutchess County.

Lorey, John. He was naturalized in Pennsylvania 11 Apr. 1761. He was from Berks County.

Lorillard, John George. He was naturalized in New York 27 Oct. 1760. He was a French Protestant yeoman from New York City.

Lorin, Peter. He was naturalized in New York 24 Nov. 1750.

Lorindine, John Baptist. He took the oath of allegiance at Mobile, West Florida 2 Oct. 1764.

Lorraine, Anthony. He took the oath of allegiance at Mobile, West Florida 2 Oct. 1764.

Losh, George. He was naturalized in Pennsylvania 24–25 Sep. 1764. He was from Northern Liberties Township, Philadelphia County.

Lott, Baltus. He was naturalized in New York 8–9 Sep. 1715. He was from Ulster County.

Lott, Engelbert. He expressed his desire to be naturalized in New Castle County, Delaware 21 Feb. 1682/3.

Lott, Engelbert. He took the oath of allegiance in Flackbush, Kings County, New York 26–30 Sep. 1687. He was a native of the colony.

Lott, Henrick. He took the oath of allegiance in Flackbush, Kings County, New York 26–30 Sep. 1687. He was a native of the colony.

Lott, Pieter. He took the oath of allegiance in Flackbush, Kings County, New York 26–30 Sep. 1687. He had been in the colony 35 years.

Lottonneau, Guillaume. He was endenized in New York 6 Feb. 1695/6.

Louck, Abraham. He was naturalized in New York 31 Jan. 1715/6. He was from Albany County.

Loucks, Diedrich. He was naturalized in New York 31 Jan. 1715/6. He was from Albany County.

Loucks, Johan Hendrick. He was naturalized in New York 3 Jan. 1715/6. He was from Albany County.

Loucks, Philip. He was naturalized in New York 17 Jan. 1715/6. He was from Albany County.

Louderbouch, Peter. He and his daughters, Catherine Louderbouch, Elizabeth Louderbouch, and Barbara Louderbouch, were naturalized in New Jersey 19 Jan. 1747/8. They were born in Germany.

Louffer, Gotlip. He was naturalized in Maryland 11 Sep. 1765. He was a German from Frederick County.

Louffer, Michael. He was naturalized in Maryland 11 Sep. 1765. He was a German from Frederick County.

Lough, Christian. He was naturalized in Pennsylvania 13 May 1768. He was from Manchester Township, York County.

Lough, Peter. He was naturalized in Pennsylvania 13 May 1768. He was from Manchester Township, York County.

Loughman, Casper. He was naturalized in Pennsylvania 14 Feb. 1729/30. He was from Lancaster County.

LoughMiller, George. He was naturalized in Frederick County, Virginia 5 May 1747.

Louillard, Peter. He was naturalized in New York 21 Apr. 1762. He was a stocking weaver from New York City and a French Protestant. [He was probably Peter Lorillard.]

Loundert, Jurich. He was naturalized in New York 14 Feb. 1715/6. He was from Albany County.

Lounhert, Philip. He was naturalized in New York 8–9 Sep. 1715. He was from Ulster County.

Lourensen, Huybert. He expressed his desire to be naturalized in New Castle County, Delaware 21 Feb. 1682/3.

Lousada, David Baruh. He was endenized in England 18 Apr. 1664. He was a Jew. He settled in Barbados.

Louzada, Aron Baruh. He was endenized in England 20 Aug. 1675. He settled in Barbados and was a Jew.

Louzada, Abraham Baruh. He was endenized in England 20 Apr. 1672. He settled in Barbados and was a Jewish merchant.

Louzada, James Baruh. He was endenized in England 16 Dec. 1687. He settled in Barbados and was a Jew.

Louzada, Moses Baruh. He was endenized in England 14 Dec. 1694. He settled in Barbados.

Loutz, George. He was naturalized in Pennsylvania 24 Sep. 1759.

Louwer, Konrat. He was naturalized in New York 27 Jan. 1770.

Lovewater, Joseph. He was naturalized in North Carolina 23 Mar. 1765. He was from Rowan County.

Lovis, Stephen. He was naturalized in Virginia 12 May 1705.

Low, Herman. He was naturalized in Maryland 11 Sep. 1765.

Lowbenback, Philip. He was naturalized in Pennsylvania 11 Apr. 1761. He was from Berks County.

Lowbougher, Christopher. He was naturalized in Pennsylvania 10 & 23 Apr. 1764. He was from Amwell, Hunterdon County, New Jersey.

Lowe, Conrod. He was naturalized in North Carolina 22 Sep. 1763. He was from Rowan County and a German.

Lowen, Jacob. He was naturalized in New York 31 Dec. 1761.

Lowen, Jury. He was naturalized in New York 31 Dec. 1761.

Lower, Christian. He was naturalized in Pennsylvania 19 May 1739. He was from Lancaster County. He also appeared as Christian Lawer.

Lower, Jacob. He was naturalized in Pennsylvania 19 May 1739. He was from Lancaster County.

Lower, Michael. He was naturalized in Pennsylvania 10 Sep. 1761. He was from Berks County.

Lowerentz, Adam. He was naturalized in New Jersey in 1750. He was from Hunterdon County.

Lowman, Bernard. He was naturalized in Pennsylvania 11 Apr. 1751. He was from York County.

Lowman, Henry. He was naturalized in Pennsylvania 11 Apr. 1761. He was from Lancaster County.

Lowness, John George. He was naturalized in Pennsylvania 10 & 23 Sep. 1764. He was from Cushahoppen Township, Bucks County.

Lows, Christopher. He was naturalized in Maryland 11 Sep. 1765. He was a German from Frederick County.

Lowtherman, John. He was naturalized in Pennsylvania 24 Sep. 1760. He was from Lancaster County.

Loy, Stephen. He was naturalized in Augusta County, Virginia 24 May 1765.

Loye, Martin. He was naturalized in North Carolina 22 Sep. 1764. He was from Rowan County and a German.

Loyer, Ad. He was naturalized in South Carolina 12 May 1748.

Loynan, Andrew. He was naturalized in Pennsylvania 24–25 Sep./5 Oct. 1767. He was from New Castle County [Delaware].

Loyse, Cornelis. He took the oath of allegiance in Boswijck, Kings County, New York 26–30 Sep. 1687. He had been in the colony 36 years.

Loyse, Pieter. He took the oath of allegiance in Boswijck, Kings County, New York 26–30 Sep. 1687. He was a native of the colony.

Lubberse, Gerrit. He took the oath of allegiance in Flackbush, Kings County, New York 26–30 Sep. 1687. He was a native of the colony.

Lubberse, Thijs. He took the oath of allegiance in Breucklijn, Kings County, New York 26–30 Sep. 1687. He had been in the colony 50 years.

Lucadon, John. He was naturalized in Virginia 12 May 1705.

Lucam, George. He was naturalized in New York 18 Oct. 1765. He was a butcher from New York City.

Lucena, Jacob. He was naturalized in Jamaica 23 Nov. 1681.

Lucena, James. He was naturalized in Rhode Island in Feb. 1761. He was from Portugal. He came with his family.

Lucken, John. He was naturalized in Pennsylvania 29 Sep. 1709. He was from Philadelphia County.

Luder, John. He was naturalized in Maryland 11 May 1774. He was a German.

Ludwick, Matthew. He was naturalized in Pennsylvania 10 & 23 Apr. 1764. He was from Macungy Township, Northampton County.

Ludwig, Christopher. He was naturalized in Pennsylvania 11 Apr. 1763. He was from Philadelphia.

Ludwig, John. He was naturalized in Pennsylvania 17 May 1770. He was from Earl Township, Lancaster County.

Luijster, Corenlis Peters. He took the oath of allegiance in Flackbush, Kings County, New York 26–30 Sep. 1687. He was a native of the colony.

Luke, Christian. He was naturalized in Pennsylvania 10 Sep. 1761. He was from Berks County.

Lukembiel, Adam. He was naturalized in Pennsylvania 10–12 Apr. 1762. He was from Berks County.

Lukenbeel, Henry. He was naturalized in Pennsylvania 11–13 Apr. 1743. He was from Philadelphia County.

Lumbardy, Peter. He was naturalized in New York 23 Dec. 1765.

Lumbrozo, Jacob. He was made a denizen in Maryland 10 Sep. 1663. He was late of Lisbon, Portugal. He was also known as John Lumbrozo.

Lund, Jacob. He was naturalized in Rhode Island in Feb. 1754. He lived in Newport and was a native of Norway. He had been in British service for several years.

Luneman, Carl. He was naturalized in New York 18 Oct. 1768. He was a carpenter from New York City.

Lung, Henry. He was naturalized in Augusta County, Virginia 16 Oct. 1765.

Lung, Nicholas. He was naturalized in Virginia 17 Apr. 1745. He was born in Sapringkn, Germany. He was a Quaker.

Lung, Philip. He was naturalized in Virginia 17 Apr. 1745. He was born in Wigsden, Germany. He was a Quaker.

Lupp, Peter. He was naturalized in New Jersey in 1770.

Lusein, Jacques. He took the oath of allegiance at Mobile, West Florida 2 Oct. 1764.

Lusher, Charles. He was naturalized in New York 16 Dec. 1737.

Luts, Henry. He was naturalized in New Jersey 7 Apr. 1761.

Lutz, Michael. He was naturalized in Pennsylvania 10–11 Apr. 1746. He was from Bucks County.

Luycasse, Jan. He was naturalized in New York 6 Dec. 1715. He was from Albany County.

Luyck, Egidius. He took the oath to the King 21–26 Oct. 1664 after the conquest of New Netherland.

Luyster, Pieter Cornelis. He took the oath of allegiance in Flackland, Kings County, New York 26–30 Sep. 1687. He had been in the colony 31 years.

Luyster, Thys Pieterse. He took the oath of allegiance in Flackland, Kings County, New York 26–30 Sep. 1687. He had been in the colony 31 years.

Lydie, Jacob. He was naturalized in Pennsylvania 24 Sep. 1753. He was from Philadelphia County.

Lydie, Jacob. He was naturalized in Pennsylvania 10 & 23 Apr. 1764. He was from Codorus Township, York County.

Lydus, Gaertruy Isabella. She was naturalized in New York 28 Feb. 1715/6. She was from Albany County.

Lydus, Maria Adrianata. She was naturalized in New York 28 Feb. 1715/6. She was from Albany County.

Lynch, Barnett. He was naturalized in Augusta County, Virginia 22 Aug. 1770.

Lynderson, Garrett. He was naturalized in Jamaica 20 June 1675.

Lyne, John. He was naturalized in Pennsylvania 11–13 Apr. 1743. He was from Lancaster County.

Lynsen, Joost. He was naturalized in New York 26 July 1715.

Lyon, Benjamin. He sought naturalization in New York 27 Nov. 1756. He was a baker.

Lyon, Jacob. He was naturalized in Jamaica 26 Feb. 1740/1. He was a Jew.

Lyon, John. He and his children, Mary Lyon, Jacob Lyon, and Elizabeth Lyon, were naturalized in Maryland 3 May 1740. He was from Prince George's County and was born in Germany.

Lype, Ulrick. He was naturalized in Pennsylvania 10–11 Apr. 1744. He was from Lancaster County.

Lyron, Lewis. He was endenized in New York 28 Oct. 1696. He was a French Protestant.

Lytner, Nathaniel. He was naturalized in Pennsylvania 24 Sep. 1741. He was from Lancaster County.

Maag, Conrad. He was naturalized in Pennsylvania 10 & 23 Apr. 1764. He was from Philadelphia.

Maag, Henry. He was naturalized in Pennsylvania 10 Apr. 1754. He was from Philadelphia County.

Maag, Jacob. He was naturalized in Pennsylvania 10–11 Apr. 1746. He was from Philadelphia.

Maag, Jacob. He was naturalized in Pennsylvania 10 Apr. 1760.

Maagg, Henrick. He was naturalized in Maryland 17 Apr. 1773. He was a German.

Maan, Bartholdus. He took the oath to the King 21–26 Oct. 1664 after the conquest of New Netherland.

Macant, Peter. He was naturalized in Virginia 12 May 1705.

Machaell, John. He was endenized in James City County, Virginia 16 Mar. 1656.

Machielse, Johannis. He took the oath of allegiance in Gravens End, Kings County, New York 26–30 Sep. 1687. He was a native of the colony.

Machlen, Jacob. He was naturalized in Pennsylvania 25 Sep. 1751. He was from Philadelphia County.

Mack, Jury. He was naturalized in New York 20 Oct. 1764.

Mackenin, Daniel. He was naturalized in Antigua 29 Apr. 1703.

Mackinel, Blassius Daniel. He was naturalized in Pennsylvania 25–27 Sep. 1740. He was from Philadelphia County.

Mackinet, Blasius Daniel. He was naturalized in Pennsylvania 6 Feb. 1730/1. He was from Philadelphia County.

Mackned, Daniel, Jr. He was naturalized in Pennsylvania 19 May 1739. He was from Philadelphia County.

Made, John. He was naturalized in Pennsylvania 11 Apr. 1761. He was from Berks County.

Madelon, Magdelen. She took the oath of allegiance at Mobile, West Florida 2 Oct. 1764.

Madis, Daniel. He was naturalized in Maryland 14 Apr. 1761.

Maduro, Isaac Levy. He was naturalized in Jamaica 14 Sep. 1694.

Maduro, Levy. He was naturalized in Jamaica 22 Nov. 1705.

Maduro, Samuel Levy. He was naturalized in Jamaica 16 Jan. 1698.

Maduro, Solomon Levi. He was naturalized in Jamaica 12 Mar. 1702/3.

Maduro, Solomon Levy. He was naturalized in Jamaica 7 Feb. 1693/4.

Maerschalck. Andries. He was naturalized in New York 26 July 1715. He was a bolter.

Maesland, Pieter. He expressed his desire to be naturalized in New Castle County, Delaware 21 Feb. 1682/3.

Magens, Jochum Melchior. He was naturalized in New York 11 Oct. 1750.

Mahault, Estienne. He was endenized in New York 10 Mar. 1686.

Mahomer, Philip. He was naturalized in Pennsylvania 11 Apr. 1761. He was from Berks County.

Mahrigen, John. He was naturalized in Pennsylvania 11 Apr. 1763. He was from Berks County.

Mahring, Woolfgang. He was naturalized in Maryland 11 Sep. 1765. He was a German from Frederick County.

Maillet, Jacques. He was an Acadian and took the oath at Annapolis in Dec. 1729.

Main, George. He was naturalized in Maryland 11 Apr. 1764. He was a German.

Main, Jeremiah. He was endenized in London 22 June 1694. He came to New York. He also appeared as Jeremiah Many.

Mainser, John. He was naturalized in New York 3 May 1755.

Mainser, Lowrens. He was naturalized in New York 3 May 1755.

Maion, Peter. He was naturalized in Jamaica 30 May 1738.

Maise de Moise, Peter. He was naturalized in Maryland 16 Nov. 1683.

Maister, Gregorius. He was naturalized in Pennsylvania 10 Apr. 1759.

Major, John. He was naturalized in Jamaica 7 July 1703. He was a practitioner of physick.

Mak, Johannes. He was naturalized in Pennsylvania 11–13 Apr. 1743. He was from Germantown.

Malason, Claud. He was an Acadian and took the oath to George II at Annapolis River, Nova Scotia in the winter of 1730.

Mallard, John. He was naturalized in Virginia 12 May 1705.

Mallard, Peter. He was naturalized in Virginia 12 May 1705.

Mallet, Stephen. He was naturalized in Virginia 12 May 1705.

Malleville, Jean. He was naturalized in New York 6 July 1723.

Malleville, Pieter. He was naturalized in New York 6 July 1723.

Mallow, Michael. He was naturalized in Augusta County, Virginia 18 May 1762.
Malthee, Francis. He was naturalized in Jamaica 9 Apr. 1745.
Man, George. He was naturalized in New York 24 Apr. 1767. He was a farmer from Orange County.
Manadoe, Peter. He and his children were naturalized in Maryland 22 Apr. 1720. He lived in Calvert County and was French.
Mancius, Georgius Wilhelmus. He was naturalized in New York 16 Dec. 1737.
Manck, Casper. He was naturalized in New York 11 Sep. 1761.
Mandell, John Christopher. He was naturalized in Jamaica 19 July 1737.
Mange, Jean. He was naturalized in Nova Scotia 5 July 1758.
Mangen, John. He was naturalized in Pennsylvania 24–25 Sep. 1764. He was from Philadelphia.
Mangen, John Ernst. He was naturalized in Pennsylvania 11 Apr. 1763. He was from Northern Liberties Township, Philadelphia County.
Manhout, Jean. He was endenized in New York 2 Apr. 1686.
Manigaud, Gabriel. He was the son of Gabriel and Marie Manigaud, natives of LaRochelle, d'Onis, France. He was naturalized in South Carolina ca. 1696.
Manigaud, Pierre. He was the son of Gabriel and Marie Manigaud, natives of LaRochelle, d'Onis, France. He was naturalized in South Carolina ca. 1696.
Manismit, Conrad. He was naturalized in Pennsylvania 24 Sep. 1760. He was from Berks County.
Mann, Christopher Hans. He was naturalized in Pennsylvania 10 Apr. 1757.
Mann, Henry. He was naturalized in Pennsylvania 24 Sep. 1762. He was from Philadelphia County.
Mann, Peter. He was naturalized in Pennsylvania 24–25 Sep. 1764. He was from Northern Liberties Township, Philadelphia County.
Mann, Philip. He was naturalized in Pennsylvania 10–14 Apr. 1747. He was from Philadelphia County.
Mannel, John. He was naturalized in New York 20 Apr. 1763. He was a husbandman from Orange County.
Mannhard, Philip. He was naturalized in New York 21 Oct. 1765. He was a house carpenter from New York City.
Manok, Jacob. He was naturalized in New York 8–9 Sep. 1715. He was from Ulster County.
Mans, Bernard. He was naturalized in Pennsylvania 24 Sep. 1762. He was from Lancaster County.
Manspile, Jacob. He was naturalized in Orange County, Virginia 24 Feb. 1742/3. He also appeared as Jacob Mansboil. He was born in Wurttemberg. He had lived in the colony seven years. He was naturalized by the General Court of the colony 15 Oct. 1745.
Mantz, Casper. He was naturalized in Pennsylvania 24 Sep. 1759.
Manuel, Claes. He took the oath of allegiance in Orange County, New York 26 Sep. 1687.
Manusmith, Christian. He was naturalized in Pennsylvania 19 May 1739. He was from Lancaster County.
Maps, Michael. He was naturalized in New Jersey 28 Apr. 1762.
Marant, Nicholas. He was naturalized in South Carolina 10 Mar. 1696/7. He was a planter.
Marberg, John Casper. He was naturalized in Pennsylvania 10–12 Apr. 1762. He was from Lancaster County.
Marbeuf, Joseph. He was born in Vielle Vigne, Bretagne, France, the son of Julien Marbeuff and Ester Robin. He was naturalized in South Carolina 10 Mar. 1696/7. He was an apothecary.
Marcellin, Mariane. She took the oath of allegiance at Mobile, West Florida 2 Oct. 1764.
March, Peter. He was naturalized in Pennsylvania 24 Sep. 1762. He was from Berks County.
Marchand, Joseph Cachet. He was naturalized in New York 24 Nov. 1750.
Marchane, John. He was naturalized in Jamaica 27 Nov. 1688.
Marche, Dina. She was naturalized in New York 6 July 1723.
Marche, Leven. He was naturalized in New York 6 July 1723.
Marchel, John. He was naturalized in New York 27 Feb. 1770.
Marchegay, Bennitt. He was made a denizen in Maryland 7 Oct. 1665. He was French.
Marcinhas, Andre. He was naturalized in New York 11 Sep. 1761.
Marckell, Martinus. He was naturalized in New York in Oct. 1740. He was a farmer from Ulster County.

Marckussen, Hans. He expressed his desire to be naturalized in New Castle County, Delaware 21 Feb. 1682/3.

Marcon, John. He was naturalized in Jamaica 26 Aug. 1714.

Mareky, Dietrick. He was naturalized in Pennsylvania 10 Apr. 1766. He was from Heidelberg Township, Lancaster County.

Maret, Carel. He was naturalized in New Jersey 8 July 1730. He was born in Germany.

Margot, Joseph. He took the oath of allegiance at Mobile, West Florida 2 Oct. 1764.

Marion, Benjamin. He was born at LaChaume, Poitou, France, the son of Jean Marion and Perinne Boutignon. His wife was Judith Baluet. Their children, born in South Carolina, were Ester Marion, Gabrielle Marion, and Benjamin Marion. They were naturalized in South Carolina ca. 1696.

Mariott, John. He was naturalized in Virginia 12 May 1705.

Mark, Conrad. He was naturalized in Pennsylvania 24 Sep. 1760. He was from Lancaster County.

Markel, Frederick. He was naturalized in New York 8–9 Sep. 1715. He was from Ulster County.

Markel, George. He was naturalized in Pennsylvania 6 Feb. 1730/1. He was from Philadelphia County.

Markert, Pieter. He was naturalized in New Jersey in 1761.

Markey, John. He was naturalized in Maryland 20 Oct. 1768.

Markle, John. He was naturalized in Pennsylvania 10 Sep. 1761. He was from Lancaster County.

Markley, Jacob. He was naturalized in Pennsylvania 24 Sep. 1753. He was from Philadelphia County.

Marklin, John. He was naturalized in Maryland 11 Sep. 1765. He was a German from Frederick County.

Marklin, Nicholas. He was naturalized in Maryland 11 Sep 1765. He was a German from Frederick County.

Markling, Christian. He was naturalized in Pennsylvania 10 Apr. 1742. He was from Philadelphia County.

Marks, Anthony. He was naturalized in New York 20 Mar. 1762.

Marks, George. He was naturalized in Pennsylvania 10 Sep. 1761. He was from Berks County.

Marks, Levy. He was naturalized in Pennsylvania 24 Sep. 1770. He was from Philadelphia. He was a Jew.

Marks, Philip. He was naturalized in New Jersey 28 Apr. 1762.

Marks, Thomas. He was naturalized in Jamaica 10 May1735. He was a free Negro.

Marks, William. He was naturalized in Pennsylvania 11 Apr. 1761. He was from Berks County.

Marlin, John. He was naturalized in New Jersey 6 Dec. 1769.

Marolff, Rudolph. He was naturalized in Pennsylvania 11–13 Apr. 1743. He was from Philadelphia County.

Marot, Philip. He was naturalized in New Jersey 28 Mar. 1749.

Marquat, Hens. He was naturalized in New York 11 Sep. 1761.

Marques, Joseph Rodrigues. He was naturalized in Jamaica 16 Aug. 1703.

Marques, Isack Rodrigues. He was naturalized in Jamaica 29 July 1690.

Marques, Isaque Rodrigues. He was endenized in New York 16 Oct. 1695. He was a merchant.

Marquetand, Lorenze. He was naturalized in Pennsylvania 10 Apr. 1760.

Marritt, Nicholas. He was naturalized in Pennsylvania 11 Apr. 1761. He was from Lancaster County.

Marseau, Jacques. He was born at Chaine, Poitou, France, the son of Gabriel Marseau and Francoise Mounart. He was naturalized in South Carolina ca. 1696.

Marsequie, Honore. He was naturalized in New York 20 May 1769. He was a merchant from New York City.

Marshall, Frederick. He was naturalized in Pennsylvania 20 Sep. 1766. He was from Saxony.

Marshall, Teterick. He was naturalized in Pennsylvania 10 Apr. 1757.

Marshon, Henry. He was naturalized in New Jersey 16 Aug. 1733. He lived in Hunterdon County.

Marstaller, Frederick. He was naturalized in Pennsylvania 19 May 1739. He was from Philadelphia County.

Marteen, James. He was naturalized in Jamaica 20 Aug. 1701.

Martell, Laurent. He was naturalized in Jamaica 13 Nov. 1756.

Martens, Jooris. He took the oath of allegiance in Breucklijn, Kings County, New York 26–30 Sep. 1687. He was a native of the colony.

Marter, Valentine. He was naturalized in Maryland 10 Apr. 1762. He was a German from Frederick County.

Martiau, Nicholas. He was endenized in England. Reference to such was made 26 Mar. 1656 in James City County, Virginia and recorded in Northampton County, Virginia 22 Nov. 1656.

Martin, Abdelo. He and his children were made denizens in Maryland 17 Mar. 1667. He was a subject of the crown of Spain.

Martin, Ambroise. He was an Acadian and took the oath of allegiance in Apr. 1730.

Martin, Baptiste. He was an Acadian and took the oath of allegiance in Apr. 1730.

Martin, Charles. He was naturalized in Maryland 29 Mar. 1775. He was a German.

Martin, Charles. He was an Acadian and took the oath to George II at Annapolis River, Nova Scotia in Dec. 1729.

Martin, Diederick. He was naturalized in Pennsylvania 10 Sep. 1761. He was from Berks County.

Martin, Etienne. He was an Acadian and took the oath to George II at Annapolis River, Nova Scotia in Dec. 1729.

Martin, Everhart. He was naturalized in Pennsylvania 25 Sep. 1758.

Martin, Frederick. He was naturalized in Pennsylvania 10 Sep. 1761. He was from Lancaster County.

Martin, George. He was naturalized in Maryland 11 Sep. 1765. He lived in Germany Township, York County, Pennsylvania and was a German.

Martin, George. He was naturalized in Pennsylvania 11 Apr. 1763. He was from Charlestown Township, Philadelphia County.

Martin, Jacob. He was naturalized in Pennsylvania 11 Apr. 1761. He was from Lancaster County.

Martin, Jacob. He took the oath of allegiance at Mobile, West Florida 2 Oct. 1764.

Martin, James. He was naturalized in London. He was the son of James Martin and his wife Mary. He was born in Rochelle, France. His certificate was recorded in Jamaica 8 Apr. 1699.

Martin, Jean. He was naturalized in New York 16 Aug. 1715. He was a yeoman from New Rochelle.

Martin, Jenda. He was naturalized in Jamaica 30 June 1731.

Martin, John. He was naturalized in New York 24 Mar. 1772.

Martin, John. He was naturalized in Virginia 12 May 1705.

Martin, John. He was endenized in Virginia 7 Nov. 1666. He was born in Denmark.

Martin, John. He was naturalized in Maryland 15 Sep. 1773. He was a German.

Martin, John. He was naturalized in Pennsylvania 24 Sep. 1753. He was from Philadelphia County.

Martin, John. He was naturalized in Pennsylvania 10 Sep. 1761. He was from Philadelphia County.

Martin, Martin. He was naturalized in Pennsylvania 10 Sep. 1761. He was from Lancaster County.

Martin, Mathieu. He took the oath of allegiance at Port Royal, Nova Scotia 16 Aug. 1695.

Martin, Michel. He was an Acadian and took the allegiance in Apr. 1730.

Martin, Michel. He was an Acadian and took the oath to George II at Annapolis River, Nova Scotia in Dec. 1729.

Martin, Moses. He was naturalized in Jamaica 24 Nov. 1724.

Martin, Nicholas. He was naturalized in Pennsylvania 24 Sep. 1755. He was from Lancaster County.

Martin, Paul. He was an Acadian and took the oath of allegiance in Apr. 1730.

Martin, Piere. He took the oath of allegiance at Mobile, West Florida 2 Oct. 1764.

Martin, Pierre. He took the oath of allegiance at Port Royal, Nova Scotia 16 Aug. 1695.

Martin, Pierre. He was an Acadian and took the oath of allegiance in Apr. 1730.

Martin, Pierre Amaitie. He was an Acadian and took the oath of allegiance in Apr. 1730.

Martin, Rene. He was an Acadian and took the oath to George II at Annapolis River, Nova Scotia in Dec. 1729.

Martin, William. He was naturalized in Virginia 7 Nov. 1766. He was a Dutchman and had previously lived on the Delaware Bay.

Martin dit Barnabe, Rene. He was an Acadian and took the oath to George II at Annapolis River, Nova Scotia Dec. 1729.

Martinez, Benjamin Vaz. He was naturalized in Jamaica in July 1690.

Martini, John. He was naturalized in South Carolina 12 May 1748.

Martins, Abraham. He was naturalized in Jamaica 29 Mar. 1704.

Martins, Leah. She was naturalized in Jamaica 31 May 1743. She was a Jewess.

Martins, Moses. He was naturalized in Jamaica in 1740–41. He was a Jew.

Martiny, Joseph. He was naturalized in Jamaica 8 Jan. 1756. He was from St. Mary's Parish.

Marton, Matthew. He was naturalized in New Jersey 6 Dec. 1769.

Marts, Bastian. He was naturalized in Maryland 6 Sep. 1765. He was a German from Frederick County.

Marts, George. He was naturalized in Maryland 11 Sep. 1765.

Marts, Theobald. He was naturalized in Maryland 15 Apr. 1761.

Martz, Peter. He was naturalized in Maryland 23 Apr. 1772. He was a German.

Mary, Christian. He was naturalized in Pennsylvania 6 Feb. 1730/1. He was from Chester County.

Maryre, James. He was naturalized in Virginia 26 Apr. 1743. He was born in France and was a clerk, i.e. a minister. He resided in Spotsylvania County and had been in Virginia seven years. He also appeared incorrectly as Johannes Maryre.

Marzahl, Philip. He was naturalized in Maryland 11 May 1774. He was a German.

Mascarene, John Paul. He was born at Castres, France, the son of John and Margaret Mascarene. He was naturalized 14 Mar. 1706/7. He came to Nova Scotia and later New England.

Mason, Christopher. He was naturalized in Pennsylvania 11 Apr. 1763. He was from Whitemarsh Township, Philadelphia County.

Mason, John. He was naturalized in Pennsylvania in Sep. 1740. He lived in Philadelphia.

Massaw, Peter. He was naturalized in Virginia 12 May 1705.

Masser, Leonard. He was naturalized in Maryland in Apr. 1749. He was from Frederick County.

Masser, Michael. He was naturalized in Pennsylvania 25 Sep. 1769. He was from Mockamixon, Bucks County.

Masserly, Daniel. He was naturalized in Pennsylvania 10–12 Apr. 1762. He was from York County.

Massier, Jaque. He was an Acadian and took the oath to George II at Annapolis River, Nova Scotia in the winter of 1730.

Masson, John. He was naturalized in New York 6 July 1723.

Massoner, Tittrick. He was naturalized in Maryland in Apr. 1749. He was from Frederick County.

Massonneau, Jacob. He was endenized 12 Sep. 1698. He came to New York.

Mast, Jacob. He was naturalized in Pennsylvania 11–13 Apr. 1743. He was from Lancaster County.

Master, Christopher. He was naturalized in Pennsylvania 10–12 Apr. 1762. He was from Berks County.

Mastin, Cornelis. He took the oath of naturalization in New York 1 Sep. 1687 in Ulster County.

Matchker, Jacob. He was naturalized in New York 24 Nov. 1750.

Mateery, Nicholas. He was naturalized in Pennsylvania 24 Sep. 1762. He was from Berks County.

Materstock, Dedrich. He was naturalized in New York 8–9 Sep. 1715. He was from Ulster County.

Mather, John. He was naturalized in Pennsylvania 11 Apr. 1761. He was from Lancaster County.

Mathews, Henry. He was naturalized in Maryland 6 June 1674. He was Swedish.

Mathews, Jacob. He and his children, George Mathews, Margarett Mathews, Maudlin Mathews, and Catherine Mathews, were naturalized in Maryland 4 June 1740. He was from Prince George's County and was born in Germany.

Mathias, Stephen. He was naturalized in Maryland 11 Apr. 1759.

Mathiason, Hendrick. He was made a denizen in Maryland 29 July 1661. He was Swedish and was late of New Amstel.

Mathiason, Mathias. He was naturalized in Maryland 22 May 1695. He was also known as Mathias Freeman. He lived in Cecil County.

Mathison, Henry. He was naturalized in Pennsylvania 25–27 Sep. 1740. He was from Philadelphia.

Mathys, Jury. He was naturalized in New York 28 Feb. 1715/6. He was from Albany County.

Matthews, John. He was naturalized in Jamaica 5 Sep. 1717. He was the son of John Matthews.

Matthews, Mary. She was naturalized in Jamaica 5 Sep. 1717. She was the daughter of John Matthews.

Matthies, John. He took the oath of naturalization in New York 1 Sep. 1687 in Ulster County.

Matthison, Matthis. He took the oath of naturalization in New York 1 Sep. 1687 in Ulster County. He was styled captain.

Matthysen, Jan. He was naturalized in New York 8–9 Sep. 1715. He was from Ulster County.

Matton, Anthony. He was naturalized in Virginia 12 May 1705.

Mattoone, John. He was naturalized in Virginia 20 Sep. 1673.

Mattos, Phinelias. He was naturalized in Jamaica 25 Aug. 1741. He was a Jew.

Mattson, Andrew. He was naturalized in Maryland 16 Nov. 1683.

Mattysen, Jan. He was naturalized in New York 8–9 Sep. 1715. He was from Ulster County.

Matulick, Gerome. He took the oath of allegiance at Mobile, West Florida 2 Oct. 1764.

Mauk, Peter. He was naturalized in Frederick County, Virginia 8 Aug. 1745. He was born in Germany.

Mauk, Peter. He was naturalized in Frederick County, Virginia 5 May 1747.

Maul, Bartholomew. He was naturalized in Pennsylvania 25–27 Sep. 1740. He was from Philadelphia County.

Maul, Conrad. He was naturalized in Pennsylvania 10–12 Apr. 1762. He was from Lancaster County.

Maupin, Gabriel. He was naturalized in Virginia 12 May 1703.

Maurer, Andreas. He was naturalized in Pennsylvania 11 Apr. 1771. He was from New Cushahoppen Township, Philadelphia County.

Maurer, Andreas. He was naturalized in Pennsylvania 11 Apr. 1771. He was from New Cushahoppen Township, Philadelphia County.

Maurer, Christian. He was naturalized in Pennsylvania 24 Sep. 1762. He was from Philadelphia County.

Maurer, George. He was naturalized in Frederick County, Virginia 14 Aug. 1767.

Maurer, George Ernst. He was naturalized in Pennsylvania 10 Sep. 1761. He was from Berks County.

Maurer, Henry. He was naturalized in Pennsylvania 11 Apr. 1763. He was from Lancaster Township, Lancaster County.

Maurer, Henry. He was naturalized in Pennsylvania 11 Apr. 1763. He was from Lancaster Township, Lancaster County.

Maurer, Philip. He was naturalized in Pennsylvania 10 Sep. 1761. He was from Lancaster County.

Mauritts, Jacob. He claimed to have been a denizen for eight years in New York in 1677.

Maurole, Joseph. He was an Acadian and took the oath of allegiance in Apr. 1730.

Mauty, John Daniel. He was naturalized in Pennsylvania 11 Apr. 1763. He was from Philadelphia.

Mauyer, John. He was naturalized in Pennsylvania 11 Apr. 1761. He was from Northampton County.

Mauze, Elias. He, his wife Elizabeth Mauze, daughter Margaret Mauze, and son Elias Mauze were endenized in England 14 Oct. 1681. They came to New York.

Mawrer, Frederick. He was naturalized in Pennsylvania 11–13 Apr. 1743. He was from Philadelphia County.

Mawrer, Jacob. He was naturalized in Pennsylvania 11–13 Apr. 1743. He was from Philadelphia County.

May, Daniel. He was naturalized in North Carolina 23 Mar. 1763. He was from Rowan County.

May, Gaspar. He was naturalized in Nova Scotia 6 July 1758.

May, George. He was naturalized in Pennsylvania 24 Sep. 1762. He was from Berks County.

May, Frederic. He was naturalized in Pennsylvania 24–25 Sep. 1764. He was from Upper Salford Township, Philadelphia County.

May, Leonard. He was naturalized in Pennsylvania 10 Apr. 1760.

May, Peter. He was naturalized in Pennsylvania 24–25 Sep. 1764. He was from Upper Hannover Township, Philadelphia County.

May, Peter. He was naturalized in New York 8–9 Sep. 1715. He was from Ulster County.

Mayer, Christian. He was naturalized in Rhode Island in May 1755 and took the oath on 10 May. He was a native of Luxembourg in Germany and was a Protestant. He made potashes in Newport.

Mayer, Felix. He was naturalized in New York 11 Sep. 1761.

Mayer, Frederick. He was naturalized in Pennsylvania 10 Apr. 1760.

Mayer, George. He was naturalized in Pennsylvania 10 Apr. 1760.

Mayer, George Nicholas. He was naturalized in Pennsylvania 25 Sep. 1752. He was from Philadelphia.

Mayer, Hans Geerlag. He was naturalized in New York 11 Sep. 1761.

Mayer, Hendrick. He was naturalized in New York 11 Sep. 1761.

Mayer, Henry. He was naturalized in Pennsylvania 10 Sep. 1761. He was from Lancaster County.

Mayer, Jacob. He was naturalized in New York 11 Sep. 1761.

Mayer, Jacob. He was naturalized in Pennsylvania 26 Feb. 1773. He was a peruke maker in Philadelphia.

Mayer, Johan Geerlag. He was naturalized in New York 11 Sep. 1761.

Mayer, Johannes. He was naturalized in New Jersey in 1768.

Mayer, Johannes. He was naturalized in Pennsylvania 24 Sep. 1746. He was from Lancaster County.

Mayer, Johannes. He was naturalized in Pennsylvania 6 Feb. 1730/1. He was from Philadelphia County.

Mayer, John Gerhard. He was naturalized in Jamaica 2 Feb. 1737/8.

Mayer, Joseph. He was naturalized in New York 11 Sep. 1761.

Mayer, Leonard. He was naturalized in Pennsylvania 10 Apr. 1760.

Mayer, Ludwick. He was naturalized in Pennsylvania 10–12 Apr. 1762. He was from York County.

Mayer, Nicholas. He was naturalized in Pennsylvania 10 Apr. 1760.

Mayer, Philip. He was naturalized in Pennsylvania 10–12 Apr. 1762. He was from Berks County.

Mayer, Solomon. He was naturalized in New York 11 Sep. 1761.

Mayer, Ulrich. He was naturalized in Pennsylvania 6 Feb. 1730/1. He was from Philadelphia County.

Mayer, Valentine. He was naturalized in Pennsylvania 11 Apr. 1761. He was from Berks County.

Maylander, John Daniel. He was naturalized in Pennsylvania 10 Sep. 1761. He was from Philadelphia County.

Maynadier, Daniel. He and his children, Daniel Maynadier and Jane Maynadier, were naturalized in Maryland 30 Oct. 1727. They were French. He was a minister. They lived in Talbot County.

Maynard, Frederick. He was naturalized in Pennsylvania 24 Sep. 1759.

Mayor, John Jeremiah. He was naturalized in Maryland 17 July 1765. He was a German from Frederick, Maryland.

Mayou, William. He was naturalized in Jamaica 25 Apr. 1693.

Mayrer, Hans Adam. He was naturalized in Pennsylvania 24 Sep. 1741. He was from Philadelphia County.

Mayster, Melchoir. He was naturalized in Pennsylvania 24 Sep. 1745. He was from Philadelphia County.

Mayz, Andreas. He was naturalized in Pennsylvania 11–13 Apr. 1743. He was from Bucks County.

Maze, Henry. He was naturalized in Augusta County, Virginia 16 Nov. 1774.

Maze, Nicholas. He was naturalized in Augusta County, Virginia 16 Nov. 1774.

Mazeres, John. He was naturalized in Virginia 12 May 1705.

Mazicq, Isaac. He was born at L'Isle of Re, France, the son of Paul Mazicq and Helesabeth Vanewick. His wife was Marianne LeSerrurier. Their daughter was Marie Anne Mazicq born in South Carolina. They were naturalized in South Carolina 10 Mar. 1696/7. He was a merchant. He also appeared as Isaac Mazyck.

Mebins, Daniel. He was naturalized in Virginia 12 May 1705.

Mecklein, John. He was naturalized in Pennsylvania 24 Sep. 1763. He was from New Hannover Township, Philadelphia County.

Mecklenburgh, Charles Ludwick. He was naturalized in Pennsylvania 10 Sep. 1761. He was from Philadelphia County.

Meddert, Henrick. He was naturalized in Maryland 3 May 1774. He was a German.

Medina, Moses de. He was naturalized in Jamaica 26 Feb. 1703. He was a Jew.

Meem, John. He was naturalized in Pennsylvania 26–27 Sep. 1743. He was from Philadelphia County.

Meenich, Jacob. He was naturalized in Pennsylvania 10 & 23 Apr. 1764. He was from Bethel Township, Berks County.

Mees, George. He was naturalized in Pennsylvania 10 Sep. 1761. He was from Lancaster County.

Meeshter, David. He was naturalized in Pennsylvania 11–13 Apr. 1743. He was from Philadelphia County.

Meesmer, Peter. He was naturalized in Pennsylvania 10 Sep. 1761. He was from Northampton County.

Meet, Pieter. He took the oath to the King 21–26 Oct. 1664 after the conquest of New Netherland.

Meeth, Philip. He was naturalized in Pennsylvania 10 Apr. 1760.

Megapolensis, Johannes. He took the oath to the King 21–26 Oct. 1664 after the conquest of New Netherland.

Megapolensis, Samuel. He took the oath to the King 21–26 Oct. 1664 after the conquest of New Netherland.

Mehl, Barbara. She was naturalized in Pennsylvania 10–12 Apr. 1762. She was from Philadelphia County.

Meily, Jacob. He was naturalized in Pennsylvania 24 Sep. 1746. He was from Lancaster County.

Meindertzen, Jan. He took the oath to the King 21–26 Oct. 1664 after the conquest of New Netherland.

Meindertzen, Jan. He took the oath to the King 21–26 Oct. 1664 after the conquest of New Netherland.

Meintzer, George. He was naturalized in Pennsylvania 10 & 23 Apr. 1764. He was from Robeson Township, Berks County.

Meintzer, John. He petitioned for naturalization in New York 16 Nov. 1739.

Meintzer, Lawrence. He petitioned for naturalization in New York 16 Nov. 1739.

Meir, Peter. He was naturalized in New Jersey in 1761. He was born in Germany. He had been in the colony seven years. He also appeared as Peter Meyer and Peter Meier.

Meixell, Martin. He was naturalized in Pennsylvania 16 May 1769. He was from Leacock Township, Lancaster County.

Melchor, John. He was naturalized in Pennsylvania 11 Apr. 1761. He was from Northampton County.

Melancon, Jean. He was an Acadian and took the oath to the King at the Mines, Pisiquit, Nova Scotia 31 Oct. 1727.

Melancon, Joseph. He was an Acadian and took the oath to the King at the Mines, Pisiquit, Nova Scotia 31 Oct. 1727.

Melancon, Paul. He was an Acadian and took the oath to the King at the Mines, Pisiquit, Nova Scotia 31 Oct. 1727.

Melancon, Philip. He was an Acadian and took the oath to the King at the Mines, Pisiquit, Nova Scotia 31 Oct. 1727.

Melanson, Amand. He was an Acadian and took the oath at Annapolis in Dec. 1729.

Melanson, Ambroise. He was an Acadian and took the oath at Annapolis in Dec. 1729.

Melanson, Charles. He was an Acadian and took the oath to George II at Annapolis River, Nova Scotia in Dec. 1729.

Melanson, Jean. He was an Acadian and took the oath of allegiance in Dec. 1729.

Melanson, Jean. He was an Acadian and took the oath of allegiance in Apr. 1730.

Melanson, Jean. He was an Acadian and took the oath of allegiance in Apr. 1730.

Melanson, Jean. He was an Acadian and took the oath of allegiance in Apr. 1730.

Melanson, Joseph. He was an Acadian and took the oath of allegiance in Apr. 1730.

Melanson, Paul. He was an Acadian and took the oath of allegiance in 31 Oct. 1727.

Melanson, Paul. He was an Acadian and took the oath of allegiance in Apr. 1730.

Melanson, Phillippe, Jr. He was an Acadian and took the oath of allegiance in Apr. 1730.

Melanson, Philippe. He was an Acadian and took the oath of allegiance in Apr. 1730.

Melanson, Pierre. He was an Acadian and took the oath to George II at the Mines, Pisiquit 31 Oct. 1727.

Melanson, Pierre. He was an Acadian and took the oath of allegiance in Apr. 1730. He was the son of Jean Melanson.

Melenson, Charle[s]. He was an Acadian and took the oath to George II at Annapolis River, Nova Scotia in Dec. 1729.

Melenson, Charles, Jr. He was an Acadian and took the oath to George II at Annapolis River, Nova Scotia in Dec. 1729.

Meleon, George. He was naturalized in Pennsylvania 24–25 Sep. 1764. He was from Mohyamensing Township, Philadelphia County.

Melford, Casper. He was naturalized in Pennsylvania 24 Sep. 1762. He was from Chester County.

Melford, John. He was naturalized in Pennsylvania 24 Sep. 1762. He was from Chester County.

Melihar, Leonard. He was naturalized in Pennsylvania in Sep. 1740. He was from Philadelphia County.

Melin, Simon. He was naturalized in New York 19 Oct. 1730.

Mell, Peter. He was naturalized in Pennsylvania 11–13 Apr. 1743. He was from Philadelphia County.

Mellado, Isaac Henriques. He was endenized in England 10 Dec. 1695. He settled in Barbados and was a Jew.

Mellanson, Baptiste. He was an Acadian and took the oath of allegiance in Apr. 1730.

Mellanson, Charles. He took the oath of allegiance at Port Royal, Nova Scotia 16 Aug. 1695.

Mellanson, Pierre. He was an Acadian and took the oath of allegiance in Apr. 1730.

Mellanson, Pierre. He was an Acadian and took the oath of allegiance in Apr. 1730.

Mellinner, Jacob. He was naturalized in Pennsylvania 11 Apr. 1761. He was from Lancaster County.

Mellon, Joseph. He took the oath of allegiance at Mobile, West Florida 2 Oct. 1764.

Mellow, David Henry. He was naturalized in New York 21 Jan. 1761. He was a mariner from New York City.

Melsbach, Nicholas. He was naturalized in New York 18 Oct. 1750. He was a farmer from Ulster County.

Melsbach, Peter. He was naturalized in New York 17 Oct. 1753. He was a farmer from Ulster County.

Melsbagh, Bartholomeus. He was naturalized in New Jersey 8 July 1730. He was born in Germany.

Melsbagh, Mathys. He was naturalized in New York 8 Nov. 1735.

Melsbagh, Philip. He was naturalized in New York 8 Nov. 1735.

Melyn, Isaac. He was endenized in New York 13 Jan. 1671/2.

Mementon, Abraham. He was naturalized in Jamaica 12 Oct. 1763.

Memin, Auguste. He was born at LaForge Nossay, Poitou, France, the son of Jean Memin and Marye Maisot. He was naturalized in South Carolina ca. 1696.

Mendes, Abigail. She was naturalized in Jamaica 29 Nov. 1743. She was a Jewess.

Mendes, Abraham DeSoza. He was endenized in London 9 Sep. 1670. He was from Jamaica.

Mendes, Abraham Pereira. He was naturalized in Jamaica 31 Aug. 1748. He was a Jew.

Mendes, Abraham. He was the [son] of Benjamin Pereira Mendes. He was naturalized in Jamaica 27 Nov. 1749/50. He was a Jew.

Mendes, David. He was naturalized in Jamaica 22 Mar. 1725/6.

Mendes, Esther. She was naturalized in Jamaica 26 Aug. 1746. She was a Jewess.

Mendes, Esther. She was naturalized in Jamaica 26 Aug. 1746. She was a Jewess.

Mendes, Esther Pereira. She was naturalized in Jamaica 23 Feb. 1742/3. She was a Jewess.

Mendes, Gabriel. He was naturalized in Jamaica 26 Aug. 1745. He was a Jew.

Mendes, Isaac. He was naturalized in Jamaica 29 Aug. 1726.

Mendes, Jacob Pereira. He was naturalized in Jamaica 23 Feb. 1742/3. He was a Jew.

Mendes, Joseph. He was endenized in England 25 Oct. 1667. He settled in Barbados and was a Jew.

Mendes, Judith. She was naturalized in Jamaica 26 Aug. 1746. She was a Jewess.

Mendes, Rachel. She was naturalized in Jamaica 26 Aug. 1746. She was a Jewess.

Mendes, Rachel Fernandes. She was naturalized in Jamaica 26 Aug. 1745. She was a Jewess.

Mendes, Raphael. He was naturalized in Jamaica 26 Feb. 1740/1. He was a Jew.

Mendes, Samuel Pereira. He was naturalized in Jamaica 21 June 1725.

Mendes, Samuel Pra. He was naturalized in Jamaica in Feb. 1748/9. He was a Jew.

Mendes, Sime. He was naturalized in Jamaica 28 Feb. 1743/4. He was a Jew.
Mendes, Solomon. He was naturalized in Jamaica 25 Oct. 1732.
Mendes, Solomon. He was naturalized in Jamaica 26 Feb. 1740/1. He was a Jew.
Mendez, David. He was naturalized in Jamaica 26 May 1742. He was a Jew.
Mendez, Abraham Rodriques. He was naturalized in Jamaica 29 July 1690.
Mendez, Jeosua Rodriques. He was naturalized in Jamaica 23 Nov. 1688.
Mendez, Moses. He was naturalized in Jamaica 20 Mar. 1720/1.
Mendez, Menasses. He was endenized in England 11 Oct. 1687. He settled in Barbados and was
     a Jew.
Mendez, Samuel. He was naturalized in Jamaica 27 May 1742.
Mendis, Jacob. He was naturalized in South Carolina 10 Mar. 1696/7. He was a merchant.
Menerran, Daniel. He was endenized in New York 23 Dec. 1695.
Menetries, David. He was naturalized in Virginia 12 May 1705.
Menfrulle, Jean. He was endenized in New York 6 Feb. 1695/6.
Meng, Melchior. He was naturalized in Pennsylvania 25 Sep. 1751. He was from Philadelphia
     County.
Meng, Peter. He was naturalized in Pennsylvania 24–25 Sep. 1764. He was from Heidelberg
     Township, Lancaster County.
Mengen, Georgius Phillippus. He was naturalized in Maryland 15 Sep. 1762. He was from
     Baltimore County.
Mengen, Peter. He was naturalized in Maryland 31 Aug. 1757.
Menges, Hieronimus. He was naturalized in New York 8–9 Sep. 1715. He was from Ulster
     County.
Menges, Johanis. He was naturalized in New York 8–9 Sep. 1715. He was from Ulster County.
Mengs, Adam. He was naturalized in Pennsylvania 24–25 Sep. 1764. He was from Lebanon
     Township, Lancaster County.
Menold, Martin. He was naturalized in New York 18 Oct. 1765. He was a shoemaker from New
     York City.
Mens, Jacob. He took the oath to the King 21–26 Oct. 1664 after the conquest of New Netherland.
Mens, Johannes. He took the oath to the King 21–26 Oct. 1664 after the conquest of New
     Netherland.
Menti, Firdinand. He was naturalized in New York 17 Jan. 1715/6. He was from Albany County.
Menton, Andrew. He was naturalized in New Jersey in 1760. He also appeared as Andreas
     Mentong. He was born in the Palatinate.
Mentries, David. He was naturalized in Virginia 12 May 1705.
Mercereau, Daniel. He petitioned for denization in New York 20 June 1695.
Mercier, Bartholomew. He was endenized in New York 17 Oct. 1685.
Mercier, Catherine. She was endenized in New York 17 Oct. 1685.
Mercier, Henry. He was endenized in New York 17 Oct. 1685.
Mercier, Isaac. He petitioned for naturalization in New York 19 Aug. 1687.
Mercier, Isaac. He petitioned for naturalization in New York 25 Oct. 1715. He was from New
     Rochelle.
Mercier, Samuel. He was endenized in New York 3 Sep. 1686.
Mercier, Susanna. She was naturalized in New York 20 Sep. 1728. She was a widow.
Merckell, Conrod. He was naturalized in Maryland 13 Apr. 1761. He was a baker in Annapolis,
     Md.
Merdele, Christoph. He was naturalized in New York 20 Mar. 1762.
Merdele, Michel. He was naturalized in New York 20 Mar. 1762.
Meriers, Peter. He was naturalized in Jamaica 30 Sep. 1709.
Merkel, Johannes. He was naturalized in New Jersey in 1764.
Merkell, George. He was naturalized in Pennsylvania 24–25 Sep. 1764. He was from Richmond
     Township, Berks County.
Merkler, Christopher. He was naturalized in New York 8–9 Sep. 1715. He was from Ulster
     County.
Merkley, Jacob. He was naturalized in New York 8 Mar. 1773.
Merkwat, Hans Jury. He was naturalized in New York 23 Dec. 1765.

Merlin, George. He was naturalized in Nova Scotia 6 July 1758.

Merlin, Paul. He was endenized in England 19 Aug. 1688. He petitioned for naturalization in New York 19 Aug. 1687.

Merllet, John Peter. He was naturalized in Jamaica 14 June 1769.

Merriott, George. He was naturalized in Frederick County, Virginia 1 Aug. 1769.

Merrit, William. He took the oath to the King 21–26 Oct. 1664 after the conquest of New Netherland.

Mers, Jan Coonraad. He was naturalized in Jamaica 28 June 1766.

Merschet, Jean Peletrau. He petitioned for naturalization in New York 19 Aug. 1687.

Mersteller, John George. He was naturalized in Pennsylvania 11 Apr. 1741. He was from Bucks County.

Mersurey, Francois. He took the oath of allegiance at Mobile, West Florida 2 Oct. 1764.

Merte, Johanis. He was naturalized in New York 8–9 Sep. 1715. He was from Ulster County. His name could also be Johanis Merle.

Mertz, John Nicholas. He was naturalized in Pennsylvania 11–13 Apr. 1743. He was from Philadelphia County.

Merviel, David. He was naturalized in Virginia 12 May 1705.

Mesias, Isaac. He was naturalized in Jamaica 26 Jan. 1703/4.

Mesinger, Michael. He was naturalized in Pennsylvania 24 Sep. 1746. He was from Philadelphia County.

Mesner, Casper. He was naturalized in Pennsylvania 11 Apr. 1761. He was from Lancaster County.

Mesner, Christian. He was naturalized in Pennsylvania 11 Apr. 1761. He was from Lancaster County.

Mesquite, Abraham Bueno de. He was endenized in Barbados 14 Dec. 1694.

Mesquita, Benjamin de. He was endenized in Jamaica 23 June 1664. He was from Portugal.

Mesquitta, Jacob Fernandes. He was naturalized in Jamaica 26 Feb. 1740/1. He was a Jew.

Mesquitta, Moses, Sr. He was naturalized in Jamaica 27 Feb. 1749/50. He was a Jew.

Messcher, Adam Machielse. He took the oath of allegiance in Gravens End, Kings County, New York 26–30 Sep. 1687. He had been in the colony 40 years.

Messersmidt, Barbara. She was naturalized in Pennsylvania 24 Sep. 1762. She was from Lancaster County.

Messias, Moses. He was naturalized in Jamaica 1 Nov. 1687.

Metayer, Elias. He was naturalized in Jamaica 29 Mar. 1708.

Methet, Charles. He was naturalized in Maryland 28 Apr. 1772. He was a German.

Metsiger, Jacob. He was naturalized in New York 17 Apr. 1750. He was a yeoman from New York City.

Mettauer, John. He was naturalized in Pennsylvania 11 Apr. 1761. He was from Lancaster County.

Mettler, George. He was naturalized in Pennsylvania 11 Apr. 1761. He was from Berks County.

Metts, Jacob. He was naturalized in Pennsylvania 6 Feb. 1730/1. He was from Philadelphia County.

Metz, Bartholomew. He was naturalized in New York 3 May 1755.

Metzer, Jacob. He sought naturalization in New York 12 Nov. 1748.

Metzer, Jacob. He was naturalized in Pennsylvania 10 Apr. 1765. He was from Lancaster Township, Lancaster County.

Metzger, George. He was naturalized in Pennsylvania 24 Sep. 1753. He was from Lancaster County.

Metzler, Daniel. He was naturalized in Maryland 10 Sep. 1762.

Metzler, John. He was naturalized in Pennsylvania 24–25 Sep. 1764. He was from Germantown Township, Philadelphia County.

Meyars, Jacob. He was naturalized in New York 16 Feb. 1771.

Meyer, Abraham. He was naturalized in Pennsylvania 11–13 Apr. 1743. He was from Philadelphia County.

Meyer, Abraham. He was naturalized in Pennsylvania 11–13 Apr. 1743. He was from Philadelphia County.

Meyer, Adolph. He was naturalized in Pennsylvania 10 Apr. 1757.

Meyer, Christian. He was naturalized in Pennsylvania 11–13 Apr. 1743. He was from Philadelphia County.

Meyer, Christian. He was naturalized in Pennsylvania 11 Apr. 1761. He was from Philadelphia County.

Meyer, Christian. He was naturalized in New York 8–9 Sep. 1715. He was from Ulster County.

Meyer, Christopher. He was naturalized in New York 30 July 1747. He was a cartman from New York City.

Meyer, Christopher, Jr. He was naturalized in Pennsylvania 11–13 Apr. 1743. He was from Philadelphia County.

Meyer, Detrick. He was naturalized in Pennsylvania 10–12 Apr. 1762. He was from York County.

Meyer, Felix. He was naturalized in New York 3 July 1759.

Meyer, Fredrich. He was naturalized in New York 8–9 Sep. 1715. He was from Ulster County.

Meyer, Friedrich. He was naturalized in Maryland 11 Apr. 1759.

Meyer, Frederick. He was naturalized in Maryland 12 Sep. 1759.

Meyer, Frederick. He was naturalized in Pennsylvania 13 May 1768. He was from Dover Township, York County.

Meyer, George. He was naturalized in Maryland 9 Apr. 1760. He was from Baltimore County.

Meyer, George. He was naturalized in Pennsylvania 11–13 Apr. 1743. He was from Philadelphia County.

Meyer, George Ludwick. He was naturalized in Pennsylvania 10–12 Apr. 1762. He was from Lancaster County.

Meyer, Gerlach. He was naturalized in New York 3 July 1759.

Meyer, Hendrich. He was naturalized in New York 28 Feb. 1715/6. He was from Albany County.

Meyer, Henrick. He was naturalized in Maryland 13 Sep. 1768. He was a German.

Meyer, Hans. He was naturalized in Pennsylvania 11–13 Apr. 1743. He was from Philadelphia County.

Meyer, Henry. He was naturalized in Pennsylvania 24 Sep. 1755.

Meyer, Isaac. He was naturalized in Pennsylvania 11–13 Apr. 1743. He was from Philadelphia County.

Meyer, Jacob. He was naturalized in Pennsylvania 11 Apr. 1761. He was from York County.

Meyer, John. He was naturalized in Maryland 14 Apr. 1762. He was a German.

Meyer, John. He was naturalized in Pennsylvania 24 Sep. 1755. He was from Berks County.

Meyer, John. He was naturalized in Pennsylvania 11 Apr. 1761. He was from Lancaster County.

Meyer, John. He was naturalized in Pennsylvania 24 Sep. 1763. He was from Shrewsbury Township, York County.

Meyer, John George. He was naturalized in Pennsylvania in Sep. 1740. He lived in Philadelphia County.

Meyer, John George. He was naturalized in Pennsylvania 24 Sep. 1760. He was from Philadelphia County.

Meyer, Thomas. He was naturalized in Pennsylvania 24–25 Sep. 1764. He was from Philadelphia.

Meyerer, Michael. He was naturalized in Maryland 17 Sep. 1751.

Meyers, Salomon. He was naturalized in New York 6 July 1723.

Meynart, Samuel. He was endenized in New York 29 July 1696.

Meyor, Peter. He was made a denizen in Maryland 22 July 1661. He was Swedish and was late of New Amstel. He brought his wife and children with him.

Michael, Christopher. He was naturalized in Maryland 28 Sep. 1763. He was a German from Frederick County.

Michael, Conrod. He was naturalized in North Carolina 22 Sep. 1763. He was from Rowan County and a German.

Michael, Andrew. He was naturalized in Maryland 11 Apr. 1764. He was a German.

Michael, Christopher. He was naturalized in Maryland 26 Sep. 1765. He was a German.

Michael, Jacob. He was naturalized in Maryland 16 Sep. 1773. He was a German.

Michael, Michael. He was naturalized in Maryland 10 Sep. 1761.

Michael, Nicholas. He was naturalized in Maryland 21 Sep. 1763. He was a German from Frederick County.

Michael, William. He was naturalized in Maryland 10 Sep. 1761.

Michaell, John. He was naturalized in Virginia in Apr. 1679. He could be identical with the John Michael of the county of Northampton County, New England [sic., i.e. Virginia] whose name was to be inserted into a naturalization bill in England on 13 June 1663.

Michaud, Abraham. He was the son of Jean and Catherine Michaud of Videdieu d'Onai, Poitou, France. His wife was Ester Michaud, the daughter of Elie and Sara Jodon, was born at L'Isle de Re, France. Their children were Jeane Michaud, Ester Michaud, and Charlotte Michaud who were born in South Carolina. They were naturalized in South Carolina ca. 1696.

Michaud, Honore. He was born at Tour de Pe, Switzerland, the son of Jean Michaud. He was naturalized in South Carolina ca. 1696.

Michaud, Pierre. He was the son of Jean and Catherine Michaud of Videdieu d'Onai, Poitou, France. His wife was Sara Michaud, daughter of Jacques and Elizabet Bertomeau, and the widow of Elie Jodon. She was born at L'Isle de Re, France. His stepson was Daniel Jodan, the son of Elie and Sara Jodon, was born at L'Isle de Re, France. They were naturalized in South Carolina ca. 1696.

Michaux, Abraham. He was naturalized in Virginia 12 May 1705.

Micheelson, Clement. He was made a denizen in Maryland 29 July 1661. He was Swedish and was late of New Amstel.

Micheelson, Jacob. He was made a denizen in Maryland 30 July 1661. He was Dutch and was late of New Amstel.

Michel, Barnett. He was naturalized in North Carolina 22 Sep. 1763. He was from Rowan County and was a German.

Michel, Francois. He was an Acadian and took the oath of allegiance in Apr. 1730.

Michel, Francois. He was an Acadian and took the oath of allegiance in Apr. 1730.

Michel, Jacob. He was naturalized in Pennsylvania 24–25 Sep./5 Oct. 1767. He was from York Township, York County.

Michel, Jacques. He took the oath of allegiance at Port Royal, Nova Scotia 16 Aug. 1695.

Michel, Joseph. He was an Acadian and took the oath of allegiance in Apr. 1730.

Michel, Louis. He was an Acadian and took the oath to the King at the Mines, Pisiquit, Nova Scotia 31 Oct. 1727.

Michel, Louis. He was an Acadian and took the oath of allegiance in Apr. 1730.

Michel, Michael. He was naturalized in Virginia 12 May 1705.

Michel, Paul. He was an Acadian and took the oath of allegiance in Apr. 1730.

Michell, Andries. He was naturalized in New York 21 Apr. 1748. He was a laborer in New York City.

Michell, Jacques. He was an Acadian and took the oath to George II at Annapolis River, Nova Scotia in Dec. 1729.

Michell, Jacques. He was an Acadian and took the oath to George II at Annapolis River, Nova Scotia in Dec. 1729.

Michell, Pierre. He was an Acadian and took the oath to George II at Annapolis River, Nova Scotia in Dec. 1729.

Michiel, Anthony. He was naturalized in New York 17 Jan. 1715/6. He was from Albany County.

Michiel, Hendrich. He was naturalized in New York 17 Jan. 1715/6. He was from Albany County.

Michiel, Hendrich, Jr. He was naturalized in New York 17 Jan. 1715/6. He was from Albany County.

Mickendurfer, Johannes. He was naturalized in Pennsylvania 11–13 Apr. 1743. He was from Bucks County.

Middag, Gerrit Aerts. He took the oath of allegiance in Breucklijn, Kings County, New York 26–30 Sep. 1687. He was a native of the colony.

Middag, John. He took the oath of naturalization in New York 1 Sep. 1687 in Ulster County.

Middagh, Joris. He was naturalized in New York 8–9 Sep. 1715. He was from Ulster County.

Middlecave, Peter. He was naturalized in Maryland 19 Oct. 1743.

Mieler, Bartell. He was naturalized in New York 6 July 1723

Mier, Gasper. He was naturalized in Maryland in 1742–1743.

Mierkin, Peter. He applied for naturalization in Pennsylvania 9 Mar. 1771. He was born in Hamburg, Germany. He was a sugar refiner. His naturalization was annulled.

Miers, Peter. He was naturalized in Pennsylvania 10 & 23 Apr. 1764. He was from Amwell, Hunterdon County, New Jersey.

Miesick, Fiet. He was naturalized in New York 17 Jan. 1715/6. He was from Albany County.

Migel, Nicolas. He was naturalized in New York 8–9 Sep. 1715. He was from Ulster County.

Migkielzen, Stoffel. He took the oath to the King 21–26 Oct. 1664 after the conquest of New Netherland.

Mikely, Jacob. He was naturalized in Pennsylvania 10 Sep. 1761. He was from Northampton County.

Mildeberger, Michael. He was naturalized in Pennsylvania 24–25 Sep. 1764. He was from Philadelphia.

Mildenbergen, Johan Adam. He was naturalized in New York 2 Aug. 1750. He was a husbandman from New York City.

Miley, George. He was naturalized in Pennsylvania 10 Sep. 1761. He was from York County.

Miley, John. He was naturalized in Pennsylvania 10 Sep. 1761. He was from Lancaster County.

Milheim, Christian. He was naturalized in Pennsylvania 10 Apr. 1760.

Miliade, Isaac Lopez. He was endenized in England 30 Nov. 1693. He settled in Barbados and was a Jew.

Mill, George. He was naturalized in Pennsylvania 13–15 Sep. 1748. He was from Philadelphia County.

Miller, Abraham. He and his children, Jacob Miller, Abraham Miller, Isaac Miller, Barbara Miller, and Louisa Miller, were naturalized in Maryland 3 May 1730. He was from Prince George's County and was born in Germany.

Miller, Adam. He was naturalized in Virginia 13 Mar. 1741/2. He was born in Shresheim, Germany.

Miller, Adam. He was naturalized in Maryland 25 Sep. 1772.

Miller, Adam. He was naturalized in Pennsylvania 11–13 Apr. 1743. He was from Lancaster County.

Miller, Adam. He was naturalized in Pennsylvania 11 Apr. 1749. He was from Philadelphia County.

Miller, Adam. He was naturalized in Pennsylvania 12 Apr. 1750. He was from Philadelphia County.

Miller, Andrew. He was naturalized in Pennsylvania 25 Sep. 1748. He was from Lancaster County.

Miller, Andrew. He was naturalized in Pennsylvania 25–26 Sep./4 Oct. 1749. He was from Philadelphia County.

Miller, Augustine. He was naturalized in Jamaica 23 Oct. 1708.

Miller, Charles. He was naturalized in Pennsylvania 30 May 1772. He was from Pipe Creek Hundred, Frederick County, Maryland.

Miller, Charles. He was naturalized in Pennsylvania 10 Sep. 1761. He was from Lancaster County.

Miller, Christian. He was naturalized in Maryland 11 Sep. 1765.

Miller, Christoffel. He was naturalized in New York 31 Dec. 1768.

Miller, Christopher. He was naturalized in Jamaica 13 Jan. 1760.

Miller, Christopher. He was naturalized in Pennsylvania 30 May 1772. He was from Pipe Creek Hundred, Frederick County, Maryland.

Miller, Conrad. He was naturalized in Pennsylvania 11 Apr. 1761. He was from Berks County.

Miller, Cornelius. He was naturalized in New York 3 May 1755.

Miller, David. He was naturalized in New York 8–9 Sep. 1715. He was from Ulster County.

Miller, Eronimus. He was naturalized in Pennsylvania 24 Sep. 1762. He was from Lancaster County.

Miller, Faltin. He was naturalized in New York 8 Mar. 1773.

Miller, Felix. He was naturalized in Pennsylvania 19 May 1739. He was from Philadelphia County.

Miller, Filb. He was naturalized in New York 8–9 Sep. 1715. He was from Ulster County.

Miller, Frederick. He was naturalized in Pennsylvania 10 Apr. 1767. He was from Frederick County, Maryland.

Miller, Frederick Casemer. He was naturalized in Pennsylvania 10 Sep. 1761. He was from Berks County.

Miller, George. He was naturalized in Pennsylvania 18 May 1739. He was from Lancaster County.

Miller, George. He was naturalized in Maryland 10 Sep. 1762.

Miller, George. He was naturalized in Pennsylvania 10 Sep. 1761. He was from Lancaster County.

Miller, George. He was naturalized in Pennsylvania 24 Sep. 1762. He was from Berks County.

Miller, Godfrey. He was naturalized in New York 24 Nov. 1750.

Miller, Gotlob. He was naturalized in Maryland 4 May 1774. He was a German.

Millet, Hans Hansen. He was naturalized in New Castle County, Delaware 21 Feb. 1682/3.

Miller, Henry. He was naturalized in Frederick County, Virginia 5 May 1747.

Miller, Henry. He was naturalized in Pennsylvania 25 Sep. 1744. He was from Philadelphia County.

Miller, Henry. He was naturalized in Pennsylvania 24–25 Sep./5 Oct. 1767. He was from Philadelphia.

Miller, Henry. He was naturalized in Pennsylvania 24 Sep. 1762. He was from Philadelphia County.

Miller, Henry. He was naturalized in Pennsylvania 11 Apr. 1763. He was from Mount Bethel Township, Northampton County.

Miller, Herman. He was naturalized in Pennsylvania 25 Mar. 1764. He was from York Township, York County.

Miller, Isaac. He was naturalized in Maryland 19 Oct. 1743.

Miller, Isaac. He was naturalized in Pennsylvania 25–27 Sep. 1740. He was from Philadelphia County.

Miller, Jacob. He was naturalized in Pennsylvania 14 Feb. 1729/30. He was from Lancaster County. He was styled black Jacob Miller.

Miller, Jacob. He was naturalized in Pennsylvania 24 Feb. 1729/30. He was from Lancaster County.

Miller, Jacob, Jr. He was naturalized in Pennsylvania 24 Feb. 1729/30. He was from Lancaster County.

Miller, Jacob. He was naturalized in Pennsylvania 11 Apr. 1741. He was from Philadelphia County.

Miller, Jacob. He was naturalized in Maryland 20 Oct. 1747.

Miller, Jacob. He was naturalized in Orange County, Virginia 24 Feb. 1742/3. He was born in the Dukedom of Wurttemburg.

Miller, Jacob, Jr. He was naturalized in Pennsylvania 14 Feb. 1729/30. He was from Lancaster County.

Miller, Jacob. He was naturalized in Pennsylvania 25–27 Sep. 1740. He was from Philadelphia County.

Miller, Jacob. He was naturalized in Pennsylvania 10 Apr. 1754. He was from Berks County.

Miller, Jacob. He was naturalized in Pennsylvania 24 Sep. 1770. He was from Bethlehem, Hunterdon County, New Jersey.

Miller, Jacob. He was naturalized in Pennsylvania 24 Sep. 1755. He was from Berks County.

Miller, Jacob. He was naturalized in Pennsylvania 11 Apr. 1761. He was from Lancaster County.

Miller, Jacob. He was naturalized in Pennsylvania 11 Apr. 1763. He was from Tolpohocken Township, Berks County.

Miller, Jacob. He was naturalized in New York 3 May 1755.

Miller, Johan. He was naturalized in New York 16 Dec. 1737.

Miller, Johan. He was naturalized in Pennsylvania 19 May 1739. He was from Philadelphia County.

Miller, Johan Christ. He was naturalized in New York 17 Jan. 1715/6. He was from Albany County.

Miller, Johannes. He was naturalized in New York in 1740–41.

Miller, Johannis. He was naturalized in New York 3 Jan. 1715/6. He was from Albany County.

Miller, John. He was naturalized in Maryland 19 Oct. 1743.

Miller, John. He was naturalized in Maryland in Apr. 1749. He was from Frederick County.

Miller, John. He was naturalized in Maryland 19 July 1765. He was a German from Frederick, Maryland.

Miller, John. He was naturalized in Maryland 11 Sep. 1765.

Miller, John. He was naturalized in Pennsylvania 11–12 Apr. 1744. He was from Lancaster County.

Miller, John. He was naturalized in Pennsylvania 24–25 Sep./5 Oct. 1767. He was from Macungy Township, Northampton County.

Miller, John. He was naturalized in Pennsylvania 10 Apr. 1766. He was from Earl Township, Lancaster County.

Miller, John. He was naturalized in Pennsylvania 10 Sep. 1761. He was from Lancaster County.

Miller, John. He was naturalized in Pennsylvania 24 Sep. 1762. He was from Berks County.

Miller, John. He was naturalized in Pennsylvania 24 Sep. 1762. He was from Lancaster County.

Miller, John. He was naturalized in New York 15 Oct. 1765. He was a doctor of physic from New York City.

Miller, John Adam. He was naturalized in Pennsylvania 24–25 Sep./5 Oct. 1767. He was from Plainfield Township, Northampton County.

Miller, John Adam. He was naturalized in Pennsylvania 25 Sep. 1758.

Miller, John Daniel. He was naturalized in New York 3 July 1759.

Miller, John Godfrey. He was naturalized in New York 3 May 1755.

Miller, John Nicholas. He was naturalized in Pennsylvania 24–25 Sep./5 Oct. 1767. He was from Plainfield Township, Northampton County.

Miller, John Frederick. He was naturalized in Halifax County, Virginia 18 Sep. 1753.

Miller, John Gerig. He was naturalized in New Jersey 8 July 1730. He was born in Germany.

Miller, John Jacob. He was naturalized in Pennsylvania 11 Apr 1761. He was from Philadelphia County.

Miller, John Peter. He was naturalized in Pennsylvania 10 & 23 Apr. 1764. He was from Upper Milford Township, Northampton County.

Miller, John Thomas. He was naturalized in New York 3 July 1759.

Miller, Leonard. He was naturalized in Pennsylvania 11–13 Apr. 1743. He was from Lancaster County.

Miller, Leonard. He was naturalized in Pennsylvania 10 Apr. 1754. He was from Lancaster County.

Miller, Leonard. He was naturalized in Pennsylvania 24 Sep. 1763. He was from Marlborough Township, Philadelphia County.

Miller, Leonard. He was naturalized in North Carolina 22 Sep. 1763. He was from Rowan County and was a German.

Miller, Lodowick. He was naturalized in Maryland 20 Oct. 1747.

Miller, Lodwig. He was naturalized in Maryland 23 Sep. 1762. He was a German from Frederick County.

Miller, Ludewic. He was naturalized in Pennsylvania 10–12 Apr. 1762. He was from York County.

Miller, Martin. He was naturalized in Pennsylvania 24–25 Sep./5 Oct. 1767. He was from Merion Township, Philadelphia County.

Miller, Martin. He was naturalized in Pennsylvania 14 Feb. 1729/30. He was from Lancaster County.

Miller, Mary Catherine. She was naturalized in New Jersey in 1769. She was the widow of John Michael Miller of Alloway Township, Salem County.

Miller, Michael. He was naturalized in Pennsylvania 25–26 Sep./4 Oct. 1749. He was from Lancaster County.

Miller, Michael. He was naturalized in Pennsylvania 24–25 Sep. 1764. He was from Cocalico Township, Lancaster County. He was a Moravian.

Miller, Michael. He was naturalized in Pennsylvania 24–25 Sep. 1764. He was from Antrim Township, Cumberland County.

Miller, Michael. He was naturalized in Pennsylvania 11 Apr. 1761. He was from Berks County.

Miller, Michael. He was naturalized in Pennsylvania 10 Apr. 1767. He was from Frederick County, Maryland.

Miller, Michael. He was naturalized in North Carolina 19 Sep. 1753. He was from Rowan County.

Miller, Nicholas. He was naturalized in Maryland 12 Apr. 1768. He was a German from Baltimore County.

Miller, Nicholas. He was naturalized in Pennsylvania 19 May 1739. He was from Lancaster County.

Miller, Paul. He was endenized in New York 29 Mar. 1693.

Miller, Paul. He was naturalized in New York 15 Nov. 1715. He was a mariner from New York City.

Miller, Peter, Jr. He was naturalized in Pennsylvania 10 Apr. 1753. He was from Philadelphia.

Miller, Philip. He was naturalized in New York in 1740–41.

Miller, Philip. He was naturalized in New York 20 Mar. 1762.

Miller, Philip. He was naturalized in Maryland 3 May 1774. He was a German.

Miller, Philip. He was naturalized in Pennsylvania 10–12 Apr. 1762. He was from York County.

Miller, Philip. He was naturalized in Pennsylvania 10–12 Apr. 1762. He was from Northampton County.

Miller, Philip Jacob. He was naturalized in Pennsylvania 10 Apr. 1767. He was from Frederick County, Maryland.

Miller, Sebastian. He was naturalized in Pennsylvania 11–13 Apr. 1743. He was from Philadelphia County.

Miller, Simon. He was naturalized in Maryland 4 Apr. 1761. He lived in Frederick County.

Miller, Valentine. He was naturalized in Pennsylvania 24 Sep. 1755. He was from Lancaster County.

Miller, Valentine. He was naturalized in Pennsylvania 24 Sep. 1762. He was from Philadelphia County.

Miller, William. He was naturalized in Pennsylvania 11 Apr. 1761. He was from Berks County.

Miller, William. He was naturalized in Pennsylvania 24–25 Sep. 1764. He was from Philadelphia.

Millet, John Peterson. He was endenized in New York 20 Apr. 1695.

Millon, Jean. He took the oath of allegiance at Mobile, West Florida 2 Oct. 1764.

Millur, Samuel. He was naturalized in New York 8 Mar. 1773.

Mills, Mary. She was granted letters of denization in Maryland 12 July 1672. She was the daughter of Peter Mills of St. Mary's County.

Mills, Peter. He was made a denizen in Maryland 23 Mar. 1668.

Mills, Peter. He was naturalized in Maryland 19 Apr. 1671. He lived in St. Mary's County and was Dutch.

Milsant, Jean Francois. He took the oath of allegiance at Mobile, West Florida 2 Oct. 1764.

Milner, Hans Michael. He was naturalized in New Jersey 8 Dec. 1744.

Mincke, Christian. He was naturalized in Pennsylvania 24–25 Sep. 1764. He was from Southwark Township, Philadelphia County.

Mincklaer, Josias. He was naturalized in New York 17 Jan. 1715/6. He was from Albany County.

Mincklaer, Killiaen. He was naturalized in New York 17 Jan. 1715/6. He was from Albany County.

Mind[e]rson, Burgar. He took the oath of naturalization in New York 1 Sep. 1687 in Ulster County.

Mindertse, Egbert. He took the oath to the King 21–26 Oct. 1664 after the conquest of New Netherland.

Minema, Benjamin. He was naturalized in New York 24 Oct. 1753. He was a clerk from Dutchess County.

Miner, Jacob. He was naturalized in Pennsylvania 24 Sep. 1755. He was from Easton Township, Easton [sic] County.

Mingle, John. He was naturalized in Pennsylvania 24 Sep. 1770. He was from Oxford, Sussex County, New Jersey.

Mininod, Francis. He was naturalized in Jamaica 23 Nov. 1699.

Mink, Christopher. He was naturalized in Pennsylvania 29 Mar. 1739. He was from Philadelphia County.

Minne, Albertt. He took the oath of allegiance in Orange County, New York 26 Sep. 1687.

Minne, Johannes. He took the oath of allegiance in Orange County, New York 26 Sep. 1687.

Minneley, Albert. He was naturalized in New York 23 Aug. 1715. He was a yeoman from Tappan.

Minot, Abraham. He was naturalized in Virginia 12 May 1705.

Minor, Doodes. He was naturalized in Virginia in Oct. 1673.

Minor, Peter. He was naturalized in Jamaica 19 May 1732.

Minser, Mark. He was naturalized in Pennsylvania 25–27 Sep. 1740. He was from Philadelphia County.

Minvielle, David. He was naturalized in England 19 Mar. 1705/6. He was the son of Peter and Paule Minvielle and was born at Montauban, France. He came to New York.

Minvielle, Gabriel. He was endenized in London 19 Aug. 1688.

Minville, Samuel de. He was naturalized in Virginia 25 Mar. 1703.

Miou, Charles. He took the oath of allegiance at Mobile, West Florida 2 Oct. 1764.

Miraill, Peter. He was naturalized in Rhode Island in Aug. 1753. He was born in France and had lately married in Newport. He had been there some years.

Miranda, Abraham Nunez. He was naturalized in Jamaica 19 Oct. 1738.

Miranda, David. He was naturalized in Jamaica 7 Dec. 1731.

Miranda, Isaac. He was naturalized in Jamaica 25 July 1735.

Miranda, Isaac Rodriques. He was naturalized in Jamaica 27 Aug. 1745. He was a Jew.

Miranda, Moses. He was naturalized in Jamaica 14 Dec. 1736.

Miranda, Moses Nunez. He was naturalized in Jamaica 15 Aug. 1745.

Miranda, Rebecca Nunes. She was naturalized in Jamaica 6 Feb. 1716/7.

Mirande, Joseph. He was naturalized in Jamaica 31 Oct. 1709.

Miratte, Jacques. He was an Acadian and took the oath of allegiance in Apr. 1730.

Mire, Abraham. He was naturalized in Pennsylvania 14 Feb. 1729/30. He was from Lancaster County.

Mire, Gasper. He was naturalized in Maryland 19 Oct. 1743.

Mire, Jacob. He was naturalized in Maryland 21 Sep. 1762. He was a German.

Mire, Jacob. He was naturalized in Pennsylvania 14 Feb. 1729/30. He was from Lancaster County.

Mire, John. He was naturalized in Maryland 15 Sep. 1762. He was from Frederick County.

Mire, John. He was naturalized in Pennsylvania 14 Feb. 1729/30. He was from Lancaster County.

Mire, Michael. He was naturalized in Pennsylvania 14 Feb. 1729/30. He was from Lancaster County.

Mire, Roody. He was naturalized in Pennsylvania 14 Feb. 1729/30. He was from Lancaster County.

Miromon, Francis. He was naturalized in Virginia 12 May 1705.

Mirry, Sebastian. He was naturalized in Pennsylvania 19 May 1739. He was from Philadelphia County.

Miseroll, Jean, Jr. He took the oath of allegiance in Boswijck, Kings County, New York 26–30 Sep. 1687. He had been in the colony 20 years.

Misersmith, John Andrew. He was naturalized in Pennsylvania 11 Apr. 1761. He was from Philadelphia County.

Mishler, Jacob. He was naturalized in Pennsylvania 10 Sep. 1761. He was from Berks County.

Mishler, Joseph. He was naturalized in Pennsylvania 10 Sep. 1761. He was from Berks County.

Misler, Ulrich. He was naturalized in Maryland 25 Oct. 1750. He was a German.

Misler, Ulrich. He was naturalized in Maryland 13 Oct. 1756. He was a German.

Mispagh, Nicholas. He petitioned for naturalization in New York 16 Nov. 1739.

Missel, Frederick. He was naturalized in Maryland 15 Apr. 1761.

Missels, Gerardus. He and his son James Missels were naturalized in Maryland 18 Oct. 1694. They also appeared as Gerardus Wessels and James Wessels.

Missersmith, Nicholas. He was naturalized in Pennsylvania 10 Sep. 1761. He was from Lancaster County.

Mitchell, George. He was naturalized in Pennsylvania 13 May 1768. He was from Dover Township, York County.

Mitchell, Jacque. He was an Acadian and took the oath to George II at Annapolis River, Nova Scotia in the winter of 1730.

Mitchell, Margaret. She was naturalized in Jamaica 17 Apr. 1728.

Mitshed, Jacob. He was naturalized in Pennsylvania 24–25 Sep. 1764. He was from Northern Liberties Township, Philadelphia County.

Mius, Charles. He was an Acadian who took the oath of allegiance at Annapolis River in Dec. 1729.

Mius, Francois. He was an Acadian who took the oath of allegiance at Annapolis River in Dec. 1729.

Mock, John. He was naturalized in Pennsylvania 11–13 Apr. 1743. He was from Philadelphia County.

Moedea, Rodriques. He was naturalized in Jamaica 1 Sep. 1742. He was a Jew.

Moelich, Andrew. He was naturalized in New Jersey in 1759.

Moelich, John. He was naturalized in New Jersey in 1759.

Moene, Jacob. He was naturalized in New York 12 July 1715. He was a chirurgeon.

Moensen, Jan. He expressed his desire to be naturalized in New Castle County, Delaware 21 Feb. 1682/3.

Moesman, Jacob Janzen. He took the oath to the King 21–26 Oct. 1664 after the conquest of New Netherland.

Moesmans, Arent Janssen. He took the oath to the King 21–26 Oct. 1664 after the conquest of New Netherland.

Mogle, Valentine. He was naturalized in Pennsylvania 11 Apr. 1761. He was from Berks County.

Mohler, Henry. He was naturalized in Pennsylvania 11 Apr. 1761. He was from Lancaster County.

Mohler, Jacob. He was naturalized in Pennsylvania 11 Apr. 1761. He was from Lancaster County.

Mohler, Ludwick. He was naturalized in Pennsylvania 11 Apr. 1761. He was from Lancaster County.

Mohlich, Gottfried. He was naturalized in New Jersey in 1747. He also appeared as Gottfried Mollick. He was from Sussex County and had been in the colony 22 years. He was born in Germany.

Mohn, John. He was naturalized in Pennsylvania 11 Apr. 1761. He was from Berks County.

Mohn, Ludwick. He was naturalized in Pennsylvania 10 Sep. 1761. He was from Berks County.

Mohn, Ulrick. He was naturalized in Pennsylvania 24 Sep. 1762. He was from Berks County.

Mohr, Andreas. He was naturalized in Pennsylvania 11 Apr. 1761. He was from Lancaster County.

Mohr, Frederick. He was naturalized in New York 11 Sep. 1761.

Mohr, Harman. He was naturalized in Pennsylvania 10 Apr. 1760.

Moke, Henry. He was naturalized in Pennsylvania 11 Apr. 1761. He was from Lancaster County.

Mol, Lambert Huybertzen. He took the oath to the King 21–26 Oct. 1664 after the conquest of New Netherland.

Moleck, Jonas. He was naturalized in New York 23 Apr. 1744. He was a baker from New York City.

Molengraff, Thomas. He took the oath to the King 21–26 Oct. 1664 after the conquest of New Netherland.

Moler, Adam. He was naturalized in Frederick County, Virginia 1 Aug. 1769.

Molich, Ehrenreich. He was naturalized in New Jersey in 1759.

Molich, Godfree. He was naturalized in New Jersey in 1757. He also appeared Godfrey Melick. He had been in the colony twenty-two years.

Molich, Johan. He was naturalized in New Jersey in 1759. He also appeared as John Moelich.

Molina, John Francis. He was naturalized in Jamaica 4 Feb. 1706.

Molina, Moses. He was naturalized in Jamaica 4 Oct. 1744.

Moll, Christopher. He was naturalized in Pennsylvania 11–13 Apr. 1743. He was from Philadelphia County.

Moll, John. He was naturalized in Pennsylvania 24 Sep. 1759.

Moll, Michael. He was naturalized in Pennsylvania 26–27 Sep. 1743. He was from Philadelphia County.

Mondes, Abraham de Soza. He was endenized in Jamaica 30 July 1670.

Monffoort, Pieter. He took the oath of allegiance in Flackland, Kings County, New York 26–30 Sep. 1687. He was a native of the colony.

Monie, Jacob. He was naturalized in New York 20 Mar. 1762.

Monis, Judah. He was naturalized in New York 28 Feb. 1715/6. He was a merchant from New York City.

Monis, Peter, Jr. He was naturalized 8–9 Sep. 1715. He was from Ulster County.

Monloy, Louis Francois. He took the oath of allegiance at Mobile, West Florida 2 Oct. 1764.

Monmemaker, Embrick. He was naturalized in Pennsylvania 24 Sep. 1762. He was from Philadelphia County.

Mong, Nicklas. He was naturalized in Maryland 12 Sep. 1764. He was a German from Frederick County.

Monsanto, Moses Mendes. He was naturalized in Jamaica 20 July 1736.

Monsanto, Raphael Molina. He was naturalized in Jamaica 13 Feb. 1761.

Monteyro, Joseph. He was naturalized in Pennsylvania 21 June 1706. He was a merchant and was born at Maderas, Portugal.

Montier, James. He and his wife were admitted into the colony of Massachusetts 1 Feb. 1691. They were French.

Montgomery, Peter. He and his sons, Francis Montgomery and John Baptists Montgomery, were naturalized in Maryland 30 Oct. 1727. They lived in Charles County and were French.

Montlemard, Maurice. He took the oath of allegiance at Mobile, West Florida 2 Oct. 1764.

Montlemard, Piere Gabriel. He took the oath of allegiance at Mobile, West Florida 2 Oct. 1764.

Monts, Bartholomew. He was naturalized in Maryland in Apr. 1749. He was from Frederick County.

Montson, Peter. He was made a denizen in Maryland 29 July 1661. He was Swedish and was late of New Amstel.

Moodye, Gyles. He was endenized in James City County, Virginia 26 Mar. 1656.

Moor, Hans. He was naturalized in Pennsylvania 19 May 1739. He was from Lancaster County.

Moor, Jacob. He was naturalized in New Jersey 8 July 1730. He was born in Germany.

Moor, Jacob. He was naturalized in Pennsylvania 10–12 Apr. 1762. He was from Northampton County.

Moor, Johan. He was naturalized in New Jersey 8 July 1730. He was born in Germany.

Moor, Michael. He was naturalized in North Carolina 23 Mar. 1765. He was from Rowan County.

Moor, Philip. He was naturalized in New York 17 Jan. 1715/6. He was from Albany County.

Moore, Blazey. He was naturalized in New York 21 Oct. 1764. He was an innholder in New York City.

Moore, Conrad. He was naturalized in Pennsylvania 24–25 Sep./5 Oct. 1767. He was from Robeson Township, Berks County.

Moore, Conradt. He was naturalized in New York 16 Feb. 1771.

Moore, Gideon. He was naturalized in Pennsylvania 24–25 Sep./5 Oct. 1767. He was from Upper Hanover Township, Philadelphia County.

Moore, Henrich. He was naturalized in New York 8–9 Sep. 1715. He was from Ulster County.

Moore, Jacob. He was naturalized in New York 20 Apr. 1769. He was a farmer outward of New York City.

Moore, Jacob. He was naturalized in New York 8 Mar. 1773.

Moore, Johannis. He was naturalized in New York 13 Mar. 1715/6. He was from Albany County.

Moore, Martin. He was naturalized in Pennsylvania 11 Apr. 1761. He was from Berks County.

Moore, Robert. He was naturalized in Jamaica 10 May 1708.

Moore, Stuffill. He was naturalized in Maryland 12 Apr. 1771. He was a German.

Morais, Abraham. He was naturalized in Jamaica 16 Nov. 1738.

Morais, Ester. She was naturalized in Jamaica 16 Nov. 1738.

Morais, Yehosuah. He was naturalized in Jamaica 6 Aug. 1690.

Morais, Samuel. He was naturalized in Jamaica 2 Mar. 1629/30.

Morales, David. He was naturalized in Jamaica 1 Aug. 1760.

Morales, Moses. He was naturalized in Jamaica 31 Aug. 1758.

Moran, Gabriel. He petitioned for naturalization from Charles County, Maryland 7 Oct. 1728.

Morant, Stephen. He was naturalized in Jamaica 16 Dec. 1734. He was a planter.

Mordecai, Mordecai M. He was naturalized in Pennsylvania in Sept.–Oct. 1765. He was a Jew.

Mordecai, Moses. He was naturalized in Pennsylvania 24–25 Sep. 1764. He was from Philadelphia.

Morgan, Adam. He was naturalized in Pennsylvania 10–14 Apr. 1747. He was from Philadelphia County.

Moreau, Rev. Jean-Baptist. He was naturalized in Nova Scotia 11 Aug. 1757.

Morehard, Jacob. He was naturalized in Pennsylvania 10 Apr. 1767. He was from Earl Township, Lancaster County.

Morey, William. He was naturalized in Pennsylvania 29 Mar. 1735. He was from Bucks County.

Morell, John. He was naturalized in Rhode Island in Aug. 1762. He had lived in Newport for several years and had married a wife there. He was a subject of the King of Spain. He took the oath 9 Sep. 1762.

Morell, Timothy. He was naturalized in Virginia 12 May 1705.

Moreno, Aaron Levy. He was naturalized in Jamaica 27 Aug. 1765.

Moreno, Rebecca. She was naturalized in Jamaica 16 Mar. 1718/9. She was also known as Rebecca Broune.

Morgan, Felix. He was naturalized in Maryland 27 Apr. 1772. He was a German.

Morgan, Sebastian. He was naturalized in Pennsylvania 10 Sep. 1761. He was from Berks County.

Morille, Jaques. He was endenized in New York 10 Mar. 1686.

Morin, Pierre. He and his wife Frances Morin were endenized in England 19 Aug. 1688. He was born at Chasteaudun, France, the son of Peter and Anne Morin.

Morino, Gabriel. He was naturalized in Jamaica 2 Mar. 1690/1.

Morissatt, Peter. He was naturalized in Virginia 12 May 1705.

Moritz, Nicholas. He was naturalized in Pennsylvania 11–13 Apr. 1743. He was from Philadelphia County.

Morkel, John. He was naturalized in New Jersey in 1764.

Morner, Quirinus. He was naturalized in Pennsylvania 24–25 Sep. 1764. He was from Brecknock Township, Lancaster County.

Morningstar, Angell. He was naturalized in Maryland 11 Apr. 1771. He was a German.

Morningstar, John. He and his children, Philip Morningstar, Elizabeth Morningstar, and Joanna Morningstar, were naturalized in Maryland 4 June 1738. He was from Baltimore County and was born in Germany.

Morrell, Mathew. He was naturalized in New York 22 Apr. 1761. He was a French Protestant and a laborer from New York City.

Morris, Christian. He was naturalized in North Carolina 22 Sep. 1763. He was from Rowan County and a German.

Morris, Samuel. He was naturalized in Frederick County, Virginia 1 Apr. 1766.

Morrison, John. He was naturalized in New York 3 May 1755.

Morrison, Thomas. He was naturalized in Jamaica 30 Apr. 1698.

Morrisset, Alexander. He petitioned to be made a citizen in New York in 1691. He was a French Protestant.

Morros, John. He was naturalized in New York 16 Aug. 1715. He was a yeoman from New Rochelle.

Mortalle, Jean Claude. He took the oath of allegiance at Mobile, West Florida 2 Oct. 1764.

Mory, Christian. He was naturalized in Pennsylvania in 1730–31. He was from Philadelphia County. He also appeared as Christian Mary.

Mose, Jacqueline. She was naturalized in Jamaica 21 Jan. 1702/3.

Moseley, Arthur. He was naturalized in Virginia *ante* 16 Sep. 1692 in order to convey lots in the borough of Norfolk. He was born in the Netherlands.

Moser, Adam. He was naturalized in Pennsylvania 11 Apr. 1749. He was from Lancaster County.

Moser, Adam. He was naturalized in Pennsylvania 19 May 1739. He was from Philadelphia County.

Moser, Adam. He was naturalized in North Carolina 22 Sep. 1763. He was from Rowan County and a German.

Moser, Bastian. He was naturalized in Pennsylvania 10 & 23 Apr. 1764. He was from Hanover Township, Philadelphia County.

Moser, Jacob. He was naturalized in Nova Scotia 5 July 1758.

Moser, Paul. He was naturalized in Pennsylvania 10 & 23 Apr. 1764. He was from New Hanover Township, Philadelphia County.

Moser, Philip. He was naturalized in Pennsylvania 24 Sep. 1760. He was from Philadelphia County.

Moses, Isaac. He was naturalized in New York 3 Feb. 1768.

Moses, Isaac. He was naturalized in New York 25 Apr. 1771. He was a merchant from New York City. He was a Jew.

Moses, Jacob. He was naturalized in New York 20 May 1769. He was a trader from New York City.

Moses, Levy. He was naturalized in New York 3 July 1759.

Moses, Simon. He was naturalized in New York 28 Feb. 1715/6. He was a merchant from New York City.

Mosser, Leonard. He was naturalized in Maryland 9 Sep. 1761. He was a weaver from Frederick County.

Mossnerl, Dieterich. He was naturalized in Maryland 15 Apr. 1761.

Motezer, John. He was naturalized in Pennsylvania 10 Sep. 1761. He was from Berks County.

Mots, Henry. He was naturalized in Pennsylvania 25–26 Sep./4 Oct. 1749. He was from Lancaster County.

Mots, Johannes. He was naturalized in New York 23 Aug. 1715. He was a yeoman from Tappan.

Motta, Abraham. He was naturalized in Jamaica 6 Sep. 1744.

Motterel, George. He was naturalized in Maryland 11 Sep. 1765.

Moule, Christoffel. He was naturalized in New York 8–9 Sep. 1715. He was from Ulster County.

Moule, Frederick. He was naturalized in New York 8–9 Sep. 1715. He was from Ulster County.

Moule, Jacob. He was naturalized in New York 8–9 Sep. 1715. He was from Ulster County.

Moulins, Abraham. He was naturalized in Virginia 12 May 1705.

Moulston, Alexander. He was naturalized in Sussex County, Delaware 28 Apr. 1683.

Mouluner, Joseph. He was naturalized in Virginia 12 May 1705.

Mounart, Francoise. She was born at Chaine, Poitou, France, the daughter of Jacques Mounart and Anne Bonneau. She was naturalized in South Carolina ca. 1696.

Mounart, Jacques. He was born at Chaine, Poitou, France, the son of Jacques Mounart and Anne Bonneau. He was naturalized in South Carolina ca. 1696.

Mounier, Pierre. He was endenized in England 9 Apr. 1687. He was born at L'Isle de Re, France, the son of Louis Mournier and Elizabeth Martineau. His wife was Louise Robinet, daughter of Louis Robinet. They were naturalized in South Carolina ca. 1696.

Mounts, Christopher. He was naturalized in Maryland 9 May 1700. He lived in Cecil County and was born of Dutch parents.

Mouratt, Peter. He was naturalized in Jamaica 26 Sep. 1684.

Moussier, Hans Jury. He was naturalized in New York 3 Jan. 1715/6. He was from Albany County.

Moussier, Jacob. He was naturalized in New York 3 Jan. 1715/6. He was from Albany County.

Mouton, Jean. He was an Acadian and took the oath of allegiance in Apr. 1730.

Mower, Jurick. He was naturalized in New York 17 Jan. 1715/6. He was from Albany County.

Moy, Christian. He was naturalized 10–12 Apr. 1762. He was from Philadelphia County.

Moy, Killian. He was naturalized in Pennsylvania 11 Apr. 1761. He was from Berks County.

Moyer, Hendrick. He was naturalized in Pennsylvania 11–13 Apr. 1743. He was from Lancaster County.

Moyer, John. He was naturalized in Pennsylvania 10 Sep. 1761. He was from Northampton County.

Moyer, John. He was naturalized in Pennsylvania 24–25 Sep. 1764. He was from Douglass Township, Philadelphia County.

Moyer, Thomas. He took the oath to the King 21–26 Oct. 1664 after the conquest of New Netherland.

Moyon, William. He was endenized in London 15 Apr. 1693. He came to New York.

Moze, Caesar. He was endenized in England 9 Apr. 1687. He came to South Carolina.

Mozey, Charles. He was naturalized in Jamaica 5 Apr. 1694.

Mueller, Michael. He was naturalized in Maryland 17 July 1765. He was a German.

Muffler, Sebastian. He was naturalized in Pennsylvania 11 Apr. 1761. He was from Philadelphia County.

Mugenbrough, Martin. He was naturalized in Maryland 6 June 1674. He was German.

Muhlenberg, Henry. He was naturalized in Pennsylvania 24 Sep. 1754. He was from Philadelphia County.

Muhlig, Christian. He was naturalized in Nova Scotia 15 Sep. 1758.

Muhlig, Gotlieb. He was naturalized in Nova Scotia 10 July 1758.

Muhlig, Henry. He was naturalized in Nova Scotia 15 Sep. 1758.

Mulder, Joseph. He was naturalized in Virginia 20 Sep. 1673.

Mulder, Joshua. He was naturalized in Virginia 22 June 1706.

Muldrup, Christian. He was naturalized in New York 3 May 1755.

Mulledaller, John. He was naturalized in New York 21 Oct. 1761. He was a cordwainer from New York City.

Mulleker, Erick. He was naturalized in Pennsylvania 11 Jan. 1683. He was formerly of New Sweden.

Muller, Adam. He was naturalized in New York 19 Oct. 1763. He was a farmer from the manor of Cortlandt.

Muller, Andries. He was naturalized in New York 19 Oct. 1763. He was a farmer from the manor of Cortlandt.

Muller, Christian. He was naturalized in Pennsylvania 25 Sep. 1751. He was from Lancaster County.

Muller, Daniel. He was naturalized in Nova Scotia 15 Sep. 1758.

Muller, Daniel. He was naturalized in Pennsylvania 25 Sep. 1751. He was from Bucks County.

Muller, Eva Maria. She was naturalized in Pennsylvania 25 Sep. 1751. She was from Lancaster County.

Muller, George. He was naturalized in New Jersey in 1750. He was from Hunterdon County. He also appeared as George Miller.

Muller, Jacob. He was naturalized in Pennsylvania 10–14 Apr. 1747. He was from Philadelphia County.

Muller, Jacob. He was naturalized in New York 29 Oct. 1762. He was a farmer from the manor of Cortlandt.

Muller, Johan Jurch. He was naturalized in New York 17 Jan. 1715/6. He was from Albany County.

Muller, John. He was naturalized in New York 29 July 1761. He was a laborer from New York City.

Muller, John. He was naturalized in New York 15 Oct. 1765. He was a doctor of physic in New York City.

Muller, Peter. He was naturalized in New York 11 Sep. 1761.

Muller, Samuel. He was naturalized in New York 17 Jan. 1715/6. He was from Albany County.

Multer, Peter. He was naturalized in New York 8 Mar. 1773.

Mumma, Peter. He was naturalized in Pennsylvania 10–12 Apr. 1762. He was from Lancaster County.

Munderbach, Johannes. He was naturalized in New York 23 Dec. 1765.

Munez, Moses. He was naturalized in Jamaica 1 Sep. 1709.

Mung, Godfret. He was naturalized in Maryland in Apr. 1749. He was from Frederick County.

Munts, Benedictus. He was naturalized in Pennsylvania 19 May 1739. He was from Philadelphia County.

Murray, Hugh. He was naturalized in Jamaica 30 Apr. 1698.

Murray, William. He was naturalized in Jamaica 25 Apr. 1698. He was a mariner.

Musafea, Jacob. He was naturalized in Jamaica 15 Jan. 1688/9.

Musch, John. He was naturalized in Pennsylvania 10 & 23 Apr. 1764. He was from Northampton County.

Musculus, William. He was naturalized in New York 23 Dec. 1765.

Muse, Charles. He was an Acadian and took the oath to George II at Annapolis River, Nova Scotia in the winter of 1730.

Muse, François. He was an Acadian and took the oath to George II at Annapolis River, Nova Scotia in the winter of 1730.

Musgrave, Francis. He was naturalized in Jamaica 30 July 1720.

Musher, Conrad. He was naturalized in Nova Scotia 4 July 1758.

Musselman, Henry. He was naturalized in Pennsylvania 14 Feb. 1729/30. He was from Lancaster County.

Musseman, Andrew. He was naturalized in Pennsylvania 26–27 Sep. 1743. He was from Lancaster County.

Musseman, Christian. He was naturalized in Pennsylvania 26–27 Sep. 1743. He was from Lancaster County.

Mussle, Hans. He was naturalized in Pennsylvania 26–27 Sep. 1743. He was from Lancaster County.

Mussleman, Samuel. He was naturalized in Pennsylvania 11–13 Apr. 1743. He was from Philadelphia County.

Muttee, Peter. He was naturalized in New York 11 Sep. 1761.

Muzelius, Fredericus. He was naturalized in New York 16 Dec. 1737.

Myar, Michael. He was naturalized in New York 16 Feb. 1771.

Myar, Peter. He was naturalized in Maryland 26 Sep. 1750.

Mye, William. He was naturalized in Pennsylvania 10–11 Apr. 1745. He was from Philadelphia County.

Myer, Christian, Jr. He was naturalized in Maryland 11–13 Apr. 1743. He was from Philadelphia County.

Myer, Christian. He was naturalized in Pennsylvania 10–14 Apr. 1747. He was from Lancaster County.

Myer, Christopher. He expressed his desire to be naturalized in New Castle County, Delaware 21 Feb. 1682/3.

Myer, Elias. He was naturalized in Pennsylvania 11–12 Apr. 1744. He was from Lancaster County.

Myer, Frederick. He was naturalized in New York 16 Feb. 1771.

Myer, Hermanus. He was naturalized in New York 20 Oct. 1764.

Myer, Jacob. He was naturalized in New York 3 May 1755.

Myer, Jacob. He was naturalized in New York 8 Mar. 1775.

Myer, Jacob. He was naturalized in Pennsylvania 26–27 Sep. 1743. He was from Bucks County.

Myer, Johannes. He was naturalized in New Jersey 21 Oct. 1754.

Myer, John. He was naturalized in Pennsylvania 24 Sep. 1762. He was from Northampton County.

Myer, John Andrew. He was naturalized in Pennsylvania 11 Apr. 1763. He was from Philadelphia.

Myer, Martin. He was naturalized in Pennsylvania 10 & 12 Apr. 1764. He was from Strasburg Township, York County.

Myer, Michael. He was naturalized in New Jersey 20 Aug. 1755.

Myer, Michael. He was naturalized in New York 16 Feb. 1771.

Myer, Solomon. He was naturalized in New York 3 May 1755.

Myer, Thomas. He was naturalized in Pennsylvania 25–27 Sep. 1740. He was from Philadelphia County.

Myer, Valentine. He was naturalized in Maryland 29 Sep. 1752.

Myerly, Baltzer. He was naturalized in Pennsylvania 11 Apr. 1761. He was from Berks County.

Myerly, David. He was naturalized in Pennsylvania 24 Sep. 1759.

Myerly, John George. He was naturalized in Pennsylvania 24 Sep. 1759.

Myers, Hyam. He was naturalized in New York 16 Jan. 1759. He was a Jewish butcher from New York City.

Myers, Manuel. He was naturalized in New York 16 Jan. 1759. He was a Jewish trader from New York City.

Myers, Mordecai. He was naturalized 24 Oct. 1771. He was a storekeeper in Charleston, South Carolina and a Jew. Gideon Dupont, Jr. and Isaac DaCosta proved his residency.

Myers, Napthaly Hart. He was naturalized in New York 27 Apr. 1764. He was a Jewish merchant from New York City.

Myers, Samuel. He was naturalized in New York 12 July 1729.

Myers, Solomon. He was naturalized in New York by the act of 1749. He was a Jewish merchant from New York City.

Myers, Solomon. He was naturalized in New York 6 July 1723.

Mylin, John. He was naturalized in Pennsylvania 14 Feb. 1729/30. He was from Lancaster County.

Mylin, Martyn. He was naturalized in Pennsylvania 14 Feb. 1729/30. He was from Lancaster County.

Mynskie, John Samuel. He, his wife Catherine Mynskie, and daughter Susannah Mynskie were naturalized in Maryland 30 Oct. 1727. He lived in Annapolis and was born in Brandenburg, Prussia. He was a blacksmith.

Myrtetus, Christopher Gideon. He was naturalized in Pennsylvania 10 Apr. 1765. He was from Philadelphia.

Nachbar, Leonhard. He was naturalized in New Jersey in 1759.

Nacks, Philip. He was naturalized in Pennsylvania 10 Sep. 1761. He was from Berks County.

Naeffen, Anna Maria. She was naturalized in Pennsylvania 26 Sep. 1748. She was from Lancaster County and was the wife of Michael Naeffen.

Naffenberger, George. He was naturalized in Pennsylvania 11–12 Apr. 1744. He was from Lancaster County.

Naffseger, Peter. He was naturalized in Pennsylvania 13 May 1771. He was from Frederick County, Maryland.

Nagel, Philip. He was naturalized in Pennsylvania 11 Apr. 1763. He was from Berks County.

Nagle, Jacob. He was naturalized in Pennsylvania 24 Sep. 1762. He was from Berks County.

Nagle, Jacob. He was naturalized in Pennsylvania 24–25 Sep. 1764. He was from Oley Township, Berks County.

Nagle, Sebastian. He was naturalized in Pennsylvania 24–25 Sep. 1764. He was from Bethel Township, Lancaster County.

Naglee, Casper. He was naturalized in Pennsylvania 10 & 23 Sep. 1764. He was from Bedminster Township, Bucks County.

Naglee, Jacob. He was naturalized in Pennsylvania 25–27 Sep. 1740. He was from Philadelphia County.

Naglee, Rudolph. He was naturalized in Pennsylvania 10 Apr. 1760.

Nale, Philip. He was naturalized in Maryland 15 Apr. 1767. He was a German.

Namias, David. He was endenized in England 27 Dec. 1662. He lived in Barbados and was a Jew. He also appeared as David Nannas and Davis Namiasi.

Nans, Rowland. He was naturalized in Maryland 17 Nov. 1682. He lived in Baltimore County.

Naph, John. He was naturalized in Maryland in Apr. 1749.

Nappinger, Andrew. He was naturalized in Pennsylvania 10 Apr. 1757.

Napthali, Isaac. His was endenized in New York in Aug. 1695.

Naquien, Francois. He was an Acadian who took the oath of allegiance in Apr. 1730.

Naquien, Jacques. He was an Acadian who took the oath of allegiance in Apr. 1730.

Narbon, Anthony. He took the oath of allegiance at Mobile, West Florida 2 Oct. 1764.

Narbona, David Lopez. He was naturalized in Jamaica 2 Oct. 1678.

Narbona, Solomon Lopez. He was naturalized in Jamaica 17 Oct. 1684.

Nare, Solomon. He was naturalized in New York by the act of 1740. He was a Jew.

Narke, Jacob. He was naturalized in New York 20 Mar. 1762.

Narvais, Isaac. He was naturalized in Jamaica 17 Nov. 1768.

Nasar, Isaac. He was naturalized in Jamaica 11 May 1704.

Nathan, Lyon. He was naturalized in Pennsylvania 11 Apr. 1763. He was from Reading Township, Berks County. He was a Jew.

Nathane, Alexander. He was naturalized in Jamaica 29 May 1750. He was a Jew.

Natzer, George Chris. He was naturalized in North Carolina 13 Sep. 1770. He was from Rowan County.

Naudin, Andrew. He and his sons, Andrew Naudin and Louis Naudin, were endenized in New York 6 Feb. 1695/6.

Navarro, Aaron. He was endenized in England 2 Aug. 1661. He settled in Barbados. He was a Jew.

Navarro, Isaac. He was endenized in London in Feb. 1699/1700. He was a merchant from Barbados and was a Jew.

Nayer, Johan Frans. He was naturalized in New York 8–9 Sep. 1715. He was from Ulster County.

Nayer, Nicolas. He was naturalized in New York 8–9 Sep. 1715. He was from Ulster County

Neace, Michael. He was naturalized in Pennsylvania 19 May 1739. He was from Bucks County.

Neaf, Henrick. He was naturalized in Maryland 11 Apr. 1760.

Neaff, Henry, Jr. He was naturalized in Pennsylvania 19 May 1739. He was from Lancaster County.

Neagley, John. He was naturalized in Pennsylvania 16 Jan. 1729/30.

Neale, Dorothy. She and her children, Anthony Neale, Henrietta Maria Neale, and James Neale, were naturalized in Maryland 1 May 1666. They were the wife and children of Capt. James Neale and were born in Spain and Portugal while Neale served there.

Neau, James. He was endenized in London 11 Mar. 1699/1700. He came to New York.

Nedmer, Anthony. He was naturalized in New York 29 Mar. 1762.

Need, Matthias. He was naturalized in Maryland 15 Apr. 1761.

Neef, Henrich. He was naturalized in Maryland 11 Apr. 1759.

Neegle, Christian. He was naturalized in Pennsylvania 10 Apr. 1754. He was from Northampton County.

Neering, John Willemsen. He expressed his desire to be naturalized in New Castle County, Delaware 21 Feb. 1682/3.

Nees, Mattheus. He was naturalized in Pennsylvania 25–27 Sep. 1740. He was from Philadelphia County.

Nees, Michael. He was naturalized in Pennsylvania 11 Apr. 1749. He was from Lancaster County.

Neese, Michael. He was naturalized in Augusta County, Virginia 16 Oct. 1765.

Neff, Jacob. He was naturalized in Pennsylvania 24–29 Sep. 1769. He was from Reading Township, Berks County.

Neff, Jacob. He was naturalized in Pennsylvania 11 Apr. 1763. He was from Oxford Township, Philadelphia County.

Neff, Rudolph. He was naturalized in Pennsylvania 11 Apr. 1763. He was from Northern Liberties Township, Philadelphia County.

Neft, Wendal. He was naturalized in Pennsylvania 13–15 Apr. 1748. He was from Philadelphia County.

Neglee, Johannes. He was naturalized in Pennsylvania 10 Apr. 1754. He was from Philadelphia County.

Negley, John. He was naturalized in Pennsylvania 14 Feb. 1729/30. He was from Philadelphia.

Nehrott, Henrick. He was naturalized in Pennsylvania 24 Sep. 1762. He was from Berks County.

Neidig, John Adam. He was naturalized in Pennsylvania 10 Sep. 1761. He was from Berks County.

Neidlin, John Christopher. He was naturalized in Pennsylvania 10–12 Apr. 1762. He was from Berks County.

Neiff, Francis. He was naturalized in Pennsylvania 14 Feb. 1729/30. He was from Lancaster County.

Neiff, Francis, Jr. He was naturalized in Pennsylvania 14 Feb. 1729/30. He was from Lancaster County.

Neiff, Henry. He was naturalized in Pennsylvania 14 Feb. 1729/30. He was from Lancaster County.

Neiff, John Henry. He was naturalized in Pennsylvania 14 Feb. 1729/30. He was from Lancaster County.

Nieff, John Henry, Jr. He was naturalized in Pennsylvania 14 Feb. 1729/30. He was from Lancaster County.

Neihawsen, Johannes. He was naturalized in Pennsylvania 25–27 Sep. 1740. He was from Philadelphia County.

Neiher, Carel. He was naturalized in New York 8–9 Sep. 1715. He was from Ulster County.

Neiss, George. He was naturalized in Pennsylvania 10 Sep. 1761. He was from Berks County.

Neiss, John. He was naturalized in Pennsylvania 24 Sep. 1762. He was from Bucks County.

Neithe, John Frederick. He was naturalized in New York 24 Nov. 1759.

Neiukirch, Johanis. He was naturalized in New York 8–9 Sep. 1715. He was from Ulster County.

Nelles, Christian. He was naturalized in New York 31 Jan. 1715/6. He was from Albany County.

Nelles, William. He was naturalized in New York 31 Jan. 1715/6. He was from Albany County.

Nelson, Ambrose. He was naturalized in Maryland 15 Nov. 1712. He lived in Baltimore County.

Nelson, Peter. He was naturalized in Pennsylvania 11 Jan. 1683. He was formerly of New Sweden.

Nengfinger, William. He was naturalized in Maryland 19 Apr. 1671. He lived in St. Mary's County and was Dutch.

Nesereau, Elias. He was naturalized in Jamaica 2 Mar. 1693/4.

Ness, George. He was naturalized in Pennsylvania 11 Apr. 1761. He was from York County.

Nessel, Martin. He was naturalized in New York 20 Mar. 1762.

Nestel, Jasper. He was naturalized in New York 20 Jan. 1776. He was from New York City.

Nett, Michael. He was naturalized in Pennsylvania 11–13 Apr. 1743. He was from Lancaster County.

Nett, Michael, Jr. He was naturalized in Pennsylvania 11–13 Apr. 1743. He was from Lancaster County.

Nesley, Ulrich. He was naturalized in Pennsylvania 25 Sep. 1751. He was from Philadelphia County.

Netf, Abraham. He was naturalized in Pennsylvania 11 Apr. 1761. He was from Lancaster County.

Netf, Jacob. He was naturalized in Pennsylvania 11 Apr. 1761. He was from Lancaster County.

Nett, Michael, Jr. He was naturalized in Pennsylvania 11–13 Apr. 1743. He was from Lancaster County.

Neufeile, Rachel. She was naturalized in New York 15 Nov. 1715. She was a widow from New Rochelle.

Neukerck, Henrick. He was naturalized in New York 8–9 Sep. 1715. He was from Ulster County.

Neuppennye, Adam. He petitioned for naturalization in New York 16 Nov. 1739.

Neus, Hans. He was naturalized in Pennsylvania 29 Sep. 1709. He was from Philadelphia County.

Neus, John. He and his sons, Matthias Neus and Cornelius Neus, were naturalized in Pennsylvania 29 Sep. 1709. They were from Philadelphia County.

Nevius, Johannes. He took the oath to the King 21–26 Oct. 1664 after the conquest of New Netherland.

Nevius, Pieter. He took the oath of allegiance in Flackland, Kings County, New York 26–30 Sep. 1687. He was a native of the colony.

New, Adam. He was naturalized in Pennsylvania 10 Sep. 1761. He was from Lancaster County.

New, Nicholas. He was naturalized in Pennsylvania 10 Sep. 1761. He was from Lancaster County.

Newcomat, John. He was naturalized in Pennsylvania 10 Sep. 1761. He was from Lancaster County.

Newcomat, Peter. He was naturalized in Pennsylvania 14 Feb. 1729/30. He was from Lancaster County.

Newcomer, John. He was naturalized in Pennsylvania 10 Sep. 1761. He was from Berks County.

Newerhouse, Andre. He was naturalized in Jamaica 3 Mar. 1723/4.

Newhard, John. He was naturalized in Jamaica 9 Aug. 1745.

Newhart, Michael. He was naturalized in Pennsylvania 10 Apr. 1759.

Newhouse, Anthony. He was naturalized in Pennsylvania 26 Sep. 1748. He was from Philadelphia County.

Newill, Wornill. He was naturalized in Jamaica 26 Jan. 1691.

Newkirk, Henry. He was naturalized in Pennsylvania 24 Sep. 1755. He was from Berks County.

Newkirk, Henry. He was naturalized in Pennsylvania 10 Sep. 1761. He was from Berks County.

Newland, John. He was naturalized in Frederick County, Virginia 1 Aug. 1769.

Newman, Augustus. He was naturalized in Rhode Island in May 1774. He was born in Saxony. In the last war he served his Majesty under Prince Ferdinand. He had come to Newport about eight years ago and a year later married. He had a child.

Newman, Christopher. He was naturalized in Pennsylvania 10 Apr. 1755. He was from Philadelphia County.

Newman, David. He was naturalized in Pennsylvania 24 Sep. 1755. He was from Philadelphia County.

Neyzard, Peter. He was naturalized in New Jersey 20 Aug. 1755.

Nicas, Jean Baptist. He took the oath of allegiance at Mobile, West Florida 2 Oct. 1764.

Nice, Dewald. He was naturalized in Pennsylvania 25–27 Sep. 1740. He was from Bucks County.

Nice, Mathias. He was naturalized in Pennsylvania 25–27 Sep. 1740. He was from Philadelphia County.

Nichola, Ludwick. He was naturalized in Pennsylvania 18 Nov. 1769. He was from Bern Township, Berks County.

Nicholas, Jacob. He was naturalized in Augusta County, Virginia 20 Aug. 1765.

215

was born at Chalais, Xaintonge, France, the son of Daniel Nicholas and
'fe was Madeleine Garillon. They were naturalized in South Carolina ca.

ᴎe was naturalized in Pennsylvania 10 Apr. 1760.
ᴊn, John. He was naturalized in Maryland 23 July 1765. He was a German.
ᴋᴄᴋ, Michael. He was naturalized in Pennsylvania 24 Sep. 1762. He was from Philadelphia County.
Nicodemus, Frederick. He was naturalized in Maryland 11 Sep. 1765.
Nicumer, Henry. He was naturalized in Maryland 15 Apr. 1772. He was a German.
Niedermardt, Conrad. He was naturalized in Pennsylvania 11 Apr. 1741. He was from Chester County.
Niep, John. He was naturalized in Pennsylvania 24 Sep. 1762. He was from Lancaster County.
Nies, Hendrick. He was naturalized in New York 22 Nov. 1715. He was from Albany County.
Niets, Hans George. He was naturalized in New York 29 July 1752. He was a farmer from Ulster County.
Nieto, Rachael Nunes. She was naturalized in Jamaica 28 Feb. 1743.
Nighat, Frederick. He was naturalized in Pennsylvania 10 Apr. 1755. He was from Northampton County.
Nisewanger, John. He was naturalized in Frederick County, Virginia 1 Apr. 1766.
Nisley, Jacob. He was naturalized in Pennsylvania 14 Feb. 1729/30. He was from Lancaster County.
Nistell, Michael. He was naturalized in New York 3 July 1759.
Nitschman, David. He was naturalized in Pennsylvania 25 Sep. 1750. He was from Bucks County. He was a Moravian.
Nixley, John. He was naturalized in Pennsylvania 24–25 Sep. 1764. He was from Philadelphia.
Noble, Anthony. He was naturalized in Pennsylvania 11–13 Apr. 1743. He was from Philadelphia. He was a painter.
Nodine, Arnold. He was endenized in New York in Nov. 1697 by Gov. Fletcher. The Privy Council declared the action void because the governor's commission did not give him the express power to grant letters of denization. He was a French Protestant.
Nodle, Ulrick. He was naturalized in Pennsylvania 11 Apr. 1763. He was from Berks County.
Noe, Peter. He was naturalized in North Carolina 23 Mar. 1763. He was from Rowan County.
Noel, Cornelius. He was endenized in Virginia 7 Nov. 1666.
Noge, Francois. He was an Acadian and took the oath of allegiance in Apr. 1730.
Nohaker, Johan. He was naturalized in Pennsylvania 19 May 1739. He was from Lancaster County.
Nold, Bernard. He was naturalized in New York 8–9 Sep. 1715. He was from Ulster County.
Noll, Antonius. He was naturalized in Maryland 31 Aug. 1757.
Noll, Francis. He was naturalized in Pennsylvania 11 Apr. 1761. He was from York County.
Noll, George. He was naturalized in Pennsylvania 13–15 Apr. 1748. He was from Lancaster County.
Noll, Martin. He was naturalized in Pennsylvania 11 Apr. 1761. He was from Philadelphia County.
Nomers, John. He was naturalized in Maryland 6 June 1674. He was Swedish.
Nones, Jacob. He was naturalized in Jamaica 9 June 1707.
Norbery, John. He was endenized in New York 17 June 1698.
Norbona, Sarah Lopez. She was naturalized in Jamaica 26 Feb. 1721/2.
Normand, Philipe. He was born at Germain, Poitou, France, the son of Philipe Normand and Jeanne Pineau. His wife was Elizabet Juin. They were naturalized in South Carolina 10 Mar. 1696/7. He was a smith.
Nonnemaker, Jacob. He was naturalized in Pennsylvania 11 Apr. 1763. He was from Hill Town Township, Bucks County.
Nowe, Louis Alexander Decaza. He was naturalized in Jamaica 22 Mar. 1724/5.
Noyman, Christopher. He was naturalized in Pennsylvania 11–13 Apr. 1743. He was from Philadelphia County.
Nummers, John. He was naturalized in New Castle County, Delaware 21 Feb. 1682/3.
Nunemaker, Jacob. He was naturalized in Maryland 11 Apr. 1764. He was a German.

Nunes, Abraham. He was naturalized in Jamaica 21 Nov. 1688.
Nunes, Abraham Rodrigues. He was naturalized in Jamaica 3 Sep. 1739.
Nunes, David. He was naturalized in Jamaica 9 Jan. 1691.
Nunes, Isaac Rodrigues. He was naturalized in Jamaica 26 Feb. 1750/1. He was a Jew.
Nunes, Jacob. He was naturalized in Jamaica 30 Nov. 1686.
Nunes, Jacob Franco. He was endenized in England 11 Oct. 1687. He was from Barbados.
Nunes, Jacob Van. He was naturalized in Jamaica 8 Apr. 1711.
Nunes, Joseph. He was endenized in London 30 May 1704. He was a resident of New York.
Nunez, Abraham. He was endenized in England 31 Oct. 1685. He settled in Barbados.
Nunez, Isaac. He was naturalized in Jamaica 6 Aug. 1741.
Nunez, Isaac Lopez. He was naturalized in Jamaica 9 May 1726.
Nunez, Isaque. He sought to be endenized 30 Aug. 1692. He was a Jew from Jamaica.
Nunez, Judeka. He was naturalized in Jamaica 26 Jan. 1703/4.
Nunez, Joshua. He was naturalized in Jamaica 29 Nov. 1743. He was a Jew.
Nunez, Joshuah. He was naturalized in Jamaica 9 Nov. 1730.
Nunez, Rachell. She was naturalized in Jamaica 27 Jan. 1703/4.
Nunez, Sarah. She was naturalized in Jamaica 31 May 1743. She was a Jewess.
Nungasser, Valentine. He was naturalized in Pennsylvania 10 Apr. 1754. He was from Philadelphia County.
Nungesser, Frederick. He was naturalized in Pennsylvania 10 Apr. 1760.
Nuss, Jacob. He was naturalized in Pennsylvania 13–15 Apr. 1748. He was from Philadelphia County.
Nutt, John. He was naturalized in North Carolina 22 Sep. 1763. He was from Rowan County and was a German.
Nutz, George. He was naturalized in Pennsylvania 24 Sep. 1760. He was from Berks County.
Nutz, Leonard. He was naturalized in Pennsylvania 24 Sep. 1746. He was from Lancaster County.
Nuytuber, Nicholas. He was naturalized in New York 10 Jan. 1715/6. He was the son of Querinus Nuytuber.
Nuytuber, Querinus. He was naturalized in New York 10 Jan. 1715/6. He was a yeoman from Phillipsburgh.
Nyer, Daniel. He was naturalized in Pennsylvania 24 Sep. 1760. He was from Philadelphia County.
Nymaster, Leonard. He was naturalized in New Jersey in 1770.
Nype, Casper. He was naturalized in Pennsylvania 11 Apr. 1761. He was from Bucks County.
Nys, Pieter. He took the oath to the King 21–26 Oct. 1664 after the conquest of New Netherland.
Oake, Jan. He took the oath of allegiance in Flackbush, Kings County, New York 26–30 Sep. 1687. He had been in the colony 36 years.
Oal, Henry. He was naturalized in Pennsylvania 11 Apr. 1752. He was from Bucks County.
Oard, John. He was naturalized in Jamaica 27 Nov. 1742.
Oasterman, John Frederick. He was naturalized in New York 16 Apr. 1750. He was a laborer from New York City.
Obb, Peter. He was naturalized in Pennsylvania 11 Apr. 1761. He was from York County.
Obe, Hendrick. He took the oath to the King 21–26 Oct. 1664 after the conquest of New Netherland.
Oberg, Peter. He was naturalized in Jamaica 26 Mar. 1760.
Oberley, Adam. He was naturalized in Pennsylvania 10–12 Apr. 1762. He was from Lancaster County.
Oberlin, John Francis. He was naturalized in Pennsylvania 24–29 Sep. 1768. He was from Bethlehem Township, Northampton County.
Oberlin, Martin. He was naturalized in Pennsylvania 24–25 Sep. 1764. He was from Bethel Township, Lancaster County.
Oberling, Rudolph. He was naturalized in Pennsylvania 24 Sep. 1757.
Obert, George. He was naturalized in New Jersey in 1770.
Obert, Peter. He was naturalized in New Jersey in 1770.
Objenti-Elias, Patchdiel. He was endenized in England 27 Dec. 1662. He was a Jew and settled in Barbados.

Occulberry, Abraham. He was naturalized in Maryland 11 Sep. 1765.

Odenbaugh, Jonas. He was naturalized in Maryland 14 Sep. 1763. He was a German.

Odenhelmer, John. He was naturalized in Pennsylvania 10–12 Apr. 1762. He was from Philadelphia County.

Odere, Isac. He was endenized in New York 23 Dec. 1695.

Oel, John Jacob. He was naturalized in New York 28 July 1743. He was a clerk from Albany County.

Oelkens, Sick. He was naturalized in New Castle County, Delaware 21 Feb. 1682/3.

Oelsen, Michiel. He expressed his desire to be naturalized in New Castle County, Delaware 21 Feb. 1682/3.

Oerter, Christopher Frederick. He was naturalized in Pennsylvania 24 Sep. 1762. He was from Northampton County.

Oertly, Henrick. He was naturalized in New York 21 Oct. 1765. He was a yeoman from New York City.

Oeth, John. He and his children were naturalized in Maryland 28 Feb. 1721/2. He lived in Anne Arundel County and was German.

Offner, Martin. He was naturalized in Pennsylvania 24 Sep. 1760. He was from Lancaster County.

Ogier, Mathieu. He was naturalized in Virginia 12 May 1705.

Ohl, Andreas. He was naturalized in Pennsylvania 24 Sep. 1754. He was from Philadelphia County.

Ohl, Michael. He was naturalized in Pennsylvania 10 Apr. 1760.

Ohleweyler, Philip. He was naturalized in Pennsylvania 24 Sep. 1763. He was from Manor Township, Lancaster County.

Oldhouse, Christian. He was naturalized in Pennsylvania 11 Apr. 1761. He was from Berks County.

Oldhouse, William. He was naturalized in Pennsylvania 10 Sep. 1761. He was from Philadelphia County.

Oleg, Sebastian. He was naturalized in Maryland 25 Mar. 1702. He lived in Anne Arundel County and was German.

Olewine, Yost. He was naturalized in Pennsylvania 24 Sep. 1755. He was from Bucks County.

Olinger, Philip. He was naturalized in Pennsylvania 24 Sep. 1762. He was from Lancaster County.

Oliver, Joseph. He was naturalized in Virginia 12 May 1705.

Oliver, Laurence. He was naturalized in Jamaica 26 Mar. 1681.

Ollivier, Pierre. He was an Acadian and took the oath of allegiance in Apr. 1730.

Olp, Bernhard. He was naturalized in New Jersey in 1761.

Omstadt, John. He was naturalized in Pennsylvania 25–27 Sep. 1740. He was from Philadelphia County.

Onckbauck, Adam. He took the oath to the King 21–26 Oct. 1664 after the conquest of New Netherland.

Onstend, George. He was naturalized in Maryland 13 Apr. 1763. He was a German from Frederick County.

Oosterhout, Teunis. He was naturalized in New York 8–9 Sep. 1715. He was from Ulster County.

Opercock, Jacob. He was naturalized in Maryland 13 Apr. 1763. He was a German from Baltimore County.

Oquein, Alexis. He was an Acadian and took the oath of allegiance in Apr. 1730.

Oquein, Anthoine. He was an Acadian and took the oath of allegiance in Apr. 1730.

Oquein, Anthoine. He was an Acadian and took the oath of allegiance in Apr. 1730.

Oquein, Charles. He was an Acadian and took the oath of allegiance in Apr. 1730.

Oquein, Jean. He was an Acadian and took the oath of allegiance in Apr. 1730.

Oquein, Joseph. He was an Acadian and took the oath of allegiance in Apr. 1730.

Oquein, Martin. He was an Acadian and took the oath of allegiance in Apr. 1730.

Oquein, Martin. He was an Acadian and took the oath of allegiance in Apr. 1730.

Oquein, Michel. He was an Acadian and took the oath of allegiance in Apr. 1730.

Oquein, Paul. He was an Acadian and took the oath of allegiance in Apr. 1730.

Oquein, Paul. He was an Acadian and took the oath of allegiance in Apr. 1730.

Oquein, Pierre. He was an Acadian and took the oath of allegiance in Apr. 1730.

Oquein, Pierre. He was an Acadian and took the oath of allegiance in Apr. 1730.
Oquein, Pierre. He was an Acadian and took the oath of allegiance in Apr. 1730.
Oquein, Rene. He was an Acadian and took the oath of allegiance in Apr. 1730.
Oquin, Rene. He was an Acadian and took the oath of allegiance in Apr. 1730.
Orange, Lewis. He was naturalized in Virginia 12 May 1705.
Orberly, Michael. He was naturalized in Pennsylvania 11 Apr. 1761. He was from Lancaster County.
Ord, William. He was naturalized in Jamaica 17 Feb. 1737/8.
Ordt, John. He was naturalized in Pennsylvania 10 Apr. 1755. He was from Northampton County.
Orendolf, Christian. He was naturalized in Pennsylvania 25 Sep. 1758.
Orilion, Charles. He was an Acadian and took the oath to George II at Annapolis River, Nova Scotia in Dec. 1729.
O'Rillon, Jean Baptist. He was an Acadian and took the oath to George II at Annapolis River, Nova Scotia in Dec. 1729.
Orish, Christopher. He was naturalized in Pennsylvania 25–26 Sep./4 Oct. 1749. He was from Lancaster County.
Orndt, Jacob. He was naturalized in Pennsylvania 24 Sep. 1753. He was from Bucks County.
Ornt, Abraham. He was naturalized in Pennsylvania 24 Sep. 1755. He was from Philadelphia County.
Ortman, Francis. He was naturalized in New York 20 May 1769.
Osier, John. He and his sons, Jacob Osier, William Osier, and John Osier, were naturalized in Maryland 30 Apr. 1736. He was from a planter from Cecil County and was born in France.
Osshyer, Anthony. He was naturalized in Pennsylvania 10 Apr. 1765. He was from Easton Township, Northampton County.
Osten, Hendrick Teno. He was naturalized in Jamaica 18 June 1720.
Osternhoudt, John, Jr. He took the oath of naturalization in New York 1 Sep. 1687 in Ulster County.
Ostertoghr, Christian. He was naturalized in Maryland 13 Apr. 1761.
Oswald, Henry. He was naturalized in Pennsylvania 11 Apr. 1763. He was from Lynn Township, Northampton County.
Oswald, Philip. He was naturalized in New York 20 May 1769.
Othason, Otho. He was naturalized in Maryland 3 Oct. 1704. He lived in Cecil County. He was born in Pennsylvania of Dutch parents who were from Gulderland, Holland.
Ott, Casper. He was naturalized in Pennsylvania 25–27 Sep. 1740. He was from Bucks County.
Ott, Frank. He was naturalized in New York 20 Mar. 1762.
Ott, Henry. He was naturalized in Pennsylvania 25–27 Sep. 1740. He was from Bucks County.
Ott, Jacob. He was naturalized in New York 18 Oct. 1765.
Ott, John George. He was naturalized in Pennsylvania 11 Apr. 1763. He was from Bristol Township, Bucks County.
Ott, Michael. He was naturalized in Maryland 11 Sep. 1765. He was a German from Frederick County.
Ott, Nicholas. He was naturalized in New Jersey in 1768.
Ott, Nicholas. He was naturalized in Pennsylvania 24 Sep. 1762. He was from York County.
Ottinger, Christopher. He was naturalized in Pennsylvania 19 May 1739. He was from Philadelphia County.
Ottinger, John Jacob. He was naturalized in Pennsylvania 11 Apr. 1761. He was from York County.
Ottman, Henry. He was naturalized in Pennsylvania 11–13 Apr. 1743. He was from Philadelphia County.
Otto, Frank. He was naturalized in New York 20 Mar. 1762.
Otto, Frans. He was naturalized in New York 20 Mar. 1762.
Otto, Gerrit. He was naturalized in New Castle County, Delaware 21 Feb. 1682/3.
Otto, John Matthew. He was naturalized in Pennsylvania 24 Sep. 1762. He was from Northampton County.
Otto, Mathias. He was naturalized in Pennsylvania in Sep. 1740. He was from Philadelphia County.
Otto, Peter. He was naturalized in Maryland 15 Apr. 1771. He was a German.

Oufensanberger, Peter. He was naturalized in Pennsylvania 24 Sep. 1755. He was from Lancaster County.

Ough, George. He was naturalized in New York 8 Mar. 1773.

Ouldson, John. He was naturalized in Maryland 9 June 1692. He lived in Kent County.

Ouldson, Peter. He was naturalized in Maryland 17 Sep. 1681.

Outgelt, Frederick. He was naturalized in New Jersey in 1770.

Outman, Johannes. He was naturalized in New York 23 Aug. 1715. He was a merchant from New York City.

Overacker, Michael. He was naturalized in New York 3 May 1755.

Overacker, Wendel. He was naturalized in New York 3 May 1755.

Overard, Peter. He was naturalized in Maryland 15 Nov. 1712. He lived in Annapolis and was a saddler. He also appeared as Peter Owerard.

Overbach, Jorg. He was naturalized in New York 8–9 Sep. 1715. He was from Ulster County.

Overbach, Peter. He was naturalized in New York 8–9 Sep. 1715. He was from Ulster County.

Overbeck, Andreas. He was naturalized in Pennsylvania 11 Apr. 1741. He was from Philadelphia County.

Overbeck, Hans George. He was naturalized in Pennsylvania 11–13 Apr. 1743. He was from Philadelphia County.

Overbeck, John Hendrick. He was naturalized in Jamaica 4 July 1722.

Overholser, Jacob. He was naturalized in Pennsylvania 11–13 Apr. 1743. He was from Philadelphia County.

Overholser, Jacob, Jr. He was naturalized in Pennsylvania 11–13 Apr. 1743. He was from Philadelphia County. He also appeared as Jacob Overhalser.

Overholster, Jacob. He was naturalized in Pennsylvania 11–13 Apr. 1743. He was from Philadelphia County.

Overholtzer, Henry. He was naturalized in Pennsylvania 11–13 Apr. 1743. He was from Philadelphia County.

Overpach, Johan Peter. He was naturalized in New York 8–9 Sep. 1715. He was from Ulster County.

Overpeck, Jacob. He was naturalized in Pennsylvania 11 Apr. 1761. He was from Berks County.

Overshield, Peter. He was naturalized in Pennsylvania 24 Sep. 1763. He was from Kingwood, West New Jersey.

Overyser, Casper. He was naturalized in New York 3 July 1759.

Owle, Carel. He was naturalized in New York 8–9 Sep. 1715. He was from Ulster County.

Owle, Henrich. He was naturalized in New York 8–9 Sep. 1715. He was from Ulster County.

Ox, Hans Adam. He was naturalized in Pennsylvania 11–13 Apr. 1743. He was from Philadelphia County.

Ox, Leonard. He was naturalized in Pennsylvania 11–13 Apr. 1743. He was from Philadelphia County.

Oxbury, Alexander. He was naturalized in New York 21 Apr. 1762. He was a cordwainer from New York City.

Pacheco, Rodrigo. He was endenized in London 12 Dec. 1711. He was a merchant of New York.

Packer, David. He was naturalized in Jamaica 4 Apr. 1682.

Packet, Daniel. He was naturalized in Maryland 15 Nov. 1712. He lived in Anne Arundel County. He was a laborer.

Packquett, Jeremy. He was naturalized in Virginia 20 Sep. 1673.

Pacquett, Daniel. He was naturalized in Maryland 11 Nov. 1709. He lived in Anne Arundel County.

Pagett, David. He, his wife Mauldin Pagett, daughter Elizabeth Pagett, and children yet unborn were naturalized in Maryland 3 Nov. 1711. He lived in Queen Anne's County and was French.

Painter, Alexander. He was naturalized in Augusta County, Virginia 16 Oct. 1765.

Painter, John. He was naturalized in New York 31 July 1760. He was a shopkeeper from New York City.

Pairtree, John. He was naturalized in Augusta County, Virginia 23 Mar. 1771.

Palache, Esther. She was naturalized in Jamaica 9 Jan. 1738/9.

Palache, Joshua. He was naturalized in Jamaica 6 July 1732.

Palier, Philip. He was naturalized in Massachusetts 7 Dec. 1731.

Palma, Giovanni. He was naturalized in Jamaica 3 July 1758.

Palmentier, Michiel. He took the oath of allegiance in Boswijck, Kings County, New York 26–30 Sep. 1687. He had been in the colony 23 years.

Palmer, Christian. He was naturalized in Pennsylvania 24 Sep. 1755. He was from Lancaster County.

Paltot, Pierre. He was endenized in New York 6 Feb. 1695/6.

Paltsgraaff, George. He was naturalized in Pennsylvania 24 Sep. 1741. He was from Philadelphia County.

Panet, Johannes. He was naturalized in New York 29 July 1762. He was from New York City.

Panetier, John. He was naturalized in Virginia 12 May 1705.

Pannibecker, Wigand. He was naturalized in Pennsylvania 11 Apr. 1761. He was from Philadelphia County.

Panz, Adam. He was naturalized in Maryland 17 July 1765. He was a German.

Para, Pieter. He took the oath of allegiance in Boswijck, Kings County, New York 26–30 Sep. 1687. He had been in the colony 28 years.

Parandier, James. He was naturalized in Maryland 22 Apr. 1720. He lived in Charles County and was French.

Parandier, John. He was naturalized in Maryland 22 Apr. 1720. He lived in Charles County and was French.

Parant, Cornelius. He was naturalized in New Jersey 21 June 1754.

Parda, Hester. She was naturalized in Jamaica 19 Nov. 1696. She was also known as Hester Browne.

Pardo, David. He was naturalized in Jamaica 3 Aug. 1696.

Pardo, Joseph. He was naturalized in Jamaica 6 Aug. 1690. He was also known as Joseph Browne.

Paredes, Abraham. He was naturalized in Jamaica 7 Nov. 1733.

Parmentier, John. He was naturalized in Virginia 12 May 1705.

Parentos, Isaac. He was naturalized in Virginia 12 May 1705.

Paris, Isaac. He was naturalized in New York 20 Mar. 1762.

Paris, Isaac, Jr. He was naturalized in New York 20 Mar. 1762.

Paris, Peter. He was naturalized in Pennsylvania 10 Apr. 1760.

Parisien, Otho. He was naturalized in New York 18 Jan. 1763. He was a French Protestant and a silversmith from New York City.

Parlner, John. He was endenized in New York 25 Nov. 1695.

Parquinett, Peter. He was naturalized in Pennsylvania 15 May 1702. He was born in Tremblade, France, the son of Andrew of Parquinett.

Parra, Judick Lopez. She was naturalized in Jamaica 17 Feb. 1734/5. She was a widow.

Parsenger, Jacob. He was naturalized in Augusta County, Virginia 16 Oct. 1765.

Part, Johannes. He was naturalized in New York 11 Sep. 1761.

Partius, Michael. He was naturalized in Pennsylvania 25 Sep. 1758.

Partridge, Judith. She was naturalized in Jamaica 18 Feb. 1707/8.

Partmess, Adam. He was naturalized in Pennsylvania 24–25 Sep. 1764. He was from Dover Township, Philadelphia County.

Pas, Charles. He was an Acadian and took the oath of allegiance in Apr. 1730.

Pasebell, Charles Theodorus. He was naturalized in Jamaica 30 Apr. 1728.

Pasquerau, Louis. He was born at Tours, France, the son of Louis Pasquerau and Madeleine Chardon. He was naturalized in South Carolina ca. 1696.

Passage, Hans George. He was naturalized in Pennsylvania 19 May 1739. He was from Philadelphia County.

Passer, John Engell. He was naturalized in Jamaica 9 Dec. 1725.

Passer, Susannah Engell. She was naturalized in Jamaica 9 Nov. 1725.

Pasteur, Jean. He was endenized in England 19 Aug. 1688. He was naturalized in Virginia 12 May 1705.

Pastorius, Francis Daniel. He was naturalized in Pennsylvania 29 Sep. 1709. He was from Philadelphia County.

Pastre, John. He was naturalized in England 10 Oct. 1688. He was in Boston, Massachusetts in 1689.

Patterson, Jacob. He was naturalized in Jamaica 7 Feb. 1770.

Patticker, Martin. He was naturalized in Pennsylvania 11 Apr. 1761. He was from Berks County.

Paul, Abraham. He was naturalized in Pennsylvania 11 Apr. 1761. He was from Lancaster County.

Paul, Andrew. He was naturalized in Pennsylvania 24 Sep. 1763. He was from Limerick Township, Philadelphia County.

Paul, John. He was naturalized in Pennsylvania 24–25 Sep./5 Oct. 1767. He was from Vincent Township, Chester County.

Pauluzen, Claes. He took the oath to the King 21–26 Oct. 1664 after the conquest of New Netherland.

Paurier, Charles. He took the oath of allegiance at Harbour Amhurst in the Magdalen Islands, Gulf of Saint Lawrence on 31 Aug. 1765. He was a native of Nova Scotia.

Paurier, Pierre. He took the oath of allegiance at Harbour Amhurst in the Magdalen Islands, Gulf of Saint Lawrence on 31 Aug. 1765. He was a native of Nova Scotia.

Payer, Leonard. He was naturalized in New York 11 Sep. 1761.

Peane, James. He, his wife Magdelen Peane, and daughter Anne Peane were naturalized in Maryland 15 Nov. 1678. They were French.

Pearshler, George. He was naturalized in Pennsylvania 24 Sep. 1763. He was from Oley Township, Berks County.

Pechin, Christopher. He was naturalized in Pennsylvania 11 Apr. 1763. He was from Philadelphia.

Pechin, Peter. He was naturalized in Pennsylvania 24 Sep. 1763. He was from Haverford Township, Chester County.

Peck, Jacob. He was naturalized in Frederick County, Virginia 5 May 1747.

Peck, Jacob. He was naturalized in Pennsylvania 10 Apr. 1760.

Pecker, John. He was naturalized in Maryland 28 Apr. 1772. He was a German.

Pecker, Peter. He was naturalized in Maryland 11 Sep. 1765.

Pecontal, Jean. He was born at Cossade, Languedoc, France, the son of Jean Pecontal and Anne Nonnelle. He was naturalized in South Carolina ca. 1696.

Peelman, Christian. He was naturalized in Pennsylvania 14 Feb. 1729/30. He was from Lancaster County.

Peer, Jacob. He was naturalized in New Jersey 8 July 1730. He was born in Germany.

Peisch, Christian. He was naturalized in Nova Scotia 6 July 1758.

Peixsoto, Joseph. He was naturalized in Jamaica 14 Apr. 1731.

Peker, Ernst. He was naturalized in New York 11 Sep. 1761.

Pele, Jean. He was the son of Pierre and Judith Pele and was born at Pais de Vaud, Switzerland. His wife was Gabrielle Pele. They were naturalized in South Carolina ca. 1696.

Pellerin, Alexandre. He was an Acadian and took the oath to George II at Annapolis River, Nova Scotia in Dec. 1729.

Pellerin, Bernarde. He was an Acadian and took the oath to George II at Annapolis River, Nova Scotia in Dec. 1729.

Pellerin, Charles. He was an Acadian and took the oath to George II at Annapolis River, Nova Scotia in Dec. 1729.

Pellerin, Etienne. He took the oath of allegiance at Port Royal, Nova Scotia 16 Aug. 1695.

Pellerin, Jean Baptist. He was an Acadian and took the oath to George II at Annapolis River, Nova Scotia in Dec. 1729.

Peltrau, Jean. He was endenized in New York 17 Sep. 1685.

Pemart, Francis. He was naturalized in New York 20 Dec. 1763.

Pena, Abraham Lopez. He was naturalized in Jamaica 12 Feb. 1756. He was from Kingston Parish.

Pence, George. He was naturalized in New Jersey in 1760. He was from Northampton, Burlington County. He had lived in the colony twenty-two years. He also appeared as Joh: George Spence.

Pence, Michael. He was naturalized in Maryland 9 Sep. 1761.

Pence, Wyrick. He was naturalized in Pennsylvania 11–12 Apr. 1744. He was from Lancaster County.

Pender, Mathias. He was naturalized in Pennsylvania in Sep. 1740. He was from Philadelphia County.

Pener, Peter. He was naturalized in Pennsylvania 25 Sep. 1750. He was from Philadelphia County.

Penheiro, Samuel Lopez. He was naturalized in Jamaica 10 Sep. 1742.

Penier, Peter. He was naturalized in New Jersey 28 Nov. 1760. He was born in Canton Bern, Switzerland. He was a lieutenant in the 62nd or Royal American Regiment of Foot. He had been in America less than five years.

Peninger, Henry. He was naturalized in Augusta County, Virginia 18 May 1762.

Peninger, Urich. He was naturalized in Pennsylvania 11 Apr. 1751. He was from Philadelphia County.

Penkick, Joseph. He was naturalized in Pennsylvania in Sep. 1740. He was from Philadelphia County.

Pennea, Rebecca. She was naturalized in Jamaica 24 Nov. 1741. She was a Jewess.

Pennebecker, Henry. He was naturalized in Pennsylvania 6 Feb. 1730/1. He was from Philadelphia County.

Penner, Veit. He was naturalized in Pennsylvania 24 Sep. 1762. He was from York County.

Penso, Jacob Alvarez. He was naturalized in Jamaica 19 Jan. 1687/8.

Pentz, Adam. He was naturalized in Maryland 13 Apr. 1763. He was a German.

Pentz, John Philip. He was naturalized in Pennsylvania 10 Apr. 1765. He was from York Township, York County.

Pepin, Paul. He was born at Grenoble, France, the son of Alexandre Pepin and Madeleine Garillon. He was naturalized in South Carolina ca. 1696.

Peppla, William. He was naturalized in Maryland 29 Apr. 1772. He was a German.

Perall, Antony. He was naturalized in Jamaica 17 Nov. 1730.

Peraro, Emanuel. He was naturalized in Massachusetts 8 Sep. 1760. He was from Portugal and was a mariner in Boston.

Perdigo, Elizabeth. She was naturalized in Jamaica 11 July 1694. She was the wife of Francis Perdigo.

Perdigo, Francis. He was naturalized in Jamaica 30 Aug. 1717.

Perdriau, Oree. He was naturalized in England 5 Apr. 1687. He had it recorded in New York 28 May 1691 and in South Carolina 1 Nov. 1698.

Perdriau, Stephen. He was naturalized in England 5 Apr. 1687. He had it recorded in New York 28 May 1691 and in South Carolina 1 Nov. 1698.

Perdo, John. He was naturalized in Pennsylvania 11–13 Apr. 1743. He was from Philadelphia County.

Perdriaux, Stephen. He was endenized in England 9 Apr. 1687. He came to New York.

Pere, John Casper. He was naturalized in New York 16 Feb. 1771.

Pereira, Abraham. He was naturalized in New York 28 Feb. 1715/6. He was a tallow chandler from New York City.

Pereira, Abraham Lopez. He was naturalized in Jamaica 15 Mar. 1709.

Pereira, Benjamin. He was naturalized in Jamaica 28 July 1693.

Pereira, Benjamin Mendes. He was naturalized in Jamaica 18 June 1772.

Pereira, David. He was naturalized in Jamaica 10 Mar. 1728/9.

Pereira, David Lopes. He was naturalized in Jamaica 19 Mar. 1693/4.

Pereira, Esther Lopes. She was naturalized in Jamaica 27 Aug. 1745. She was a Jewess.

Pereira, Isaac. He was naturalized in Jamaica 1 Nov. 1687.

Pereira, Isaac, Jr. He was naturalized in Jamaica 3 Oct. 1711.

Pereira, Isaac Mendes. He was naturalized in Jamaica 30 Aug. 1761.

Pereira, Isaac Rodriques. He was naturalized in Jamaica 26 Dec. 1746.

Pereira, Jacob. He was naturalized in Jamaica 7 May 1716.

Pereira, Jacob Lopez. He was naturalized in Jamaica 20 Feb. 1699.

Pereira, Jacob Soraes. He was naturalized in Jamaica 22 Feb. 1725/6.

Pereira, Joseph Soares. He was naturalized in Jamaica 21 Aug. 1733.

Pereira, Moses. He was naturalized in Jamaica 23 Mar. 1699/1700.

Pereira, Rachel Fernandes. She was naturalized in Jamaica 26 Aug. 1746. She was a Jewess.

Pereira, Rachell. She was naturalized in Jamaica 6 Apr. 1709.

Pereira, Rebecka. She was naturalized in Jamaica 21 Apr. 1740. She was the wife of Joseph Pereira.

Pereira, Sarah. She was naturalized in Jamaica 17 Dec. 1723.

Peres, Peter. He was naturalized in Pennsylvania 10–12 Apr. 1762. He was from York County.

Pereyra, Abraham. He was naturalized in Jamaica 8 June 1685.

Pereyra, Menaseh. He was naturalized in Jamaica 29 July 1690.

Pereyra, Moseh. He was endenized in London 17 Feb. 1670/1. He was a merchant from Barbados.

Perksdole, Nicodemus. He was born in Frederick County, Virginia 1 Aug. 1769.

Pernette, Jos. He was naturalized in Nova Scotia 22 Sep. 1758.

Perodeau, Guillaume. He was endenized in New York 2 Sep. 1685.

Peronneau, Henry. He was born at LaRochelle, France, the son of Samuel Peronneau and Jeanne Collin. He was naturalized in South Carolina 10 Mar. 1696/7. He was a merchant.

Perot, James. He was endenized in London 24 June 1703. He came to New York.

Perry, Christian. He was naturalized in Pennsylvania 12 Apr. 1750. He was from Chester County.

Perry, John. He was naturalized in Jamaica 26 Apr. 1753.

Pertsch, Andrew. He was naturalized in Pennsylvania 24–25 Sep. 1764. He was from Philadelphia.

Peru, Peter. He was naturalized in Virginia 12 May 1705.

Pesaro, Thomas. He was naturalized in Jamaica 29 July 1702.

Peschaire, Francis. He was naturalized in Jamaica 14 Nov. 1704.

Peteet, John. He took the oath of naturalization in New York 1 Sep. 1687 in Ulster County.

Petel, John. He was naturalized in Massachusetts 12 Apr. 1731.

Peteneau, John. He was naturalized in South Carolina 10 Mar. 1696/7.

Peter, Abraham. He was naturalized in Pennsylvania 11–13 Apr. 1743. He was from Philadelphia County.

Peter, Henry. He was naturalized in Pennsylvania 24 Sep. 1762. He was from York County.

Peter, Ingle. He was naturalized in Pennsylvania 11–13 Apr. 1743. He was from Philadelphia County.

Peter, Johannes. He was naturalized in Pennsylvania 11 Apr. 1761. He was from Philadelphia County.

Peteriz, Jan Dewit. He was naturalized in New York 20 Sep. 1728.

Peterman, Jacob. He was naturalized in Pennsylvania 11 Apr. 1763. He was from Philadelphia County.

Peters, Christian. He was naturalized in Maryland 8 Aug. 1729. He lived in Cecil County and was German.

Peters, Gerhard. He was naturalized in Pennsylvania 6 Feb. 1730/1. He was from Philadelphia County.

Peters, Godfrey. He was naturalized in New Jersey 8 July 1730. He was born in Germany.

Peters, Hendrick. He was naturalized in Pennsylvania 25–27 Sep. 1740. He was from Philadelphia County.

Peters, Jacob. He was naturalized in Pennsylvania 25–27 Sep. 1740. He was from Philadelphia County.

Peters, Peter. He was naturalized in Pennsylvania 25–27 Sep. 1740. He was from Philadelphia County.

Petersen, Adam. He was naturalized in New Castle County, Delaware 21 Feb. 1682/3.

Petersen, Hans. He was naturalized in New Castle County, Delaware 21 Feb. 1682/3.

Peterson, Carell. He expressed his desire to be naturalized in New Castle County, Delaware 21 Feb. 1682/3.

Peterson, Christian. He was naturalized in Virginia in Mar. 1675/6.

Peterson, Cornelius. He was naturalized in Maryland 6 June 1674. He was Swedish.

Peterson, Cornelius. He was naturalized in Jamaica 7 Aug. 1706.

Peterson, George. He was naturalized in New York 17 Apr. 1744. He was a sugar baker from New York City.

Peterson, Hans. He was naturalized in Maryland 6 June 1674. He was Danish. He also appeared as Hance Peterson.

Peterson, Jacob. He was made a denizen in North Carolina in Mar. 1697/8. He had been an inhabitant of the English government for seventeen years and had previously lived in Maryland where he received his denization on 2 Nov. 1677.

Peterson, Jacob. He took the oath to the King 21–26 Oct. 1664 after the conquest of New Netherland.

Peterson, Jacob. He was naturalized in Augusta County, Virginia 21 Nov. 1764.

Peterson, John. He was naturalized in Virginia in Oct. 1673.

Peterson, Mathias. He and his son, Peter Peterson, were naturalized in Maryland 19 Apr. 1671. They lived in Talbot County and were Dutch.

Peterson, Mathias. He and his children were naturalized in Maryland 6 Nov. 1685.

Petit, [——]. He was a Roman Catholic priest and took the oath of allegiance at Port Royal, Nova Scotia 16 Aug. 1695.

Petit, Joshua. He was naturalized in Virginia 12 May 1705.

Petit, John. He was endenized in Virginia 7 Nov. 1666. He was born in France. He had a family of children. He was from York County. He also appeared as John Peteete.

Petitot, Denis. He took the oath of allegiance at Port Royal, Nova Scotia 16 Aug. 1695.

Petitot dit St. Scemes, Reny. He was an Acadian and took the oath to George II at Annapolis River, Nova Scotia in the winter of 1730.

Petitpass, Claude. He took the oath of allegiance at Port Royal, Nova Scotia 16 Aug. 1695.

Petre, Antoine. He was an Acadian and took the oath of allegiance in Apr. 1730.

Petre, Claude. He was an Acadian and took the oath of allegiance in Apr. 1730.

Petre, Claude. He was an Acadian and took the oath of allegiance in Apr. 1730.

Petre, Claude. He was an Acadian and took the oath of allegiance in Apr. 1730.

Petre, Jacob. He was naturalized in Pennsylvania 10–12 Apr. 1762. He was from Bucks County.

Petre, Jean. He was an Acadian and took the oath of allegiance in Apr. 1730.

Petre, Jean. He was an Acadian and took the oath of allegiance in Apr. 1730.

Petre, Jean, Jr. He was an Acadian and took the oath of allegiance in Apr. 1730.

Petre, Jean Baptiste. He was an Acadian and took the oath to George II at Annapolis River, Nova Scotia in the winter of 1730.

Petre, Joseph. He was an Acadian and took the oath of allegiance in Apr. 1730.

Petre, Pierre. He was an Acadian and took the oath of allegiance in Apr. 1730.

Petri, George. He was naturalized in Pennsylvania 24 Sep. 1762. He was from Lancaster County.

Petrie, Johan Coenraet. He was naturalized in New York 22 Nov. 1715. He was from Albany County.

Petrie, William. He was naturalized in New York 27 Jan. 1770.

Petters, Andries. He took the oath of naturalization in New York 1 Sep. 1687 in Ulster County.

Petterson, Cornelis. He took the oath of naturalization in New York 1 Sep. 1687 in Ulster County.

Pett[e]rson, John. He took the oath of naturalization in New York 1 Sep. 1687 in Ulster County.

Petterson, Petter. He took the oath of naturalization in New York 1 Sep. 1687 in Ulster County.

Peydleman, Dedrick. He was naturalized in Pennsylvania 11–13 Apr. 1743. He was from Philadelphia County.

Pfatteger, Martin. He was naturalized in Pennsylvania 10 Sep. 1761. He was from Berks County.

Pfaffhauser, Jacob. He was naturalized in Nova Scotia 5 July 1758.

Pfeffer, Michael. He was naturalized in New York 23 Aug. 1715. He was a laborer from New York City.

Pfeiffer, Daniel. He was naturalized in Pennsylvania 10 & 23 Apr. 1764. He was from Amwell, Hunterdon County, New Jersey.

Pfeiffer, Henrick. He was naturalized in Maryland 13 Sep. 1758.

Pfiefer, Jacob. He was naturalized in New Jersey in 1775. He lived in Gloucester County. He was born in Germany. He also appeared as Jacob Phifer.

Pfiffer, Jacob. He was naturalized in Maryland 3 Sep. 1765. He was a German from Sharpsburgh, Maryland.

Pfister, Casper. He was naturalized in Pennsylvania 24 Sep. 1763. He was from Lampeter Township, Lancaster County.

Pfister, George Adam. He was naturalized in Pennsylvania 10–12 Apr. 1762. He was from Philadelphia County.

Pfister, Henrick. He was naturalized in Maryland 10 Apr. 1762. He was a German from Anne Arundel County.

Pfister, Jacob. He was naturalized in Pennsylvania 10 Apr. 1754. He was from Philadelphia County.

Pflubach, Jacob. He was naturalized in Maryland 11 Apr. 1759.

Pfotezer, George. He was naturalized in Pennsylvania 11 Apr. 1761. He was from Lancaster County.

Phaisant, John James. He was naturalized in Virginia 12 May 1705.

Phannet, Andrew. He was endenized in New York 6 Feb. 1695/6.

Pheger, John. He was naturalized in New Jersey 20 Aug. 1755.

Phenus, Philip. He was naturalized in New York 31 July 1766. He was a tailor from New Town, Queens County.

Phifester, Francis. He was naturalized in New York 24 Mar. 1772.

Phile, Frederic. He was naturalized in Pennsylvania 26 Feb. 1773. He was a practitioner of physic in Philadelphia.

Philip, Valentine. He was naturalized in Pennsylvania 10 Apr. 1765. He was from Rockland Township, Bucks County.

Philips, Jonas. He was naturalized in New York 25 Apr. 1771. He was a merchant from New York City.

Philips, John. He was naturalized in Pennsylvania 24 Sep. 1762. He was from Berks County.

Philips, Nicholas. He was naturalized in Maryland 16 Apr. 1761.

Philips, Nicholas. He was naturalized in New Jersey 28 Apr. 1762.

Philips, Nicolas. He was naturalized in New York 17 Jan. 1715/6. He was from Albany County.

Philips, Peter. He was naturalized in New York 17 Jan. 1715/6. He was from Albany County.

Phillipeaux, Jean Baptist. He took the oath of allegiance at Mobile, West Florida 2 Oct. 1764.

Philpock, John. He was naturalized in Maryland 9 Sep. 1761. He was from Anne Arundel County.

Phister, John. He was naturalized in Pennsylvania 25 Sep. 1769. He was from Northampton Township, Bucks County.

Picar, Louis. He was naturalized in South Carolina in ca. 1696.

Pickenpagh, Leonard. He was naturalized in Maryland 29 Sep. 1762. He was a German from Frederick County.

Pickle, Henry. He was naturalized in Augusta County, Virginia 18 May 1762.

Pickle, Ludwick. He was naturalized in Pennsylvania 24 Sep. 1755. He was from Philadelphia County.

Pickle, Tobias. He was naturalized in Pennsylvania 19 May 1739. He was from Lancaster County.

Pickler, Mark. He was naturalized in Maryland 19 Oct. 1743.

Picot, Michel. He was an Acadian who took the oath of allegiance at Annapolis River in Dec. 1729.

Piecus, George. He was naturalized in Pennsylvania 10–12 Apr. 1762. He was from Philadelphia County.

Pieler, Adam. He was naturalized in Nova Scotia 5 July 1758.

Pier, Harrama. He took the oath of naturalization in New York 1 Sep. 1687 in Ulster County.

Pieter, Abraham. He took the oath to the King 21–26 Oct. 1664 after the conquest of New Netherland.

Pieters, Reintse. He took the oath to the King 21–26 Oct. 1664 after the conquest of New Netherland. He was from Blosart.

Pieterse, Cornelis. He took the oath of allegiance in Flackbush, Kings County, New York 26–30 Sep. 1687. He was a native of the colony.

Pieterse, Lefferd. He took the oath of allegiance in Flackbush, Kings County, New York 26–30 Sep. 1687. He had been in the colony 27 years.

Pieterse, Marten. He took the oath of allegiance in Gravens End, Kings County, New York 26–30 Sep. 1687. He was a native of the colony.

Pietersen, Samuel. He expressed his desire to be naturalized in New Castle County, Delaware 21 Feb. 1682/3.

Pietersen, Thomas. He was naturalized in New Castle County, Delaware 7 Aug. 1683. He was a Norman.

Pietersenproot, Jan. He expressed his desire to be naturalized in New Castle County, Delaware 21 Feb. 1682/3.

Pieterzen, Albert. He took the oath to the King 21–26 Oct. 1664 after the conquest of New Netherland. He was a trumpeter.

Pieterzen, Nathanael. He took the oath to the King 21–26 Oct. 1664 after the conquest of New Netherland.

Piffer, Joseph. He was naturalized in Pennsylvania 24 Sep. 1763. He was from Springfield Township, Philadelphia County.

Pignott, Michell. He was an Acadian and took the oath to George II at Annapolis River, Nova Scotia in the winter of 1730.

Pilet, Philip. He was naturalized in New York 27 Jan. 1770.

Pimmitt, John. He was naturalized in Virginia in Apr. 1679.

Pinaud, Paul. He was naturalized in New York 26 July 1715. He was a laborer.

Pincherio, Abraham Lopez. He was naturalized in Jamaica 13 Jan. 1724/5.

Pinckly, John. He was naturalized in Maryland 14 Apr. 1760. He also appeared as John Binckly.

Pineau, Jacques. He was endenized in England 28 Dec. 1687. He came to Rhode Island and later settled in Lebanon, Connecticut where he was made a freeman.

Pingart, Jeane. She was naturalized in Jamaica 27 July 1682.

Pingeman, Hans. He was naturalized in Pennsylvania 29 Mar. 1735. He was from Philadelphia County.

Pinkley, Joannes. He was naturalized in Pennsylvania 19 May 1739. He was from Lancaster County.

Pinson, James. He was naturalized in Virginia 12 May 1705.

Pintard, Anthony. He was a French Protestant and applied for denization in 1691 in New York.

Pintard, Gabriel. He was naturalized in Jamaica 30 July 1690.

Pinto, Abraham. He was naturalized in New York 28 Feb. 1715/6. He was a merchant from New York City.

Pinto, Daniel Rodriques. He was naturalized in Jamaica 16 Sep. 1734.

Pinto, Isaac. He was naturalized in Jamaica 11 Jan. 1710/11.

Pinto, Jacob. He was naturalized in Jamaica 13 Nov. 1710.

Pinto, Joseph. He was naturalized in Jamaica 29 Apr. 1728.

Pinto, Joseph Jesurum. He was naturalized in New York 22 Jan. 1766. He was a Jewish minister from New York City.

Piper, John Michael. He was naturalized in Pennsylvania 10 & 23 Apr. 1764. He was from Philadelphia.

Piper, William. He was naturalized in Maryland 14 Sep. 1763.

Pisel, Peter. He was naturalized in Pennsylvania 25 Sep. 1751. He was from Philadelphia County.

Pitre, Jean Baptiste. He was an Acadian who took the oath of allegiance at Annapolis River in Dec. 1729.

Pitt, Jacob. He was naturalized in New York 3 July 1718.

Pitt, Jan. He was naturalized in New York 3 July 1718.

Pitting, Lodwick. He was naturalized in Pennsylvania 29 Mar. 1735. He was from Philadelphia County.

Pitting, Martin. He was naturalized in Pennsylvania 29 Mar. 1735. He was from Philadelphia County.

Plank, Adam. He was naturalized in New York 16 Feb. 1771.

Plansz, Johannes. He was naturalized in New York 11 Sep. 1761.

Plantin, John. He was naturalized in New York 19 Dec. 1765.

Plas, Johan Hend. He was naturalized in New York 17 Jan. 1715/6. He was from Albany County

Pleninger, Matthias. He was naturalized in New Jersey in 1766. He was born in Germany and had been in the colony sixteen years.

Pletel, Johannes Jacob. He, his wife Anne Elizabeth Pletel, and daughters Catharine Pletel, Margaret Pletel, and Anne Sarah Pletel, were endenized in London 25 Aug. 1708. They came to New York.

Pletz, Cornelius. He was naturalized in Jamaica 3 Apr. 1760.

Pleyson, John. He was naturalized in Jamaica 26 May 1701.

Plieger, Tobias. He was naturalized in Pennsylvania 24 Sep. 1763. He was from Lancaster Township, Lancaster County.

Pliler, Jacob. He was naturalized in Pennsylvania 10 & 23 Apr. 1764. He was from Alsace Township, Lancaster County.

Plockhoy, Cornelis. He was naturalized in Sussex County, Delaware 28 Apr. 1683.

Plum, George. He was naturalized in Pennsylvania 24–25 Sep. 1764. He was from Philadelphia.

Plum, Ludwig. He was naturalized in Pennsylvania 10–14 Apr. 1747. He was from Philadelphia County.

Plutner, Michael. He was naturalized in Pennsylvania 24 Sep. 1762. He was from Philadelphia County.

Pluvier, Cornelius. He took the oath to the King 21–26 Oct. 1664 after the conquest of New Netherland.

Poast, John Johnson. He took the oath of naturalization in New York 1 Sep. 1687 in Ulster County.

Pocke, Adam. He was naturalized in New Jersey 20 Aug. 1755.

Poger, George. He was naturalized in Pennsylvania 25 Sep. 1747. He was from Philadelphia County.

Poh, John Jacob. He was naturalized in Pennsylvania 24 Sep. 1762. He was from Berks County.

Poideuin, Anthoine. He was born in Menthenon, Gaule, France and was the son of Anthoinne Poideuin and Gabrielle Berou. His wife was Marguerite DeBourdos, a native of Grenoble in Dofine, France, the daughter of Jacque DeBourdos and Madelenne Garilian. They were naturalized in South Carolina ca. 1696. Compare with Poiteum.

Poinier, Peter. He was naturalized in New Jersey 17 Mar. 1713/4. He was a native of France and a Protestant. He also appeared as Peter Remuer and Peter Romier.

Poinset, Pierre, Sr. He was born at Soubize, France, the son of Pierre and Marie Poinset. He was naturalized in South Carolina 10 Mar. 1696/7. He was a smith.

Poinset, Pierre, Jr. He was born at Soubize, France, the son of Pierre Poinset, Sr., and Sara Foucherau. His wife was Anne Gobard. They were naturalized in South Carolina 10 Mar. 1696/7. He was a smith.

Poirier, Jean. He was an Acadian and took the oath of allegiance in Apr. 1730.

Poirier, Jean. He was an Acadian and took the oath of allegiance in Apr. 1730.

Poirier, Jean. He was an Acadian and took the oath of allegiance in Apr. 1730.

Poirier, Joseph. He was an Acadian and took the oath of allegiance in Apr. 1730.

Poirier, Joseph. He was an Acadian and took the oath of allegiance in Apr. 1730.

Poirier, Louis. He was an Acadian and took the oath of allegiance in Apr. 1730.

Poirier, Michel. He was an Acadian and took the oath of allegiance in Apr. 1730.

Poirier, Michel. He was an Acadian and took the oath of allegiance in Apr. 1730.

Poirier, Michel. He was an Acadian and took the oath of allegiance in Apr. 1730. He was styled "de France."

Poirier, Pierre. He was an Acadian and took the oath of allegiance in Apr. 1730.

Poirier, Rene. He was an Acadian and took the oath of allegiance in Apr. 1730.

Poiteuin, Anthonie, He was a native of Orsemont, Gaule, France, the son of Jacque Poiteuin and Jenne Modemen. His wife was Gabrielle Berou, a native of Ormey, Bause, the daughter of Utrope Berou and Andree LeProu. They were naturalized in South Carolina 10 Mar. 1696/7. He was a weaver.

Poiteuin, Pierre. He was born in Menthenon, Gaule, France, son of Anthoinne Poiteuin and Gabrielle Berou. He was naturalized in South Carolina 10 Mar. 1696/7. He was a planter.

Poiteum, Anthonie. He was born at Maintenon, France, the son of Anthoine Poiteum and Gabrielle Berou. His wife was Margueritte DeBordeaux. They were naturalized in South Carolina 10 Mar. 1696/7. He was a weaver. Compare with Poideuin.

Poker, Jacob. He was naturalized in Frederick County, Virginia 4 Mar. 1766.

Polander, Abigail. She was naturalized in Jamaica 27 Oct. 1737. She was the wife of Joseph Polander, merchant.

Polander, Abigail. She was naturalized in Jamaica 16 Nov. 1752. She was a widow.

Polander, Eleazer. He was naturalized in Jamaica 29 June 1714.

Polfer, Michael. He was naturalized in New York 3 May 1755.

Polfer, Peter. He was naturalized in New York 3 May 1755.

Polhemius, Daniel. He took the oath of allegiance in Flackbush, Kings County, New York 26–30 Sep. 1687. He was a native of the colony.

Pollman, John William. He was naturalized in New Jersey 20 June 1765.

Polsell, Peter. He was naturalized in Maryland 15 Apr. 1761.

Polt, Michael. He was naturalized in New York 3 July 1766.

Poltz, Michael. He was naturalized in New York 3 May 1755.

Pommier, Francis. He was naturalized in Virginia 12 May 1705.

Pontius, Adam. He was naturalized in New York 3 July 1759.

Pontius, Christian. He was naturalized in New York 21 Apr. 1762. He was a tailor from New York City.

Pontius, John. He was naturalized in Pennsylvania 10–12 Apr. 1762. He was from Berks County.

Pontius, Nicholas. He was naturalized in Pennsylvania 24 Sep. 1762. He was from Berks County.

Pooderbach, George. He was naturalized in Pennsylvania 24–29 Sep. 1768. He was from Frederick County, Maryland.

Poor, Pieter. He was naturalized in North Carolina 23 Mar. 1763. He was from Rowan County.

Pope, John Grisman. He was naturalized in Maryland 10 Apr. 1762. He was a German from Frederick County.

Pope, Robert. He was naturalized in Jamaica 20 Jan. 1748/9.

Popelsdorf, William. He was naturalized in New York 8 Nov. 1735.

Popp, Conrad. He was naturalized in Pennsylvania 24–25 Sep. 1764. He was from Brecknock Township, Lancaster County.

Popp, Nicholas. He was naturalized in Pennsylvania 10 Apr. 1765. He was from Bedminster Township, Bucks County.

Popp, Peter. He was naturalized in Pennsylvania 24–25 Sep. 1764. He was from Brecknock Township, Lancaster County.

Popplesdorf, Albertus. He was naturalized in New Jersey 20 Aug. 1755.

Porcher, Isaac. He was born at St. Severe in Berry, France, the son of Isaac Porcher and Suzanne Ferre. His wife was Claude Cheriny. Their children, Isaac Porcher, Pierre Porcher, Madelaine Porcher, and Claude Porcher, were born in England and South Carolina. They were naturalized in South Carolina *ca.* 1696.

Poree, Peter. He was naturalized in Rhode Island 3 Aug. 1763. He came from the French West Indies to Newport.

Porell, —. He was naturalized in South Carolina *ca.* 1696.

Porlier, Baptiste. He was an Acadian who took the oath of allegiance at Annapolis River in Dec. 1729.

Portello, Ester. She was naturalized in Jamaica 12 Mar. 1721/2.

Porteus, James. He was naturalized in Orange County, Virginia 2 May 1744. He was a native of Stockholm, Sweden.

Porto, Abraham Gomez. He was naturalized in Jamaica 21 Jan. 1684/5.

Porto, Ester Gomes. She was naturalized in Jamaica 28 May 1707.

Pos, Lodowick. He took the oath to the King 21–26 Oct. 1664 after the conquest of New Netherland.

Pos, Willem. He took the oath of allegiance in Breucklijn, Kings County, New York 26–30 Sep. 1687. He was a native of the colony.

Post, Daniel. He was naturalized in New York 17 Jan. 1715/6. He was from Albany County.

Post, Frederick. He was naturalized in Pennsylvania 10 Apr. 1760.

Post, Johan Hend. He was naturalized in New York 17 Jan. 1715/6. He was from Albany County.

Potell, Jean. He was born at Diepe, France, the son of Nicholas Potell and Marye Bruguet. His wife was Madeleine Pepin. Their children, Pierre Potell, Jacques Potell, and Jean Potell, were born in South Carolina. They were naturalized in South Carolina *ca.* 1696.

Potelo, Aron. He was naturalized in Jamaica 22 Feb. 1702.

Pott, Conrod. He was naturalized in Maryland 10 Sep. 1760.

Pott, John. He was naturalized in Pennsylvania 24 Sep. 1759.

Pott, William. He was naturalized in Pennsylvania 11–13 Apr. 1743. He was from Lancaster County.

Potts, George. He was naturalized in Pennsylvania 10 Apr. 1767. He was from Bethel Township, Lancaster County.

Potts, Ludwick. He was naturalized in Maryland 18 Sep. 1764. He was a German.

Poucher, Anthony. He was naturalized in New York 11 Sep. 1761.

Poulsen, Justa. He was naturalized in New Castle County, Delaware 21 Feb. 1682/3.

Poulsen, Oele. He expressed his desire to be naturalized in New Castle County, Delaware 21 Feb. 1682/3.

Poulson, Andrew. He was naturalized in Maryland 6 Nov. 1685. He was alias Andrew Mullock.

Poulson, Henry. He was naturalized in Jamaica 13 Mar. 1759. He was a sea captain.

Pountenay, Henry. He was naturalized in New York 27 Mar. 1716. He was a butcher from New York City.

Poupar, Michel. He was an Acadian and took the oath of allegiance in Apr. 1730.

Poussum, Lawrance. He was naturalized in Maryland 14 Sep. 1763. He was a German.

Pouston, John. He was made a denizen in Maryland 4 Mar. 1663/4. He was a subject of Scotland.

Poutcher, Tunis. He was naturalized in New York 3 May 1755.

Powell, Barnard. He was naturalized in Maryland 11 Sep. 1765.

Powell, Philip. He was naturalized in Maryland 11 Sep. 1765.

Power, Henry. He was naturalized in Maryland 10 Apr. 1762. He was a German from Frederick County.

Powers, George. He was naturalized in New York 20 May 1769.

Powlas, Powlas. He took the oath of naturalization in New York 1 Sep. 1687 in Ulster County.

Powlason, Powlas, Jr. He took the oath of naturalization in New York 1 Sep. 1687 in Ulster County.

Powlis, Jacob. He was naturalized in Maryland 15 Apr. 1763. He was a German from Frederick County.

Powlus, Adam. He was naturalized in Pennsylvania 11 Apr. 1763. He was from Windsor Township, York County.

Powlus, Michael. He was naturalized in Pennsylvania 11 Apr. 1763. He was from Windsor Township, York County.

Powser, Michael. He was naturalized in Pennsylvania 10–12 Apr. 1762. He was from Berks County.

Poyas, John Ernst. He was naturalized in South Carolina 24 Oct. 1741.

Poyshert, Peter. He was naturalized in New York 21 Oct. 1765. He was a blacksmith from New York City.

Predix, Anthony. He was naturalized in Jamaica 26 Mar. 1719.

Preniman, Adam. He was naturalized in Pennsylvania 14 Feb. 1729/30. He was from Lancaster County.

Preniman, Christian. He was naturalized in Pennsylvania 14 Feb. 1729/30. He was from Lancaster County.

Preniman, Christopher. He was naturalized in Pennsylvania 14 Feb. 1729/30. He was from Lancaster County.

Prett, Peter. He was naturalized in Pennsylvania 10–14 Apr. 1747. He was from Lancaster County.

Prette, Isaac Lopes. He was naturalized in Jamaica 25 Aug. 1741. He was a Jew.

Prettiker, Hans Jacob. He was naturalized in New Jersey 28 Apr. 1762.

Prevot, Peter. He was naturalized in Virginia 12 May 1705.

Price, Augustine. He was naturalized in Augusta County, Virginia 16 Oct. 1765.

Price, Conrad. He was naturalized in Pennsylvania 25 Sep. 1753. He was from Berks County.

Priegel, Hans Jorg. He was naturalized in New York 8–9 Sep. 1715. He was from Ulster County.

Prien, Christopher. He was naturalized in New York 3 July 1759.

Priggs, John. He was naturalized in Maryland 21 Oct. 1756. He was a resident of Prince George's County. He was a German.

Prijean, Charles. He was an Acadian and took the oath to George II at Annapolis River, Nova Scotia in Dec. 1729.

Prijean, François. He was an Acadian and took the oath to George II at Annapolis River, Nova Scotia in Dec. 1729.

Prijean, Honore. He was an Acadian and took the oath at Annapolis in Dec. 1729.

Prijean, Jean. He was an Acadian and took the oath at Annapolis in Dec. 1729.

Prijean, Joseph. He was an Acadian and took the oath at Annapolis in Dec. 1729.

Prijean, Pierre. He was an Acadian and took the oath to George II at Annapolis River, Nova Scotia in Dec. 1729.

Prijeant, Francois. He was an Acadian and took the oath of allegiance in Apr. 1730.

Pril, Isaac Fernandes. He was naturalized in Jamaica 26 Feb. 1740/1. He was a Jew.

Prioleau, Elias. He was granted denization in England 15 April in the third year of the reign of King James II. Elias Prioleau was a clergyman. The certificate also covered his wife Jane Prioleau and their children, Elias Prioleau and Jane Prioleau. They were from France. Elias Prioleau and his daughter Jane Prioleau were naturalized in South Carolina 3 June 1697. Elias Prioleau was a son of Samuel Prioleau and Jeanne Merlat. He was born in Xaintaonge, France, and his wife, Jeanne Burgeaud, was born on the Isle of Re. Their daughter, Jeanne Prioleau, was born in St. Jean d'Angely. Their other children, Samuel Prioleau, Marie Prioleau, and Ester Prioleau, were born in Carolina.

Priper, Ernst. He was naturalized in Nova Scotia 6 July 1758.

Proback, Hieronimus. He was naturalized in Pennsylvania 10–12 Apr. 1762. He was from Lancaster County.

Porbasco, Christopffel. He took the oath of allegiance in Flackbush, Kings County, New York 26–30 Sep. 1687. He has been in the colony 35 years.

Probst, Adam. He was naturalized in Pennsylvania 10 Apr. 1760.

Probst, Jacob. He was naturalized in Pennsylvania 13 May 1771. He was from York, York County.

Probst, Martin. He was naturalized in Pennsylvania 24 Sep. 1762. He was from Berks County.

Proctor, Henry. He was naturalized in Pennsylvania 10 Apr. 1760.

Proper, Johan Frederick. He was naturalized in New York 22 Nov. 1715. He was from Albany County.

Proper, Johan Joseph. He was naturalized in New York 22 Nov. 1715. He was from Albany County.

Proper, Johan Pieter. He was naturalized in New York 22 Nov. 1715. He was from Albany County.

Props, Michael. He was naturalized in Augusta County, Virginia 18 May 1762.

Propst, Michael. He was naturalized in Pennsylvania 10 Sep. 1761. He was from Berks County.

Propst, Valentine. He was naturalized in Pennsylvania 10 Sep. 1761. He was from Berks County.

Prosius, Peter. He was naturalized in New York 20 Mar. 1762.

Protzman, Adam. He was naturalized in Pennsylvania 10–12 Apr. 1762. He was from Philadelphia County.

Protzman, Lawrence. He was naturalized in Maryland 12 Apr. 1759. He lived in Frederick County and was a potter.

Protzman, Lewis. He was naturalized in Maryland 7 May 1767. He was a German from Frederick County.

Prou, Cyprian. He was naturalized in Virginia ca. 1704.

Prou, Jean. He was the son of Moyse and Sara Prou and was born in Poitou, France. His wife, Jeane, was dead. His children were Jeane Prou, Jean Prou, and Charlotte Prou. They were naturalized in South Carolina ca. 1696.

Proud, John. He was naturalized in New Jersey in 1775. He was born in Germany.

Provorist, Benjamin. He took the oath of naturalization in New York 1 Sep. 1687 in Ulster County.

Provost, Johannes. He took the oath to the King 21–26 Oct. 1664 after the conquest of New Netherland. He was from Albany.

Prutzman, Jacob. He was naturalized in Pennsylvania 10–12 Apr. 1762. He was from Northampton County.

Pry, George. He was naturalized in Pennsylvania 25 Sep. 1751. He was from Philadelphia County.

Pryl, Dewaeld. He was naturalized in New York 3 Jan. 1715/6. He was from Albany County.

Pruys, Claas Danielson. He expressed his desire to be naturalized in New Castle County, Delaware 21 Feb. 1682/3.

Pryjean, Honoré. He was an Acadian and took the oath to George II at Annapolis River, Nova Scotia in the winter of 1730.

Pryjean, Honore. He was an Acadian and took the oath of allegiance in Apr. 1730.

Pryjean, Jean. He was an Acadian and took the oath to George II at Annapolis River, Nova Scotia in the winter of 1730.

Pucheo, Moses Israel. He was endenized in England 27 Dec. 1661. He settled in Barbados. He was a Jew. He also appeared as Moses Israel Pacho.

Puchie, Mathias. He was naturalized in Maryland 15 Sep. 1761. He was from Frederick County.

Puff, Valentine. He was naturalized in Pennsylvania 10 Apr. 1755. He was from Philadelphia County.

Pulver, Johannis Wm. He was naturalized in New York 17 Jan. 1715/6. He was from Albany County.

Puschart, John George. He was naturalized in New York 25 Nov. 1727.

Putman, Andrew. He was naturalized in Maryland 24 Sep. 1762. He was a German from Frederick County.

Putts, Michael. He was naturalized in Pennsylvania 11 Apr. 1761. He was from Bucks County.

Putts, William. He was naturalized in Pennsylvania 29 Sep. 1709. He was from Philadelphia County.

Pygel, Jacob. He was naturalized in New York 20 Mar. 1762.

Pynes, Giles. He was naturalized in Jamaica 6 Feb. 1757.

Pypper, David. He was naturalized in New York 18 Apr. 1749. He was a tailor from New York City.

Quackenboss, Wouter. He was naturalized in New York 6 Dec. 1715. He was from Albany County.

Quantein, Isaac. He was naturalized in New York 16 Aug. 1715. He was a yeoman from the Manor of Pelham.

Quartstillwag, Johannes. He was naturalized in Pennsylvania 11–13 Apr. 1743. He was from Philadelphia County.

Queraud, Joshua. He was naturalized in New York 4 Oct. 1715. He was a blacksmith from New York City.

Quessi, Jean. He was an Acadian and took the oath to George II at Annapolis River, Nova Scotia in Dec. 1729.

Quick, Teunis Thomazen. He took the oath to the King 21–26 Oct. 1664 after the conquest of New Netherland.

Quick, Thomas. He took the oath of naturalization in New York 1 Sep. 1687 in Ulster County.

Quincie, Michel. He was an Acadian and took the oath of allegiance in Apr. 1730.

Quintard, Isaac. He was endenized in London 24 June 1703. He came to New York.

Quintero, Francisco. He was naturalized in Jamaica 7 Jan. 1747/8.

Quithlot, John. He was naturalized in New York 16 Feb. 1771.

Quitinio, David. He was naturalized in Jamaica 19 Feb. 1690/1.

Quixano, Aaron Mendes. He was naturalized in Jamaica 17 Jan. 1701/2.

Quixano, Abraham Mendes. He was naturalized in Jamaica 6 Aug. 1690.

Quixano, Moses Mendez. He was naturalized in Jamaica 20 May 1700.

Quodman, Jacob. He was naturalized in Jamaica 12 July 1688.

Quodman, Peter. He was naturalized in Jamaica 4 June 1675.

Rabbold, John Jacob. He was naturalized in Pennsylvania 11 Apr. 1761. He was from Berks County.

Rabine, Nicholas. He was naturalized in Pennsylvania 25–27 Sep. 1740. He was from Philadelphia County.

Rack, Georg Jacob. He was naturalized in Maryland 9 Apr. 1760. He lived in Baltimore Maryland.

Racois, Etienne. He was an Acadian and took the oath of allegiance in Apr. 1730.

Radd, John Cunrad. He was naturalized in Pennsylvania 26–27 Sep. 1743. He was from Philadelphia County.

Radeback. Henry. He was naturalized in Pennsylvania 24 Sep. 1759.

Radeback, Michael. He was naturalized in Pennsylvania 10 Apr. 1760.

Radenheimer, Peter. He was naturalized in New Jersey in 1763. He had lived in the colony seven years. He was born in Germany.

Radin, John Henry. He was naturalized in Pennsylvania 10 Sep. 1761. He was from Lancaster County.

Radmaker, Ulrich. He was naturalized in Pennsylvania 11 Apr. 1761. He was from Berks County.

Radwitzer, John. He was naturalized in Pennsylvania 29 Sep. 1709. He was from Philadelphia County.

Raeber, John. He was naturalized in Pennsylvania 11 Apr. 1761. He was from Berks County.

Raff, Frederick. He was naturalized in New York 20 Dec. 1763.

Raff, John. He was naturalized in New York 20 Dec. 1763.

Ragg, Precilla. She was naturalized in Jamaica 28 Nov. 1753. She was a free Negro.

Raiguel, Abraham. He was naturalized in Pennsylvania 10 Sep. 1761. He was from Lancaster County.

Raim, Peter. He was naturalized in North Carolina 22 Mar. 1764. He was from Rowan County and a German. His name may have been Peter Rezim.

Raisner, Casper. He was naturalized in New York 3 July 1759.

Ralph, Francis. He was naturalized in New Jersey 6 Dec. 1769.

Ram, John. He was naturalized in New York 23 Dec. 1763.

Ramalho, Isaac. He was naturalized in Jamaica in 25 Nov. 1740. He was a Jew.

Ramalho, Leah. She was naturalized in Jamaica 23 Feb. 1742/3. She was a Jewess.

Rambo, Gunner. He was naturalized in Pennsylvania 11 Jan. 1683. He was formerly of New Sweden.

Rambo, Peter. He was naturalized in Pennsylvania 11 Jan. 1683. He was formerly of New Sweden.

Ramichen, Conrad. He was naturalized in Nova Scotia 5 July 1758.

Ramos, Isaac. He was naturalized in Jamaica 15 July 1684.

Ramsaur, Dietheric. He was naturalized in Pennsylvania 25–26 Sep./4 Oct. 1749. He was from Philadelphia County.

Ramsaur, Henry. He was naturalized in Pennsylvania 13–15 Apr. 1748. He was from Philadelphia County.

Ran, Jacob. He was naturalized in Pennsylvania 11 Apr. 1761. He was from Berks County.

Ranck, Hans George. He was naturalized in New York 29 July 1752. He was a shoemaker from Ulster County.

Randeker, John. He was naturalized in New York 26 July 1769. He was a cartman from New York City.

Rankel, Cornelius. He was naturalized in New York 11 Sep. 1761.

Ranzell, Justus. He was naturalized in New Jersey 20 Aug. 1755.

Ranzier, Frederick. He was naturalized in New York 29 July 1762. He was a cooper from New York City.

Rapine, Anthony. He was naturalized in Virginia 12 May 1705.

Rapp, Bernard. He was naturalized in Pennsylvania 24 Sep. 1762. He was from Philadelphia County.

Rapp, Peter. He was naturalized in Pennsylvania 10 Apr. 1760.

Rapp, Philip Henry. He was naturalized in Pennsylvania 11 Apr. 1761. He was from Philadelphia County.

Rappe, Gabriel. He was endenized in England 9 Apr. 1687. He promised allegiance to the King and obedience to William Penn in Pennsylvania 10 Sep. 1685. He was styled captain.

Raquier, Jacob. He promised allegiance to the King and obedience to William Penn in Pennsylvania 10 Sep. 1685.

Rashoon, Stephen. He and his children were naturalized in Maryland 3 Nov. 1711. He lived in Talbot County.

Rasper, Johannis. He was naturalized in New York 20 Dec. 1763.

Ratenhouwer, Godfrey. He was naturalized in New York 20 Mar. 1762.

Ratfoun, Christian. He was naturalized in Pennsylvania 18 Nov. 1768.

Rathe, John Jacob. He was naturalized in Pennsylvania 26–27 Sep. 1743. He was from Philadelphia County.

Rathget, Henry. He was naturalized in New Jersey in 1762. He was born in Sweden. He had been in the colony twenty years. He was from Cumberland County.

Ratier, Jacob. He, his wife Jael Ratier, and her son, Anrold Naudin, were endenized in England 8 May 1697. They came to New York.

Rattenhausen, Garret. He was naturalized in Pennsylvania 25–27 Sep. 1740. He was from Philadelphia County.

Ratuit, Mathew. He was naturalized in Jamaica 12 Nov. 1719.

Rau, Andreas. He was naturalized in Maryland 9 Sep. 1761.

Rauch, Michael. He was naturalized in Pennsylvania 11–13 Apr. 1743. He was from Lancaster County.

Rauchin, John. He was naturalized in Jamaica 3 Mar. 1703.

Rauensauner, John. He was naturalized in Pennsylvania 10 & 23 Apr. 1764. He was from Rockland Township, Berks County.

Rauh, Jacob. He was naturalized in Maryland 10 Sep. 1760.

Raush, Nicholas. He was naturalized in Pennsylvania 11 Apr. 1749. He was from Philadelphia County.

Rautforin, Frederick. He was naturalized in Pennsylvania 10 Sep. 1761. He was from Lancaster County.

Ravaud, Daniel. He was naturalized in New York 6 Mar. 1715/6. He was a weaver from New York City.

Ravenel, Rene. He was the son of Daniel Ravenel and Marie Ravenel of Vitre, Bretagne, France. His wife was Charlotte Ravenel, the daughter of —— de St. Julien of Malacre and born at Vitre, Bretagne, France. Their children were Jeanne Charlotte Ravenel, Daniel Ravenel, and Rene Ravenel born in South Carolina. They were naturalized in South Carolina ca. 1696.

Raybuck, John. He was naturalized in Maryland 21 Sep. 1762. He was a German.

Rayman, William. He was naturalized in Maryland 24 Oct. 1728. He lived in Annapolis and was a German. He came from the Rhenish Palatinate.

Raymel, Philip. He was naturalized in Maryland 11 Sep. 1765. He was a German from Frederick County.

Raymon, Isaac. He was naturalized in New York 16 Aug. 1715. He was a yeoman from New Rochelle.

Raymond, Baptiste. He was an Acadian and took the oath to George II at Annapolis River, Nova Scotia in Dec. 1729.

Raymond, Francois. He was an Acadian and took the oath to George II at Annapolis River, Nova Scotia Dec. 1729.

Rawn, Casper. He was naturalized in Pennsylvania 10 Apr. 1765. He was from New Providence Township, Philadelphia County.

Reager, Burket. He was naturalized in Frederick County, Virginia 2 Mar. 1768.

Real, George. He was naturalized in North Carolina 22 Sep. 1763. He was a German and from Rowan County.

Ream, Everard. He was naturalized in Pennsylvania 14 Feb. 1729/30. He was from Lancaster County.

Rebanstock, Johannes. He was naturalized in Pennsylvania 29 Sep. 1709. He was from Philadelphia County.

Rebant, Daniel. He was naturalized in Virginia 12 May 1705.

Reber, Andreas. He was naturalized in New York 5 Nov. 1745. He was a shopkeeper from New York City.

Reber, Christoffel. He was naturalized in Maryland 21 Sep. 1764. He was a German.

Reber, John. He was naturalized in Pennsylvania 13 May 1768. He was from Heidelberg Township, Berks County.

Reber, Lawrence. He was naturalized in Pennsylvania 24 Sep. 1762. He was from Berks County.

Reble, Conrad. He was naturalized in Pennsylvania 29 Mar. 1735. He was from Philadelphia County.

Rebone, John. He was naturalized in Pennsylvania 10 Apr. 1765. He was from Philadelphia.

Rechter, Andries. He was naturalized in New York 8–9 Sep. 1715. He was from Ulster County.

Redd, Adam. He was naturalized in Pennsylvania 10 Apr. 1753. He was from York County.

Reddel, —. He took the oath to the King 21–26 Oct. 1664 after the conquest of New Netherland.

Reddonnell, William. He was naturalized in Jamaica 13 Aug. 1690.

Redecker, Henry. He was naturalized in New York 31 Dec. 1768.

Reder, Adam. He was naturalized in Pennsylvania 25–27 Sep. 1740. He was from Philadelphia County.

Reder, Michael. He was naturalized in Pennsylvania 24 Sep. 1741. He was from Philadelphia County.

Redick, Andrew. He was naturalized in New Jersey 20 Aug. 1755.

Redkey, Nicholas. He was naturalized in Jamaica 15 Apr. 1730.

Redwal, Philip. He was naturalized in Pennsylvania 25–27 Sep. 1740. He was from Philadelphia County.

Reeber, William. He was naturalized in Maryland 11 Sep. 1765. He was a German from Frederick County.

Reebcamp, Charles. He was naturalized in Pennsylvania 19 May 1739. He was from Philadelphia County.
Reebcamp, Justis. He was naturalized in Pennsylvania 19 May 1739. He was from Philadelphia County.
Reech, Henry. He was naturalized in Pennsylvania 11 Apr. 1761. He was from Lancaster County.
Reed, Adam. He was naturalized in Pennsylvania 19 May 1739. He was from Philadelphia County.
Reed, Caspar. He was naturalized in Pennsylvania 19 May 1739. He was from Lancaster County.
Reed, Elias. He was naturalized in Pennsylvania 11 Apr. 1761. He was from Berks County.
Reehl, Frederick. He was naturalized in Maryland 11 Sep. 1765. He was a German from Frederick County.
Reehldown, Daniel. He was naturalized in Pennsylvania 24 Sep. 1755. He was from Lancaster County.
Reel, Mathias. He was naturalized in Pennsylvania 11 Apr. 1749. He was from Bucks County.
Reel, William. He was naturalized in Pennsylvania 11 Apr. 1761. He was from York County.
Reem, Baltzer. He was naturalized in Pennsylvania 11 Apr. 1761. He was from Berks County.
Reem, Christopher. He was naturalized in Pennsylvania 11 Apr. 1761. He was from Lancaster County.
Reemer, Frederick. He was naturalized in Pennsylvania 10 & 23 Apr. 1764. He was from Codorus Township, York County.
Rees, Adam. He was naturalized in Maryland 10 Sep. 1760.
Rees, Adries. He took the oath to the King 21–26 Oct. 1664 after the conquest of New Netherland.
Rees, Deitrick. He was naturalized in Pennsylvania 24–25 Sep. 1764. He was from Philadelphia.
Rees, Henry. He was naturalized in Pennsylvania 11 Apr. 1761. He was from Northampton County.
Rees, Jacob. He was naturalized in Pennsylvania 24 Sep. 1760. He was from Bucks County.
Rees, John George. He was naturalized in Pennsylvania 25 Sep. 1758.
Rees, John Martin. He was naturalized in Pennsylvania 10 & 23 Sep. 1764. He was from Philadelphia.
Rees, Lawrence. He was naturalized in Pennsylvania 10 Apr. 1760.
Rees, William. He was naturalized in New York 17 Jan. 1715/6. He was from Albany County.
Reeser, Baltzazar, Jr. He was naturalized in Pennsylvania 19 May 1739. He was from Philadelphia.
Reeser, William. He was naturalized in Pennsylvania 10 Sep. 1761. He was from Berks County.
Reesinger, John Adam. He was naturalized in Maryland 7 May 1767. He was a German from Frederick County.
Reezer, George. He was naturalized in Pennsylvania 11–13 Apr. 1743. He was from Philadelphia County.
Reezer, Henrick. He was naturalized in Pennsylvania 11–13 Apr. 1743. He was from Lancaster County.
Reezer, Matthew. He was naturalized in Pennsylvania 24–25 Sep. 1764. He was from Lancaster Township, Lancaster County. He was a Moravian.
Reezer, Philip. He was naturalized in Pennsylvania 11 Apr. 1761. He was from Berks County.
Reezer, Ulrick. He was naturalized in Pennsylvania 11–13 Apr. 1743. He was from Bucks County.
Reezer, William. He was naturalized in Pennsylvania 11–13 Apr. 1743. He was from Lancaster County.
Regault, Christopher. He was naturalized in Virginia 20 Sep. 1763.
Regher, Peter. He was naturalized in Maryland 12 Apr. 1771. He was a German.
Reght-Meyer, Coonraedt. He was naturalized in New York 22 June 1734.
Regler, Andreas. He was naturalized in New York 21 Apr. 1762. He was a butcher from New York City.
Rehfus, Johannes. He was naturalized in Nova Scotia 5 July 1758.
Rehm, George. He was naturalized in Pennsylvania 11 Apr. 1761. He was from Berks County.
Rehm, Peter, Sr. He was naturalized in Pennsylvania 10 Sep. 1761. He was from Lancaster County.
Rehm, Peter, Jr. He was naturalized in Pennsylvania 10 Sep. 1761. He was from Lancaster County.

Reiber, Leonard. He was naturalized in Pennsylvania 10–14 Apr. 1747. He was from Philadelphia County.

Reible, William. He was naturalized in Pennsylvania 26 Feb. 1773. He was a trader from Philadelphia.

Reichart, Jacob. He was naturalized in Maryland 12 Sep. 1759. He lived in Baltimore, Maryland.

Reid, Henry. He was naturalized in Pennsylvania 11 Apr. 1751. He was from Philadelphia County.

Reid, Philip. He was naturalized in Pennsylvania 24 Sep. 1741. He was from Philadelphia County.

Reidy, Jacob. He was naturalized in Pennsylvania 11 Apr. 1751. He was from Philadelphia County.

Reif, Conrad. He was naturalized in Pennsylvania 6 Feb. 1730/1. He was from Philadelphia County.

Reif, Jacob. He was naturalized in Pennsylvania 6 Feb. 1730/1. He was from Philadelphia County.

Reif, John George. He was naturalized in Pennsylvania 6 Feb. 1730/1. He was from Philadelphia County.

Reif, John George, Jr. He was naturalized in Pennsylvania 6 Feb. 1730/1. He was from Philadelphia County.

Reif, Peter. He was naturalized in Pennsylvania 6 Feb. 1730/1. He was from Philadelphia County.

Reiff, Hans. He was naturalized in Pennsylvania 11–13 Apr. 1743. He was from Philadelphia County.

Reiffschneider, Sebastian. He was naturalized in Pennsylvania 29 Mar. 1735. He was from Philadelphia County.

Reiffshnieder, Michael. He was naturalized in Pennsylvania 11 Apr. 1763. He was from Dublin Township, Philadelphia County.

Reiger, George. He was naturalized in Pennsylvania in Sep. 1740. He was from Philadelphia County.

Reiger, Jacob Frederick. He was naturalized in Pennsylvania 24 Sep. 1741. He was from Lancaster County.

Reighart, Ulrick. He was naturalized in Pennsylvania 24 Sep. 1762. He was from Lancaster County.

Reighter, Peter. He was naturalized in Pennsylvania 10–12 Apr. 1762. He was from Lancaster County.

Reigler, Andreas. He was naturalized in New York 11 Sep. 1761.

Reijnierse, Auke. He took the oath of allegiance in Flackbush, Kings County, New York 26–30 Sep. 1687. He was a native of the colony.

Reik, Herman. He was naturalized in Pennsylvania 11 Apr. 1761. He was from Berks County.

Reimer, John Francis. He was naturalized in Pennsylvania 10–12 Apr. 1762. He was from Lancaster County.

Reinberg, Andrew. He was naturalized in Pennsylvania in Sep. 1740. He lived in Philadelphia County.

Reiner, George. He was naturalized in Pennsylvania 11 Apr. 1761. He was from Northampton County.

Reinhard, Georg. He was naturalized in Maryland 12 Sep. 1759.

Reinhard, George. He was naturalized in Pennsylvania 10 Sep. 1761. He was from Lancaster County.

Reinhard, Godfrey. He was naturalized in Pennsylvania 10 Apr. 1772. He was from Tewksbury, Hunterdon County, New Jersey.

Reinhart, Wersel Laser. He took the oath of allegiance at Mobile, West Florida 2 Oct. 1764.

Reinhold, Christopher Henry. He was naturalized in Pennsylvania 10 Apr. 1760.

Reinhold, George Christopher. He was naturalized in Pennsylvania 10 Sep. 1761. He was from Philadelphia County.

Reinier, Pieter. He took the oath to the King 21–26 Oct. 1664 after the conquest of New Netherland.

Reinoutzen, Reinout. He took the oath to the King 21–26 Oct. 1664 after the conquest of New Netherland.

Reintzel, Valentine. He was naturalized in Pennsylvania 10 & 23 Apr. 1764. He was from Tulpehocken Township, Berks County.

Reinwald, Christopher. He was naturalized in Pennsylvania 11–13 Apr. 1743. He was from Philadelphia County.

Reinwalt, Christopher. He was naturalized in Pennsylvania 10 Apr. 1755. He was from Philadelphia County.

Reinwalt, George. He was naturalized in Pennsylvania 24 Sep. 1745. He was from Philadelphia County.

Reip, Valentine. He was naturalized in Maryland 23 Apr. 1772. He was a German.

Reis, Henry. He was naturalized in Maryland 10 Sep. 1760.

Reis, Margaret. She was naturalized in Pennsylvania 26 Sep. 1748. She was from Lancaster County and was the wife of Michael Reis.

Reis, Michael. He was naturalized in Pennsylvania 10–14 Apr. 1747. He was from Lancaster County.

Reiser, Jacob. He was naturalized in Pennsylvania 10–11 Apr. 1746. He was from Lancaster County.

Reiser, Paul. He was naturalized in Pennsylvania 10 Apr. 1760.

Reislin, Matthew. He was German and was naturalized in Maryland 15 Oct. 1742.

Reiss, George. He was naturalized in Pennsylvania 10 Sep. 1761. He was from Philadelphia County.

Reiter, Paul. He was naturalized in New York 3 July 1759.

Reiter, Paul. He was naturalized in New York 11 Sep. 1761.

Reitter, Michael. He was naturalized in Pennsylvania 11 Apr. 1749. He was from Philadelphia County.

Relje, Johannis. He was naturalized in New York 8–9 Sep. 1715. He was from Ulster County.

Remarse, Johann. He was naturalized in New York 27 July 1721.

Rembert, Andrew. He was the son of Francois Rembert and Judith Rembert and was of Pont en Royan, Daufine, France. His wife was Anne Rembert, daughter of Jean and Louise Bressan. Their children, Anne Rembert, Andre Rembert, Gerosme Rembert, Pierre Rembert, Susane Rembert, and Jeane Rembert, were born in South Carolina. They were naturalized in South Carolina ca. 1696.

Remespergher, George. He was naturalized in Maryland 14 Apr. 1761.

Remey, Jacob. He was naturalized 29 Sep. 1680. He had his certificate recorded in Westmoreland County, Virginia 8 Oct. 1702.

Remich, Lawrence. He was naturalized in Pennsylvania 11 Apr. 1761. He was from Philadelphia County.

Remick, Daniel. He was naturalized in Pennsylvania 10 Apr. 1754. He was from Northampton County.

Remmy, John. He was naturalized in New York 21 Oct. 1761. He was a potter in New York City.

Remsberger, Paul. He was naturalized in Pennsylvania 19 May 1739. He was from Lancaster County.

Remsberger, Stephen. He was naturalized in Pennsylvania 19 May 1739. He was from Lancaster County.

Remschberger, Stephen. He was naturalized in Maryland 14 Apr. 1761. He was from Frederick County.

Remsen, Abram. He took the oath of allegiance in Breucklijn, Kings County, New York 26–30 Sep. 1687. He was a native of the colony.

Remsen, Adam Leonard. He was naturalized in New York 24 Mar. 1772.

Remsen, Daniel. He took the oath of allegiance in Flackbush, Kings County, New York 26–30 Sep. 1687. He was a native of the colony.

Remsen, Jacob. He took the oath of allegiance in Flackbush, Kings County, New York 26–30 Sep. 1687. He was a native of the colony.

Remsen, Jan. He took the oath of allegiance in Flackbush, Kings County, New York 26–30 Sep. 1687. He was a native of the colony.

Remsen, Jeronimus. He took the oath of allegiance in Breucklijn, Kings County, New York 26–30 Sep. 1687. He was a native of the colony.

Remssen, Jooris. He took the oath of allegiance in Flackbush, Kings County, New York 26–30 Sep. 1687. He was a native of the colony.

Remssen, Rem. He took the oath of allegiance in Flackbush, Kings County, New York 26–30 Sep. 1687. He was a native of the colony.

Remue, Francois. He took the oath of allegiance at Mobile, West Florida 2 Oct. 1764.

Remy, Abraham. He was naturalized in Virginia 12 May 1705.

Renau, Jean. He was endenized in New York in Oct. 1697.

Renaud, Ely. He was naturalized in Jamaica 16 Oct. 1742.

Reneau, Mary. She was naturalized in New York 20 Sep. 1728. She was the wife of Andrew Reneau.

Reneau, Stephen. He was naturalized in New York 2 Aug. 1715. He was a boatman from New Rochelle.

Rengleman, Christopher. He was naturalized in North Carolina 26 Sep. 1767. He was from Rowan County. His name has also been given as Christopher Rendleman.

Rengleman, John. He was naturalized in North Carolina 26 Sep. 1767. He was from Rowan County. His name has also been given as John Rendleman.

Renn, Bernhard. He was naturalized in Pennsylvania 11–13 Apr. 1743. He was from Philadelphia County.

Rennau, Heinrich. He, his wife Joanna Rennau, son Heinrich Rennau, and son Lourentz Rennau were endenized in London 25 Aug. 1708. They came to New York.

Renner, Adam. He was naturalized in Maryland 11 Sep. 1765.

Renner, Frederick Christian. He was naturalized in New York 16 Jan. 1771. He was a sugar baker from New York City.

Renner, George. He was naturalized in Pennsylvania 10 Apr. 1772. He was from Whitpain Township, Philadelphia County.

Renner, George Bless. He was naturalized in Pennsylvania 11 Apr. 1761. He was from Lancaster County.

Reno, Jacob. He was naturalized in Pennsylvania 24 Sep. 1763. He was from Philadelphia.

Renoroy, —. He took the oath of allegiance at Mobile, West Florida 2 Oct. 1764.

Rentz, Peter. He and his sons, Joseph Rentz, John Rentz, and Andrew Rentz, were naturalized in Maryland 31 Aug. 1739. He was born in Germany.

Renzlaer, Jeremias. He took the oath to the King 21–26 Oct. 1664 after the conquest of New Netherland.

Renzlaer, Richard. He took the oath to the King 21–26 Oct. 1664 after the conquest of New Netherland.

Reorher, Godfret. He was naturalized in Pennsylvania 25–26 Sep./4 Oct. 1749. He was from Lancaster County.

Reppert, Peter. He was naturalized in Pennsylvania 10 Apr. 1765. He was from New Britain Township, Bucks County.

Rerigh, William. He was naturalized in Pennsylvania 19 May 1739. He was from Philadelphia County. He also appeared as William Rerig.

Resio, Jeronimo Rodriques. He was endenized in Barbados in Feb. 1663.

Resler, Hantill. He was naturalized in New Jersey 21 Oct. 1754.

Resler, Jacob. He was naturalized in New York 21 Oct. 1761. He was a tallow chandler from New York City.

Resler, Teunis. He was naturalized in New York 17 Jan. 1753. He was a baker from New York City.

Reslvi, John. He was naturalized in Pennsylvania 24 Sep. 1762. He was from Lancaster County.

Ressler, George. He was naturalized in Pennsylvania 11 Apr. 1761. He was from Berks County.

Ressor, Bernard. He was naturalized in Pennsylvania 14 Feb. 1729/30. He was from Lancaster County. He also appeared as Bernard Reser.

Reti, Peter. He was naturalized in Pennsylvania 10–12 Apr. 1762. He was from Berks County.

Retter, Tobias. He was naturalized in Pennsylvania 11 Apr. 1761. He was from Lancaster County.

Reuss, Nicolas. He was naturalized in Jamaica 25 July 1730.

Reuter, Michael. He was naturalized in Pennsylvania 10 Apr. 1760.

Revera, Jacob Rodrigues. He was naturalized in New York 21 Jan. 1746/7. He was a Jewish merchant from New York City.

Reycken, Reinier. He took the oath to the King 21–26 Oct. 1664 after the conquest of New Netherland.

Reydenaure, Nicholas. He was naturalized in Maryland 6 Oct. 1768. He was a German from Frederick County.

Reyer, Martin. He was naturalized in Pennsylvania 24 Sep. 1741. He was from Philadelphia County.

Reyer, Sebastian. He was naturalized in Pennsylvania 11–13 Apr. 1743. He was from Lancaster County.

Reyer, Stophel. He was naturalized in Pennsylvania 24–25 Sep./5 Oct. 1767. He was from Bethel Township, Berks County.

Reyerse, Adriaen. He took the oath of allegiance in Flackbush, Kings County, New York 26–30 Sep. 1687. He had been in the colony 41 years.

Reyfenburger, Jurich. He was naturalized in New York 14 Feb. 1715/6. He was from Albany County.

Reyley Burghart. He was naturalized in Maryland 15 Sep. 1763. He was a German.

Reyley, John. He was naturalized in Maryland 15 Sep. 1763. He was a German.

Reyling, Valentine. He was naturalized in New Jersey in 1761.

Reyly, Martin. He was naturalized in Pennsylvania 24 Sep. 1766.

Reymer, Frederick. He was naturalized in Pennsylvania 29 Mar. 1735. He was from Philadelphia County.

Reynaud, Benjamin. He and his wife, Mary Reynaud, were endenized in England 31 March in the fourth year of the reign of King James II. Nicolas Haywood attested to their papers in London, England 5 Apr. 1688. He had their certificate recorded in Stafford Co., Va. 2 Oct. 1688. Later he had it recorded in North Carolina in July 1698. He had settled in Currituck Precinct.

Reynaud, John. He was naturalized in Jamaica 1 Nov. 1731.

Reynaud, Lewis. He, his wife Anne Reynaud, and their children, Lewis Reynaud and Sarah Reynaud, were endenized in England in Mar. 1688. He had their certificate recorded in Stafford County, Virginia 2 Oct. 1688. [The surname became Reno in America.]

Reyner, Christian. He was naturalized in Pennsylvania 24 Sep. 1763. He was from Upper Milford Township, Northampton County.

Reynhard, Daniel. He was naturalized in Pennsylvania 10–12 Apr. 1762. He was from Philadelphia County.

Rezer, Baltes. He was naturalized in Pennsylvania 25–27 Sep. 1740. He was from Philadelphia County.

Rezer, Jacob. He was naturalized in Pennsylvania 11 Apr. 1761. He was from Berks County.

Rezer, Philip. He was naturalized in Pennsylvania 11 Apr. 1761. He was from Berks County.

Rezio, Abraham Levi. He was endenized in Barbados 25 Oct. 1667.

Rezio, Antonio Rodrigues. He was endenized in England 11 July 1661. He settled in Barbados. He was a Jew.

Rezio, Isaac. He was naturalized in Jamaica 4 May 1691.

Rezio, Jeronimo Rodrigues. He was endenized in London 20 Feb. 1662/3. He was from Barbados. He was a Jew.

Rheinhard, Valentin. He was naturalized in Maryland 12 Apr. 1758. He lived in Manheim Township.

Rhien, John Jacob. He was naturalized in Pennsylvania 11 Apr. 1763. He was from Strasburg Township, York County.

Rhinehart, Valentine. He was naturalized in New York 29 July 1762. He was an innholder from New York City.

Rhinelander, William. He was naturalized in New York 31 July 1754. He was a yeoman from New York City.

Rhode, Philip. He was naturalized in Pennsylvania 11 Apr. 1761. He was from Lancaster County.

Rhora, Jacob. He was naturalized in Pennsylvania 26–27 Sep. 1743. He was from Lancaster County.

Rhora, John. He was naturalized in Pennsylvania 26–27 Sep. 1743. He was from Lancaster County.

Rhuell, Gustav. He was naturalized in New York 16 Dec. 1737.

Rhutt, Sebastian. He was naturalized in Pennsylvania 11 Apr. 1761. He was from Berks County.

Rhyma, John. He was naturalized in New York 8 Mar. 1773.

Rhyne, Honnicol. He was naturalized in New York 8 Mar. 1773.

Rhyne, Michael. He was naturalized in Pennsylvania 24 Sep. 1741. He was from Lancaster County.

Ribas, Menashe. He was naturalized in Jamaica 24 Nov. 1741. He was a Jew.

Ribbeau, James. He was naturalized in Virginia 12 May 1705.

Ribeaudeau, Clode. He was an Acadian and took the oath to George II at Annapolis River, Nova Scotia in the winter of 1730.

Ribeaudeaux, Michel. He was an Acadian and took the oath to George II at Annapolis River, Nova Scotia in the winter of 1730.

Rebeiro, Isaac. He was naturalized in Jamaica 17 July 1693.

Ribiero, Abraham. He was naturalized in Jamaica in 25 Nov. 1740. He was a Jew.

Riblet, Abraham. He was naturalized in Pennsylvania 11 Apr. 1761. He was from Lancaster County.

Ribot, Charles. He was endenized in New York 10 Dec. 1694.

Ribot, Francis. He was naturalized in Virginia 12 May 1705. He was born in France.

Ribouleau, Nicholas. He promised allegiance to the King and obedience to William Penn 10 Sep. 1685 in Pennsylvania.

Ribouteau, Gabriel. He was born at Lachaume, Poitou, France, the son of Estienne Ribouteau and Catherine Girardot. He was naturalized in South Carolina ca. 1696.

Rice, Daniel. He was naturalized in Pennsylvania 10 & 23 Apr. 1764. He was from Darby Township, Philadelphia County.

Rice, Gasper. He was naturalized in Maryland 11 Sep. 1765.

Rice, Hannis. He was naturalized in New York 11 Sep. 1761.

Rice, Mathias. He was naturalized in Lunenburg County, Virginia 2 Aug. 1748.

Rich, Jacob. He was naturalized in Pennsylvania 10 Apr. 1760.

Rich, Stephen. He and his children were naturalized in Maryland 14 Nov. 1713. He was a carpenter from Queen Anne County.

Rich, Thomas. He was naturalized in North Carolina 22 Mar. 1764. He was from Rowan County and a German.

Richair, Peter. He was naturalized in Jamaica 9 Oct. 1734.

Richard, Alexandre. He took the oath of allegiance at Port Royal, Nova Scotia 16 Aug. 1695.

Richard, Alexandre. He was an Acadian and took the oath of allegiance in Apr. 1730.

Richard, Baptiste. He was an Acadian and took the oath of allegiance in Apr. 1730.

Richard, Francois. He was an Acadian and took the oath to George II at Annapolis River, Nova Scotia in Dec. 1729.

Richard, Jacques. He was an Acadian and took the oath of allegiance in Apr. 1730.

Richard, James. He was naturalized in Maryland 4 June 1744. He lived in Baltimore and was born in Rochelle, France.

Richard, Jermain. He was an Acadian and took the oath of allegiance in Apr. 1730.

Richard, John. He was naturalized in Pennsylvania 11 Apr. 1744. He was from Philadelphia County.

Richard, John Frederick. He was naturalized in Pennsylvania in Sep. 1740. He was from Philadelphia County.

Richard, Joseph. He was an Acadian and took the oath to George II at Annapolis River, Nova Scotia in Dec. 1729.

Richard, Joseph. He was an Acadian and took the oath to George II at Annapolis River, Nova Scotia in Dec. 1729.

Richard, Martin. He took the oath of allegiance at Port Royal, Nova Scotia 16 Aug. 1695.

Richard, Martin. He was an Acadian and took the oath of allegiance in Apr. 1730.

Richard, Martin. He was an Acadian and took the oath of allegiance in Apr. 1730.

Richard, Michel. He was an Acadian and took the oath to George II at Annapolis River, Nova Scotia in Dec. 1729.

Richard, Michel. He was an Acadian and took the oath to George II at Annapolis River, Nova Scotia in Dec. 1729.

Richard, Michel. He was an Acadian and took the oath of allegiance in Apr. 1730.

Richard, Michel. He was an Acadian and took the oath of allegiance in Apr. 1730.

Richard, Michel. He was an Acadian and took the oath of allegiance in Apr. 1730.

Richard, Michel. He was an Acadian and took the oath to George II at Annapolis River, Nova Scotia in Dec. 1729.

Richard, Paulus. He took the oath to the King 21–26 Oct. 1664 after the conquest of New Netherland.

Richard, Pierre. He was an Acadian and took the oath to the King at the Mines, Pisiquit, Nova Scotia 31 Oct. 1727.

Richard, Pierre. He was an Acadian and took the oath to the King at the Mines, Pisiquit, Nova Scotia 31 Oct. 1727.

Richard, Pierre. He was an Acadian and took the oath to George II at Annapolis River, Nova Scotia in Dec. 1729.

Richard, Pierre. He was an Acadian and took the oath of allegiance in Apr. 1730.

Richard, Pierre. He was an Acadian and took the oath of allegiance in Apr. 1730.

Richard, Pierre. He was an Acadian and took the oath of allegiance in Apr. 1730.

Richard, Pierre. He was an Acadian and took the oath of allegiance in Apr. 1730.

Richard, Rene. He was an Acadian and took the oath to the King at the Mines, Pisiquit, Nova Scotia 31 Oct. 1727.

Richard, Rene. He was an Acadian and took the oath to George II at Annapolis River, Nova Scotia in the winter of 1730.

Richard, Rene. He was an Acadian and took the oath of allegiance in Apr. 1730.

Richard, Samuel. He was naturalized in New York 3 July 1718.

Richard dit Lefou, Mitchell. He was an Acadian and took the oath to George II at Annapolis River, Nova Scotia in the winter of 1730.

Richards, Adam. He was naturalized in Pennsylvania 10 Apr. 1765. He was from East Caln Township, Chester County.

Richards, Benjamin. He was naturalized in Jamaica 29 July 1709.

Richards, James. He was naturalized in Maryland 24 Sep. 1762. He was from Baltimore County.

Richart, John. He was naturalized in Pennsylvania 24 Sep. 1762. He was from Philadelphia County.

Richart, Joseph. He was naturalized in New York 8–9 Sep. 1715. He was from Ulster County.

Riche, Michael. He was naturalized in New York 16 Feb. 1771.

Richeop, Christian. He was naturalized in Pennsylvania 24 Sep. 1755. He was from Philadelphia County.

Richers, John Michael. He was naturalized in Pennsylvania 20 May 1769.

Richmans, Harman. He was naturalized in New Jersey 28 Mar. 1719. He was from Monmouth County.

Richtmeyer, Jorg. He was naturalized in New York 16 Dec. 1737.

Richwin, George. He was naturalized in Pennsylvania 11 Apr. 1763. He was from Upper Dublin Township, Philadelphia County.

Rickabacker, Adam. He was naturalized in Pennsylvania 10 Sep. 1761. He was from Lancaster County.

Ricke, Henry. He was naturalized in Pennsylvania 26–27 Sep. 1743. He was from Bucks County.

Rickley, William. He was naturalized in Virginia 28 Oct. 1745. He was born in Canton Berne, Switzerland.

Ricks, Christopher. He was naturalized in Pennsylvania 24 Sep. 1771. He was from East Caln Township, Chester County.

Rickstine, Christian. He was naturalized in Pennsylvania 10 & 23 Apr. 1764. He was from Maiden Creek Township, Berks County.

Ridder, Barent Joosten. He took the oath of allegiance in New Uijtrceht, Kings County, New York 26–30 Sep. 1687. He had been in the colony 35 years.

Ridenaur, Henry. He was naturalized in Maryland 11 Apr. 1753.

Ridenaur, Matthias. He was naturalized in Maryland 11 Apr. 1753.

Ridenaur, Peter. He was naturalized in Maryland 11 Apr. 1753.

Riebell, Georg. He was naturalized in New Jersey in 1759. He also appeared as George Rubell and George Revell. He was born in Germany.

Riecher, Gabriel. He was naturalized in Pennsylvania 10 Apr. 1758.

Riegeler, Leonarat. He was naturalized in New York 6 Dec. 1746.

Rieger, George. He was naturalized in Pennsylvania 24 Sep. 1760. He was from Berks County.

Rieger, Joannes Bartholomew. He was naturalized in Pennsylvania in Sep. 1740. He was a Lutheran minister from Lancaster County.

Riely, John. He was naturalized in Pennsylvania 11 Apr. 1763. He was from Philadelphia.
Riemesnyder, Hendrick. He was naturalized in New York 20 Mar. 1762.
Rien, David. He was naturalized in Pennsylvania 11Apr. 1761. He was from Berks County.
Ries, Andreas. He was naturalized in Maryland 11 Apr. 1764. He was a German from Frederick County.
Ries, John. He was naturalized in New York 20 Apr. 1769. He was a farmer.
Ries, Thomas. He was naturalized in Maryland 11 Apr. 1764. He was a German from Frederick County.
Riess, John. He was naturalized in Pennsylvania 10 Sep. 1761. He was from Northampton County.
Riet, Michiel Goewy. He was naturalized in New York 13 Mar. 1715/6. He was from Albany County.
Rietmeyer, Henry. He was naturalized in Pennsylvania 25 Sep. 1758.
Rietz, Anthony. He was naturalized in Pennsylvania 24–25 Sep. 1764. He was from York Township, Philadelphia County.
Rife, Abraham. He was naturalized in Pennsylvania 10–11 Apr. 1746. He was from Philadelphia County.
Rifel, Adam. He was naturalized in Pennsylvania 25 Sep. 1750. He was from Philadelphia County.
Righart, Christopher. He was naturalized in Pennsylvania 24–25 Sep. 1764. He was from Lancaster Township, Lancaster County. He was a Moravian.
Righter, Peter. He was naturalized in Pennsylvania 19 May 1739. He was from Philadelphia County.
Rightmeyer, Coenradt. He was naturalized in New York in Oct. 1740. He was a farmer from Ulster County.
Rightmier, Coenraet. He was naturalized in New York 22 June 1734.
Rightmire, Johan Ludowick. He was naturalized in New Jersey 8 July 1730. He was born in Germany.
Rigor, John. He was naturalized in Maryland 11 Apr. 1764. He was a German.
Rihtmeyer, Jorg. He was naturalized in New York 16 Dec. 1737.
Rijcken, Hendrick. He took the oath of allegiance in Flackbush, Kings County, New York 26–30 Sep. 1687. He had been in the colony 24 years.
Rim, George. He was naturalized in New York 11 Sep. 1761.
Rinamon, Christopher. He was naturalized in Maryland 26 Sep. 1765. He was a German.
Rind, John. He was naturalized in Maryland 9 Sep. 1761. He was from Anne Arundel County.
Rinehard, George. He was naturalized in Pennsylvania 11 Apr. 1761. He was from Northampton County.
Rinehart, Abraham. He was naturalized in Maryland 8 Sep. 1768. He was a German.
Rinehart, Henry. He was naturalized in Pennsylvania 24–25 Sep. 1764. He was from Philadelphia.
Rineil, Henry. He was naturalized in Pennsylvania 10 Sep. 1761. He was from Lancaster County.
Riner, Estienne. He was an Acadian who took the oath to the King at the Mines, Pisiquit 31 Oct. 1727.
Ring, Christopher. He was naturalized in New York 3 May 1755.
Ringer, Mathias. He was naturalized in Pennsylvania 11–13 Apr. 1743. He was from Philadelphia County.
Ringland, John Christian. He was naturalized in New York 3 Feb. 1768. He was a boatman from Ulster County.
Ringle, Lawrence. He was naturalized in New York 8 Mar. 1773.
Ringsdorp, Johannes. He was naturalized in New York 8–9 Sep. 1715. He was from Ulster County.
Rininger, John Marks. He was naturalized in Pennsylvania 10 Sep. 1761. He was from Philadelphia County.
Rinker, Henry. He was naturalized in Pennsylvania 29 Mar. 1735. He was from Bucks County.
Rinker, Jacob. He was naturalized in Frederick County, Virginia 2 June 1767.
Riortean, Jean. He was endenized in New York 22 Oct. 1697.
Ripat, Nieles Neelsen. He expressed his desire to be naturalized in New Castle County, Delaware 21 Feb. 1682/3.

Ripley, Elizabeth. She was naturalized in Jamaica 23 Feb. 1737/8.

Rippel, Lawrence David. He was naturalized in Pennsylvania 10–12 Apr. 1762. He was from York County.

Ris, Daniel. He was naturalized in Jamaica 29 July 1690. He was a doctor.

Risher, Peter. He and his children, Daniel Risher, Susannah Risher, and Elizabeth Risher, were naturalized in Maryland 4 June 1738. He was from Baltimore County and was born in Germany.

Rislar, Jacob. He was naturalized in New York 21 Oct. 1761. He was a tallow chandler from New York City.

Risler, Tunis. He was naturalized in New York 17 Jan. 1753. He was a baker from New York City.

Risner, Tobias. He was naturalized in Maryland 13 Apr. 1763. He was a German.

Ritchy, Gregory. He was naturalized in Pennsylvania 11 Apr. 1763. He was from Whitemarsh Township, Philadelphia County.

Ritenauer, John. He was naturalized in Pennsylvania 24–25 Sep. 1764. He was from Tulpehocken Township, Berks County.

Ritenauer, Nicholas. He was naturalized in Pennsylvania 24–25 Sep. 1764. He was from Lancaster Township, Lancaster County.

Ritman, David. He was naturalized in New York 21 Apr. 1762. He was a carpenter from New York City.

Ritman, Michael. He was naturalized in New York 20 Apr. 1763. He was a weaver from New York City.

Ritschart, Uti. He was naturalized in Pennsylvania 10–12 Apr. 1762. He was from Berks County.

Ritsman, Johannis. He was naturalized in New York 11 Sep. 1761.

Ritter, Barbara. She was naturalized in Pennsylvania 10 Sep. 1761. She was from Berks County.

Ritter, Barbara. She was naturalized in Pennsylvania 10 Sep. 1761. She was from Berks County.

Ritter, Caspar. He was naturalized in Pennsylvania 10 Apr. 1754. He was from Northampton County.

Ritter, George. He was naturalized in Pennsylvania 10–11 Apr. 1745. He was from Philadelphia County.

Ritter, Henrick. He was naturalized in Pennsylvania 25–27 Sep. 1740. He was from Bucks County.

Ritter, Henry. He was naturalized in New York 10 Apr. 1759. He was a cordwainer from New York City.

Ritter, Jacob. He was naturalized in Maryland 12 Sep. 1764. He was a German from Frederick County.

Ritter, Ludovicus. He was naturalized in Maryland 11 Sep. 1765.

Ritter, Michael. He was naturalized in Pennsylvania 25–27 Sep. 1740. He was from Philadelphia County.

Ritter, Michael. He was naturalized in New York 19 Apr. 1759. He was a tailor from New York City.

Ritter, Peter. He was naturalized in Pennsylvania in Sep. 1740. He was from Philadelphia County.

Ritz, Christian. He was naturalized in Pennsylvania 24–25 Sep. 1764. He was from Lancaster County.

Ritzema, Rudolphus. He was naturalized in New York 3 July 1766.

Rivera, Abraham Rodregos. He was naturalized in New York 17 June 1726.

Rivera, Jacob Rodrigues. He was naturalized in New York 21 Jan. 1746. He was a Jewish merchant from New York City.

Rivet, Michel. He was an Acadian and took the oath of allegiance in Apr. 1730.

Riz, Hanah Lopes. She was naturalized in Jamaica 30 Aug. 1743. She was a Jewess.

Roab, Christopher. He was naturalized in Pennsylvania 19 May 1739. He was from Philadelphia County.

Roadarmill, John. He was naturalized in Pennsylvania 24 Sep. 1768. He was from Richmond Township, Berks County.

Roades, Henry. He was naturalized in Maryland in Apr. 1749. He was from Frederick County.

Roadrok, Andrew. He was naturalized in Maryland 26 Sep. 1761.

Roan, Charles Martin. He was naturalized in New Jersey 28 Apr. 1762.

Roan, Henry. He was naturalized in North Carolina 13 Sep. 1770. He was from Rowan County.

Roar, Jacob. He was naturalized in Pennsylvania 11 Apr. 1751. He was from Bucks County.

Rob, Christopher. He was naturalized in New Jersey 6 Dec. 1769.

Robat, Johannes. He took the oath of allegiance at Mobile, West Florida 2 Oct. 1764.

Robert, Daniel. He was endenized in London 3 July 1705. He came to New York.

Robert, James. He was naturalized in Maryland 17 Dec. 1708. He lived in Calvert County and was French Protestant.

Robert, John. He was naturalized in Virginia 12 May 1705.

Robert, Pierre. He was the son of Daniel Robert and Marie Robert of St. Imier, Switzerland. His wife was Jeanne Robert, the daughter of Jean Bayer and Susane Bayer of Bale, Switzerland. Their son Pierre Robert was born in Bale, Switzerland. They were naturalized in South Carolina *ca.* 1696.

Roberts, Martha. She was naturalized in Jamaica 6 Jan. 1756. She was from St. Catherine's Parish.

Roberts, Vincent. He was naturalized in New Jersey 28 Mar. 1719. He was born in France.

Robichau, Alexandre. He was an Acadian and took the oath to George II at Annapolis River, Nova Scotia Dec. 1729.

Robichaux, Charles. He took the oath of allegiance at Port Royal, Nova Scotia 16 Aug. 1695.

Robichaux, Prudent. He took the oath of allegiance at Port Royal, Nova Scotia 16 Aug. 1695.

Robichaux, Prudent. He was an Acadian and took the oath to George II at Annapolis River, Nova Scotia Dec. 1729.

Robillard, Peter. He was naturalized in Jamaica *ca.* 1700.

Robin, Francois. He took the oath of allegiance at Port Royal, Nova Scotia 16 Aug. 1695.

Robinson, Barns. He was naturalized in New York 24 Nov. 1750.

Robishau, Alexandre. He was an Acadian and took the oath of allegiance in Apr. 1730.

Robishau, Charles. He was an Acadian and took the oath of allegiance in Apr. 1730.

Robishau, François. He was an Acadian and took the oath to George II at Annapolis River, Nova Scotia Dec. 1729.

Robishau, Francois. He was an Acadian and took the oath of allegiance in Apr. 1730.

Robishau, Francois. He was an Acadian and took the oath of allegiance in Apr. 1730.

Robishau, Jean. He was an Acadian and took the oath of allegiance in Apr. 1730.

Robishau, Joseph. He was an Acadian and took the oath to George II at Annapolis River, Nova Scotia in Dec. 1729.

Robishau, Joseph. He was an Acadian and took the oath of allegiance in Apr. 1730.

Robishau, Joseph, Jr. He was an Acadian and took the oath of allegiance in Apr. 1730.

Robishau, Louis. He was an Acadian and took the oath of allegiance in Apr. 1730.

Robishau, Pierre. He was an Acadian and took the oath to George II at Annapolis River, Nova Scotia in Dec. 1729.

Robishau, Pierre. He was an Acadian and took the oath to George II at Annapolis River, Nova Scotia in Dec. 1729.

Robishau, Pierre. He was an Acadian and took the oath of allegiance in Apr. 1730.

Robishau, Prudent, Jr. He was an Acadian and took the oath to George II at Annapolis River, Nova Scotia in the winter of 1730.

Roblez, Jacob David de. He sought to be endenized 30 Aug. 1692 in Jamaica. He was a Jew.

Rochon, Augustin. He took the oath of allegiance at Mobile, West Florida 2 Oct. 1764.

Rochon, Piere. He took the oath of allegiance at Mobile, West Florida 2 Oct. 1764.

Rochon, Piere. He took the oath of allegiance at Mobile, West Florida 2 Oct. 1764.

Rockeberger, George Adam. He was naturalized in Pennsylvania 10–12 Apr. 1762. He was from Philadelphia County.

Rockefelter, Johan Peter. He and his two sons, Peter Rockefelter and Johannes Rockefelter, were naturalized in New Jersey in 8 July 1730. He was born in Germany.

Rocky, Henry. He was naturalized in Pennsylvania 24 Sep. 1762. He was from Lancaster County.

Rocquet, Jean. He took the oath of allegiance at Mobile, West Florida 2 Oct. 1764.

Roct, Christian. He was naturalized in Maryland 11 Sep. 1765.

Rod, Jacob. He was naturalized in Maryland 12 Sep. 1764. He was a German.

Rodarmarle, Christian. He was naturalized in Pennsylvania 25 Sep. 1744. He was from Philadelphia County.

Rodarmarle, Paul. He was naturalized in Pennsylvania 25 Sep. 1744. He was from Philadelphia County.

Roddonell, Elizabeth. She was naturalized in Jamaica 29 July 1709. She was the wife of William Roddenell.

Rode, John. He was naturalized in Pennsylvania 10–12 Apr. 1762. He was from Philadelphia County.

Rode, John Jacob. He was naturalized in Pennsylvania 11 Apr. 1761. He was from Philadelphia County.

Rode, Philip. He was naturalized in Pennsylvania 24 Sep. 1762. He was from Berks County.

Rodebach, George. He was naturalized in Pennsylvania 24 Sep. 1762. He was from Berks County.

Rodebach, Peter. He was naturalized in Pennsylvania 24 Sep. 1762. He was from Berks County.

Rodeges, Abraham. He was naturalized in Jamaica 30 Nov. 1732.

Rodenbach, Johannes. He was naturalized in New Jersey in 1750. He was from Hunterdon County. He also appeared as Johanes Rodebach.

Rodenbeler, Philip. He was naturalized in Maryland 11 Apr. 1764. He was a German.

Roderick, Lodwig. He was naturalized in Maryland 23 Sep. 1762. He was a German from Frederick County.

Rodermell, Peter. He was naturalized in Pennsylvania 11–13 Apr. 1743. He was from Lancaster County.

Rodermill, Christopher. He was naturalized in Pennsylvania 24 Sep. 1762. He was from York County.

Rodrigues, Daniel. He was naturalized in Jamaica in Dec. 1721.

Rodrigues, Isaac. He was naturalized in Jamaica 4 Aug. 1719.

Rodrigues, Isaac. He was naturalized in New York 6 July 1723.

Rodrigues, Isaac Raphael. He was naturalized in New York 16 Dec. 1737.

Rodrigues, Moses. He was naturalized in Jamaica 26 Feb. 1740/1. He was a Jew. He also appeared as Moses Roderiques.

Rodriguez, Alphonso. He was endenized in England 16 Dec. 1687. He settled in Barbados and was a Jew.

Rodriques, Isaac. He was naturalized in Jamaica 1 Dec. 1710.

Rodriques, Moses. He was naturalized in Jamaica 26 Aug. 1746. He was a Jew.

Rodriques, Moses. He was naturalized in Jamaica 9 Aug. 1704.

Rodte, Woolrick. He was naturalized in Pennsylvania 14 Feb. 1729/30. He was from Lancaster County.

Rody, John. He was naturalized in Pennsylvania in Sep. 1740. He was from Bucks County.

Roelands, Robert. He was naturalized in Maryland 8 May 1669. He was born in Brabant, Holland.

Roeloffs, Teunis. He took the oath of allegiance in Orange County, New York 26 Sep. 1687.

Roeloffs, Amte. She was naturalized in Jamaica 11 Aug. 1687. She was the wife of Jacob Roelofs.

Roelofs, Jacob. He was naturalized in Jamaica 11 Aug. 1687.

Roelofzen, Boele. He took the oath to the King 21–26 Oct. 1664 after the conquest of New Netherland.

Roelofzen, Jan. He took the oath to the King 21–26 Oct. 1664 after the conquest of New Netherland.

Roemin, Simon Janzen. He took the oath to the King 21–26 Oct. 1664 after the conquest of New Netherland.

Roemin, Simon Janzen. He took the oath of naturalization in Gravens End, Kings County, New York 26–30 Sep. 1687. He had been in the colony for 34 years.

Roesinkranc, Sander. He took the oath of naturalization in New York 1 Sep. 1687 in Ulster County.

Roesslie, Conrad. He was naturalized in Pennsylvania 10–12 Apr. 1762. He was from Northampton County.

Roeters, Abraham. He was naturalized in New York 6 July 1723.

Roeters, Susanna. She was naturalized in New Jersey 8 July 1730. She was the daughter of Abraham and Sophia Roeters and was born in Amsterdam, Holland. Her sister, Christina Elrington, the widow of Francis Elrington, was naturalized at the same time.

Roettig, Christoph. He was naturalized in New York 20 Mar. 1762.

Roff, Jacob. He was naturalized in Pennsylvania 24 Sep. 1753. He was from Philadelphia.

Roge, John. He was naturalized in New York 24 Jan. 1740/1. He was a merchant from New York City.

Roger, John. He was naturalized in Virginia 12 May 1705.

Roggen, Frans Petrus. He was naturalized in New York 20 Oct. 1764.

Roggen, John Jacob. He was naturalized in New York 20 Oct. 1764.

Rohefeller, Diel. He was naturalized in New York 16 Dec. 1737.

Roher, Jacob. He was naturalized in Pennsylvania 10 Sep. 1761. He was from Lancaster County.

Rohot, Johannes. He took the oath of allegiance at Mobile, West Florida 2 Oct. 1764.

Rohr, John Andrew. He was naturalized in Pennsylvania 11 Apr. 1761. He was from Philadelphia County.

Rohr, John Frederick. He was naturalized in Pennsylvania 10 Apr. 1758.

Rohr, Rudolph. He was naturalized in Maryland 17 July 1765. He was a German.

Rohrback, Christian. He was naturalized in Pennsylvania 10 Sep. 1761. He was from Lancaster County.

Rohrer, John. He was naturalized in Pennsylvania 21 Nov. 1769. He was from Lancaster Township, Lancaster County.

Roistrock, John. He was naturalized in Pennsylvania 11 Apr. 1751. He was from Bucks County.

Rokheffeller, Johannis Petrus. He was naturalized in New York 21 Oct. 1761. He was a farmer from Camp, Albany County.

Rokheffeller, Simon. He was naturalized in New York 21 Oct. 1761. He was a farmer from Camp, Albany County.

Rokkenfelder, Christian. He was naturalized in New York 18 Oct. 1750. He was a blacksmith from Ulster County.

Rolland, John Abraham. He was endenized in London 29 Sep. 1698. He came to New York.

Rolland, Peter. He was endenized in London 29 Sep. 1698. He came to New York.

Roller, John. He was naturalized in Maryland 11 Sep. 1765. He was a German from Frederick County.

Romar, Michael. He was naturalized in Maryland in Apr. 1749. He was from Frederick County.

Romich, Adam. He was naturalized in Pennsylvania 29 Mar. 1735. He was from Philadelphia County.

Romig, Frederick. He was naturalized in Pennsylvania 10 Apr. 1753. He was from Northampton County.

Romkes, Bruin. He was naturalized in Nova Scotia 5 July 1758.

Romler, Leonhart. He was naturalized in Pennsylvania 19 May 1739. He was from Lancaster County.

Ronckel, Joset. He was naturalized in Maryland 11 Apr. 1760.

Ronis, Thomas. He was naturalized in New York 8–9 Sep. 1715. He was from Ulster County.

Ronkill, John. He was naturalized in New York 3 May 1755.

Ronlaff, John. He was naturalized in New York 8 Mar. 1773.

Roodt, Paul. He was naturalized in Pennsylvania 22–24 Nov. 1773. He was from Frederick County, Maryland.

Roof, Anthony. He was naturalized in Maryland 11 Sep. 1765. He was a German from Frederick County.

Roop, Bernhard. He was naturalized in Pennsylvania 24–25 Sep. 1764. He was from Philadelphia.

Roorbagh, Johannes. He was naturalized in New York 17 June 1726.

Roos, Adrien. He was naturalized in New York 2 Dec. 1689. He was 42 years old and a farmer from Ulster County.

Roos, Arrie. He took the oath of naturalization in New York 1 Sep. 1687 in Ulster County.

Roos, Christian. He was naturalized in Maryland 11 Sep. 1765. He was a German from Frederick County.

Roos, Francis. He was naturalized in Pennsylvania 11 Apr. 1741. He was from Philadelphia County.

Roos, Gerret. He was endenized in New York 19 July 1715. He was a baker.

Roos, Gerrit Janzen. He took the oath to the King 21–26 Oct. 1664 after the conquest of New Netherland.

Roos, Guert. He was naturalized in New York 19 July 1715. He was a cordwainer.

Roos, Heyman. He was naturalized in New York before 1715. He was 45 years old and a shoemaker from Hurly, Ulster County.

Roos, Heymon. He took the oath of naturalization in New York 1 Sep. 1687 in Ulster County.

Roos, John. He took the oath of naturalization in New York 1 Sep. 1687 in Ulster County.

Roos, Lodowick. He was naturalized in New York 31 July 1754. He was a German.

Roos, Pieter. He was naturalized in New York 8–9 Sep. 1715. He was from Hurly, Ulster County.

Roosevelt, Johannes. He was naturalized in New York 20 Oct. 1764. He was a chirurgeon.

Roosinffelt, Claes. He took the oath of naturalization in New York 1 Sep. 1687 in Ulster County.

Rop, Michael. He was naturalized in Maryland 29 Sep. 1762. He was a German from Frederick County.

Ropost, Bernard. He was naturalized in Pennsylvania 10 Sep. 1761. He was from Berks County.

Roppert, Adam. He was naturalized in Pennsylvania 10–12 Apr. 1762. He was from Lancaster County.

Rorback, Jacob. He was naturalized in Maryland 16 Sep. 1765. He was a German.

Roreback, Reinhard. He was naturalized in Pennsylvania 11 Apr. 1761. He was from Berks County.

Rorer, Frederick. He was naturalized in Maryland 11 Sep. 1760. He lived in Frederick County and was a German. He was a Mennonist.

Rorig, Hindrick. He was naturalized in New York 11 Sep. 1761.

Rorrer, Jacob. He was naturalized in Maryland 20 Oct. 1747.

Rorer, John. He was naturalized in Maryland 10 Sep. 1762.

Ros, Wilhelm. He was naturalized in New York 26 Mar. 1762.

Rose, Arnold. He was naturalized in Pennsylvania 11 Apr. 1763. He was from Philadelphia.

Rose, Johanis Peter. He was naturalized in New York 15 Oct. 1765. He was a shoemaker from Albany County.

Rose, Peter. He and his wife Johanna Rose were endenized in London 25 Aug. 1708. They came to New York.

Rosekrans, Abraham. He was naturalized in New York 29 Mar. 1762.

Rosekrans, Jacob Dirckse. He took the oath of allegiance in Boswijck, Kings County, New York 26–30 Sep. 1687. He was a native of the colony.

Rosenbergh, Benjamin. He was naturalized in Maryland 25–27 Sep. 1740. He was from Philadelphia County.

Rosendahl, Nicholas. He was naturalized in Jamaica 6 July 1739.

Rosenkrans, Dirck. He was naturalized in New York 8–9 Sep. 1715. He was from Ulster County.

Rosenplater, John Herman. He was naturalized in Maryland 11 Sep. 1765.

Ross, Caesar. He was naturalized in Jamaica 28 Nov. 1744.

Ross, Jacob. He was naturalized in New York 22 June 1734.

Ross, Johannes. He was naturalized in New Jersey 21 Oct. 1754.

Ross, Wilhelm. He was naturalized in New York 20 Mar. 1762.

Rossel, Henry. He was naturalized in New York 20 Apr. 1769. He was a tanner from outside of New York City.

Rossell, Jacob. He was naturalized in Pennsylvania 11 Apr. 1763. He was from Tolpohocken Township, Berks County.

Rossener, Jorg. He was naturalized in New York 11 Sep. 1761.

Rosset, John. He was naturalized in Virginia 12 May 1705.

Rost, Erhard. He was naturalized in Pennsylvania 10 Sep. 1761. He was from Berks County.

Roster, John. He was naturalized in Maryland 11 Apr. 1759.

Rosty, Christoph. He was naturalized in Nova Scotia 5 July 1758.

Rosty, Killian. He was naturalized in Nova Scotia 5 July 1758.

Rosyberger, Henry. He was naturalized in Pennsylvania 11–13 Apr. 1743. He was from Philadelphia County.

Rot, Daniel. He was naturalized in Pennsylvania 11 Apr. 1761. He was from Northampton County.

Rote, Conrad. He was naturalized in Pennsylvania 10 Sep. 1761. He was from Berks County.

Rotenberger, Nicholas. He was naturalized in Pennsylvania 11 Apr. 1761. He was from Northampton County.

Roth, Francis. He was naturalized in Pennsylvania 10 Apr. 1754. He was from Northampton County.

Roth, Jacob. He was naturalized in Pennsylvania 10 Sep. 1761. He was from Philadelphia County.

Roth, Johan Jacob. He was naturalized in Pennsylvania 19 May 1739. He was from Philadelphia County.

Roth, Johannes. He was naturalized in Pennsylvania 6 Feb. 1730/1. He was from Chester County.

Roth, John Joseph. He was naturalized in Pennsylvania 10 Sep. 1761. He was from Philadelphia County.

Rother, Jacob. He was naturalized in New York 11 Sep. 1761.

Rott, John George. He was naturalized in Pennsylvania 11 Apr. 1749. He was from Bucks County.

Rotter, Herick. He was naturalized in Pennsylvania 10–14 Apr. 1747. He was from Bucks County.

Rotter, Elias. He was naturalized in Pennsylvania 10 Apr. 1755. He was from Berks County.

Rou, Nikals. He was naturalized in New York 8–9 Sep. 1715. He was from Ulster County.

Rou, Paul. He was naturalized in Jamaica 30 July 1690.

Rouch, Johann Caspar. He was naturalized in New York 17 Jan. 1715/6. He was from Albany County.

Rouch, John. He was naturalized in Maryland 11 Sep. 1765.

Rouderbush, George. He was naturalized in Pennsylvania 24–25 Sep. 1764. He was from Upper Hannover Township, Philadelphia County.

Rougeon, Peter. He was naturalized in New York 21 Apr. 1762. He was a ship carpenter from New York City and a French Protestant.

Rougon, Peter. He was naturalized in New York 3 July 1759.

Roup, George. He was naturalized in Pennsylvania in Sep. 1740. He was from Bucks County.

Roup, Peter. He was naturalized in Pennsylvania in Sep. 1740. He was from Bucks County.

Rous, Lucas. He was naturalized in Pennsylvania 10 Apr. 1760.

Rouse, John. He was naturalized in New Jersey 28 Apr. 1762.

Rouse, Peter. He was naturalized in Jamaica 28 Nov. 1749.

Rouset, David. He was naturalized in New York 1 Nov. 1715. He was a leather dresser from New York City.

Rousett, John. He was naturalized in Jamaica 3 Oct. 1720.

Rousman, Johannis. He was naturalized in New York 22 Nov. 1715. He was from Albany County.

Roussett, Peter. He was naturalized in Jamaica 18 June 1718.

Roux, James. He was naturalized in Virginia 12 May 1705.

Row, Erhard. He was naturalized in Maryland 11 Sep. 1765. He was a German from Frederick County.

Row, Hans Jurch. He was naturalized in New York 17 Jan. 1715/6. He was from Albany County.

Row, Jacob. He was naturalized in Pennsylvania 10 Apr. 1765. He was from Philadelphia.

Row, John Martin. He was naturalized in Pennsylvania 11 Apr. 1763. He was from Philadelphia.

Row, John Maurice. He was naturalized in Pennsylvania 10 Sep. 1761. He was from Lancaster County.

Rowk, Philip. He was naturalized in Pennsylvania 24–25 Sep. 1764. He was from Upper Hannover Township, Philadelphia County.

Rowland, David. He was naturalized in Jamaica 10 Dec. 1688.

Rowland, Jacob. He was naturalized in Pennsylvania 10 Sep. 1761. He was from Lancaster County.

Rowse, George. He was naturalized in Pennsylvania 6 Feb. 1730/1. He was from Philadelphia County.

Rowx, Timothy. He was naturalized in Virginia 12 May 1705.

Roy, Charles. He was an Acadian and took the oath to George II at Annapolis River, Nova Scotia in Dec. 1729.

Roy, Jean. He was an Acadian and took the oath to the King at the Mines, Pisiquit, Nova Scotia 31 Oct. 1727.

Roy, Jean. He was an Acadian and took the oath of allegiance in Apr. 1730.

Roy, John Guy. He petitioned for naturalization in Virginia 19 Apr. 1705. It was granted 12 May 1705. He also appeared as John Guy Rey.

Roy, Philippe. He was an Acadian and took the oath of allegiance in Apr. 1730.

Roy, Rene. He was an Acadian and took the oath of allegiance in Apr. 1730.

Royer, Bastian. He was naturalized in Pennsylvania 14 Feb. 1729/30. He was from Lancaster County.

Royer, Noel, Sr. He was born in Tours, France, the son of Sebastien Royer and Marie Rendon. His wife was Madeleine Saunier who was born at Chateleraulx. She was the daughter of Jacques Saunier and Judith Baudon. Their children were Pierre Royer, Madeleine Royer, and Marie Royer who were born in Tours, France. They were naturalized in South Carolina ca. 1696.

Royer, Noel, Jr. He was born in Tours, France, the son of Noel Royer and Madeleine Saunier. His wife was Judith Giton who was born at Voulte, Dauphinee, France. They were naturalized in South Carolina 10 Mar. 1696/7. He was a weaver.

Rozilini, Onorio. He was naturalized in Maryland 8 Aug. 1732. He lived in Annapolis and was born in the Venetian territories.

Rubbert, Lehnhart. He was naturalized in Pennsylvania 10 Sep. 1761. He was from Berks County.

Rubel, Ulrich. He was naturalized in Pennsylvania 29 Mar. 1735. He was from Bucks County.

Rubell, Johannis Casparus. He was naturalized in New York 23 Dec. 1765.

Rubley, Jacob. He was naturalized in Pennsylvania 11 Apr. 1751. He was from Lancaster County.

Ruch, Frederich. He was naturalized in New York 8–9 Sep. 1715. He was from Ulster County.

Ruch, Frederich, Jr. He was naturalized in New York 8–9 Sep. 1715. He was Ulster County.

Ruch, George. He was naturalized in Pennsylvania 10–11 Apr. 1746. He was from Bucks County.

Ruch, Jacob. He was naturalized in Pennsylvania 10–11 Apr. 1746. He was from Philadelphia County.

Ruch, Michael. He was naturalized in Pennsylvania 10–11 Apr. 1746. He was from Bucks County.

Rucker, Peter. He petitioned for naturalization in Virginia 24 Apr. 1704. He also appeared as Peter Ruckes.

Ruckstool, Solomon. He was naturalized in Pennsylvania 24 Sep. 1763. He was from Upper Salford Township, Philadelphia County.

Rudesill, Andrew. He was naturalized in Pennsylvania 10–12 Apr. 1762. He was from York County.

Rudey, Dedrick. He was naturalized in Pennsylvania in Sep. 1740. He was from Bucks County.

Rudht, Henry. He was naturalized in Pennsylvania 11–13 Apr. 1743. He was from Philadelphia County.

Rudisilly, Jacob. He was naturalized in Pennsylvania 11 Apr. 1761. He was from York County.

Rudisilly, Lewis. He was naturalized in Pennsylvania 13 May 1768. He was from Codorus Township, York County.

Rudman, Andreas. He was naturalized in Pennsylvania 20 July 1701. He was a clerk and was born in Geste, Sweden, the son of John Rudolph.

Rudolf, Leonard Chris'. He was naturalized in Nova Scotia 11 Sep. 1758.

Rudolph, Andrew. He was naturalized in North Carolina 22 Sep. 1763. He was from Rowan County and a German.

Rudolph, Johannes. He was naturalized in Pennsylvania 24 Sep. 1746. He was from Philadelphia County.

Rudy, Daniel. He was naturalized in Pennsylvania 24 Sep. 1760. He was from Lancaster County.

Rudy, John. He was naturalized in Pennsylvania 10 Sep. 1761. He was from Lancaster County.

Ruebel, Johannes. He was naturalized in Maryland 12 Sep. 1759.

Ruet, George. He was naturalized in Maryland 20 Sep. 1765. He was a German.

Ruet, Jacob. He was naturalized in Maryland 20 Sep. 1765. He was a German.

Ruetlinger, Henry. He was naturalized in Pennsylvania 10 Apr. 1769. He was from Bristol Township, Bucks County.

Ruff, Johan Christian. He was naturalized in New York 20 Mar. 1762.

Ruff, Michael. He was naturalized in Maryland 12 Sep. 1753.

Ruffer, Peter. He was naturalized in Frederick County, Virginia 4 Aug. 1768.

Ruger, Frederick. He was naturalized in New York 20 Apr. 1763. He was a carman in New York City.

Rule, Hammond. He was naturalized in Jamaica 28 Aug. 1679.

Rule, Peter. He was naturalized in Pennsylvania in Sep. 1740. He was from Bucks County.

Rulland, John. He took the oath of naturalization in New York 1 Sep. 1687 in Ulster County.

Rulleau, John. He was naturalized 20 Mar. 1707/8 in England. He was the son of John and Mary Rulleau and was born at Saumien, Saintonge, France. He settled in New York.

Rumfeldt, Henry. He was naturalized in Pennsylvania 11 Apr. 1741. He was from Bucks County.

Rumman, Jacob. He was naturalized in Pennsylvania 11 Apr. 1761. He was from Philadelphia County.

Runchel, Joset. He was naturalized in Maryland 11 Apr. 1759.

Runck, Jacob. He was naturalized in New Jersey in 1763. He had been in the colony seven years. He was from Germany.

Rung, Henry. He was naturalized in Pennsylvania 11 Apr. 1763. He was from Lancaster Township, Lancaster County.

Rungle, Jacob. He was naturalized in Maryland 11 Sep. 1765. He was a German from Frederick County.

Runk, John. He was naturalized in Pennsylvania 11 Apr. 1761. He was from Berks County.

Runk, Philip. He was naturalized in Pennsylvania 24 Sep. 1760. He was from Lancaster County.

Runkett, John. He was naturalized in Pennsylvania 11 Apr. 1761. He was from Berks County.

Runkett, Nicholas. He was naturalized in Pennsylvania 11 Apr. 1761. He was from Berks County.

Runyoe, John Peter. He was naturalized in Pennsylvania 10 Apr. 1767. He was from Bedminster Township, Bucks County.

Rup, Hans. He was naturalized in Pennsylvania 6 Feb. 1730/1. He was from Philadelphia County.

Rup, Jacob. He was naturalized in Maryland 12 Apr. 1771. He was a German.

Rupe, John. He was naturalized in Pennsylvania 11 Apr. 1761. He was from Lancaster County.

Rupert, George. He was naturalized in New York 27 Jan. 1770.

Rupp, John. He was naturalized in Pennsylvania 24 Sep. 1763. He was from Philadelphia.

Rupp, Peter. He was naturalized in Pennsylvania 25 Sep. 1758.

Ruppert, Adam. He was naturalized in New York 3 July 1759.

Ruppert, Francis. He was naturalized in New York 3 July 1759.

Rurs, Hendrick. He was naturalized in New York 20 Mar. 1762.

Rush, Conrad. He was naturalized in Pennsylvania 11 Apr. 1761. He was from Philadelphia County.

Rush, John. He was naturalized in Pennsylvania 25–27 Sep. 1740. He was from Philadelphia County.

Rush, John. He was naturalized in New York 16 Feb. 1771. He was a farmer from Bergen County, New Jersey.

Rush, Michael, Sr. He was naturalized in Pennsylvania 10 Sep. 1761. He was from Berks County.

Rush, Michael, Jr. He was naturalized in Pennsylvania 10 Sep. 1761. He was from Berks County.

Russ, David. He was naturalized in New York 11 Sep. 1761.

Russ, Michael. He was naturalized in Maryland 11 Sep. 1765. He was from Frederick County.

Russel, William. He was naturalized in New York 19 Dec. 1766.

Russell, Michael. He was naturalized in New York 3 July 1759.

Rust, Nicholas. He was naturalized in Jamaica 10 Nov. 1701.

Ruth, Christian. He was naturalized in Pennsylvania 10 Apr. 1755. He was from Northampton County.

Ruth, Christian. He was naturalized in Pennsylvania 11 Apr. 1761. He was from Berks County.

Ruth, Jacob. He was naturalized in Pennsylvania 11 Apr. 1761. He was from Berks County.

Ruth, Michael. He was naturalized in Pennsylvania 11 Apr. 1761. He was from Berks County.

Ruth, Peter. He was naturalized in Pennsylvania 11 Apr. 1761. He was from Berks County.

Rutsen, Jacob. He was naturalized in New York 8–9 Sep. 1715. He was from Ulster County.

Rutsen, Johon. He was naturalized in New York 8–9 Sep. 1715. He was from Ulster County.

Rutt, Peter. He was naturalized in Pennsylvania 19 May 1739. He was from Lancaster County.

Rutt, William. He was naturalized in Pennsylvania 10 Apr. 1760.

Rutter, Francis. He was naturalized in Pennsylvania 10 Apr. 1753. He was from Berks County.

Rutter, George. He was naturalized in Pennsylvania 10 Apr. 1753. He was from Berks County.

Ruttinghuysen, Claus. He was naturalized in Pennsylvania 29 Sep. 1709. He was from Philadelphia County.

Rutton, Abraham. He took the oath of naturalization in New York 1 Sep. 1687 in Ulster County.

Ruyter, Henrich. He was naturalized in New York 8–9 Sep. 1715. He was from Ulster County.

Ryall, John. He was naturalized in Pennsylvania 11–12 Apr. 1744. He was from Lancaster County.

Ryan, Lodowick. He was endenized in Maryland 22 June 1771. He was born in Germany.

Rychart, George. He was naturalized in Pennsylvania 10 Apr. 1765. He was from Lower Saucon Township, Northampton County.

Ryer, Michael. He was naturalized in Pennsylvania 25–27 Sep. 1740. He was from Philadelphia County.

Ryledorfes, Henry. He was naturalized in Pennsylvania 24 Sep. 1762. He was from Berks County.

Rynard, Johnis. He took the oath of allegiance in Orange County, New York 26 Sep. 1687.

Rynlander, Bernard. He was naturalized in New York 21 Apr. 1750. He was a tanner from Westchester County.

Rypell, John. He was naturalized in New York 28 Feb. 1715/6. He was a baker from New York City.

Rysdyck, Isaac. He was naturalized in New York 3 July 1766.

Ryst, John. He was naturalized in New York 20 Mar. 1762.

Ryswick, John. He was naturalized in Pennsylvania 11 Apr. 1761. He was from Northampton County.

Saand, Christian. He was naturalized in New York 20 Apr. 1773. He was from Skohary Township.

Sabbatier, Peter. He was naturalized in Virginia 12 May 1705.

Sabee, Leonhard. He was naturalized in Maryland 9 Sep. 1761.

Sable, Leonard. He was naturalized in Pennsylvania 10–12 Apr. 1762. He was from York County.

Sacerdote, Moses Vitta. He was naturalized in Jamaica 26 Oct. 1730.

Saciller, John. He was naturalized in Massachusetts 7 Dec. 1731.

Sacombel, Louis. He was naturalized in New York 17 June 1726.

Sahler, Peter. He was naturalized in Pennsylvania 24 Sep. 1762. He was from York County.

Saiger, Frederick. He was naturalized in Pennsylvania 11 Apr. 1761. He was from Lancaster County.

Sailer, Valentine. He was naturalized in Pennsylvania 10 Apr. 1765. He was from Providence Township, Philadelphia County.

Sailor, Abraham. He was naturalized in Pennsylvania 25–27 Oct. 1740. He was from Philadelphia County.

Sailor, Balthazar. He was naturalized in Pennsylvania in Sep. 1740. He was from Philadelphia County.

Sailor, George. He was naturalized in Pennsylvania 11–13 Apr. 1743. He was from Philadelphia County.

Sailor, Philip. He was naturalized in Pennsylvania 10 Sep. 1761. He was from Berks County.

St. Clemens, John. He was endenized in Barbados 13 Feb. 1671. He was a native of France.

St. Gaudens, Peter. He was naturalized in New York 6 Mar. 1715/6. He was a yeoman from New Rochelle.

St. John, John Hector. He was naturalized in New York 23 Dec. 1765.

St. Julien, Louis de. He was born at Vitre, France, the son of Pierre St. Julien and Jeanne LeFebure. He was naturalized in South Carolina ca. 1696.

St. Julien, Pierre de. He was born at Vitre, Bretagne, France and was the son of Pierre St. Julien and Jeanne LeFebure. His wife was Damaris Elizabeth LeSerurier. Their children, Pierre St. Julien and Jacques St. Julien, were born in South Carolina. The family was naturalized in South Carolina ca. 1696.

St. Leger, Thomas. He was naturalized in South Carolina 1 June 1702. He was the son of Stephen de Bacolon by Mary his wife and was born at St. Leger in Guienne, France.

St. Lorain, Gabriel. He took the oath of allegiance at Mobile, West Florida 2 Oct. 1764.

St. Sceine, Denis. He was an Acadian and took the oath to George II at Annapolis River, Nova Scotia in the winter of 1730.

St. Sceine, Denis. He was an Acadian and took the oath at Annapolis in Dec. 1729.

St. Sceine, Denis. He was an Acadian and took the oath at Annapolis in Dec. 1729.

Sait, David. He was naturalized in New York 20 Mar. 1762.

Saiz, Johannes Michael. He was naturalized in New York 17 Oct. 1753. He was a baker from New York City.

Salat, Jean. He took the oath of allegiance at Port Royal, Nova Scotia 16 Aug. 1695.

Salback, Jacob. He was naturalized in Pennsylvania 24 Sep. 1763. He was from Berwick Township, York County.

Salback, Jermi. He was naturalized in New York 8–9 Sep. 1715. He was from Ulster County.

Saldana, Abraham Dovall. He was naturalized in Jamaica 28 Feb. 1743/4. He was a Jew.

Saldana, Solomon. He was naturalized in Jamaica 27 May 1746. He was a Jew.

Saldano, Jacob Carrello. He was naturalized in Jamaica 19 Aug. 1751.

Salem, Andrew. He was naturalized in Pennsylvania 11 Jan. 1683. He was formerly of New Sweden.

Sallady, Frederick. He was naturalized in Pennsylvania 11 Apr. 1763. He was from Earl Township, Lancaster County.

Salmonsmiller, Ludwick. He was naturalized in Maryland 11 Sep. 1765. He lived in Manheim Township, York County, Pennsylvania.

Salom, David. He was naturalized in Jamaica 26 Feb. 1740/1. He was a Jew.

Salom, Esther. She was naturalized in Jamaica 27 Aug. 1745. She was a Jewess.

Salomonsiller, Ludwick. He was naturalized in Maryland 11 Sep. 1765. He lived in Manheim Township, York County, Pennsylvania.

Salsbergh, Michael. He was naturalized in New York 31 Dec. 1768.

Salsby, William. He was naturalized in Jamaica 16 Feb. 1684.

Saltogeber, Andreas. He was naturalized in Pennsylvania 10 Sep. 1761. He was from Lancaster County.

Salver, Rudolph. He was naturalized in Pennsylvania 10–11 Apr. 1745. He was from Bucks County.

Saman, Ludwick. He was naturalized in Pennsylvania 11 Apr. 1761. He was from Berks County.

Samler, John. He was naturalized in New York 20 May 1769. He was a sugar refiner from New York City.

Sampoxo, Rachell Gomez. She was naturalized in Jamaica 30 Mar. 1709.

Sampson, Guillaume. He was an Acadian and took the oath of allegiance in Apr. 1730.

Samson, Daniell. He was naturalized in New York 16 Aug. 1715. He was a yeoman from the manor of Pelham.

Samuel, Levy. He was naturalized in New York in 1740–41. He was a Jew.

Samuells, Samuell. He expressed his desire to be naturalized in New Castle County, Delaware 21 Feb. 1682/3.

Sanches, Abraham. He was naturalized in Jamaica 25 May 1742.

Sanches, Abraham. He was naturalized in Jamaica 26 Aug. 1746. He was a Jew.

Sanches, Benjamin. He was naturalized in Jamaica 26 Aug. 1746. He was a Jew.

Sanchez, Sarah. She was naturalized in Jamaica 23 Feb. 1742/3. She was a Jewess.

Sancombell, Louis. He was naturalized in New York 17 June 1726.

Sander, Hendrick. He was naturalized in New York 11 Sep. 1761.

Sanders, Peter. He and his children were naturalized in Maryland 3 Nov. 1711. He lived in Talbot County.

Sanderzen, Thomas. He took the oath to the King 21–26 Oct. 1664 after the conquest of New Netherland.

Sandots, Leonard. He was naturalized in New York 3 July 1759.

Sanger, Henry. He was naturalized in Pennsylvania 11 Apr. 1761. He was from Berks County.

Sanpaio, Abraham Gomes. He was naturalized in Jamaica 4 Nov. 1701.

Santwoord, Cornelis. He was naturalized in New York 6 July 1723.

Sarazen, Stephen. He was naturalized in Virginia 12 May 1705.

Sarayna, Abraham. He was naturalized in Jamaica 14 Feb. 1721/2.

Sarich, Stephen. He was naturalized in New Jersey 10 Mar. 1762.

Sarmer, Lodowick. He was naturalized in Pennsylvania 10 Apr. 1760.

Sartor, Jacob. He and his sons, Johannes Sartor and Hendrick Sartor, were naturalized in New Jersey 8 July 1730. They were born in Germany.

Sarver, John. He was naturalized in Pennsylvania 10 Apr. 1754. He was from Berks County.

Sarzedas, Rachel. She was naturalized in Jamaica 24 Feb. 1746/7. He was a Jew.

Sasmanhausen, Emanuel. He was naturalized in Pennsylvania 11–13 Apr. 1743. He was from Philadelphia County.

Sasportas, Samuel. He was endenized in England 16 Dec. 1687. He settled in Barbados and was a Jew.

Sassamanhaure, Johannes. He was naturalized in Pennsylvania 11 Apr. 1763. He was from Greenwich Township, Berks County.

Sassin, Francis. He was naturalized in Virginia 12 May 1705.

Satzedo, David Lopes. He was naturalized in Jamaica 3 Apr. 1722.

Sauer, Henry. He was naturalized in Pennsylvania 10 Apr. 1760.

Saull, Adam. He was naturalized in New Jersey in 1765. He was born in Germany and had been in the colony eleven years.

Saum, Nicholas. He was naturalized in Maryland 3 Sep. 1765. He was a German from Sharpsburgh, Maryland.

Saunder, Henry. He was naturalized in Pennsylvania 11–12 Apr. 1744. He was from Lancaster County.

Sauner, Pierre. He was naturalized in Nova Scotia 5 July 1758. His name may have been Pierre Launer.

Saurbeck, George. He was naturalized in New Jersey 7 Dec. 1769.

Sauter, John George. He was naturalized in Pennsylvania 10–12 Apr. 1762. He was from Philadelphia County.

Sauter, Philip. He was naturalized in New Jersey in 1757. He was from Cumberland County. He was from Germany and had been in the colony 24 years.

Sauthier, Claude Joseph. He was naturalized in New York 24 Mar. 1772.

Sauvoye, Germain. He took the oath of allegiance at Port Royal, Nova Scotia 16 Aug. 1695.

Savoie, Andre. He was an Acadian and took the oath of allegiance in Apr. 1730.

Savoie, Jean. He was an Acadian and took the oath of allegiance in Apr. 1730.

Savoie, Germain. He was an Acadian and took the oath of allegiance at Annapolis in Dec. 1729.

Savoie, Germain, cadet. He was an Acadian and took the oath of allegiance at Annapolis in Dec. 1729.

Savoir, Charles. He was an Acadian and took the oath of George II at Annapolis River, Nova Scotia in Dec. 1729.

Savoir, Germain. He was an Acadian and took the oath to George II at Annapolis River, Nova Scotia in Dec. 1729.

Savoir, Jean. He was an Acadian and took the oath to George II at Annapolis River, Nova Scotia in the Dec. 1729.

Savoir, Paul. He was an Acadian and took the oath to George II at Annapolis River, Nova Scotia in Dec. 1729.

Savoir Cobett, Germain. He was an Acadian and took the oath to George II at Annapolis River, Nova Scotia in Dec. 1729.

Savoy, Isacq. He was naturalized in New Castle County, Delaware 21 Feb. 1682/3.

Savoye, Germain. He took the oath of allegiance at Port Royal, Nova Scotia 16 Aug. 1695.

Sawler, John. He was naturalized in Pennsylvania 10 Apr. 1760.

Sax, Johan Peter. He was naturalized in New York 2 Aug. 1750. He was a farmer from Albany County.

Sax, Johannes Michael. He was naturalized in New York 17 Oct. 1753. He was a baker from New York City.

Saxe, Michael. He was naturalized in New York 20 Oct. 1764.

Say, John. He was naturalized in Virginia 12 May 1705.

Sayler, Matthew. He was naturalized in Maryland 10 Apr. 1762. He was a German from Anne Arundel County.

Sbrecker, Coenraad. He was naturalized in New York 11 Sep. 1761.

Sbrecker, George. He was naturalized in New York 11 Sep. 1761.

Sbrecker, Martin. He was naturalized in New York 11 Sep. 1761.

Scamper, Peter. He was naturalized in Maryland 17 May 1701. He lived in Prince George's County.

Schaaf, Casper. He was naturalized in Maryland 11 Apr. 1761.

Schaafbanck, Pieter. He took the oath to the King 21–26 Oct. 1664 after the conquest of New Netherland.

Schaak, Jurian Hansen. He was naturalized in New York 29 Nov. 1745.

Schaber, Andreas. He was naturalized in Pennsylvania 10–12 Apr. 1762. He was from Berks County.

Schack, Caspar. He was naturalized in New Jersey in 1758. He had lived in New Jersey 19 years.

Schad, Theodorus. He was naturalized in New York 11 Sep. 1761.

Schad, Ulrick. He was naturalized in New York 11 Sep. 1761.

Schaefer, Casper. He was naturalized in New Jersey in 1764.

Schaefer, Christian. He was naturalized in Maryland 14 Sep. 1763. He was a German.

Schaefer, David. He was naturalized in Pennsylvania 24 Sep. 1763. He was from Shrewsbury Township, York County.

Schaers, Alexander. He took the oath of allegiance in Breucklijn, Kings County, New York 26–30 Sep. 1687. He was a native of the colony.

Schafer, Hendrick. He was naturalized in New York 8 Mar. 1773.

Schafer, Maria Catharina. She was naturalized in New York 20 Jan. 1776. She was the widow of Jost Schafer. She was a member of the German Church in Lebanon, West New Jersey.

Schaff, Philip. He was naturalized in New York 1 Aug. 1750. He was a brass founder from New York City.

Schaffelberger, Caspar. He was naturalized in Nova Scotia 5 July 1758.

Schaffer, Adam. He was naturalized in New Jersey in 1761. He had lived in America twenty-two years and in New Jersey seven years. He was from Germany.

Schaffer, John. He was naturalized in Pennsylvania 10 & 23 Apr. 1764. He was from Amwell, Hunterdon County, New Jersey.

Schaffer, Mattheus. He was naturalized in New York 3 July 1759.

Schaffer, Nicholas. He was naturalized in New York 3 July 1759.

Shafter, Jacob. He was naturalized in Maryland 11 May 1774. He was a German.

Schaid, Charles. He was naturalized in Pennsylvania 10–12 Apr. 1762. He was from Lancaster County.

Schain, Peter. He was naturalized in Pennsylvania 24 Sep. 1762. He was from Berks County.

Schainer, John. He was naturalized in Pennsylvania 24–25 Sep. 1764. He was from Douglass Township, Philadelphia County.

Schairer, Michael. He was naturalized in Pennsylvania 24 Sep. 1745. He was from Lancaster County.

Schal, Johannes. He was naturalized in New York 3 July 1759.

Schall, Frederick. He was naturalized in New York 20 Mar. 1762.

Schall, Johannes. He was naturalized in New York 11 Sep. 1761.

Schall, Joseph. He was naturalized in Maryland 9 Sep. 1772. He was a German.

Schaltz, Jacen Christian. He was naturalized in New York 20 May 1769.

Schamp, Pieter. He took the oath of allegiance in Boswijck, Kings County, New York 26–30 Sep. 1687. He had been in the colony 15 years.

Schanck, George. He was naturalized in Pennsylvania 24–25 Sep. 1764. He was from Lancaster Township, Lancaster County.

Schappert, Nicholas. He was naturalized in Pennsylvania 11 Apr. 1761. He was from Berks County.

Scharffenstein, John. He was naturalized in New Jersey in 1761. He also appeared as John Sparpestein.

Schaub, Andrew. He was naturalized in Pennsylvania 10–12 Apr. 1762. He was from Lancaster County.

Schaub, Christopher. He was naturalized in Pennsylvania 11 Apr. 1761. He was from Lancaster County.

Schaub, Peter. He was naturalized in Pennsylvania 10 Sep. 1761. He was from Lancaster County.

Schaut, Henry. He was naturalized in Pennsylvania 6 Feb. 1730/1. He was from Philadelphia County.

Schavas, Nicholas. He was naturalized in Pennsylvania 24 Sep. 1762. He was from York County.

Schaws, John Adam. He was naturalized in Pennsylvania 11 Apr. 1721. He was from Philadelphia County.

Schebely, Leonard. He was naturalized in Maryland 21 Sep. 1764. He was a German.

Schee, Hermann. He was naturalized in Maryland 25 Mar. 1702. He lived in Cecil County and was of Dutch parents.

Scheffer, Frederick. He was naturalized in New York 11 Oct. 1715. He was from Albany County.
Scheffer, George. He was naturalized in Maryland 21 Sep. 1764. He was a German.
Scheffer, George. He was naturalized in Pennsylvania 24–25 Sep. 1764. He was from Germantown Township, Philadelphia County.
Scheffer, George Frederick. He was naturalized in Pennsylvania 10 Apr. 1765. He was from Rockland Township, Berks County.
Scheffer, Philip. He was naturalized in New York 3 Jan. 1715/6. He was from Albany County.
Scheffer, Reynhaert. He was naturalized in New York 11 Oct. 1715. He was from Albany County.
Scheider, Abraham. He was naturalized in Pennsylvania 24–25 Sep. 1764. He was from Tulpehocken Township, Berks County.
Scheidler, George. He was naturalized in Maryland 19 Oct. 1743. He was from Manaquice.
Scheimer, Jacob. He was naturalized in Pennsylvania 6 Feb. 1730/1. He was from Philadelphia County.
Schel, Christian. He was naturalized in New York 11 Sep. 1761.
Schel, Christoph. He was naturalized in New York 21 Oct. 1765. He was a cartman from New York City.
Schelde, Carle. He was naturalized in New York 20 Mar. 1762.
Schell, Carle. He was naturalized in Maryland 16 Apr. 1760. He lived in Frederick, Maryland.
Schell, Christian. He was naturalized in New York 20 Dec. 1763.
Schell, Christian. He was naturalized in New York 20 Oct. 1764.
Schell, Johannes. He was naturalized in New York 20 Dec. 1763.
Schell, Johannes. He was naturalized in New York 20 Oct. 1764.
Schellmeir, George. He was naturalized in Pennsylvania 11 Apr. 1761. He was from Philadelphia County.
Schempos, Dirck. He was naturalized in New York 8–9 Sep. 1715. He was from Ulster County.
Schenerhinger, Mathew. He was naturalized in New York 23 Oct. 1765. He was a hatter from New York City.
Schenck, Andrew. He was naturalized in Nova Scotia 10 July 1758.
Schenck, Jan Martense. He took the oath of allegiance in Flackland, Kings County, New York 26–30 Sep. 1687. He had been in the colony 37 years.
Schenck, Jan Roeloffs. He took the oath of allegiance in Flackland, Kings County, New York 26–30 Sep. 1687. He was a native of the colony.
Schenck, Marten Roeloffe. He took the oath of allegiance in Flackland, Kings County, New York 26–30 Sep. 1687. He was a native of the colony.
Schencke, Johanas. He took the oath of naturalization in New York 1 Sep. 1687 in Ulster County.
Schenkel, Henry. He was naturalized in New Jersey in 1759.
Schenkel, Henry. He was naturalized in Nova Scotia 10 July 1758.
Schenkel, Martin. He was naturalized in Pennsylvania 6 Feb. 1730/1. He was from Philadelphia County.
Schepfell, Michael. He was naturalized in Maryland 31 Sep. 1763. He was a German from Frederick County.
Schepmoes, Dirck. He was naturalized in New York 8–9 Sep. 1715. He was from Ulster County.
Scherer, Daniel. He was naturalized in New Jersey in 1761.
Schermiller, Gotlieb. He was naturalized in Nova Scotia 10 July 1758.
Scherp, Jurich Emrig. He was naturalized in New York 17 Jan. 1715/6. He was from Albany County.
Scherpe, Andries Hanse. He was naturalized in New York 27 Apr. 1716. He was from Albany County.
Scherts, Jurch. He was naturalized in New York 31 Jan. 1715/6. He was from Albany County.
Scheun, Catharine. She was naturalized in Pennsylvania 11 Apr. 1761. She was from Berks County.
Schever, Harme. He was naturalized in New York 20 Mar. 1762.
Schever, Hendrick. He was naturalized in New York 8–9 Sep. 1715. He was from Ulster County.
Schick, Christian. He was naturalized in New York 16 Feb. 1771.
Schief, William. He was naturalized in New York 11 Oct. 1765. He was from Albany County.
Schieffer, Jacob. He was naturalized in New York 22 Nov. 1715. He was from Albany County.

Schieffer, Nicolas. He was naturalized in New York 11 Oct. 1715. He was from Albany County.

Schierts, Andries. He was naturalized in New York 6 Dec. 1715. He was from Albany County.

Schiets, Hans Adam. He was naturalized in New York 22 Nov. 1715. He was from Albany County.

Schiets, Johannis. He was naturalized in New York 22 Nov. 1715. He was from Albany County.

Schilp, Peter. He was naturalized in Pennsylvania 24 Sep. 1762. He was from Northampton County.

Schinck, George. He was naturalized in New York 16 Feb. 1771.

Schinckigh, Bernard. He was endenized in England 15 Sep. 1664. He was a merchant residing in Barbados.

Schith, Jacob. He was naturalized in New York 16 Feb. 1771.

Schivelbergh, Johannes. He took the oath to the King 21–26 Oct. 1664 after the conquest of New Netherland.

Schlatter, Michael. He was naturalized in Pennsylvania 11 Apr. 1763. He was from Springfield Township, Philadelphia County.

Schley, George. He was naturalized in Maryland 16 Sep. 1762. He was a German from Frederick County.

Schley, Thomas. He was naturalized in Pennsylvania 24 Sep. 1760. He was from Frederick County, Maryland.

Schleydorn, Henry. He was naturalized in Pennsylvania 25–27 Sep. 1740. He was from Philadelphia.

Schlichtern, Eva Catharina. She was naturalized in Pennsylvania 24–25 Sep. 1764. She was from Philadelphia.

Schliedorn, Henrick. He was naturalized in New York 27 July 1721.

Schlod, George. He was naturalized in Jamaica 24 Nov. 1716

Schlonecker, Michael. He was naturalized in Pennsylvania 10 Apr. 1760.

Schlonecker, Michael, Jr. He was naturalized in Pennsylvania 10 Apr. 1760.

Schlorpp, Peter. He was naturalized in Maryland 15 Sep. 1762. He was from Frederick County.

Schloss, Andreas. He was naturalized in Maryland 17 Apr. 1761.

Schlosser, George. He was naturalized in Pennsylvania 10 Apr. 1759.

Schlothaver, Nicholas. He was naturalized in Maryland 31 Aug. 1757.

Schmaal, Adam. He was naturalized in Pennsylvania 24 Sep. 1762. He was from York County.

Schmare, Martin. He was naturalized in Maryland 9 Apr. 1760. He lived in Baltimore County.

Schmetzer, Adam. He was naturalized in Maryland 3 May 1769. He was a German from Frederick County.

Schmick, John Jacob. He was naturalized in Pennsylvania 10 & 23 Apr. 1764. He was from Bethlehem Township, Northampton County.

Schmid, Georg. He was naturalized in Maryland 9 Sep. 1761.

Schmid, John Philip. He was naturalized in Pennsylvania 10 Sep. 1761. He was from Berks County.

Schmid, Michael. He was naturalized in Maryland 13 Apr. 1763. He was a German from Frederick County.

Schmidt, Edward. He was naturalized in Maryland 14 Sep. 1763.

Schmidt, Henry. He was naturalized in Pennsylvania 21 Nov. 1770. He was from Hempfield Township, Lancaster County.

Schmidt, Henry, Sr. He was naturalized in Pennsylvania 24 Sep. 1763. He was from Frederick Township, Philadelphia County.

Schmidt, Henry, Jr. He was naturalized in Pennsylvania 24 Sep. 1763. He was from Upper Hannover Township, Philadelphia County.

Schmidt, Jacob. He was naturalized in Nova Scotia 5 July 1758.

Schmidt, Johan Jurch. He was naturalized in New York 17 Jan. 1715/6. He was from Albany County.

Schmidt, Nicholas. He sought naturalization in New Jersey in the 18th century.

Schmidt, Peter. He was naturalized in Nova Scotia 10 July 1758.

Schmit, Andreas. He was naturalized in Maryland 16 Sep. 1773. He was a German.

Schmit, Elizabeth. She was naturalized in Maryland 16 Sep. 1773. She was a German.

Schmuck, Peter. He was naturalized in New Jersey 28 Mar. 1749. He was born in France.

Schmyer, Philip. He was naturalized in Pennsylvania 11–13 Apr. 1743. He was from Bucks County.

Schnabel, John. He was naturalized in Pennsylvania 10–12 Apr. 1762. He was from Berks County.

Schnauber, Johann Heinrich. He was naturalized in New Jersey in 1764.

Schnauber, Johannes. He was naturalized in New Jersey in 1764.

Schneider, Adam. He was naturalized in New Jersey in 1764. He was born in Germany.

Schneider, Christian. He was naturalized in Pennsylvania 11 Apr. 1761. He was from Philadelphia County.

Schneider, Conrad. He was naturalized in Pennsylvania 11 Apr. 1749. He was from Philadelphia County.

Schneider, Conrad. He was naturalized in Pennsylvania 11 Apr. 1761. He was from Berks County.

Schneider, Conrad. He was naturalized in Pennsylvania 24–25 Sep. 1764. He was from Philadelphia.

Schneider, Daniel. He was naturalized in New York 20 Oct. 1747. He was a yeoman from Ulster County.

Schneider, Henrich. He was naturalized in New York 20 Mar. 1762.

Schneider, Henry. He was naturalized in Pennsylvania 29 Mar. 1735. He was from Bucks County.

Schneider, Jacob. He was naturalized in Pennsylvania 11 Apr. 1761. He was from York County.

Schneider, Johannes. He was naturalized in Pennsylvania 11 Apr. 1761. He was from Berks County.

Schneider, Martin. He was naturalized in Pennsylvania 24 Sep. 1762. He was from Lancaster County.

Schneider, Michael. He was naturalized in Pennsylvania 30 May 1769. He was from Heidelberg Township, Berks County.

Schneider, Peter. He was naturalized in Pennsylvania 29 Mar. 1735. He was from Bucks County.

Schneider, Simon. He was naturalized in Pennsylvania 21 Nov. 1770. He was from Lancaster, Lancaster County.

Schneider, Valentine. He was naturalized in Pennsylvania 11 Apr. 1761. He was from Lancaster County.

Schneider, William. He was naturalized in New York 19 Jan. 1774. He was a baker from New York City.

Schneizer, Jacob. He was naturalized in Pennsylvania 10–12 Apr. 1762. He was from Lancaster County.

Schnepf, Johann Peter. He was naturalized in Maryland 10 Sep. 1760.

Schnepf, Johannes Peter. He was naturalized in Maryland 19 Sept. 1761.

Schneyder, Daniel. He was naturalized in Pennsylvania 24–25 Sep. 1764. He was from Bethel Township, Berks County.

Schneyder, Jacob. He was naturalized in New York 11 Sep. 1761.

Schnitzhaus, John Adolphus. He was naturalized in Jamaica 17 Oct. 1765.

Schnuck, Francis. He was naturalized in Pennsylvania 11 Apr. 1761. He was from Philadelphia.

Schnuck, Francis. He was naturalized in Pennsylvania 11 Apr. 1761. He was from Philadelphia County.

Schoeck, Adam. He was naturalized in Maryland 10 Sep. 1760.

Schoenberger, Philip. He was naturalized in Pennsylvania 24 Sep. 1762. He was from Philadelphia County.

Schoals, John. He was naturalized in New York 31 July 1750. He was a mariner from New York City.

Scholdies, Johannis. He was naturalized in New York 31 Jan. 1715/6. He was from Albany County.

Scholl, Johannes. He was naturalized in Pennsylvania 29 Sep. 1709. He was from Philadelphia County.

Scholl, Michael. He was naturalized in Maryland 13 Apr. 1763. He was a German from Frederick County.

Scholl, Peter. He was naturalized in Pennsylvania 11 Apr. 1749. He was from Bucks County.

Scholl, Philip Peter. He was naturalized in Pennsylvania 10 & 23 Apr. 1764. He was from Maxatawny Township, Berks County.

Scholl, Simon Peter. He was naturalized in Pennsylvania 11 Apr. 1763. He was from Lynn Township, Northampton County.

Scholtz, Christopher. He was naturalized in Pennsylvania 11–13 Apr. 1743. He was from Philadelphia County.

Scholtz, George, Jr. He was naturalized in Pennsylvania 11–13 Apr. 1743. He was from Philadelphia County.

Scholtz, Melchior. He was naturalized in Pennsylvania 11–13 Apr. 1743. He was from Philadelphia County.

Scholtze, David. He was naturalized in Pennsylvania 29 Mar. 1735. He was from Philadelphia.

Scholtze, George. He was naturalized in Pennsylvania 29 Mar. 1735. He was from Philadelphia.

Schoner, Daniel. He was naturalized in Pennsylvania 29 Mar. 1735. He was from Philadelphia County.

Schonmaker, Egbert. He was naturalized in New York 8–9 Sep. 1715. He was from Ulster County.

Schonmaker, Jochem. He was naturalized in New York 8–9 Sep. 1715. He was from Ulster County.

Schonnert, Frederick. He was naturalized in New York 18 Oct. 1765. He was a shopkeeper from New York City.

School, Michael. He was naturalized in Maryland 13 Apr. 1763. He was a German from Frederick County.

School, Peter. He was naturalized in Pennsylvania 29 Sep. 1709. He was from Philadelphia County.

Schoop, Gabriel. He was naturalized in Pennsylvania 11 Apr. 1761. He was from Berks County.

Schoot, John. He was naturalized in Pennsylvania 10 Apr. 1772. He was from Hatfield Township, Philadelphia County.

Schop, John. He was naturalized in Pennsylvania 11 Apr. 1761. He was from Berks County.

Schorer, Christian. He was naturalized in New York 8 Mar. 1773.

Schoron, John. He was naturalized in Pennsylvania 10–12 Apr. 1762. He was from York County.

Schotler, Garret. He was naturalized in New York 20 May 1769.

Schott, John. He was naturalized in Pennsylvania 10 Apr. 1772. He was from Hatfield Township, Philadelphia County.

Schough, Andreas. He was naturalized in New York 16 Feb. 1771.

Schouster, Nicholas. He was naturalized in Pennsylvania 24 Sep. 1763. He was from Shrewsbury Township, York County.

Schoute, Andreas. He was naturalized in Pennsylvania 10 Sep. 1761. He was from Northampton County.

Schrack, John Jacob. He was naturalized in Pennsylvania 6 Feb. 1730/1. He was from Philadelphia County.

Schrack, John Joseph. He was naturalized in Pennsylvania 6 Feb. 1730/1. He was from Philadelphia County.

Schrack, Philip. He was naturalized in Pennsylvania 6 Feb. 1730/1. He was from Philadelphia County.

Schrain, John Nicholas. He was naturalized in Pennsylvania 10–12 Apr. 1762. He was from York County.

Schram, Fredrich. He was naturalized in New York 8–9 Sep. 1715. He was from Ulster County

Schram, George. He was naturalized in Pennsylvania 24 Sep. 1762. He was from York County.

Schram, Henrich. He was naturalized in New York 8–9 Sep. 1715. He was from Ulster County.

Schram, Johanis. He was naturalized in New York 8–9 Sep. 1715. He was from Ulster County.

Schredy, Martin. He was naturalized in Pennsylvania 10 Sep. 1761. He was from Lancaster County.

Schreffler, Henry. He was naturalized in Pennsylvania 18–20 May 1772. He was from Reading Township, Berks County.

Schreiber, Albertus. He was naturalized in New York 8–9 Sep. 1715. He was from Ulster County.

Schreiber, Stephen. He was naturalized in New York 20 Apr. 1774. He was from Montgomery Ward of New York City.

Schreit, Jorg Adam. He was naturalized in New York 7–8 Sep. 1715. He was from Ulster County.

Schreyck, Johannes. He was naturalized in Pennsylvania 26–27 Sep. 1743. He was from Lancaster County.

Schreyer, Frederick. He was naturalized in Pennsylvania 24–25 Sep. 1764. He was from Philadelphia.

Schriener, Nicholas. He was naturalized in Pennsylvania 11 Apr. 1761. He was from Philadelphia County.

Schrink, Peter. He was naturalized in Maryland 18 Sep. 1762. He was a German.

Schrocker, Johan Adam. He was naturalized in Pennsylvania 11 Apr. 1741. He was from Philadelphia County.

Schroff, Christopherus. He was naturalized in Maryland 3 May 1774. He was a German.

Schropp, Mathew. He was naturalized in Pennsylvania 24 Sep. 1762. He was from Northampton County.

Schuck, Johan Jacob. He was naturalized in Jamaica 4 Oct. 1716.

Schuen, Catharina. She was naturalized in Pennsylvania 11 Apr. 1761. She was from Berks County.

Schuerman, Conraet. He was naturalized in New York 17 Jan. 1715/6. He was from Albany County.

Schuffi, Johannes. He was naturalized in Maryland 17 Apr. 1773. He was a German.

Schug, Peter. He was naturalized in Pennsylvania 24 Sep. 1762. He was from Philadelphia County.

Schuhntz, George. He was naturalized in Pennsylvania 24 Sep. 1760. He was from Berks County.

Schuhntz, Jacob. He was naturalized in Pennsylvania 24 Sep. 1760. He was from Berks County.

Schui, Ludwick. He was naturalized in Pennsylvania 10 Sep. 1761. He was from Lancaster County.

Schuiler, Philip. He was naturalized in New Jersey in 1759. He was from Germany.

Schuler, Gabriel. He was naturalized in Pennsylvania 29 Sep. 1709. He was from Philadelphia County. He also appeared as Gabriel Senter.

Schuler, Lawrence. He was naturalized in New York 19 Dec. 1766.

Schultz, Casparus. He was naturalized in New York 17 Oct. 1744. He was a farmer from Dutchess County.

Schumaker, Bartholomew. He was naturalized in Maryland 29 Sep. 1764. He was a German.

Schumaker, George. He was naturalized in New Jersey 13 Apr. 1763. He was a German from Frederick County.

Schuneman, Herman. He was endenized in London 25 Aug. 1705. He was to go to New York. He was a German Lutheran.

Schuong, Johannes. He was naturalized in New York 8 Nov. 1735.

Schupp, George. He was naturalized in Pennsylvania 10 Sep. 1761. He was from Lancaster County.

Schurck, David. He was naturalized in Pennsylvania 11 Apr. 1761. He was from Lancaster County.

Schurri, Johannes. He was naturalized in New York 18 Oct. 1750. He was a blacksmith from Dutchess County.

Schuster, Jacob. He was naturalized in Pennsylvania 24–25 Sep./5 Oct. 1767. He was from Nantmill Township, Chester County.

Schutt, Jacob. He took the oath of naturalization in New York 1 Sep. 1687 in Ulster County.

Schutt, John. He took the oath of naturalization in New York 1 Sep. 1687 in Ulster County.

Schutt, William. He took the oath of naturalization in New York 1 Sep. 1687 in Ulster County.

Schutts, Phillip. He was naturalized in New York 16 Dec. 1737.

Schutz, Conrad. He was naturalized in Pennsylvania 24–25 Sep. 1767. He was from Upper Hannover Township, Philadelphia County.

Schutz, Mathias, Jr. He was naturalized in Pennsylvania 25–27 Sep. 1740. He was from Philadelphia.

Schutze, Johann Michael. He was naturalized in New York 12 July 1715. He was a tailor.

Schwaartz, Abraham. He was naturalized in Pennsylvania 6 Feb. 1730/1. He was from Philadelphia County.

Schwachhammer, Conrad. He was naturalized in New Jersey in 1750. He was from Hunterdon County.

Schwachhammer, Samuel. He was naturalized in New Jersey in 1759. He was born in Germany.

Schwanger, Paul. He was naturalized in Pennsylvania 24 Sep. 1762. He was from Philadelphia County.

Schwantz, George. He was naturalized in Pennsylvania 24 Sep. 1760. He was from Lancaster County.

Schwartz, George. He was naturalized in New Jersey in 1750. He was from Hunterdon County.

Schwartz, Otho William. He was naturalized in Nova Scotia 11 Sep. 1758.

Schwartz, Valentine. He was naturalized in Maryland 9 Sep. 1761. He was from Frederick County.

Schwartz, William. He was naturalized in Maryland 14 Apr. 1762. He was a German.

Schwarzwalder, Martin. He was naturalized in New Jersey in 1764.

Schwas, John Adam. He was naturalized in Pennsylvania 11 Apr. 1752. He was from Philadelphia County.

Schwaub, Jacob. He was naturalized in Pennsylvania 10 Sep. 1761. He was from Lancaster County.

Schweeter, George. He was naturalized in Pennsylvania 10 Sep. 1761. He was from Lancaster County.

Schweetzer, Christian. He was naturalized in Pennsylvania 24 Sep. 1762. He was from Lancaster County.

Schweiger, Nicholas. He was naturalized in Pennsylvania 10 Sep. 1761. He was from Berks County.

Schweighauser, John Conrad. He was naturalized in Pennsylvania 10 Apr. 1757.

Schweitzer, Henry. He was naturalized in Pennsylvania 10 Apr. 1756. He was from Manheim Township, Lancaster County.

Schweinhart, George. He was naturalized in Maryland in Oct. 1743.

Schwenck, Conrod. He was naturalized in Maryland 6 Sep. 1769. He was a German.

Schwenk, Martin. He was naturalized in Pennsylvania 11 Apr. 1761. He was from Northampton County.

Schwisser, Herman. He was endenized in London 25 Aug. 1708. He came to New York.

Schwisser, Lorentz. He, his wife, Anne Catherine Schwisser, and daughter Johanne Schwisser, were endenized in London 25 Aug. 1708. They came to New York.

Schyck, Jacob. He was naturalized in Pennsylvania 11 Apr. 1761. He was from Philadelphia County.

Schyet, Anthony. He was naturalized in New York 11 Oct. 1715.

Sclabach, Henry. He was naturalized in Pennsylvania 10 Sep. 1761. He was from Lancaster County.

Scotzer, Martin. He was naturalized in Frederick County, Virginia 5 Sep. 1769.

Scruyver, Jan. He took the oath to the King 21–26 Oct. 1664 after the conquest of New Netherland.

Seabalt, John. He was naturalized in New York 27 Jan. 1770.

Seacrist, Henry. He was naturalized in Frederick County, Virginia 3 Mar. 1768.

Sealand, Heibort. He took the oath of naturalization in New York 1 Sep. 1687 in Ulster County.

Seaman, Jonathan. He was naturalized in Frederick County, Virginia 6 May 1766.

Sebas, John. He was naturalized in New York 3 July 1759.

Sebastian, Michael. He was naturalized in Pennsylvania in Sep. 1740. He was from Philadelphia County.

Seber, Jacob. He was naturalized in New York 27 Jan. 1770.

Secabough, Peter. He was naturalized in Frederick County, Virginia 1 Aug. 1769.

Secq, Moses. He was admitted into the colony of Massachusetts 1 Feb. 1691. He was French.

Seeber, Jacob. He was naturalized in New York 11 Sep. 1761.

Seeber, Jacob, Jr. He was naturalized in New York 11 Sep. 1761.

Seeber, William. He was naturalized in New York 11 Sep. 1761.

Seecher, Jacob. He was naturalized in Pennsylvania 24 Sep. 1763. He was from Upper Milford Township, Northampton County.

Seeggrist, Bartholomew. He was naturalized in Pennsylvania 10 Sep. 1761. He was from Lancaster County.

Sees, Balthazar. He was naturalized in Pennsylvania 10–11 Apr. 1745. He was from Lancaster County.

Seesholtz, David. He was naturalized in Pennsylvania 19 May 1739. He was from Philadelphia County.

Seeu, Cornelis Jansse. He took the oath of allegiance in Flackbush, Kings County, New York 26–30 Sep. 1687. He had been in the colony 27 years.

Segedorp, Harme. He was naturalized in New York 3 Jan. 1715/6. He was from Albany County.

Seger, Christian. He was naturalized in Pennsylvania 11 Apr. 1761. He was from Northampton County.

Seger, Mathius. He was naturalized in New Jersey in 1761. He also appeared as Mathias Sagor.

Seger, Samuel. He was naturalized in Pennsylvania 11 Apr. 1761. He was from Northampton County.

Segrist, Valentine. He was naturalized in Maryland 25 Sep. 1772.

Seibb, Christopher. He was naturalized in Pennsylvania 24 Sep. 1745. He was from Philadelphia County.

Seibert, Wendel. He was naturalized in Pennsylvania 24–25 Sep./5 Oct. 1767. He was from Bethel Township, Berks County.

Seibt, Casper. He was naturalized in Pennsylvania 25–26 Sep./4 Oct. 1749. He was from Philadelphia County.

Seibt, David. He was naturalized in Pennsylvania 11–13 Apr. 1743. He was from Philadelphia County.

Seidel, John. He was naturalized in New York 3 July 1759.

Seidel, Nathaniel. He was naturalized in Pennsylvania 10–12 Apr. 1762. He was from Northampton County.

Seidle, John. He was naturalized in Pennsylvania 10 Apr. 1757.

Seidler, Gottlieb. He was naturalized in Nova Scotia 5 July 1758.

Seidler, Matthias. He was naturalized in Pennsylvania 10 Sep. 1761. He was from Lancaster County.

Seigarsar, Felix. He was naturalized in Maryland 7 Sep. 1763. He was a German.

Seigerist, Jacob. He was naturalized in Pennsylvania 11 Apr. 1761. He was from York County.

Seigle, Goliffe. He was naturalized in Pennsylvania 10 Apr. 1757.

Seigler, Johannes. He was naturalized in Pennsylvania 11–13 Apr. 1743. He was from Philadelphia County.

Seijl, Jacob. He was naturalized in Pennsylvania 29 Mar. 1735. He was from Philadelphia.

Seiler, Jacob. He was naturalized in Maryland 15 Sep. 1763. He was a German.

Seiple, John Lobwick. He was naturalized in Pennsylvania 10–11 Apr. 1746. He was from Philadelphia.

Seitenbender, Henry. He was naturalized in Pennsylvania 10 Apr. 1764. He was from Cumru Township, Berks County.

Seitz, Wendle. He was naturalized in Maryland 11 Sep. 1765.

Seix, Hendrick. He was naturalized in New York 11 Oct. 1715. He was from Albany County.

Seixas, Isaac. He was naturalized in New York 4 Nov. 1745. He was a Jewish merchant from New York City.

Seixas, Jacob Mendes. He was naturalized in Jamaica 26 Feb. 1750/1. He was a Jew.

Selbach, Anroldus. He was naturalized in New York 3 July 1759.

Selbach, Johan Peter. He was naturalized in New York 3 July 1759.

Sell, George. He was naturalized in Pennsylvania 10 Sep. 1761. He was from Berks County.

Sellen, Henry. He was naturalized in Pennsylvania 29 Sep. 1709. He was from Philadelphia County.

Seller, John. He was naturalized in Augusta County, Virginia 16 Oct. 1765.

Seller, Philip Henrick. He was naturalized in Pennsylvania in Sep. 1740. He was from Bucks County.

Sellers, James. He was naturalized in Jamaica 18 Aug. 1675.

Sellinger, William. He was naturalized in Pennsylvania 5 Mar. 1725/26. His name also appeared as William Seliger. He was born in Germany.

Selser, Wyrick. He was naturalized in Pennsylvania 10 Apr. 1765. He was from Tulpehocken Township, Berks County.

Seltzer, Jacob. He was naturalized in Pennsylvania 10 Apr. 1765. He was from Heidelberg Township, Berks County.

Seltzer, Jacob. He was naturalized in Pennsylvania 6 Feb. 1730/1. He was from Philadelphia County.

Semmer, John. He was naturalized in Maryland in Sep. 1751.

Sempill, Josyn. He expressed his desire to be naturalized in New Castle County, Delaware 21 Feb. 1682/3.

Senably, Henry. He was naturalized in Maryland 21 Sep. 1764. He was a German.

Seneschaud, Daniel. He was the son of Jonas and Jeane Seneschaud of St. Maixant, Poitou, France. His wife, Magdelaine Seneschaud, was the daughter of Daniel and Marie Ardouin of Gemoset, Xaintonge, France. Their daughter, Elizabeth Seneschaud, was born in South Carolina. They were naturalized in South Carolina ca. 1696.

Seng, Philip. He was naturalized in Pennsylvania 11 Apr. 1761. He was from Lancaster County.

Senghaar, Caspar. He was naturalized in Pennsylvania 24 Sep. 1762. He was from Lancaster County.

Senior, Joseph. He was endenized in England 27 Nov. 1671. He settled in Barbados and was a Jew.

Sens, Christianus. He was naturalized in Maryland 15 Sep. 1762. He was from Baltimore County.

Sensebach, Johan Teunis. He sought naturalization in New York 31 Oct. 1739.

Sensebach, Phillipus. He was naturalized in New York 18 Oct. 1750. He was a farmer from Ulster County.

Sensenbach, Jacob. He was naturalized in New York 8 Nov. 1735.

Sensenig, Christian. He was naturalized in Pennsylvania 25 Sep. 1747. He was from Lancaster County.

Sensfelder, Philip. He was naturalized in Pennsylvania 10 Apr. 1765. He was from Philadelphia.

Sensibach, Frederick. He was naturalized in New York by the act of 1740.

Sensibach, John Christ. He was naturalized in New York by the act of 1740.

Sentiny, John. He was naturalized in New Jersey 20 Aug. 1755.

Senzeman, John. He was naturalized in Pennsylvania 11 Apr. 1761. He was from Lancaster County.

Sequira, Abraham Henriques. He was naturalized in Jamaica 26 May 1741. He was a Jew.

Sequira, Isaac Henriques. He was naturalized in Jamaica 26 Feb. 1740/1. He was a Jew.

Sere, Noel. He was born at Luminie, Brie, France, the son of Claude Sere and Ester Guillet. His wife was Catherine Challiou. She also appeared as Catherine Challion, daughter of Louis Challion and Benoite Pitauer. She was born at Lyon, France. Their children, Noel Sere and Marguerite Sere, were born in South Carolina. They were naturalized in South Carolina 10 Mar. 1696/7. He was a weaver. He also appeared as Noel Serre.

Sereno, Solomon Mendez. He was endenized in England 28 June 1682. He was a merchant and settled in Barbados.

Serjanton, John. He was naturalized in Virginia 12 May 1705.

Serra, Antonio Gomez. He was naturalized in Jamaica 26 Feb. 1703. He was a Jew.

Serrano, Ishac. He was endenized in London 25 May 1664. He was a merchant from Barbados.

Servant, Bertram. He was endenized in Virginia 3 Oct. 1667.

Servant, Bertram. He was naturalized in Elizabeth City County, Virginia 28 Nov. 1698. He was a native of France. He was 66 years of age and had been a resident of Elizabeth City County for 38 years. on 22 Mar. 1697/8.

Server, Jacob. He was naturalized in Pennsylvania in Sep. 1740. He was from Bucks County.

Server, Johan Jacob. He was naturalized in New York 17 Jan. 1715/6. He was from Albany County.

Server, Marte. He was naturalized in New York 17 Jan. 1715/6. He was from Albany County.

Server, Tobias. He was naturalized in New York 20 Apr. 1763. He was a husbandman from Orange County.

Servis, Christopher. He was naturalized in New York 11 Sep. 1761.

Servis, Peter. He was naturalized in New York 11 Sep. 1761.

Serwaes, Thys. He took the oath of allegiance in Orange County, New York 26 Sep. 1687.

Sesmez, Jean. He was an Acadian and took the oath of allegiance in Apr. 1730.

Sessenning, Jacob. He was naturalized in Pennsylvania 11–13 Apr. 1743. He was from Lancaster County.

Setefan, Johannes. He was naturalized in New York 3 July 1759.

Seth, Jacob. He was naturalized in Maryland 26 Apr. 1684.

Sevenbergh, Christian. He was naturalized in New York 3 May 1755.

Sever, Jacob. He was naturalized in New York 11 Sep. 1761.

Seville, John. He was naturalized in Jamaica 30 [?] 177[?]. His certificate was recorded 2 Feb. 1771.

Sexton, John. He was naturalized in Frederick County, Virginia 4 Mar. 1766.

Seybert, Johan Jacob. He was naturalized in New York 13 Mar. 1715/6. He was from Albany County.

Seybert, Johan Martin. He was naturalized in New York 13 Mar. 1715/6. He was from Albany County.

Seydall, Nicholas. He was naturalized in Pennsylvania 24 Sep. 1762. He was from Berks County.

Seydel, John Nicholas. He was naturalized in Pennsylvania 25 Sep. 1751. He was from Philadelphia County.

Seydig, John Philip. He was naturalized in Pennsylvania 24 Sep. 1762. He was from Philadelphia County.

Seydle, Ernast Sigomond. He was naturalized in Pennsylvania 10 Apr. 1754. He was from Berks County.

Seyler, Jacob. He was naturalized in Pennsylvania 24 Sep. 1762. He was from Lancaster County.

Seyn, Petter. He was naturalized in New York 23 Aug. 1715. He was a yeoman from Tappan.

Shaad, Theodorus. He was naturalized in New York 3 July 1759.

Shaad, Ulrick. He was naturalized in New York 3 July 1759.

Shaaf, George. He was naturalized in Pennsylvania 10 Apr. 1765. He was from Philadelphia.

Shaaf, Peter. He was naturalized in Pennsylvania 24 Sep. 1762. He was from Lancaster County.

Shabecker, Martin. He was naturalized in Pennsylvania 25–27 Sep. 1740. He was from Philadelphia County.

Shadaire, Valentine. He was naturalized in Pennsylvania 24 Sep. 1762. He was from Lancaster County.

Shadron, Henry. He was naturalized in Pennsylvania 20 May 1769. He was from York Township, York County.

Shadwell, David. He was naturalized in New York 16 Feb. 1771.

Shadwell, Michael. He was naturalized in New York 16 Feb. 1771.

Shafer, Baltzer. He was naturalized in Pennsylvania 10–12 Apr. 1762. He was from Lancaster County.

Shafer, Hendrick. He was naturalized in New York 8 Mar. 1773.

Shafer, Johannes. He was naturalized in Pennsylvania 11 Apr. 1741. He was from Philadelphia County.

Shaff, George. He was naturalized in Pennsylvania 10 Apr. 1765. He was from Philadelphia.

Shaffer, Adam. He was naturalized in Pennsylvania 19 May 1739. He was Bucks County.

Shaffer, David. He was naturalized in Pennsylvania 10 Apr. 1757.

Shaffer, Jacob. He was naturalized in Pennsylvania 19 Mar. 1739. He was from Lancaster County.

Shaffer, Johannes. He was naturalized in Pennsylvania 6 Feb. 1730/1. He was from Philadelphia County.

Shaffer, Philip. He was naturalized in Pennsylvania 24 Sep. 1745. He was from Lancaster County.

Shaffer, Philip Jacob. He was naturalized in Maryland 11 Sep. 1765. He was a German from Frederick County.

Shaffer, Michael. He was naturalized in Pennsylvania 24 Sep. 1762. He was from Northampton County.

Shaffner, Casper. He was naturalized in Pennsylvania 26–27 Sep. 1743. He was from Lancaster County.

Shaffner, Jacob. He was naturalized in Pennsylvania 10 Sep. 1761. He was from Lancaster County.

Shafter, Jacob. He was naturalized in Maryland 11 May 1774. He was a German.

Shaid, Jacob. He was naturalized in Pennsylvania 11–13 Apr. 1743. He was from Bucks County.

Shall, George. He was naturalized in Pennsylvania 10 Sep. 1761. He was from Berks County.

Shallas, Theobald. He was naturalized in Pennsylvania 24 Sep. 1763. He was from Mount Pleasant Township, York County.

Shally, Charles. He was naturalized in Pennsylvania 11 Apr. 1761. He was from Lancaster County.

Shally, Ludwick. He was naturalized in Pennsylvania 10 Sep. 1761. He was from Lancaster County.

Shallos, Valentine. He was naturalized in Pennsylvania 10 Apr. 1758.

Shamback, George. He was naturalized in Pennsylvania 11 Apr. 1761. He was from Philadelphia County.

Shamback, Valentine. He was naturalized in Pennsylvania 11 Apr. 1763. He was from New Providence Township, Philadelphia County.

Shandler, George. He was naturalized in Pennsylvania 10 Sep. 1761. He was from Berks County.

Shank, Henry. He was naturalized in Pennsylvania 24 Sep. 1754. He was from Lancaster County.

Shank, John. He was naturalized in Pennsylvania 14 Feb. 1729/30. He was from Lancaster County. He was styled "Big" John Shank.

Shank, Michael. He was naturalized in Pennsylvania 14 Feb. 1729/30. He was from Lancaster County.

Shantz, Jacob. He was naturalized in Pennsylvania 12 Apr. 1750. He was from Philadelphia County.

Shantz, Jacob. He was naturalized in Pennsylvania 11 Apr. 1761. He was from Lancaster County.

Shapher, Philip. He was naturalized in New York 20 Mar. 1762.

Sharen, Jacob. He was naturalized in Pennsylvania 24 Sep. 1759.

Sharff, Conrad. He was naturalized in Pennsylvania 24 Sep. 1741. He was from Lancaster County.

Sharp, Philip. He was naturalized in Pennsylvania 25–27 Sep. 1740. He was from Philadelphia County.

Sharpe, George. He was naturalized in New York 27 Jan. 1770.

Sharpe, George. He was naturalized in North Carolina 22 Sep. 1764. He was from Rowan County and a German.

Sharpe, Henry. He was naturalized in North Carolina 22 Sep. 1764. He was from Rowan County and a German.

Sharpe, Jacob. He was naturalized in New York 4 Oct. 1715. He was from Kingsbury, Dutchess County and was a yeoman.

Sharpenstein, Christijan. He was naturalized in New Jersey in 1757. He had been in the colony 32 years. He was born in Germany. He also appeared as Christian Sharp.

Sharpenstein, Johannes Peter. He was naturalized in New Jersey in 1750. He was from Hunterdon County.

Sharpenstein, Moritz. He was naturalized in New Jersey in 1750. He was from Hunterdon County.

Sharpenstein, Paul. He was naturalized in New Jersey in 1750. He also appeared as Paul Sharbenstein. He was from Hunterdon County.

Sharpentin, Matthias. He was naturalized in New Jersey 8 Dec. 1744.

Shaul, Sebastian. He was naturalized in Maryland 16 Sep. 1762. He was a German from Frederick County.

Shauman, John. He was naturalized in Pennsylvania 10–12 Apr. 1762. He was from York County.

Shauman, John. He was naturalized in New York 3 July 1759.

Shaura, John. He was naturalized in Maryland 12 Sep. 1759.

Shaver, Bartholomew. He was naturalized in Pennsylvania 19 May 1739. He was from Lancaster County.

Shaver, Frederick. He was naturalized in Pennsylvania 24 Sep. 1753. He was from Berks County.

Shaver, Henry. He was naturalized in Pennsylvania 24–25 Sep./5 Oct. 1767. He was from Charlestown Township, Chester County.

Shaver, John. He was naturalized in Maryland 29 Mar. 1775. He was a German.

Shaver, Michael. He was naturalized in Pennsylvania 24 Sep. 1753. He was from Berks County.

Shaver, Peter. He was naturalized in Pennsylvania 24 Sep. 1753. He was from Berks County.

Shawn, Leonard. He was naturalized in Maryland 14 Apr. 1762. He was a German.

Sheafer, Peter. He was naturalized in Maryland 15 Apr. 1761.

Sheaff, Henry. He was naturalized in Pennsylvania 26 Feb. 1773. He was a grocer from Philadelphia.

Sheaff, William. He was naturalized in Pennsylvania 26 Feb. 1773. He was a grocer from Philadelphia.

Sheaffer, Frederick. He was naturalized in Pennsylvania 23 Nov. 1773. He was from Lancaster, Lancaster County.

Shecktell, Michael. He was naturalized in Pennsylvania 11 Apr. 1763. He was from Reading Township, Berks County.

Shedoran, John Leonard. He was naturalized in Pennsylvania 10–12 Apr. 1762. He was from York County.

Sheefer, George. He was naturalized in Pennsylvania 10 Sep. 1761. He was from Berks County.

Sheener, Melchior. He was naturalized in Pennsylvania 11 Apr. 1761. He was from Philadelphia County.

Scheerham, Christoffel. He was naturalized in New York 31 Dec. 1768.

Shees, Peter. He was naturalized in Maryland 11 Sep. 1765. He was a German from Frederick County.

Sheets, Jacob. He was naturalized in New York 8 Mar. 1773.

Sheffer, Alexander. He was naturalized in Pennsylvania 10 Apr. 1758.

Sheffer, Andreas. He was naturalized in Pennsylvania 10 Apr. 1760.

Sheffer, Detrick. He was naturalized in Pennsylvania 10 Sep. 1761. He was from Berks County.

Sheffer, Frederick. He was naturalized in Pennsylvania 11 Apr. 1761. He was from Northampton County.

Sheffer, George. He was naturalized in Pennsylvania 11 Apr. 1761. He was from Berks County.

Sheffer, George. He was naturalized in Pennsylvania 10 Sep. 1761. He was from Berks County.

Sheffer, George Jacob. He was naturalized in Pennsylvania 10 Apr. 1765. He was from Codorus Township, York County.

Sheffer, Jacob. He was naturalized in Pennsylvania 11 Apr. 1761. He was from Berks County.

Sheffer, John. He was naturalized in Pennsylvania 11–12 Apr. 1744. He was from Lancaster County.

Sheffer, Nicholas. He was naturalized in Maryland 11 Sep. 1765.

Sheffer, Yost. He was naturalized in Pennsylvania 10 Apr. 1766. He was from Hunterdon County, New Jersey.

Sheibele, Casper. He was naturalized in Pennsylvania 10 Apr. 1766. He was from Lancaster Township, Lancaster County.

Sheirer, Henry. He was naturalized in Pennsylvania 10–12 Apr. 1762. He was from Berks County.

Shelbert, Peter. He was naturalized in Pennsylvania 11–13 Apr. 1743. He was from Philadelphia County.

Shell, Casper. He was naturalized in Pennsylvania 10 Apr. 1767. He was from Donegal Township, Lancaster County.

Shell, Peter. He was naturalized in Pennsylvania 19 May 1739. He was from Lancaster County.

Shellenberg, Henry. He was naturalized in Pennsylvania 11 Apr. 1749. He was from Philadelphia County.

Shellery, Ulrich. He was naturalized in Maryland 11 May 1774. He was a German.

Shelley, Abraham. He was naturalized in Pennsylvania 11–13 Apr. 1743. He was from Bucks County.

Shelliberger, John. He was naturalized in Pennsylvania 25–27 Sep. 1740. He was from Philadelphia County.

Shellich, Adam. He was naturalized in Pennsylvania 10 Apr. 1765. He was from Paradise Township, York County.

Shellig, John Philip. He was naturalized in Pennsylvania 25–27 Sep. 1740. He was from Philadelphia County.

Shellman, John. He was naturalized in Maryland 16 Apr. 1761.

Shelts, Charles. He was naturalized in New York 24 Nov. 1750.

Shenck, Roeloff Martense. He took the oath of allegiance in Flackland, Kings County, New York 26–30 Sep. 1687. He had been in the colony 37 years.

Shenckell, Henry. He was naturalized in Pennsylvania 24–25 Sep./5 Oct. 1767. He was from Coventry Township, Chester County.

Shenigh, Fredrick. He was naturalized in New York 23 Dec. 1765.

Shenk, Henry. He was naturalized in Pennsylvania 11 Apr. 1761. He was from Lancaster County.

Shenkell, Frederick. He was naturalized in Pennsylvania 24–25 Sep. 1764. He was from Philadelphia.

Shepfell, Michael. He was naturalized in Maryland 21 Sep. 1763. He was a German from Frederick County.

Sheppard, George. He was naturalized in Pennsylvania 24–25 Sep. 1764. He was from Philadelphia.

Shepperd, Gasper. He was naturalized in New Jersey in 1764.

Sherer, Bernard. He was naturalized in Pennsylvania 11 Apr. 1763. He was from Whitpain Township, Philadelphia County.

Sherer, Ulrick. He was naturalized in Pennsylvania 24 Sep. 1741. He was from Philadelphia County.

Sherer, Valentine. He was naturalized in Pennsylvania 10 Sep. 1761. He was from Philadelphia County.

Sherer, Valentine. He was naturalized in Pennsylvania 11 Apr. 1763. He was from Whitpain Township, Philadelphia County.

Sheretele, Bernard. He was naturalized in Pennsylvania 11 Apr. 1761. He was from Berks County.

Sherick, Casper. He was naturalized in Pennsylvania 25–26 Sep./4 Oct. 1749. He was from Lancaster County.

Sherman, Philip Adam. He was naturalized in Pennsylvania 11 Apr. 1761. He was from Berks County.

Sherp, Jacob. He was naturalized in New York 3 May 1755.

Sherp, John. He was naturalized in New York 3 May 1755.

Sherp, Michael. He was naturalized in New York 3 May 1755.

Sherpenstone, Jacob. He was naturalized in New York 20 Dec. 1763.

Sherper, Abraham. He was naturalized in Pennsylvania 24 Sep. 1760. He was from Berks County.

Sherrer, Ulrick. He was naturalized in Pennsylvania 11–13 Apr. 1743. He was from Philadelphia County.

Sherrick, Joseph. He was naturalized in Pennsylvania 12 Apr. 1750. He was from Lancaster County.

Shertzer, Jacob. He was naturalized in Pennsylvania 11 Apr. 1761. He was from Lancaster County.

Shervitz, Arnold. He was naturalized in Pennsylvania 21 Nov. 1770. He was from Hannover Township, Lancaster County.

Shewen, Henry. He was naturalized in Pennsylvania 24 Sep. 1755. He was from Berks County.

Sheyer, Teunis. He was naturalized in New York 13 Mar. 1715/6. He was from Albany County.

Shibely, Christian. He was naturalized in Pennsylvania 24 Sep. 1759.

Shibler, Christopher. He was naturalized in Pennsylvania 24 Sep. 1754. He was from Philadelphia County.

Shick, Ludwick. He was naturalized in Pennsylvania 11 Apr. 1761. He was from Philadelphia County.

Shicker, Mary. She was naturalized in Jamaica 22 Oct. 1717. She was the wife of Francis Shicker.

Shideacre, Valentine. He was naturalized in Maryland 18 Apr. 1760.

Shield, Charles. He was naturalized in Maryland 14 Sep. 1763. He was a German.

Shiesler, George. He was naturalized in Pennsylvania 24 Sep. 1762. He was from Berks County.

Shiff, George. He was naturalized in New York 8 Mar. 1773.

Shild, Michel Harder. He was naturalized in New Jersey in 1759.

Shiller, John Dennis. He was naturalized in New Jersey in 1759.

Shimel, William. He was naturalized in Pennsylvania 10 Apr. 1760.

Shindledeker, Jacob. He was naturalized in Maryland 10 Sep. 1760.

Shingle, Lawrence. He was naturalized in Maryland 11 Sep. 1765.

Shinkel, Johan Hendrich. He was naturalized in New York 17 Jan. 1715/6. He was from Albany County.

Shinkel, Jonas. He was naturalized in New York 17 Jan. 1715/6. He was from Albany County.

Shitfer, Nicholas. He was naturalized in Pennsylvania 11 Apr. 1761. He was from Berks County.

Shitz, Peter. He was naturalized in Pennsylvania 24 Sep. 1759.

Shive, George. He was naturalized in Pennsylvania 11 Apr. 1749. He was from Philadelphia County.

Shleetzer, Jacob. He was naturalized in Maryland 11 Sep. 1765. He was a German from Frederick County.

Shleher, George Casper. He was naturalized in Pennsylvania 11–13 Apr. 1743. He was from Philadelphia County.

Shlichter, John. He was naturalized in Pennsylvania 10–11 Apr. 1746. He was from Philadelphia County.

Shilley, Jacob. He was naturalized in Maryland 16 Sep. 1765.

Shilling, Jacob, Sr. He was naturalized in Maryland 31 Aug. 1757.

Shilling, Jacob, Jr. He was naturalized in Maryland 1 Sep. 1757.

Shingle, Frederick. He was naturalized in Pennsylvania 10 Sep. 1761. He was from Lancaster County.

Shingler, Jost. He was naturalized in Pennsylvania 11–13 Apr. 1743. He was from Philadelphia County.

Shinnholser, Johannes. He was naturalized in Pennsylvania 11–13 Apr. 1743. He was from Chester County.

Shipley, Martin. He was naturalized in New Jersey 21 Oct. 1754.

Shirman, Simon. He was naturalized in Pennsylvania 24 Sep. 1746. He was from Lancaster County.

Shissler, Adam. He was naturalized in Maryland 18 July 1759.

Shittler, Ludwick. He was naturalized in Pennsylvania 10 Apr. 1765. He was from Frederick Township, Philadelphia County.

Shitz, Peter. He was naturalized in Pennsylvania 24 Sep. 1759.

Shitz, Tillmar. He was naturalized in Pennsylvania 10 Sep. 1761. He was from Lancaster County.

Shive, Martin. He was naturalized in New Jersey in 1759. He was born in Germany.

Shlatter, Martin. He was naturalized in Pennsylvania 10 Apr. 1765. He was from Upper Merion Township, Philadelphia County.

Shloug, Jacob. He was naturalized in Pennsylvania 19 May 1739. He was from Lancaster County.

Shloy, John. He was naturalized in Maryland 13 Sep. 1758.

Shloy, John. He was naturalized in Maryland 11 Apr. 1759.

Shmeck, John. He was naturalized in Pennsylvania 24 Sep. 1760. He was from Berks County.

Shmidt, Adam. He was naturalized in Nova Scotia 10 July 1758.

Shmith, Cannerah. He was naturalized in Maryland 17 Sep. 1751.

Shnebely, Conrad. He was naturalized in Maryland 11 Sep. 1765.

Shneck, George. He was naturalized in Pennsylvania 10 Apr. 1765. He was from Philadelphia.

Shneeke, John. He was naturalized in Pennsylvania 24 Sep. 1755. He was from Lancaster County.

Shneider, Conrad. He was naturalized in Maryland 15 Sep. 1761. He was from Frederick County.

Shneider, John Adam. He was naturalized in Pennsylvania 11 Apr. 1761. He was from Philadelphia County.

Shneider, Leonard. He was naturalized in Pennsylvania 11 Apr. 1763. He was from Upper Salford Township, Philadelphia County.

Shneider, Michael. He was naturalized in Maryland 15 Sep. 1761. He was from Frederick County.

Shnyder, Jacob. He was naturalized in Pennsylvania 10 Apr. 1767. He was from Frederick County, Maryland.

Shock, John. He was naturalized in Pennsylvania 11 Apr. 1761. He was from Berks County.

Shocklier, Henry. He was naturalized in Pennsylvania 19 May 1739. He was from Philadelphia County.

Shoe, Godfried. He was naturalized in New York 27 Jan. 1770.

Shoe, Johan Wm. He was naturalized in New York 17 Jan. 1715/6. He was from Albany County.

Shoe, Johannis. He was naturalized in New York 17 Jan. 1715/6. He was from Albany County.

Shoe, Martinus. He was naturalized in New York 17 Jan. 1715/6. He was from Albany County.

Shoeck, Adam. He was naturalized in Maryland 24 Aug. 1760.

Shoemaker, Adam. He was naturalized in Pennsylvania 10 & 23 Apr. 1764. He was from Upper Milford Township, Northampton County.

Shoemaker, Frederick. He was naturalized in Pennsylvania 10 & 23 Apr. 1764. He was from Upper Milford Township, Northampton County.

Shoemaker, George. He was naturalized in Pennsylvania 29 Sep. 1709. He was from Philadelphia County.

Shoemaker, Godfried. He was naturalized in New York 11 Sep. 1761.

Shoemaker, Isaac. He was naturalized in Pennsylvania 29 Sep. 1709. He was from Philadelphia County.

Shoemaker, Jacob. He was naturalized in New York 22 Nov. 1715. He was from Albany County.

Shoemaker, Jacob. He was naturalized in Pennsylvania 29 Sep. 1709. He was from Philadelphia County.

Shoemaker, Jacob. He was naturalized in Pennsylvania 11–13 Apr. 1743. He was from Philadelphia County.

Shoemaker, Jacob. He was naturalized in Pennsylvania 10 Sep. 1761. He was from Lancaster County.

Shoemaker, John Jacob. He was naturalized in Pennsylvania 10 Apr. 1760.

Shoemaker, Peter. He was naturalized in Pennsylvania 29 Sep. 1709. He was from Philadelphia County.

Shoemaker, Peter. He was naturalized in Pennsylvania 24 May 1771. He was from Cocalico Township, Lancaster County.

Shoemaker, Thomas. He was naturalized in New York 22 Nov. 1715. He was from Albany County.

Shoemaker, Yost. He was naturalized in Pennsylvania 11 Apr. 1761. He was from Berks County.

Shol, Coenrad. He was naturalized in New York 31 Dec. 1768.

Shol, Johannes. He was naturalized in New York 31 Dec. 1768.

Sholeberger, Frederick. He was naturalized in Pennsylvania 11 Apr. 1763. He was from Greenwich Township, Berks County.

Sholl, Christian. He was naturalized in Maryland 16 Apr. 1761.

Sholtz, George. He was naturalized in Pennsylvania 10 Apr. 1760.

Shook, Lawrence. He was naturalized in Pennsylvania 25 May 1770. He was from Frederick County, Maryland.

Shoop, Jacob. He was naturalized in Maryland 11 Sep 1765. He was from Mt. Pleasant Township, York County.

Shope, Martin. He was naturalized in Maryland 19 Oct. 1743. He was a Quaker.

Shopf, Henry. He was naturalized in New York 11 Sep. 1761.

Shorn, George. He was naturalized in Pennsylvania 25–27 Sep. 1740. He was from Philadelphia County.

Short, John. He was naturalized in Maryland 24 Sep. 1765. He was a German.

Short, John. He was naturalized in Pennsylvania 11 Apr. 1752. He was from Bucks County.

Shott, Christian. He was naturalized in Maryland 15 Apr. 1761.

Shotter, John. He was naturalized in Pennsylvania 11 Apr. 1761. He was from Lancaster County.

Shou, John. He was naturalized in Maryland 15 Sep. 1762. He was from Frederick County.

Shoub, Henry. He was naturalized in Pennsylvania 19 May 1739. He was from Philadelphia County.

Shoul, George. He was naturalized in Pennsylvania 11 Apr. 1761. He was from Philadelphia County.

Shouman, William. He was naturalized in New York 16 Feb. 1771.

Shoure, Adam. He was naturalized in New York 8–9 Sep. 1715. He was from Ulster County.

Shoure, Michael. He was naturalized in New York 8–9 Sep. 1715. He was from Ulster County.

Shous, Frederick. He was naturalized in Pennsylvania 10 Apr. 1760.

Shover, Henry. He was naturalized in Maryland 11 Apr. 1761. He lived in Frederick County.

Shover, Peter. He was naturalized in Maryland 21 Apr. 1773. He was a German.

Shover, Simon. He was naturalized in Maryland 1 Oct. 1767. He was a German.

Shower, Michael. He was naturalized in Pennsylvania 11 Apr. 1761. He was from Berks County.

Shownower, Hans. He was naturalized in Pennsylvania 11–12 Apr. 1744. He was from Lancaster County.

Shrager, Gerrart, Jr. He was naturalized in Pennsylvania 25–27 Sep. 1740. He was from Philadelphia County.

Shrager, Gossen. He was naturalized in Pennsylvania 25–27 Sep. 1740. He was from Philadelphia County.

Shreeder, George. He was naturalized in Pennsylvania 10 Apr. 1765. He was from Weissenberg Township, Northampton County.

Shreib, Hiernonimus. He was naturalized in New York 8–9 Sep. 1715. He was from Ulster County.

Shreiber, Conrod. He was naturalized in Maryland 15 Sep. 1762. He was from Baltimore County.

Shreider, Simon. He was naturalized in New York 27 Jan. 1770.

Shreider, William. He was naturalized in Maryland 31 Aug. 1757.

Shreiner, Hans Adam. He was naturalized in Pennsylvania 19 May 1739. He was from Lancaster County.

Shreiner, John Valentine. He was naturalized in Pennsylvania 25 Sep. 1750. He was from Lancaster County.

Shreiner, Philip. He was naturalized in Pennsylvania 25 Sep. 1750. He was from Lancaster County.

Shreyer, Godfrey. He was naturalized in Jamaica 6 July 1732.

Shreyer, Sarah. She was naturalized in Jamaica 20 Sep. 1737. She was a free mulatto.

Shriber, Peter. He was naturalized in Pennsylvania 24 Sep. 1762. He was from York County.

Shrict, John. He was naturalized in Pennsylvania 24 Sep. 1763. He was from Cumru Township, Berks County.

Shrier, George. He was naturalized in Maryland 19 Oct. 1743.

Shrier, Jacob. He was naturalized in Maryland 19 Oct. 1743.

Shrier, John. He was naturalized in Maryland 19 Oct. 1743.

Shrier, Nicholas. He was naturalized in Maryland in 1742–1743.

Shrifer, Joseph. He was naturalized in New York 8–9 Sep. 1715.

Shrim, John. He was naturalized in Maryland 13 Apr. 1761.

Shriner, Abraham. He was naturalized in Pennsylvania 10 Sep. 1761. He was from Bucks County.

Shriner, Martin. He was naturalized in Pennsylvania 24 Sep. 1760. He was from Lancaster County.

Shriver, Andrew. He was naturalized in Maryland 19 Oct. 1743.

Shriver, George. He was naturalized in Maryland 1742–1743.

Shriver, Lutwick. He was naturalized in Maryland 19 Oct. 1743.

Shrunck, Lawrence. He was naturalized in Pennsylvania 10–12 Apr. 1762. He was from Berks County.

Shryber, John. He was naturalized in Pennsylvania 10 Sep. 1761. He was from Lancaster County.

Shuatterly, Michael. He was naturalized in New Jersey 8 June 1751.

Shubart, Augustus. He was naturalized in Pennsylvania 10 Apr. 1767. He was from Philadelphia.

Shubert, David. He was naturalized in Pennsylvania 24 Sep. 1745. He was from Philadelphia County.

Shubert, John Michael. He was naturalized in Pennsylvania 10–12 Apr. 1762. He was from Philadelphia County.

Shubert, Nicholas. He was naturalized in Pennsylvania 24 Sep. 1760. He was from Northampton County.

Shuder, Adam. He was naturalized in Pennsylvania 25 Sep. 1753. He was from Northampton County.

Shueman, Philip. He was naturalized in Pennsylvania 11 Apr. 1763. He was from Lynn Township, Northampton County.

Shuet, Conrad. He was naturalized in Maryland 15 Sep. 1762. He was from Frederick County.

Shukes, Christian. He was naturalized in Pennsylvania 11 Apr. 1761. He was from Bucks County.

Shulleberg, Ulrich. He was naturalized in Pennsylvania 12 Apr. 1750. He was from Lancaster County.

Shults, Andrew. He was naturalized in Pennsylvania 14 Feb. 1729/30. He was from Lancaster County.

Shults, Charles. He sought naturalization in New York 12 Nov. 1748.

Shultz, Christian. He was naturalized in New York 16 Feb. 1771.

Shultz, George. He was naturalized in Pennsylvania 11–13 Apr. 1743. He was from Philadelphia County.

Shultz, George. He was naturalized in Pennsylvania 25 Sep. 1758.

Shultz, Gregorius. He was naturalized in Pennsylvania 11 Apr. 1761. He was from Northampton County.

Shultz, Jacob. He was naturalized in Pennsylvania 24 Sep. 1762. He was from York County.

Shultz, John. He was naturalized in Jamaica 10 Dec. 1701.

Shultz, John. He was naturalized in Pennsylvania 25 Sep. 1753. He was from York County.

Shultz, John. He was naturalized in Pennsylvania 10 Apr. 1760.

Shultz, John. He was naturalized in Pennsylvania 10 Sep. 1761. He was from Lancaster County.

Shultz, John. He was naturalized in Pennsylvania 24 Sep. 1762. He was from York County.

Shultz, Martin. He was naturalized in Pennsylvania 26–27 Sep. 1743. He was from Lancaster County.

Shultz, Samuel. He was naturalized in Pennsylvania 10 Sep. 1761. He was from Berks County.

Shulz, Daniel. He was naturalized in Maryland 11 Sep. 1765. He was a German from Frederick County.

Shuman, Jacob. He was naturalized in Pennsylvania 24 Sep. 1762. He was from Berks County.

Shurger, Simon. He was naturalized in New York 19 Dec. 1766.

Shurter, Frederick. He was naturalized in New York 23 Dec. 1765.

Shuttler, Mathew. He was naturalized in Jamaica 13 Mar.1752.

Shutz, Conrad. He was naturalized in Pennsylvania 11 Apr. 1751. He was from Philadelphia County.

Shutz, Henry. He was naturalized in Pennsylvania 11 Apr. 1751. He was from Philadelphia County.

Shutz, Mathias. He was naturalized in Pennsylvania 25–27 Sep. 1740. He was from Philadelphia.

Shutz, Philip. He was naturalized in Pennsylvania 11 Apr. 1744. He was from Lancaster County.

Shuymer, Mattys. He was naturalized in New York 8–9 Sep. 1715. He was from Ulster County.

Shwamle, John. He was naturalized in New Jersey in 1761. He lived in Cumberland County and had lived in New Jersey fourteen years. He also appeared as Johannes Schwamley.

Shwartz, Andreas. He was naturalized in Pennsylvania 11 Apr. 1763. He was from Strasburg Township, York County.

Shwartz, Frederick. He was naturalized in Maryland 11 Sep. 1765. He was a German from Frederick County.

Shwegheler, George. He was naturalized in Maryland 14 Sep. 1763. He was a German.

Shweikert, Peter. He was naturalized in New York 3 July 1759.

Shwenk, Caspar. He was naturalized in Maryland 11 Sep. 1765. He was a German from Frederick County.

Shwingle, George. He was naturalized in Pennsylvania 11 Apr. 1761. He was from Lancaster County.

Shwope, John. He was naturalized in Pennsylvania 14 Feb. 1729/30. He was from Lancaster County.

Shyer, Adam. He was naturalized in Pennsylvania 10 Apr. 1767. He was from Exeter Township, Philadelphia County.

Sibell, Henry. He was naturalized in Maryland 22 Apr. 1773. He was a German.

Sibert, George. He was naturalized in Pennsylvania 10–12 Apr. 1762. He was from Berks County.

Sibert, Jacob. He was naturalized in Frederick County, Virginia 2 Oct. 1765.

Sibrant, Haire alias William. He was endenized in London 20 Feb. 1662/3. He was from Barbados.

Sickel, George David. He was naturalized in Pennsylvania 10 & 23 Sep. 1764. He was from Philadelphia County.

Sickle, John David. He was naturalized in Pennsylvania 25 Sep. 1744. He was from Philadelphia County.

Sickneer, Jacob. He was naturalized in New York 21 Feb. 1715/6. He was 11 years old and a son of Apollonia Sickneer.

Sicks, John. He was made a denizen in Maryland 30 Jan. 1663/4. He was German and was late of England.

Sieble, John. He was naturalized in Pennsylvania 25 Sep. 1751. He was from Lancaster County.

Siechrist, Henry. He was naturalized in Pennsylvania 24–25 Sep. 1764. He was from Rapho Township, Lancaster County.

Sieder, Jacob. He was naturalized in Pennsylvania 11 Apr. 1761. He was from Berks County.

Sieder, Michael. He was naturalized in Pennsylvania 11 Apr. 1761. He was from Northampton County.

Sieffert, Johannes. He was naturalized in New York 11 Sep. 1761.

Siegeler, Pieter. He was naturalized in New York 3 July 1759.

Sielie, Jacob. He was naturalized in New York 20 Oct. 1764.

Siemon, Anthony. He was naturalized in New York 11 Sep. 1761.

Siemon, Johan Wm. He was naturalized in New York 17 Jan. 1715/6. He was from Albany County.

Siemon, John. He was naturalized in New York 8 Mar. 1773. He was from New York City.

Siex, Hendrick. He was naturalized in Maryland in Oct. 1748.

Sifert, Michael. He was naturalized in Pennsylvania 11 Apr. 1761. He was from Chester County.

Sigfried, Hans. He was naturalized in Pennsylvania 6 Feb. 1730/1. He was from Philadelphia County.

Sights, Michael. He was naturalized in Pennsylvania 10 Apr. 1767. He was from Bedminster Township, Chester County.

Signe, Nicholas. He was naturalized in New Jersey 8 July 1730. He was born in Germany.

Sigourney, Andrew, Sr. He was naturalized in Massachusetts 12 Apr. 1731.

Sigueria, Ester Henriques. She was naturalized in Jamaica 16 Feb. 1731/2.

Silva, David, Jr. He was naturalized in Jamaica 5 Dec. 1752.

Silva, David Gomez. He was naturalized in Jamaica 24 Aug. 1732.

Silva, David Rodrigues. He was naturalized in Jamaica 25 Feb. 1760.

Silva, Haim Rodrigues. He was naturalized in Jamaica 4 Dec. 1772.

Silva, Isaac Gomes. He was naturalized in Jamaica 23 Feb. 1742/3. He was a Jew.

Silva, Joshua Gomez. He was naturalized in Jamaica 26 May 1742. He was a Jew.

Silva, Sarah Lopez. She was naturalized in Jamaica 13 Nov. 1752.

Silvera, Moses. He was naturalized in Jamaica 24 Feb. 1684/5.

Silvester, Constant. He was naturalized in England 29 Dec. 1660. He was born in Amsterdam, Holland, the son of Giles and Mary Silvester. The said Giles Silvester was a native of Salisbury, England. He came to New York.

Silvester, Giles. He was naturalized in England 29 Dec. 1660. He was born in Amsterdam, Holland, the son of Giles and Mary Silvester. He came to New York.

Silvester, Joshua. He was naturalized in England 29 Dec. 1660. He was born in Amsterdam, Holland, the son of Giles and Mary Silvester. He came to New York.

Silvester, Nathaniel. He was naturalized in England 29 Dec. 1660. He was born in Amsterdam, Holland, the son of Giles and Mary Silvester. He came to New York.

Silvester, Peter. He was naturalized in Northumberland County, Virginia 17 Sep. 1656. He was born at Amsterdam, Holland, son of Giles Silvester, a native of Salisbury, England.

Simailleau, Jean. He was endenized in New York in Oct. 1697. He was a French Protestant.

Simerman, Peter. He was naturalized in Pennsylvania 25 Sep. 1751. He was from Lancaster County.

Simkan, Pieter. He took the oath to the King 21–26 Oct. 1664 after the conquest of New Netherland.

Simmons, Anthony. He was naturalized in New York 11 Sep. 1761.

Simmons, Isaac. He was naturalized in Maryland 20 Oct. 1747.

Simon, Andre. He was an Acadian and took the oath to George II at Annapolis River, Nova Scotia in Dec. 1729.

Simon, Andre. He was an Acadian and took the oath of allegiance at Annapolis in Dec. 1729.

Simon, Andre. He was an Acadian and took the oath of allegiance at Annapolis in Dec. 1729.

Simon, Augustin. He was naturalized in Virginia 12 May 1705.

Simon, Charles. He was an Acadian and took the oath to George II at Annapolis River, Nova Scotia in Dec. 1729.

Simon, Casper. He was naturalized in Pennsylvania in Sep. 1740. He was from Philadelphia County.

Simon, Johannes. He was naturalized in Nova Scotia 5 July 1758.

Simon, Joseph. He was naturalized in Pennsylvania 25–26 Sep./4 Oct. 1749. He was from Lancaster. He was a Jew.

Simon, Michael. He was naturalized in Pennsylvania 24 Sep. 1754. He was from Philadelphia County.

Simon, Peter. He was naturalized in Rhode Island in Aug. 1751. He lived in Newport, R.I. and was a merchant. He was born in France.

Simons, Claes. He took the oath of allegiance in Breucklijn, Kings County, New York 26–30 Sep. 1687. He was a native of the colony.

Simons, Joseph. He was naturalized in New York 16 Feb. 1771.

Simons, Walter. He was naturalized in Pennsylvania 29 Sep. 1709. He was from Philadelphia County.

Simonse, Peter. He took the oath of allegiance in New Uijtrceht, Kings County, New York 26–30 Sep. 1687. He was a native of the colony.

Simonssen, Aert. He took the oath of allegiance in Breucklijn, Kings County, New York 26–30 Sep. 1687. He was a native of the colony.

Simpson, Ann. She was naturalized in Jamaica 21 Sep. 1719.

Simson, Joseph. He was naturalized in New York 6 July 1723.

Simson, Joseph. He was naturalized in New York by the act of 1740. He was a Jewish merchant from New York City.

Simson, Martin. He was naturalized in New York 16 Feb. 1771.

Sin, Henry. He was naturalized in Maryland in Apr. 1749. He was from Frederick County.

Sing, Leonard. He was naturalized in Pennsylvania 11 Apr. 1751. He was from Philadelphia County.

Singer, Caspar. He was naturalized in Pennsylvania 19 May 1739. He was from Philadelphia County.

Singhaas, Michael. He was naturalized in Pennsylvania 10 Sep. 1761. He was from Philadelphia County.

Sink, Jacob. He was naturalized in North Carolina 22 Mar. 1764. He was from Rowan County and a German.

Sinn, George Christian. He was naturalized in Pennsylvania 10 Apr. 1760.

Sinn, Jacob. He was naturalized in Maryland 11 Apr. 1764. He was a German.

Sinnexen, Broer. He was naturalized in New Castle County, Delaware 21 Feb. 1682/3.

Sinseback, Johan Teunis. He was naturalized in New York 20 Oct. 1747. He was a yeoman from Ulster County.

Sinsel, Frederick. He was naturalized in Pennsylvania 24–25 Sep. 1764. He was from Oley Township, Berks County.

Siorts, Cornelius. He was naturalized in Pennsylvania 29 Sep. 1709. He was from Philadelphia County.

Sipherson, Marcus. He was made a denizen in Maryland 22 July 1661. He was Swedish and was late of New Amstel.

Sire, Guillaume. He was an Acadian and took the oath of allegiance in Apr. 1730.

Sire, Jean. He was an Acadian and took the oath of allegiance in Apr. 1730.

Sire, Jean. He was an Acadian and took the oath of allegiance in Apr. 1730.

Sire, Louis. He was an Acadian and took the oath of allegiance in Apr. 1730.

Sire, Michel. He was an Acadian and took the oath of allegiance in Apr. 1730.

Sire, Paul. He was an Acadian and took the oath of allegiance in Apr. 1730.

Sire, Pierre. He was an Acadian and took the oath of allegiance in Apr. 1730.

Sire, Pierre. He was an Acadian and took the oath of allegiance in Apr. 1730.

Sirley, Jacob Barnard. He was naturalized in Frederick County, Virginia 1 Nov. 1768.

Sistera, Gabriel. He was naturalized in Connecticut in May 1773. He lived in New London. He was a native of Barcelona, Spain.

Sites, Peter. He was naturalized in Pennsylvania 10 Apr. 1753. He was from Lancaster County.

Sitzman, Christian. He was naturalized in Pennsylvania 11 Apr. 1761. He was from Bucks County.

Skans, Johannis. He was naturalized in New York 3 Jan. 1715/6. He was from Albany County.

Skink, George. He was naturalized in New York 27 Jan. 1770.

Slacker, George. He was naturalized in Pennsylvania 25 Sep. 1751. He was from Philadelphia County.

Slager, Ernst. He was naturalized in Maryland 9 Apr. 1760. He lived in Baltimore County.

Slagtergaal, Hendrick. He was naturalized in Jamaica 31 May 1748.

Slatter, Casper. He was naturalized in Pennsylvania 11 Apr. 1761. He was from Bucks County.

Slaremaker, Mathias. He was naturalized in Pennsylvania 14 Feb. 1729/30. He was from Lancaster County.

Slayback, David. He was naturalized in New Jersey 7 Apr. 1761.
Slaymaker, Lawrence. He was naturalized in Pennsylvania 11–13 Apr. 1743. He was from Lancaster County.
Slecht, Cornelis. He took the oath of naturalization in New York 1 Sep. 1687 in Ulster County.
Slecht, Matthies. He took the oath of naturalization in New York 1 Sep. 1687 in Ulster County.
Sleeger, Adam. He was naturalized in Pennsylvania 25 Sep. 1758.
Sleght, Barent. He took the oath of allegiance in Breucklijn, Kings County, New York 26–30 Sep. 1687. He was a native of the colony.
Sleght, Daniel. He was naturalized in New York 20 May 1769.
Sleght, Hendrick. He took the oath of allegiance in Breuckljin, Kings County, New York 26–30 Sep. 1687. He had been in the colony 35 years.
Sleght, Hendrick. He was naturalized in New York 20 Oct. 1764.
Sleigh, Henry. He was naturalized in Pennsylvania 24 Sep. 1762. He was from Berks County.
Sleighter, Gallus. He was naturalized in Pennsylvania 10–12 Apr. 1762. He was from Philadelphia County.
Sleighter, Henry. He was naturalized in Pennsylvania 11 Apr. 1761. He was from Philadelphia County.
Sleighty, Christian. He was naturalized in Pennsylvania 10 Apr. 1760.
Sleycomb, George. He was naturalized in Maryland 11 June 1697. He was German.
Sleyter, Peter. He was naturalized in Maryland 26 Apr. 1684.
Slichtenhorst, Gerrit. He took the oath to the King 21–26 Oct. 1664 after the conquest of New Netherland.
Slick, John. He was naturalized in Maryland 11 Sep. 1765.
Slickting, Nicholas. He was naturalized in Pennsylvania 11 Apr. 1763. He was from Berks County.
Sliegle, Christopher, Sr. He was naturalized in Pennsylvania 20 May 1768. He was from Berwick Township, York County.
Sligh, Jacob. He was naturalized in Maryland in Apr. 1749. He was from Frederick County.
Sligh, Thomas. He was naturalized in Maryland in Apr. 1749. He was from Frederick County.
Sliker [?], Francis. He was naturalized in Jamaica 15 June 1695.
Slim, Peter. He was naturalized in New Jersey 6 Dec. 1769.
Slingloff, Henry. He was naturalized in Pennsylvania 29 Mar. 1735. He was from Philadelphia County.
Slipplear, George. He was naturalized in Pennsylvania 11 Apr. 1751. He was from Lancaster County.
Sloss, Richard. He was naturalized in Jamaica 17 May 1703.
Slowder, Christian. He was naturalized in Maryland 10 Sep. 1772.
Sluiter, Jacob, Jr. He was naturalized in Maryland 18 Oct. 1694.
Sluitt[er], Claes Claes. He took the oath of naturalization in New York 1 Sep. 1687 in Ulster County.
Sluyter, Hendrick. He was naturalized in Maryland 18 Oct. 1694.
Sly, Jacob. He was naturalized in Maryland 11 Sep. 1765.
Smack, Hendrick Matthysse. He took the oath of allegiance in New Uijtrceht, Kings County, New York 26–30 Sep. 1687. He had been in the colony 33 years.
Small, Jacob. He was naturalized in New York 28 July 1773. He was a blacksmith from New York City.
Small, Michael. He was naturalized in Pennsylvania 11 Apr. 1749. He was from Lancaster County.
Small, Michael. He was naturalized in Pennsylvania 11 Apr. 1761. He was from Philadelphia County.
Smalling, William. He was naturalized in Jamaica 30 Nov. 1762.
Smatt, Matthias. He was naturalized in Maryland 13 Apr. 1763. He was a German.
Smedes, Benjamin. He was naturalized in New York 8–9 Sep. 1715. He was from Ulster County.
Smedis, John. He took the oath of naturalization in New York 1 Sep. 1687 in Ulster County.
Smidt, Balthazar. He was naturalized in Pennsylvania 24–25 Sep. 1764. He was from Philadelphia.

Smidt, Carl. He was naturalized in Maryland 14 Apr. 1762. He was a German.

Smidt, George. He was naturalized in Maryland 9 Sep. 1761. He was from Frederick County.

Smidt, Jacob. He was naturalized in Maryland 9 Sep. 1761. He was from Frederick County.

Smidt, John. He was naturalized in Pennsylvania 11 Apr. 1761. He was from Philadelphia County.

Smidt, Nicholas. He was naturalized in Pennsylvania 24–29 Sep. 1769. He was from Colebrookdale Township, Berks County.

Smidt, Peter. He was naturalized in Pennsylvania 10 Apr. 1753. He was from Lancaster County.

Smidt, Peter. He was naturalized in Pennsylvania 11 Apr. 1763. He was from Heidelberg Township, Berks County.

Smit, Bastian. He was naturalized in Pennsylvania 6 Feb. 1730/1. He was from Philadelphia County.

Smit, Casper. He was naturalized in Pennsylvania 10–12 Apr. 1762. He was from Berks County.

Smit, Johan Christ. He was naturalized in New York 3 Jan. 1715/6. He was from Albany County.

Smith, Abraham. He was naturalized in Pennsylvania 26–27 Sep. 1743. He was from Lancaster County.

Smith, Adam. He was naturalized in Pennsylvania 10 Apr. 1765. He was from Hatfield Township, Philadelphia County.

Smith, Adam. He was naturalized in North Carolina 22 Sep. 1763. He was from Rowan County and was a German.

Smith, Adam. He was naturalized in North Carolina 22 Sep. 1764. He was from Rowan County and was a German.

Smith, Adam Meichel. He was naturalized in New York 27 Apr. 1716. He was from Albany County.

Smith, Andrew. He was naturalized in Pennsylvania 24 Sep. 1755. He was from Philadelphia County.

Smith, Andrew. He was naturalized in Pennsylvania 24 Sep. 1762. He was from York County.

Smith, Barent. He was naturalized in New York 27 July 1768. He was a tailor from New York City.

Smith, Bastian. He was naturalized in Pennsylvania in 1730–31. He was from Philadelphia County.

Smith, Bernard. He was naturalized in Pennsylvania 24 Sep. 1762. He was from Northampton County.

Smith, Casper. He was naturalized in Maryland 21 May 1756.

Smith, Christopher. He was naturalized in Pennsylvania 11 Apr. 1741. He was from Philadelphia County.

Smith, Christopher. He was naturalized in Pennsylvania 11 Apr. 1761. He was from Berks County.

Smith, Christopher. He was naturalized in Pennsylvania 10 Sep. 1761. He was from Philadelphia County.

Smith, Christopher. He was naturalized in New York 3 May 1755. He was from New York City.

Smith, Daniel. He was naturalized in Pennsylvania 24 Sep. 1762. He was from Berks County.

Smith, Coenraad. He was naturalized in New York 11 Sep. 1761.

Smith, Coenraed. He was naturalized in New York 17 Jan. 1715/6. He was from Albany County.

Smith, Conradt. He was naturalized in New York 27 Jan. 1770.

Smith, Daniel. He was naturalized in New York 21 Apr. 1748. He was a laborer from New York City.

Smith, David. He was naturalized in Maryland 29 Sep. 1762. He was a German from Frederick County.

Smith, David. He was naturalized in North Carolina 22 Sep. 1763. He was from Rowan County and a German.

Smith, Eberhard. He was naturalized in Pennsylvania 11 Apr. 1763. He was from Weiseberg Township, Northampton County.

Smith, Emperor. He was made a denizen in Maryland 17 Feb. 1762. He was Dutch.

Smith, Francis. He was naturalized in Pennsylvania 24–25 Sep. 1764. He was from Heidelberg Township, Lancaster County.

Smith, Frederick. He was naturalized in New Jersey 6 Dec. 1769.

Smith, Frederick. He was naturalized in North Carolina 22 Sep. 1763. He was from Rowan County and a German.

Smith, Frederick. He was naturalized in Pennsylvania in Sep. 1740. He lived in Philadelphia.

Smith, Gasper. He was naturalized in North Carolina 22 Sep. 1763. He was from Rowan County and was a German.

Smith, George. He was naturalized in Maryland in Apr. 1749.

Smith, George. He was naturalized in Frederick County, Virginia 1 Aug. 1769.

Smith, Henry. He was naturalized in Pennsylvania 19 May 1739. He was from Philadelphia County.

Smith, Henry. He was naturalized in Maryland in Apr. 1749. He was from Frederick County.

Smith, Henry. He was naturalized in Pennsylvania 24 Sep. 1755. He was from Lancaster County.

Smith, Henry. He was naturalized in Pennsylvania 24 Sep. 1762. He was from York County.

Smith, Henry. He was naturalized in Pennsylvania 24–25 Sep. 1764. He was from Philadelphia.

Smith, Henry. He was naturalized in New York 31 Dec. 1768.

Smith, Henry. He was naturalized in New York 8 Mar. 1773.

Smith, Jacob. He was naturalized in Maryland in Apr. 1749. He was from Frederick County.

Smith, Jacob. He was naturalized in Maryland 10 Apr. 1762. He was a German from Anne Arundel County.

Smith, Jacob. He was naturalized in Maryland 21 Sep. 1762. He was a German.

Smith, Jacob. He was naturalized in Pennsylvania 26–27 Sep. 1743. He was from Philadelphia County.

Smith, Jacob. He was naturalized in Pennsylvania 11 Apr. 1761. He was from Northampton County.

Smith, Johan. He was naturalized in New York 8 Mar. 1773.

Smith, Johan Adam. He was naturalized in New York 17 Jan. 1715/6. He was from Albany County.

Smith, Johan Chris., Jr. He was naturalized in New Jersey 8 Dec. 1744.

Smith, Johan Georg. He was naturalized in New York 8–9 Sep. 1715. He was from Ulster County.

Smith, Johan Hendrick. He was naturalized in New York 11 Sep. 1761.

Smith, Johan Nicholas. He was naturalized in New York 11 Sep. 1761.

Smith, Johan Petter. He was naturalized in New Jersey in 1750. He was from Hunterdon County.

Smith, Johan Willem. He was naturalized in New York 16 Nov. 1739.

Smith, Johannes. He was naturalized in New York 11 Sep. 1761.

Smith, Johannes. He was naturalized in Pennsylvania 19 May 1739. He was from Philadelphia County.

Smith, John. He was naturalized in Jamaica 15 Nov. 1742.

Smith, John. He was naturalized in Maryland 6 Oct. 1768. He was a German from Frederick County.

Smith, John. He was naturalized in New York 24 Nov. 1750.

Smith, John. He was naturalized in New York 31 Dec. 1768.

Smith, John. He was naturalized in New York 16 Feb. 1771.

Smith, John. He was naturalized in New York 16 Feb. 1771.

Smith, John. He was naturalized in Pennsylvania 29 Sep. 1709. He was from Philadelphia County.

Smith, John. He was naturalized in Pennsylvania 10 Apr. 1766. He was from Hunterdon County, New Jersey.

Smith, John Conradt. He was naturalized in New York 8 Mar. 1773.

Smith, John George. He was naturalized in Maryland in Apr. 1749. He was from Frederick County.

Smith, John Henry. He was naturalized in Pennsylvania 24–25 Sep. 1764. He was from Tulpehocken Township, Berks County.

Smith, Joseph. He was naturalized in Maryland 3 May 1740. He was from Prince George's County and was born in Germany.

Smith, Joseph. He was naturalized in Pennsylvania 11 Apr. 1741. He was from Philadelphia County.

Smith, Joseph. He was naturalized in Pennsylvania 24–25 Sep. 1764. He was from Greenwich, Sussex County, New Jersey.

Smith, Lambert. He was naturalized in New York 22 Aug. 1715. He was a yeoman from Tappan.

Smith, Leonhart. He was naturalized in Pennsylvania 19 May 1739. He was from Philadelphia County.

Smith, Martin. He was naturalized in New York 3 July 1759.

Smith, Mathias. He was naturalized in Pennsylvania 11 Apr. 1751. He was from Lancaster County.

Smith, Matthias. He was naturalized in New York 3 May 1755. He was from New York City.

Smith, Matthias. He was naturalized in Pennsylvania 11 Apr. 1761. He was from Berks County.

Smith, Matthias. He was naturalized in Pennsylvania 11 Apr. 1763. He was from Upper Dublin Township, Philadelphia County.

Smith, Matteys. He was naturalized in New Jersey 8 July 1730. He was born in Germany.

Smith, Melchior. He was naturalized in Pennsylvania 10 Apr. 1760.

Smith, Michael. He was naturalized in New York 24 Nov. 1750.

Smith, Michael. He was naturalized in Pennsylvania 10 Apr. 1755. He was from Northampton County.

Smith, Nicolas. He was naturalized in New York 8–9 Sep. 1715. He was from Ulster County.

Smith, Nicolas. He was naturalized in New York 17 Jan. 1715/6. He was from Albany County.

Smith, Peter. He was naturalized in Maryland 3 May 1740. He was from Prince George's County and was born in Germany.

Smith, Peter. He was naturalized in New York 22 Nov. 1715. He was from Albany County.

Smith, Peter. He was naturalized in New York 17 Jan. 1715/6. He was from Albany County.

Smith, Peter. He was naturalized in Pennsylvania 14 Feb. 1729/30. He was from Lancaster County.

Smith, Peter. He was naturalized in Pennsylvania 24–25 Sep. 1764. He was from Germantown.

Smith, Peter. He was naturalized in Pennsylvania 24–25 Sep./5 Oct. 1767. He was from Bethel Township, Lancaster County.

Smith, Philip. He was naturalized in Maryland 4 Apr. 1761. He lived in Frederick County.

Smith, Philip. He was naturalized in Maryland 13 Apr. 1761.

Smith, Philip. He was naturalized in Maryland 10 Sep. 1762.

Smith, Philip. He was naturalized in Maryland 13 Apr. 1763. He was a German.

Smith, Philip. He was naturalized in Maryland 11 Sep. 1765. He was a German from Frederick County.

Smith, Philip. He was naturalized in New York 31 Dec. 1768.

Smith, Philip. He was naturalized in New York 8 Mar. 1773.

Smith, Poulus. He was naturalized in New York 8–9 Sep. 1715. He was from Ulster County.

Smith, Roderick. He was naturalized in Pennsylvania 12 Apr. 1750. He was from Chester County.

Smith, Rowland. He was naturalized in Pennsylvania 19 May 1739. He was from Philadelphia County.

Smith, Wilhelmus. He was naturalized in New York 11 Sep. 1761.

Smith, William. He was naturalized in New York 8–9 Sep. 1715. He was from Ulster County.

Smith, William. He was naturalized in New York 18 Oct. 1750. He was a blacksmith from Ulster County.

Smith, William. He was naturalized in Pennsylvania 11–13 Apr. 1743. He was from Philadelphia County.

Smith, William. He was naturalized in Pennsylvania 10 Apr. 1772. He was from Philadelphia.

Smith, Zacharis. He was naturalized in New York 29 Oct. 1750.

Smithers, Christopher. He was naturalized in Maryland 3 May 1704. He lived in Annapolis. He was German and was a tailor by trade.

Smiths, Michael. He was naturalized in Pennsylvania in 5 Mar. 1725/6. He was born in Germany.

Smitt, Jonas. He was naturalized in New York 22 Nov. 1715.

Smoker, Christian. He was naturalized in Pennsylvania 10 Sep. 1761. He was from Lancaster County.

Smose, John. He was naturalized in Pennsylvania 11–13 Apr. 1743. He was from Lancaster County.

Smoutz, Abram. He was naturalized in Pennsylvania 10 Sep. 1761. He was from Lancaster County.

Snably, Conrod. He was naturalized in Maryland 4 Sep. 1765. He was a German from Frederick County.

Snaering, George. He was naturalized in Pennsylvania 10–12 Apr. 1762. He was from Philadelphia County.

Snap, John. He was naturalized in Frederick County, Virginia 5 Nov. 1746.

Snap, John, Jr. He was naturalized in Frederick County, Virginia 5 Nov. 1746.

Snap, Lawrence. He was naturalized in Frederick County, Virginia 5 Nov. 1746.

Snavely, Henry. He was naturalized in Maryland 30 Sep. 1762. He was a German from Frederick County.

Sneck, George, Jr. He was naturalized in New York 8 Mar. 1773.

Snediker, Christiaen. He took the oath of allegiance in Flackbush, Kings County, New York 26–30 Sep. 1687. He was a native of the colony.

Snediker, Gerrit. He took the oath of allegiance in Flackbush, Kings County, New York 26–30 Sep. 1687. He was a native of the colony.

Sneeder, Christian. He was naturalized in Pennsylvania 10 Sep. 1761. He was from Lancaster County.

Sneffle, Jacob. He was naturalized in Pennsylvania 26–27 Sep. 1743. He was from Lancaster County.

Sneibly, John. He was naturalized in Pennsylvania 11 Apr. 1761. He was from Lancaster County.

Sneider, Andreas. He was naturalized in New York 3 July 1759.

Sneider, Christopher. He was naturalized in New York 23 Oct. 1741.

Sneider, Jacob. He was naturalized in Maryland 10 Sep. 1760.

Sneider, John. He was naturalized in Pennsylvania 24 Sep. 1759.

Sneider, John. He was naturalized in Pennsylvania 11 Apr. 1761. He was from Northampton County.

Sneider, John George. He was naturalized in Pennsylvania 10 Apr. 1760.

Sneider, Philip. He was naturalized in Pennsylvania 10 & 23 Apr. 1764. He was from Lower Saucon Township, Northampton County.

Sneider, William. He was naturalized in New York 3 July 1759.

Snell, Jacob. He was naturalized in New York 11 Oct. 1715. He was from Albany County.

Snevely, Jacob. He was naturalized in Pennsylvania 14 Feb. 1729/30. He was from Lancaster County.

Snevely, Jacob, Jr. He was naturalized in Pennsylvania 14 Feb. 1729/30. He was from Lancaster County.

Snevely, John. He was naturalized in Pennsylvania 14 Feb. 1729/30. He was from Lancaster County.

Snevely, John Jacob. He was naturalized in Pennsylvania 14 Feb. 1729/30. He was from Lancaster County.

Sneyder, Henderick. He was naturalized in New York 17 Apr. 1750. He was a cartman from New York City.

Sneyder, Hendrick. He was naturalized in New York 17 Jan. 1715/6. He was from Albany County.

Sneyder, Jacob. He was naturalized in New York 17 Jan. 1715/6. He was from Albany County.

Sneyder, Johan. He was naturalized in New York 14 Feb. 1715/6. He was from Albany County.

Sneyder, Johan Joest. He was naturalized in New York 14 Feb. 1715/6. He was from Albany County.

Sneyder, Johan Wm. He was naturalized in New York 17 Jan. 1715/6. He was from Albany County.

Sneyder, Michael. He was naturalized in New York 11 Sep. 1761.

Sneyder, Willem. He was naturalized in New York 17 Jan. 1715/6. He was from Albany County.

Snider, Christian. He was naturalized in Pennsylvania 25–27 Sep. 1740. He was from Philadelphia County.

Snider, Christopher. He was naturalized in New Jersey 8 July 1730. He was born in Germany.

Snider, Frederick. He was naturalized in Maryland 13 Apr. 1763. He was a German.

Snider, George. He was naturalized in Maryland 13 Apr. 1763. He was a German.

Snider, George. He sought naturalization in New Jersey in the 18th century.

Snider, Henry. He was naturalized in Maryland 10 Apr. 1770.

Snider, Henry. He was naturalized in Pennsylvania 25 Sep. 1750. He was from Lancaster County.

Snider, John. He was naturalized in Maryland 11 Sep. 1765. He was a German from Frederick County.

Snider, John. He was naturalized in Pennsylvania 10 Sep. 1761. He was from Berks County.

Snider, John Wilhelm. He was naturalized in New York 8–9 Sep. 1715. He was from Ulster County.

Snider, Johannes. He was naturalized in Pennsylvania 25–27 Sep. 1740. He was from Philadelphia County.

Snider, Martin. He was naturalized in Maryland 13 Apr. 1763. He was a German.

Snider, Martinus. He was naturalized in New York in Oct. 1740. He was a farmer from Ulster County.

Snider, Peter. He was naturalized in Pennsylvania 25–27 Sep. 1740. He was from Bucks County.

Snieder, Filliep. He was naturalized in New Jersey 8 Dec. 1744.

Snievly, John. He was naturalized in Pennsylvania 24 Sep. 1746. He was from Lancaster County.

Snoble, Casper. He was naturalized in Pennsylvania 10 Sep. 1761. He was from Berks County.

Snoek, Hendrick. He was naturalized in New Jersey 8 July 1730. He was born in Germany.

Snoek, Johan Willem. He was naturalized in New Jersey 8 July 1730. He was born in Germany.

Snoffer, John. He was naturalized in New Jersey in 1764.

Snoffer, John Henry. He was naturalized in New Jersey in 1764.

Snook, Adam. He was naturalized in New Jersey 20 Aug. 1755.

Snook, John. He was naturalized in New Jersey in 1768.

Snous, Johannes. He was naturalized in New York 3 July 1759.

Snug, Johannes Henry. He was naturalized in New Jersey 8 Dec. 1744.

Snyder, Anthony. He was naturalized in Pennsylvania 10 Sep. 1761. He was from Lancaster County.

Snyder, Charles. He was naturalized in Pennsylvania 10 Sep. 1761. He was from Lancaster County.

Snyder, Georg. He was naturalized in New York 8–9 Sep. 1715. He was from Ulster County.

Snyder, George. He was naturalized in New York 31 Dec. 1761.

Snyder, Hendrick. He was naturalized in New York 24 Nov. 1750.

Snyder, Hendrick. He was naturalized in New York 21 Apr. 1769. He was a farmer from Orange County.

Snyder, Henry. He was naturalized in Pennsylvania 19 May 1739. He was from Philadelphia County.

Snyder, Jacob. He was naturalized in Pennsylvania 24–25 Sep. 1764. He was from Germantown.

Snyder, Johanis. He was naturalized in New York 8–9 Sep. 1715. He was from Ulster County.

Snyder, John. He was naturalized in New Jersey 3 June 1763.

Snyder, John. He was naturalized in Pennsylvania 6 Feb. 1730/1. He was from Philadelphia County.

Snyder, John Henry. He was naturalized in Pennsylvania 11–13 Apr. 1743. He was from Philadelphia County.

Snyder, John Ruef. He was naturalized in Pennsylvania 10 Sep. 1761. He was from Berks County.

Soares, Joseph. He was naturalized in Jamaica 24 Nov. 1741. He was a Jew.

Soares, Leah. She was naturalized in Jamaica 24 Nov. 1741. She was a Jewess.

Soarez, Aron Jacob. He sought to endenized 30 Aug. 1692. He was a Jew from Jamaica.

Soarez, Jacob Levy. He was naturalized in Jamaica 16 Mar. 1690/1.

Sobell, William. He was naturalized in New York 31 Dec. 1768.

Soblet, Abraham. He was naturalized in Virginia 12 May 1705.

Soblet, James. He was naturalized in Virginia 12 May 1705.

Soblet, Peter. He was naturalized in Virginia 12 May 1705.

Sobrih, Gasper. He was naturalized in Virginia 12 May 1705.

Soey, Yoes. He was naturalized in New York 6 July 1723.

Sohl, Peter. He was naturalized in Pennsylvania 10 Apr. 1767. He was from Heidelberg Township, Berks County.

Soldener, George. He was naturalized in Maryland in Apr. 1749. He was from Frederick County.

Sole, Detrick. He was naturalized in Pennsylvania 10–12 Apr. 1762. He was from Berks County.

Sole, Henry. He was naturalized in Pennsylvania 10–12 Apr. 1762. He was from Berks County.

Solis, Abraham DaSilva. He was naturalized in Jamaica 13 Oct. 1687. He was a distiller.
Soll, Johan. He was naturalized in New York 8 Mar. 1773.
Sollaegre, John. He was naturalized in Virginia 12 May 1705.
Solomon, Jonas. He was naturalized in New York 27 Oct. 1763. He was a Jewish merchant from New York City.
Solomon, Joseph. He was naturalized in Pennsylvania 11 Apr. 1751. He was from Lancaster County. He was a Jew.
Solomons, Levy. He was naturalized in New York 3 May 1755.
Somer, Ludwick. He was naturalized in Maryland 11 Sep. 1765. He was a German from Frederick County.
Somie, Jacques. He was an Acadian who took the oath of allegiance at the Mines, Pisiquit, Nova Scotia 31 Oct. 1727.
Somie, Pierre. He was an Acadian who took the oath of allegiance at the Mines, Pisiquit, Nova Scotia 31 Oct. 1727.
Somie, Rene. He was an Acadian who took the oath of allegiance at the Mines, Pisiquit, Nova Scotia 31 Oct. 1727.
Sommer, John. He was naturalized in Maryland 17 Sep. 1751.
Sommer, Michael. He was naturalized in Pennsylvania 10–12 Apr. 1762. He was from York County.
Sommervill, Elizabeth. She was naturalized in Jamaica 12 Feb. 1693/4.
Somner, Peter Nicholaus. He was naturalized in New York 20 Mar. 1762.
Somy, Peter. He was naturalized in Pennsylvania 13–15 Apr. 1748. He was from Lancaster County.
Sonfrank, Jacob. He was naturalized in Maryland 8 Sep. 1764. He was a German.
Sonies, Joseph. He was naturalized in Jamaica 28 May 1707.
Sonn, George. He was naturalized in Pennsylvania 24 Sep. 1760. He was from York County.
Sontag, Adam. He was naturalized in Pennsylvania 10–12 Apr. 1762. He was from Berks County.
Sonts, Dedrick. He was naturalized in New York 8–9 Sep. 1715. He was from Ulster County.
Sooy, Joost. He was naturalized in New Jersey 26 Mar. 1719. He also appeared as Yoos Sooge.
Sooy, Yoos. He was naturalized in New York 6 July 1723.
Sorbiere, John. He was naturalized in Jamaica 23 Feb. the first year of Queen Anne.
Sornberger, Georg Jacob. He was naturalized in New York 23 Oct. 1741.
Sornier, Etienne. He was an Acadian and took the oath of allegiance in Apr. 1730.
Sornier, Jacques. He was an Acadian and took the oath to George II at the Mines, Pisiquit 31 Oct. 1727.
Sornier, Jacques. He was an Acadian and took the oath of allegiance in Apr. 1730.
Sornier, Louis. He was an Acadian and took the oath of allegiance in Apr. 1730.
Sornier, Pierre. He was an Acadian and took the oath to George II at the Mines, Pisiquit 31 Oct. 1727.
Sornier, Pierre. He was an Acadian and took the oath of allegiance in Apr. 1730.
Sornier, Rene. He was an Acadian and took the oath to George II at the Mines, Pisiquit 31 Oct. 1727.
Sornier, Rene. He was an Acadian and took the oath of allegiance in Apr. 1730.
Souber, George. He was naturalized in Pennsylvania 29 Mar. 1735. He was from Philadelphia County.
Souber, John. He was naturalized in Pennsylvania 29 Mar. 1735. He was from Philadelphia County.
Souber, Peter. He was naturalized in Pennsylvania 29 Mar. 1735. He was from Philadelphia County.
Souder, Christian. He was naturalized in Pennsylvania 25 Sep. 1747. He was from Philadelphia County.
Souder, Felix. He was naturalized in Maryland 11 Sep. 1765. He was a German from Frederick County.
Souder, Jacob. He was naturalized in Pennsylvania 6 Feb. 1730/1. He was from Bucks County.
Soulard, Peter. He was naturalized in New Jersey 31 July 1740. He was born in France.
Soullice, John. He was naturalized in New York 27 Sep. 1715. He was a baker from New York City.

Soumain, Simeon. He was endenized in New York 18 Apr. 1695.

Sousa, Isaque Rodriguez de. He sought to be endenized 30 Aug. 1692. He was a Jew from Jamaica.

Souso, Anthonij. He took the oath of allegiance in Breucklijn, Kings County, New York 26–30 Sep. 1687. He had been in the colony 5 years.

Souter, Henry. He was naturalized in Pennsylvania 10 Apr. 1760.

Souter, Jacob. He was naturalized in Pennsylvania 25–27 Oct. 1740. He was from Philadelphia County.

Souther, Christopher. He was naturalized in Maryland 20 Oct. 1768.

Soville, John. He was naturalized in Virginia 12 May 1705.

Sowass, Henry. He was naturalized in Pennsylvania 11 Apr. 1761. He was from Berks County.

Sowder, George Thomas. He was naturalized in Pennsylvania 11–12 Apr. 1744. He was from Lancaster County.

Sower, Phillip. He was naturalized in North Carolina 22 Mar. 1764. He was from Rowan County and a German.

Sowers, Christopher. He was naturalized in Pennsylvania 14 Feb. 1729/30. He was from Lancaster County.

Sowreshler, Hegmerick. He was naturalized in New York 8–9 Sep. 1715. He was from Ulster County.

Spach, Jonas. He was naturalized in New York 21 Oct. 1741.

Spachius, Philip. He was naturalized in New Jersey in 1775. He was born in Germany.

Spahr, John George. He was naturalized in Pennsylvania 10–12 Apr. 1762. He was from York County.

Spaler, Johannes. He was naturalized in New York 22 June 1734.

Spamagle, Luywick. He was naturalized in Pennsylvania 11 Apr. 1763. He was from Whitemarsh Township, Philadelphia County.

Span, Adam. He was naturalized in New York 8–9 Sep. 1715. He was from Ulster County.

Spangler, Bolser. He was naturalized in Pennsylvania 11 Apr. 1752. He was from York County.

Spann, Adam. He was naturalized in Pennsylvania 10 Apr. 1758.

Spanseiler, George. He was naturalized in Pennsylvania 10 Apr. 1762. He was from York County.

Sparr, Michael. He was naturalized in Pennsylvania 20 May 1769. He was from Dover Township, York County.

Sparre, Seweren Frank. He was naturalized in Jamaica 27 Feb. 1754. He was from St. Catherine's Parish.

Spaught, Adam. He was naturalized in Maryland in Apr. 1749. He was from Frederick County.

Spear, George. He was naturalized in Augusta County, Virginia 21 Aug. 1770.

Spear, Leonard. He was naturalized in Pennsylvania 11 Apr. 1763. He was from Worcester Township, Berks County.

Spear, Philip. He was naturalized in Pennsylvania 11 Apr. 1761. He was from Philadelphia County.

Spease, Conrod. He was naturalized in Maryland 13 Apr. 1761. He lived in Frederick County.

Speck, William. He was naturalized in Pennsylvania 11–13 Apr. 1743. He was from Philadelphia County.

Speder, Daniel. He was naturalized in New York 18 Oct. 1749. He was a cartman from New York City.

Speech, Conradt. He was naturalized in Pennsylvania 24 Sep. 1755. He was from Philadelphia County.

Speecher, Henry. He was naturalized in Pennsylvania 11 Apr. 1761. He was from York County.

Speedler, Jacob. He was naturalized in Pennsylvania 10 Sep. 1761. He was from Lancaster County.

Spees, Jacob. He was naturalized in Pennsylvania 10 Apr. 1765. He was from Bethel Township, Berks County.

Speiht, John Peter. He was naturalized in Pennsylvania 25 Sep. 1751. He was from Philadelphia County.

Speike, David. He was naturalized in North Carolina 22 Sep. 1763. He was from Rowan County and a German.

Speiss, Victor. He was naturalized in Pennsylvania 11 Apr. 1761. He was from Berks County.

Spencer, Zacheriah. He was German and was naturalized in Maryland 13 Oct. 1742.

Spengle, Daniel. He was naturalized in Maryland 1 Oct. 1767. He was a German.

Spengler, Bernard. He was naturalized in Pennsylvania 24 Sep. 1762. He was from York County.

Spengler, Henry. He was naturalized in Pennsylvania 11 Apr. 1763. He was from York Township, York County.

Spengler, John Christopher. He was naturalized in Pennsylvania 11 Apr. 1761. He was from Berks County.

Spengler, Mathias. He was naturalized in Maryland 16 Apr. 1761.

Spengler, Michael. He was naturalized in Pennsylvania 11 Apr. 1761. He was from Lancaster County.

Sperbeck, Martin. He was naturalized in New York 11 Sep. 1761.

Sperry, Peter. He was naturalized in Frederick County, Virginia 2 Oct. 1765.

Speykerman, Bastiaen. He was naturalized in New York 13 Mar. 1715/6. He was from Albany County.

Spice, Peter. He was naturalized in Frederick County, Virginia 12 Aug. 1767.

Spick, Frederick Tendle. He was naturalized in New Jersey 8 Dec. 1744.

Spickerman, Johan Harme. He was naturalized in New York 31 Jan. 1715/6. He was from Albany County.

Spickler, Martin. He was naturalized in Pennsylvania 11 Apr. 1761. He was from Lancaster County.

Spiegel, Michael. He was naturalized in Pennsylvania 10 Apr. 1759.

Spiegle, Frederick. He was naturalized in Pennsylvania 24 Sep. 1760. He was from Northampton County.

Spiegle, John Remigius. He was naturalized in Pennsylvania 11 Apr. 1761. He was from Philadelphia County.

Spies, John Philip. He was naturalized in New York 21 Oct. 1761. He was a cordwainer from New York City.

Spies, Ludwic. He was naturalized in Pennsylvania 24–25 Sep. 1764. He was from Dover Township, Philadelphia County.

Spigelaer, Jan. He took the oath of allegiance in Flackbush, Kings County, New York 26–30 Sep. 1687. He had been in the colony 25 years.

Spikeler, Jacob. He was naturalized in Pennsylvania 10 Sep. 1761. He was from Lancaster County.

Spiker, Julius. He was naturalized in Frederick County, Virginia 4 Sep. 1765.

Spindler, Jacob. He was naturalized in Maryland 14 Sep. 1770. He was a German.

Spindler, Ludwig. He was naturalized in Nova Scotia 5 July 1758.

Spingler, George. He was naturalized in Pennsylvania 26–27 Sep. 1743. He was from Philadelphia County.

Spingler, George Jacob. He was naturalized in Pennsylvania 11 Apr. 1741. He was from Philadelphia County.

Spingler, Jacob. He was naturalized in New York 3 July 1759.

Spingler, John Balthas. He was naturalized in New York 3 July 1739.

Spingler, Rudolph. He was naturalized in Pennsylvania 24 Sep. 1762. He was from York County.

Spinner, Ulrick. He was naturalized in Pennsylvania 11 Apr. 1761. He was from Bucks County.

Spittal, Joseph. He was naturalized in Pennsylvania 10 Apr. 1765. He was from Douglass Township, Philadelphia County.

Spittlemyer, Adam. He was naturalized in Pennsylvania 11 Apr. 1761. He was from Berks County.

Spittler, John. He was naturalized in Maryland 10 Apr. 1770. He was from Baltimore County.

Spitzfarden, Benedict. He was naturalized in Pennsylvania 24 Sep. 1762. He was from Lancaster County.

Spitznagle, Baltzer. He was naturalized in Pennsylvania 10–12 Apr. 1762. He was from Philadelphia County.

Spohn, Henry. He was naturalized in Pennsylvania 11 Apr. 1761. He was from Berks County.

Spoon, Michael. He was naturalized in Pennsylvania 11–13 Apr. 1743. He was from Philadelphia County.

Spore, John. He was naturalized in Pennsylvania 11 Apr. 1763. He was from Lancaster Township, Lancaster County.

Spornheir, William. He was naturalized in New York 11 Sep. 1761.

Sporry, Jacob. He was naturalized in Nova Scotia 5 July 1758.

Spory, Jacob. He was naturalized in New York 31 July 1770. He was a gardener from New York City.

Spotz, William. He was naturalized in Pennsylvania 11 Apr. 1761. He was from Lancaster County.

Sprangenbergh, Johannes. He was naturalized in New York 3 July 1759.

Sprecher, Georg. He was naturalized in New York 11 Sep. 1761.

Spreeker, George. He was naturalized in Pennsylvania 10 Apr. 1758.

Spreen, John. He was endenized in London 20 Feb. 1662/3. He was from Barbados.

Spregher, Jacob Andrew. He was naturalized in Pennsylvania 10 Apr. 1765. He was from Lancaster Township, Lancaster County.

Spring, Philip. He was naturalized in Pennsylvania 10 Sep. 1761. He was from Berks County.

Springer, Charles. He was naturalized in Pennsylvania 23 July 1701. He was born in Stockholm, Sweden, the son of Christopher Springer.

Springer, Silvester. He was naturalized in New York 3 Feb. 1768. He was a tobacconist from New York City.

Sproegel, John Henry. He was naturalized in Pennsylvania 3 Apr. 1705. He was a brother of Lodwick Christian Sproegel. He was born in Quedlinburg, Prussia, the son of John Henry Sproegel. The surname also appeared as Sproeyle.

Sproegel, Lodwick Christian. He was naturalized in Pennsylvania 3 Apr. 1705. He was a brother of John Henry Sproegel.

Spycher, Peter. He was naturalized in Pennsylvania 25 Sep. 1747. He was from Philadelphia County.

Spyes, Peter. He was naturalized in New York 13 Mar. 1715/6. He was from Albany County.

Spygelaar, Jan. He took the oath to the King 21–26 Oct. 1664 after the conquest of New Netherland.

Spyker, Benjamin. He was naturalized in Pennsylvania 24 Sep. 1753. He was from Lancaster County.

Spyker, John. He was naturalized in Pennsylvania 24 Sep. 1755. He was from Lancaster County.

Sramt, Henrich. He was naturalized in New York 8–9 Sep. 1715. He was from Ulster County.

Sramt, Michel. He was naturalized in New York 8–9 Sep. 1715. He was from Ulster County.

Srum, Michael. He was naturalized in New York 20 May 1769.

Staalcop, Carell. He expressed his desire to be naturalized in New Castle County, Delaware 21 Feb. 1682/3.

Staalcop, Jan, Jr. He expressed his desire to be naturalized in New Castle County, Delaware 21 Feb. 1682/3.

Staats, Isabella. She was naturalized in New York 28 Feb. 1715/6. She was from Albany County.

Staats, Jan Janse. He took the oath of allegiance in Breucklijn, Kings County, New York 26–30 Sep. 1687. He was a native of the colony.

Staats, Johannes. He was naturalized in New York 17 Oct. 1744. He was a farmer from Dutchess County.

Staats, Pieter. He took the oath of allegiance in Breucklijn, Kings County, New York 26–30 Sep. 1687. He was a native of the colony.

Staats, Pieter Janse. He took the oath of allegiance in Breucklijn, Kings County, New York 26–30 Sep. 1687. He was a native of the colony.

Stable, Christopher. He was naturalized in Maryland in Apr. 1749. He was from Frederick County.

Stadelmyer, David. He was naturalized in Maryland 7 May 1767. He was a German from Frederick County.

Stadleman, William. He was naturalized in Pennsylvania 10–12 Apr. 1762. He was from Philadelphia County.

Stadler, Christopher. He was naturalized in Pennsylvania 26–27 Sep. 1743. He was from Bucks County.

Stadler, Jacob. He was naturalized in Pennsylvania 24–25 Sep. 1764. He was from Philadelphia.

Stadler, Thomas. He was naturalized in Maryland 25 Apr. 1771. He was a German from Charles County.

Staets, Abraham. He took the oath to the King 21–26 Oct. 1664 after the conquest of New Netherland.

Staffer, Philip. He was naturalized in Pennsylvania 10 Sep. 1761. He was from Lancaster County.

Stagg, Ann. She was naturalized in New Jersey 8 July 1730. She was born in Germany.

Stagner, John Barnet. He was naturalized in Rowan County, North Carolina 13 July 1763.

Staiger, Adam. He was naturalized in Pennsylvania 24–25 Sep. 1764. He was from Lebanon Township, Lancaster County.

Stailey, Joseph. He was naturalized in North Carolina 22 Sep. 1763. He was from Rowan County and was a German.

Staily, John. He was naturalized in Pennsylvania 11 Apr. 1761. He was from Lancaster County.

Stain, Sebastian. He was naturalized in Pennsylvania 24 Sep. 1755. He was from Lancaster County.

Stairer, Joseph. He was naturalized in New York 20 May 1769.

Stalcop, Jan Andriesse. He expressed his desire to be naturalized in New Castle County, Delaware 21 Feb. 1682/3.

Staley, Jacob. He was naturalized in Maryland 19 Oct. 1743.

Staley, Ulrick. He was naturalized in Pennsylvania 10 Apr. 1757.

Stall, Adam. He was naturalized in Maryland 19 Oct. 1743.

Stall, Henrick. He was naturalized in Maryland 21 Sep. 1764. He was a German.

Stall, Jacob. He was naturalized in Maryland 3 Sep. 1765. He was a German.

Stallcop, Andries. He was naturalized in New Castle County, Delaware 21 Feb. 1682/3.

Staller, Michael. He was naturalized in New York 24 Mar. 1772.

Stalls, Caspar. He was naturalized in Pennsylvania 29 Sep. 1709. He was from Philadelphia County.

Stam, Adam. He was naturalized in Maryland 1 Oct. 1767. He was a German from Frederick County.

Stam, George. He was naturalized in New York 11 Sep. 1761.

Stam, George, Jr. He was naturalized in New York 11 Sep. 1761.

Stam, Jacob. He was naturalized in Pennsylvania 24 Sep. 1742. He was from York County.

Stam, Lourens. He was naturalized in New York 11 Sep. 1761.

Stam, Werner. He was naturalized in Pennsylvania 10–12 Apr. 1762. He was from Berks County.

Stambach, Jacob. He was naturalized in Pennsylvania 10–12 Apr. 1762. He was from York County.

Stambaugh, Christian. He was naturalized in Pennsylvania 11–12 Apr. 1744. He was from Bucks County.

Stamber, Christopher. He was naturalized in Maryland 13 Sep. 1758.

Stamm, George. He was naturalized in New York 3 July 1759.

Staneman, Rudolph. He was naturalized in New Jersey 20 Aug. 1755.

Staner, Christian. He was naturalized in Pennsylvania 14 Feb. 1729/30. He was from Lancaster County.

Staningar, George. He was naturalized in Pennsylvania 26–27 Sep. 1743. He was from Bucks County.

Stannert, Lewis. He was naturalized in Pennsylvania 11 Apr. 1771. He was from Whitemarsh Township, Philadelphia County.

Stapell, Johan Jacob. He was naturalized in New York 20 May 1769.

Star, Henry. He was naturalized in Pennsylvania 24 Sep. 1755. He was from Berks County.

Starck, Jurgen. He was naturalized in Jamaica 4 July 1730.

Starn, Adam. He was naturalized in New York 31 Jan. 1715/6. He was from Albany County.

Starn, Jacob. He was naturalized in New Jersey in 1757. He had been in the colony 17 years. He was born in Germany.

Starnher, George. He was naturalized in Pennsylvania 11 Apr. 1761. He was from Philadelphia County.

Staug, Philip. He was naturalized in Pennsylvania 24 Sep. 1763. He was from Lower Salford Township, Philadelphia County.

Stay, Frederick. He was naturalized in Pennsylvania 24 Feb. 1729/30. He was from Lancaster County.

Stayley, George. He was naturalized in Pennsylvania 24 Sep. 1762. He was from Lancaster County.

Steegler, Gerrard. He was naturalized in Pennsylvania 10 & 23 Apr. 1764. He was from Strasburg Township, York County.

Steck, Nicholas. He was naturalized in New York 3 May 1755.

Stedlin, Frederick. He was naturalized in Jamaica 25 Feb. 1760.

Steeble, Simon. He was naturalized in Maryland 11 Sep. 1765.

Steel, Christopher. He was naturalized in Pennsylvania 24–25 Sep./5 Oct. 1767. He was from Manheim Township, York County.

Steel, Henry. He was naturalized in Pennsylvania 10 Apr. 1760.

Steel, Roelof. He was naturalized in New York 11 Oct. 1715. He was from Albany County.

Steelman, John Hans. He was naturalized in Maryland 19 Oct. 1695. He lived in Cecil County.

Steelman, John. He was naturalized in Maryland 19 Oct. 1695. He lived in Cecil County.

Steenbach, Anthony. He was naturalized in New York 19 Oct. 1748. He was a baker from New York City.

Steenrnier, Bastian. He was naturalized in New York 11 Apr. 1761.

Steenwick, Cornelius B. He took the oath to the King 21–26 Oct. 1664 after the conquest of New Netherland.

Steer, Christian. He was naturalized in Pennsylvania 24 Sep. 1763. He was from Upper Milford Township, Bucks County.

Steer, Conrad. He was naturalized in Pennsylvania 10 Sep. 1761. He was from Bucks County.

Steeselmyer, Stephan. He was naturalized in Pennsylvania 10 Apr. 1765. He was from Frederick Township, Philadelphia County.

Stegar, Franics. He was granted leave to have a patent of 400 acres in Virginia on 4 May 1745 before his naturalization.

Stehly, Elizabeth. She was naturalized in Maryland 16 Sep. 1773. She was German.

Stehr, Mathias. He was naturalized in Pennsylvania 29–30 May 1772. He was from York, York County.

Stehr, William. He was naturalized in Pennsylvania 10 Sep. 1761. He was from Lancaster County.

Steidel, Nathaniel. He was naturalized in Pennsylvania 10–12 Apr. 1762. He was from Northampton County.

Steigle, Henry William. He was naturalized in Pennsylvania 10 Apr. 1760.

Steigh, Christopher. He was naturalized in Pennsylvania 11 Apr. 1761. He was from Lancaster County.

Stein, Henricus. He was naturalized in Maryland 15 Sep. 1762. He was from Baltimore County.

Stein, Jacob. He was naturalized in Pennsylvania 11 Apr. 1761. He was from Berks County.

Stein, Ulrich. He was naturalized in Frederick County, Virginia 4 Aug. 1747.

Steinbrinner, Jacob. He was naturalized in New York 18 Oct. 1750. He was a blacksmith from New York City.

Steiner, George. He was naturalized in Maryland 14 Sep. 1763. He was a German from Frederick County.

Steiner, Jacob. He was naturalized in Maryland 17 July 1765. He was a German.

Steiner, Johannes. He was naturalized in Pennsylvania 11–13 Apr. 1743. He was from Chester County.

Steinmetz, Daniel. He was naturalized in Pennsylvania 19 May 1739. He was from Philadelphia County.

Steinmetz, Nickolaus. He was naturalized in New Jersey in 1758. He had been in the colony 26 years.

Steinstaeuffer, Daniel. He was naturalized in Maryland 14 Apr. 1762. He was a German.

Steinwas, Arnold. He was naturalized in New York 8 Mar. 1773.

Steirer, Joseph. He was naturalized in New York 20 May 1769.

Steitz, George. He was naturalized in Pennsylvania 19 May 1739. He was from Lancaster County.

Stellenwarf, Peter. He sought naturalization in New Jersey 4 Apr. 1722.

Stellingwerf, Pieter. He was naturalized in New York 6 July 1723.

Stemm, Conrad. He was naturalized in Pennsylvania 11–13 Apr. 1743. He was from Philadelphia County.

Stence, Jacob. He was naturalized in Pennsylvania 24 Sep. 1762. He was from York County.

Stenger, Conrad. He was naturalized in Pennsylvania 24 Sep. 1763. He was from Rockhill Township, Bucks County.

Stephan, Andreas. He was naturalized in Maryland 12 Sep. 1764. He was a German from Frederick County.

Stephan, Leonard. He was naturalized in Maryland 11 Sep. 1765. He was a German from Frederick County.

Stephan, Peter. He was naturalized in Orange County, Virginia in that part designed to become Frederick County on 21 Oct. 1743. He had lived there more than seven years. He was a native of Heidelberg, Germany.

Stephany, John Sebastian. He was naturalized in New York 3 July 1759.

Stephens, Lawrence. He was naturalized in Frederick County, Virginia 4 Aug. 1747.

Sterback, Yost. He was naturalized in Pennsylvania 11 Apr. 1761. He was from York County.

Sterenbergen, Johan B. He was naturalized in New York 31 Jan. 1715/6. He was from Albany County.

Stern, Jacob. He was naturalized in Maryland 19 Oct. 1743.

Stetler, Johan. He was naturalized in Pennsylvania 19 May 1739. He was from Lancaster County.

Stettler, Henry. He was naturalized in Pennsylvania 25–27 Sep. 1740. He was from Philadelphia County.

Stettler, Valentine John. He was naturalized in Pennsylvania in 1739. He was from Lancaster County.

Stevens, Judith. She was naturalized in Jamaica 25 July 1733.

Stevense, Jan. He took the oath of allegiance in Flackland, Kings County, New York 26–30 Sep. 1687. He had been in the colony 27 years.

Stevense, Luycas. He took the oath of allegiance in Flackland, Kings County, New York 26–30 Sep. 1687. He had been in the colony 27 years.

Stever, Baltzer. He was naturalized in Pennsylvania 11–12 Apr. 1744. He was from Bucks County.

Steyer, Tobias, Sr. He was naturalized in Pennsylvania 24 Nov. 1769. He was from Manheim Township, York County.

Steyger, Niecolas. He was naturalized in New York 14 Feb. 1715/6. He was from Albany County.

Steyger, Stephanis. He was naturalized in New York 8–9 Sep. 1715. He was from Ulster County.

Steyler, Nicholas. He was naturalized in Pennsylvania 11–13 Apr. 1743. He was from Bucks County.

Stickel, Lenhart. He was naturalized in New York 8–9 Sep. 1715. He was from Ulster County.

Sticken, Dirck. He took the oath to the King 21–26 Oct. 1664 after the conquest of New Netherland.

Sticker, Adam. He was naturalized in Pennsylvania 10 Apr. 1760.

Stickle, Valentine. He was naturalized in Pennsylvania 25 Sep. 1751. He was from Philadelphia County.

Sticklen, John. He was naturalized in New York 20 May 1769.

Stickling, Niecolas. He was naturalized in New York 14 Feb. 1715/6. He was from Albany County.

Stiddem, Adam. He expressed his desire to be naturalized in New Castle County, Delaware 21 Feb. 1682/3.

Stiddem, Erasmus. He expressed his desire to be naturalized in New Castle County, Delaware 21 Feb. 1682/3.

Stiddem, Lucas. He expressed his desire to be naturalized in New Castle County, Delaware 21 Feb. 1682/3.

Stiddem, Lulof. He expressed his desire to be naturalized in New Castle County, Delaware 21 Feb. 1682/3.

Stiddem, Tymen. He expressed his desire to be naturalized in New Castle County, Delaware 21 Feb. 1682/3.

Stiemer, Anthony. He was naturalized in Pennsylvania 10 & 23 Apr. 1764. He was from Germantown, Philadelphia County.

Stienfurt, Balthasar. He was naturalized in Pennsylvania 11 Apr. 1763. He was from Philadelphia.
Stienmetz, Henry. He was naturalized in Pennsylvania 11 Apr. 1763. He was from Philadelphia.
Stienmetz, Valentine. He was naturalized in Pennsylvania 11 Apr. 1761. He was from Northampton County.
Stiep, Marten. He was naturalized in New York 31 Jan. 1715/6.
Stierwald, Peter. He was naturalized in Pennsylvania 11 Apr. 1763. He was from Northern Liberties Township, Philadelphia County.
Stiever, Baltus. He was naturalized in New York 17 Jan. 1715/6. He was from Albany County.
Stigar, Jordan. He was naturalized in Maryland 22 Apr. 1773. He was a German.
Stiger, Andreas. He was naturalized in Maryland 13 Sep. 1758.
Stiger, Andrew. He was naturalized in Maryland 11 Apr. 1759.
Stighter, Conrad. He was naturalized in Pennsylvania 10 Sep. 1761. He was from Berks County.
Stigleman, Jacob. He was naturalized in Pennsylvania 10 & 23 Apr. 1764. He was from Lancaster Township, Lancaster County.
Still, Cornelys Jacobzen. He took the oath to the King 21–26 Oct. 1664 after the conquest of New Netherland.
Stille, Axell. He was made a denizen in Maryland 29 July 1661. He was Swedish and was late of New Amstel.
Stille, Axell. He was naturalized in Maryland 6 June 1674. He was Swedish.
Stiller, John. He was naturalized in Pennsylvania 11 Jan. 1683. He was formerly of New Sweden.
Stineman, John. He was naturalized in Pennsylvania 11–13 Apr. 1743. He was from Philadelphia County.
Stiop, Marten. He was naturalized in New York 31 Jan. 1715/6. He was from Albany County.
Stior, Philip. He was naturalized in Pennsylvania 11–13 Apr. 1743. He was from Lancaster County.
Stites, Michael. He was naturalized in Pennsylvania 11 Apr. 1761. He was from Philadelphia County.
Stober, Hans Ulrick. He was naturalized in Pennsylvania 11–13 Apr. 1743. He was from Philadelphia County.
Stober, Valentine. He was naturalized in Pennsylvania 25–26 Sep./4 Oct. 1749. He was from Lancaster County.
Stober, Philip. He was naturalized in Pennsylvania 11 Apr. 1761. He was from Lancaster County.
Stocke, Abraham. He was naturalized in Northumberland County, Virginia 17 Sep. 1656. He was born in Calais, France but was of Dover, County Kent, England, the son of Robert Stocke of Scotland.
Stoever, John Casper. He was naturalized in Pennsylvania 24 Sep. 1741. He was from Lancaster County.
Stofel, Henry. He was naturalized in Maryland 1 Sep. 1757.
Stoffelse, Dirck. He took the oath of allegiance in Flackland, Kings County, New York 26–30 Sep. 1687. He had been in the colony 30 years.
Stoffelse, Gerrit. He took the oath of allegiance in New Uijtrceht, Kings County, New York 26–30 Sep. 1687. He had been in the colony 36 years.
Stofflat, Michael. He was naturalized in Pennsylvania 10 Apr. 1765. He was from Philadelphia.
Stohler, Isaac. He was naturalized in Pennsylvania 10 & 23 Apr. 1764. He was from Manchester Township, York County.
Stohler, Sebastian. He was naturalized in Pennsylvania 11 Apr. 1761. He was from Lancaster County.
Stokey, John. He was naturalized in Pennsylvania 24 Sep. 1760. He was from Lancaster County.
Stoler, George. He was naturalized in Pennsylvania 11 Apr. 1761. He was from Lancaster County.
Stoler, John. He was naturalized in Maryland 13 Apr. 1762. He was a German.
Stoler, Werther. He was naturalized in Maryland 12 Sep. 1764. He was a German.
Stoll, John Jacosa. He took the oath of naturalization in New York 1 Sep. 1687 in Ulster County.
Stoll, Pieter Janzell. He took the oath to the King 21–26 Oct. 1664 after the conquest of New Netherland.
Stoller, Michael. He was naturalized in New York 20 Dec. 1763.
Stoller, Michael. He was naturalized in New York 8 Mar. 1773.

Stolnaker, George. He was naturalized in Pennsylvania 10 Apr. 1755. He was from Northampton County.

Stoltz, Niclaus. He was naturalized in Maryland 13 Apr. 1763. He was a German.

Stombaugh, Philip. He was naturalized in Pennsylvania 29–30 May 1772. He was from Frederick County, Maryland.

Stomf, Hans Jury. He was naturalized in New York 31 Jan. 1715/6. He was from Albany County.

Stone, Abraham. He was naturalized in Pennsylvania 10 & 23 Apr. 1764. He was from Cocalico Township, York County.

Stone, Henry. He was naturalized in Augusta County, Virginia 18 May 1762.

Stone, John. He was naturalized in Maryland 11 Sep. 1765. He was a German from Frederick County.

Stone, John. He was naturalized in New York 27 Jan. 1770.

Stone, John. He was naturalized in Pennsylvania 11 Apr. 1749. He was from Lancaster County.

Stone, John George. He was naturalized in Pennsylvania 10 Apr. 1760.

Stone, John Leonard. He was naturalized in Pennsylvania 25–27 Sep. 1740. He was from Philadelphia County.

Stone, Leonard. He was naturalized in Pennsylvania 10 Apr. 1754. He was from Lancaster County.

Stone, Ludwic. He was naturalized in Pennsylvania 24–25 Sep. 1764. He was from Lancaster Township, Lancaster County. He was a Moravian.

Stoneburner, Leonard. He was naturalized in Pennsylvania 24–25 Sep. 1764. He was from Germantown.

Stoneman, Christian. He was naturalized in Pennsylvania 14 Feb. 1729/30. He was from Lancaster County.

Stoneman, Johan George. He was naturalized in Pennsylvania 11–13 Apr. 1743. He was from Philadelphia County.

Stoneman, Joseph. He was naturalized in Pennsylvania 14 Feb. 1729/30. He was from Lancaster County.

Stoner, Conrod. He was naturalized in North Carolina 22 Sep. 1764. He was from Rowan County and a German.

Stoner, Jacob. He and his sons, John Stoner and Jacob Stoner, were naturalized in Maryland 3 May 1740. He was from Prince George's County and was born in Germany.

Stoner, John. He was naturalized in Pennsylvania 12 Apr. 1750. He was from Chester County.

Stoner, Rudolph. He was naturalized in Pennsylvania 26–27 Sep. 1743. He was from Lancaster County.

Stonetz, Leonard. He was naturalized in New Jersey in 1758. He lived in Salem County and had been in the colony 26 years. He also appeared as Leonard Steinmetz.

Stonmetz, Jacob. He was naturalized in Pennsylvania 11 Apr. 1761. He was from Philadelphia County.

Stooker, Michael. He was naturalized in Maryland 28 Sep. 1762. He was a German from Frederick County.

Stooner, Jacob. He was naturalized in Pennsylvania 10–12 Apr. 1762. He was from Lancaster County.

Stoothoff, Gerret Elberts. He took the oath of allegiance in Flackland, Kings County, New York 26–30 Sep. 1687. He was a native of the colony.

Stoppelbert, Peter. He was naturalized in New York 17 Jan. 1715/6. He was from Albany County.

Storck, Nicolaus. He was naturalized in Nova Scotia 10 July 1758.

Stork, Jacob. He was naturalized in Pennsylvania 24–29 Sep. 1749. He was from Ridley Township, Chester County.

Storm, Dirck. He took the oath of allegiance in Orange County, New York 26 Sep. 1687.

Storm, John. He was endenized in Maryland 22 June 1771. He was born in Germany.

Storm, John George. He was naturalized in Pennsylvania 13 May 1771. He was from Frederick County, Maryland.

Storme, Vansel. He was naturalized in Maryland 15 Apr. 1761.

Stouber, John William. He was naturalized in Maryland 13 Apr. 1762. He was a German.

Stouck, Werner. He was naturalized in Pennsylvania 24 Sep. 1762. He was from Berks County.

Stoude, Martin. He was naturalized in Maryland 14 Apr. 1762. He was a German.

Stouffer, Daniel. He was naturalized in Pennsylvania 11–13 Apr. 1743. He was from Philadelphia County.

Stouffer, John. He was naturalized in Pennsylvania 21 Nov. 1769. He was from Lampeter Township, Lancaster County.

Stouffer, John. He was naturalized in Pennsylvania 10 Sep. 1761. He was from Lancaster County.

Stough, Jacob. He was naturalized in Pennsylvania 10–12 Apr. 1762. He was from Berks County.

Stough, Frederick. He was naturalized in Pennsylvania 10 & 23 Apr. 1764. He was from Dover Township, York County.

Stough, George. He was naturalized in Pennsylvania 10 & 23 Apr. 1764. He was from Dover Township, York County.

Stoupher, Urick. He was naturalized in Pennsylvania 10–11 Apr. 1745. He was from Lancaster County.

Stout, Adam. He was naturalized in Pennsylvania 25 Sep. 1747. He was from Philadelphia County.

Stout, George. He was naturalized in Pennsylvania 10 Apr. 1755. He was from Northampton County.

Stout, Jacob. He was naturalized in Pennsylvania 11 Apr. 1751. He was from Bucks County.

Stout, Matthias. He was naturalized in Pennsylvania 11 Apr. 1761. He was from Berks County.

Stout, Michael. He was naturalized in Pennsylvania 11 Apr. 1761. He was from Berks County.

Stoutenbergh, Pieter. He took the oath to the King 21–26 Oct. 1664 after the conquest of New Netherland.

Stove, Jacob. He was naturalized in Pennsylvania 10 Apr. 1760.

Stover, Christian. He was naturalized in Pennsylvania 24 Sep. 1763. He was from Lampeter Township, Lancaster County.

Stover, Jacob, Jr. He was naturalized in New York 3 May 1755.

Stover, John Casper. He was naturalized in Pennsylvania 29 Mar. 1735. He was from Chester County.

Stover, Martin. He was naturalized in Pennsylvania 11 Apr. 1761. He was from Lancaster County.

Stowber, Christian. He was naturalized in New York 8 Nov. 1737.

Stowfer, Christian. He was naturalized in Pennsylvania 25–27 Sep. 1740. He was from Philadelphia County.

Stowss, Baltser. He was naturalized in Pennsylvania 10 Apr. 1765. He was from Philadelphia.

Stoy, Ulrick. He was naturalized in Pennsylvania 10 Apr. 1754. He was from Berks County.

Stoy, William. He was naturalized in Pennsylvania 11 Apr. 1761. He was from Lancaster County.

Strabb, Casper. He was naturalized in Pennsylvania 10 & 23 Apr. 1764. He was from Alsace Township, Berks County.

Strainer, William. He was naturalized in Pennsylvania 11 Apr. 1761. He was from Philadelphia County.

Strasser, John Nicholas. He was naturalized in Pennsylvania 11 Apr. 1763. He was from Albany Township, Berks County.

Straube, John William. He was naturalized in Pennsylvania in Sep. 1740. He was from Philadelphia County.

Straubell, Zachariah. He was naturalized in Maryland 11 Sep. 1763. He was a German.

Straum, Benedict. He was naturalized in Pennsylvania 24 Sep. 1741. He was from Philadelphia County.

Straus, Albright. He was naturalized in Pennsylvania 10 Apr. 1755. He was from Berks County.

Strauss, Bernard. He was naturalized in Pennsylvania 24 Sep. 1762. He was from Northampton County.

Strebell, John. He was naturalized in New York 26 Oct. 1764. He was a farmer from Albany County.

Strecher, Matthias. He was naturalized in Pennsylvania 10 Sep. 1761. He was from Lancaster County,

Strecher, Matthias, Jr. He was naturalized in Pennsylvania 10 Sep. 1761. He was from Lancaster County.

Streeter, John Philip. He was naturalized in Pennsylvania 25–27 Sep. 1740. He was a Lutheran minister in Bucks County.

Streetman, Martin. He was naturalized in New Jersey 20 Aug. 1755.

Streher, Peter. He was naturalized in Pennsylvania 11 Apr. 1761. He was from York County.

Streiber, Conrad. He was naturalized in Pennsylvania 10 Apr. 1760.

Streing, Daniel. He, his wife Charlotte Streing, and children Peter Streing, Mathew Streing, Mary Streing, and Ann Streing were endenized in England 25 Mar. 1688. They came to South Carolina.

Streit, Godfried. He was naturalized in New York 20 Oct. 1758. He was a cordwainer from New York City. He had resided in New Jersey five years, in Pennsylvania about eighteen months, and in New York one year and eight months.

Streit, Johan Friederick. He was naturalized in New York 8–9 Sep. 1715. He was from Ulster County.

Strepers, John, Sr. He was naturalized in Pennsylvania 29 Sep. 1709. He was from Philadelphia County.

Strepers, William. He was naturalized in Pennsylvania 29 Sep. 1709. He was from Philadelphia County.

Strever, Joachim. He was naturalized in Maryland 10 Sep. 1762.

Streyper, George. He was naturalized in Pennsylvania 24–25 Sep. 1764. He was from Philadelphia.

Stricker, Elias. He was naturalized in Pennsylvania 10–14 Apr. 1747. He was from Philadelphia.

Stricker, John. He was naturalized in Pennsylvania 10–14 Apr. 1747. He was from Philadelphia.

Stricker, Melchior. He was naturalized in Pennsylvania 10 Apr. 1765. He was from Forks Township, Northampton County.

Stricklan, Henry. He was naturalized in New Jersey 6 Dec. 1769.

Strickler, Andrew. He was naturalized in Pennsylvania 25 Sep. 1744. He was from Lancaster County.

Strickler, Henry. He was naturalized in Pennsylvania 25 Sep. 1750. He was from Lancaster County.

Striepers, Peter Hendrick. He was naturalized in New Jersey 20 June 1765.

Striepers, Peter Hendrick. He was naturalized in Pennsylvania 20 Sep. 1766. He was born a subject of the King of Prussia.

Strijcker, Jacob. He took the oath of allegiance in Flackland, Kings County, New York 26–30 Sep. 1687. He had been in the colony 36 years.

Strijker, Gerrit Janse. He took the oath of allegiance in Flackbush, Kings County, New York 26–30 Sep. 1687. He has been in the colony 35 years.

Striker, Michael. He was naturalized in Maryland 10 Sep. 1760.

Stripe, David. He was naturalized in Pennsylvania 11 Apr. 1749. He was from Lancaster County.

Stroder, William. He was naturalized in New Jersey in 1768.

Strook, Michel. He was naturalized in New York 10 Mar. 1762.

Stroop, Johanis. He was naturalized in New York 8–9 Sep. 1715. He was from Ulster County.

Stroop, John. He was naturalized in Pennsylvania 24–25 Sep. 1764. He was from Philadelphia.

Stroud, Adam. He was naturalized in Augusta County, Virginia 22 Mar. 1769.

Stroup, William. He was naturalized in Frederick County, Virginia 6 June 1753.

Strycker, Jan. He took the oath of allegiance in Flackbush, Kings County, New York 26–30 Sep. 1687. He had been in the colony 35 years.

Strycker, Pieter. He took the oath of allegiance in Flackbush, Kings County, New York 26–30 Sep. 1687. He was a native of the colony.

Stuart, Philip William. He was naturalized in New York 8 Mar. 1773.

Stuart, Thomas. He was naturalized in Jamaica 2 May 1698. He was a bachelor in surgery.

Stubarare, Peter. He was naturalized in New York 23 Oct. 1765. He was a stocking weaver from New York City.

Stuber, George. He was naturalized in New York 24 Apr. 1767. He was a tailor from New York City.

Stuble, Christopher. He was naturalized in New York 8 Mar. 1773.

Stuck, Conrad. He was naturalized in Pennsylvania 21 May 1770. He was from Codorus Township, York County.

Stucky, Jacob. He was naturalized in New Jersey 28 Apr. 1762.

Stucky, Simon. He was naturalized in Pennsylvania 10 Apr. 1767. He was from Frederick County, Maryland.

Stuke, Jacob. He was naturalized in Pennsylvania 11 Apr. 1761. He was from Philadelphia County.

Stull, Jacob. He was naturalized in Maryland 20 Oct. 1742.

Stull, Mathias. He was naturalized in Maryland 3 May 1774. He was a German.

Stump, Adam. He was naturalized in Pennsylvania 11–13 Apr. 1743. He was from Lancaster County.

Stump, Caspar. He was naturalized in Pennsylvania 19 May 1739. He was from Lancaster County.

Stump, Christian. He was naturalized in Pennsylvania 11–13 Apr. 1743. He was from Lancaster County.

Stump, George. He was naturalized in Pennsylvania 24 Sep. 1755. He was from Philadelphia County.

Stump, Johannes. He was naturalized in Pennsylvania 11–13 Apr. 1743. He was from Lancaster County.

Stump, John. He and his children, John Stump and Henry Stump, were naturalized in Maryland 18 Oct. 1738. He was from Cecil County and was born in Germany.

Stumra, Adam. He was naturalized in Pennsylvania 11 Apr. 1761. He was from Berks County.

Stute, Anthony. He sought naturalization in New Jersey in the 18th century.

Stute, Anthony, Jr. He sought naturalization in New Jersey in the 18th century.

Stutzman, Jacob. He was naturalized in Pennsylvania 10 Apr. 1767. He was from Cumberland County, Maryland.

Stutzman, Martin. He was naturalized in Pennsylvania 10 Apr. 1753. He was from Berks County.

Stuyvesant, Pieter G. He took the oath to the King 21–26 Oct. 1664 after the conquest of New Netherland.

Styer, John. He was naturalized in Pennsylvania 11 Apr. 1763. He was from Hunterdon County, New Jersey.

Styers, John. He was naturalized in New York 20 Oct. 1764.

Styers, John. He was naturalized in New York 19 Dec. 1766.

Stykelkan, Mense. He was made a denizen in Maryland 8 May 1675. He was Dutch.

Styner, Frederick. He was naturalized in Pennsylvania 11–13 Apr. 1743. He was from Philadelphia County.

Suber, William, Jr. He was naturalized in New York 3 July 1759.

Subrink, Cornelis. He took the oath of allegiance in Breucklijn, Kings County, New York 26–30 Sep. 1687. He was a native of the colony.

Sueiter, Jacobus Peter. He was naturalized in New York 8 Nov. 1735.

Sueverdiz, Carl. He was naturalized in New York 3 July 1759.

Suldrick, David. He was naturalized in Pennsylvania 24–25 Sep. 1764. He was from Lower Merrion Township, Philadelphia County.

Sullinger, Christopher. He was naturalized in Pennsylvania 10 Sep. 1761. He was from Lancaster County.

Sulsback, Philip. He was naturalized in Pennsylvania 11 Sep. 1761. He was from Philadelphia County.

Sumer, John. He was naturalized in Maryland 15 Apr. 1761.

Sumer, John. He was naturalized in Pennsylvania 10–12 Apr. 1762. He was from Philadelphia County.

Summer, Valentine. He was naturalized in Maryland 18 Apr. 1760.

Summers, Jacob. He was naturalized in North Carolina 22 Sep. 1764. He was from Rowan County and a German.

Super, Philip. He was naturalized in Pennsylvania 10 Apr. 1766. He was from Haverford Township, Chester County.

Supinger, Ulrick. He was naturalized in Pennsylvania 10 Sep. 1761. He was from Lancaster County.

Surett, Piere. He was an Acadian and took the oath to George II at Annapolis River, Nova Scotia in Dec. 1729.

Surface, Nicholas. He was naturalized in Pennsylvania 10 Sep. 1761. He was from Lancaster County.

Surface, Philip. He was naturalized in Pennsylvania 11 Apr. 1763. He was from Philadelphia.

Surget, Peter. He was naturalized in New York 27 Jan. 1770.

Surzedas, Abraham. He was naturalized in Jamaica 11 Jan. 1738/9.

Surzedas, Abraham. He was naturalized in Jamaica 24 Feb. 1746/7. He was a Jew.

Susholt, Melchior. He was naturalized in Pennsylvania 26–27 Sep. 1743. He was from Philadelphia County.

Suss, George. He was naturalized in Maryland 7 May 1767. He was a German from Frederick County.

Suts, Baltus. He was naturalized in New York 8–9 Sep. 1715. He was from Ulster County.

Suylandt, Huybert. He was naturalized in New York 8–9 Sep. 1715. He was from Ulster County.

Suzane, Frances. He was naturalized in Jamaica 16 Jan. 1748/9.

Swadley, Mark. He was naturalized in Augusta County, Virginia 18 May 1762.

Swank, George. He was naturalized in Pennsylvania 24 Sep. 1755. He was from Philadelphia County.

Swanson, Andrew. He was naturalized in Pennsylvania 11 Jan. 1683. He was formerly of New Sweden. [His true identity was Andries Svenson.]

Swanson, Swan. He was naturalized in Pennsylvania 11 Jan. 1683. He was formerly of New Sweden. [His true identity was Sven Svenson.]

Swanson, Wollis [Wolle]. He was naturalized in Pennsylvania 11 Jan. 1683. He was formerly of New Sweden. [His true identity was Olle Svenson.]

Swardtwout, Thomas. He took the oath of naturalization in New York 1 Sep. 1687 in Ulster County.

Swarts, Andrew. He was naturalized in Maryland 13 Apr. 1763. He was a German.

Swartwoudt, Anthony. He took the oath of naturalization in New York 1 Sep. 1687 in Ulster County.

Swartwout, Rollof. He took the oath of naturalization in New York 1 Sep. 1687 in Ulster County.

Swartz, Andreas. He was naturalized in Pennsylvania 11–13 Apr. 1743. He was from Philadelphia County.

Swartz, Charles. He was naturalized in Pennsylvania 10 Apr. 1754. He was from Philadelphia County.

Swartz, Conrad. He was naturalized in Pennsylvania 10 Sep. 1761. He was from Lancaster County.

Swartz, Henry. He was naturalized in Pennsylvania 11 Apr. 1761. He was from Berks County.

Swartz, Jacob. He was naturalized in Pennsylvania 11–13 Apr. 1743. He was from Bucks County.

Swartz, Michael. He was naturalized in Pennsylvania 13 May 1768. He was from Upper Dublin Township, Philadelphia County.

Swartz, Nicholas. He was naturalized in Pennsylvania 10 Sep. 1761. He was from Berks County.

Swartz, Peter. He was naturalized in New York 19 Oct. 1763. He was a farmer from Cortland Manor.

Swartz, Peter. He was naturalized in Pennsylvania 11–13 Apr. 1743. He was from Philadelphia County.

Swartz, Peter. He was naturalized in Pennsylvania 10 & 23 Apr. 1764. He was from Philadelphia.

Swartzbach, Adam. He was naturalized in Pennsylvania 11 Apr. 1761. He was from Berks County.

Swartzhoupt, John. He was naturalized in Pennsylvania 10–12 Apr. 1762. He was from Berks County.

Sweeten, Ouzeel. He was endenized in New York 4 Nov. 1692.

Swegger, Wendell. He was naturalized in Pennsylvania 11–13 Apr. 1743. He was from Lancaster County.

Sweigle, David. He was a surgeon and was naturalized in Antigua 12 Dec. 1700.

Sweinhart, George. He was naturalized in Maryland 19 Oct. 1743. He also appeared as George Schweinhart. He was from Manaquice.

Swenk, Casper. He was naturalized in Maryland 11 Sep. 1765. He was a German from Frederick County.

Sweitts, Cornelius. He took the oath of naturalization in New York 1 Sep. 1687 in Ulster County.

Swenk, Nicholas. He was naturalized in Pennsylvania 24 Sep. 1755. He was from Philadelphia County.

Swenke, Jacob. He was naturalized in Pennsylvania 10 Apr. 1754. He was from Philadelphia County.

Swere, John. He was naturalized in New York 6 Dec. 1715. He was a joiner from New York City.

Swickack, Philip. He was naturalized in Pennsylvania 11–12 Apr. 1744. He was from Lancaster County.

Swinehart, George. He was naturalized in Pennsylvania 10 Apr. 1755. He was from Berks County.

Swinehart, Michael. He was naturalized in Pennsylvania 24 Sep. 1755. He was from Philadelphia County.

Swineyard, John. He was naturalized in Maryland 4 Nov. 1724. He lived in Baltimore County and was French.

Swing, Johannes. He was naturalized in Pennsylvania 11–13 Apr. 1743. He was from Philadelphia County.

Swing, Ludowick. He was naturalized in North Carolina 23 Mar. 1763. He was from Rowan County.

Swingle, Nicholas. He was naturalized in Pennsylvania 24 Sep. 1754. He was from Lancaster County.

Swingle, Nicholas. He was naturalized in Pennsylvania 10 Apr. 1755. He was from Berks County.

Swingle, Nicholas. He was naturalized in Pennsylvania 10 Apr. 1755. He was from Bucks County.

Swink, Henry. He was naturalized in New Jersey 28 Apr. 1762.

Switts, Cornelius. He was naturalized in New York 8–9 Sep. 1715. He was from Ulster County.

Switzer, John. He was naturalized in Pennsylvania 10 Sep. 1761. He was from Berks County.

Swoab, George. He was naturalized in Pennsylvania 18 Nov. 1768. He was from Paradise Township, York County.

Swoope, Michael. He was naturalized in Pennsylvania 12 Apr. 1750. He was from York County.

Swope, George. He was naturalized in Pennsylvania 11–12 Apr. 1744. He was from Lancaster County.

Swormstedt, Christian. He was naturalized in Maryland 4 Nov. 1710. He was a German and a surgeon. He lived in Calvert County.

Swortsweller, Christian. He was naturalized in Pennsylvania 10 Apr. 1765. He was from Earl Township, Lancaster County.

Swortwelder, Martin. He was naturalized in New Jersey in 1764.

Syberberg, Christian. He was naturalized in New Jersey 28 Apr. 1762.

Sybrandt, John. He was naturalized in New York 25 Nov. 1727.

Sycard, Ambroise. He and his sons, Ambroise Sycard, Daniel Sycard, and Jacques Sycard, were endenized in New York 6 Feb.1695/6.

Sydeman, Jacob. He was naturalized in Maryland 15 Apr. 1761.

Syfert, Adam. He was naturalized in Pennsylvania 21 May 1770. He was from Dover Township, York County.

Syffert, Johannes. He was naturalized in New York 3 July 1759.

Sylvius, John. He was naturalized in Jamaica 4 Mar. 1712/13.

Symon, Andrew. He was an Acadian and took the oath to George II at Annapolis River, Nova Scotia in the winter of 1730.

Symonys, Harmanus. He was naturalized in New York 24 July 1724.

Syserson, Marcus. He was naturalized in Maryland 6 June 1674. He was Swedish.

Sysinger, George. He was naturalized in Pennsylvania 10 Sep. 1761. He was from Berks County.

Sysinger, Nicholas. He was naturalized in Pennsylvania 25 Sep. 1758.

Tacke, Cornelis. He took the oath of naturalization in New York 1 Sep. 1687 in Ulster County.

Tades, Michiel. He took the oath to the King 21–26 Oct. 1664 after the conquest of New Netherland.

Tadrick, Christian. He was naturalized in New York 11 Sep. 1761.

Taft, Nicholas. He was naturalized in New York 3 May 1755.

Tallenbok, Samuel. He was naturalized in Maryland 13 Apr. 1763. He was a German from Frederick County.

Tampie, Etiene. He was naturalized in South Carolina ca. 1696. [Compare the entry of Estienne Tample.]

Tample, Estienne. He was born at Xaintonge, France, the son of Estienne Tample and Jeanne Prinseaud. His wife was Marie DuBosc. They were naturalized in South Carolina ca. 1696. [Compare the entry of Etiene Tampie.]

Tampleran, Jean. He was naturalized in Jamaica 6 Sep. 1731.

Tanner, Jacob. He was naturalized in Nova Scotia 5 July 1758.

Tanner, Michael. He was naturalized in Maryland 12 Sep. 1764. He was a German.

Tannewolf, Jacob Frederick. He was naturalized in Maryland 16 Apr. 1760. He was from Frederick, Maryland.

Tappan, Christian. He was naturalized in Pennsylvania 11–13 Apr. 1743. He was from Lancaster County.

Tasht, Jacob. He was naturalized in Pennsylvania 10 & 23 Apr. 1764. He was from Marlborough Township, Philadelphia County.

Tatwiler, Jacob. He was naturalized in Pennsylvania 11–13 Apr. 1743. He was from Bucks County.

Tausehek, Casper. He was naturalized in New York 20 Mar. 1762.

Tauvron, Estienne. He was born at L'Isle de Re, France, the son of Jacques Tauvron and Marie Brigeaud. His children were Madeleine Tauvron born at L'Isle de Re, France and Ester Tauvron born at Plymouth, Massachusetts. They were naturalized in South Carolina ca. 1696.

Tauvron, Marie. She was born at L'Isle of Re, France, the daughter of Jacques Tauvron and Marie Brigeaud. Her son was Moyse LeBreun. They were naturalized in South Carolina ca. 1696. Her husband was Moyse LeBreun.

Tavares, David. He was naturalized in Jamaica 7 May 1716.

Tavares, David, Jr. He was naturalized in Jamaica 4 Feb. 1746/7.

Tawers, John. He was naturalized in Maryland 3 May 1704. He lived in Cecil County. He also appeared as John Jawart, John Jeaurt, and John Jawert.

Taxstieder, Jury. He was naturalized in New York 3 Jan. 1715/6. He was from Albany County.

Taylor, Daniel. He was naturalized in Pennsylvania 24 Sep. 1766.

Taylor, John. He was naturalized in Pennsylvania 14 Feb. 1729/30. He was from Lancaster County.

Taylor, John. He was naturalized in Pennsylvania 24 Sep. 1759.

Taylor, Michael. He was naturalized in Maryland 29 Nov. 1774. He was a German.

Taymist, John. He was naturalized in Pennsylvania 24–25 Sep. 1764. He was from Lower Milford Township, Bucks County.

Tayne, Isacq. He expressed his desire to be naturalized in New Castle County, Delaware 21 Feb. 1682/3.

Teal, Christian. He was naturalized in Maryland 14 Sep. 1763. He was a German.

Teaser, Peter. He was naturalized in Maryland 21 Sep. 1764. He was a German.

Teetz, John Frederick. He was naturalized in Pennsylvania 11 Apr. 1763. He was from Philadelphia.

Tegarden, William. He was naturalized in Maryland 11 Sep. 1765.

Teller, Benjamin. He was naturalized in Jamaica 9 Oct. 1706.

Tellez, Isaac. He was naturalized in Jamaica 16 Aug. 1694.

Tellez, Jacob. He was naturalized in Jamaica 5 Jan. 1694/5.

Tellieur, Jacob. He was endenized in New York 25 Sep. 1685.

Telp, George. He was naturalized in Pennsylvania 24 Sep. 1756.

Templeman, Conrad. He was naturalized in Pennsylvania 11–13 Apr. 1743. He was from Lancaster County.

Tenbrock, Wessell. He took the oath of naturalization in New York 1 Sep. 1687 in Ulster County.

Ten Broeck, Dirk Wessels. He was naturalized in New York 14 Feb. 1715/6. He was from Albany County.

Tendler, John. He was naturalized in Pennsylvania 24 Sep. 1760. He was from Lancaster County.

TenEyck, Coenraut. He took the oath to the King 21–26 Oct. 1664 after the conquest of New Netherland.

Tenni, Jacob. He was naturalized in New York 17 Oct. 1749. He was a cartman from New York City.

Terhuen, Jan Albertse. He took the oath of allegiance in Flackland, Kings County, New York 26–30 Sep. 1687. He was a native of the colony.

Terriot, Bonaventure. He took the oath of allegiance at Port Royal, Nova Scotia 16 Aug. 1695.

Terriot, Charles. He was an Acadian and took the oath of allegiance in Apr. 1730.

Terriot, Charles. He was an Acadian and took the oath of allegiance in Apr. 1730.

Terriot, Claude. He took the oath of allegiance at Port Royal, Nova Scotia 16 Aug. 1695.

Terriot, Claude. He was an Acadian and took the oath to the King at the Mines, Pisiquit, Nova Scotia 31 Oct. 1727.

Terriot, Claude. He was an Acadian and took the oath of allegiance in Apr. 1730.

Terriot, Claude. He was an Acadian and took the oath of allegiance in Apr. 1730.

Terriot, Claude. He was an Acadian and took the oath of allegiance in Apr. 1730.

Terriot, Francois. He was an Acadian and took the oath of allegiance in Apr. 1730.

Terriot, Francois. He was an Acadian and took the oath of allegiance in Apr. 1730.

Terriot, Germain, Sr. He was an Acadian and took the oath to the King at the Mines, Pisiquit, Nova Scotia 31 Oct. 1727.

Terriot, Germain. He was an Acadian and took the oath of allegiance in Apr. 1730.

Terriot, Germain. He was an Acadian and took the oath of allegiance in Apr. 1730.

Terriot, Jacques. He was an Acadian and took the oath to the King at the Mines, Pisiquit, Nova Scotia 31 Oct. 1727.

Terriot, Jacques. He was an Acadian and took the oath of allegiance in Apr. 1730.

Terriot, Jean. He was the son of Jean Terriot. He was an Acadian and took the oath to the King at the Mines, Pisiquit, Nova Scotia 31 Oct. 1727.

Terriot, Jean. He was an Acadian and took the oath to the King at the Mines, Pisiquit, Nova Scotia 31 Oct. 1727.

Terriot, Jean. He was an Acadian and took the oath to the King at the Mines, Pisiquit, Nova Scotia 31 Oct. 1727.

Terriot, Jean. He was an Acadian and took the oath of allegiance in Apr. 1730.

Terriot, Jean. He was an Acadian and took the oath of allegiance in Apr. 1730.

Terriot, Jean. He was an Acadian and took the oath of allegiance in Apr. 1730.

Terriot, Jean. He was an Acadian and took the oath of allegiance in Apr. 1730.

Terriot, Jean. He was an Acadian and took the oath of allegiance in Apr. 1730.

Terriot, Jermain. He was an Acadian and took the oath of allegiance in Apr. 1730.

Terriot, Joseph. He was an Acadian and took the oath to the King at the Mines, Pisiquit, Nova Scotia 31 Oct. 1727.

Terriot, Joseph. He was an Acadian and took the oath of allegiance in Apr. 1730.

Terriot, Joseph. He was an Acadian and took the oath of allegiance in Apr. 1730.

Terriot, Pierre. He was an Acadian and took the oath of allegiance in Apr. 1730.

Terriot, Pierre. He was an Acadian and took the oath of allegiance in Apr. 1730.

Terro, Jacob, Jr. He was naturalized in New York by the act of 1740. He was a Jew from Ulster County.

Terse, Augustin. He was naturalized in Jamaica 9 June 1753.

Ter Willegen, Jan. He was naturalized in New York 8–9 Sep. 1715. He was from Ulster County.

Tesschemaker, Petrus. He expressed his desire to be naturalized in New Castle County, Delaware 21 Feb. 1682/3.

Tesson, Marie. She was naturalized in New York 6 Dec. 1746.

Tesson, Nicholas. He was naturalized in New York 6 Dec. 1746.

Tetard, John Peter. He was naturalized in New York 21 Apr. 1762. He was a clerk from New York City and a French Protestant.

Tetern, Sibald. He was naturalized in Pennsylvania 24 Sep. 1762. He was from Bucks County.

Teunizen, Jan. He took the oath to the King 21–26 Oct. 1664 after the conquest of New Netherland.

Texer, John. He was naturalized in Jamaica 24 Oct. 1719.

Thauvee, Andre. He was endenized in England 10 July 1696. He came to New York.

Thauvet, Marie Susanne. She was naturalized in New York 6 Mar. 1715/6. She was a widow from New Rochelle.

Theil, John. He was naturalized in New York 11 Sep. 1761.

Theil, Philipp. He was naturalized in Maryland 9 Apr. 1760. He lived in Baltimore, Maryland.

Thelaball, James. He was naturalized in Virginia 28 Nov. 1683. He was born in France.

Theriate, Dominick. He was naturalized in Virginia 20 Sep. 1763.

Therousde, Jacob. He petitioned to be naturalized in New York 19 Aug. 1687.

Therunet, Andre. He petitioned to be naturalized in New York 19 Aug. 1687.

Theunisen, Jan. He took the oath of allegiance in Breucklijn, Kings County, New York 26–30 Sep. 1687. He was a native of the colony.

Theunissen, Denijs. He took the oath of allegiance in Flackbush, Kings County, New York 26–30 Sep. 1687. He was a native of the colony.

Thevou, Abraham. He was naturalized in New York 8–9 Sep. 1715. He was from Ulster County.

Thevou, Daniel. He was naturalized in New York 8–9 Sep. 1715. He was from Ulster County.

Thibaudeau, Pierre. He took the oath of allegiance at Port Royal, Nova Scotia 16 Aug. 1695.

Thibodeau, Claude. He was an Acadian who took the oath of allegiance at Annapolis River in Dec. 1729.

Thibodeau, Michel. He was an Acadian who took the oath of allegiance at Annapolis River in Dec. 1729.

Thibodeau, Jean Baptiste. He was an Acadian who took the oath of allegiance at Annapolis River in Dec. 1729.

Thibodo, Antoine. He was an Acadian and took the oath of allegiance in Apr. 1730.

Thibodo, Paul. He was an Acadian and took the oath of allegiance in Apr. 1730.

Thibodo, Pierre. He was an Acadian and took the oath of allegiance in Apr. 1730.

Thibodo, Rene. He was an Acadian and took the oath of allegiance in Apr. 1730.

Thibou, Louis. He was born at Orleans, France, the son of Jean Thibou and Marie Callard. His wife was Charlotte Mariette. Their children were Louis Thibou and Charlotte Thibou born in Paris, France; Jacob Thibou and Louise Thibou born in South Carolina; Gabrielle Thibou born in London, England; and Isaac Thibou born in New York. They were naturalized in South Carolina 10 Mar. 1696/7. He was a merchant. He also appeared as Lewis Thisbou.

Thies, Michael. He was naturalized in Pennsylvania 24 Sep. 1757.

Thilbeaurt, Jean. He was naturalized in Virginia 12 May 1705.

Thom, Henrick. He was naturalized in Maryland 11 Sep. 1765. He was a German from Frederick County.

Thoma, Durst. He was naturalized in Pennsylvania 11 Apr. 1761. He was from Lancaster County.

Thomas, Andries. He was naturalized in New York 8–9 Sep. 1715. He was from Ulster County.

Thomas, Christian. He and his son, Henry Thomas, were naturalized in Maryland 3 May 1740. He was from Prince George's County and was born in Germany.

Thomas, Christian. He was naturalized in Pennsylvania 11 Jan. 1683. He was formerly from New Sweden.

Thomas, Dorst. He was naturalized in Pennsylvania 10 Sep. 1761. He was from Lancaster County.

Thomas, Frederick. He was naturalized in Maryland 17 July 1765. He was a German.

Thomas, Hans Jury. He was naturalized in New York 22 Nov. 1715. He was from Albany County.

Thomas, Hendrick. He was naturalized in Maryland 3 May 1740. He was from Prince George's County and was born in Germany.

Thomas, Jean. He was born at St. Jean d'Angeley, St. Onge, France, the son of Jean Thomas and Anne Dupon. He was naturalized in South Carolina ca. 1696.

Thomas, Johan Stoffel. He was naturalized in New York 8–9 Sep. 1715. He was from Ulster County.

Thomas, Johannes. He was naturalized in Pennsylvania 24 Sep. 1753. He was from Lancaster County.

Thomas, John. He was naturalized in South Carolina 10 Mar. 1696/7.

Thomas, John. He was naturalized in Virginia 12 May 1705.

Thomas, John. He was naturalized in Orange County, Virginia 28 Jan. 1742/3. He was a native of Nieuberg, Bishopric of Speyer, Germany.

Thomas, John. He was naturalized in Maryland 17 Apr. 1759.

Thomas, Mathieu. He was naturalized in New York 6 Dec. 1746.

Thomas, Michael. He was naturalized in Maryland in Apr. 1749. He was from Frederick County.

Thomas, Valentine. He was naturalized in Maryland 17 Apr. 1759.

Thomassen, Oele. He was naturalized in New Castle County, Delaware 21 Feb. 1682/3. He also appeared as Oliver Thomassen.

Thomour, John. He was naturalized in London. He was the son of Peter Thomour and his wife Mary. He was born in Rochelle, France. His certificate was recorded in Jamaica in 1707.

Thompson, Cornelius. He was naturalized in New Jersey 30 Nov. 1723. He was born in the Duchy of Holelsein [?Holstein].

Thompson, Martha. She was naturalized in Jamaica 20 Sep. 1737. She was a free Negro.

Thopf, Deitrick. He was naturalized in Pennsylvania 24 Sep. 1762. He was from Lancaster County.

Thorian, Scher. He was naturalized in Lunenburg County, Virginia 1 Sep. 1746.

Thoroulde, Dorotia. He was endenized in New York 14 June 1686.

Thoroulde, Jacob. He was endenized in New York 14 June 1686.

Thoroulde, Marianne. She was endenized in New York 15 June 1686.

Thyssen, Hendrick. He took the oath of allegiance in Breucklijn, Kings County, New York 26–30 Sep. 1687. He had been in the colony 21 years.

Thyssen, Pieter. He took the oath of allegiance in New Uijtrceht, Kings County, New York 26–30 Sep. 1687. He was a native of the colony.

Tibaudo, Alexandre. He was an Acadian and took the oath to the King at the Mines, Pisiquit, Nova Scotia 31 Oct. 1727.

Tibaudo, Antoine. He was an Acadian and took the oath to the King at the Mines, Pisiquit, Nova Scotia 31 Oct. 1727.

Tibaudo, Jean. He was an Acadian and took the oath to the King at the Mines, Pisiquit, Nova Scotia 31 Oct. 1727.

Tibaudo, Jean Batiste. He was an Acadian and took the oath to the King at the Mines, Pisiquit, Nova Scotia 31 Oct. 1727.

Tibaudo, Jean Baptiste. He was an Acadian and took the oath to the King at the Mines, Pisiquit, Nova Scotia 31 Oct. 1727.

Tibaudo, Rene. He was an Acadian and took the oath to the King at the Mines, Pisiquit, Nova Scotia 31 Oct. 1727.

Tibo, Louis. He was an Acadian and took the oath to George II at Annapolis River, Nova Scotia in Dec. 1729.

Tibodeau, Jean Baptiste. He was an Acadian and took the oath of allegiance in Apr. 1730.

Tibodo, Alexandre. He was an Acadian and took the oath of allegiance in Apr. 1730.

Tibodo, Antonie. He was an Acadian and took the oath to George II at Annapolis River, Nova Scotia in Dec. 1729.

Tibodo, Antoine. He was an Acadian and took the oath at Annapolis in 1729.

Tibodo, Antoine. He was an Acadian and took the oath of Annapolis in 1729.

Tibodo, Charles. He was an Acadian and took the oath of allegiance in Apr. 1730. He was the son of Jean Tibodo.

Tibodo, Entoine. He was an Acadian and took the oath to George II at Annapolis River, Nova Scotia in Dec. 1729.

Tibodo, Jean. He was an Acadian and took the oath of allegiance in Apr. 1730.

Tibodo, Jean. He was an Acadian and took the oath of allegiance in Apr. 1730.

Tibodo, Jean Baptist. He was an Acadian and took the oath to George II at Annapolis River, Nova Scotia in the winter of 1730.

Tibodo, J[ean] B[aptiste]. He was an Acadian and took the oath of allegiance in Apr. 1730.

Tibodo, J[ean] B[aptiste], Jr. He was an Acadian and took the oath of allegiance in Apr. 1730.

Tibodo, Jermain. He was an Acadian and took the oath of allegiance in Apr. 1730. He was the son of Francois Tibodo.

Tibodo, Joseph. He was an Acadian and took the oath of allegiance in Apr. 1730.

Tibodo, Pierre. He was an Acadian and took the oath to George II at Annapolis River, Nova Scotia in Dec. 1729.

Tibodo, Pierre. He was an Acadian and took the oath of allegiance in Apr. 1730.

Tibodo, Pierre. He was an Acadian and took the oath of allegiance in Apr. 1730.

Tibodo, Phillipe. He was an Acadian and took the oath of allegiance in Apr. 1730.

Tick, Conrad. He was naturalized in Maryland 10 Apr. 1762. He was a German from Anne Arundel County.

Tick, William. He was naturalized in Maryland 6 June 1674. He was born in Amsterdam, Holland.

Ticke, William. He was made a denizen in Maryland 19 Apr. 1669. He was late of Amsterdam, Holland.

Tickel, Michael. He was naturalized in Maryland 11 Sep. 1765.

Tickensheets, William. He was naturalized in Maryland 11 Sep. 1765.

Tiedeman, Jacobus. He was naturalized in New York 24 Nov. 1750.

Tiefenbach, Michael. He was naturalized in Maryland 12 Sep. 1759. He lived in Baltimore, Maryland.

Tiefendorph, Jacob. He was naturalized in New York 3 May 1755.

Tiegel, William. He was naturalized in New York 31 Dec. 1768.

Tiel, Ananias. He was naturalized in New York 22 Nov. 1715. He was from Albany County.

Tiel, Asmus. He was naturalized in Nova Scotia 5 July 1758.

Tiel, John. He was naturalized in Nova Scotia 15 Sep. 1758.

Tiel, Martin. He was naturalized in New York 17 Jan. 1715/6. He was from Albany County.

Tier, Daniel. He was naturalized in New York 20 Apr. 1769. He was a cartman from New York City and a French Protestant.

Tierckse, Thomas. He took the oath of allegiance in New Uijtrceht, Kings County, New York 26–30 Sep. 1687. He had been in the colony 35 years.

Tiers, Daniel. He was naturalized in New York 21 Jan. 1762. He was a laborer from New York City and a French Protestant.

Tiers, John Henry. He was naturalized in New York 22 Apr. 1761. He was a laborer from New York City and a French Protestant.

Tiers, Magdalen. She was naturalized in New York 21 Jan. 1762. She was a spinster from New York City. She was a French Protestant.

Tiers, Mathew. He was naturalized in New York 21 Jan. 1762. He was a blacksmith from New York City and a French Protestant.

Tik, Nicholas. He was naturalized in Pennsylvania 11 Apr. 1763. He was from Berks County.

Tilheaver, Michael. He was naturalized in New Jersey 9 Dec. 1744.

Tiller, Caspar. He was naturalized in Pennsylvania 19 May 1739. He was from Lancaster County.

Tilling, Casper. He was naturalized in Pennsylvania 10 Sep. 1761. He was from Lancaster County.

Tillingen, George. He was naturalized in Maryland 13 Apr. 1763. He was a German from Frederick County.

Tillinger, Lodowick. He was naturalized in Pennsylvania 24 Sep. 1759.

Tillon, Vincent. He was endenized in England 3 July 1701. He came to New York.

Tillou, Peter. He, his wife Anne Tillon, and children Suzanna Tillon, Francis Tillon, and John Tillon, and kinswoman were endenized in England 14 Oct. 1681. He petitioned to be naturalized in New York in 1691. He was a French Protestant. Both spellings of the surname appear in the records.

Timanus, Jacob. He was naturalized in Pennsylvania 10 Apr. 1755. He was from Philadelphia.

Timberman, Conrad. He was naturalized in Pennsylvania 11 Apr. 1749. He was from Philadelphia County.

Timberman, Mathias. He was naturalized in Maryland 14 Sep. 1763. He was a German.

Timmer, Thomas. He was naturalized in New York 20 Sep. 1728.

Timmerman, Henry. He was naturalized in New York 31 July 1771. He was a mason from Albany County.

Timmerman, Jacob. He was naturalized in New York 3 Jan. 1715/6. He was from Albany County.

Timmerman, Nicholas. He was naturalized in New York 19 Dec. 1766.

Timmor, Wiet. He was naturalized in New York 8 Nov. 1735.

Tinker, Peter. He was naturalized in North Carolina 22 Sep. 1763. He was from Rowan County and was a German.

Tipolet, Mary Magdaline. She was naturalized in Maryland 8 Sep. 1772. She was a German.

Titlma, Johanna Sophia. She was naturalized in New York 6 July 1723. She was the widow of Jacobus Dekey, late of New York City.

Titmore, John. He was naturalized in Pennsylvania 24 Sep. 1759.

Tise, Matthias. He was naturalized in Pennsylvania 19 May 1739. He was from Lancaster County.

Tittenhoffer, Paul. He was naturalized in Pennsylvania 19 May 1739. He was from Lancaster County.

Tivanni, Antoni. He was naturalized in New York 12 July 1715. He was a periwig-maker.

Tobias, Christian. He was naturalized in New York 20 Dec. 1763.

Tobias, Christopher. He was naturalized in New York 31 Dec. 1761.

Tobias, Christopher. He was naturalized in New York 23 Jan. 1762. He was a Quaker yeoman from Queens County.

Tobias, Joseph. He was naturalized in South Carolina 26 Nov. 1741. He was a Jew.

Tobiassen, Theunis. He took the oath of allegiance in Breucklijn, Kings County, New York 26–30 Sep. 1687. He was a native of the colony.

Tobie, Yost. He was naturalized in Pennsylvania 11 Apr. 1761. He was from Berks County.

Toersen, Oele. He was naturalized in New Castle County, Delaware 21 Feb. 1682/3.

Tofelor, Peter. He was naturalized in Maryland 18 July 1759.

Toffeller, George. He was naturalized in Maryland 11 Apr. 1764. He was a German.

Toftman, Martin. He was naturalized in Maryland 11 Sep. 1765. He was a German from Frederick County.

Toil, Philip. He was naturalized in Maryland 10 Sep. 1760.

Tolle, John Frederick. He was naturalized in New York 27 Jan. 1770.

Tom, Michael. He was naturalized in Maryland 29 Nov. 1774. He was a German.

Toms, Catharine. She was naturalized in Pennsylvania 24–29 Sep. 1768. She was from Frederick County, Maryland.

Tomy, Martin. He was naturalized in Pennsylvania 10 Apr. 1758.

Tonneau, Abraham. He petitioned to be naturalized in New York in 1691. He was a French Protestant.

Tonneman, Pieter. He took the oath to the King 21–26 Oct. 1664 after the conquest of New Netherland.

Toopes, Henry. He was naturalized in Pennsylvania 24 Sep. 1753. He was from Lancaster County.

Tordine, Henry. He was naturalized in Maryland in Apr. 1749. He was from Frederick County.

Toreson, Andrew. He was made a denizen in Maryland 22 July 1661. He was Swedish and was late of New Amstel.

Toreward, Martin. He was naturalized in Pennsylvania 10 Apr. 1765. He was from Lancaster Township, Lancaster County.

Torez, Sarah Lopez. She was naturalized in Jamaica 26 Jan. 1703/4.

Torian, Scher. He was naturalized in Virginia 1 Sep. 1746. He was from Lunenburg County.

Torpel, Gottfried. He was naturalized in Nova Scotia 5 July 1758.

Torquett, Humphrey. He was naturalized in South Carolina 10 Mar. 1696/7. He was a shipwright.

Torquett, Paul. He was naturalized in South Carolina 10 Mar. 1696/7. He was a shipwright.

Torres, Abraham Lopez. He was naturalized in Jamaica 18 Jan. 1753.

Torres, David. He was naturalized in Jamaica 26 Feb. 1740/1. He was a Jew.

Torres, Jacob. He was naturalized in Jamaica 1 July 1730.

Torres, Jacob Lopez. He was naturalized in Jamaica 28 July 1684.

Torres, Rachael. She was naturalized in Jamaica 22 Nov. 1735. She was the wife of Jacob Torres, a merchant.

Torres, Reina. She was naturalized in Jamaica 28 Feb. 1743/4. She was a Jewess.

Tossen, Lasse Oesen. He was naturalized in New Castle County, Delaware 21 Feb. 1682/3.

Tossen, Mathias Laersen. He expressed his desire to be naturalized in New Castle County, Delaware 21 Feb. 1682/3.

Tossen, Oele Oelsen. He was naturalized in New Castle County, Delaware 21 Feb. 1682/3.

Toulon, Nicholas. He was naturalized in New York 18 Jan. 1764. He was a mariner from New Rochelle, Westchester County and a French Protestant.

Toulson, Andrew. He was naturalized in Maryland 19 Apr. 1671. He lived in Baltimore County and was Swedish.

Tour, Lucien. He was an Acadian and took the oath to George II at Annapolis River, Nova Scotia in the winter of 1730.

Toura, Moses. He was naturalized in Jamaica 3 Feb. 1684/5.

Tournier, Stephen. He was naturalized in Virginia 12 May 1705.

Touro, Abraham. He was naturalized in Jamaica 20 Feb. 1703/4.

Touro, Issac. He was naturalized in Jamaica 22 Feb. 1702.

Touro, John. He was naturalized in Jamaica 23 Feb. 1720/1.

Touro, Rachell. She was naturalized in Jamaica 10 May 1709.

Tourtelot, Abraham. He and his children James Tourtelot, Jacob Tourtelot, Moses Tourtelot, and John Tourtelot were endenized in England 16 Dec. 1687. They came to Massachusetts.

Touton, Jean. He came to Virginia in 1662 and was endenized there. He sought citizenship in Massachusetts 29 June 1687. He was born in France.

Towenhower, Godfried. He was naturalized in Pennsylvania 24–25 Sep. 1764. He was from Coventry Township, Chester County.

Towgood, Samuel. He was a mariner and died in Jamaica. He gave his estate to two sons, Robert Towgood and John Towgood who were infants. The two sons were declared naturalized in the event that there would be any dispute about their place of nativity. They were naturalized in Jamaica 9 June 1732.

Trable, Moses. He was naturalized in Pennsylvania 11 Apr. 1761 He was from Philadelphia.

Trabueq, Anthony. He was naturalized in Virginia 12 May 1705.

Tracsler, Jeremiah. He was naturalized in Pennsylvania 11 Apr. 1752. He was from Bucks County.

Tracy, Nathaniel. He was naturalized in Northumberland County, Virginia 17 Sep. 1656. He was born in Rotterdam, Holland, son of John Tracy.

Tracy, Richard. He was naturalized in Northumberland County, Virginia 17 Sep. 1656. He was born in Rotterdam, Holland, son of John Tracy.

Tracy, Stephen. He was naturalized in Northumberland County, Virginia 17 Sep. 1656. He was born in Rotterdam, Holland, son of John Tracy.

Trahan, Alexandre. He was an Acadian and took the oath of allegiance in Apr. 1730. He was styled "captain."

Trahan, Alexandre. He was an Acadian and took the oath of allegiance in Apr. 1730.

Trahan, Charles. He was an Acadian and took the oath of allegiance in Apr. 1730.

Trahan, Etien. He was an Acadian and took the oath of allegiance in Apr. 1730.

Trahan, Etienne. He was an Acadian and took the oath to George II at the Mines, Pisiquit 31 Oct. 1727.

Trahan, Francois. He was an Acadian and took the oath to George II at the Mines, Pisiquit 31 Oct. 1727.

Trahan, Francois. He was an Acadian and took the oath of allegiance in Apr. 1730.

Trahan, Guillaume. He was an Acadian and took the oath to George II at the Mines, Pisiquit 31 Oct. 1727.

Trahan, Guillaume. He was an Acadian and took the oath of allegiance in Apr. 1730.

Trahan, Jean. He was an Acadian and took the oath to George II at the Mines, Pisiquit 31 Oct. 1727.

Trahan, Jean. He was an Acadian and took the oath of allegiance in Apr. 1730.

Trahan, Jean. He was an Acadian and took the oath of allegiance in Apr. 1730.

Trahan, Jean. He was an Acadian and took the oath of allegiance in Apr. 1730.

Trahan, Jean Baptiste. He was an Acadian and took the oath of allegiance in Apr. 1730.

Trahan, Joseph. He was an Acadian and took the oath of allegiance in Apr. 1730.

Trahan, Joseph. He was an Acadian and took the oath of allegiance in Apr. 1730.

Trahan, Joseph. He was an Acadian and took the oath of allegiance in Apr. 1730.

Trahan, Paul. He was an Acadian and took the oath of allegiance in Apr. 1730.

Trahan, Pierre. He was an Acadian and took the oath to George II at the Mines, Pisiquit 31 Oct. 1727.

Trahan, Pierre. He was an Acadian and took the oath of allegiance in Apr. 1730.

Trahan, Pierre. He was an Acadian and took the oath of allegiance in Apr. 1730.

Trahan, Rene. He was an Acadian and took the oath of allegiance in Apr. 1730.

Trajer, George. He was naturalized in Maryland 13 Sep. 1770. He was a German from Baltimore County.

Tranberg, Peter. He was naturalized in New Jersey in 1739. He was born in Sweden.

Traphager, Hendrick. He took the oath of naturalization in New York 1 Sep. 1687 in Ulster County.

Traphager, Johanas. He took the oath of naturalization in New York 1 Sep. 1687 in Ulster County.

Traphager, William, Jr. He took the oath of naturalization in New York 1 Sep. 1687 in Ulster County.

Trapp, Philip. He was naturalized in Pennsylvania 11 Apr. 1761. He was from Northampton County.

Trautman, John. He was naturalized in Pennsylvania 25 Sep. 1751. He was from Lancaster County.

Trautman, Michael. He was naturalized in Maryland 7 May 1767. He was a German from Frederick County.

Traverrie, Peter. He was endenized in New York 22 July 1695.

Traxel, Johan Peter. He was naturalized in Pennsylvania 26 Sep. 1748. He was from Bucks County.

Traxell, Daniel. He was naturalized in Pennsylvania 11 Apr. 1761. He was from Northampton County.

Traxell, John Nicholas. He was naturalized in Pennsylvania 11 Apr. 1761. He was from Northampton County.

Traxell, Michael. He was naturalized in Pennsylvania 11 Apr. 1761. He was from Northampton County.

Treber, Anton. He was naturalized in Nova Scotia 5 July 1758.

Treber, John. He was naturalized in Pennsylvania 11 Apr. 1761. He was from Lancaster County.

Treber, Nicholas. He was naturalized in Pennsylvania 11 Apr. 1761. He was from Lancaster County.

Treichel, Elias Lewis. He was naturalized in Pennsylvania 10 Apr. 1767. He was from Philadelphia.

Tremble, Jean. He was endenized in New York in Oct. 1697. He was a French Protestant.

Trencle, Christopher. He was naturalized in Pennsylvania 25 Sep. 1750. He was from Lancaster County.

Tresnac, Matis. He took the oath of allegiance at Mobile, West Florida 2 Oct. 1764.

Tressler, David. He was naturalized in Pennsylvania 10 Sep. 1761. He was from Lancaster County.

Tressly, George. He was naturalized in Pennsylvania 10 Apr. 1767. He was from Lower Dublin Township, Philadelphia County.

Trevor, Johan Peter. He was naturalized in New York 8–9 Sep. 1715. He was from Ulster County.

Trewbey, Christopher. He was naturalized in Pennsylvania 25–27 Sep. 1740. He was from Bucks County.

Trexler, Peter. He was naturalized in Pennsylvania 6 Feb. 1730/1. He was from Philadelphia County.

Trezevant, Daniel. He was the son of Theodore Trezevant and Susanne Menou and was born at Authon, Perche, France. His wife was Susanne Maulard who was born at Chanseville, Basse, France, the daughter of Lubin Maulard and Gabrielle Berou. They were naturalized in South Carolina 10 Mar. 1696/7. He was a weaver.

Trezevant, Daniel. He was the son of Daniel Trezevant and Susanne Maulard and was born at Menthenon, Gaule, France. He was naturalized in South Carolina 10 Mar. 1696/7. He was a weaver.

Tribblebess, Jacob. He was naturalized in Pennsylvania 24 Sep. 1760. He was from Berks County.

Tricktenhengst, Johannes. He was naturalized in Pennsylvania 24 Sep. 1741. He was from Philadelphia County.

Triel, Jacques. He took the oath of allegiance at Port Royal, Nova Scotia 16 Aug. 1695.

Trigueul, Pierre. He was an Acadian and took the oath of allegiance in Apr. 1730.

Triller, William. He sought naturalization in New Jersey in the 18th century.

Trimmer, Johannes. He was naturalized in New Jersey 8 Dec. 1744.

Trimmer, Matthias. He was naturalized in New Jersey 8 Dec. 1744.

Trimper, George. He was naturalized in New York 3 May 1755.

Trinmer, Andrew. He was naturalized in New Jersey 20 Aug. 1755.

Tristan, Simon. He was endenized in London 20 Mar. 2 James II. He came to Massachusetts.

Tristan, Simon. He was naturalized in Jamaica 13 Feb. 1701/2.

Trois, David Nunis. He was naturalized in Jamaica in Feb. 1748/9. He was a Jew.

Trois, Ester Nunes. She was naturalized in Jamaica 28 Nov. 1749. She was a Jew.

Trollett, Michael. He was naturalized in Rhode Island in Oct. 1752. He was a merchant in Newport and was a Protestant.

Trombouer, Andreas. He was naturalized in Pennsylvania 19 May 1739. He was from Philadelphia County.

Trombouer, Jacob. He was naturalized in Pennsylvania 19 May 1739. He was from Philadelphia County.

Trompoor, Johanis Jacob. He was naturalized in New York 8–9 Sep. 1715. He was from Ulster County.

Trompoor, Nicolas. He was naturalized in New York 8–9 Sep. 1715. He was from Ulster County.

Trone, George. He was naturalized in Pennsylvania 10 Sep. 1761. He was from York County.

Trouillart, Laurent Philippe. He was naturalized in South Carolina *ca.* 1698. He was born at Fette, Regnault Roidam, the son of Pierre and Marie Trouillart; his wife was Madeleine Maslet or Madeleine Masset who was born in the same place; their daughters Elizabet Trouillart and Madeleine Trouillart were born in South Carolina. His father was professor of theology.

Trout, Hendrick. He and his son, Jacob Trout, were naturalized in Maryland 3 May 1740. He was from Prince George's County and was born in Germany.

Troutman, Leonard. He was naturalized in Maryland 15 Apr. 1761. He was a German.

Troutman, George. He was naturalized in Pennsylvania 10–12 Apr. 1762. He was from Lancaster County.

Troutman, Peter. He was naturalized in Maryland 24 Sep. 1765.

Troxle, Abraham. He was naturalized in Maryland 5 May 1768. He was a German from Frederick County.

Troys, Hannah. She was naturalized in Jamaica 8 Sep. 1717. She was the wife of Jacob Troys.

Truby, Andries. He was naturalized in New York 6 July 1723.

Truckenmiller, John. He was naturalized in Pennsylvania 11 Apr. 1763. He was from Philadelphia.

Truckenmiller, Sebastian. He was naturalized in Pennsylvania 11 Apr. 1763. He was from Upper Milford Township, Northampton County.

Truell, Philip. He was naturalized in Maryland 10 May 1774. He was a German.

Trumbole, Andrew. He was naturalized in Pennsylvania in Sep. 1740. He was from Philadelphia County.

Trumper, Harmanus. He was naturalized in New York 21 Apr. 1769. He was a farmer from Orange County.

Tryer, Frederick. He was naturalized in Maryland 9 Sep. 1761. He was from Frederick County.

Tshoudee, Winebert. He was naturalized in Pennsylvania 10 Apr. 1760.

Tubben, Henry. He was naturalized in Pennsylvania 29 Sep. 1709. He was from Philadelphia County.

Tuchman, Stephen. He was naturalized in Maryland 15 Sep. 1762. He was from Baltimore County.

Tuchmannus, Peter. He was naturalized in Maryland 15 Sep. 1758. He had come from Alsace eight years ago.

Tueter, Daniel. He was naturalized in New York 31 July 1765. He was a silversmith from New York City.

Tule, John Godfried. He was naturalized in Pennsylvania 11 Apr. 1763. He was from Northern Liberties Township, Philadelphia County.

Tull, Pieter Pieterse. He took the oath of allegiance in Flackland, Kings County, New York 26–30 Sep. 1687. He had been in the colony 30 years.

Tundell, George. He was naturalized in New York 16 Feb. 1771.

Tunies, Jury. He took the oath of naturalization in New York 1 Sep. 1687 in Ulster County.

Tunis, Arrian. He took the oath of naturalization in New York 1 Sep. 1687 in Ulster County.

Tunis, Abraham. He was naturalized in Pennsylvania 29 Sep. 1709. He was from Philadelphia County.

Tunis, Claes. He took the oath of naturalization in New York 1 Sep. 1687 in Ulster County.

Tups, Oswal. He was naturalized in Maryland 11 Sep. 1765.

Turck, Isaac. He was endenized in London 25 Aug. 1708. He also appeared as Isaac Zurck. He came to New York.

Turner, Anne. He was naturalized in Jamaica 15 Aug. 1709.

Turner, George. He was naturalized in Maryland 15 Apr. 1761.

Turner, John. He was naturalized in Maryland 15 Sep. 1761. He was from Frederick County.

Turner, Katherine. She was naturalized in Jamaica 28 Jan. 1700. She was a widow.

Turner, Thomas. He was naturalized in Maryland 19 Apr. 1671. He lived in Anne Arundel County and was born in Middlebourgh, Province of Zealand.

Turpin, Jean. He was an Acadian and took the oath of allegiance in Apr. 1730.

Tusse, Jan. He was naturalized in New York 16 Aug. 1715. He was a yeoman from New Rochelle.

Tutwieler, John. He was naturalized in Pennsylvania 10 Sep. 1761. He was from Lancaster County.

Tuymen, Hermann. He was naturalized in Pennsylvania 29 Sep. 1709. He was from Philadelphia County.

Tyler, Andries. He took the oath to the King 21–26 Oct. 1664 after the conquest of New Netherland.

Tyler, John Baptist. He was naturalized in Maryland 19 Apr. 1706. He lived in Prince George's County. He was Dutch.

Tyler, William. He took the oath to the King 21–26 Oct. 1664 after the conquest of New Netherland.

Tymot, Juryan. He was naturalized in New York 8–9 Sep. 1715. He was from Ulster County.

Tynges, Jacob. He was naturalized in New York 8 Mar. 1773.

Tysen, Matthias. He was naturalized in Pennsylvania 29 Sep. 1709. He was from Philadelphia County.

Tyson, Reinier. He was naturalized in Pennsylvania 29 Sep. 1709. He was from Philadelphia County.

Tysse, Peter. He was naturalized in Pennsylvania 11 Apr. 1761. He was from Northampton County.

Tzoller, John. He was naturalized in Pennsylvania 24–25 Sep. 1764. He was from Hannover Township, Philadelphia County.

Tzyle, John. He was naturalized in Pennsylvania 11 Apr. 1763. He was from Lancaster Township, Lancaster County.

Ubben, Barnard. He was made a denizen in Maryland 17 Feb. 1662. He was Dutch. He brought his wife and children with him.

Uhl, Christian Reinhart. He was naturalized in Pennsylvania 10 Apr. 1760.

Uhland, John Frederick. He was naturalized in Pennsylvania 10 Sep. 1761. He was from Philadelphia County.

Uhle, Christopher. He was naturalized in Orange County, Virginia 28 Jan. 1742/3. He was born in Wurttemburg. He had been in the colony seven years.

Uhler, Anastasius. He was naturalized in Pennsylvania 10 Sep. 1761. He was from Lancaster County.

Uhler, Valentine. He was naturalized in Pennsylvania 24 Sep. 1762. He was from Northampton County.

Uhlum, Jacob. He was naturalized in Pennsylvania 24 Sep. 1762. He was from Philadelphia County.

Uin, Helias. He was naturalized in New York 8–9 Sep. 1715. He was from Ulster County.

Ulderey, Stephen. He and his children, Stephen Ulderey, George Ulderey, Daniel Ulderey, John Ulderey, Elizabeth Ulderey, and Susanna Ulderey, were naturalized in Maryland 4 June 1738. He was from Baltimore County and was born in Germany.

Uler, Deter. He was naturalized in Pennsylvania 10 Apr. 1760.

Ulius, Henry. He was naturalized in Pennsylvania 10–12 Apr. 1762. He was from York County.

Ullendorf, Charles. He was naturalized in Pennsylvania 24 Sep. 1762. He was from Northampton County.

Ulman, Melger. He was naturalized in Nova Scotia 10 July 1758. [His forename was Melchior.]

Ulmer, Christian. He was naturalized in Jamaica 21 May 1736. He was an organist.

Ulrich, Caspar. He was naturalized in Pennsylvania 29 Mar. 1735. He was from Philadelphia.

Ulrich, George. He was naturalized in Pennsylvania 24–25 Sep. 1764. He was from Heidelberg Township, Lancaster County.

Ulrich, Matheus. He was naturalized in Maryland 11 Apr. 1759.

Ulrich, Peter. He was naturalized in Maryland 13 Sep. 1758.

Ulrich, Peter. He was naturalized in Pennsylvania 24 Sep. 1742. He was from Philadelphia County.

Ulrich, Philip. He was naturalized in Pennsylvania 24–25 Sep. 1764. He was from Blockley Township, Philadelphia County.

Ulrick, Frederick. He was naturalized in Pennsylvania 10 Apr. 1766. He was from Rockland Township, Berks County.

Ulrick, Jacob. He was naturalized in Maryland 15 Apr. 1772. He was a German.

Ulrick, Stephen. He was naturalized in Pennsylvania 25–27 Sep. 1740. He was from Philadelphia County.

Ulrick, Stephen. He was naturalized in Pennsylvania 10 Apr. 1767. He was from Frederick County, Maryland.

Umborne, Philip. He was naturalized in Pennsylvania 10 Sep. 1761. He was from Lancaster County.

Unander, Erick. He was naturalized in Pennsylvania 30 Nov. 1759. He was born in Sweden and was the minister of the Swedes congregation at Wilmington, Delaware. He had resided in the area eleven years.

Underkoffer, Jacob. He was naturalized in Pennsylvania 10 Apr. 1765. He was from Frederick Township, Philadelphia County.

Unfersaht, John. He was naturalized in Pennsylvania 10 Apr. 1758.

Ungefare, John Martin. He and his children, George Ungefare, Francis Ungefare, and Catherine Ungefare, were naturalized in Maryland 4 June 1738. He was from Baltimore County and was born in Germany.

Unger, Henry. He was naturalized in Maryland 10 Sep. 1760.

Ungerer, Henrick. He was naturalized in Maryland 9 Sep. 1761.

Ungne, Peter. He was admitted into the colony of Massachusetts 1 Feb. 1691. He was French.

Unrook, George. He was naturalized in Pennsylvania 19 May 1739. He was from Lancaster County.

Unruh, John. He was naturalized in Pennsylvania 11 Apr. 1763. He was from Bristol Township, Philadelphia County.

Unruw, Valentine. He was naturalized in Pennsylvania 11–12 Apr. 1744. He was from Lancaster County.

Unseld, Frederick. He was naturalized in Maryland in Apr. 1749.

Uplinger, Christian. He was naturalized in Pennsylvania 10 Sep. 1761. He was from Lancaster County.

Uplinger, Nicholas. He was naturalized in Pennsylvania 11–13 Apr. 1743. He was from Philadelphia County.

Upp, Philip. He was naturalized in Pennsylvania 11 Apr. 1761. He was from Lancaster County.

Urich, Valentine. He was naturalized in Pennsylvania 10–11 Apr. 1745. He was from Lancaster County.

Urinson, Cornelius. He was made a denizen in Maryland 22 July 1661. He was Swedish and was late of New Amstel.

Urinson, John. He was made a denizen in Maryland 22 July 1661. He was Swedish and was late of New Amstel.

Urledick, Valentine. He was naturalized in Pennsylvania 10–12 Apr. 1762. He was from Berks County.

Ury, Michael. He and his children were naturalized in Maryland 6 Nov. 1725. He lived in Prince George's County and was Greek.

Uselman, Valentine. He was naturalized in Maryland in Apr. 1749. He was from Frederick County.

Uslee, Petter Meinardeau. He promised allegiance to the King and obedience to William Penn in Pennsylvania 10 Sep. 1683.

Usler, Adam. He was naturalized in Nova Scotia 6 July 1758.

Usselman, Valentine. He was naturalized in Maryland 6 Sep. 1765. He was a German from Frederick County.

Ute, John. He was naturalized in New York 18 Oct. 1750. He was a butcher from New York City.

Utrz, Jacob. He was naturalized in New Jersey 8 Dec. 1744.

Uttrey, Jacob. He was naturalized in Pennsylvania 25–27 Sep. 1740. He was from Philadelphia.

Utz, Jacob. He was naturalized in New Jersey 31 Aug. 1757.

Vacois, Estienne. He was an Acadian who took the oath of allegiance 31 Oct. 1727.

Valandra, Peter. He was naturalized in Jamaica 24 May 1684.

Valck, Jan. He expressed his desire to be naturalized in New Castle County, Delaware 21 Feb. 1682/3.

Valck, Sybrant. He expressed his desire to be naturalized in New Castle County, Delaware 21 Feb. 1682/3.
Valckenburgh, Vallentyn. He was naturalized in New York 8–9 Sep. 1715.
Valentia, Abigail. She was naturalized in Jamaica 1 June 1744. She was a Jewess.
Valentia, David. He was naturalized in Jamaica 1 June 1744. He was a Jew.
Valentine, George. He was naturalized in Maryland 15 Sep. 1758. He came from Germany seven years ago.
Valescure, John. He was naturalized in Jamaica 2 Feb. 1706/7.
Vallade, Peter. He was naturalized in New York 21 Apr. 1762. He was a French Protestant merchant from New York City.
Vallarde, Mary Elizabeth. She was naturalized in New York 25 Nov. 1751.
Vallarde, Piere. He was naturalized in New York 25 Nov. 1751.
Valle, Jacob DeFonseca. He was naturalized in Jamaica 20 Aug. 1690.
Valleau, Isaias. He was naturalized in New York 6 July 1723.
Valleij, Jesely. He took the oath of naturalization in New York 1 Sep. 1687 in Ulster County.
Vallentine, Simon. He was naturalized in South Carolina 10 Mar. 1696/7. He was a merchant.
Vallet, Peter. He was naturalized in Jamaica 10 Aug. 1708.
Vallette, Elie. He was naturalized in Maryland 2 May 1764. He was a German.
Vallick, Martin. He was naturalized in Orange County, Virginia 28 Jan. 1742/3.
Vallos, Estienne. He petitioned to be naturalized in New York 19 Aug. 1687.
Valton, John. He was naturalized in Virginia 12 May 1705.
Valverde, Abraham. He was endenized in England 1 Feb. 1696. He settled in Barbados. He was also known as Abraham Green.
VanAcar, Marinos. He took the oath of naturalization in New York 1 Sep. 1687 in Ulster County.
VanAerts Daalen, Cornelis Simonsen. He took the oath of allegiance in Flackland, Kings County, New York 26–30 Sep. 1687. He was a native of the colony.
VanAerts Daalen, Simon Janse. He took the oath of allegiance in Flackland, Kings County, New York 26–30 Sep. 1687. He had been in the colony 34 years.
VanAken, Henry. He was naturalized in Pennsylvania 29 Mar. 1739. He was from Philadelphia.
VanAken, Marinus. He was naturalized in New York 8–9 Sep. 1715. He was from Ulster County.
Vanall, Matthew. He was naturalized in South Carolina 20 Jan. 1741/2.
Vanallen, Peter. He was naturalized in New Jersey 29 May 1756.
VanAma, Jochyam. He took the oath of naturalization in New York 1 Sep. 1687 in Ulster County.
VanAmach, Theunis Janse. He took the oath of allegiance in Flackland, Kings County, New York 26–30 Sep. 1687. He had been in the colony 14 years.
Vanbagh, George William. He was naturalized in New Jersey 20 Aug. 1755.
VanBebber, Matthias. He was naturalized in Pennsylvania 29 Sep. 1709. He was from Philadelphia County.
VanBeek, Gerrit Jansen. He was naturalized in New Castle County, Delaware 21 Feb. 1682/3.
Vanbell, Peter. He was a free denizen in St. Christopher 13 July 1699.
VanBeverhoudt, Adriaan. He took the oath of citizenship in Georgia on or before 6 Aug. 1754. He was late of St. Croix. He had three sons one of whom was John VanBeverhoudt. [Lucas VanBeverhoudt and Isebrandt may have been the names of the other two, but the record does not identify them.]
VanBeverhoudt, Berand Langemack. He was naturalized in New York 24 Nov. 1750.
VanBeverhoudt, Bertrand. He was naturalized in New York 24 Nov. 1750.
VanBeverhoudt, Claudius. He was naturalized in New York 24 Nov. 1750.
VanBeverhoudt, Johanes. He was naturalized in New York 24 Nov. 1750.
VanBeverhoudt, John. He took the oath of citizenship in Georgia on or before 6 Aug. 1754. He was late of St. Croix. He was the son of Adriaan VanBeverhoudt.
VanBeverhoudt, Margaret. She was naturalized in New York 24 Nov. 1750.
VanBiber, Isaac. He was naturalized in Maryland 25 Mar. 1702. He lived in Cecil County and was of Dutch parents.
VanBiber, Mathias. He was naturalized in Maryland 25 Mar. 1702. He lived in Cecil County and was of Dutch parents.
VanBueren, Willem Jacobs. He took the oath of allegiance in Flackbush, Kings County, New York 26–30 Sep. 1687. He had been in the colony 38 years.

VanBommel, Hendrick. He took the oath to the King 21–26 Oct. 1664 after the conquest of New Netherland.

VanBommel, Jan Hendrickzen. He took the oath to the King 21–26 Oct. 1664 after the conquest of New Netherland.

VanBorcklo, Jan Willemsen. He took the oath of allegiance in Gravens End, Kings County, New York 26–30 Sep. 1687. He was a native of the colony.

VanBosch, Jan Wouterse. He took the oath of allegiance in Flackbush, Kings County, New York 26–30 Sep. 1687.

VanBrent, Joost Rutsen. He took the oath of allegiance in New Uijtrceht, Kings County, New York 26–30 Sep. 1687. He was a native of the colony.

VanBrugh, Carel. He took the oath to the King 21–26 Oct. 1664 after the conquest of New Netherland.

VanBrugh, Johannes. He took the oath to the King 21–26 Oct. 1664 after the conquest of New Netherland.

VanBrunt, Cornelis Rustsen. He took the oath of allegiance in New Uijtrecht, Kings County, New York 26–30 Sep. 1687. He was a native of the colony.

VanBrunt, Rooth Joosten. He took the oath of allegiance in New Uijtrceht, Kings County, New York 26–30 Sep. 1687. He had been in the colony 34 years.

VanBrussum, Egbert. He took the oath to the King 21–26 Oct. 1664 after the conquest of New Netherland.

VanBueren, Jacob Willem. He took the oath of allegiance in Flackbush, Kings County, New York 26–30 Sep. 1687. He had been in the colony 38 years.

VanBurgh, Arent Jansen. He was naturalized in Delaware 21 Feb. 1682/3. He was from New Castle.

VanBurkelo, Herman. He was naturalized in Maryland 18 Oct. 1694.

VanBush, Hendrick Johnson. He took the oath of naturalization in New York 1 Sep. 1687 in Ulster County.

VanBuytenhuysen, Jan Gerritzen. He took the oath to the King 21–26 Oct. 1664 after the conquest of New Netherland.

VanCampen, Lambert Hendrickzen. He took the oath to the King 21–26 Oct. 1664 after the conquest of New Netherland.

VanCassant, Isaac. He took the oath of allegiance in Flackbush, Kings County, New York 26–30 Sep. 1687. He has been in the colony 35 years.

VanCleeff, Jan. He took the oath of allegiance in New Uijtrceht, Kings County, New York 26–30 Sep. 1687. He had been in the colony 34 years.

VanCortland, Oloffe Stevenzen. He took the oath to the King 21–26 Oct. 1664 after the conquest of New Netherland.

VanCouwehooven, Gerrit Willemsen. He took the oath of allegiance in Flackland, Kings County, New York 26–30 Sep. 1687. He was a native of the colony.

VanCouwenhooven, Willem Gerritse. He took the oath of allegiance in Flackland, Kings County, New York 26–30 Sep. 1687. He was a native of the colony.

VanCouwenhoven, Johannes. He took the oath to the King 21–26 Oct. 1664 after the conquest of New Netherland.

VanDalfsen, Jan. He was naturalized in New York 23 Aug. 1715. He was a weaver. He was from Tappan.

VanDalsen, Willem. He was naturalized in New York 1 Aug. 1745. He was a schoolmaster from New York City. His name might be Willem VanDalsemo.

VandenBurgh, Arent Jansen. He was naturalized in New Castle County, Delaware 21 Feb. 1682/3.

VandenBurgh, Hendrik. He was naturalized in New Castle County, Delaware 21 Feb. 1682/3.

VanDenHam, Henry. He was naturalized in New York 15 Jan. 1750/1. He was a vintner from New York City.

Vanderberg, Frans. He was naturalized in New York 24 July 1724.

Vanderbilt, Aris. He took the oath of allegiance in Flackbush, Kings County, New York 26–30 Sep. 1687. He was a native of the colony.

Vanderbilt, Jacob. He took the oath of allegiance in Flackbush, Kings County, New York 26–30 Sep. 1687. He was a native of the colony.

Vanderbrats, Volkert. He took the oath of allegiance in Breucklijn, Kings County, New York 26–30 Sep. 1687. He was a native of the colony.

Vanderbreets, Juriaen. He took the oath of allegiance in Breucklijn, Kings County, New York 26–30 Sep. 1687. He was a native of the colony.

VanderBush, Lowranc. He took the oath of naturalization in New York 1 Sep. 1687 in Ulster County.

VanDerCleffe, Dirck. He took the oath to the King 21–26 Oct. 1664 after the conquest of New Netherland.

VanderCoelen, Reyniers. He expressed his desire to be naturalized in New Castle County, Delaware 21 Feb. 1682/3.

VanDerGaegh, Cornelius. He was naturalized in Pennsylvania 29 Sep. 1709. He was from Philadelphia County.

Vandergrifft, Nicolase. He took the oath of allegiance in New Uijtrceht, Kings County, New York 26–30 Sep. 1687. He was a native of the colony.

VanDerGrist, Paulus Leendertzen. He took the oath to the King 21–26 Oct. 1664 after the conquest of New Netherland.

VanDerHeggen, Jacob Gaetshalck. He and his son, Gaetschalck VanDerHeggen, were naturalized in Pennsylvania 29 Sep. 1709. They were from Philadelphia County.

Vanderheyden, Mathias. He expressed his desire to be naturalized in New Castle County, Delaware 21 Feb. 1682/3.

Vanderheyden, Mathias. He was naturalized in Maryland 9 June 1692. He lived in Cecil County.

Vanderlyn, Pieter. He was naturalized in New York 24 June 1719.

Vandermij, Tielman. He took the oath of allegiance in New Uijtrceht, Kings County, New York 26–30 Sep. 1687. He had been in the colony 13 years.

Vandernote, Michaell. He was made a denizen in Maryland 30 July 1661. He was Dutch and was late of New Amstel.

Vanderpool, Isaac Isaacus. He was endenized in London 2 Aug. 1732. He was from St. Christopher.

Vanderpool, John. He was endenized in London 2 Nov. 1730. He was from St. Christopher.

VanDerSchuyren, Willem. He took the oath to the King 21–26 Oct. 1664 after the conquest of New Netherland.

VanDerSluys, Reinier. He and his son Adrian VanDerSluys were naturalized in Pennsylvania 29 Sep. 1709. They were from Philadelphia County.

VanderVeer, Cornelis. He was naturalized in New Castle County, Delaware 21 Feb. 1682/3.

Vanderveer, Jacob. He was naturalized in New Castle County, Delaware 21 Feb. 1682/3.

VanderVeer, Jan Cornelissen. He took the oath of allegiance in Flackbush, Kings County, New York 26–30 Sep. 1687. He was a native of the colony.

VanDerVin, Hendrick Janzen. He took the oath to the King 21–26 Oct. 1664 after the conquest of New Netherland.

Vandervolgen, Claes. He was naturalized in New York 11 Oct. 1715. He was from Albany County.

Vanderwait, Conrad. He was naturalized in Pennsylvania 24 Sep. 1763. He was from Northern Liberties Township, Philadelphia County.

Vanderwater, Abraham. He was endenized in New York 17 Oct. 1685.

Vandeventer, Cornelis Janse. He took the oath of allegiance in New Uijtrceht, Kings County, New York 26–30 Sep. 1687. He was a native of the colony.

VanDeventer, Jan. He took the oath of allegiance in New Uijtrceht, Kings County, New York 26–30 Sep. 1687. He had been in the colony 25 years.

VandeWater, Benjamin. He took the oath of allegiance in Breucklijn, Kings County, New York 26–30 Sep. 1687. He was a native of the colony.

VanDeWater, Hendrick. He took the oath to the King 21–26 Oct. 1664 after the conquest of New Netherland.

VandeWater, Jacobus. He took the oath of allegiance in Breucklijn, Kings County, New York 26–30 Sep. 1687. He had been in the colony 29 years.

Vanderwerf, Richard. He and his son, John Roeloffs Vanderwerf, were naturalized in Pennsylvania 29 Sep. 1709. They were from Philadelphia County.

VanDick, Arrent. He took the oath of naturalization in New York 1 Sep. 1687 in Ulster County.

Vandijck, Achias Janse. He took the oath of allegiance in Breucklijn, Kings County, New York 26–30 Sep. 1687. He was a native of the colony 36 years.

Vandijck, Jan Janse. He took the oath of allegiance in New Uijtrceht, Kings County, New York 26–30 Sep. 1687. He had been in the colony 35 years.

Vandijck, Karel Janse. He took the oath of allegiance in New Uijtrceht, Kings County, New York 26–30 Sep. 1687. He had been in the colony 35 years.

VanDitmaertz, Jan. He took the oath of allegiance in Flackbush, Kings County, New York 26–30 Sep. 1687. He was a native of the colony.

Vandoverage, Henry Fayson. He was naturalized in Virginia 21 Sep. 1671.

Vandreson, John. He was naturalized in New Jersey 31 July 1740. He was from Holland.

Vandriesen, Petrus. He was naturalized in New York 11 Oct. 1715. He was from Albany County.

Vanduyn, Cornelis Gerris. He took the oath of allegiance in New Uijtrceht, Kings County, New York 26–30 Sep. 1687. He was a native of the colony.

Vanduyn, Denijs Gerrisse. He took the oath of allegiance in New Uijtrceht, Kings County, New York 26–30 Sep. 1687. He was a native of the colony.

VanDuyn, Gerrit Cornelis. He took the oath of allegiance in New Uijtrceht, Kings County, New York 26–30 Sep. 1687. He had been in the colony 28 years.

VanDyck, Claes Thomas. He took the oath of allegiance in Breucklijn, Kings County, New York 26–30 Sep. 1687. He was a native of the colony.

VanDyck, Hendrick. He took the oath to the King 21–26 Oct. 1664 after the conquest of New Netherland.

Vandyck, Johanes. He was naturalized in New York 6 Dec. 1746.

VanDyckhuys, Jan Theunis. He took the oath of allegiance in Flackland, Kings County, New York 26–30 Sep. 1687. He had been in the colony 34 years.

VanElsland, Claes, Jr. He took the oath to the King 21–26 Oct. 1664 after the conquest of New Netherland.

VanElsland, Claes, Sr. He took the oath to the King 21–26 Oct. 1664 after the conquest of New Netherland.

VanEtta, Jacob. He took the oath of naturalization in New York 1 Sep. 1687 in Ulster County.

VanEtta, John. He took the oath of naturalization in New York 1 Sep. 1687 in Ulster County.

VanEtten, Jan. He was naturalized in New York 8–9 Sep. 1715. He was from Ulster County.

VanFleitt, Gerrit. He took the oath of naturalization in New York 1 Sep. 1687 in Ulster County.

VanFleitt, John. He took the oath of naturalization in New York 1 Sep. 1687 in Ulster County.

VanFlyeren, Jeron. He was naturalized in New York 28 Feb. 1715/6. He was from Ulster County.

Vanfossen, John. He was naturalized in Pennsylvania 25–27 Sep. 1740. He was from Philadelphia County.

VanFredinborch, Isack. He took the oath of naturalization in New York 1 Sep. 1687 in Ulster County.

VanFredingborch, William. He took the oath of naturalization in New York 1 Sep. 1687 in Ulster County.

Vangagehelm, John Frederick. He was naturalized in Frederick County, Virginia 5 May 1747.

VanGelder, Ary. He was naturalized in New York 3 July 1759.

VanGelder, Jan. He took the oath to the King 21–26 Oct. 1664 after the conquest of New Netherland.

VanGilst, James. He was naturalized in Rhode Island 10 June 1766. He was a merchant in Newport. He was from the Netherlands. He came with his family.

VanHaeren, Isaac. He was naturalized in New York 24 Nov. 1750.

VanHaerlem, Jan. He took the oath to the King 21–26 Oct. 1664 after the conquest of New Netherland.

VanHarlingen, Johannes Martinus. He was naturalized in New York 6 July 1723.

Vanharlinghen, Johannes Martinus. He was naturalized in New Jersey 31 July 1740. He was born in the Netherlands.

VanHeeck, John. He was naturalized in Maryland 8 May 1669. He was born in Virginia.

VanHertsbergen, Johannes. He was naturalized in New York 19 July 1715. He was a merchant.

VanHeythusen, Gerard. He was naturalized in London 29 Dec. 1660. He was the son of Bernhard Vanheythusen and was born at Waert in Brabant. He resided in St. Martin's Orgars Parish. He later came to New York.

VanHoven, Hendryck. He was endenized in New York 9 June 1698.

VanIngen, Dirck. He was naturalized in New York 31 Dec. 1768.

VanKampen, Jan, He was naturalized in New York 8–9 Sep. 1715. He was from Ulster County.

VanKerck, Jan, Sr. He took the oath of allegiance in New Uijtrceht, Kings County, New York 26–30 Sep. 1687. He had been in the colony 24 years.

VanKerck, Jan, Jr. He took the oath of allegiance in New Uijtrceht, Kings County, New York 26–30 Sep. 1687. He was a native of the colony.

VanKinswilder, Geertruyda. She was naturalized in New York 29 Oct. 1730. He was the wife of Herman Winkler.

VanKleeff, Cornelis. He took the oath of allegiance in New Uijtrceht, Kings County, New York 26–30 Sep. 1687. He was a native of the colony.

VanLaar, Arien. He took the oath to the King 21–26 Oct. 1664 after the conquest of New Netherland.

VanLaar, Stoffel. He took the oath to the King 21–26 Oct. 1664 after the conquest of New Netherland.

Vanlandigam, Michaell. He was naturalized in Virginia in Oct. 1673.

Vanlashant, Christian. He was naturalized in Pennsylvania 10 Apr. 1755. He was from Philadelphia County.

Vanlashy, John. He was naturalized in Pennsylvania 11 Apr. 1761. He was from Lancaster County.

Vanlear, John George. He was naturalized in Pennsylvania 25–27 Sep. 1740. He was from Chester County.

Vanleer, Bernard. He was naturalized in Pennsylvania 5 Mar. 1725/6. He was born in Germany.

VanLoo, John. He was naturalized in New York 6 July 1723.

VanMeteeren, Kreijn Janse. He took the oath of allegiance in New Uijtrceht, Kings County, New York 26–30 Sep. 1687. He had been in the colony 24 years.

VanNesten, Pieter. He took the oath of allegiance in Breucklijn, Kings County, New York 26–30 Sep. 1687. He had been in the colony 40 years.

VanNimwegen, Harmanis. He was naturalized in New York 8–9 Sep. 1715. He was from Ulster County.

VanNuys, Auke Janse. He took the oath of allegiance in Flackbush, Kings County, New York 26–30 Sep. 1687. He had been in the colony 36 years.

VanOblinis, Peter. He was naturalized in New York 13 Dec. 1715. He was a yeoman from New York City.

VanOlinda, Peter. He was naturalized in New York 27 Apr. 1716. He was from Albany County.

VanOsternhoudt, John Johnson. He took the oath of naturalization in New York 1 Sep. 1687 in Ulster County.

VanPelt, Aert Theunissen. He took the oath of allegiance in New Uijtrceht, Kings County, New York 26–30 Sep. 1687. He was a native of the colony.

VanPelt, Anthony. He took the oath of allegiance in New Uijtrceht, Kings County, New York 26–30 Sep. 1687. He had been in the colony 24 years.

VanPelt, Wouter. He took the oath of allegiance in New Uijtrceht, Kings County, New York 26–30 Sep. 1687. He had been in the colony 24 years.

VanPetten, Claes. He was naturalized in New York 17 Jan. 1715/6. He was from Albany County.

VanRanst, Gerrit. He was naturalized in New York 19 July 1715. He was a painter.

VanRanst, Pieter. He was naturalized in New York 13 Dec. 1715. He was a sailmaker from New York City.

VanRuyven, Cornelius. He took the oath to the King 21–26 Oct. 1664 after the conquest of New Netherland.

VanSantvoord, Cornelius. He was naturalized in New York 6 July 1723.

VanSchuiller, Philip Peterson. He took the oath to the King 21–26 Oct. 1664 after the conquest of New Netherland.

VanSevenhove, John. He was endenized in New York 19 Apr. 1693.

VanSichgelen, Ferdinandus. He took the oath of allegiance in Flackland, Kings County, New York 26–30 Sep. 1687. He had been in the colony 35 years.

VanSiegelen, Renier. He took the oath of allegiance in Gravens End, Kings County, New York 26–30 Sep. 1687. He was a native of the colony.

Vansintern, Isaac. He was naturalized in Pennsylvania 6 Feb. 1730/1. He was from Philadelphia County.

VanSollingen, Johannes. He was naturalized in New York 27 July 1721.

V[an]Steenwicke, Albert Johnson. He took the oath of naturalization in New York 1 Sep. 1687 in Ulster County.

VanStodt, Jacob Lowr. He was naturalized in Northumberland County, Virginia 17 Sep. 1656. He was born in Holland but had been an inhabitant of Yonghall, Ireland.

VanSutphen, Dirck Janse. He took the oath of allegiance in New Uijtrceht, Kings County, New York 26–30 Sep. 1687. He had been in the colony 36 years.

VanSwaringen, Garrett. He, his wife Barbarah DeBarrette, and their children, Elizabeth Vanswaringen and Zacharias Vanswaringen, were naturalized in Maryland 8 May 1669. He was born in Reensterdwan, Holland. She was born in Valenciennes, the Low Countries when under Spanish control, and their children in New Amstel.

VanTaerling, Floris. He was naturalized in New York 6 July 1723.

VanTaerlingh, Jan. He was naturalized in New York 24 June 1719.

VanTaerlingh, Nicholaus. He was naturalized in New York 17 June 1726.

VanTexel, John. He took the oath of allegiance in Orange County, New York 26 Sep. 1687.

VanTricht, Gerrit. He took the oath to the King 21–26 Oct. 1664 after the conquest of New Netherland.

VanVarick, Jacobus. He was naturalized in New York 2 Aug. 1715. He was a bolter from New York City.

VanVliet, Dirck Jansn. He took the oath of allegiance in Flackbush, Kings County, New York 26–30 Sep. 1687. He had been in the colony 23 years.

VanVliet, Jan Dircks. He took the oath of allegiance in Flackbush, Kings County, New York 26–30 Sep. 1687. He had been in the colony 23 years.

VanVoorhuijs, Albert Courten. He took the oath of allegiance in Flackland, Kings County, New York 26–30 Sep. 1687. He was a native of the colony.

VanVoorhuys, Court Stevense. He took the oath of allegiance in Flackland, Kings County, New York 26–30 Sep. 1687. He had been in the colony 27 years.

VanVoorhuys, Gerrit Courten. He took the oath of allegiance in New Uijtrceht, Kings County, New York 26–30 Sep. 1687. He was a native of the colony.

VanWickelen, Evert Janssen. He took the oath of allegiance in Flackland, Kings County, New York 26–30 Sep. 1687. He had been in the colony 23 years.

VanWien, Hendrick. He took the oath of naturalization in New York 1 Sep. 1687 in Ulster County.

VanWijck, Theodorus. He took the oath of allegiance in Flackbush, Kings County, New York 26–30 Sep. 1687. He was a native of the colony.

VanWyck, Cornelis Barense. He took the oath of allegiance in Flackbush, Kings County, New York 26–30 Sep. 1687. He had been in the colony 27 years.

VanWyck, Johannes. He was naturalized in New York 22 June 1734.

Varambaugh, Francois. He was naturalized in South Carolina 14 Aug. 1744.

Varetanger, Jacob Hendrickzen. He took the oath to the King 21–26 Oct. 1664 after the conquest of New Netherland.

Varick, Rudolphus. He was endenized in New York 29 July 1686.

Vas, Diederick. He was naturalized in New York 8–9 Sep. 1715. He was from Ulster County.

Vas, Petrus. He was naturalized in New York 8–9 Sep. 1715. He was from Ulster County.

Vas, Pierre. He was endenized in New York 6 Feb. 1695/6.

Vassall, Anna. She was naturalized in Jamaica 20 July 1685.

Vechten, Claes Arense. He took the oath of allegiance in Breucklijn, Kings County, New York 26–30 Sep. 1687. He had been in the colony 27 years.

Vechten, Hendrick. He took the oath of allegiance in Breucklijn, Kings County, New York 26–30 Sep. 1687. He had been in the colony 27 years.

Vedderlin, Johannes. He was naturalized in New York 22 June 1734.

Veerman, Harman. He was naturalized in New York 4 Oct. 1698.

Vega, Rice. He was naturalized in Jamaica 27 Aug. 1745. He was a Jew.

Veillard, Peter. He was naturalized in Maryland 15 Sep. 1762. He was a German. He was from Manochasy.

Veillon, John. He petitioned for naturalization in Virginia 24 Apr. 1704.

Veillon, John James. He was naturalized in Virginia *ca.* 1704.

Velden, Hieronimus. He was naturalized in New York by the act of 1740.

Veldtman, Geertruyda. She was naturalized in New York 14 Oct. 1732.

Veldtman, Hans. He was naturalized in New York 14 Oct. 1732.

Veldtman, Hendrick. He was naturalized in New York 14 Oct. 1732.

Veldtman, John. He was naturalized in New York 31 July 1754. He was a farmer from Richmond County.

Veldtman, Maria. She was naturalized in New York 14 Oct. 1732.

Veller, Flip. He was naturalized in New York 8–9 Sep. 1715. He was from Ulster County.

Venrick, Mathias. He was naturalized in Pennsylvania 10–11 Apr. 1745. He was from Lancaster County.

Venus, Philip. He was naturalized in Pennsylvania 11 Apr. 1763. He was from York Township, York County.

Venus, Philip. He was naturalized in New York 3 July 1766.

Verbrack, Nicholas. He was naturalized in Maryland 26 Apr. 1684. He was master of a ship. He also appeared as Nicholas Verbraach.

Verbynen, Peter. He was naturalized in Pennsylvania 29 Sep. 1709. He was from Philadelphia County.

Verdon, Thomas. He took the oath of allegiance in Breucklijn, Kings County, New York 26–30 Sep. 1687. He was a native of the colony.

Verdress, John. He was naturalized in Maryland 19 Oct. 1743.

Verdris, Valentine. He was naturalized in Maryland 25 Sep. 1743.

Vergereau, Bertram Gideon. He was naturalized in New York 27 Sep. 1715. He was from New York City.

Verhoof, Jan Gerritsen. He expressed his desire to be naturalized in New Castle County, Delaware 21 Feb. 1682/3.

Verhoofe, Cornelis. He was naturalized in Sussex County, Delaware 28 Apr. 1683.

Vankerck, Barent. He took the oath of allegiance in New Uijtrceht, Kings County, New York 26–30 Sep. 1687. He was a native of the colony.

Verkerck, Roeloff. He took the oath of allegiance in Flackbush, Kings County, New York 26–30 Sep. 1687. He had been in the colony 24 years.

Vermoon, Jacob. He took the oath to the King 21–26 Oct. 1664 after the conquest of New Netherland.

Vernezobre, Christopher Abraham. He was naturalized in New York 20 Oct. 1764.

VerNoij, Cornelis. He took the oath of naturalization in New York 1 Sep. 1687 in Ulster County.

Vernooy, Cornelis. He was naturalized in New York 8–9 Sep. 1715. He was from Ulster County.

Verntheusel, Martin. He was naturalized in Pennsylvania 24 Sep. 1760. He was from Lancaster County.

Verplank, Abraham. He took the oath to the King 21–26 Oct. 1664 after the conquest of New Netherland.

Verschier, Wouter Gysbert. He took the oath of allegiance in Boswijck, Kings County, New York 26–30 Sep. 1687. He had been in the colony 38 years.

Verschuer, Hendrick. He took the oath of allegiance in Boswijck, Kings County, New York 26–30 Sep. 1687. He was a native of the colony.

VerSchuer, Jochem. He took the oath of allegiance in Boswijck, Kings County, New York 26–30 Sep. 1687. He was a native of the colony.

Vertreese, Frederick. He was naturalized in Maryland in Apr. 1749. He was from Frederick County.

Vertreese, Jacob. He was naturalized in Maryland in Apr. 1749. He was from Frederick County.

Vertress, Hartman. He was naturalized in Maryland 7 May 1767. He was a German from Frederick County.

Verveel, Daniel. He took the oath to the King 21–26 Oct. 1664 after the conquest of New Netherland.

Vetter, Jacob. He was naturalized in Pennsylvania 11–13 Apr. 1743. He was from Philadelphia County.

Vetter, Lucas. He was naturalized in New York 3 July 1759.

Vezien, John. He was naturalized in New York 19 July 1715. He was a gardener.

Vickersheim, Adam. He was naturalized in Maryland 5 Oct. 1769. He was a German from Frederick County. He had been in the county about twelve years.

Victor, Frederick. He was naturalized in Maryland 24 Apr. 1762. He lived in Annapolis.

Vidal, Charles. He took the oath of allegiance at Mobile, West Florida 2 Oct. 1764.

Videaul, Pierre. He was born at LaRochelle, France, the son of Pierre Videaul and Madelaine Burgaud. His wife was Janne Elizabeth Videaul. Their daughter Janne Elizabeth Videaul was born in London, England. Their other children, Pierre Nicholas Videaul, Marianne Videaul, and Marthe Ester Videaul, were born in South Carolina. He was naturalized in South Carolina 10 Mar. 1696/7. He also appeared as Peter Videau.

Videt, Jan. He took the oath to the King 21–26 Oct. 1664 after the conquest of New Netherland.

Vierselius, George Andreas. He was naturalized in New Jersey in 1764. He was born in Hesse-Darmstadt. He had been in the colony six years. He lived in Hunterdon County.

Viest, Jacob. He was naturalized in Pennsylvania 10 Sep. 1761. He was from York County.

Viez, Francis. He was naturalized in Jamaica 14 June 1737.

Vigera, John Frederick. He was naturalized in Pennsylvania 11 Apr. 1751. He was from Philadelphia County.

Vignan, Jordain. He was naturalized in Jamaica 10 Sep. 1731.

Vignaud, Anne. She was born at Porte des Barques, Xanintongue, France and was the widow of Charles Faucheraud. Her children were Anne Faucheraud and Gedson Faucheraud, both born at Porte des Barques, and Marie Faucheraud born in England. They were naturalized in South Carolina ca. 1696.

Vignes, Adam. He was naturalized in Virginia 12 May 1705.

Villepontoux, Peter. He, his wife Jane Villepontoux, and children Peter Villepontoux, Marie Villepontoux, and Jane Villepontoux were naturalized in England 5 Mar. 1690/1.

Villeroze, Jean Mitchell. He took the oath of allegiance at Mobile, West Florida 2 Oct. 1764.

Vinceen, Joseph. He was an Acadian and took the oath to George II at the Mines, Pisiquit, Nova Scotia 31 Oct. 1727. He also appeared as Joseph Vincent.

Vincent, Adrian. He took the oath to the King 21–26 Oct. 1664 after the conquest of New Netherland.

Vincent, Anth. He was an Acadian and took the oath of allegiance in Apr. 1730.

Vincent, Augustin Nicholas. He took the oath of allegiance at Mobile, West Florida 2 Oct. 1764.

Vincent, Clement. He was an Acadian and took the oath of allegiance in Apr. 1730.

Vincent, Francis. He, his wife Anna Vincent, and children Anna Vincent and Francis Vincent were endenized in England 14 Oct. 1681.

Vincent, Joseph. He was an Acadian and took the oath of allegiance in Apr. 1730.

Vincent, Michel. He was an Acadian and took the oath to the King at the Mines, Pisiquit, Nova Scotia 31 Oct. 1727.

Vincent, Michel. He was an Acadian and took the oath of allegiance in Apr. 1730.

Vincent, Pierre. He was an Acadian and took the oath to the King at the Mines, Pisiquit, Nova Scotia 31 Oct. 1727. He was styled "le fils."

Vincent, Pierre. He was an Acadian and took the oath to the King at the Mines, Pisiquit, Nova Scotia 31 Oct. 1727.

Vincent, Pierre, Sr. He was an Acadian and took the oath of allegiance in Apr. 1730.

Vincent, Rene. He was an Acadian and took the oath of allegiance in Apr. 1730.

Vincler, Abraham. He was naturalized in Virginia in Apr. 1679.

Vinder, Abraham. He was naturalized in Virginia in Apr. 1679.

Vinera, Daniel Rodrigues. He was naturalized in New York by the act of 1740. He was a Jew.

Ving, Jan. He took the oath to the King 21–26 Oct. 1664 after the conquest of New Netherland.

Vinger, Johannis. He was naturalized in New York 17 Jan. 1715/6. He was from Albany County.

Vingler, Philips. He was naturalized in New York 17 Jan. 1715/6. He was from Albany County.

Vink, Andries. He was naturalized in New York 22 Nov. 1715. He was from Albany County.

Vink, Christian. He was naturalized in New York 3 Jan. 1715/6. He was from Albany County.

Virselius, George Andreas. He was naturalized in New Jersey 28 Nov. 1760. He had been in the colony six years. He was born in Hessen-Darmstadt. He lived in Hunterdon County.

Vis, Jacob. He took the oath to the King 21–26 Oct. 1664 after the conquest of New Netherland.

Vischer, Johannis. He was naturalized 8–9 Sep. 1715. He was from Ulster County.

Visser, Theunis. He sought naturalization in New York 1 Sep. 1731.

Vitte, Peter. He was naturalized in Virginia 12 May 1705.

Vizea, Rebecca Nunez. She was naturalized in Jamaica 23 Feb. 1747/8.

Voediren, Johan Bernard. He was naturalized in New York 27 July 1721.

Voerman, Jacob. He was naturalized in New York 8–9 Sep. 1715. He was from Ulster County.

Vogdes, Reinard. He was naturalized in Pennsylvania 11–13 Apr. 1743. He was from Philadelphia County.

Vogel, Andrew. He was naturalized in Maryland 15 Apr. 1761.

Vogel, John. He was naturalized in New York 19 Oct. 1735. He was a vintner from New York City.

Voght, Christian. He was naturalized in Pennsylvania 10 & 23 Apr. 1764. He was from Lancaster Township, Lancaster County.

Vogler, John Frederick. He was naturalized in Maryland 11 Sep. 1764. He was a German from Frederick County.

Vogler, John. He was naturalized in Pennsylvania 25–27 Sep. 1740. He was from Philadelphia County.

Vogt, Andrew. He was naturalized in Virginia 20 Oct. 1744. He was a native of Carlsbad, Germany.

Vogt, Jacob. He was naturalized in New Jersey 20 Aug. 1755.

Vogt, John Jacob. He was naturalized in Pennsylvania 10 & 23 Apr. 1764. He was from Paradise Township, York County.

Vogt, John Paul. He was naturalized in Virginia 20 Oct. 1744. He was a native of Frankfort, Germany.

Vogt, Valentine. He was naturalized in Pennsylvania 10 Sep. 1761. He was from Philadelphia County.

Vogt, Walter. He was naturalized in New Jersey in 1764.

Vokes, Walton. He was naturalized in New Jersey in 1764.

Volck, Andreas. He, his wife Anna Catharine Volck, daughter Anne Gertrude Volck, son George Hieronemus Volck, daughter Maria Barbara Volck, and daughter Anne Catharine Volck were endenized in London 25 Aug. 1708. They came to New York.

Volck, Andrew. He was naturalized in New York 8–9 Sep. 1715. He was from Ulster County.

Volck, George. He was naturalized in Pennsylvania 24 Sep. 1760. He was from Berks County.

Volck, Johannis Bartel. He was naturalized in New York 3 Feb. 1768.

Volckertsen, Peter. he was naturalized in Delaware 21 Feb. 1682/3. He was from New Castle County.

Volk, Ulrich. He was naturalized in Maryland 13 Apr. 1763. He was a German.

Vollenwyser, Jacob. He was naturalized in New York 11 Sep. 1761.

Vollert, Jost. He was naturalized in Pennsylvania 10 Apr. 1755. He was from Northampton County.

Vollhardt, Philip. He was naturalized in Maryland 8 Sep. 1768. He was a German from Baltimore, Maryland.

Volmar, John. He was naturalized in New York 3 May 1755.

Voloux, James. He was naturalized in South Carolina 20 Jan. 1741.

Volts, Melgert. He was naturalized in New York 3 Jan. 1715/6.

Volz, Johan Jost. He was naturalized in New York 8 Mar. 1773.

Vonck, Bartholomew. He was endenized in New York 6 Apr. 1697.

Vonherwiyt, Jacob. He was naturalized in Pennsylvania 25 Sep. 1747. He was from Philadelphia County.

Vonk, Peter. He was naturalized in New York 3 Apr. 1716. He was a yeoman from Orange County.

Vonk, Pieter. He was naturalized in New York 22 Nov. 1715. He was from Albany County.

Voogt, William. He was naturalized in New York 24 Nov. 1750.

Vos, Johannes. He was naturalized in New Jersey 3 June 1763.

Voshee, Daniel. He was naturalized in New York 23 Oct. 1765. He was a tobacco cutter from New York City.

Voss, Jurian. He was naturalized in New York 19 Oct. 1763. He was a farmer from the manor of Cortlandt.

Voyer, John. He was naturalized in Virginia 12 May 1705.

Vries, Cornelis Jansen. He expressed his desire to be naturalized in New Castle County, Delaware 21 Feb. 1682/3.

Vroman, Adam. He was naturalized in New York 22 Nov. 1715.

Vulgamot, Joseph. He was naturalized in Maryland 20 Oct. 1747.

Wacker, Jacob. He was naturalized in Maryland 11 Sep. 1765. He was a German from Frederick County.

Wacker, Jacob. He was naturalized in Maryland 11 Sep. 1765. He was a German from Frederick County.

Wacker, Jost. He was naturalized in Maryland 7 Sep. 1768. He was a German.

Wacks, Henry. He was naturalized in Pennsylvania 10 Apr. 1767. He was from Alsace Township, Philadelphia County.

Wacks, Peter. He was naturalized in Pennsylvania 10 Apr. 1767. He was from Bern Township, Philadelphia County.

Wagenar, Fallerus. He was naturalized in New York 3 July 1759.

Wagenar, M. Tobias. He was naturalized in Pennsylvania 10–14 Apr. 1747. He was from Philadelphia County. He was a minister.

Wagener, Andrew. He was naturalized in New Jersey in 1764.

Wagener, Ludwick. He was naturalized in Augusta County, Virginia 18 May 1763.

Wagener, Michael. He was naturalized in Maryland 3 Mar. 1758.

Wager, Mary. She was naturalized in Jamaica 15 Sep. 1742. She was a free Negro.

Waggamore, Henry. He was naturalized in Virginia 20 Sep. 1673.

Waggenaer, Peter. He was naturalized in New York 31 Jan. 1715/6. He was from Albany County.

Waggenor, Reubart. He was naturalized in Jamaica 8 Oct. 1736.

Waggoner, Christopher. He was naturalized in Pennsylvania 11 Apr. 1761. He was from Northampton County.

Waggoner, Frederick. He was naturalized in New York 27 Jan. 1770.

Waggoner, George. He was naturalized in Pennsylvania 11 Apr. 1761. He was from Berks County.

Waggoner, Henry. He was naturalized in Pennsylvania 24 Sep. 1762. He was from Lancaster County.

Waggoner, Jacob. He was naturalized in New York 16 Feb. 1771.

Waggoner, Philipina. She was naturalized in Pennsylvania 11 Apr. 1771. She was from Philadelphia.

Waggoner, Yost. He was naturalized in Pennsylvania 10–12 Apr. 1762. He was from Lancaster County.

Waggonerz, Jacob. He was naturalized in New York 9 Mar. 1773.

Wagle, John. He was naturalized in Pennsylvania 24 Sep. 1754. He was from Lancaster County.

Wagman, Christopher. He was naturalized in Pennsylvania 24 Sep. 1760. He was from Lancaster County.

Wagner, Adam. He was naturalized in Pennsylvania 11 Apr. 1761. He was from Berks County.

Wagner, Christopher. He was naturalized in Pennsylvania 25–26 Sep./4 Oct. 1749. He was from Philadelphia County.

Wagner, Christopher. He was naturalized in Pennsylvania 11 Apr. 1761. He was from Berks County.

Wagner, Jacob. He was naturalized in Pennsylvania 11 Apr. 1761. He was from Berks County.

Wagner, Jacob. He was naturalized in Pennsylvania 11 Apr. 1761. He was from York County.

Wagner, Jacob. He was naturalized in Pennsylvania 10 & 23 Apr. 1764. He was from Macungy Township, Northampton County.

Wagner, John. He was naturalized in Pennsylvania 10 Apr. 1753. He was from Berks County.

Wagner, Wilhelm. He was naturalized in Pennsylvania 10 Apr. 1765. He was from New Jersey.

Wagner, Yost. He was naturalized in Pennsylvania 11 Apr. 1761. He was from Berks County.

Wagonar, Elias. He was naturalized in Pennsylvania 11–13 Apr. 1743. He was from Philadelphia County.

Wagoner, Casper. He was naturalized in Maryland 11 Sep. 1765. He was a German from Frederick County.

Wagoner, Harman. He was naturalized in New Jersey 20 Aug. 1755.

Wagoner, Melker. He was naturalized in Pennsylvania 24 Sep. 1753. He was from Philadelphia County.

Wagoner, Michael. He was naturalized in Maryland 20 Sep. 1760.

Wagoner, Sebastian. He was naturalized in Pennsylvania 11–13 Apr. 1743. He was from Chester County.

Waidle, Frederick. He was naturalized in Pennsylvania 24 Sep. 1760. He was from Lancaster County.

Wainwood, Godfrey. He was naturalized in Rhode Island in Aug. 1772. He was a baker and a native of Prussia. He lived in Newport and came to the colony several years earlier with his family.

Wakerley, Abraham. He was naturalized in Pennsylvania 11 Apr. 1763. He was from Springfield Township, Philadelphia County.

Walber, Johan Peter. He was naturalized in Pennsylvania 24 Sep. 1742. He was from Bucks County.

Walber, Peter. He was naturalized in Pennsylvania 11–13 Apr. 1743. He was from Bucks County.

Walber, Nicholas. He was naturalized in Pennsylvania 25–27 Sep. 1740. He was from Bucks County.

Walburn, Herman. He was naturalized in Pennsylvania 19 May 1739. He was from Lancaster County.

Walck, Stephen Franciscus. He was naturalized in Pennsylvania 10 Apr. 1767. He was from Robinson Township, Berks County.

Waldenborg, Charles. He was naturalized in Virginia 12 May 1705.

Walder, Henry. He was naturalized in Pennsylvania 11 Apr. 1763. He was from Strasburg Township, York County.

Walder, Jacob. He was naturalized in Maryland 17 July 1765. He was a German from Frederick, Maryland.

Waldhawer, Christopher. He was naturalized in Pennsylvania 10 Sep. 1761. He was from Lancaster County.

Waldhawer, George. He was naturalized in Pennsylvania 10 Sep. 1761. He was from Lancaster County.

Waldner, Lutwick. He was naturalized in Maryland 17 Sep. 1764. He was a German.

Waldorph, Jacob. He was naturalized in New York 3 May 1755.

Waldorph, William. He was naturalized in New York 3 May 1755.

Waldron, Daniel. He took the oath of allegiance in Boswijck, Kings County, New York 26–30 Sep. 1687. He had been in the colony 35 years.

Waldron, Resolveert. He took the oath to the King 21–26 Oct. 1664 after the conquest of New Netherland.

Waldschmith, John. He was naturalized in Pennsylvania 11 Apr. 1761. He was from Berks County.

Walk, Martin. He was naturalized in Orange County, Virginia 15 Oct. 1745. He was born in the Dukedom of Wurttemberg. He had been in the colony seven years.

Walker, George. He was naturalized in Pennsylvania 10 & 23 Apr. 1764. He was from Philadelphia.

Walker, John. He was naturalized in Pennsylvania 24 Sep. 1760. He was from Philadelphia County.

Walker, Mary. She was naturalized in Jamaica 10 Oct. 1763.

Walkick, Frederick. He was naturalized in Pennsylvania 24 Sep. 1760. He was from Berks County.

Wall, Henry. He was naturalized in Maryland 10 Apr. 1762.

Wall, John. He was naturalized in Pennsylvania 24 Sep. 1762. He was from York County.

Wallace, Willim Peter. He was naturalized in New York 20 Mar. 1762.

Wallborn, Christian. He was naturalized in Pennsylvania 10 Sep. 1761. He was from Lancaster County.

Walldorft, Andonni. He was naturalized in New Jersey in 1759. He also appeared as Anthony Waldorf. He was born in Germany.

Waller, Jacob. He was naturalized in Maryland in Apr. 1749.

Walliser, Michal. He was naturalized in New York 16 Feb. 1771.

Wallraven, Hendrik. He expressed his desire to be naturalized in New Castle County, Delaware 21 Feb. 1682/3.

Wallwyn, Elizabeth. She was naturalized in Jamaica 8 Dec. 1730.

Walraeven, Gysbert. He expressed his desire to be naturalized in New Castle County, Delaware 21 Feb. 1682/3.

Walsh, William. He was naturalized in New Jersey in 1759.

Walt, Oswald. He was naturalized in Pennsylvania in Sep. 1740. He was from Philadelphia County.

Walter, Henrick. He was naturalized in Maryland 11 Sep. 1765.

Walter, Henry. He was naturalized in Pennsylvania 11 Apr. 1752. He was from Lancaster County.

Walter, Jacob. He was naturalized in Pennsylvania in Sep. 1740. He was from Philadelphia County.

Walter, Jacob. He was naturalized in Pennsylvania 11 Apr. 1763. He was from Codorus Township, York County.

Walter, Jacob. He was naturalized in Pennsylvania 24 Sep. 1763. He was from Tulpehockin Township, Berks County.

Walter, Jacob. He was naturalized in New York 3 May 1755.

Walter, Jacob. He was naturalized in New York 16 Feb. 1771.

Walter, Jacob. He was naturalized in New York 8 Mar. 1773.

Walter, Johannes. He was naturalized in New York 16 Feb. 1771.

Walter, Johannes Franciscus. He was naturalized in New York 14 Oct. 1732.

Walter, John. He was naturalized in New York 11 Sep. 1761.

Walter, Martin. He was naturalized in Pennsylvania 11 Apr. 1763. He was from Northern Liberties Township, Philadelphia County.

Walter, Michael Charles. He was naturalized in New Jersey in 1764. He resided in Cumberland County and had been in the colony fourteen years. He also appeared as Carl Walder. He was born in Germany.

Walter, Philip. He was naturalized in Pennsylvania 10 Apr. 1765. He was from Macungy Township, Northampton County.

Waltir, Matthew. He was naturalized in Pennsylvania 24–25 Sep. 1764. He was from Marlborough Township, Philadelphia County.

Waltmayer, George. He was naturalized in New York 3 May 1755.

Walts, Reinhard. He was naturalized in Maryland 20 Apr. 1771. He was a German.

Walz, Coenraed. He was naturalized in New York 20 Mar. 1762.

Wambelt, John George. He was naturalized in Pennsylvania 11–13 Apr. 1743. He was from Bucks County.

Wambold, Frederick. He was naturalized in Pennsylvania 25 Sep. 1750. He was from Frederick County.

Wamboldt, Peter. He was naturalized in Nova Scotia 5 July 1758.

Wannemaker, Bernard. He was naturalized in Pennsylvania 24 Sep. 1762. He was from Northampton County.

Wannemaker, Max. He was naturalized in Pennsylvania 24 Sep. 1762. He was from Northampton County.

Wanner, Lodwich. He was naturalized in New York 31 Jan. 1715/6. He was from Albany County.

Wanshaer, Anthony. He took the oath of allegiance in Flackland, Kings County, New York 26–30 Sep. 1687. He was a native of the colony.

Wanshaer, Jan. He took the oath to the King in New York 21–26 Oct. 1664 after the conquest of New Netherland. He was from St. Abuin.

Ward, John Michaell. He was naturalized in Jamaica 21 Mar. 1700/1.

Warley, Daniel. He was naturalized in Pennsylvania 25–27 Sep. 1740. He was from Philadelphia County.

Warnaer, Christophel. He was naturalized in New York 13 Mar. 1715/6. He was from Albany County.

Warner, Andreas. He was naturalized in Pennsylvania 11 Apr. 1761. He was from Philadelphia County.

Warner, Conrad. He was naturalized in Nova Scotia 6 July 1758.
Warner, Henrich. He was naturalized in Pennsylvania 25–27 Sep. 1740. He was from Philadelphia County.
Warner, Henry. He was naturalized in New Jersey 20 Aug. 1755.
Warner, Michael. He was naturalized in New York 8 Mar. 1773.
Warner, Nicholas. He was naturalized in Maryland 12 Apr. 1759.
Warraven, Johan Adolph. He was naturalized in New York 28 Feb. 1715/6. He was from Albany County.
Wart, Jacob. He was naturalized in Pennsylvania 25 Sep. 1751. He was from Bucks County.
Wartham, Adam. He was naturalized in Pennsylvania 12 Apr. 1750. He was from Philadelphia County.
Waspie, John. He was naturalized in Pennsylvania 11 Apr. 1761. He was from Philadelphia County.
Watchel, George. He was naturalized in New York 31 Dec. 1761.
Waterhouse, Elizabeth. She was naturalized in Jamaica 12 Aug. 1695. She was also known as Elizabeth Homings.
Waterman, George. He was naturalized in Pennsylvania 11–12 Apr. 1744. He was from Lancaster County.
Watsell, John. He was naturalized in New York 24 Nov. 1750.
Watz, Martin. He was naturalized in Pennsylvania 25 Sep. 1751. He was from Lancaster County.
Wayger, Barent. He was naturalized in New York 3 May 1755.
Wayger, Everard. He was naturalized in New York 3 May 1755.
Wayger, Hans Jury. He was naturalized in New York 3 May 1755.
Wayger, Leonard. He was naturalized in New York 3 May 1755.
Wealer, Henry. He was naturalized in Pennsylvania 24 Sep. 1763. He was from Paradise Township, York County.
Weaver, Adam. He was naturalized in Pennsylvania 24–25 Sep. 1764. He was from Bensalem Township, Berks County.
Weaver, Christian. He was naturalized in Maryland 3 Sep. 1765. He was a German.
Weaver, Conrad. He was naturalized in Pennsylvania 24 Sep. 1759.
Weaver, George. He was naturalized in Maryland 1 May 1773. He was a German from Frederick County.
Weaver, George. He was naturalized in Pennsylvania 14 Feb. 1729/30. He was from Lancaster County.
Weaver, George. He was naturalized in Pennsylvania 11 Apr. 1761. He was from Philadelphia County.
Weaver, Hendrick. He petitioned for naturalization in New York 16 Nov. 1739.
Weaver, Henry. He was naturalized in Pennsylvania 14 Feb. 1729/30. He was from Lancaster County.
Weaver, Henry. He was naturalized in Pennsylvania 11 Apr. 1761. He was from Northampton County.
Weaver, Jacob. He was naturalized in Pennsylvania 14 Feb. 1729/30. He was from Lancaster County.
Weaver, Jacob. He was naturalized in Pennsylvania 24–25 Sep. 1764. He was from Northern Liberties Township, Philadelphia County.
Weaver, Johannis. He was naturalized in New York 20 Dec. 1763. He was a tailor from Orange County.
Weaver, John. He was naturalized in Pennsylvania 14 Feb. 1729/30. He was from Lancaster County.
Weaver, John. He was naturalized in Pennsylvania 24 Sep. 1757.
Weaver, John. He was naturalized in Pennsylvania 24 Sep. 1762. He was from Lancaster County.
Weaver, Mathias. He was naturalized in Pennsylvania 10 Apr. 1760.
Weaver, Michael. He was naturalized in Pennsylvania 24–25 Sep. 1764. He was from Northern Liberties Township, Philadelphia County.
Weaver, Nicholas. He was naturalized in Pennsylvania in 4 Mar. 1763. He was a tailor from the Duchy of Deuxponts [i.e. Zweibrucken], Germany.

Weber, Adam. He was naturalized in Pennsylvania 11 Apr. 1751. He was from Philadelphia County.

Weber, Andreas. He was naturalized in Pennsylvania 10 Sep. 1761. He was from Northampton County.

Weber, Christian. He was naturalized in Pennsylvania 29 Mar. 1735. He was from Philadelphia County.

Weber, Friderick. He was naturalized in New Jersey. He had been in the British colonies fourteen years the last seven of which were in New Jersey. He was from Germany. He also appeared as Friedrich Waber.

Weber, George. He was naturalized in Pennsylvania 11 Apr. 1761. He was from Lancaster County.

Weber, Herman. He was naturalized in Pennsylvania 11 Apr. 1761. He was from Berks County.

Weber, Jacob. He, his wife Anne Elizabeth Weber, daughter Eve Elizabeth Weber, and daughter Eve Maria Weber were endenized in London 25 Aug. 1708. They came to New York.

Weber, Johannes. He was naturalized in New York 23 Oct. 1741.

Weber, John. He was naturalized in Maryland 11 Apr. 1761.

Weber, John. He was naturalized in Pennsylvania 10 Apr. 1772. He was from Gwinedth Township, Philadelphia County.

Weber, Leonard. He was naturalized in Pennsylvania 24–25 Sep./5 Oct. 1767. He was from Gwinedth Township, Philadelphia County.

Weber, Leonnard. He was naturalized in Maryland 5 May 1768. He was a German from Frederick County.

Weber, Manus. He was naturalized in Pennsylvania 24–25 Sep. 1764. He was from Rockland Township, Bucks County.

Weber, Michael. He was naturalized in Pennsylvania 24 Sep. 1762. He was from Lancaster County.

Weber, Michael. He was naturalized in New York 21 Oct. 1765. He was a shoemaker from New York City.

Weber, Philip. He was naturalized in Pennsylvania 11 Apr. 1763. He was from York Township, York County.

Weber, Tobias. He was naturalized in Pennsylvania 10–12 Apr. 1762. He was from Philadelphia County.

Weber, Valentine. He was naturalized in Pennsylvania 10–12 Apr. 1762. He was from Lancaster County.

Weck, George. He was naturalized in Pennsylvania 24–25 Sep. 1764. He was from Philadelphia.

Wedell, George. He was naturalized in Maryland 15 Sep. 1772. He was a German.

Wederstrandt, Conrad Theodore. He was endenized in Maryland 3 May 1764. He was born in France.

Weeber, Johan Henry. He was naturalized in Pennsylvania 19 May 1739. He was from Philadelphia County.

Weeber, John. He was naturalized in Pennsylvania 10 Apr. 1765. He was from Philadelphia.

Weeder, Johannis Joost. He was naturalized in New York 20 Mar. 1762.

Weedick, Henry. He was naturalized in Virginia 20 Sep. 1673.

Weeks, Christian. He was naturalized in Pennsylvania 11 Apr. 1761. He was from Berks County.

Weeland, Thomas. He was naturalized in Orange County, Virginia 15 Oct. 1745. He was born in the Dukedom of Wurttemberg.

Ween, William. He was naturalized in New Jersey in 1750. He was from Hunterdon County.

Weesener, Henry. He was naturalized in New York 28 Feb. 1715/6. He was a yeoman from Orange County.

Weesener, Johannes. He was naturalized in New York 28 Feb. 1715/6. He was a yeoman from Orange County.

Weesner, Mathias. He was naturalized in Maryland 15 Sep. 1772. He was a German.

Weetmore, Ulrick. He was naturalized in Pennsylvania 10 Sep. 1761. He was from Lancaster County.

Weever, Hendrick. He was naturalized in New Jersey 8 July 1730. He was born in Germany.

Weever, Jacob. He was naturalized in New York 8–9 Sep. 1715. He was from Ulster County.

Weever, William. He was naturalized in Jamaica 4 Mar. 1762.

Wegele, Johan Michel. He was naturalized in New York 8–9 Sep. 1715. He was from Ulster County.

Weger, Jacob. He was naturalized in New York 11 Sep. 1761.

Weiber, Bless. He was naturalized in Pennsylvania 11 Apr. 1761. He was from Philadelphia County.

Weiber, Michael. He was naturalized in Pennsylvania 29 Mar. 1735. He was from Bucks County.

Weiberick, Andrew. He was naturalized in Pennsylvania 24 Sep. 1763. He was from Lancaster Township, Lancaster County.

Weible, John. He was naturalized in Maryland 3 Sep. 1765. He was a German.

Weichell, Johan Michael. He was naturalized in Pennsylvania 11–13 Apr. 1743. He was from Philadelphia County.

Weider, Michael. He was naturalized in Pennsylvania 10 Apr. 1765. He was from York Township, York County.

Weiderhold, Adolf. He was naturalized in Nova Scotia 5 July 1758.

Weidler, Michael. He was naturalized in Pennsylvania 29 Mar. 1735. He was from Chester County.

Weidman, Abraham. He was naturalized in Pennsylvania 10 Sep. 1760. He was from Lancaster County.

Weidman, Christopher. He was naturalized in Pennsylvania 24 Sep. 1760. He was from Lancaster County.

Weidman, Michael. He was naturalized in Pennsylvania 24 Sep. 1763. He was from Douglas Township, Philadelphia County.

Weidner, Dichius. He was naturalized in Pennsylvania 11 Apr. 1761. He was from Berks County.

Weidner, George. He was naturalized in Pennsylvania 11 Apr. 1761. He was from Berks County.

Weidner, Lazarus. He was naturalized in Pennsylvania 11 Apr. 1761. He was from Berks County.

Weifer, Christopher. He was naturalized in Pennsylvania 11–13 Apr. 1743. He was from Philadelphia County.

Weig, Baltzer. He was naturalized in Pennsylvania 10–12 Apr. 1762. He was from Philadelphia County.

Weigand, Michael. He, his wife Anne Maria Weigand, son George Weigand, and son Tobias Weigand and daughter, Anne Marie Weigand, were endenized in London 25 Aug. 1708. They came to New York.

Weigert, Hans George. He was naturalized in Pennsylvania 29 Mar. 1735. He was from Philadelphia County.

Weigieser, Andreas. He was naturalized in New York 3 July 1759.

Weigner, Christopher. He was naturalized in Pennsylvania 11–13 Apr. 1743. He was from Philadelphia County.

Weigner, Conrad. He was naturalized in Pennsylvania 10–14 Apr. 1747. He was from Philadelphia County.

Weigner, Hans. He was naturalized in Pennsylvania 11–13 Apr. 1743. He was from Philadelphia.

Weigner, Melchior. He was naturalized in Pennsylvania 11–13 Apr. 1743. He was from Philadelphia County.

Weijnants, Pieter. He took the oath of allegiance in Breucklijn, Kings County, New York 26–30 Sep. 1687. He was a native of the colony.

Weikart, George. He was naturalized in Pennsylvania 24–25 Sep. 1764. He was from Tulpehocken Township, Berks County.

Weiker, John Philip. He was naturalized in New Jersey in 1764.

Weil, Friedrich. He was naturalized in Nova Scotia 5 July 1758.

Weiland, Petriem. He was naturalized in Pennsylvania 10 Apr. 1760.

Weild, George. He was naturalized in Maryland 28 Sep. 1763. He was a German from Frederick County.

Weiler, Andrew. He was naturalized in Pennsylvania 24 Sep. 1762. He was from Berks County.

Weimar, Frederick. He was naturalized in Maryland 16 Sep. 1762. He was a German from Frederick County.

Weimarin, Marie. She and her daughter, Catharine Weimarin, were endenized in London 25 Aug. 1708. They came to New York.

Weimer, Bernard. He was naturalized in Maryland 20 May 1736. He was from Baltimore County and was born in Germany.

Wein, Michael. He was naturalized in Pennsylvania 24–25 Sep. 1764. He was from Philadelphia.

Weine, Jacob. He was naturalized in Pennsylvania 10–11 Apr. 1745. He was from Bucks County.

Weinert, Nich. He was naturalized in Maryland 9 Sep. 1761.

Weinhold, Nicholas. He was naturalized in Pennsylvania 10 Sep. 1761. He was from Lancaster County.

Weinneimer, Philip. He was naturalized in Pennsylvania 11 Apr. 1761. He was from Philadelphia County.

Weir, Andrew. He was naturalized in Pennsylvania 24 Sep. 1763. He was from Manchester Township, York County.

Weir, Philip. He was naturalized in New Jersey in 1750.

Weis, Adam. He was naturalized in Maryland 10 Sep. 1760.

Weis, Henrick. He was naturalized in Maryland 16 Apr. 1760. He lived in Frederick, Maryland.

Weis, Jacob. He was naturalized in Maryland 23 Apr. 1772. He was a German.

Weise, Johann Caspar. He was naturalized in Jamaica 30 June 1764.

Weisel, Frederick. He was naturalized in Pennsylvania 10–12 Apr. 1762. He was from Bucks County.

Weisenthal, Charles Frederick. He was naturalized in Maryland 20 Nov. 1771. He had lived in Baltimore more than twelve years. He was a physician and a German.

Weisenthall, Charles. He was naturalized in Maryland 12 Sep. 1765. He was a German from Baltimore County.

Weiser, Conrad. He was naturalized in Pennsylvania 11–12 Apr. 1744. He was from Lancaster County.

Weishammer, Jacob. He was naturalized in Jamaica 23 Nov. 1693.

Weisman, John. He was naturalized in Pennsylvania 11 Apr. 1761. He was from Philadelphia County.

Weiss, Frederick. He was naturalized in New York 3 July 1759.

Weiss, Frederick. He was naturalized in Pennsylvania 24 Sep. 1762. He was from Lancaster County.

Weiss, George Michael. He was naturalized in Pennsylvania 10 Sep. 1761. He was from Lancaster County.

Weiss, Jacob. He was naturalized in Pennsylvania 12 Apr. 1750. He was from Philadelphia County. He was a Moravian.

Weiss, Lewis. He was naturalized in Pennsylvania in 9 Mar. 1763. He was from Prussia.

Weiss, Matthias. He was naturalized in Pennsylvania 10–12 Apr. 1762. He was from Northampton County.

Weiss, Philip. He was naturalized in Pennsylvania 10 Sep. 1761. He was from Berks County.

Weissman, George Philip. He was naturalized in Pennsylvania 11 Apr. 1763. He was from Philadelphia.

Weitzel, Paul. He was naturalized in Pennsylvania 10–12 Apr. 1762. He was from Lancaster County.

Weitzel, Wemer. He was naturalized in Pennsylvania 10–12 Apr. 1762. He was from Berks County.

Weitzell, Frederick. He was naturalized in Pennsylvania 10–12 Apr. 1762. He was from Berks County.

Weiver, Henericus. He was naturalized in Maryland 16 Apr. 1773. He was a German.

Welchenbach, Reinhard. He was naturalized in Maryland 12 Sep. 1764. He was a German from Frederick County.

Weld, Jacob. He was naturalized in Pennsylvania 10 Sep. 1761. He was from Lancaster County.

Welder, Martin Swort. He was naturalized in New Jersey in 1764.

Weller, George. He sought naturalization in New Jersey in the 18th century.

Weller, George. He was naturalized in Pennsylvania 10 Apr. 1760.

Weller, Hieronimus. He was naturalized in New York 8–9 Sep. 1715. He was from Ulster County.

Weller, Jacob. He was naturalized in Maryland 15 Apr. 1761.

Weller, Jacob. He was naturalized in Maryland 9 Sep. 1761.

Wellker, George. He was naturalized in Pennsylvania 24 Sep. 1741. He was from Philadelphia County.

Wellmens, Jacobus. He was naturalized in Jamaica 25 Apr. 1753.

Welp, Gerrit. He was naturalized in New York 20 Oct. 1764. He was a painter from New York City.

Welseld, Martin, Sr. He was naturalized in Maryland in Apr. 1749.

Welseld, Martin, Jr. He was naturalized in Maryland in Apr. 1749.

Welsh, Jacob. He was naturalized in Pennsylvania 24 Sep. 1762. He was from York County.

Welsh, Michael. He was naturalized in Pennsylvania 24 Sep. 1762. He was from York County.

Welshance, Joseph. He was naturalized in Pennsylvania 10 Apr. 1760.

Welty, Andrew. He was naturalized in Maryland 11 Apr. 1759.

Wemer, Philip. He was naturalized in New York 3 July 1759.

Wendell, John. He was naturalized in New York 31 Dec. 1768.

Wenery, Francis. He was naturalized in Pennsylvania 25 Sep. 1751. He was from Lancaster County.

Wenger, Henry. He was naturalized in Pennsylvania 11–13 Apr. 1743. He was from Philadelphia County.

Wenger, Peter. He was naturalized in Pennsylvania 24 Sep. 1770. He was from Nantmill Township, Chester County.

Wenk, Casper. He was naturalized in Pennsylvania 10–12 Apr. 1762. He was from Berks County.

Wenss, Jorg. He was naturalized in New York 16 Dec. 1737.

Wentz, Peter. He was naturalized in Pennsylvania 6 Feb. 1730/1. He was from Philadelphia County.

Wentz, Philip. He was naturalized in Pennsylvania 10 Sep. 1761. He was from Philadelphia County.

Wentz, Valentine. He was naturalized in Maryland 15 Sep. 1762. He was from Baltimore County.

Werfield, George. He was naturalized in Pennsylvania 25 Sep. 1753. He was from Lancaster County.

Werfield, Melchior. He was naturalized in Pennsylvania 25 Sep. 1753. He was from Lancaster County.

Werner, Peter. He was naturalized in Pennsylvania 25 Sep. 1751. He was from Lancaster County.

Werns, Conrad. He was naturalized in Pennsylvania 11 Apr. 1761. He was from Lancaster County.

Werns, George. He was naturalized in Pennsylvania 11 Apr. 1761. He was from Lancaster County.

Werntz, Leonard. He was naturalized in Pennsylvania 10 Apr. 1766. He was from Northern Liberties Township, Philadelphia County.

Werryfields, Jacob. He was naturalized in Pennsylvania 24–25 Sep./5 Oct. 1767. He was from Frederick County, Maryland.

Wersehler, Mauritius. He was naturalized in Maryland 9 Apr. 1760. He lived in Baltimore, Maryland.

Wert, Henry. He was naturalized in Pennsylvania 10–12 Apr. 1762. He was from York County.

Wert, Johannes. He was naturalized in New York 3 July 1759.

Wertchen, Christian. He was naturalized in New Jersey 20 Aug. 1755.

Wertchen, William. He was naturalized in New Jersey 20 Aug. 1755.

Werth, Johann Jacob. He was naturalized in New York 29 July 1752. He was a doctor of physic from Schohary, Albany County.

Werts, Peter. He was naturalized in New Jersey 20 Aug. 1755.

Wertz, Jacob. He was naturalized in Pennsylvania 10–12 Apr. 1762. He was from Cumberland County.

Weshenback, Henry. He was naturalized in Maryland 21 Sep. 1764. He was a German.

Wesner, Adam. He was naturalized in New York 3 Apr. 1716. He was the son of Johannes Wesner from Orange County. The surname also appears as Weesener.

Wesner, John. He was naturalized in Pennsylvania 10–12 Apr. 1762. He was from Berks County.

Wesner, Martin. He was naturalized in Pennsylvania 10–12 Apr. 1762. He was from Berks County.

Wessels, Gerrardus. He expressed his desire to be naturalized in New Castle County, Delaware 21 Feb. 1682/3.

Wessels, Hendrick. He was naturalized in New York 29 Nov. 1745.

Wessels, Herman. He took the oath of allegiance to the King 21–26 Oct. 1664 after the conquest of New Netherland.

Wessels, Warner. He took the oath to the King 21–26 Oct. 1664 after the conquest of New Netherland.

Wesselse, Jacobus. He was naturalized in New York 6 July 1723.

Wesselzen, David. He took the oath to the King 21–26 Oct. 1664 after the conquest of New Netherland.

Westbrock, Johanas. He took the oath of naturalization in New York 1 Sep. 1687 in Ulster County.

Westbroeck, Johannes. He was naturalized in New York before 1715. He was a shoemaker from Kingston, Ulster County.

Westbrook, Dirrick. He took the oath of naturalization in New York 1 Sep. 1687 in Ulster County.

Westbury, Catherine. She was naturalized in Jamaica 22 Nov. 1716.

Westerberger, Paul. He was naturalized in Pennsylvania 24–25 Sep./5 Oct. 1767. He was from Frederick County, Maryland.

Westerhouse, William. He was endenized in Virginia 1 Apr. 1658. He was a Dutchman.

Westerlo, Elidardus. He was naturalized in New York 11 Sep. 1761.

Westermeyer, John. He was naturalized in New York 26 July 1769. He was a baker from New York City.

Westfalin, Abl. He took the oath of naturalization in New York 1 Sep. 1687 in Ulster County.

Westfalin, Claes. He took the oath of naturalization in New York 1 Sep. 1687 in Ulster County.

Westfalin, Johannas. He took the oath of naturalization in New York 1 Sep. 1687 in Ulster County.

Westfallin, Symon. He took the oath of naturalization in New York 1 Sep. 1687 in Ulster County.

Westgo, Francis. He was naturalized in Pennsylvania 11 Apr. 1761. He was from Northampton County.

Westhoffer, Valentine. He was naturalized in Pennsylvania 10 Apr. 1755. He was from Lancaster County.

Westinghaver, Christopher. He was endenized in Maryland 22 June 1771. He was born in Germany.

Westor, John. He was naturalized in Pennsylvania 14 Feb. 1729/30. He was from Philadelphia.

Westphal, Fredrick. He was naturalized in New York 18 Oct. 1774. He was from New York City.

Wetterhan, John. He was naturalized in New York 27 July 1774. He was from New York City.

Wetzel, Jacob. He was naturalized in Pennsylvania 11 Apr. 1749. He was from Bucks County.

Wetzel, Martin. He was naturalized in Maryland 13 Sep. 1764. He was a German from Frederick, Maryland.

Wever, Jacob. He was naturalized in New York 8–9 Sep. 1715. He was from Ulster County.

Wever, Nicholas. He was naturalized in New York 11 Oct. 1715. He was from Albany County.

Weyant, Magiel. He was naturalized in New York 8–9 Sep. 1715. He was from Ulster County.

Weygand, John Albert. He was naturalized in New York 21 Aug. 1767. He was from New York City and had been a minister in New York about sixteen years.

Weybrecht, Martin. He was naturalized in Pennsylvania 19 May 1739. He was from Lancaster County.

Weybrethe, Martin. He was naturalized in Pennsylvania 10 Apr. 1756. He was from Manheim Township, Lancaster County.

Weymer, Godfrey. He was naturalized in New Jersey in 1764. He also appeared as Gottfried Weimer. He was born in Germany and had been in the colony eleven years.

Weyniger, Hans Gerhard. He was naturalized in New York 14 Feb. 1715/6. He was from Albany County.

Weyniger, Uldrich. He was naturalized in New York 14 Feb. 1715/6. He was from Albany County.

Weyrick, George. He was naturalized in Pennsylvania 19 May 1739. He was from Lancaster County.

Weys, Andrew. He was naturalized in New York 18 Oct. 1744. He was a carpenter from Dutchess County.

Weytman, Hans Marte. He was naturalized in New York 31 Jan. 1715/6. He was from Albany County.

Wezler, Martain. He was naturalized in Maryland 19 Oct. 1743. He was from Manaquice.

Whadell, Johannes. He was naturalized in New York 3 July 1759.

Wheeler, John. He was made a denizen in Maryland 29 July 1661. He was Swedish and was late of New Amstel.

Whelsale, Nicholas. He was naturalized in Maryland in Apr. 1749. He was from Frederick County.

Whetstone, Henry. He was naturalized in Pennsylvania 11–13 Apr. 1743. He was from Philadelphia County.

Whertonbacker, Bernard. He was naturalized in Maryland 15 Apr. 1763. He was a German from Frederick County.

Whightman, Jacob. He was naturalized in Pennsylvania 11 Apr. 1751. He was from Philadelphia County.

Whisler, Thomas. He was naturalized in New Jersey 6 Dec. 1769.

Whisther, Martin. He was naturalized in Maryland in 1743–1744.

Whistler, Jacob. He was naturalized in Pennsylvania 24 Sep. 1755. He was from Lancaster County.

Whitehead, Isaiah. He was naturalized in Pennsylvania 24 Sep. 1762. He was from Lancaster County.

Whiteman, Hendrick. He was naturalized in New York 18 Oct. 1750.

Whiteman, Henry. He was naturalized in New York 3 May 1755.

Whiteman, Jacob. He was naturalized in New York 31 Dec. 1761.

Whitman, Frederick. He was naturalized in Maryland 16 Apr. 1760.

Whitman, George. He was naturalized in Pennsylvania 24 Sep. 1760. He was from Lancaster County.

Whitman, Jacob. He was naturalized in Pennsylvania 10 Apr. 1754. He was from Philadelphia County.

Whitmer, Jacob. He was naturalized in Pennsylvania 24 Sep. 1762. He was from Lancaster County.

Whitmire, Michael. He was naturalized in Maryland 10 Sep. 1762.

Whitmore, Christian. He was naturalized in Pennsylvania 24–25 Sep./5 Oct. 1767. He was from Frederick County, Maryland.

Whitmore, Jacob. He was naturalized in Pennsylvania 24 Sep. 1760. He was from Lancaster County.

Whitmore, Peter. He was naturalized in New York 8 Mar. 1773.

Whitsett, Adam. He was naturalized in Orange County, North Carolina 22 Sep. 1770.

Whitsett, Henry. He was naturalized in Orange County, North Carolina 22 Sep. 1770.

Whitton, John. He was naturalized in Augusta County, Virginia 18 May 1774.

Whole, Isaac. He was naturalized in Pennsylvania 24 Sep. 1753. He was from Lancaster County.

Whole, Wendall. He was naturalized in Pennsylvania 24 Sep. 1753. He was from Lancaster County.

Wick, Johan. He was naturalized in New York 11 Sep. 1761.

Wickhuysen, Pieter. He was naturalized in New York 8–9 Sep. 1715. He was from Ulster County.

Wicknar, John. He was naturalized in Maryland 11 Sep. 1765.

Widder, Augustine. He was naturalized in Pennsylvania 10 Sep. 1761. He was from Lancaster County.

Widenar, Adam. He was naturalized in Pennsylvania 11–13 Apr. 1743. He was from Philadelphia County.

Widenar, George Adam. He was naturalized in Pennsylvania 11–13 Apr. 1743. He was from Philadelphia County.

Widerstein, Henry. He was naturalized in New York 20 Dec. 1763.

Widerstein, Henry. He was naturalized in New York 20 Oct. 1764.

Widman, John. He was naturalized in Pennsylvania 11 Apr. 1749. He was from Lancaster County.

Widtner, John. He was naturalized in Pennsylvania 11–13 Apr. 1743. He was from Philadelphia County.

Widtner, John George. He was naturalized in Pennsylvania 11–13 Apr. 1743. He was from Philadelphia County.

Wieck, Paul. He was naturalized in Jamaica 28 Jan. 1762.

Wiederief, Daniel. He was naturalized in Frederick County, Virginia 4 Aug. 1747.

Wiedershein, Daniel. He was naturalized in New York 23 Oct. 1765. He was a butcher from New York City.

Wiederwax, Hendrick Christophel. He was naturalized in New York 22 Nov. 1715. He was from Albany County.

Wiederwax, Johan And. He was naturalized in New York 22 Nov. 1715. He was from Albany County.

Wiedman, Philip. He was naturalized in Pennsylvania 11 Apr. 1763. He was from Lynn, Northampton County.

Wiegel, Christopher. He was naturalized in Pennsylvania 24–25 Sep. 1764. He was from Douglass Township, Berks County.

Wiemer, Andries. He was naturalized in New York 31 Dec. 1761.

Wierman, Jacob. He was naturalized in Pennsylvania 11–13 Apr. 1743. He was from Philadelphia County.

Wierpack, Nicholas. He was naturalized in Pennsylvania 11 Apr. 1761. He was from Bucks County.

Wies, Killean. He was naturalized in Pennsylvania 25 Sep. 1751. He was from Philadelphia County.

Wiest, Conraet. He was naturalized in New York 8–9 Sep. 1715. He was from Ulster County.

Wiest, Jacob. He was naturalized in Pennsylvania 24–25 Sep. 1764. He was from Oley Township, Berks County.

Wiggell, John. He was naturalized in Maryland 10 Sep. 1761.

Wightman, Martin. He was naturalized in Pennsylvania 25–27 Sep. 1740. He was from Lancaster.

Wigil, Sebastian. He was naturalized in Maryland 13 Apr. 1763. He was a German.

Wigmore, Jacob. He was naturalized in New Jersey 10 Mar. 1762.

Wigner, Abraham. He was naturalized in Pennsylvania 20 Sep. 1745. He was from Philadelphia County.

Wigner, George. He was naturalized in Pennsylvania 20 Sep. 1745. He was from Philadelphia County.

Wijckoff, Claes Pieterse. He took the oath of allegiance in Flackland, Kings County, New York 26–30 Sep. 1687. He was a native of the colony.

Wijckoff, Gerrit Pieterse. He took the oath of allegiance in Flackland, Kings County, New York 26–30 Sep. 1687. He was a native of the colony.

Wijckoff, Hendrick Pieterse. He took the oath of allegiance in Flackland, Kings County, New York 26–30 Sep. 1687. He was a native of the colony.

Wijckoff, Jan Pieterse. He took the oath of allegiance in Flackland, Kings County, New York 26–30 Sep. 1687. He was a native of the colony.

Wijckoff, Pieter Claasen. He took the oath of allegiance in Flackland, Kings County, New York 26–30 Sep. 1687. He had been in the colony 51 years.

Wijnhart, Cornelis. He took the oath of allegiance in New Uijtrceht, Kings County, New York 26–30 Sep. 1687. He had been in the colony 30 years.

Wild, Abraham. He was naturalized in Pennsylvania 10 Apr. 1760.

Wild, Caspar. He was naturalized in Jamaica 11 Aug. 1737.

Wild, Hillary. He was naturalized in Jamaica 18 Apr. 1732.

Wild, Jacob. He was naturalized in Maryland 12 Sep. 1753.

Wild, Nicholas. He was naturalized in Pennsylvania 24 Sep. 1762. He was from York County.

Wildbahne, Charles Frederick. He was naturalized in Pennsylvania 24–25 Sep. 1764. He was from Heidelberg Township, York County.

Wilde, John. He was endenized in Maryland 22 June 1771. He was born in Germany.

Wildemann, Jacob. He was naturalized in Maryland 10 Apr. 1770.

Wileman, Rachell. She was naturalized in New York 3 Apr. 1716. She was the wife of Henry Wileman of New York City.

Wiligas, Jan. He was naturalized in New York 26 July 1715. He was a turner.

Wilhelm, Ann Catharina. She was naturalized in Pennsylvania 10 Apr. 1760.

Wilhelm, Henry. He was naturalized in Pennsylvania 10 Apr. 1755. He was from Northampton County.

Wilhelm, Jacob. He was naturalized in Pennsylvania 11–12 Apr. 1744. He was from Lancaster County.

Wilhelm, Jacob. He was naturalized in Pennsylvania 10 Apr. 1760.

Wilhelm, Johannes. He was naturalized in Pennsylvania 19 May 1739. He was from Philadelphia County.

Wilhelm, Michael. He was naturalized in Pennsylvania 10 Apr. 1754. He was from Northampton County.

Wilhite, John. He was naturalized in Orange County, Virginia 24 Feb. 1742/3. He was a native of the Electorate of Mentz. He also appeared as John Wilhoid.

Wilhite, Tobias. He was naturalized in Orange County, Virginia 24 Feb. 1742/3. He was a native of the Elector of Mentz. He also appeared as Tobias Wilhoid.

Wilhyde, Frederick. He was naturalized in Maryland in Apr. 1749. He was from Frederick County.

Wiliard, Theobald. He was naturalized in Maryland 10 Apr. 1760. He was from Frederick County.

Wilk, George. He was naturalized in Maryland 11 Sep. 1765.

Will, Christian. He was naturalized in New York 18 Oct. 1769.

Will, Gerhard. He was naturalized in Pennsylvania 10–12 Apr. 1762. He was from Berks County.

Will, Hendrick William. He was naturalized in New York 16 Dec. 1737.

Will, Henry. He was naturalized in New York 21 Oct. 1761. He was a pewterer from New York City.

Will, John. He was naturalized in New York 3 July 1759.

Will, John Michel. He was naturalized in New York 31 Oct. 1745. He was a cordwainer from New York City.

Will, Michael. He was naturalized in Maryland 19 Oct. 1743.

Will, Philip. He was naturalized in New York 21 Oct. 1761. He was a pewterer from New York City.

Will, William. He was naturalized in New York 16 Dec. 1737.

Willanger, Lodowick. He was naturalized in Pennsylvania 11–12 Apr. 1744. He was from Philadelphia County.

Willemse, Henrick. He took the oath of allegiance in Flackbush, Kings County, New York 26–30 Sep. 1687. He had been in the colony 38 years.

Willemse, Johannis. He took the oath of allegiance in Flackland, Kings County, New York 26–30 Sep. 1687. He had been in the colony 25 years.

Willemse, Willem. He took the oath of allegiance in Gravens End, Kings County, New York 26–30 Sep. 1687. He had been in the colony 30 years.

Willemsen, Dirk. He expressed his desire to be naturalized in New Castle County, Delaware 21 Feb. 1682/3.

Willemsen, Pieter. He took the oath of allegiance in Flackbush, Kings County, New York 26–30 Sep. 1687. He was a native of the colony.

Willemson, Abram. He took the oath of allegiance in Flackland, Kings County, New York 26–30 Sep. 1687. He had lived in the colony 25 years.

Willemzen, Ratger. He took the oath to the King 21–26 Oct. 1664 after the conquest of New Netherland.

Willerips, Hans. He took the oath of allegiance at Mobile, West Florida 2 Oct. 1764.

Willhelm, Nicolaus. He was naturalized in Maryland 12 Sep. 1764. He was a German from Frederick County.

Williams, Johann Nicholaus, Sr. He was naturalized in Maryland 14 Apr. 1762. He was a German.

Williams, Johann Nicholaus, Jr. He was naturalized in Maryland 14 Apr. 1762. He was a German.

Williams, John. He was naturalized in Jamaica 23 Mar. 1699/1700.

Williams, John. He was naturalized in Pennsylvania 24 Sep. 1756.

Williams, Mary. She was naturalized in Jamaica 13 Nov. 1726.

Williamson, John. He took the oath of naturalization in New York 1 Sep. 1687 in Ulster County. He was styled the German.

Williard, Elias. He was naturalized in Maryland 14 Apr. 1770. He was a German from Frederick County.

Willkens, Claes. He took the oath of allegiance in Flackbush, Kings County, New York 26–30 Sep. 1687. He had been in the colony 25 years.

Willower, Christian. He was naturalized in Pennsylvania 11 Apr. 1749. He was from Bucks County.

Wilson, Elizabeth. She was naturalized in Jamaica 12 Mar. 1729/30. She was a free Negro.

Wilson, Robert. He was naturalized in Jamaica 17 Sep. 1717. He was a free Negro.

Wiltbanck, Halmainas. He was naturalized in Sussex County, Delaware 28 Apr. 1683.

Winckle, John. He was naturalized in New York 11 Sep. 1761.

Wincoop, Gerritt. He took the oath of naturalization in New York 1 Sep. 1687 in Ulster County.

Wincoope, Evert. He took the oath of naturalization in New York 1 Sep. 1687 in Ulster County.

Wincop, Johanas. He took the oath of naturalization in New York 1 Sep. 1687 in Ulster County.

Windemude, George. He was naturalized in New Jersey in 1764. He also appeared as George Windemuth.

Windle, Augustine. He was naturalized in Frederick County, Virginia 5 May 1747.

Windle, Christopher. He was naturalized in Frederick County, Virginia 5 May 1747.

Windle, Christopher. He was naturalized in Frederick County, Virginia 14 Aug. 1767.

Windle, Mathias. He was naturalized in Pennsylvania 10–11 Apr. 1745. He was from Philadelphia County.

Windle, Valentine. He was naturalized in Frederick County, Virginia 5 May 1747.

Windle, Valentine. He was naturalized in Frederick County, Virginia 14 Aug. 1767.

Windrich, Baltus. He was naturalized in New York 8–9 Sep. 1715. He was from Ulster County.

Winegardner, Nicholas. He was naturalized in Pennsylvania 10 Sep. 1761. He was from Lancaster County.

Wineling, Jacob. He sought naturalization in New Jersey in the 18th century.

Winer, John. He was naturalized in Pennsylvania 11–13 Apr. 1743. He was from Philadelphia County.

Winger, Lazarus. He was naturalized in Pennsylvania 24 Sep. 1755. He was from Berks County.

Wingher, John. He was naturalized in Pennsylvania 11 Apr. 1761. He was from Lancaster County.

Wingher, Joseph. He was naturalized in Pennsylvania 11 Apr. 1761. He was from Lancaster County.

Wingleblegh, Peter. He was naturalized in Pennsylvania 10 Apr. 1767. He was from Bethel Township, Lancaster County.

Winkler, Hans Willem VanKinswilder. He was naturalized in New York 29 Oct. 1730.

Winkler, Herman. He was naturalized in New York 29 Oct. 1730.

Winkler, Jacomina Gaertruyda Isabella. She was naturalized in New York 29 Oct. 1730.

Winkler, Lewis Adolph. He was naturalized in New York 29 Oct. 1730.

Winkler, Maria Magtelda. She was naturalized in New York 29 Oct. 1730.

Winkler, Nicolass Verkuyle. He was naturalized in New York 29 Oct. 1730.

Winnacker, Jacob. He was naturalized in New Jersey 8 June 1751.

Winniy, Petter. He took the oath of naturalization in New York 1 Sep. 1687 in Ulster County.

Winster, Pieter. He took the oath to the King 21–26 Oct. 1664 after the conquest of New Netherland.

Wint, Andrew. He was naturalized in Pennsylvania 25 Sep. 1752. He was from Northampton County.

Winter, George. He was naturalized in New Jersey 6 Dec. 1769.

Winter, George. He was naturalized in Pennsylvania 25 Sep. 1740. He was from Philadelphia County.

Winter, Hendrick. He was naturalized in New Jersey 8 Dec. 1744.

Winter, Hendrick. He was naturalized in New York 17 Jan. 1715/6. He was from Albany County.

Winter, Martin. He was naturalized in Maryland 15 Sep. 1761. He was from Baltimore County.

Winteroth, Casparus. He was naturalized in Maryland 11 Apr. 1753.

Winters, Eva Martia. She was the widow of George Winters of Frederick County. She was naturalized in Maryland 11 Apr. 1764.

Winthrop, Balthazar. He was naturalized in New York 23 Oct. 1755. He was a mariner from New York City.

Wintringor, Barnard. He was naturalized in Pennsylvania 10 & 23 Apr. 1764. He was from Hilltown, Bucks County.

Wirking, Jacob. He was naturalized in Pennsylvania 24–25 Sep. 1764. He was from Philadelphia.

Wirmley, John. He was naturalized in Pennsylvania 10–12 Apr. 1762. He was from Lancaster County.

Wirt, Casper. He was naturalized in Maryland 21 Apr. 1763. He was a German.

Wirt, Jacob. He was naturalized in Maryland 21 Apr. 1763. He was a German.

Wirth, Frederick. He was naturalized in Pennsylvania 10 Apr. 1760.

Wirth, Philip. He was naturalized in Pennsylvania 24–25 Sep. 1764. He was from Union Township, Berks County.

Wirtz, William. He was naturalized in Pennsylvania 11 Apr. 1761. He was from Lancaster County.

Wise, Francis. He and his children, Mary Wise, Jacob Wise, and Elizabeth Wise, were naturalized in Maryland 3 May 1740. He was from Prince George's County and was born in Germany.

Wise, Henry. He was naturalized in Maryland 16 Apr. 1761.

Wise, Jacob. He was naturalized in Pennsylvania 11–13 Apr. 1743. He was from Philadelphia County.

Wise, Jacob. He was naturalized in Pennsylvania 11–13 Apr. 1743. He was from Philadelphia County.

Wise, Jacob, Jr. He was naturalized in Pennsylvania 11–13 Apr. 1743. He was from Philadelphia County.

Wisecarver, John. He was naturalized in Frederick County, Virginia 1 Aug. 1769.

Wiser, David. He was naturalized in Pennsylvania 11–13 Apr. 1743. He was from Philadelphia County.

Wiser, Phillip. He was naturalized in North Carolina 22 Sep. 1763. He was from Rowan County and was a German.

Wisham, Conrad. He was naturalized in Pennsylvania 21 May 1770. He was from Dover Township, York County.

Wishong, Simon. He was naturalized in Pennsylvania 24 Sep. 1762. He was from Lancaster County.

Wislar, Jacob. He was naturalized in Pennsylvania 11–13 Apr. 1743. He was from Philadelphia County.

Wiss, Detrick. He was naturalized in Maryland 3 Sep. 1765. He was a German from Sharpsburgh, Maryland.

Wisshaar, George. He was naturalized in Maryland 11 Sep. 1765. He was a German from Frederick County.

Wist, Jacob. He was naturalized in Pennsylvania 24 Sep. 1762. He was from Berks County.

Wistar, Caspar. He was naturalized in Pennsylvania in 1724. He was from Germany.

Wistar, John. He was naturalized in Pennsylvania 25–27 Sep. 1740. He was from Philadelphia.

Wister, Casper. He was naturalized in New Jersey 31 July 1740. He was born in Germany.

Wister, Casper. He was naturalized in Pennsylvania 25–27 Sep. 1740. He was from Philadelphia.

Wister, John. He was naturalized in Pennsylvania 14 Feb. 1729/30. He was from Philadelphia County.

Wister, John. He was naturalized in Pennsylvania 25–27 Sep. 1740. He was from Philadelphia.

Wither, Christopher. He was naturalized in Pennsylvania 10 Sep. 1761. He was from Lancaster County.

Witherick, George. He was naturalized in New York 8 Mar. 1773.

Witherick, Michael. He was naturalized in New York 8 Mar. 1773.

Witman, Christopher. He was naturalized in Pennsylvania 19 May 1739. He was from Philadelphia County.

Witmer, Adam. He was naturalized in Pennsylvania 19 May 1739. He was from Lancaster County.

Witmer, Benjamin. He was naturalized in Pennsylvania 19 May 1739. He was from Lancaster County.

Witmur, Peter. He was naturalized in New York 16 Feb. 1771.

Witner, Henry. He was naturalized in North Carolina 19 Sep. 1753. He was from Rowan County.

Witrick, Adam. He was naturalized in Pennsylvania 24 Sep. 1754. He was from Lancaster County.

Witt, Volkert. He took the oath of allegiance in Boswijck, Kings County, New York 26–30 Sep. 1687. He was a native of the colony.

Wittberger, John Peter. He was naturalized in Pennsylvania 11 Apr. 1761. He was from Philadelphia County.

Witterhold, Charles. He was naturalized in Pennsylvania 11 Apr. 1763. He was from Germantown, Philadelphia County.

Witterick, Martin. He was naturalized in Maryland 28 Sep. 1762. He was a German from Frederick County.

Witthart, Johannes. He took the oath to the King 21–26 Oct. 1664 after the conquest of New Netherland.

Wittmyer, John Michael. He was naturalized in Maryland 7 May 1767. He was a German from Frederick County.

Witz, Charles. He was naturalized in Pennsylvania 11 Apr. 1761. He was from Philadelphia County.

Wob, Walter. He was naturalized in New Jersey 6 Dec. 1769.

Woerbel, Johannes, Sr. He was naturalized in Maryland 10 Sep. 1760.

Woerbel, Johannes, Jr. He was naturalized in Maryland 10 Sep. 1760.

Woertman, Dirck Janse. He took the oath of allegiance in Breucklijn, Kings County, New York 26–30 Sep. 1687. He had been in the colony 40 years.

Woester, Simon. He was naturalized in New York 3 May 1755.

Wohlfarht, Adam. He was naturalized in Maryland 6 Oct. 1768. He was a German from Frederick County.

Wohlfart, Conrad. He was naturalized in Pennsylvania 10 Sep. 1761. He was from Lancaster County.

Wohlgemuth, Hannes. He was naturalized in New York 11 Sep. 1761.

Wohlhaupter, Gottlieb. He sought naturalization in New York 27 Nov. 1756.

Wohlheber, John. He was naturalized in Pennsylvania 13 May 1768. He was from Tolpohocken Township, Berks County.

Wohner, Peter. He was naturalized in Maryland 15 Sep. 1762. He was from Frederick County.

Wold, Andrew. He was naturalized in Pennsylvania 25 Sep. 1744. He was from Philadelphia County.

Wolegamode, Samuel. He was naturalized in Pennsylvania 24–25 Sep./5 Oct. 1767. He was from Frederick County, Maryland.

Wolf, Andrew. He was naturalized in Pennsylvania 25 Sep 1744. He was from Philadelphia County.

Wolf, Anthony. He was naturalized in Pennsylvania 24 Sep. 1763. He was from Manchester Township, York County.

Wolf, Barnet. He was naturalized in Pennsylvania 10–12 Apr. 1762. He was from Lancaster County.

Wolf, Coenraed. He was naturalized in New York 20 May 1769.

Wolf, George. He was naturalized in Pennsylvania 10 Apr. 1760.

Wolf, George. He was naturalized in Pennsylvania 11 Apr. 1761. He was from Berks County.

Wolf, Hendrick. He was naturalized in Maryland 15 Sep. 1758. He was from Hundsbach ad Rhinum.

Wolf, Henrick. He was naturalized in Pennsylvania 10 Apr. 1760.

Wolf, Henry. He was naturalized in Pennsylvania 11 Apr. 1761. He was from Berks County.

Wolf, Jacob. He was naturalized in Pennsylvania 16 May 1769. He was from Donegal Township, Lancaster County.

Wolf, Johannes. He was naturalized in New York 8 Mar. 1773.

Wolf, John. He was naturalized in Pennsylvania 10 Apr. 1760.

Wolf, John. He was naturalized in Pennsylvania 10–12 Apr. 1762. He was from York County.

Wolf, John. He was naturalized in Pennsylvania 10–12 Apr. 1762. He was from Philadelphia County.

Wolf, John Christopher Frederick. He was naturalized in Pennsylvania 10 Sep. 1761. He was from Philadelphia County.

Wolf, Michael. He was naturalized in New Jersey in 1772. He was born in Germany. He was from Greenwich Township, Gloucester County. He had been a member of St. Michael's Church in Philadelphia for the last seventeen years.

Wolf, Michael. He was naturalized in Pennsylvania 11 Apr. 1761. He was from Lancaster County.

Wolf, Samuel. He was naturalized in Pennsylvania 11 Apr. 1761. He was from Lancaster County.

Wolf, Peter. He was naturalized in Pennsylvania 18 Nov. 1768. He was from Manchester Township, York County.

Wolfart, Ludwick. He was naturalized in Pennsylvania 10 Sep. 1761. He was from Lancaster County.

Wolfe, Frederick. He was naturalized in New York 16 Feb. 1771.

Wolfe, John Peter. He was naturalized in Pennsylvania 10–12 Apr. 1762. He was from York County.

Wolfersberger, John. He was naturalized in Pennsylvania 10 Sep. 1761. He was from Lancaster County.

Wolfersparger, John. He was naturalized in Pennsylvania 11–12 Apr. 1744. He was from Lancaster County.

Wolfert, Johannes. He was naturalized in Pennsylvania 10–14 Apr. 1747. He was from Lancaster County.

Wolfesberger, Frederick. He was naturalized in Pennsylvania 11 Apr. 1761. He was from Lancaster County.

Wolff, Johan David. He was naturalized in New York 29 Oct. 1730.

Wolff, John. He was naturalized in Pennsylvania 10–12 Apr. 1762. He was from York County.

Wolff, Peter. He was naturalized in Pennsylvania 11 Apr. 1761. He was from Lancaster County.

Wolfhart, Nicholas. He was naturalized in Pennsylvania 10 Apr. 1760.

Wolfort, Michael. He was naturalized in Pennsylvania 10 Apr. 1765. He was from West New Jersey.

Wolgemooth, Johannes. He was naturalized in New York 3 July 1759.

Wolhaupter, David. He was naturalized in New York 23 Apr. 1765. He was a turner from New York City.

Wolhaupter, Gottliep. He was naturalized in New York 3 July 1759.

Wollasen, Johon Petter. He was naturalized in New York 8–9 Sep. 1715. He was from Ulster County.

Wolleben, Fillib. He was naturalized in New York 8–9 Sep. 1715. He was from Ulster County.

Wolleben, Johann Jacob. He was naturalized in New York 8–9 Sep. 1715. He was from Ulster County.

Wolleben, Peter. He was naturalized in New York 8–9 Sep. 1715. He was from Ulster County.

Wolleven, Vallentyn. He was naturalized in New York 8–9 Sep. 1715. He was from Ulster County.

Womelsdorff, Daniel. He was naturalized in Pennsylvania 10–14 Apr. 1747. He was from Philadelphia County.

Womer, John Michael. He was naturalized in Pennsylvania 11 Apr. 1761. He was from Berks County.

Wommer, Michael. He was naturalized in Pennsylvania 11 Apr. 1761. He was from Berks County.

Wonderly, Egydius. He was naturalized in New York 20 Apr. 1763. He was a joiner from New York City.

Wonnemacher, Conrad. He was naturalized in Pennsylvania 24–25 Sep./5 Oct. 1767. He was from Hanover Township, Philadelphia County.

Wonsidler, Philip. He was naturalized in Pennsylvania 24 Sep. 1763. He was from Lower Milford Township, Bucks County.

Wood, George. He was naturalized in Pennsylvania 25–27 Sep. 1740. He was from Philadelphia County.

Wood, John. He was naturalized in Pennsylvania 25–27 Sep. 1740. He was from Philadelphia County.

Woodring, Peter. He was naturalized in Pennsylvania 11 Apr. 1752. He was from Bucks County.

Woolf, Adam. He was naturalized in Maryland 17 Apr. 1759.

Woolf, Garrett. He was naturalized in Maryland 30 Oct. 1727. He lived in Annapolis and was a shoemaker.

Woolf, John. He, his wife Hannah, and children Annalesse Woolf, Hanna Woolf, and Peter Woolf were naturalized in Maryland 30 Oct. 1727. He lived in Annapolis and was a shoemaker.

Woolf, John. He was naturalized in Maryland 13 Apr. 1763. He was a German from Frederick County.

Woolf, John George. He was naturalized in Pennsylvania 24–25 Sep./5 Oct. 1767. He was from Tolpehocken Township, Berks County.

Woolf, Mauldin. She was naturalized in Maryland 30 Oct. 1727. She was a spinster.

Woolf, Michael. He was naturalized in Maryland 23 Apr. 1772. He was a German.

Woolf, Paul. He was naturalized in Maryland 10 Sep. 1762.

Woolfin, Christoph. He was naturalized in Maryland 28 Sep. 1763. He was a German from Frederick County.

Woolfinger, Bernard. He was naturalized in Pennsylvania 25–27 Sep. 1740. He was from Philadelphia County.

Woolford, George. He was naturalized in Pennsylvania 25 Sep. 1751. He was from Lancaster County.

Woolfkull, Henry. He was naturalized in Pennsylvania 24 Sep. 1760. He was from Lancaster County.

Woolman, John. He was naturalized in Pennsylvania 24–25 Sep./5 Oct. 1767. He was from Horsham Township, Philadelphia County.

Woolrice, George. He was naturalized in New York 20 May 1769.

Woolrich, Coonrod. He was naturalized in Augusta County, Virginia 18 May 1762.

Woolring, Abraham. He was naturalized in Pennsylvania 10 Apr. 1742. He was from Bucks County.

Woolslegle, John. He was naturalized in Pennsylvania 14 Feb. 1729/30. He was from Lancaster County.

Wooph, Martin. He was naturalized in Maryland 21 Sep. 1763. He was a German from Frederick County.

Workhard, George. He was naturalized in New York 21 Oct. 1762. He was a baker from New York City.

Workhiser, Nicholas. He was naturalized in Pennsylvania 10 Apr. 1765. He was from Worcester Township, Philadelphia County.

Working, Nicholas. He was naturalized in Pennsylvania 10 Apr. 1765. He was from Conewago Township, York County.

Worman, Henry. He was naturalized in Pennsylvania 29–30 May 1772. He was from Sam's Creek, Frederick County, Maryland.

Worn, Martin. He was naturalized in Pennsylvania 24–25 Sep. 1764. He was from Philadelphia.

Wottering, John Daniel. He was naturalized in Maryland 9 Sep. 1761 He was from Frederick County and was a farmer and carpenter.

Wouterzen, Egbert. He took the oath to the King 21–26 Oct. 1664 after the conquest of New Netherland.

Wouterzen, Jan. He took the oath to the King 21–26 Oct. 1664 after the conquest of New Netherland.

Wourterzen, Willem. He took the oath to the King 21–26 Oct. 1664 after the conquest of New Netherland.

Woynat, Corenlis. He was naturalized in New York 22 Nov. 1715. He was a boatman from New York City.

Wrangler, Charles Magnus. He was naturalized in Pennsylvania in 4 Mar. 1763. He was born in Sweden and was a doctor of divinity.

Wreckerle, Emanuel Frederick. He was naturalized in Pennsylvania 10 Apr. 1760.

Wrightnomer, Nicholas. He was naturalized in Maryland 20 Oct. 1747. He also appeared as Nicholas Ridenaur.

Writter, Barthol. He was naturalized in Pennsylvania 25–27 Sep. 1740. He was from Philadelphia County.

Wunder, John George. He was naturalized in Pennsylvania 24 Sep. 1763. He was from Reading Township, Berks County.

Wurman, John. He was naturalized in Pennsylvania 11 Apr. 1761. He was from Bucks County.

Wurtman, Hans Harmon. He was naturalized in New York 8–9 Sep. 1715. He was from Ulster County.

Wyand, Wendal. He was naturalized in Pennsylvania 11–13 Apr. 1743. He was from Philadelphia County.

Wyatt, James. He was naturalized in Jamaica 20 Dec. 1700.

Wyghel, Adam. He was naturalized in Maryland 15 Apr. 1761.

Wykerline, Paul. He was naturalized in Pennsylvania 25–27 Sep. 1740. He was from Philadelphia County.

Wyerman, Hans. He was naturalized in Pennsylvania 11–13 Apr. 1743. He was from Philadelphia County.

Wyerman, Hans, Jr. He was naturalized in Pennsylvania 11–13 Apr. 1743. He was from Philadelphia County.

Wyerman, Henrick. He was naturalized in Pennsylvania 25 Sep. 1747. He was from Bucks County.

Wyler, Jacob. He was naturalized in Pennsylvania 11 Apr. 1761. He was from Berks County.

Wyland, Peter. He was naturalized in Pennsylvania 11 Apr. 1761. He was from Lancaster County.

Wymer, John. He was naturalized in Maryland in Apr. 1749. He was from Frederick County.

Wynkoop, Johannis. He was naturalized in New York 8–9 Sep. 1715. He was from Ulster County.

Wyse, Andries. He was naturalized in New York 16 Nov. 1739.

Wyster, Hendrick. He was naturalized in Jamaica 11 [torn] 1738.

Yackell, Abraham. He was naturalized in Pennsylvania 11–13 Apr. 1743. He was from Philadelphia County.

Yager, Adam. He was naturalized in Virginia 19 Sep. 1730. He was born at Fulkenston near Dusseldorf.

Yager, Hendrick. He was naturalized in New Jersey 8 July 1730. He was born in Germany.

Yager, Johannes. He was naturalized in New Jersey 8 July 1730. He was born in Germany.

Yager, John Casper. He was naturalized in Pennsylvania 10 Sep. 1761. He was from Philadelphia County.

Yager, Johannes Peter. He was naturalized in New Jersey 8 July 1730. He was born in Germany.

Yager, Nicholas. He was naturalized in Virginia 13 July 1722. He was born at Wichersbach, Hesse. He lived in Spotsylvania County.

Yager, Peter. He was naturalized in New Jersey 20 Aug. 1755.

Yahn, John. He was naturalized in Pennsylvania 11 Apr. 1763. He was from New Hannover Township, Philadelphia County.

Yaiger, Jacob. He was naturalized in Pennsylvania 24 Sep. 1759.

Yaigle, Baltzer. He was naturalized in Pennsylvania 10 Apr. 1759.

Yaisser, Frederick. He was naturalized in Pennsylvania 24 Sep. 1760. He was from Lancaster County.

Yakell, Abraham. He was naturalized in Pennsylvania 11–13 Apr. 1743. He was from Germantown.

Yakell, Balthazar. He was naturalized in Pennsylvania 11–13 Apr. 1743. He was from Bucks County.

Yakell, Christopher. He was naturalized in Pennsylvania 11–13 Apr. 1743. He was from Philadelphia County.

Yakell, John. He was naturalized in Pennsylvania 11–13 Apr. 1743. He was from Bucks County.

Yanzen, Gerrit Stavast. He took the oath to the King 21–26 Oct. 1664 after the conquest of New Netherland.

Yanzen, Martin. He took the oath to the King 21–26 Oct. 1664 after the conquest of New Netherland.

Yare, Benedict. He was naturalized in New Jersey 3 June 1763.

Ydaniah, Joseph. He was naturalized in Jamaica 20 Aug. 1681.

Yeacle, Christopher. He was naturalized in Pennsylvania 11–13 Apr. 1743. He was from Germantown.

Yeager, Andreas. He was naturalized in Pennsylvania 10 & 23 Apr. 1764. He was from New Hanover Township, Philadelphia County.

Yeager, John. He was naturalized in Pennsylvania 24–25 Sep./5 Oct. 1767. He was from Frederick County, Maryland.

Yeck, Martin. He was naturalized in Pennsylvania 10 Sep. 1761. He was from Lancaster County.

Yeildinbrand, Adam. He was naturalized in Maryland 28 Sep. 1763. He was a German from Frederick County.

Yerb, Jacob. He was naturalized in Pennsylvania 24 Sep. 1753. He was from Lancaster County.

Yerb, John. He was naturalized in Pennsylvania 24 Sep. 1753. He was from Lancaster County.

Yerger, Andrew. He was naturalized in Pennsylvania 10 Sep. 1761. He was from Philadelphia County.

Yerger, Thomas. He was naturalized in Pennsylvania 10 Sep. 1761. He was from Philadelphia County.

Yerkhas, Anthony. He was naturalized in Pennsylvania 14 Feb. 1729/30. He was from Philadelphia.

Yerkhas, Herman. He was naturalized in Pennsylvania 14 Feb. 1729/30. He was from Philadelphia.

Yoacham, Jacob. He was naturalized in Pennsylvania 10 Sep. 1761. He was from Philadelphia County.

Yoachum, Michael. He was naturalized in Pennsylvania 13–15 Apr. 1748. He was from Philadelphia County.

Yoel, Henry. He was naturalized in Maryland 3 Sep. 1765. He was a German.

Yoh, George. He was naturalized in Pennsylvania 11 Apr. 1761. He was from Berks County.

Yoh, Michael. He was naturalized in Pennsylvania 10 Sep. 1761. He was from Philadelphia County.

Yoke, John. He was naturalized in Pennsylvania 24 Sep. 1759.

Yoncker, Rudolph. He was naturalized in New York 3 July 1759.

Yoner, Jacob. He was naturalized in Pennsylvania 26 Sep. 1748. He was from Lancaster County.

Yoner, Nicholas. He was naturalized in Pennsylvania 13 May 1771. He was from Frederick County, Maryland.

Yong, George. He was naturalized in Maryland 3 May 1774. He was a German.

Yordan, John George. He was naturalized in New York 3 July 1759.

Yordea, Peter. He was naturalized in Pennsylvania 14 Feb. 1729/30. He was from Lancaster County.

Yorger, Martin. He was naturalized in Pennsylvania 11 Apr. 1761. He was from Philadelphia County.

Yost, Andrew. He was naturalized in Pennsylvania 20 May 1771. He was from Brecknock Township, Berks County.

Yost, Casper. He was naturalized in Pennsylvania 24 Sep. 1760. He was from Lancaster County.

Yost, Francis. He was naturalized in Pennsylvania 10 Apr. 1755. He was from Berks County.

Yost, Jacob. He was naturalized in Pennsylvania 11 Apr. 1761. He was from Philadelphia County.

Yost, John. He was naturalized in Pennsylvania 11 Apr. 1761. He was from Philadelphia County.

Yost, Michael. He was naturalized in Pennsylvania 10 & 23 Apr. 1764. He was from Bedminster Township, Bucks County.

Yost, Nicholas. He was naturalized in Pennsylvania 24 Sep. 1755. He was from Berks County.

Yost, Nicholas. He was naturalized in Pennsylvania 10 Sep. 1761. He was from Berks County.

Yost, Philip. He was naturalized in Pennsylvania 24 Sep. 1755. He was from Philadelphia County.

Youmer, Detrick. He was naturalized in Pennsylvania 10 & 23 Apr. 1764. He was from Macungy Township, Northampton County.

Young, Adam. He was naturalized in Pennsylvania 11 Apr. 1761. He was from Berks County.

Young, Adolph. He was naturalized in New York 11 Sep. 1761.

Young, Anthony. He was naturalized in Jamaica 30 Nov. 1723.

Young, Barnard. He was naturalized in Maryland in Apr. 1749. He was from Frederick County.

Young, Christian. He was naturalized in New York 20 Mar. 1762.

Young, Conrad. He was naturalized in Maryland 21 Sep. 1762. He was a German.

Young, David. He was naturalized in Maryland 19 Oct. 1743.

Young, George Jacob. He was naturalized in Pennsylvania 10 Apr. 1754. He was from Philadelphia County.

Young, Hendrick. He was naturalized in Pennsylvania 11 Apr. 1749. He was from Philadelphia County.

Young, Henry. He was naturalized in Pennsylvania 10 Apr. 1760.

Young, Isaac. He was naturalized in Pennsylvania 25 Sep. 1758.

Young, Jacob. He was naturalized in New Jersey 20 Aug. 1755.

Young, Jacob. He was naturalized in Maryland 10 Apr. 1761.

Young, Jacob. He was naturalized in Pennsylvania 11 Apr. 1761. He was from Berks County.

Young, Johan. He was naturalized in New Jersey 8 July 1730. He was born in Germany.
Young, John. He was naturalized in Maryland in 1749. He was from Frederick County.
Young, John. He was naturalized in New Jersey 21 Oct. 1754.
Young, John Nicholas. He was naturalized in Pennsylvania 11 Apr. 1761. He was from Philadelphia County.
Young, Martin. He was naturalized in Pennsylvania 10 Sep. 1761. He was from Berks County.
Young, Mary. She was naturalized in Jamaica 17 Dec. 1735.
Young, Peter. He was naturalized in Maryland in Apr. 1749. He was from Frederick County.
Young, Peter. He was naturalized in Pennsylvania 10 Apr. 1766. He was from Hunterdon County, New Jersey.
Young, Peter. He was naturalized in New York 27 Jan. 1770.
Young, Philip. He was naturalized in New Jersey 6 June 1751.
Young, Philip. He was naturalized in Pennsylvania 10 Apr. 1765. He was from Philadelphia.
Young, Pieter. He was naturalized in New Jersey 8 July 1730. He was born in Germany.
Young, Rowland. He was naturalized in Pennsylvania 24 Sep. 1762. He was from Berks County.
Young, Tebald. He was naturalized in New York 3 Jan. 1715/6. He was from Albany County.
Young, Tunis. He was naturalized in New Jersey 20 Aug. 1755.
Young, Valentine. He was naturalized in Pennsylvania 11 Apr. 1761. He was from Berks County.
Young, Valentine. He was naturalized in Pennsylvania 11 Apr. 1761. He was from Northampton County.
Young, William. He was naturalized in Pennsylvania 11 Apr. 1751. He was from Philadelphia County.
Youngblood, Peter. He and his children, William Youngblood, Peter Youngblood, Sarah Youngblood, and Mary Youngblood, were naturalized in Maryland 6 Mar. 1739. He was from Prince George's County and was born in Germany.
Younger, Lewis. He was naturalized in Maryland 10 Apr. 1762. He was a German from Anne Arundel County.
Younger, Michael. He was naturalized in North Carolina 22 Sep. 1763. He was from Rowan County and a German.
Youngman, Johan Dedrick. He was naturalized in Pennsylvania 11 Apr. 1741. He was from Philadelphia County.
Youse, Frederick. He was naturalized in Pennsylvania 10–12 Apr. 1762. He was from York County.
Youst, Harmond. He was naturalized in Maryland 14 Apr. 1770. He was a German from Frederick County.
Ysaaks, Abraham. He was naturalized in New York 6 July 1723.
Yund, George. He was naturalized in Pennsylvania 11 Apr. 1761. He was from Lancaster County.
Yung, Pilus. He was naturalized in New York 16 Dec. 1737.
Yunken, Henry. He was naturalized in Pennsylvania 24 Sep. 1760. He was from Philadelphia.
Yzadro, Jacob Baruch. He was naturalized in Jamaica 15 June 1708.
Yzedro, Sarah Baruh. She was naturalized in Jamaica 22 June 1714.
Zaatzmentzhoussen, Joest Hendrick. He was naturalized in Pennsylvania 6 Feb. 1730/1. He was from Philadelphia County.
Zacharias, Daniel. He was naturalized in Maryland 11 Apr. 1759.
Zacharias, Daniel. He was naturalized in Maryland 11 Apr. 1760.
Zacharias, Daniel. He was naturalized in Maryland 10 Sep. 1760.
Zacharias, Johannes. He was naturalized in Pennsylvania 19 May 1739. He was from Philadelphia County.
Zackarias, Mathias. He was naturalized in Maryland 10 Sep. 1762.
Zachariass, Daniel. He was naturalized in Pennsylvania 11 Apr. 1761. He was from Berks County.
Zadouski, Anthony. He was naturalized in Pennsylvania 29 Mar.1735. He was from Philadelphia County.
Zanger, John Peter. He was naturalized in New Jersey 31 July 1740. He was born in Germany.
Zantzinger, Paul. He was naturalized in New Jersey in 1750. He was from Hunterdon County. He also appeared as Paul Zanzinger.
Zapff, Daniel. He was naturalized in Maryland 14 Sep. 1763. He was a German.

Zank, Henry. He was naturalized in Pennsylvania 11 Apr. 1761. He was from Lancaster County.

Zebb, Peter. He was naturalized in Maryland 9 Sep. 1761.

Zeegaard, Andries. He was naturalized in New York 20 Dec. 1763.

Zeegaerd, Andries. He was naturalized in New York 31 Dec. 1761.

Zeeger, Michael. He was naturalized in New York 3 May 1755.

Zeegle, Frederick. He was naturalized in Pennsylvania 10 Sep. 1761. He was from Lancaster County.

Zeegler, Philip. He was naturalized in Pennsylvania 24 Sep. 1763. He was from Upper Salford Township, Philadelphia County.

Zeh, Michael. He was naturalized in Pennsylvania 24 Sep. 1763. He was from Philadelphia.

Zeigler, Jacob. He was naturalized in Pennsylvania 10 Apr. 1760.

Zeigler, Ludwick. He was naturalized in Pennsylvania 11 Apr. 1761. He was from Lancaster County.

Zeigler, Philip. He was naturalized in Pennsylvania 10 Apr. 1760.

Zeisberger, David. He was naturalized in Pennsylvania 10 & 23 Apr. 1764. He was from Bethlehem Township, Northampton County.

Zeister, Michael. He was naturalized in Pennsylvania 24 Sep. 1760. He was from Berks County.

Zeiwizt, George. He was naturalized in Pennsylvania 29 Mar. 1735. He was from Bucks County.

Zenger, John. He was naturalized in New York 17 June 1726.

Zenger, John Peter. He and his children were naturalized in Maryland 27 Oct. 1720. He lived in Kent County and was a printer. He was born in the Upper Palatinate on the Rhine.

Zenger, John Peter. He was naturalized in New York 6 July 1723.

Zentbower, Martin. He was naturalized in Maryland 1 Oct. 1767. He was a German from Frederick County.

Zerch, Baltzer. He was naturalized in Pennsylvania 10–12 Apr. 1762. He was from Berks County.

Zibberling, Bernth. He was naturalized in New York 8–9 Sep. 1715. He was from Ulster County.

Ziebach, Bartholomew. He was naturalized in Pennsylvania 10 Apr. 1765. He was from Tulpehocken Township, Berks County.

Ziegerfoss, Andrew. He was naturalized in Pennsylvania 24–25 Sep./5 Oct. 1767. He was from Springfield Township, Bucks County.

Ziegler, Christopher. He was naturalized in New Jersey in 1769. He was born in Germany.

Ziegler, Gotthart. He was naturalized in New York 3 July 1759.

Ziegler, Michael. He was naturalized in Pennsylvania 6 Feb. 1730/1. He was from Philadelphia County.

Ziegler, Wilhelm. He was naturalized in Pennsylvania 29 Mar. 1735. He was from Philadelphia.

Zigler, George. He was naturalized in Maryland 14 Sep. 1763. He was a German from Frederick County.

Zimmer, Jeremiah. He was naturalized in Pennsylvania 11 Apr. 1763. He was from Brecknock Township, Berks County.

Zimmerman, Abraham. He was naturalized in Pennsylvania 29 Mar. 1735. He was from Philadelphia County.

Zimmerman, Adam. He was naturalized in New Jersey in 1764. He was born in Germany.

Zimmerman, Christopher. He was naturalized in Pennsylvania 6 Feb. 1730/1. He was from Philadelphia County.

Zimmerman, Christopher. He was naturalized in Pennsylvania 24–25 Sep./5 Oct. 1767. He was from Philadelphia.

Zimmerman, George. He was naturalized in Maryland 14 Apr. 1762. He was a German.

Zimmerman, George. He was naturalized in Maryland 14 Sep. 1763. He was a German.

Zimmerman, George. He was naturalized in Pennsylvania 24 Sep. 1741. He was from Philadelphia County.

Zimmerman, George. He was naturalized in Pennsylvania 24 Sep. 1762. He was from Berks County.

Zimmerman, Gottlieb Abraham. He was naturalized in Pennsylvania in 1735. He was from Philadelphia County.

Zimmerman, Henry. He was naturalized in New York 21 Oct. 1765. He was a carpenter from New York City.

Zimmerman, John. He was naturalized in Virginia 19 Apr. 1745. He was born at Saltzfeld, Germany. He lived in Orange County. He was also known as John Carpenter.

Zimmerman, John. He was naturalized in Pennsylvania 11–13 Apr. 1743. He was from Lancaster County. He was also known as John Carpenter.

Zimmerman, Joseph. He was naturalized in New Jersey in 1760. He had been in the colony thirty-two years. He was born in Germany.

Zimmerman, Jost. He was naturalized in Maryland 21 Sep. 1764. He was a German.

Zimmerman, Michael. He was naturalized in Pennsylvania 24 Sep. 1762. He was from Berks County.

Zimmerman, Sebastian. He was naturalized in Maryland 13 Sep. 1758.

Zinck, Johan Casper. He sought naturalization in New York 27 Nov. 1756.

Zinn, John. He was naturalized in Pennsylvania 11 Apr. 1761. He was from York County.

Zinn, Philip Jacob. He was naturalized in Pennsylvania 10 Sep. 1761. He was from York County.

Zinser, Michael. He was naturalized in Pennsylvania 10–12 Sep. 1762. He was from Philadelphia County.

Zipperling, Bernhert, Jr. He was naturalized in New York 8–9 Sep. 1715. He was from Ulster County.

Zipperling, Frederik. He was naturalized in New York 8–9 Sep. 1715. He was from Ulster County.

Zipperling, Michael. He was naturalized in New York 8–9 Sep. 1715. He was from Ulster County.

Zirwer, Johannes. He was naturalized in Pennsylvania 29 Mar. 1735. He was from Philadelphia County.

Zoll, Henrich. He was naturalized in Maryland 14 Apr. 1762. He was a German from Frederick County.

Zoller, Jacob. He was naturalized in Maryland 11 Sep. 1765.

Zoller, John. He was naturalized in Pennsylvania 24–25 Sep. 1764. He was from Upper Hannover Township, Philadelphia County.

Zollinger, Andreas. He was naturalized in New York 11 Sep. 1761.

Zollinger, Caspar. He was naturalized in New York 11 Sep. 1761.

Zollinger, Ulrick. He was naturalized in Pennsylvania 10 Apr. 1760.

Zouberbuhler, Sebastian. He was naturalized in Nova Scotia 4 July 1758.

Zueringher, Johannes. He was naturalized in New York 17 Apr. 1750. He was a yeoman from New York City.

Zurbucher, Henrich. He was naturalized in Maryland 14 Apr. 1762. He was a German.

Zuvelt, Georg. He was naturalized in New York 8–9 Sep. 1715. He was from Ulster County.

Zuvelt, George Adam. He was naturalized in New York 8–9 Sep. 1715. He was from Ulster County.

Zuzan, Piere. He took the oath of allegiance at Mobile, West Florida 2 Oct. 1764.

Zweerts, Constantinus. He was naturalized in Jamaica 30 June 1764.

Zyer, Matthias. He was naturalized in Maryland 11 Sep. 1765. He was a German from Frederick County.

Appendix
Some Naturalizations in New France

—— [blank], ——. He was naturalized in May 1710.

—— [blank], Abel. He was a native of England and was naturalized 22 March 1732.

—— [blank], Andre. He lived with Guillaume Lemieux at Bellechase. He was naturalized in May 1710.

—— [blank], Jean. He was native of Ireland and lived at Petite-Riviere near Quebec. He had married a French wife, and had a family. He was naturalized in May 1710.

—— [blank], Jean. He was called the Irishman. He was naturalized in May 1710.

—— [blank], Jean-Baptiste. He lived on the coast of Beaupre near Quebec. He had married a French wife, and had a family. He was naturalized in May 1710.

—— [blank], Marie. She was from Ireland and was naturalized in May 1710.

—— [blank], Marie Ann. She was from England and was naturalized in May 1710.

—— [blank], Richard. He was naturalized in May 1710.

Alleyn, Madeleine. She was from England and was naturalized in May 1710.

Arnold, Jean. He was naturalized in June 1713.

Aubrey dit Larose, Germain. He was from Ireland. He was naturalized in May 1710.

Banistoe, Jean. He was naturalized in June 1713.

Bizard, Jacques. He was naturalized 1 Mar. 1687.

Board, Abel-Joseph. He was a native of London, England; resided at Pointe-aux-Trembles; had married a French wife, and had a family. He was naturalized in May 1710.

Brake, Louise Gabrielle. She was from England and was naturalized in May 1710.

Brojon [?], Marie-Charlotte. She was from England and was naturalized in May 1710.

Brook, Marie. She was from England and was naturalized in May 1710.

Buraff, Thomas. He was naturalized in June 1713.

Byrne, Denis. He was a native of Ireland and was naturalized in June 1713.

Carool [?], Jean-Baptiste. He was a native of Ireland; lived at Lavaltrie; had married a French wife; and had a family. He was naturalized in May 1710.

Carter, Yvan. He was naturalized in May 1710.

Clements, Edouard. He was naturalized in June 1713.

Christiason, Marie-Anne-Louise. She was born in New Netherland and had married a Frenchman, Moyse Dupuy, and came with him into Canada in the year of the peace. She lived at Laprairie and had five or six children. She was naturalized in May 1710.

Coss, Elisabeth. She was from England and was naturalized in May 1710.

Cout, Madeline. She was from England and was naturalized in May 1710.

Crony dit Saint-Jean, Jean. He was from Ireland and was naturalized in May 1710.

David, Charles. He was naturalized in June 1713.

Davis, Helene. She was from England and was naturalized in May 1710.

Dennis, Jean. He was naturalized in June 1713.

Dian, Victor-Thomas. He was naturalized in June 1713.

Dicker, Jean-Louis. He was naturalized in May 1710.

Dixon, Robert. He was naturalized in June 1713.

Drew, Marie-Anne. She was naturalized in June 1713.

Drody, Marie. She was from England and was naturalized in May 1710.

Dunkin, Catherine. She was from England and was naturalized in May 1710.

Fanef, Claude-Mathias. He was from England and lived in Montreal. He was naturalized in March 1714.

Faremont, Mathias-Claude. He was naturalized in May 1710.

Feltz, Charles-Joseph-Alexandre-Ferdinand. He was a German surgeon major in the troops at Montreal. He was naturalized 3 Feb. 1758.

Finn, Martha. She was from England and was naturalized in May 1710.

Fisk, Daniel. He was naturalized in June 1713.

Flechier, Edouard. He was naturalized in June 1713.

Fray, Andre. He was naturalized in May 1710.

Furie, Marie-Francoise. She was from England and was naturalized in May 1710.

Goffurier, Marie-Jeanne. She was from England and was the widow of Thomas Left. She was naturalized in May 1710.

Grechill, Joseph. He was naturalized in June 1713.

Hammon, Marie-Francoise. She was from England and was naturalized in May 1710.

Hastinger, Joseph. He was from the coast of Beaupre. He was naturalized in May 1710.

Hind, Joseph. He was naturalized in May 1710.

Hind, Joseph. He was from the coast of Beaupre. He was naturalized in May 1710. He was a brother of Joseph Hind. [second of the name]

Holond, Jean. He was a native of Ireland and was naturalized in June 1713.

Huss, Anne. She was from England and was naturalized in May 1710.

Huss, Antoine-Nicolas. He was naturalized in May 1710.

Huss, Thomas. He was naturalized in May 1710.

Hust, Elisabeth. She was from England and was naturalized in May 1710.

Hutchin, Nicolas. He was naturalized in May 1710.

Jamesie, Guillaume. He was a native of England; resided at Pointe-aux-Trembles; had married a French wife; and had a family. He was naturalized in May 1710.

Jefferys, Thomas. He was naturalized in June 1713.

Jordan, Gabriel. He was from Quebec. He was naturalized in May 1710.

Jordan, Marie-Anne. She was from England and was naturalized 13 April 1740.

Kalogg, Joseph. He was naturalized in May 1710.

Kay, Marguerite Kerwin. She was from England and was married to a sergeant in the troops named Chevalier. She was naturalized in May 1710.

Komball, Marie-Louise. She was from England and was naturalized in May 1710.

Lamax, Marie-Elisabeth. She was from England and was naturalized in May 1710.

Laza, Jean. He was a native of Ireland; lived at Montreal; was married to an English wife; and had eight children. He was naturalized in May 1710.

Leiyter, Jacques. He was naturalized in June 1713.

Lemaire dit Saint-Germain, Charles. He was from Ireland; lived at Lachine; had married a French wife; and had a family. He was naturalized in May 1710.

Littlefiver, Pierre Augustin. He was naturalized in May 1710.

Loeman, Marie. She was widow of —— Howe. She was naturalized in June 1713.

Lord, Anne. She was from England and had married 8abaphton [?] Holet dit Laviolette, tisserand, and lived at Villemarie. She was naturalized in May 1710.

Lorey, Jacques. He was naturalized in June 1713.

Lucas, Simon. He was naturalized in June 1713.

Maddox, Daniel. He was from England and was naturalized in June 1713.

Menning, Charles. He was naturalized in June 1713.

Messy, Benjamin. He was naturalized in May 1710.

Mistrot, Marie-Ursule. She was from England and had married Charles Boisboi. She lived at Saint-Francois. She was naturalized in May 1710.

Montass, Philippe. He was naturalized in May 1710.

Neilson, Richard. He was a native of New England; resided at Saint-Francois; had married a French wife; and had a family. He was naturalized in May 1710.

Ohe, Jean-Baptiste. He was a native of Ireland; lived at Montreal; had married a French wife; and had a family. He was naturalized in May 1710.

Otis, Jean. He was naturalized in June 1713.

Otis, Jean-Baptiste. He was a native of New England; lived on the coast of Beaupre; had married a French wife; and had a family. He was naturalized in May 1710.

Otis, Paul. He was from Villemarie. He was naturalized in May 1710.

Otis, Rose. She was from England and was married. She was naturalized in May 1710.

Otom, Christin. She was from England and came to Canada with her mother. She had married Louis LeBran, menuisier, and lived at Villemarie. She was naturalized in May 1710.

Parsons, Catherine. She was from New England and was naturalized in June 1713.

Pearse, Richard. He was naturalized in June 1713.

Perrinn, Guillaume. He was naturalized in June 1713.

Pillsbury, Jacques. He was naturalized in June 1713.

Pilman, Marie-Louise. She was from England and was the widow of Etienne William. She lived at Quebec. She was naturalized in May 1710.

Power [?], Joseph. He was naturalized in May 1710.

Price, Louis. He was naturalized in May 1710.

Priser, Elisabeth. She was from England and had married Jean Fournavan. She lived at Villemarie and had two children. She was naturalized in May 1710.

Reed, Jean. He was naturalized in June 1713.

Ricard, Jean. He was from the seminary at Quebec. He was naturalized in May 1710.

Robert, Joseph. He was naturalized in June 1713.

Ruff, Isaac. He was naturalized in June 1713.

Sayer, Marie-Joseph. She was from England and was naturalized in May 1710.

Scavler, Michel. He was naturalized in May 1710.

Scothoir, Jean. He was naturalized in June 1713.

Sergeant, Louis-Philippe. He was naturalized in May 1710.

Shoulder, Thomas. He was naturalized in June 1713.

Shrurer, Marie. She was from England and had married a man named Paquet. She lived near Quebec and had several children. She was naturalized in May 1710.

Sloutz, Jean. He was naturalized in May 1710.

Sloutz, Joseph. He was naturalized in May 1710.

Stebbens, Jacques-Charles. He was naturalized in May 1710.

Steward, Charles. He was naturalized in June 1713.

Stillet, Thomas. He was naturalized in June 1713.

Stobberer, Marguerite. She was from England and had married Jean des Noyons, a sergeant in the troops, and had a family. She was naturalized in May 1710.

Stobbon, Louise-Therese. She was from England and was naturalized in May 1710.

Stoze [?], Marie. She was from England and was naturalized in May 1710.

Stozer, Marie-Priscille. She was from England and was naturalized in May 1710.

Stroton, Hervey. He was naturalized in May 1710.

Strouds, Gilles. He was a native of London, England and was naturalized 30 Apr. 1749.

Sylvain, Thimothe. He was a native of Ireland and was naturalized 7 March 1724.

Tailor, Guillaume. He was from Villemarie. He was naturalized in May 1710.

Taybol [?], Marguerite. She was from England and was naturalized in May 1710.

Taylor, Charles. He was naturalized in June 1713.

Taylor, Richard. He was naturalized in June 1713.

Thomas, Claude. He was from England and was naturalized 1 June 1753.

Thomas, Jean. He was a native of Bristol, England, had married a French wife, and had two children. He was naturalized in May 1710.

Urtozer, Marie-Francoise. She was married to Jean Berger, painter, and lived at Villemarie. She was naturalized in May 1710.

Uso, Jean. He was a native of England. He was naturalized in May 1710.

Villieu, Sebastien de. He was naturalized in June 1668.

Waber, Marie-Elisabeth. She was from England and was naturalized in May 1710.

Wardaway, Jeanne. She was from England and was naturalized in June 1713.

Warren, Madeleine. She was from England and was the wife of Philippe Robitaille, tonnelier; lived at Villemarie; and had four children. She was naturalized in May 1710.

Washton [?], Marie. She was from England and was the wife of Jean Laska [?], a native of Ireland. She lived at the isle of Montreal and had three children. She was naturalized in May 1710.

White, Guillaume. He was naturalized in June 1713.

Wilding, Guillaume. He was naturalized in June 1713.

Willet, Jean. He was naturalized in June 1713.

William, Marie-Madeleine. She was from England and had married a man named Vildaigre, garde-port, at Quebec. She was naturalized in May 1710.

Willis, Marie. She was a woman of Pierre Derisy, merchant in Quebec. She was naturalized 27 January 1722.

Wilson, Madeleine. She was from England, had married a man named Chevalier, perruquier, lived at Quebec, and had a family. She was naturalized in May 1710.

Wood, Christophe. He was naturalized in June 1713.

Index

This index lists only those persons mentioned within the entries—such as children, spouses, and parents—as well as all names in the Appendix. It **does not** include the names of the main subjects, which are arranged alphabetically in the text.